Manuel Knoll, Stephen Snyder, Nurdane Şimşek (Eds.)
New Perspectives on Distributive Justice

New Perspectives on Distributive Justice

Deep Disagreements, Pluralism, and the Problem of Consensus

Edited by
Manuel Knoll, Stephen Snyder, Nurdane Şimşek

DE GRUYTER

ISBN 978-3-11-071023-6
e-ISBN (PDF) 978-3-11-053736-9
e-ISBN (EPUB) 978-3-11-053620-1

Library of Congress Control Number: 2018958556

Bibliographic information published by the Deutsche Nationalbibliothek
The Deutsche Nationalbibliothek lists this publication in the Deutsche Nationalbibliografie;
detailed bibliographic data are available on the Internet at http://dnb.dnb.de.

© 2020 Walter de Gruyter GmbH, Berlin/Boston
This volume is text- and page-identical with the hardback published in 2019.
Printing and binding: CPI books GmbH, Leck

www.degruyter.com

Table of Contents

List of Abbreviations —— IX

Manuel Knoll/Stephen Snyder/Nurdane Şimşek
Introduction: Two Opposing Conceptions of Distributive Justice —— 1

Part I: Deep Disagreements

Manuel Knoll
Deep Disagreements on Social and Political Justice: Their Meta-Ethical Relevance and the Need for a New Research Perspective —— 23

Ulrich Steinvorth
Are There Irreconcilable Conceptions of Justice? Critical Remarks on Isaiah Berlin —— 53

Michael Haus
Equality beyond Liberal Egalitarianism: Walzer's Contribution to the Theory of Justice —— 71

Giovanni Giorgini
Stuart Hampshire and the Case for Procedural Justice —— 91

Bertjan Wolthuis
Public Reason in Circumstances of Pluralism —— 109

Manuel Knoll/Nurdane Şimşek
Does Rawls's First Principle of Justice Allow for Consensus? A Note —— 127

Part II: Ancient Perspectives and Critiques of the Centrality of Justice

Francisco L. Lisi
Aristotle on Natural Right —— 133

Eckart Schütrumpf
What Is "Just in Distribution" in Aristotle's *Nicomachean Ethics* and *Politics* – Too Much Justice, Too Little Right —— 151

Christoph Horn
Justice in Ethics and Political Philosophy: A Fundamental Critique —— 171

Chandran Kukathas
Justicitis —— 187

Part III: The Problem of Consensus

Alberto L. Siani
Rawls on Overlapping Disagreement and the Problem of Reconciliation —— 207

Chong-Ming Lim
Public Reason, Compromise within Consensus, and Legitimacy —— 225

Ulrike Spohn
From Consensus to Modus Vivendi? Pluralistic Approaches to the Challenge of Moral Diversity and Conflict —— 243

Manon Westphal
What Bonds Citizens in a Pluralistic Democracy? Probing Mouffe's Notion of a *Conflictual* Consensus —— 259

Michał Rupniewski
Citizenship, Community, and the Rule of Law: With or Without Consensus? —— 275

Peter Caven
Political Liberalism: The Burdens of Judgement and Moral Psychology —— 291

Part IV: Expanding the Perspective on Obligations

Angela Kallhoff
John Rawls and Claims of Climate Justice: Tensions and Prospects —— 311

Annette Förster
Assistance, Emergency Relief and the Duty Not to Harm – Rawls' and Cosmopolitan Approaches to Distributive Justice Combined —— 329

Bill Wringe
Global Collective Obligations, Just International Institutions and Pluralism —— 345

Stephen Snyder
Intergenerational Justice in the Age of Genetic Manipulation —— 361

Part V: Diversifying the Perspective

Kok-Chor Tan
The Contours of Toleration: A Relational Account —— 385

Chad Van Schoelandt/Gerald Gaus
Constructing Public Distributive Justice: On the Method of Functionalist Moral Theory —— 403

Elena Irrera
Respect as an Object of Equal Distribution? Opacity, Individual Recognition and Second-Personal Authority —— 423

Maria Dimitrova
Responsibility and Justice: Beyond Moral Egalitarianism and Rational Consensus —— 441

Tom Bailey
Habermas's and Rawls's Postsecular Modesty —— 449

Part VI: The Difference Principle

Peter Koller
A Defense of the Difference Principle beyond Rawls —— 469

Aysel Demir
Marxist Critiques of the Difference Principle —— 487

Part VII: **The Economic Perspective: Adam Smith**

Jeffrey Young
Justice, Equity, and Distribution: Adam Smith's Answer to John Rawls's Difference Principle — 505

Barry Stocker
Statism and Distributive Injustice in Adam Smith — 523

Notes on Contributors — 541

Author Index — 545

Subject Index — 551

List of Abbreviations

Aristotle

EN Nicomachean Ethics
Met. Metaphysics
Phys. Physics
Pol. Politics
Rhet. Rhetoric
Top. Topics

Cicero

Rep. De re publica

Habermas, Jürgen

FH The Future of Human Nature

Plato

Gorg. Gorgias
Leg. Laws
Menx. Menexenus
Prot. Protagoras
Resp. Republic

Rawls, John

JF Justice as Fairness
LP The Law of Peoples
PL Political Liberalism
TJ A Theory of Justice

Smith, Adam

LJ Lectures on Jurisprudence
TMS The Theory of Moral Sentiments

https://doi.org/10.1515/9783110537369-001

WN *Wealth of Nations*

Other abbreviations

DP   Difference Principle
GRT Global Resource Taxation
IPCC Intergovernmental Panel on Climate Change
OR   Opacity Respect (Model)

Manuel Knoll/Stephen Snyder/Nurdane Şimşek
Introduction: Two Opposing Conceptions of Distributive Justice

The concept of distributive justice and its history are far more complex than most contemporary scholars are aware of. In recent decades, it has become commonplace within the discourse to equate "distributive justice" with "social justice."[1] However, this equation is quite modern and does not capture the meaning of "distributive justice" in the tradition of Plato and Aristotle. In its modern sense, distributive justice mainly refers to a just distribution of the goods and responsibilities of a society among its members. For John Rawls, the "principles of social justice" not only "provide a way of assigning rights and duties in the basic institutions of society" but also "define the appropriate distribution of the benefits and burdens of social cooperation" (1971, § 1, p. 4).[2] With his famous two principles of justice as fairness, Rawls achieved – as it is usually acknowledged – "a remarkably precise *definition* of 'distributive justice' in its modern sense" (Fleischacker 2004, p. 114, cf. 111).[3] As Samuel Fleischacker convincingly demonstrates in his *Short History of Distributive Justice*, this definition is distinctively modern and cannot be found in the ancient and medieval world. Indeed, the backgrounds of the world of antiquity and that of our own may be too great to bridge, bringing into question the alleged universality of philosophical concepts. Despite this – and though in the course of history, accounts of justice

---

[1] Miller 2003, p. 1f.; Hayek 2013, p. 226f. For Friedrich A. von Hayek's and David Miller's accounts of the origin of the term "social justice" see Hayek 2013, p. 329f., fn. 8, and Miller 2003, p. 3f., 269–270. Vol. 2 of Hayek's book *Law, Legislation and Liberty* is titled *The Mirage of Social Justice* (2013, p. 167). For Hayek, the term "social justice" is empty and meaningless and thus a mirage because "[s]trictly speaking, only human conduct can be called just or unjust": "To apply the term 'just' to circumstances other than human actions or the rules governing them is a category mistake" (2013, pp. 198, 232). In a free market economy, the market is a spontaneous and impersonal process. Therefore, the outcome of the market can neither be just nor unjust and needs no correction by a central authority (2013, pp. 231–236; cf. Hayek 1990, Barry 1995, p. 169, and Kersting 2000, p. 61). With his central argument against "social justice," Hayek wants to fight the socialist threat to the "values of a free civilization": "So long as the belief in 'social justice' governs political action, this process must progressively approach nearer and nearer to a totalitarian system" (2013, pp. XIX, 228 230, 232).
[2] For Miller, when "we talk and argue about social justice," we "are discussing how the good and bad things in life should be distributed among the members of a human society" (2003, p. 1).
[3] Four years before Rawls' *A Theory of Justice* appeared in 1971, he published an important article called "Distributive Justice" (1967).

https://doi.org/10.1515/9783110537369-002

emerge that may ring truer for our time – the specters of Aristotle and Rawls remain in contention throughout this volume.

Distributive justice in its modern sense is connected to the ideal of the welfare state. The main task of a welfare state is to provide minimal provisions for a good life to all its citizens. This requires a certain redistribution of wealth and income from the rich to the poor, from the talented to the untalented, and from the fortunate to the unfortunate. Rawls justifies such redistributions with his "difference principle" that has to be understood – despite some scholarly objections to this interpretation – as the principle of the welfare state (cf. Knoll 2013).[4] For good reasons, Rawls is perceived as a "welfare-state liberal" or as the philosopher of Social Democracy (Sandel 1982, p. 66).[5] Rawls' difference principle is inextricably linked to his "principle of redress." The principle of redress is "the principle that undeserved inequalities call for redress; and since inequalities of birth and natural endowment are undeserved, these inequalities are to be compensated for" (Rawls 1971, § 17, p. 100). The basic two moral claims of Rawls' arguments for the welfare state are negative: persons deserve neither to be born in a privileged family nor to be gifted with skills and talents by nature (cf. Rawls 1971, §§ 17, 48; pp. 104, 311). The principle of redress negates such undeserved inequalities between people and aims at establishing equality among them as far as possible and reasonable through state redistributions. The difference principle is not identical with the principle of redress. But like the latter, its intention is to compensate for undeserved social and natural inequalities and, in particular, to mitigate "the arbitrary effects of the natural lottery" (Rawls 1971, §§ 12, 17; pp. 74, 101). If one wishes to configure the social system in a way that "no one gains or loses from his arbitrary place in the distribution of natural assets or his initial position in society without giving or receiving compensating advantages in return," one is "led to the difference principle" (Rawls 1971, § 17, p. 102). According to the difference principle, those who "have been favored by nature, whoever they are, may gain from their good fortune only on terms that improve the situation of those who have lost out" (Rawls 1971, § 17, p. 101). One main problem of Rawls' argument for the welfare state is, however, that even if it were possible to deny individuals their privileged claim to their natural gifts, this would not amount to society's claim on them. If there were

---

4 According to Rawls' difference principle, "social and economic inequalities are to be arranged so that they are [...] to the greatest benefit of the least advantaged" (1971, § 46, p. 302; cf. 1999, § 46, p. 266, and 2001, § 13, p. 42f.). For a defense of the difference principle and its main idea, see Koller in this volume. For a Marxist critique of the difference principle, see Demir in this volume.

5 Jonathan Wolff mentions the "left-wing welfarism defended by Rawls" (1991, p. 1).

no strong moral bonds of community and solidarity between individuals, society's claim to their natural gifts would be as random and arbitrary as that of the individuals.[6] However, in view of Rawls' and a number of other modern authors' defense of the welfare state, Fleischacker is certainly right when he declares that distributive justice

> in its modern sense calls on the state to guarantee that property is distributed throughout society so that everyone is supplied with a certain level of material means. Debates about distributive justice tend to center on the amount of means to be guaranteed and on the degree to which state intervention is necessary for those means to be distributed (Fleischacker 2004, p. 4).

In her article "Aristotelian Social Democracy," Martha Nussbaum claimed that in his time Aristotle was already a defender of the welfare state (1990). However, her attempt to substantiate this anachronistic claim was not convincing. For several reasons, Aristotle's ancient political philosophy is incompatible with Nussbaum's "Social Democracy" (cf. Knoll 2014, Mulgan 2000). For Aristotle, distributive justice has nothing to do with what today is called "social justice."[7] For him, distributive justice mainly regulates a just distribution of political offices and the recognition or honor that citizens can gain through exercising them.[8] This is why in Book V of the *Nicomachean Ethics*, in which he introduces distributive justice as one form of particular justice, he gives only a brief outline of this

---

[6] For this serious objection to Rawls' theory, which is just one of many, see Sandel 1984, p. 89 f. According to Robert Nozick, another severe critic of Rawls, people have a claim to their natural gifts even though they don't deserve them: "It is not true, for example, that a person earns Y (a right to keep a painting he's made, praise for writing *A Theory of Justice*, and so on) only if he's earned (or otherwise *deserves*) whatever he used (including natural assets) in the process of earning Y. Some of the things he uses he just may *have*, not illegitimately. It needn't be that the foundations underlying desert are themselves deserved, *all the way down*" (Nozick 1974, p. 225). For a compelling critique of Rawls' denial of "the reality of desert" and of the existence of deserving people, see Walzer 1983, p. 260 f.; cf. Nozick 1974, p. 214.
[7] Similar to Nussbaum, Rawls erroneously and anachronistically claims that Aristotle "has a conception of social justice" (Rawls 1971, p. 11). However, Aristotle mentions the distribution of money among the members of the political community in the context of distributive justice one time (*EN* V 5, 1130b31).
[8] The term "distributive justice" goes back to Thomas of Aquinas' term "*iustitia distributiva*." For a critique of this term and its usage for Aristotle's political philosophy, see Schütrumpf in this volume. For a response to an earlier version of Schütrumpf's position, see Knoll 2011, pp. 414–417.

political kind of justice (*EN* V 5, 1130b30 – 34; *EN* V 6, 1131a18 – b24). Aristotle extends and refines this outline in the *Politics* starting with Book III.[9]

For Aristotle, distributive justice is a form of justice that is not blindfolded; it allots the political offices in view of the qualities of the citizens. As different citizens have different qualities, they should be allotted unequal shares. According to one of Aristotle's two distributive principles, only equals should get equal shares, while those unequal should be allotted unequal shares. In a just distribution, these shares should be bestowed on citizens in proportion to their different qualities, or as Aristotle puts it, in proportion to their unequal "merit" or "worth" (*axia*).[10] Aristotle's second distributive principle defines a just distribution as one "according to merit" (*kat' axian*). This means that every citizen gets allotted equal shares in proportion to his unequal worth or merit. Like Plato, Aristotle calls this form of equality, which he favors and opposes to "numeric" or "arithmetic" equality, "proportional" or "geometrical" equality (*EN* V 6, 1131a18 – b24; cf. *Leg.* 6, 757a – e; *Gorg.* 508a, 490b – e).[11]

Already in the *Nicomachean Ethics*, Aristotle delineates the above-mentioned formal principles of distributive justice and refers to the political dispute concerning how to give them content and make them concrete: "For everyone agrees that what is just in distribution must be according to merit in some sense. But they do not all refer to the same sort of merit: for democrats it is freedom, for supporters of oligarchy it is wealth, for others it is noble birth, and for aristocrats it is virtue" (*EN* V 6, 1131a25 – 29).[12] Citizens have different political convictions. Therefore, they substantially disagree about the criterion or standard that is appropriate for measuring merit. In the quotation, Aristotle mentions four groups with funda-

---

[9] In the *Politics*, Aristotle refers two times to the short account of distributive justice that he gave in the *Nicomachean Ethics* (*Pol.* III 9, 1280a16 – 25; *Pol.* III 12, 1282b18 – 23).
[10] Only in a few English editions of the *Nicomachean Ethics* and the *Politics* is the term "*axia*" translated with "worth." Usually it is rendered with "merit." All trans. from *EN* and *Pol.* in this introduction are M.K.'s
[11] For the relation of Plato's theory of distributive justice to Aristotle's, see Knoll in this volume pp. 27–31 and Knoll 2010.
[12] In his *Short History of Distributive Justice*, Samuel Fleischacker incorrectly claims that the above-mentioned political dispute about the appropriate standard of merit concerns citizenship and not – as is actually the case – political power (Fleischacker 2004, p. 19). In ancient oligarchies or aristocracies, the poor or common people were citizens but had no political power. Fleischacker also erroneously claims that both wealth and noble birth are the specific standards of oligarchy (Fleischacker 2004, p. 19). However, Aristotle clearly links oligarchy to wealth and treats noble birth as an independent standard of merit and as a separate claim to political power. The reason for his misconception is that Fleischacker neglects Aristotle's treatment of distributive justice in the *Politics* (Fleischacker 2004, pp. 5, 13 – 16, 19 – 20). This is also the case with David Miller's speculations about the scope of distributive justice in Aristotle (2003, p. 2).

mentally different political convictions and their four corresponding standards of merit. It is noteworthy that for Aristotle the true aristocrats are those who hold "virtue" (*arête*) to be the appropriate standard of merit and not the members of the unnamed fourth group who favor "noble birth." While the criteria "wealth," "virtue," and "noble birth" allow a gradation of "more" and "less," people are either free as citizens or – Aristotle's contrast to "freedom" (*eleutheria*) – they are slaves, foreigners or resident aliens.[13]

In Book III of the *Politics*, Aristotle takes up the issue of the political dispute regarding the appropriate standard of merit, giving reasons for his own position. He concedes that in the political quarrel over how political offices should be distributed, freedom, wealth, noble birth, and virtue can be regarded for some reasons as justified claims. But none of the claims of the four political convictions in question is "absolutely justified" (*Pol.* III 13, 1283a29–31). In the political dispute relating to the just distribution of offices and the appropriate standard of merit, all four political groups or parties can put forward valid arguments. The supporters of an oligarchic conception of distributive justice, who Aristotle equates with the rich, argue that they are "usually more reliable in matters of contract" and that they "have a larger share of the land," which is "to the benefit of the public" (*Pol.* III 9, 1280a25–31; *Pol.* III 13, 1283a31–33). Because of these merits, they hold an unequal share in the distribution of political power to be just and claim that an oligarchy, in which the offices are distributed in proportion to "wealth" (*plutos*), is the appropriate "political system" (*politeia*). Aristotle criticizes this position, stating that one cannot derive conclusively from the single particular inequality of wealth a general inequality that could justify an oligarchic political system. The argument of the supporters of oligarchy would be convincing if the end of the *polis* were wealth. But for Aristotle, this is not the true goal of a political community (*Pol.* III 9, 1280a22–31; *Pol.* V 1, 1301a31–36).

The adherents of a democratic conception of distributive justice argue that all male citizens are equal because they are all born as free men. Because of this, they hold it to be just if both the poor and the rich get an equal share in political power and claim that a democracy is the appropriate political system. Aristotle criticizes this position, stating that one cannot derive conclusively from the single particular equality of freedom a general equality that could justify a democratic political system (*Pol.* III 9, 1280a22–31; *Pol.* V 1, 1301a28–36). The argument of the democrats would be convincing if the true goal of the *polis* were freedom, but this an idea that Aristotle rejects.

---

[13] For more detailed interpretations of these four criteria or standards, see Keyt 1991, pp. 243–247, and Knoll 2016, pp. 70–73.

Contrary to supporters of both democratic and oligarchic conceptions of distributive justice, the members of the good families refer to their "noble birth" (*eugeneia*). They argue that they are citizens to a greater degree than those of low birth, that good birth is honored in every community, and that descendants of good parents are likely to be better than children of the low-born because noble birth is the virtue of the family. With these arguments, the better-born claim they are justified in getting a larger share of political power than the low-born (*Pol.* III 13, 1283a33–37).

The above given reconstruction of the arguments of the supporters of oligarchy, of the democrats, and of the well-born shows that each conception of distributive justice is linked with its corresponding political system. Each conception justifies the distribution of political power that characterizes its corresponding political system. Aristotle understands the different political systems – with the exception of tyranny – as embodiments of different conceptions of distributive justice.[14] In the *Politics*, he presents several arguments for his preference for the aristocratic conception that holds "political virtue" (*politikê aretê*) to be the appropriate measure of merit and the most justified claim for political power. Aristotle's main reason for this preference is that political virtue contributes substantially to reaching the good life or "human flourishing" (*eudaimonia*), the true goal of the *polis*. Because of the close link between the four conceptions of distributive justice and their respective political systems, in regard to his political convictions, Aristotle has to be classified as a supporter of aristocracy.[15] For Aristotle, the best political system is a true aristocracy in which the morally and intellectually best men rule.[16]

---

[14] Cf. Keyt 1991, p. 238; Miller 1995, p. 79; Mulgan 1991, p. 310.

[15] For reconstructions of Aristotle's arguments for the conception of distributive justice he favors, see Keyt 1991, pp. 247–259, and Knoll 2016, pp. 73–86; cf. Miller 1995, p. 127. David Keyt distinguishes between an aristocratic and an Aristotelian conception of distributive justice. The latter has a standard of merit that includes not only virtue but wealth and freedom (Keyt 1991, pp. 247, 259). To be sure, the Aristotelian standard of merit embraces wealth and freedom, but this is true for the aristocratic standard as well. As a consequence, there is no need to introduce an additional Aristotelian standard or conception of distributive justice. Keyt's interpretation leads to an inconsistency within the analysis of his paper. Keyt claims correctly that Aristotle's best *polis* is a "true aristocracy," which "embodies the Aristotelian conception of distributive justice" (Keyt 1991, p. 260). As each political system embodies its corresponding conception, it is only sound to understand the conception contained in aristocracy as an aristocratic conception of distributive justice.

[16] Cf. Bates 2003, p. 97; Chuska 2000, p. 322f.; Keyt 1991, pp. 260–270; Knoll 2016, pp. 87–94; Miller 1995, p. 192. For a critique of a different line of interpretation that understands Aristotle's best political system as a mixed government, which he calls "polity" (*politeia*), and the literature on this issue, see Knoll 2016, pp. 60, 87–94.

Rawls claims that his approach to distributive justice does "tally with tradition" and in particular with Aristotle's account of justice (1971, § 2, p. 10). Contrary to this claim, he devotes an entire section of *A Theory of Justice* to explain why justice as fairness rejects "the notion of distribution according to virtue" and the view that "moral desert" or "moral worth" should play a role in determining distributive shares (1971, § 48, pp. 310–315). In the section, he pronounces "certainly to the extent that the *precept of need* is emphasized, moral worth is ignored" (1971, § 48, p. 312; our italics). A distribution of goods and benefits according to need is the central principle of the welfare state.[17] Rawls is aware of that. In his chapter on the "Background Institutions for Distributive Justice," he declares that "the government guarantees a social minimum" to citizens for which the "transfer branch" is responsible (1971, § 43, pp. 274–276). This branch or institution "guarantees a certain level of well-being and honors the *claims of need*" (1971, § 43, p. 276 f.; our italics).[18] In order to do this, the welfare state requires considerable revenues and thus a redistribution of income and wealth. This should be done by the "distribution branch" that is responsible for acquiring these revenues through taxation (1971, § 43, p. 277 f.). For Robert Nozick, one of the most important critics of Rawls' theory, redistributions and proportional taxes on expenses and income in order to finance the welfare state are unjust: "Taxation of earning from labor is on a par with forced labor. Some persons find this claim obviously true: taking the earnings of *n* hours labor is like taking *n* hours from the person; it is like forcing the person to work *n* hours for another's purpose" (1974, p. 179).[19]

For Aristotle, the appropriate measure of merit is political virtue. On the contrary, Rawls rejects merit as a standard of distributive justice: "The criterion to each according to his virtue would not, then, be chosen in the original position" (1971, § 48, p. 313, cf. p. 310). Of course, for Rawls this criterion does not mainly refer to the distribution of political power but more generally to the distribution of primary goods like income and wealth. While Rawls rejects a distribution of income according to merit or to natural talents and skills, in the "case of

---

17 Cf. Miller 2003, p. 225 f.; Walzer 1984, pp. 64–94.
18 For Rawls, "the precept of need is left to the transfer branch" (1971, § 47, p. 309).
19 In *Anarchy, State, and Utopia*, Nozick advocates an entitlement theory of justice. This theory is a clear antithesis to Rawls' conception of justice: "From the point of view of an entitlement theory, redistribution is a serious matter indeed, involving, as it does, the violation of people's rights" (1974, p. 168; cf. Barry 1995, p. 173 f.). Steinvorth, in this volume, develops and defends the thesis that we can rationally arbitrate between Rawls' and Nozick's conceptions of justice.

wages" he accepts kindred "common sense precepts of justice" like the "precepts to each according to his effort and to each according to his contribution" in order to increase economic wealth (1971, § 47, p. 304 f.). However, in a just society these precepts have to be adjusted by the overriding *precept of need*. Just as Rawls assigns priority to his first principle of justice, which calls for an equal distribution of rights and liberties, the *precept of need* has priority over the above-mentioned "common sense precepts of justice." Therefore, it is not surprising that Rawls cautiously expresses his support for Marx's precept "from each according to his ability, to each according to his needs" (1971, § 47, p. 305; cf. Marx 2009, p. 11).[20] For Aristotle, a distribution according to need, in particular when it is not linked to the contributions to the *polis*, would seem unjust.

Aristotle's political theory of merit and Rawls' defense of the welfare state are not only opposed in their respective distributive principles but in their underlying images of humanity. According to Rawls' moral and normative conception of the person, all persons are equal as *moral persons*.[21] His conception of the person is a central feature of his theory because he claims that "the capacity for moral personality is a sufficient condition for being entitled to equal justice" (Rawls 1971, § 77, p. 505). This is the main reason why Rawls' theory of distributive justice starts out from strict egalitarianism.[22] The belief in human equality,

---

[20] Rawls declares, with caution, that this "precept is cited by Marx in his *Critique of the Gotha Program*" (1971, § 47, fn. 33, p. 305). However, Marx declares that this precept is for a "higher phase of communist society" (Marx 2009, p. 11). In regard to Marx's precept, Rawls pronounces, "It is even possible to elevate one of these precepts, or some combination of them, to the level of a first principle, as when it is said: from each according to his ability, to each according to his needs" (1971, § 47, p. 305). However, later in the section, he stresses the "subordinate place of common sense norms" and declares "None of these precepts can be plausibly raised to a first principle" (1971, § 47, p. 307). For an interpretation of Marx's precept and its role for Rawls' theory of justice, see Knoll in this volume pp. 33–39.

[21] Moral persons "are distinguished by two features: first they are capable of having (and are assumed to have) a conception of their good (as expressed by a rational plan of life); and second they are capable of having (and are assumed to acquire) a sense of justice, a normally effective desire to apply and to act upon the principles of justice, at least to a minimum degree" (Rawls 1971, § 77, p. 505).

[22] Rawls' two principles of justice are derived from "a more general conception of justice that can be expressed as follows. All social values – liberty and opportunity, income and wealth, and the bases of self-respect – are to be distributed equally unless an unequal distribution of any, or all, of these values is to everyone's advantage" (1971, § 11, p. 62). Rawls' general conception expresses a *"presumption* in favour of equality." It is a "substantive egalitarian principle of justice which assumes that all departures from equality have to be morally justified" (Barry 1995, p. 153).

which goes back to the Sophists, Stoics, Christianity, and Kant, is a central basis of contemporary egalitarianism. In a publication that is intended to contribute to the fight for equality, the members of the *Equality Studies Centre at University College Dublin* pronounce, "Basic equality is the cornerstone of all egalitarian thinking: the idea that at some very basic level all human beings have equal worth and importance, and are therefore equally worthy of concern and respect" (Baker/Lynch/Cantillon/Walsh 2009, p. 23).[23] On the contrary, for Aristotle, persons have extremely different moral worth corresponding to the degree in which they have developed their ethical virtues and their "prudence" (*phronêsis*) or in which they have perfected their character and their practical reason.[24] These differences in moral worth or merit are the crucial differences that determine the appropriate shares in political distributions. Similar to Aristotle, for John Kekes, a contemporary critic of egalitarianism, virtuous and vicious or good and evil persons have different human worth.[25]

Despite their contrasts, Aristotle's and Rawls' approaches to distributive justice each suffer from a similar shortcoming. Both refer only to the distribution of a very limited amount of goods. Aristotle primarily focuses on political offices or political power and the recognition that citizens can gain through exercising them. Rawls is just concerned with the primary goods liberty, rights, income, wealth, opportunities, and self-respect. However, a society distributes more goods than those mentioned above, and likewise there are more distributive principles than those referred to by Aristotle and Rawls. A more pluralistic approach to distributive justice has been presented in 1983 by Michael Walzer in *Spheres of Justice*. Like Rawls, Walzer calls for a strong welfare state (1983, pp. 90, 318). Walzer argues convincingly that "the first and most important distributive question" is how a political community distributes membership (1983, p. 31).[26] The importance of this social good becomes apparent if one considers the fate of stateless persons and refugees. It also becomes evident in regard to

---

23 For the cardinal role of respect and self-respect for Rawls' and Walzer's theories of justice, see Knoll 2017.
24 As for Aristotle, for Plato, all persons have extremely different human worth. For Plato, persons can be as different as reason, the highest part of the soul, and the appetites, the lowest part of the soul.
25 Kekes 1997, p. 120. In his book *Facing Evil*, Kekes tackles evil not as a metaphysical or religious problem but as a worldly one. In the book, he defines "*evil as undeserved harm*" (1990, p. 4). For him, persons are unequal in a moral sense: "To avoid misunderstanding, let me emphasize that the merit to which I believe human worth is proportional is moral, not merit based on birth, talents, membership in some social group, or inheritances" (1990, p. 122).
26 For the distributive principle that Walzer holds to be appropriate for the allocation of membership, see Snyder 2014.

the fact that citizens enjoy several other social goods like security and welfare. Similar to Rawls, for Walzer, welfare should be distributed "to each according to his socially recognized needs" (1983, p. 91; cf. p. 25). In his chapter "Office," Walzer pronounces that offices[27] should be allotted to qualified applicants and introduces a subtle distinction between qualification and desert (1983, pp. 135–139). Desert is the "crucial standard for public honor" and such honors, like the Nobel Prize, should go to the persons who deserve them (1983, p. 259; cf. Miller 2003, pp. 131–155). Another important social good is education. Walzer distinguishes between basic and higher education. The former should be "distributed equally to every child" according to the distributive principle "need" because "all future citizens need an education" (1983, pp. 206, 203). For higher education, on the contrary, students have to qualify "by some display of interest and capacity" (1983, pp. 209, 203). In his chapter "Political Power," Walzer argues that in democracies all citizens should have equal voting rights and the right for active political participation. Greater political power, however, should be distributed only to those citizens who make "the most persuasive argument" (1983, pp. 309, 304). These are just some examples for Walzer's pluralistic approach to distributive justice that is able to recognize and combine distributions according to both arithmetic and proportional equality and according to both distributive principles "merit" and "need."[28]

In *Anarchy, State, and Utopia*, Robert Nozick writes, "Political philosophers now must either work within Rawls' theory or explain why not… It is impossible to read Rawls' book without incorporating much, perhaps transmuted, into one's own deepened view" (1974, p. 183). True, the general trend of the essays collected in this volume is to acknowledge a debt to Rawls, but many will follow Nozick's second option, which is to explain why they do not work within Rawls' theoretical framework. The point of departure, for the first set of essays concerning deep disagreements, is the problem of whether there can be a consensus on philosophical notions of justice. The essays immediately following are critical of the centrality allotted to a normative concept of distributive justice in ancient and contemporary theories of justice. The next group of writers seeks to improve the Rawlsian concept of consensus, exploring how the problem of political con-

---

[27] Walzer defines an office "as any position in which the political community as a whole takes an interest, choosing the person who holds it or regulating the procedures by which he is chosen" (1983, p. 129). In his chapter "Office," Walzer's primary argument does not concern political offices but certain jobs that require special qualifications. Political offices and positions are chiefly discussed in the chapter "Political Power."

[28] For Walzer's approach to distributive justice, see section 3 of Haus in this volume.

sensus is reached in the face of deep and actual differences in political aims. The remaining essays focus on ways that distributive justice applies to environmental, international, and intergenerational obligations, articulate new perspectives on what distributive justice actually means, attempt to reform or criticize Rawls' difference principle, and assess distributive justice from the economic perspective of Adam Smith.

The essays concerning deep disagreements revolve around the question of whether consensus on social and political conceptions of justice can be reached. *Manuel Knoll* denies this possibility. He argues for a new research perspective on social and political justice and suggests focusing on the analysis of the causes of deep disagreements on justice. Theoreticians, such as Rawls, aim at a consensus on justice that is impossible to achieve. In fact, the root of practical-political conflict often lies in unbridgeable conceptions of justice. Knoll substantiates his claims by examining a number of ancient, modern, and contemporary concepts of justice, showing how they are irreconcilable. Based on this, he concludes that the causes behind deep disagreements would be a better topic of study than consensus, sketching several such causes. Finally, Knoll focuses on the meta-ethical relevance of his results and rejects moral realism and cognitivism based on the *argument from deep disagreements on justice*. Ulrich Steinvorth and Michael Haus argue that irreconcilable accounts of justice and equality can be resolved by looking at the underlying goods they seek to distribute. *Steinvorth* sees disagreement stemming from incompatible goods, while Haus holds that the problem stems from the criteria of distribution. Steinvorth begins by citing Berlin's statement that "ends equally ultimate, equally sacred" can nonetheless be irreconcilable, and he strives to find reconciliation in goods that are irreducibly social. Steinvorth sees an incompatibility of aims in Nozick and Rawls, who pursue justice in different sets of goods, which makes agreement on its terms impossible. Steinvorth defines irreducibly social goods as those which acknowledge the co-dependent nature of our species, focusing on social recognition. Recognizing a set of common social goods shows a way to mediate between Rawls and Nozick, and Steinvorth spells out what the upshot might be for political philosophy. For *Haus*, questions regarding management of disagreements among those assumed equal and autonomous and handling of reasonable views outside of the egalitarian perspective show an underlying contradiction in egalitarian thought, which, nonetheless, is a driving force in Western political thought. Still, Haus defends the ideal of equality, seeking a resolution in line with Michael Walzer's "complex equality," an analysis of how distribution of goods is based on criteria specific to each sphere. Deep conceptual disagreements are held in check by the "shared understandings" and "social meanings" implicit in principles of membership, and by reducing domination, problems at the core of liberal egalitarianism can be overcome.

Giovanni Giorgini is also critical of conceptions of justice too closely tied to accounts of subjective capacities (such as Rawls') that in the end are rooted in comprehensive worldviews. To avoid disagreement over the myriad forms of the good life, following Hampshire, Giorgini argues that a procedural account of justice is needed. The notion of distributive justice would stand above the fray, acting as an umpire. Procedure is the only reasonable way to resolve disputes involving a plurality of worldviews. Along similar lines, *Bertjan Wolthuis* contends that Rawls' account of public reason is underwritten by a moralistic notion of distributive justice fundamentally incompatible with the agonistic climate of the actual political deal-making process. Seeking an adequate notion of public reason, he examines Habermas' notion of public opinion and Aristotle's account of "*endoxa*," or reputable things. In the end, Wolthuis finds that Aristotle's concept of *endoxa* provides realists with a more viable alternative to Rawls' and Habermas' accounts of public reason because it is neither tied to the shared convictions of welfare liberalism nor settled on before the argumentation begins. It is standard of what is reasonable that can be formed in the process of the negotiation. *Manuel Knoll* and *Nurdane Şimşek* make the point that Rawls' "consensus approach" to political justice is circular. This is the case both for his contractarian and coherence methods. In the end, Rawls' pretense of consensus becomes a distraction; the answer to the problem of consensus is found instead in the causes of our disagreements.

The next section's essays question the critical centrality of the concept of justice in philosophical debates and even in our social organization. Francisco Lisi and Eckart Schütrumpf criticize the normative notion of justice attributed to the ancients by contemporary theorists. The common contention, *Lisi* argues, that Aristotle's philosophy entails a notion of natural law, is an error. Contrary to Plato, for Aristotle, justice is a strictly human venture. Rather than referring to the divine, Aristotle strives to differentiate the realm of the divine from the realm of the human. Aristotle's political writings connect the right kind of constitution with the right kind of people. Lisi finds no inherent cosmic function in this idea of justice. The job of the legislator is not to discern a natural rule but to ensure that the legislation fits with the natural dispositions of those who are legislated. According to *Schütrumpf*, a normatively grounded account of distributive justice cannot be derived from Aristotle's *Politics*. Most writings on Aristotle's *Politics* do not properly distinguish "justice" (*dikaiosunē*) and "what is just" (*to dikaion*); the normative concept of justice, as an overarching virtue employed in the *polis*, is actually derived from Aristotle's discussion of doing what is just or right in reciprocity or distribution. "What is just" in the latter sense does not imply any justice in the person and does not amount to a normative account of justice akin to a virtue. To synthesize a general principle of normative justice from its sparse mention in the *Nicomachean Ethics* and the *Politics* results in an abstraction that does not adequately explain the details of the application of "what is just"; seeking an account of distributive justice in Aristotle's writings is "much ado about nothing." *Christoph Horn* takes aim at the "primacy thesis": contemporary theories viewing justice as the defining normative component of ethical and political philosophy. This false view originates in the writings of Mill and Rawls, both who take justice to be the most significant factor of their normative theories. Horn uses several examples and semantic arguments to show that justice does not penetrate the core of morality. Generally, justice refers to lawfulness and fairness, often not intersecting with moral violations such as murder and torture in cases where the law condones them, and in honor and fairness among thieves, what is "just" is not linked to their immoral actions. Like Horn, *Chandran Kukathas* argues that justice is an oversold, overburdened, theoretical, and normative commodity. The result of the incursion of the academy's expansive notion of justice into our everyday world is "Justicitis." Covering too many aspects of our lives, justice's conceptual proliferation does little to improve day-to-day life. The problem, a la Rawls, is that given the pride of place justice has among the virtues and in "moral and political reflection," even the slightest injustice is not tolerated. Kukathas proposes a Humean alternative that does not view justice as society's foundation; rather, it emerges "spontaneously" out of a stable social condition when parties come together without explicit agreement. Justice, seen as such, would not place normative obligations above stability and more vital needs.

The essays that follow explore the problem of consensus in terms of alternatives to Rawls. Each writer is looking for a better explanation for how, in light of our deep disagreements, we nonetheless are able to reach some form of political consensus. *Alberto Siani* takes issue with Rawls' attempt to philosophically ground a universal principle of justice on unanimous rational agreement. He pursues instead a "dissident" view that does not emphasize overlapping consensus, instead stressing political liberalism's reliance on "overlapping disagreement," which can never be resolved by philosophical means. This, Siani argues, is because philosophical reconciliation is not grounded in a theory of rationality; rather, it brings to light the aspects of opposing but potentially legitimate views that can be forged into an overlapping consensus. Here is where Siani sees the legitimacy of political liberalism, and perhaps also a principle of justice.

Chong-Ming Lim, Ulrike Spohn, and *Manon Westphal* consider consensus as a form of *modus vivendi. Lim* examines overlapping consensus in order to show that political compromises are at its root. He assesses the appeal to public reason from the perspectives of citizens' plural comprehensive views. In using public reason, citizens may have to engage in different sorts of compromise, and situating such compromises in the broader context of citizens' relationship with each other, Lim argues that public reason liberalism may not offer a necessary standard for evaluating the legitimacy of political decisions. *Spohn* examines Charles Taylor's and John Gray's critiques of Rawls' overlapping consensus, investigating solutions to problems of value pluralism in terms of dialogical and agonistic variants of *modus vivendi*. Underneath Rawls' account of overlapping consensus, Taylor recognizes a broad-based "dissensus" that must be reconciled; members of democratic societies must engage in dialogue and compromise. Gray sees in Rawls' freestanding justification for overlapping consensus the privileging of a single comprehensive view that might not reflect liberal values. For Spohn, while both accounts are flawed, they show how nuanced notions of *modus vivendi* might resolve conflict in the face of deep disagreement. *Westphal* presents Chantal Mouffe's "conflictual consensus" as an alternative to Rawls' overlapping consensus. The public reasons that should unite in reality tend to be a force of division. It is the deep disagreements at the core of democratic societies, Mouffe argues, that actually bring about political "consensus"; consensus on the meaning of normative principles is never reached. Such a unity is illusory, held together through a negative delineation forming identities around what various parties collectively oppose. Westphal concedes that using Mouffe's model, no consensus could be reached, but a compromise would be available if a mechanism like hers, sensitive to asymmetries of power, could be put in place.

Michal Rupniewski and Peter Caven look to alternatives to the Rawlsian consensus that address the burdens of judgment. *Rupniewski* relocates Rawls' notion of justice to the pragmatic realm of a citizen's commitment to the rule of law. What he calls "the rule of law consensus" integrates the strength of our commitments, and the burdens of judgment, better than overlapping consensus: through the criteria of membership, from the perspective of "the rule of law consensus," agreements are still subject to the burdens of judgment. In this sense, justice is subjected to a hermeneutical process, situated not as a regulative ideal but practically grounded in the desire to remain within the collective. This stops short of *modus vivendi*, insofar as one's self-understanding is wrapped up in the actual commitment to rule of law within the political unit. *Caven* holds that Rawls has inadequately grounded the burdens of judgment. This could reduce overlapping consensus to little more than a *modus vivendi*. Agreements, for Rawls, can be reached despite parties not sharing underlying moral principles. The inappropriateness of using exclusive worldviews when trying to reach agreements leads us to accept the burdens of judgment. But, per Caven, Rawls' burdens of judgment do not provide internal reasons for accepting reasonable pluralism; people would agree for the wrong reasons. Looking to moral psychology shows how affect-based dispositions are at the root of much moral disagreement. For Caven, this vindicates the burdens of judgment and strengthens the case for political liberalism.

The topic of obligations moves the volume's essays away from deep disagreement and consensus, expanding the discussion of distribution to a new level by examining issues of international, intergenerational, and climate justice. *Angela Kallhoff* discusses how the increasingly scarce resources of the environment should be handled globally in terms of a distributive paradigm. For Kallhoff, though Rawls' theory of justice is not explicitly equipped to address environmental justice, his notion of distributive justice is relevant to its central concerns. Applying Rawls' theory to environmental justice encounters problems in his conception of the "objective circumstances of justice," the "distributive paradigm," and "value pluralism." Still, for Kallhoff, Rawls' theory of justice can be beneficial for environmental justice by showing how individual perspectives can be superseded for higher principles of fairness and by providing theories of environmental justice with background assumptions used to establish reasonable goals, moral responsibility, and a prioritization mechanism. Annette Förster and Bill Wringe write on how international duties of distribution might be grounded. *Förster* examines the replacement of the difference principle with the duty of assistance in Rawls' *The Law of Peoples*, which is a further elaboration of Rawls' domestic theory to the international realm. Rawls does not feel that the bonds of membership that bind citizens to the difference principle would hold in international relations. He argues, nonetheless, that the duty of assistance to others would hold. Förster defends Rawls' substitution, but with Pogge, agrees that without an account of a history of nations, Rawls' theory lacks the demand of co-responsibility, and the principle of assistance would need to be updated to reflect this if it were to adequately substitute the difference principle. *Wringe* analyzes the plausibility of the concept of collective obligations and how they might be fulfilled by individual members of collectives through their support of institutions having the potential to redress collective needs. The basic right of sustenance clarifies how individual and collective obligations can be connected, showing that unstructured collectives – such as everyone alive – can fulfill a global collective obligation. The right to sustenance could be coherently asserted if collective global obligation were recognized as the "obligation-bearer of last resort." This would form the basis for a transcendental argument supporting the idea of global obligation falling on an unstructured body such as the "global collective." *Stephen Snyder* considers intergenerational justice, not in terms of distribution of scarce goods to future generations, but in light of what electively changing the genome might do to the self-identification of future members. Using Habermas' argument that changing the human genome could undermine the moral basis of the species, Snyder examines how a contractualist theory of intergenerational justice should, or could, take into account 1) species-obligations and 2) the necessary presupposition of species-obligation persisting into the future.

In the next set of essays, the writers provide diverse perspectives on problems related to distributive justice. *Kok-Chor Tan* examines the structure of liberal toleration. Toleration is a normative stance entailing an evaluative dualism. Agents first perceive states of affairs they do not approve of; in toleration the action of another is accepted within the relational context, despite normatively rejecting it. Without basic disapproval of a given state of affairs, there is nothing to tolerate. Tolerance is distributive insofar as different levels of moral critique are applied to others depending on their relation to us – immediate family, friend, colleague, or simply fellow citizen. What is acceptable for a fellow citizen might be absolutely unacceptable for immediate family. Thus, for Tan, our notion of justice is underwritten by a consensus on the rules of interaction we will tolerate. *Chad Van Schoelandt* and *Gerald Gaus* propose a functionalist reading of Rawls' theory of distributive justice, which they hold is warranted insofar as people employ notions of justice to achieve some practical aim. But for this, metrics that more accurately measure distributive results are needed, like monetary gain. Agreeing with moral philosophers who find this metric lacking, the flexible usage of the metric of monetary gain is appropriate for functionalism. Other metrics provide more informational completeness but are functionally unusable due to problems with measurement. The final aim of their investigation of the cooperative structure of Rawls' political consensus provides the framework for an ongoing "progressive research agenda." *Elena Irrera* makes the case for an account of political justice that moves beyond the distribution of income, wealth, and social position. The principle of respect is an essential component of a system of justice, and it must be better integrated into institutional systems of distribution if the injustices of the dominant culture are to be addressed. Irrera does not disagree with accounts that advocate for better distribution of the more easily measurable metrics of money and power, but argues that the alternative index of respect is needed in order that it can become its own distributive object. Irrera's aims are to better articulate what this object is and to suggest how it might be implemented. *Maria Dimitrova* is critical of the notion of impartiality embedded within Rawls' notion of justice. Rawls, per Dimitrova, views society as a system of independent social-cooperation and wants to show that his account of justice is able to "legitimate" the modern political constitutional government. But the universal and impartial stance taken within Rawls' "original position" does not take responsibility and obligation to others into account because justice is understood to be an autonomous achievement. It presents a universal rule, obliging one to a command, and not a responsibility to the other. This, Dimitrova concludes, undermines his theory of justice because it is the responsibility of the institution to the other that makes its normative value concrete. *Tom Bailey* examines "postsecular modesty" in the writings of Habermas and Rawls. This becomes apparent as their writings shifted away from their earlier, more stringent, secular stances that excluded religious arguments from the public sphere. In later writings, Rawls and Habermas acknowledge room for religion in the public sphere and public sphere discourse, but the political framework undergirding liberal democracies must remain secular. Despite this, Bailey argues that their later "postsecular" writings imply that their frameworks for achieving political justification and the grounds on which they are based – deliberative rationality for Habermas and mutual respect for Rawls – have no ultimate authority over religious or other alternatives.

Rawls' difference principle is the topic of the subsequent section, defended by Peter Koller and critiqued by Aysel Demir. *Koller* finds that Rawls' arguments, as presented over the years, are not adequate to support the claims of the difference principle. Nonetheless, it presents a cogent principle of socio-economic justice, and Koller makes the case for a modified version. The revised difference principle can justify unavoidable social inequalities if the social-economic system is organized in the following way: the benefits of inequality to the less well-off must be weighted higher than those of the more well-off, such that the inequalities do not exceed what is needed in maintaining the balance in favor of the less well-off. This version of the difference principle would stand on firmer ground while not losing any of its power as an original and valuable conception of social justice. *Demir* presents a Marxist critique of Rawls' difference principle, arguing that it exacerbates exploitive inequalities already embedded in the capitalist framework. Demir focuses on Marx's principle "from each according to his ability, to each according to his needs," contrasting it with Rawls' difference principle, stating that anyone who profits from social inequality may do so only if it also benefits the worse off. The basic contrast is that Rawls aims at equal treatment, and the Marxists at equalization. These approaches to distribution, for Demir, are not just irreconcilable: the Rawlsian principle further propagates the injustice of the capitalist system by institutionalizing inequality and deepening class conflict.

The final two essays focus on distribution from the economic perspective of Adam Smith. *Jeffrey Young* challenges the commonly held notion that Smith's body of work does not address normative issues of distributive justice. Young addresses what he perceives to be Rawls' view that Smith's utilitarian-leaning economic theory does not speak to the well-being of the people. While Rawls' theory of justice is clearly a theory of distributive justice, it is less clear that this would be the case for Smith, who distinguishes commutative from distributive justice and counts only the former under his theory of justice. Nonetheless, Young argues that normative comments on the well-being of the majority, found throughout Smith's writings, constitute a secondary theme that speaks strongly to matters of distributive justice. *Barry Stocker* seeks to displace contemporary "progressive" attempts to bring Smith into the fold of thinkers supporting a form of state intervention favoring the welfare of its poorest members through distributive justice. The misconceptions of contemporary thinkers come from what some see as the contradictory claims of Smith's moral and legal writings and his theory of state. These equivocations imply that Smith's moral support of the poorest element at a meta-level underwrites a sort of state-led redistribution of wealth because Smith does claim that the happiness of the majority of the people is the highest indicator of a state's flourishing. Stocker argues that despite the validity of pointing to Smith's support of those at the lowest economic level, it never amounts to redistribution of wealth, especially to the poorest.

Bibliography

Baker, John/Lynch, Kathleen/Cantillon, Sara/Walsh, Judy (2009): *Equality. From Theory to Action*. Second edition. Houndmills: Palgrave Macmillan.

Barry, Norman P. (1995): *An Introduction to Modern Political Theory*. Third revised and expanded edition. Houndsmills: Macmillan (first edition 1981).

Bates, Clifford Angell, Jr. (2003): *Aristotle's "Best Regime". Kingship, Democracy, and the Rule of Law*. Baton Rouge: LSU Press.

Chuska, Jeff (2000): *Aristotle's Best Regime. A Reading of Aristotle's "Politics" VII. 1–10*. Lanham, Cumnor Hill: University Press of America.

Fleischacker, Samuel (2004): *A Short History of Distributive Justice*. Cambridge, MA: Harvard University Press.

Hayek, Friedrich A. v. (1990): "The Atavism of Social Justice". In: Hayek, Friedrich A. v.: *New Studies in Philosophy, Politics, Economics and the History of Ideas*. London: Routledge (first published 1978), pp. 57–68.

Hayek, Friedrich A. v. (2013): *Law, Legislation and Liberty. A New Statement of the Liberal Principles of Justice and Political Economy*. With a new foreword by Paul Kelly. London, New York: Routledge (first published 1976).

Kekes, John (1990): *Facing Evil*. Princeton: Princeton University Press.

Kekes, John (1997): *Against Liberalism*. Ithaca, London: Cornell University Press.

Kersting, Wolfgang (2000): *Theorien der sozialen Gerechtigkeit*. Stuttgart: Metzler.

Keyt, David (1991): "Aristotle's Theory of Distributive Justice". In: Keyt, David/Miller, Fred D. Jr. (Eds.): *A Companion to Aristotle's "Politics"*. Cambridge, Oxford: Blackwell, pp. 238–278.
Knoll, Manuel (2010): "Die distributive Gerechtigkeit bei Platon und Aristoteles". In: *Zeitschrift für Politik* (ZfP) 1, pp. 3–30.
Knoll, Manuel (2011): "Die *Politik* des Aristoteles – Aufsatzsammlung oder einheitliches Werk? Replik auf Eckart Schütrumpfs Erwiderung". In: *Zeitschrift für Politik* (ZfP) 4, pp. 410–423.
Knoll, Manuel (2013): "An Interpretation of Rawls's Difference Principle as the Principle of the Welfare State". In: *Sofia Philosophical Review* 7. No. 2, pp. 5–33.
Knoll, Manuel (2014): "How Aristotelian is Martha Nussbaum's 'Aristotelian Social Democracy'?" In: *Rivista di Filosofia* 2, pp. 207–222.
Knoll, Manuel (2016): "The Meaning of Distributive Justice for Aristotle's Theory of Constitutions". In: *ΠΗΓΗ/FONS. Revista electrónica de estudios sobre la civilizatión clásica y su recepción* (OJS, www.uc3 m.es/pege). Vol. 1, pp. 57–97.
Knoll, Manuel (2017): "The Cardinal Role of Respect and Self-Respect for Rawls's and Walzer's Theories of Justice". In: Giorgini, Giovanni/Irrera, Elena (Eds.): *The Roots of Respect. A Historic-Philosophical Itinerary*. Berlin, Boston: De Gruyter, pp. 207–227.
Marx, Karl (2009): *Critique of the Gotha Programme*. London: Dodo Press.
Miller, David (2003): *Principles of Social Justice*. Third printing, Cambridge, MA: Harvard University Press (first published 1999).
Miller, Fred D. Jr. (1995): *Nature, Justice, and Rights in Aristotle's "Politics"*. Oxford: Clarendon Press.
Mulgan, Richard (1991): "Aristotle's Analysis of Oligarchy and Democracy". In: Keyt, David/Miller, Fred D. Jr. (Eds.): *A Companion to Aristotle's "Politics"*. Cambridge, Oxford: Blackwell, pp. 307–322.
Mulgan, Richard (2000): "Was Aristotle an 'Aristotelian Social Democrat'?" In: *Ethics* 111. No. 1, pp. 79–101.
Nozick, Robert (1974): *Anarchy, State, and Utopia*. New York, Oxford: Basic Books/Basil Blackwell.
Nussbaum, Martha (1990): "Aristotelian Social Democracy". In: Douglass, R. Bruce/Mara, Gerald M./Richardson, Henry S. (Eds.): *Liberalism and the Good*. New York, London: Routledge, pp. 203–252.
Rawls, John (1967): "Distributive Justice". In: Laslett, Peter/Runciman, W.G. (Eds.): *Philosophy, Politics, and Society*. Oxford: Blackwell, pp. 58–82.
Rawls, John (1971): *A Theory of Justice*. Cambridge, MA: Belknap Press of Harvard University Press.
Rawls, John (1999): *A Theory of Justice*. Revised edition. Cambridge, MA: Belknap Press of Harvard University Press.
Rawls, John (2001): *Justice as Fairness. A Restatement*. Kelly, Erin (Ed.). Cambridge, MA, London: Belknap Press of Harvard University Press.
Rawls, John (2005): *Political Liberalism*. Expanded edition. New York: Columbia University Press.
Sandel, Michael J. (1982): *Liberalism and the Limits of Justice*. Cambridge: Cambridge University Press.

Sandel, Michael J. (1984): "The Procedural Republic and the Unencumbered Self". In: *Political Theory* 12. No. 1, pp. 81–96.

Snyder, Stephen (2014): "Mitgliedschaft als soziales Gut und Rahmenbedingung für gerechte Verteilungen". In: Knoll, Manuel/Spieker, Michael (Eds.): *Michael Walzer: Sphären der Gerechtigkeit. Ein kooperativer Kommentar.* Preface by M. Walzer. Staatsverständnisse 29. Stuttgart: Steiner, pp. 73–91.

Walzer, Michael (1983): *Spheres of Justice. A Defense of Pluralism and Equality.* New York: Basic Books.

Wolff, Jonathan (1991): *Robert Nozick. Property, Justice and the Minimal State.* Cambridge, Oxford: Polity Press/Basil Blackwell.

Part I: Deep Disagreements

Manuel Knoll
Deep Disagreements on Social and Political Justice: Their Meta-Ethical Relevance and the Need for a New Research Perspective*

Abstract: This article starts off with a historical section showing that deep disagreements among notions of social and political justice are a characteristic feature of the history of political thought. Since no agreement or consensus on distributive justice is possible, the article argues that political philosophers should – instead of continuously proposing new normative theories of justice – focus on analyzing the reasons, significance, and consequences of such kinds of disagreements. The next two sections are analytical. The first sketches five possible reasons for deep disagreements among notions of social and political justice. The second discusses the meta-ethical relevance of the lack of consensus on justice and rejects ethical realism and cognitivism based on *the argument from deep disagreements*.

1 The need for a new research perspective on social and political justice

Following Neo-Kantians like Jürgen Habermas and in particular John Rawls, leading contemporary political philosophers aim at some form of consensus or rational agreement on justice.[1] Rawls conceives of this as a consensus concern-

---

* For their astute and helpful comments on this article I thank Thomas Schramme, Stephen Snyder, Andreas Urs Sommer, and Bertjan Wolthuis.
1 Nussbaum understands her capabilities approach as "a partial theory of social justice" that "aspires to be the object of an Overlapping Consensus" (2011, pp. 40, 93, cf. pp. 79, 91). In line with Ronald Dworkin, Will Kymlicka even claims that all contemporary theories of justice agree on "equality as a value" (2002, p. 4; cf. Haus in this volume). In several of his writings, Jürgen Habermas holds that unimpeded discourses and arguments based on communicative reason are generally able to solve disagreements and lead to consensus in moral issues (1991; cf. Wolthuis in this volume). Like discourse, consensus is a central value of modern proponents of deliberative democracy who believe that deliberations ideally aim at rational agreement. In response to this, Jeremy Waldron states "that in the real world, even after deliberation, people will continue to disagree in good faith about the common good, and about the issues of policy, principle, justice, and right which we expect a legislature to deliberate upon" (1999, p. 93, cf. p. 91f.).

ing an "initial choice situation" for principles of justice, as a rational agreement on which principles to choose, or as an "overlapping consensus" that a pluralist society should reach with regard to a political conception of justice (1971, § 4, §§ 20ff.; pp. 18, 118ff.; 2005, IV §§ 1–8, pp. 133–172). For Rawls, citizens' consensus on principles of justice is an essential feature of a "well-ordered society" (1971, § 1, p. 4f.; 2005, I § 6, p. 35). However, the notion that a consensus on social and political justice could be achieved was questionable from the start. This was made evident by Robert Nozick's immediate and strong disagreement with Rawls's fundamental moral conviction that the inequalities of natural endowments are undeserved and call for social redress or compensation (Nozick 1974, pp. 168f., 225, 228). Likewise, no agreement can be reached about Rawls's claim that individuals are equal as moral persons (Rawls 1971, pp. 19, 505). Going back to Aristotle, John Kekes argued that people who habitually harm others have a lower moral worth than those who habitually do good (Kekes 1990, pp. 121–123). From this perspective, Rawls's rationalist creed that all persons can be convinced by the same arguments and must therefore reach a rational consensus on principles of justice becomes highly questionable (Rawls 1971, p. 139).

This article argues for the need of a shift of the research perspective on social and political justice. Its first aim is to show that no consensus on justice is possible. The article demonstrates that many convictions and conceptions concerning social and political justice are not only opposed to each other, but that there exist deep disagreements between them. Deep disagreements are disagreements that cannot be resolved through the use of reasons and arguments (cf. Fogelin 2005, pp. 8, 11).[2] As a consequence of deep disagreements on social and political justice, political philosophers should redirect their efforts. Instead of continuously proposing and defending new normative theories of justice, they ought rather research the reasons, significance, and consequences of such kinds of disagreements and find out how to cope with them. In order to progress, innovative political thought has to move beyond the idea of the consensus. This move is also necessary because many political conflicts are caused by or can be derived from disagreements on social and political justice that can – in the worst cases – lead to violent conflicts and even civil wars.[3]

---

[2] Fogelin's 1985 article sparked controversies on deep and peer disagreements. For a summary of the debates and literature on the epistemology of disagreement see Siegel 2013.

[3] The arguments of this article proceed mainly on the conceptual level. However, this level is closely linked to the level of "practical politics". Philosophical conceptions of social and political justice usually depart from "practical" social and political issues and attempt to think through such issues "theoretically" or defend a specific conception of justice. However, it is

Insights regarding deep disagreements on social and political justice can be found, as early as 1984, in Dagmar Herwig's systematic study on justice – her "Habilitationsschrift" – that received little attention (Herwig 1984). Herwig's study shows that two opposing models of justice – "equal treatment" (*Gleichbehandlung*) and "equalization" (*Egalisierung*) – can be traced throughout the history of political thought.[4] In *Justice and Interpretation* (1993), Gorgia Warnke questioned the "ideal of political consensus" from the perspective of the "hermeneutic or interpretative turn" in political philosophy and argued that there are "disagreements between equally well-justified interpretations" (Warnke 1993, p. VIIf.).[5] Also Stuart Hampshire's *Justice is Conflict* and Jeremy Waldron's *Law and Disagreement* depart from disagreements on justice and the divergent conceptions of justice prevailing in society (Hampshire 1999; Waldron 1999). Waldron laments that contemporary philosophers are contributing mainly to existing disagreements concerning justice, of which there are many, instead of pondering their significance: "it is rare to find a philosopher attempting to come to terms with disagreements about justice within the framework of his own political theory" (Waldron 1999, p. 1f.).

For Hampshire, all "modern societies are, to a greater or lesser degree, morally mixed, with rival conceptions of justice, conservative and radical, flaring into open conflict and needing arbitration" (Hampshire 1999, p. 38). These kinds of conflicts about "substantial justice" cannot be overcome but are not a defect. Harmony and consensus are, according to Hampshire, unrealistic goals. The best we can hope for are institutions and procedures that realize "procedural justice" and a fair "adjudication of conflicts" (Hampshire 1999, pp. 29, 45). Procedural justice is usually "imperfect and not ideal", leading to compromise and not to consensus (Hampshire 1999, pp. 39, 42–43). Hampshire requires from all "moral enemies" to follow the principle "that contrary views of what is just and fair are allowed equal hearing, equal access, in the city or state, and that

---

not only philosophers, but also "ordinary" citizens, who have a sense of justice and conceptions of social and political justice that motivate their political actions. Sometimes citizen's conceptions of justice are informed by philosophical theory and theorists usually hope to influence "practical politics".

4 For a critical account of Herwig's view see Steinvorth in this volume.

5 One of the political theorists with whom Warnke substantiates her supposition of a hermeneutic turn is Michael Walzer and his claim that all social goods should be distributed according to their "social meanings" or citizen's "common understanding" of these goods (Walzer 1983, pp. XIV, 8–12, 312f.). From Warnke's perspective, there is disagreement on justice because meanings of social goods must be understood or interpreted and there are many different and justifiable ways to do this.

no one conception of substantial justice in society is imposed by domination and by the threat of force" (Hampshire 1999, pp. 46, 29–46).[6]

In section 2 (2.1–2.3) this article lays out several of the insurmountable disagreements on just distributions and a just society. This section will demonstrate that from the ancient world to the present day two fundamentally opposed basic conceptions of social and political justice can be traced in Western political thought. In modern terminology, these two irreconcilable conceptions can be characterized as egalitarian and non-egalitarian notions of social and political justice. While champions of egalitarian justice negate the natural and social inequalities of people and hold that it is just to establish arithmetic, numeric or simple equality, non-egalitarians or proportionalists like Plato, Aristotle or Nietzsche conceive of a just distribution of goods as proportional to existing inequalities. For non-egalitarians or champions of proportional justice, it is just to allot equal shares only to equals, not to everyone. The historical sketches in section 2 allow for a more detailed comprehension of the various aspects of the irreconcilable pluralism and conflict within conceptions of justice. Based on this understanding, section 3 sketches five possible reasons for deep disagreements among notions of social and political justice. This is intended as a first and preliminary step towards a better understanding of deep disagreements on justice. Section 4 briefly discusses the meta-ethical relevance of these irreconcilable disagreements. The section argues that statements about a just distribution or a just society do not refer to objective moral facts like ethical realists hold and cannot claim objective moral truth like cognitivists assert. As a consequence of the irreconcilable pluralism and conflict within conceptions of justice, we have to adopt a form of ethical relativism or skepticism that could be called "ethico-political relativism" or "ethico-political skepticism".

---

6 For Hampshire's case for procedural justice see Giorgini in this volume.

2 From ancient to contemporary philosophy: The irreconcilable pluralism and conflict of conceptions of social and political justice

2.1 Egalitarian versus proportional justice in Plato and Aristotle

Plato's and Aristotle's writings contain valuable insights regarding opposing conceptions of distributive justice and the corresponding political systems that can be derived from them. The views of these ancient philosophers on political justice have played a vital role in shaping Western political thought. Their influence can still be traced in the irreconcilable conceptions of social and political justice found in contemporary philosophy. Going back to the Pythagoreans, in the *Gorgias* and the *Laws* Plato distinguishes between two concepts of equality. One kind of equality he calls equality of "measures, weights and numbers", the other one the "most genuine" and "best" equality (*Leg.* VI 757b; Plato 1997, p. 1433). Both forms of equality are inextricably linked to distributive justice, which Plato understands as political justice. Since Aristotle, the first form of equality is called "arithmetic" or "numeric" equality. In modern democracies this form of equality is realized and manifested in the principle "one citizen, one vote". Michael Walzer calls this form of equality "simple equality".[7] For Plato, legislators implement this form of equality when they "distribute equal awards by lot" (*Leg.* VI 757b; Plato 1997, p. 1433; cf. *Leg.* III 690c). This was the way in which most political offices were distributed in ancient democracies. As an aristocratic political thinker who defends the rule of the morally and intellectually best men, Plato rejects the democratic and egalitarian claim that a distribution of political power should allot equal shares to all male citizens (cf. Knoll 2017a).

The second form of equality is distinguished by Plato as a divine form of equality (*Leg.* VI 757b). In the *Gorgias*, Plato calls this form of equality "geometrical equality" (508a, cf. 490b–e). Geometrical equality is proportional equality. In order to politically apply it one needs

> to grant much to the great and less to the less great, adjusting what you give to take account of the real nature of each – specifically, to confer high recognition on great virtue, but when

---

[7] "Simple equality is a simple distributive condition, so that if I have fourteen hats and you have fourteen hats, we are equal" (Walzer 1983, p. 18).

you come to the poorly educated in this respect, to treat them as they deserve. We maintain, in fact, that statesmanship consists of essentially this – strict justice (*Leg.* VI 757c; Plato 1997, p. 1433).

In this crucial and condensed passage Plato presents his theory of proportional justice, which is a political theory of distributive justice. It contains most of the building blocks of Aristotle's theory of distributive justice and in particular of the conception of political justice he prefers, which is an aristocratic conception focusing on political virtue (cf. Knoll 2010; Knoll 2017b). As the context of the passage elucidates, by addressing the distribution of recognition Plato a fortiori addresses the distribution of political offices and power. For him, such distribution should proceed according to proportional equality. Before political power is distributed, citizens need to be distinguished according to the criteria "virtue" (*arête*) and "education" (*paideia*) (cf. Aristotle: *Pol.* III 13, 1283a25; all trans. from *Pol.* and *EN* are M.K.s). The passage elucidates that Plato holds citizens to be quite unequal in these two respects. Political power should be allotted in proportion to the unequal amount of virtue and education citizens actually have. This is in line with his earlier mention of seven opposing "claims" (*axiômata*) used to justify ruling. There Plato pronounces that the "most important claim" is the one according to which "the ignorant man should follow the leadership of the wise and obey his orders" (*Leg.* III 690d; Plato 1997, p. 1379). Plato's distributive principle for political offices is "To each in proportion to his virtue and education". This principle implies that it is just to allot equal shares only to equally virtuous and educated citizens, not to everyone.

Plato's theory of political justice is embodied in the "political system" (*politeia*) he outlines in the *Laws*. Despite his clear preference for proportional or geometrical justice, he argues for a mixture of the two forms of equality and a mixed constitution. However, like the political system Plato outlined in the *Republic*, the one of the *Laws* has a strong aristocratic character that makes sure that all important political offices are distributed to the morally and intellectually best citizens (cf. Knoll 2017a). Plato's mixed constitution includes the equality of "measures, weights and numbers" only for reasons of the stability of the political community. About the mixture of the two forms of equality, he declares, "So though force of circumstances compels us to employ both sorts of equality, we should employ the second [...] as little as possible" (*Leg.* VI 757e; Plato 1997, p. 1433). Plato's political concession to the champions of democracy does not mean, however, that egalitarian justice is in general logically consistent with proportional justice. Egalitarianism and proportionalism manifest not only opposing but irreconcilable moral convictions about political justice. Before substantiating this thesis, it seems natural to include Aristotle's political theory of distributive justice in the discussion because Aristotle further develops and clarifies Plato's theory of two forms of equality and justice.

Aristotle's political theory of merit has already been extensively treated in the introduction to this volume. Therefore, here it suffices to focus on his report and analysis of disagreements on political justice and political systems. In the *Nicomachean Ethics*, Aristotle identifies a just distribution of political power with a distribution "according to merit" (*kat' axian*) (*EN* V 6, 1131a24–26). However, citizens with different political convictions substantially disagree with each other on how to measure merit. The democrats favor "freedom" as the appropriate criterion of merit, the supporters of oligarchy "wealth", the aristocrats "virtue" (*arête*), and an unnamed fourth group "noble birth" (*EN* V 6, 1131a27–29). In the *Nicomachean Ethics*, like later in the *Politics*, Aristotle distinguishes between four different conceptions of distributive justice: the democratic, the oligarchic and the aristocratic conception, and an undesignated fourth conception. Each of these conceptions is linked with its corresponding political system and justifies its specific distribution of political power. To argue that every free-born male citizen should get an equal share in political power is identical with the defense of democracy. To advocate the distribution of political offices in proportion to wealth is the same as to support oligarchy. To argue that political power should be given only to virtuous citizens is identical with the defense of aristocracy.[8] Aristotle shares Plato's aristocratic political preferences. The best political system he outlines in Books VII and VIII of the *Politics* is a true aristocracy and embodies the aristocratic conception of political justice (cf. Knoll 2016, pp. 87–94). For Aristotle, the political dispute over the appropriate criterion of merit and the appropriate conception of distributive justice is, in the end, a quarrel over the appropriate political system.

This result of Aristotle's analysis is not only theoretically relevant. Rather, the close link between disagreements on political justice and disagreements on political systems elucidates the huge practical and political significance of his analysis. The reason for this is that such kinds of disagreements can lead to seditions, revolutions and civil wars. Therefore, it is not surprising that "upheaval" or "revolution" (*stasis*) is the topic of Book V of the *Politics*. In Book V, Aristotle argues that the general motive for sedition or political revolution is that citizens are outraged and get angry when they perceive the distribution of polit-

---

[8] The "distribution of honors according to virtue (*kat' aretên*) seems to be the most characteristic trait of aristocracy; for virtue is the defining criterion of aristocracy, as wealth is the criterion for oligarchy, and free birth of democracy" (*Pol.* IV 8, 1294a9–11). For a reconstruction of the different arguments of the supporters of the four different conceptions of distributive justice see the introduction to this volume.

ical power to be unjust, and therefore want to change the political system of their *polis* or state.[9] For Aristotle, the disagreements between, say, supporters of an oligarchic conception of justice and oligarchy and champions of a democratic conception and democracy are a form of deep disagreements. It is not possible to convince either group through the use of reasons and arguments. This is also demonstrated by the many bloody upheavals and civil wars that happened after and during the horrific Peloponnesian War, in which Athens endorsed the democratic and Sparta the anti-democratic or oligarchic forces (cf. Thucydides III 82; Gehrke 1985). If Aristotle's analysis of deep disagreements on political justice and their inextricable link to deep disagreements on political systems is correct, he developed a political theory that does not only allow us to better understand several of the political revolutions that happened throughout history but also several of the political conflicts that keep happening in contemporary political systems.

In the *Nicomachean Ethics*, Aristotle interprets a just distribution of political power in general as a distribution "according to merit". For him, the source of disagreements on political justice is not this principle but the four opposing interpretations of merit. In the *Politics*, however, he opposes "numeric" or "arithmetic" (*gar arithmô*) equality like Plato to equality "according to merit" (*kat' axian*) (V 1, 1301b29f.; VI 2, 1317b4; cf. Plato, *Leg.*, VI 751d).[10] This opposition equals to the fundamental antagonism between arithmetic and proportional equality and justice. *Proportional justice*, which applies proportional equality, and *egalitarian justice*, which implements arithmetic equality, are not only opposites but are in general logically irreconcilable. They mutually exclude each other and represent two competing and contradictory understandings of justice that are connected to different sets of rules. This means that they cannot both be applied to solve the same distribution problem without nullifying each other (cf. Herwig 1984, pp. 97–99). Either justice is equality *only for equals* or (in an exclusive sense) *for all* (equals and unequals). The formal principle of proportional justice determines that *only equals* should get equal shares, while unequals should be allotted unequal shares. This formal principle is only in one case rec-

---

[9] Ronald Polansky points out: "Since the disposition fostering change or sedition is ultimately the sense of injustice in distribution in the community, this must be the most general of all the causes operative in change" (Polansky 1991, p. 335). The main anthropological basis of Aristotle's theory of political revolutions is the human sense of justice (*Pol.* I 2, 1253a15–18; cf. Knoll 2016, p. 75f.).
[10] For Aristotle, "absolute justice" (*haplos dikaion*) is "according to merit" (*Pol.* V 1, 1301b35f.). For his preferences for an aristocratic conception of distributive justice and for a true aristocracy see the introduction to this volume and Knoll 2017b.

oncilable with the formal principle of egalitarian justice that determines that *all* should get equal shares: in the case that everyone is equal. If in a distribution of political power there are unequal citizens like rich and poor ones, an oligarchic conception of proportional justice requires allotting unequal shares to them in proportion to their unequal wealth. For oligarchic justice, to distribute equal shares in such a case would be unjust.[11] From the perspective of democratic justice, however, a distribution of unequal shares is unjust. Democratic justice, which is egalitarian justice, requires allotting equal shares to every citizen, which can be achieved through a universal and equal suffrage. Census suffrage, which is based on oligarchic justice, is unjust from the prevailing modern perspective of egalitarian justice. It is noteworthy that after the French Revolution, which had equality, liberty and fraternity written on its banner, still two out of three draft constitutions (1791 and 1795) excluded the poor male citizens from the right to vote for the National Assembly. For elections to the Prussian state parliament census suffrage, the three-class franchise, was reestablished after the revolution 1848/49 and stayed valid until 1918.

2.2 The rise of egalitarian justice in modernity and the opposition of the champions of proportional justice

The vast majority of French citizens in the 18th century perceived the distribution of social goods and privileges in the *ancient régime* to be unjust. This was certainly one of the reasons for the French Revolution. This revolution was an important breakthrough for the rise of egalitarian justice. Since 1789, an increasing struggle for different forms of equality has become a central feature of modernity. According to an early egalitarian conception, social and political justice is achieved when everyone gets allotted equal rights. This idea goes back to the ancient conception of democratic justice, to some sophists, to the stoics, and to the Christian idea that all souls are equal in the eyes of God.[12] In the ancient world,

---

11 If there were virtuous and non-virtuous citizens who had claims in the same distribution, to distribute equal shares would also be unjust from the perspective of an aristocratic conception of justice. Aristocratic justice requires allotting unequal shares to citizens in proportion to their unequal virtue. However, if the most virtuous citizens were poor, such a distribution would be unjust from the perspective of oligarchic justice.
12 In a remarkable passage, Friedrich Nietzsche, a fierce opponent of the rise of egalitarian justice, pronounces, "The poisonous doctrine 'equal rights for everyone' – Christianity disseminated this the most thoroughly". For Nietzsche, the French Revolution and other revolutions go back to the egalitarian "belief in the 'privileges of the majority'" and thus to "*Christian* value

egalitarian justice primarily justified the claim for equal political participation of all male citizens. In the modern world, egalitarians call not only for an equal right to participate in the political life for all adult citizens but especially for equal civil and human rights. The egalitarian claim that everyone should have equal rights and liberties is also expressed by John Rawls's first principle of justice (Rawls 1971, p. 302).

Such egalitarian claims, however, have been opposed by several 19th-century philosophers. In his conception of social and political justice, Friedrich Nietzsche draws on the non-egalitarian or proportionalist views of Plato and Aristotle, claiming that a just distribution must allot goods in proportion to existing inequalities and allot equal shares only to equals, not to everyone:

> The doctrine of equality! ... But no poison is more poisonous than this: because it *seems* as if justice itself is preaching here, while in fact it is the *end* of justice ... 'Equality for the equal, inequality for the unequal' – that is what justice would *really* say: along with its corollary, 'never make the unequal equal' (*Twilight of the Idols*, Skirmishes § 48, Nietzsche 2005, p. 221 f.).

Like Plato and Aristotle, Nietzsche is convinced that people are not only fundamentally unequal but also extremely different in worth and rank. Therefore they should not be allotted equal but unequal rights. Persons with higher value deserve prerogatives and privileges. This is the reason why Nietzsche often contemplates rank orders and the appropriate criteria for establishing them. Similar to how Plato and Aristotle conceive the close relationship between political justice and the *polis*, Nietzsche's conception of proportional justice is embodied in his notion of a well-ordered state or society (cf. Knoll 2017c). Concerning political justice, like Plato and Aristotle, John Stuart Mill defends proportionalism by advocating a distribution of unequal voting rights according to people's unequal "value" and "worth" of their opinions to be measured by their unequal virtue, intelligence and knowledge (2001, chap. 8, pp. 163, 169 f.).

Before 1789, most of the favored positions in French society were distributed based on aristocratic privileges and thus on noble birth and inheritance. One slogan the revolutionaries used to oppose the *ancient régime* demanded "The career open to talents". The demand for *equal opportunity*[13] was at least ideally a demand for equal chances for *all* talents. However, this claim for egalitarian justice

---

judgments these revolutions are translating into blood and crimes!" (*The Anti-Christ* § 43; Nietzsche 2005, p. 40).

13 The demand that careers should be open to talents and that equal talents should have equal opportunities goes as far back as to the meritocracy Plato outlines in his *Republic* (cf. III, 415b–c).

was connected to claims and demands for proportional justice. The favored positions should not be distributed to *all* applicants but in proportion to individual merit or desert. An applicant deserves a position if he or she possesses certain qualities that allow us to anticipate "a future performance in which that quality is displayed" (Miller 2003, p. 137). This way of distributing the favored positions is the modern version of Plato's and Aristotle's claims that the political offices should be allotted "according to merit" (*kat' axian*). For Plato and Aristotle, the main reward for performing well in political offices was the "honor" or "recognition" (*timê*) the officeholders received from their fellow citizens (cf. *Pol.* III 10, 1281a31). In the modern world, the performance principle justifies high wages for talented and well-trained persons who perform well in their jobs. Such persons deserve not only a high wage but also recognition in proportion to their contributions to society. In distributing rewards, the performance principle applies proportional justice and gives to each according to his or her contribution. If two persons produce equivalent performances, then they deserve the same rewards. If a third person performs significantly better than those two, she deserves a higher reward in proportion to her better performance.

Connected to the rise of egalitarian justice, in the last years of the 18th century a different and distinctively modern principle of distributive justice appeared on the political stage. It was either the radical egalitarian "Gracchus" Babeuf, the leader of a failed coup attempt against the Directory in 1796, or Johann Gottlieb Fichte who "first explicitly proclaimed that justice requires the state to redistribute goods to the poor" (Fleischacker 2004, pp. 76, 160 f.). According to Babeuf, every man has received from nature "an *equal right* to enjoy all the goods" and the "aim of society is to defend this *equality*" (in Birchall 1997, p. 166; italics M.K.). In Western history, this was the "first definitive expression" of the "notion of distributive justice" in the modern sense (Fleischacker 2004, p. 55). The modern notion of distributive justice is inextricably linked to the welfare state and to the principle of a distribution of goods according to need (cf. the introduction to this volume). This latter principle, which is the distributive principle of the welfare state, can be applied in society jointly with the merit principle: "A society can give people what they deserve but also set resources aside to cater to needs" (Miller 2003, p. 155). This combination of principles is realized, at least to some extent or in imperfect form, in most modern welfare states.

Today, a society that distributes both rewards according to merit and some basic goods according to need is often welcomed as a just society (cf. Miller 2003, pp. 93, 200 f., 245). However, this contemporary conviction about social justice was firmly opposed by Karl Marx. In his 1875 *Critique of the Gotha Program*, Marx claims that in "a higher phase of communist society" labor duties and social wealth would be distributed by applying the principle "From each according to his ability, to each according to his needs!" (Marx 2009, p. 11). In the literature, it is a controversial issue as to whether Marx's principle has to be interpreted as his principle of distributive justice (cf. Geras 1989; Rawls 2007, pp. 335–372). For the purposes of this article it is not necessary to meddle in this debate and to embark on an extensive Marx-exegesis. It is enough to note that there are good reasons to understand Marx's principle as a principle of distributive justice. After introducing his principle and after expounding the considerations that lead him to postulate it, Marx declares that he now dealt enough with the issue of a "'fair distribution'" (*gerechte Verteilung*) (Marx 2009, p. 11). That Marx's principle is essentially a principle of distributive justice is also demonstrated by the fact that contemporary political philosophers treat the "needs principle"[14] as such. In his theory of distribute justice, Michael Walzer defends the claim that basic social goods like security, health care or, more generally, welfare should be allotted in proportion to "socially recognized needs" (1983, pp. 25f., 64–94). This principle is not an egalitarian principle because it aims at proportional equality and therefore allows for justified inequalities. Like Walzer, David Miller outlines a pluralistic theory of distributive justice that recognizes *need*, *desert*, and *equality* as principles and "criteria of social justice" (2003, pp. 41, 93, 245).

In his *Critique of the Gotha Program*, the draft program of the United Workers' Party of Germany, Marx distinguishes two phases of communist society. Despite the fact that in the earlier period social privileges and class differences are abolished, it is "still stamped with the birthmarks" of the capitalist society from which it emerges (2009, p. 8). In this socialist period every working individual receives – after indispensable deductions – back from society "means of consumption" exactly in proportion to her contribution measured by her "individual quantum of labor" (2009, p. 8f.). Like the exchange of commodities in capitalist society, it is an "exchange of equal values". For Marx, such a socialist organization of society has several inevitable "defects" and is "stigmatized by a bourgeois limitation" (2009, p. 8f.). If people are merely measured and rewarded by the "*equal standard*" of their labor contribution to society, they will receive *unequal shares* of the social wealth. The reason for this is that "one man is superior to another physically, or mentally, and supplies more labor in the same time, or can labor for a longer time". The performance principle "tacitly recognizes unequal individual endowment, and thus productive capacity, as a natural privi-

---

[14] Norman Geras designates Marx's whole principle "From each according to his ability, to each according to his needs!" as the "needs principle" (1989, p. 221). However, it is more appropriate to apply this designation only to the second part of Marx's principle: "To each according to his needs!"

lege" (2009, p. 9f.). There is another reason why Marx rejects the performance principle. A distribution of social wealth in proportion to labor contributions leads to further inequalities because unequal individuals – "one worker is married, another is not; one has more children than another, and so on and so forth" – have unequal needs. This means that a worker who is a bachelor with no family will be significantly wealthier than a worker who has large needs due to the large family she is responsible for (2009, p. 10).

These are the considerations that lead Marx to postulate the principle "From each according to his ability, to each according to his needs!" that should regulate distributions in the final phase of communist society. This principle uncouples – and this is its crucial point – what individual citizens contribute to society with their labor and their natural endowments from the distributive claims they have to the sum-total of the fruits of society's labor. For Marx, the distribution of social wealth should be independent from unequal labor contributions and should be exclusively based on unequal individual needs. It seems likely that Babeuf's egalitarian convictions that every man has an *equal right* to all the goods and that society has to aim at this *equality* is the base for Marx's principle (Birchall 1997, pp. 95f., 166). This principle could mean that in "a higher phase of communist society" in which "all the springs of co-operative wealth flow more abundantly" a relatively unproductive worker who has large needs due to her large family receives significantly more means of consumption from society than a relatively productive worker who is a bachelor with no family (Marx 2009, p. 11).

From the perspective of the performance or merit principle, however, it is extremely unjust if those persons who contribute more to society receive significantly less than those who contribute less. However, Marx does not acknowledge or approve the "bourgeois" performance principle at all. His own distributive principle is not only irreconcilable with the performance principle but nullifies it or, in the case just mentioned, even allows it to be reversed. For Marx, the distribution of social wealth should be exclusively based on unequal needs. Between the advocates of the performance or merit principle and Marx exists a deep disagreement on social justice.

An important modern witness to the irreconcilability of conceptions of social and political justice is the sociologist and philosopher Max Weber. Weber's view on justice is part of his general view that modernity is characterized by an irresolvable pluralism and struggle of values. Views similar to Weber's were pronounced by Isaiah Berlin who holds that the "normal human situation" is that "ends equally ultimate, equally sacred" and "entire systems of value" "come into collision without possibility of rational arbitration" (Berlin 2013, p. 94; cf.

pp. 94–99).[15] For Weber, a distinctive trait of the modern world is the existence not only of irreconcilable conceptions of the good but of justice.[16] Facing such a situation, each individual has to make a personal decision about which of the competing values she wants to choose and cherish. Weber persuasively states about social justice that,

> The implications of the postulate of "justice" cannot be decided unambiguously by any ethic. Whether one, for example – as would correspond most closely with the views expressed by Schmoller – owes much to those who achieve much or whether one should demand much from those who accomplish much; whether one should, e.g., in the name of justice [...] accord great opportunities to those with eminent talents or whether on the contrary (like Babeuf) one should attempt to equalize the injustice of the unequal distribution of mental capacities through the rigorous provision that talented persons, whose talent gives them prestige, must not utilize their better opportunities for their own benefit – these questions cannot be definitely answered. The ethical problem in most social-political issues is, however, of this type (Weber 1949, p. 15f.).

According to Weber, there is no possibility for a rational solution to deep disagreements on social and political justice. Though moral philosophers can give arguments for their conceptions of justice, they cannot deliver an ultimate and undisputable rational grounding for any of their different normative theories. For the conflict between opposing values and ends there exists "no (rational or empirical) scientific procedure of any kind whatsoever which can provide us with a decision" (Weber 1949, p. 19; cf. Gölz 1978).

2.3 Contemporary disagreements between supporters of egalitarian and proportional justice

In today's world, the performance principle and meritocracy are still advocated by political philosophers (cf. Miller 2003, pp. 177–202). However, most contemporary political theorists are endorsing egalitarian justice. In the tradition of Babeuf and Marx, contemporary egalitarians like Ronald Dworkin and Richard Arneson claim that a just society has to establish some form of arithmetic or numeric equality like "equality of resources" or "equality of opportunity for welfare" (cf. Cohen 1989). The goal of egalitarian justice is – if this is compatible

---

[15] For a critique of Berlin's value pluralism see Steinvorth in this volume.
[16] From Weber's perspective, Rawls's move to come to terms with the opposing conceptions of the good by striving for a consensus on a political conception of justice and a just social framework that allows these conception to coexist does not work.

with upholding other values like liberty – to make people more equal in these respects. Following Dworkin's suggestion "that the idea that each person matters equally is at the heart of all plausible political theories", Will Kymlicka pronounces that "each theory shares the same 'egalitarian plateau'" (Kymlicka 2002, p. 4; cf. Haus in this volume). However, there are still contemporary political philosophers like John Kekes who publish serious treatises like *The Illusions of Egalitarianism* (2003), which argue *Against Liberalism* (1997). Going back to Aristotle, Kekes claims "that the worth of human beings varies with their moral merit" and that "justice makes the right" to resources "contingent on what their recipients deserve" (1997, p. 120). Kekes defends proportional justice and deeply disagrees with the liberal and egalitarian conception of justice. Other philosophers such as Harry Frankfurt argue that equality is morally irrelevant and propose that we should rather focus on non-relational standards like distributing a sufficient amount of goods to everyone (Frankfurt 1988, 2015; cf. Krebs 2000).

John Rawls, whose defense of the welfare state has already been treated at length in the introduction to this volume, starts off his theory of distributive justice from a "substantive egalitarian principle of justice which assumes that all departures from equality have to be morally justified" (Barry 1995, p. 153). In some crucial aspects, Rawls's position on social justice comes close to Babeuf's and Marx's views. Like Marx, he opposes recognizing "unequal individual endowment, and thus productive capacity, as a natural privilege" (Marx 2009, p. 10). Considering this closeness and Rawls's extensive studies of Marx's view on justice, it could even be argued that he appropriates Marx's view and elaborates it (Rawls 2007, pp. 335–372).[17] As a champion of egalitarian justice, Rawls negates the natural and social inequalities of people. For him, no one "deserves his greater natural capacity nor merits a more favorable starting place in society". Rawls's intuition about social justice is, "Those who have been favored by nature, whoever they are, may gain from their good fortune only on terms that improve the situation of those who have lost out" (1971, § 17, p. 101f.). Based on this central intuition, from which he develops his difference principle, Rawls advocates a strong welfare state that redistributes income and wealth from the well-off members of society to the least advantaged ones (cf. Knoll 2013). As already expounded in the introduction to this volume, Rawls rejects a distribution of primary goods like income and wealth according to merit and advocates, like Marx, a distribution according to need. However, if it comes to wages, Rawls allows, in contrast to Marx, inequalities based on efforts and contributions in

---

[17] For the claim of a deep disagreement between Marx's principle of distributive justice and Rawls's difference principle see Demir in this volume.

order to create incentives to work more or more efficiently (1971, §§ 43, 47 f., pp. 276 f., 304 f., 309, 312). Rawls's egalitarian goal is, nevertheless, to make people more equal concerning certain primary goods like rights, liberties, opportunities, income, wealth, and self-respect.

An opposing conception of social justice and of a just political order has been introduced by the libertarian Robert Nozick. For his political thought, like for Rawls's, individual rights are central. However, he strongly disagrees with the (im-)moral core of Rawls's view. According to Nozick, even if people might not deserve their natural endowments, they still rightfully own them and have a justified claim to them (1974, p. 225). Therefore, he strongly disagrees with Rawls's conception of social justice that regards people's "natural talents as a common asset" and "treats people's abilities and talents as resources for others" (1974, p. 228; cf. pp. 30, 33, 172; cf. Rawls 1971, p. 101). Rawls's view equals to introducing "a head tax on assets and abilities" (1974, p. 229). For Nozick, a just society is not allowed to redistribute resources from the rich to the poor as this violates people's rights. Nozick himself develops an "entitlement theory of justice" that goes back to Locke and the reductionist early modern view that distributive justice concerns mainly the just appropriation and just transfer of property (1974, pp. 153, 149–182; cf. Kersting 2000, pp. 47–53). In a well-known polemic statement, Nozick, the advocate of a minimal state, objects to Rawls's ideal of an extensive welfare state and to the redistributions it requires: "Taxation of earnings from labor is on a par with forced labor. Some persons find this claim obviously true: taking the earnings of n hours labor is like taking n hours from the person; it is like forcing the person to work n hours for another's purpose" (1974, p. 169).

The deep disagreements between Rawls's and Nozick's views on social justice could be interpreted as a resumption of the deep disagreements between advocates of the performance or merit principle and Marx's views on social justice. While Nozick argues for a version of "political individualism" and the performance principle, Rawls defends "political communalism" and a distribution of goods that should be primarily based on the needs of the least advantaged citizens.[18] As a non-egalitarian, Nozick has no problem with social inequality and defends an unequal distribution of wealth and income in proportion to labor contributions based on unequal natural endowments and efforts. On the contrary, Rawls aims at socially compensating for the natural and social inequalities

---

[18] In his contribution to this volume, Ulrich Steinvorth argues for the thesis that we can rationally arbitrate between Rawls's and Nozick's conceptions of justice. Steinvorth characterizes Rawls's view as "political communalism". For good reasons he prefers this term to "political communism".

and at establishing the highest possible level of social equality. However, while Marx calls for a distribution of social wealth independent from labor contributions, Rawls concedes some unequal rewards and wages based on efforts and contributions.

3 Reasons for deep disagreements among notions of social and political justice

The preceding analysis of the history of political thought on distributive justice demonstrates that deep disagreements among notions of social and political justice are one of its characteristic features. From antiquity to the present day we can observe disagreements on values, just distributions and a just society that cannot be resolved through the use of reasons and arguments. Perhaps the only progress in this history is the emergence of the modern notion of distributive justice that is connected to the welfare state and a distribution of basic goods according to need (cf. Fleischacker 2004). However, the conflict between egalitarian and non-egalitarian or proportional justice cannot be resolved by attributing the conflicting views to different historical periods and by claiming a "moral progress" towards egalitarianism (cf. Herwig 1984).[19] As the preceding analysis demonstrates, the fundamentally opposed two basic conceptions of social and political justice can be traced both in antiquity and in modernity.

There are good reasons to suppose with Aristotle and Rawls that all human beings possess a "sense of justice" (*Pol.* I 2, 1253a14–18; Rawls 1971, § 4, § 39, § 77; pp. 19, 243, 505). Small children somehow notice when they or others are treated unjustly. However, as adults opposing intuitions of what constitutes a just distribution and a just political order are formed. As a first and preliminary step toward a better understanding of such disagreements, this section sketches five possible reasons that can explain them. This sketch and the exact relationship between these reasons have to be elaborated through detailed analyses in future research.

(1) For Hampshire, moral conflict is inevitable because *human imagination*, which makes us unique individuals, causes us to develop not only different notions of a good and happy life but different moral outlooks (1983; 1999, pp. 18, 30, 68; cf. Giorgini in this volume).

---

[19] For arguments against a Hegelian historical or evolutionary solution of disagreements see Ribeiro 2011, pp. 18–21.

(2) In *Spheres of Justice*, Walzer bases his theory of justice on the meanings of social goods in particular societies (1983). From this perspective, disagreement can be explained by the fact that several different interpretations of these meanings are possible and justifiable (Warnke 1993).[20]

(3) A classical approach to explaining disagreements on justice can be found in the Marxist tradition. From this perspective, *justice is based on class interest*. Philosophical disagreements regarding just distributions and just political orders can be understood by tracing them back to the social or economic position of the theoretician. For Marx, the "economic structure of society" is "the real foundation" "on which arises a legal and political superstructure and to which correspond definite forms of social consciousness". It is human's "social existence that determines their consciousness" (1987, p. 263). According to Marx's view, a conception of justice generalizes a particular social position or expresses the particular interest of one social class. The position of the less favored social classes suggests an egalitarian view according to which it is just to establish a good deal of social equality and to redistribute the income of the privileged classes. On the contrary, the social position and interest of the privileged classes prompt a non-egalitarian view that conceives of a just distribution of social goods as one in proportion to existing inequalities. This approach to explaining the disagreements on social and political justice assumes that moral judgments on justice are not an independent phenomenon but can be reduced to objective interests that go along with different social positions. An argument for this approach is that it takes into account human egoism. Rawls had good reasons to situate the parties who decide on principles of justice "behind a veil of ignorance" (1971, § 24, p. 136). Such an information deficit about one's own social position and natural endowments prevents people from making choices in their personal interest and is intended to lead to impartial decisions. However, it can be shown empirically – consider Marx, Engels and most members of the Frankfurt School – that not all theoreticians advocate their "objective class interests".

(4) A fourth approach to explaining disagreements on justice could be called a *cognitive approach*. This approach can be illustrated by an important change in Rawls's view. In *A Theory of Justice*, Rawls defends a Kantian understanding of reason as a general or universal faculty. For him, the parties who decide about principles of justice in the initial situation of equality are "similar rational and similarly situated", and therefore "each is convinced by the same arguments" (1971, § 25, p. 139). On the contrary, in *Political Liberalism*, Rawls concedes "dif-

---

20 Cf. footnote 5 of this article.

ficulties in arriving at agreement in judgment" or the reality of "reasonable disagreement" which is "disagreement between reasonable persons" (2005, II § 2, pp. 55, 58). Now Rawls acknowledges as a "general fact" of "the political culture of a democratic society" that "many of our most important judgments are made under conditions where it is not expected that conscientious persons with full powers of reason, even after free discussion, will all arrive at the same conclusion" (2005, I § 6, p. 36; II § 2, p. 58). Rawls denotes the causes or sources of reasonable disagreements as "the burdens of judgment"[21] and presents an open list: Evidence is difficult to evaluate, the overall weight of the manifold relevant (normative) considerations on both sides of an issue is hard to assess, our concepts are vague and therefore we must rely on interpretations and judgments about interpretations, our moral and political judgments are shaped by our disparate life experiences, it is difficult to select among our moral and political values and to prioritize them (2005, II § 2, pp. 55–57). Generally speaking, "Different conceptions of the world can reasonably be elaborated from different standpoints and diversity arises in part from our distinct perspectives" (2005, II § 2, p. 58). With his burdens-of-judgment argument Rawls wants to explain the modern pluralism of "reasonable comprehensive religious, philosophical, and moral doctrines" (2005, I § 6, p. 36; II § 3, pp. 54f., 60).[22] There is evidence for "attributing to Rawls the belief that issues of justice are *not* subject to the burdens of judgment" (Waldron 1999, p. 152). However, this exemption cannot be justified. The burdens of judgment can also be "used to characterize our political deliberations, including our deliberations about rights and justice, as well as ethics, religion, etc." (Waldron 1999, p. 112). The burdens of judgment can partly explain our deep disagreements on social and political justice. By admitting "reasonable disagreements", Rawls unintentionally undermines his ideas of an overlapping consensus on a political conception of justice and of a possible agreement on principles of social justice (cf. Waldron 1999, p. 151f.; for a realist notion of reasonableness see Wolthuis in this volume).

The cognitive approach to explaining the causes of disagreements on justice can and should, of course, be pursued beyond Rawls's discussion of the burdens of justice. This approach points toward a broader investigation of human reason.

---

[21] For the burdens of judgment see also Peter Caven's and Michal Rupniewski's contributions to this volume.

[22] "The evident consequence of the burdens of judgment is that reasonable persons do not all affirm the same comprehensive doctrine" (2005, II § 3, p. 60). Rawls also declares, "These burdens of judgment are of first significance for a democratic idea of tolerance" (2005, II § 2, p. 58; cf. Introduction, p. XXIVf.). An understanding of the sources or causes of the modern pluralism of comprehensive doctrines should make it easier to tolerate the doctrines one disapproves.

Why do philosophers constantly disagree with each other? Why are they only rarely convinced by each other's arguments? Considering that "philosophy is the *business* of disagreement", it is "very surprising" that until today philosophy has not "worked out a fairly sophisticated account of disagreement" (Ribeiro 2011, p. 3). In the terminology of Jean-François Lyotard's *The Differend*, there exists a conflict or "differend" (*différend*) between egalitarian and non-egalitarian conceptions of social and political justice (1988). For Lyotard, like other conflicts, this one cannot be decided because there is no rule for a judgment that can be applied to both conceptions. Highly relevant for future research on the cognitive causes for disagreements are also the contemporary debates on deep and peer disagreements (Fogelin 2005, Siegel 2013).

(5) A fifth approach to explaining disagreements on conceptions of justice focuses on the *opposing images of humanity* connected to them. According to this approach, disagreements on justice can be explained by a clash of the underlying conceptions of man. In the language of Fogelin's *Logic of Deep Disagreements*, the conflicting convictions that humans are either *equal* or (in an exclusive sense) *unequal*, or rather that either the one or the other matters, are the "underlying principles" or "framework propositions" that can surface as the reasons that create the disagreements on justice (2005, p. 8).[23] For non-egalitarians like Plato, Aristotle, and Nietzsche, human beings are fundamentally unequal and have unequal value. On the contrary, for egalitarians all human beings have equal worth, and are therefore equally worthy of concern and respect. For Plato, people can be as different as reason, the highest part of the soul, and the appetites, the lowest part of the soul. For Aristotle, person's different human value corresponds to the degree in which they have perfected their ethical virtues, their character, and their practical and theoretical reason. Based on people's different worth and rank, for Plato, Aristotle, and Nietzsche it is just to distribute equal shares only to equals, not to everyone. On the contrary, based on their conviction of human equality, egalitarians aim at establishing more equal-

---

[23] One of Fogelin's examples for deep disagreements is the abortion debate: "Parties on opposite sides of the debate can agree on a wide range of biological facts" and also "on the sanctity of human life" (2005, p. 8). However, "the central issue of the abortion debate is the moral status of the fetus", and in regard to this issue the one party believes that at conception or shortly afterwards "an immortal soul enters into the fertilized egg" and the other party does not. There is no way of solving such a disagreement through the use of reasons and arguments because of the irreconcilable belief systems that the disagreement is based on (2005, p. 8f.). For a critique of Fogelin's "Wittgensteinian view" of the "limits of reason" see Siegel 2013, pp. 16–21; cf. Ribeiro 2011, pp. 7–9.

ity among persons.[24] For non-egalitarians, just distributions should correspond to natural inequalities, for modern egalitarians they should move beyond such inequalities towards more equality (cf. Herwig 1984, p. 202). If deep disagreements on just distributions and just political orders can be explained primarily through disagreements about the equality or inequality of human beings, future research has to examine the reasons for deep disagreements about human nature.

4 The meta-ethical relevance of deep disagreements among notions of social and political justice

The linguistic turn in the philosophy of the 20th century lead to a new branch of moral philosophy called meta-ethics. This new discipline does not defend any normative principles or ethical theories but investigates the nature of morality and the meaning of moral statements and judgments. What do we mean when we claim that something is right, good or just? Are we referring to moral facts and moral truth or do we just express our personal, or our society's, feelings, thoughts, and attitudes? Meta-ethics analyzes more than just moral language and arguments; it also analyses the ontological and epistemological questions connected to them. "Ethical realists" claim that moral statements and judgments refer to moral facts or an objective moral reality, anti-realists (called moral skeptics, ethical relativists or ethical subjectivists) deny this. "Cognitivists" maintain that moral judgments can be true or false and that there is such a thing as moral knowledge. "Non-cognitivists" reject the idea that moral knowledge is possible.

The preceding demonstration that deep disagreements among notions of social and political justice are a characteristic feature of the history of political thought is significant for meta-ethics. The reason for this is that the existence of such deep disagreements is a strong argument against ethical realism and cognitivism. More than two thousand years of intense philosophical research on justice – our central moral, social and political virtue – has neither uncovered objective truth about the matter nor led to any agreement among scholars. Looking at it the other way round, deep disagreements among notions of social and political justice exist because there are no objective moral reality and no moral

---

[24] Cf. Sommer 2016, pp. 42f., 66f. For a more detailed account of the opposing images of humanity see the introduction to this volume, p. 8f.

facts. There is nothing in the world to back up *one* of the conflicting philosophical views on justice and no procedure using moral facts to solve moral disagreements and to show that one view is wrong and one is right. If the *argument against moral realism from deep disagreements* is persuasive, we attain a sixth reason for explaining deep disagreements among notions of social and political justice. The *philosophical* argument that the existence of deep disagreements on justice refutes ethical realism is similar to the well-known *sociological* argument from relativity, which it complements.

Let's start with some preliminary meta-ethical observations and considerations. If we analyse ordinary moral language and thought, we notice that it usually contains claims about objective moral facts. We frequently exclaim, "This is not just!" However, the fact that our moral statements and judgments make such claims does not prove that moral facts or objective values exist. As John L. Mackie put it: "The claim to objectivity, however ingrained in our language and thought, is not self-validating" (1977, p. 35). Despite their claims to objectivity, our moral statements and judgments could still just express our subjective moral feelings, thoughts, desires, and attitudes. As Mackie argues, the "supposed objectivity of moral qualities" could arise from "the projection or objectification of moral attitudes" (1977, p. 42). Just as we tend to read our feelings into the objects, for example by ascribing a fungus that disgusts us the quality of foulness, we project our subjective moral feelings, desires, and attitudes into the world (1977, p. 42). Furthermore, invoking an objective moral reality could simply have the strategic function to make our subjective judgments appear stronger and more authoritative. Consider children who say that they really *need* something, which just expresses that they really *want* it. For Mackie, moral claims pointing to something "objectively descriptive" are "all false" (1977, p. 35). Mackie supports this "error theory" mainly with "the argument from relativity and the argument from queerness" and claims that the latter is more important than the former (1977, pp. 35–42).

The philosophical *argument from queerness* has an ontological part: "If there were objective values, then they would be entities or qualities or relations of a very strange sort, utterly different from anything else in the universe" (1977, p. 38). Examples for such queer entities are Plato's forms and in particular his form of the good. Plato was an ethical realist and cognitivist. The argument from queerness also has an epistemological part. If objective moral facts existed, it would be very difficult to explain how we could access them: "Correspondingly, if we were aware of them, it would have to be by some special faculty of moral perception or intuition, utterly different from our ordinary ways of knowing everything else" (1977, p. 38). In a recent counter to the argument from queerness, Julian Nida-Rümelin defends an ethical realism that is ontologically agnostic

(2016, pp. 91–136). However, this does not leverage out the argument. The ethical realist who both claims that moral facts exist and that we can somehow access them has the burden of proof. If we are to accept the belief that objective values are part of the structure of the world, we should be able to track or comprehend their nature and their place in this world.[25] Likewise, someone who claims an empirical fact, say, the existence of centaurs, should be able to prove their existence to the skeptic. If the moral skeptic needs to identify moral facts with an inaccessible metaphysical or divine reality like the one usually associated with Plato's form of the good, she has good reasons to doubt their existence.

The sociological *argument from relativity* goes back to the sophist Protagoras who was informed about the variation in customs and moral codes from one culture to another by the historian Herodotus. From this, Protagoras concluded that in moral matters there are no universal truths. However, for good reasons he argued that some moral beliefs are more beneficial than others (Plato: *Theaetetus* 166e–167d, 172a/b, 177d/e).[26] Today, based on history, anthropology, ethnology, and sociology, descriptive morality informs us about the wide range of diversity in moral beliefs. This diversity and the existence of all kinds of moral disagreements – on values, a good life, the common good, politics, abortion, euthanasia, animal rights, and on and on – are the premises of the argument from relativity.[27] This argument claims both that moral diversity and disagreement suggest "that there are no absolute universal moral standards binding on all men at all times" and that the validity of moral beliefs and principles depends on their cultural or even on their individual acceptance[28] (Ladd 1985, pp. 1, 3). This argument against ethical realism "has some force simply because the actual variations in the moral

---

[25] For Nida-Rümelin, it is an undeniable normative fact that murder is morally wrong (2016, pp. 124, 130). To be sure, this is a universally shared moral judgment or belief and there are universally shared reasons to think that murder is morally wrong. However, in order to substantiate the view that beyond these judgments, beliefs and reasons there exists such a thing as an objective moral fact to which they refer would require an additional proof.

[26] Plato deeply disagreed with Protagoras's ethical relativism or skepticism. His own theory that the philosopher can achieve the truth about objective forms of justice and the good that exist separate from the sensual world is an attempt to refute Protagoras's view that in these matters there are no universal truths because justice and moral goodness varies from one culture to another. Plato's student Aristotle, however, deeply disagreed with Plato that such forms exist.

[27] Moral disagreements are embedded in a wider set of religious and philosophical disagreements.

[28] The position that the validity of moral beliefs and principles depends on their cultural acceptance is called "conventional ethical relativism". The more radical position is "subjective ethical relativism" that bases the validity of moral beliefs and principles on the "acceptance by an individual agent" (Pojman/Fieser 2012, p. 16).

codes are more readily explained by the hypothesis that they reflect ways of life than by the hypothesis that they express perceptions, most of them seriously inadequate and badly distorted, of objective values" (Mackie 1977, p. 37). If moral truth exists, contradicting norms and values cannot be likewise true. The enormous amount of existing moral diversity and disagreement suggests that no moral view can be understood as the apprehension of the *one* objective moral truth (cf. Birnbacher 2003, p. 391 f.; Waldron 1999, p. 177).

The *argument* against ethical realism *from deep disagreements on justice* is above all a philosophical argument. It is not just an argument concerning ethics but as well political philosophy.[29] This argument is not primarily based on societies' or cultures' disagreements on moral codes or distributions in the political community but on disagreements among researchers and scholars. Even if we suppose that philosophers' judgments about a just distribution or just society are influenced by their own personal and cultural backgrounds, their disagreements supposedly go deeper and are more rational than "common" people's and societies' disagreements on values and moral codes. Philosopher's views are not only based on their "considered judgments"[30] on justice but on elaborated theories that they defend with carefully constructed arguments. According to an old-fashioned view, philosophy is committed to finding out the truth. However, after more than two thousand years of continuous philosophical disagreements on social and political justice, it is very likely that no objective truth about justice exists. Considering the enormous amount of past philosophical efforts, there is no reason for optimism that the lack of consensus could change in the future (cf. Ribeiro 2011, pp. 18–21).

Of course, the mere fact of continuous deep disagreements on justice does not conclusively rule out the possibility that an objective moral reality or moral truth exists. Hypothetically, supporters of proportional justice like Plato could have been able to perceive the truth and all egalitarians could have distorted or false views on justice or vice versa. However, the burden-of-proof argument also applies to these cases. Neither Plato nor other moral realists were able to demonstrate the existence of an objective moral reality. Similarly, as Waldron puts it, "moral disagreement remains a continuing difficulty for realism, even

---

[29] For Aristotle, justice is a moral or ethical virtue that is also applied in arguments about political distributions (cf. Knoll 2016). Similarly, for Rawls and other contemporary philosophers, political philosophy is applied moral philosophy. There are good reasons for this view and for understanding justice claims as moral claims.
[30] Rawls defines "considered judgments" as those "judgments in which our moral capacities are most likely to be displayed without distortion". They are "rendered under conditions favorable to the exercise of the sense of justice" (Rawls 1971, § 9, p. 47).

it does not entail its falsity, so long as the realist fails to establish connections between the idea of objective truth and the existence of procedures for resolving disagreement" (1999, p. 177). In mainstream sciences, practitioners disagree with each other, say, about aspects of climate change, but there is some agreement on the methods and procedures how to settle or resolve such disagreements. However, "*nothing remotely comparable*" exists among moralists or moral philosophers (Waldron 1999, p. 178). Waldron's argument from the lack of consensus on how to solve moral disagreements is connected to the burden-of-proof argument. Both arguments are part of the philosophical argument against moral realism from deep disagreements. Combined with the arguments from queerness and from relativity, this results in a very strong case against moral realism and cognitivism.[31]

5 Conclusion

This article has demonstrated that deep disagreements among notions of social and political justice are a characteristic feature of the history of political thought. Despite the fact that today there is much more consensus on democracy than a hundred years ago, disagreements on political justice linger on (cf. Knoll/Şimşek in this volume). This article has also shown that the fact of deep disagreements on justice yields important arguments for the case of the moral skeptic or ethical relativist against the moral realist and cognitivist. Considering that deep disagreements among notions of social and political justice concern both ethics and political philosophy, it would be most appropriate to denote the position defended here as ethico-political relativism or ethico-political skepticism (for the relation of disagreements to relativism and skepticism see Ribeiro 2011, pp. 9–11).

This article has only sketched six reasons that explain deep disagreements among notions of social and political justice. Future research needs to elaborate on this sketch and analyze the exact relationship between these reasons. Equally important is the question of how to cope with deep disagreements on justice. Considering that such disagreements can lead to violent conflicts and civil wars, this task is of serious practical and political relevance. Conventional ethical relativists often claim that their theory supports the value of tolerance (cf.

---

[31] Ronald Dworkin claims "that there is often a single right answer to complex questions of law and political morality" and rejects the "no-right-answer" thesis (1978, p. 279f.). However, the argument from deep disagreements on social and political justice demonstrates that Dworkin's view cannot be upheld.

Pojman/Fieser 2012, p. 20 f.). However, deep disagreements on justice lead rather to enmity among the supporters of egalitarianism and proportionalism. The least we can ask for is that the opposed parties of such conflicts respect the fact that reasonable disagreements on justice exist. This means that they should not oversimplify the matter by degrading the opponent as ignorant, backward, prejudiced, unintelligent, and such like (cf. Waldron 1999, p. 111; Ribeiro 2011, pp. 7–11).[32]

To be sure, many actual political conflicts are caused or can be derived from disagreements on social and political justice. This is especially true when firm moral and political convictions are involved as it is the case in quarrels between liberals and conservatives, generally speaking, between the political "left" and "right". Considering that justice is the most important moral, social, and political virtue, it is even possible to define these terms based on the corresponding egalitarian or non-egalitarian convictions about social and political justice. Similar ideas have been expressed by Noberto Bobbio in his small study *Left and Right* (1997). According to Bobbio, the political convictions of the "left" and "right" are not only connected to egalitarian or non-egalitarian views of justice, but to opposing images of humanity that go along with them (cf. section 3 of this article). The hypothesis that followers of German political parties on the left share egalitarian views and adherents of German political parties on the right non-egalitarian views, has been successfully verified applying empirical research (Fichtner 2012).

Disagreement has become a new research interest among scholars with different backgrounds. Deep disagreements exist not only among notions of social and political justice and among ethicists, but among philosophers in general (Ribeiro 2011). There are new controversies on deep and peer disagreements and a debate on the epistemology of disagreement (cf. Siegel 2013). Political scientists engage in conflict research and we certainly see a lot of political and moral disagreement in domestic politics and international relations. It would be desirable, if future research focused more on the various commonalities and connections of the different forms of disagreement.

---

[32] According to Waldron, respecting disagreement "need not involve rejecting the premise about the singularity of truth; that is, it need not involve anything like relativism. Respect has to do with how we treat each other's *beliefs* about justice in circumstances where none of them is self-certifying, not how we treat the truth about justice itself" (1999, p. 111).

Bibliography

Barry, Norman P. (1995): *An Introduction to Modern Political Theory.* Third revised and expanded edition. Houndsmills: Macmillan (first edition 1981).
Berlin, Isaiah (2013): "The Originality of Machiavelli" (first published 1972). In: Berlin, Isaiah: *Against the Current. Essays in the History of Ideas.* Henry Harvey (Ed.). Princeton, Oxford: Princeton University Press (second edition, first published 1979), pp. 33–100.
Birchall, Ian H. (1997): *The Spectre of Babeuf.* Houndsmills, New York: Macmillan/St. Martin's Press.
Birnbacher, Dieter (2003): *Analytische Einführung in die Ethik.* Berlin, New York: De Gruyter.
Bobbio, Noberto (1997): *Left and Right. The Significance of a Political Distinction.* Chicago: University of Chicago Press (first published 1993).
Cohen, Gerald A. (1989): "On the Currency of Egalitarian Justice". In: *Ethics 99,* pp. 906–944.
Dworkin, Ronald (1978): *Taking Right Seriously.* With a new appendix and a response to critics. Cambridge, MA: Harvard University Press.
Fichtner, Georg (2012): *Die gerechtigkeitstheoretischen Grundlagen der politischen Begriffe "links" und "rechts".* Munich: Grin.
Fleischacker, Samuel (2004): *A Short History of Distributive Justice.* Cambridge, MA: Harvard University Press.
Fogelin, Robert J. (2005): "The Logic of Deep Disagreements". In: *Informal Logic* 25. No. 1, pp. 3–11 (first published 1985).
Frankfurt, Harry G. (1988): "Equality as a Moral Ideal". In: Frankfurt, Harry G.: *The Importance of What We Care about. Philosophical Essays.* Cambridge: Cambridge University Press, pp. 134–158.
Frankfurt, Harry G. (2015): *On Inequality.* Princeton, Oxford: Princeton University Press.
Gehrke, Hans-Joachim (1985): *Stasis. Untersuchungen zu den inneren Kriegen in den griechischen Staaten des 5. und 4. Jahrhunderts.* Munich: Beck.
Geras, Norman (1989): "The Controversy about Marx and Justice". In: Callinicos, Alex (Ed.): *Marxist Theory.* Oxford: Oxford University Press, pp. 211–267.
Gölz, Walter (1978): *Begründungsprobleme der praktischen Philosophie.* Stuttgart-Bad Cannstatt: Fromann-Holzboog.
Habermas, Jürgen (1991): *Erläuterungen zur Diskursethik.* Frankfurt a. M.: Suhrkamp.
Hampshire, Stuart (1983): *Morality and Conflict.* Oxford: Basil Blackwell.
Hampshire, Stuart (1999): *Justice is Conflict.* London: Duckworth.
Herwig, Dagmar (1984): *Gleichbehandlung und Egalisierung als konkurrierende Modelle von Gerechtigkeit. Eine systematische Analyse.* Munich: Fink.
Kekes, John (1990): *Facing Evil.* Princeton: Princeton University Press.
Kekes, John (1997): *Against Liberalism.* Ithaca, London: Cornell University Press.
Kekes, John (2003): *The Illusions of Egalitarianism.* Ithaca, London: Cornell University Press.
Kersting, Wolfgang (2000): *Theorien der sozialen Gerechtigkeit.* Stuttgart: Metzler.
Knoll, Manuel (2010): "Die distributive Gerechtigkeit bei Platon und Aristoteles". In: *Zeitschrift für Politik* (ZfP) 1, pp. 3–30.
Knoll, Manuel (2013): "An Interpretation of Rawls's Difference Principle as the Principle of the Welfare State". In: *Sofia Philosophical Review* 7. No. 2, pp. 5–33.

Knoll, Manuel (2016): "The Meaning of Distributive Justice for Aristotle's Theory of Constitutions". In: *ΠΗΓΗ/FONS. Revista electrónica de estudios sobre la civilizatión clásica y su recepción* (OJS, www.uc3 m.es/pege), Vol. 1, pp. 57–97.
Knoll, Manuel (2017a): "Platons Konzeption der Mischverfassung in den *Nomoi* und ihr aristokratischer Charakter". In: Knoll, Manuel/Lisi, Francisco L. (Eds.): *Platons "Nomoi". Die politische Herrschaft von Vernunft und Gesetz*. Staatsverständnisse 100. Baden Baden: Nomos, pp. 23–48.
Knoll, Manuel (2017b): "Aristóteles y el pensamiento político aristocrático". Renato Cristi (Trans.). In: *Revista de Filosofía* 73, pp. 87–106.
Knoll, Manuel (2017c): "The Übermensch as Social and Political Task: A Study in the Continuity of Nietzsche's Political Thought". In: Knoll, Manuel/Stocker, Barry (Eds.): *Nietzsche as Political Philosopher*. Berlin, Boston: De Gruyter (first published 2014), pp. 239–266.
Krebs, Angelika (Ed.) (2000): *Gleichheit oder Gerechtigkeit. Texte der neuen Egalitarismuskritik*. Frankfurt a.M.: Suhrkamp.
Kymlicka, Will (2002): *Contemporary Political Philosophy. An Introduction*. Second edition. Oxford: Oxford University Press.
Ladd, John (Ed.) (1985): *Ethical Relativism*. Lanham, New York, London: University Press of America (first published 1973).
Lyotard, Jean-François (1988): *The Differend. Phrases in Dispute*. Georges Van Den Abbeele (Trans.). Manchester: Manchester University Press (first published Paris 1983).
Mackie, John L. (1977): *Ethics. Inventing Right and Wrong*. London: Penguin.
Marx, Karl (1987): *A Contribution to the Critique of Political Economy*. In: Marx, Karl/Engels, Friedrich: *Collected Works*. Vol. 29, Moscow: Progress Publishers.
Marx, Karl (2009): *Critique of the Gotha Programme*. London: Dodo Press.
Mill, John Stuart (2001): *Considerations on Representative Government*. London: Electric Book Company.
Miller, David (2003): *Principles of Social Justice*. Third printing. Cambridge, MA: Harvard University Press (first published 1999).
Nida-Rümelin, Julian (2016): *Humanistische Reflexionen*. Frankfurt a.M.: Suhrkamp.
Nietzsche, Friedrich (2005): *The Anti-Christ, Ecce Homo, Twilight of the Idols, and Other Writings*. Aaron Ridley/Judith Norman (Eds.); J. Norman (Trans.). Cambridge Texts in the History of Philosophy. Cambridge: Cambridge University Press.
Nozick, Robert (1974): *Anarchy, State, and Utopia*. Oxford: Basic Books.
Nussbaum, Martha (2011): *Creating Capabilities. The Human Development Approach*. Cambridge: Belknap Press of Harvard University Press.
Plato (1997): *Laws*. T.J. Saunders (Trans.). In: Plato, *Complete Works*. J.M. Cooper (Ed.). Indianapolis, Cambridge: Hackett.
Pojman, Louis P./Fieser, James (2012): *Ethics. Discovering Right and Wrong*. Seventh edition. Belmont, CA: Wadsworth Cengage Learning.
Polansky, Ronald (1991): "Aristotle on Political Change". In: Keyt, David/Miller, Fred D. Jr. (Eds.): *A Companion to Aristotle's "Politics"*, Cambridge, Oxford: Blackwell, pp. 322–345.
Rawls, John (1971): *A Theory of Justice*. Cambridge, MA: Belknap Press of Harvard University Press.

Rawls, John (2005): *Political Liberalism*. Expanded edition. New York: Columbia University Press.

Rawls, John (2007): *Lectures on the History of Political Philosophy*. Samuel Freeman (Ed.). Cambridge, MA, London: Belknap Press of Harvard University Press.

Ribeiro, Brian (2011): "Philosophy and Disagreement". In: *Crítica. Revista Hispanoamericana de Filosofía* 43. No. 127, pp. 3–25.

Siegel, Harvey (2013): "Argumentation and the Epistemology of Disagreement". In: *OSSA Conference Archive*, Paper 157.

Sommer, Andreas Urs (2016): *Werte. Warum man sie braucht, obwohl es sie nicht gibt.* Stuttgart: Metzler.

Waldron, Jeremy (1999): *Law and Disagreement*. Oxford: Oxford University Press.

Walzer, Michael (1983): *Spheres of Justice. A Defense of Pluralism and Equality*. New York: Basic Books.

Warnke, Claudia (1993): *Justice and Interpretation*. Cambridge, MA: MIT Press.

Weber, Max (1949): "The Meaning of 'Ethical Neutrality' in Sociology and Economics". In: Weber, Max: *On the Methodology of the Social Sciences*. Edward Shills/Henry Finch (Trans. and Eds.). Glencoe, IL: The Free Press of Glencoe.

Ulrich Steinvorth
Are There Irreconcilable Conceptions of Justice? Critical Remarks on Isaiah Berlin

Abstract: To test Berlin's claim that there are "ends equally ultimate, equally sacred" and yet incompatible, I examine the conceptions of justice held by Rawls and Nozick as paradigms of possible irreconcilability, defined as incompatibility without prospect of rational arbitration. Against the ideas that conceptions of justice result from class interests, as Marxists claim, or from "principally different interpretations of and stances on existence", as the political theorist Dagmar Herwig suggests, I argue we can rationally arbitrate between the conceptions of justice of Rawls and Nozick if we take account of social goods that cannot be reduced to products of individual production. Showing how it is possible to rationally arbitrate between Rawls and Nozick, I spell out a few of the consequences for political philosophy. I close by adding a note on the irreconcilability of Plato's conception of justice with that of Thrasymachus, arguing that it is even a weaker witness to Berlin's claim than the alleged irreconcilability between Rawls and Nozick.

1 Are there irreconcilable conceptions of justice?

Are there irreconcilable conceptions of justice? This is what Isaiah Berlin implies when he praises

> Machiavelli's cardinal achievement ... his *de facto* recognition that ends equally ultimate, equally sacred, may contradict each other, that entire systems of value may come into collision without possibility of rational arbitration, ... not merely in exceptional circumstances, as ... the clash of Antigone and Creon or in the story of Tristan – but (this was surely new) as part of the normal human situation (Berlin 2013, section IV).

Value pluralism abolishes belief in one universal truth, but, for Berlin, this abolition is progress:

> So long as only one ideal is the true goal, it will always seem to men that no means can be too difficult, no price too high, to do whatever is required to realize the ultimate goal. Such certainty is one of the great justifications of fanaticism, compulsion, persecution. But ... if rationality and calculation can be applied only to means or subordinate ends, but never to ultimate ends; then ... the path is open to empiricism, pluralism, toleration, compromise. Toleration is historically the product of the realization of the irreconcilability of equally

https://doi.org/10.1515/9783110537369-004

> dogmatic faiths, and the practical improbability of complete victory of one .... (Berlin 2013, section IV).

However it is *historically* dubious whether toleration is "the product of the realization of the irreconcilability of equally dogmatic faiths, and the practical improbability of complete victory of one", rather than a resignation to what is understood to be only a temporary impossibility, namely, to force people into believing what they do not want to believe. *Logically*, toleration cannot be defended without attacking intolerant states, religions and individuals. We cannot consistently preach toleration without intolerance against the intolerant, as little as we can defend liberty without attacking suppressors. Therefore, consistent tolerance is incompatible at least with some forms of value pluralism. It presupposes recognition of a universally valid idea of justice that sets limits to toleration.

Nonetheless, despite this fatal objection, Berlin's claim remains persuasive. The reason is not difficult to find. The same political philosophers who insist on one universal truth have argued for what seem to be irreconcilable conceptions of justice. The conceptions of justice they have argued for are incompatible not just because of differences that could be easily cleared up with some discussion. Rather, these differences are incompatible because there is no rational way to arbitrate among them. In this special sense, the conceptions of justice proposed by Plato and Aristotle, as those of Hobbes and Locke, are not irreconcilable. Their basic model of justice is the same. In the case of Plato and Aristotle, it's a society that allows everyone to use their talents; in the case of Hobbes and Locke, it's a society that secures for everyone the maximum of liberty. Once the ancient and the modern couples recognize their common basic models of justice, they will be able to clear up their differences through rational argument.

In contrast, at first sight, the differences between the ancient and the modern couple, between Plato and Aristotle on the one side and Hobbes and Locke on the other, may seem irreconcilable. However, they may prove reconcilable, seeing as the two couples may agree that there is a maximum of liberty if and only if everyone has the opportunity to freely use their talents. In light of this, there seems to be a rational way to arbitrate even between them.

Yet, the conception of justice (or injustice) held by the sophist Thrasymachus (as we know him from Plato) is indeed irreconcilable with the conceptions of justice of Plato and Aristotle, and likewise of Hobbes and Locke. The sophist bases his conception on an interest in power that is entirely alien to the idea that justice must allow everyone the use of their talents or a maximum of liberty. In fact, his conception is the very denial of the expectation that the ordinary use of the term *justice* seems to imply, namely that in a just society everyone can have a good life or at least is respected. So how can there be a rational arbitration between Thrasymachus and Plato? Thus, the irreconcilability of Thrasymachus' conception of justice with those of most other political philosophers does seem to bear witness to the truth of Berlin's value pluralism.

Before looking at the case of Thrasymachus and Plato, let's look at another candidate for a pair of irreconcilable conceptions of justice, the team of Rawls and Nozick. Although colleagues at the same university and offspring of rather similar social conditions, the latter understands justice as the protection of private property and the former as equal distribution in the interest of everyone, leaving only a limited place for private property. Isn't this as irreconcilable as the difference between Thrasymachus and Plato?

However, I claim that the traditional idea of a universal truth, or a universal justice, is not as weak as is often believed. I am going to argue that,
(a) we can rationally arbitrate between Rawls and Nozick,
(b) Marx and Dagmar Herwig who may seem to agree with Berlin cannot support Berlin,
(c) rational arbitration for Rawls and Nozick implies basic changes in political philosophy, and
(d) the irreconcilability between Thrasymachus and Plato does not support Berlin.

2 The irreconcilability of individualism and commonalism

Rawls describes his principles of justice as

> a special case of a more general conception of justice that can be expressed as follows: All social values – liberty and opportunity, income and wealth, and the bases of self-respect – are to be distributed equally unless an unequal distribution of any, or all, of these values is to everyone's advantage. Injustice, then, are simply inequalities that are not to the benefit of all (Rawls 1972, p. 62, cf. p. 303).

Consider what this means: if I work less than you, you get more income only if your surplus benefits me. Is this just? Don't we have something like an inviolable right to the product of our labor?

Nozick followed this intuition when he opposed to Rawls an alternative approach:

> Individuals have rights, and there are things no person or group may do to them (without violating their rights). So strong and far-reaching are these rights that they raise the ques-

tion of what, if anything, the state and its officials may do. How much room do individuals leave for the state? (Nozick 1974, p. ix).

Will not everyone who is cheated out of the fruits of their labor agree with Nozick? How can it be just to redistribute what we have honestly acquired? Nozick defended capitalism, but his view is the basis of the *labor movement* that fought for just wages, that is, for the assignment of the value of the products to the producers. Nozick's conception of justice also conforms to those of Hobbes, Locke, Kant and other liberals who summed justice up in the *harm principle*, the prohibition on the restriction of anyone's liberty unless their liberty restricts someone else's.

Moreover, the right to appropriate the fruits of one's labor is analog to the right to make healthy adult agents responsible for their actions and the duty to take responsibility for one's actions. If our actions are bad, we'll be punished; if they are productive, property is our reward. Even Thrasymachus' claim that justice is the right to take what you can get could be reconciled with Nozick *if* he universalized his claim, declaring that everyone has the right to take what they can get if they do not prevent anyone else from using the same right (but he wouldn't accept the universalizability condition).

In fact, Nozick's conception of justice is an updated version of *political individualism*. It seems it must be backed by everyone for whom the individual is prior to society and society exists for the individual rather than the other way around. Thus, Nozick's conception of justice is well supported by both our intuitions of justice and the history of political philosophy.

However, the very author who based his justice theory on moral intuitions, John Rawls, contradicts Nozick, as he regards everything distributable as something to be equally distributed unless the unequal distribution benefits the poorer ones. On the other hand, Rawls' conception of justice finds support in the writings of Plato and Aristotle, as well as Hegel and Marx, who like Rawls regarded the goods that can be distributed in a society as something no individual has a natural right to appropriate. Just as Nozick's conception of justice is an updated version of political individualism, Rawls' conception is an updated version of what we may call *political commonalism*. I prefer to call it *commonalism* rather than *communism* to indicate that it does not imply a communism of the kind that socialist and communist parties and states tried to realize but only the idea that important parts of a society's resources are its common property.

Can political commonalism really not be supported by widespread moral intuitions? Certainly it can as far as we can be convinced that, as Aristotle claimed, society, or more precisely, the *polis*, is prior to the household and the individual (*Pol.* I 2, 1253a18 f.). This, however, is not a popular thesis today. Nonetheless, we have to concede that in the past it did seem very convincing to many people. Today, there still are quite a few people, even if not strongly represented in contemporary politics, who adhere to the idea that important parts of a society's assets are common property, and that, as individuals depend on such property, society is prior to the individual.

Moreover, there are two facts that should stop us from rejecting Rawls' justice conception.

First, Rawls denies neither the harm principle nor the idea of individual liberty. He even declares this idea his first principle of justice, which reads:

> Each person is to have an equal right to the most extensive basic liberty compatible with a similar liberty for others (1971, p. 60).

Rawls (1971, p. 61) even declares that this principle has priority over his second justice principle that corresponds to his "more general conception of justice". The second principle of justice reads:

> Social and economic inequalities are to be arranged so that they are both (a) reasonably expected to be to everyone's advantage, and (b) attached to positions and offices open to all (1971, p. 60).[1]

The problem, though, is that it is difficult to see how this priority, and Rawls's general conception of justice that requires "all social values" to be equally distributed unless inequality benefits everyone, is compatible with his "equal right to the most extensive basic liberty compatible with a similar liberty for others". For your liberty is strongly restricted if you get a higher salary for longer work only if it benefits me too. Or if we argue that if you got more salary, than this is incompatible with "a similar liberty for" me, then most people certainly wouldn't want such liberty.

Second and more instructively, if we understand the *social values*, which Rawls says must be distributed equally, not as any distributable good, but as goods that are *irreducibly social*, then Rawls can become convincing. Irreducibly social values are goods that can only be provided by society, not by a single individual. I provisionally define an *irreducibly social value or good* as a good having all of the following properties:

(1) It results from the fact that we are social animals that somehow need one another.

---

[1] This is Rawls's preliminary formulation, followed later by more explicit ones. I rely on the preliminary version because it is short and gives us Rawls' idea better than the explicit versions.

(2) I can have more or less of it, so I can be justly and unjustly treated relating to it.
(3) It cannot be distributed and appropriated like a commodity, as it has no exchange value.
(4) It makes it possible to produce goods that can have exchange value and be appropriated.

If there are irreducibly social goods in the sense defined, and if all goods produced in societies owe their production to the existence of such social goods, then we may find a rational argument proving that no product is appropriable by a natural right but only under the Rawlsian condition that it must benefit every member of society.

If we find such an argument, we can rationally arbitrate between Rawls and Nozick, judging Rawls' theory of justice true as far as his principle of equal distribution applies to irreducibly social goods only, and judging Nozick's theory of justice true as far as it applies to goods only that have been produced by individuals and can be assigned as the product of identifiable individuals. In the same way, we can rationally arbitrate between the *political individualism* and *political commonalism* that Nozick and Rawls have reformulated. Their conceptions of justice, hence the difference between the most important among the competing conceptions of justice in the history of philosophy, would not be irreconcilable. We could rationally solve age-old conflicts of ideas.

Yet before deliberating the possibility of such an argument, let's have a look at Marx, who is often considered to believe in the irreconcilability of conceptions of justice, as he often assigns them to economic interests, and another less well known author who did claim the irreconcilability of conceptions of justice.

3 Marx's and Herwig's explanations

Marx no doubt contributed to the view that justice is based on class interests. Thus, in his much quoted Preface to *A Contribution to the Critique of Political Economy* of 1859 he said that

> In the social production of their existence, men inevitably enter into definite relations, which are independent of their will, namely relations of production appropriate to a given stage in the development of their material forces of production. The totality of these relations of production constitutes the economic structure of society, the real foundation, on which arises a legal and political superstructure and to which correspond definite forms of social consciousness. The mode of production of material life conditions the general process of social, political and intellectual life (1987, p. 263).

Nonetheless, Marx stuck to the contrary idea that theories of politics and justice are true or false for universally valid reasons. For evidence of this claim, I refer here only to his and Engels' *Communist Manifesto* (Ch. 1):

> Just as ... at an earlier period, a section of the nobility went over to the bourgeoisie, so now a portion of the bourgeoisie goes over to the proletariat, and in particular, a portion of the bourgeois ideologists, who have raised themselves to the level of comprehending theoretically the historical movement as a whole (1970, p. 43).

Though born into the bourgeoisie, Marx and Engels sided with the proletariat, despite their bourgeois pride and prejudice that made them dislike most proletarians. What made them thus side was not an interest but a reason. As their historiography in their *Communist Manifesto* shows, their reason is that the class interests of the proletariat allow more individuals to use and develop their capabilities than the class interests of the bourgeoisie. Judging societies and their conceptions of justice by the *standard of how much they allow individuals to develop their capabilities*, they use a criterion of progress and moral superiority that Plato, Aristotle, Hobbes, Locke and Kant have also used. That they raise themselves to the level of comprehending history means they evaluate societies and class interests by a criterion accepted by many past and present philosophers. They judge the proletarian class interest to be objectively better than the bourgeois class interest because it allows more people to develop their capabilities.

Despite its use by so many philosophers, this criterion of progress has the weak point of allowing different interpretations of progress, depending on *which capabilities* are to be developed in the first place, *who decides* what one's capabilities are, *how* they are used and developed, and how important the *number of people* using their capabilities is. These differences cannot be rationally arbitrated by an appeal to progress. Though not always, sometimes the differences are important. Therefore, as long as we do not agree on a universally valid interpretation of the standard of the development of people's capabilities or talents, the use of this criterion of progress is insufficient for rational arbitration between incompatible conceptions of justice, much as, together with other criteria, it may be of help.

It can no longer be claimed that only the Marxists and Berlin reject the rational arbitration of values. Rather, this disbelief has been the prevailing view among contemporaries as well. Values and moral rules are widely considered to be relative to specific, rather than universal, social and mental conditions. It is worth having a look at Dagmar Herwig, a little known German political theorist, because she provides a theoretical basis for justice relativism that we can use to defend Berlin's claim that there are irreconcilable values, including conceptions of justice such as those of Rawls and Nozick.

Herwig argues that equality has been conceived in two incompatible ways, as *Gleichbehandlung, equal treatment*, and as *Egalisierung, equalization*. *Equal treatment* requires everyone to treat anyone appropriately according to human nature and reason. This approach has been chosen by most philosophers: the sophists, Plato and Aristotle, the Stoics, Hobbes, Rousseau and other representatives of "individualist natural law", and many contemporary theorists; all of them protecting talents. *Equalization* aims at making individuals as equal as possible, setting no limit to their equalization. Herwig argues the utopians from Thomas Morus in the early 16th century to Cabet's *Communist Creed* of 1842 defended it. The ancient Christians also supported this notion (Herwig 1984, pp. 134–143, though she refers only to passages in the New Testament that she claims demand *equalization*), and in present times it has become a sort of fashion (Herwig 1984, pp. 144–160, 90–97, 28–49).

Equal treatment, like political individualism, measures justice by the adequacy of an action to a law of reason that requires of everyone equal respect to anyone. Yet *equalization* differs from political commonalism, as commonalism does set limits to equalization, appealing, like equal treatment, to a law of reason or nature or a similar principle that forbids unconditional equalization. This is particularly obvious in Rawls, whose first justice principle secures everyone's liberty. In fact, Herwig, when discussing Rawls, praises him for his going beyond her two models (Herwig 1984, pp. 2 and 22–27).

Herwig's interest is to prove and describe, rather than to explain, the irreconcilability of her two models. Yet she does provide an explanation for how the tensions between the two models of justice "broke up already among the sophists" (1984, p. 110). Although all sophists appealed to *nature* as the right source for just laws, they drew opposite conclusions. Hippias and Antiphon postulated unrestricted equality, while Gorgias and Thrasymachus argued for privileges for the strong. "The discrepancy", she explains,

> is not contingent on different premises, but rather ... on different viewpoints towards the same object. People are taken, on the one hand as members of a *species*, as *Gattungswesen*; on the other, as *individuals*. In the former case, the concept of nature is related to the species: all humans are members of the same biological species and as such, by natural necessity, have the same general properties of the species. As congeners, as *Gattungswesen*, all of them are equal. In the latter case, the concept of nature is related to man as an individual. Thus, this interpretation arrives at the very contrary result ... Both judgments have the same relative validity, a validity relative to the viewpoint chosen. They become questionable and attackable only if claimed to be absolutely valid for further argumentation (Herwig 1984, pp. 103–106).

Herwig explains the two models as two understandings of the "concept of nature", one that takes people "as members of a *species*, as *Gattungswesen*" and one that takes them "as *individuals*". I wonder how "different viewpoints towards the same object" can be "not contingent on different premises", but this claim underlines her crucial point. Her point is that the two models are "equally legitimate responses to the most imperfect human nature and its social manifestations" (Herwig 1984, p. 2); "rooted in principally different interpretations of and stances on existence [*zwei in grundsätzlich verschiedenen Existenzauslegungen und -haltungen wurzelnde Modelle von Gerechtigkeit*]" (Herwig 1984, p. 204).[2]

However, *are* they "equally legitimate responses"? How can the fact that humans are members of the human species allow deducing that laws should promote equalization, as it belongs to the human species that its members have different talents? Equalization is not a legitimate response to human nature at all. Rather, equalization resulted, as Herwig herself says, from special ideas about equality that some Christians adhered to, while the utopians drew on the indignation at the crass inequalities of their epochs rather than on principles equally legitimate as the principles of equal treatment.

In fact, Herwig's starting point was the discussion of equality in the late 1960s and 70s in Germany. The discussion rallied around the slogan *Dare more democracy (Mehr Demokratie wagen)*. The dialogue, of both similar and contrary ideas, made up, as Herwig called it, a "woolly network" ("verworrenes Netzwerk", Herwig 1984, p. 1), that cried out for the clarification she strove to articulate. Today, though, equalization is no longer a live option. Nearly every political theorist rejects aiming at unlimited equalization. Nearly everyone insists that individuals should develop their individual talents. Everyone abhors the equalization depicted in black utopias such as *1984* and *Brave New World*. The Christian idea of equalization that Herwig promotes as a serious opponent to equal treatment lacks textual evidence in ancient authors. She herself gives equalization a low rank when she points to equalization theory's conceptual confusion (Herwig 1984, pp. 3ff.) and concedes that she considers the models to be "not equivalent as theories" ("theoretisch ungleichwertig", Herwig 1984, p. 2), obviously preferring the model of equal treatment. Hence, as equalization, in the unspecified sense of her equalization model, lacks convincingness, her explanation of irreconcilable conceptions is also not convincing.

---

[2] Cf. Herwig 1984, p. 49f. Here she is critical of explaining the irreconcilability by differences between ancient and modern societies or between philosophical and religious thinking, to which the two conceptions might be assigned.

4 Irreducibly social goods and Rawlsian social values

As neither Marx nor Herwig can support Berlin's claim that there be "ends equally ultimate, equally sacred", we find support for arbitrating between the positions of Rawls and Nozick, asking whether there are irreducibly social values in the sense provisionally defined.

The first thing to recognize is that in his general conception of justice, Rawls lists as social values "liberty and opportunity, income and wealth, and the bases of self-respect". These values are not irreducibly social goods. Contrary to condition (1) in the above definition, they do not necessarily result from the fact that we are social animals somehow in need of one another. For I can have income, such as a harvest, also if I act alone. Likewise, I can have wealth and opportunity and liberty if I am alone. I likely can also have self-respect when I exist alone as the only human in the world. I might compare myself with animals and, taking pride in my superior intelligence, develop self-respect. In any case, although in cooperation I can produce more wealth, I can produce some alone.

Therefore, it is fair enough, as individualists demand, to regard the cooperative product as a result of the different contributions of the cooperators, and the cooperators as the owners of exactly that part of the value of the product that corresponds to the value of their cooperative contributions. It seems also fair enough to assume that every producer has a natural right to appropriate the value of their product. Of course, it would be illegitimate if you did not get more income than me if your labor was longer.

Nonetheless, there are irreducibly social goods only society can provide. The most important ones are social recognition, a good that psychologists, pedagogues and historians recognize as basic for human life, and the synergies of interaction, a good recognized as basic for modern societies in economics and administration.

As things are, we are not the only human in the world but living with other humans and, exempting perhaps some outliers, are in need of recognition coming from at least some of them; otherwise we don't find satisfaction or meaning in life. So, in terms of the four points laid out above at the end of section 2 regarding irreducibly social values or goods, social recognition is a good that results from the fact that we are social animals in need of one another, as required by property (1). It's also a good of which I can have more or less, so I can be unjustly treated in relation to social recognition, as required by property (2). Yet it is not an exchangeable product. Although identifiable individuals can give me the social recognition I need, it cannot be exchanged as commodities can. If I pay for social recognition, it's not recognition I get. Social recognition is not a commodity and cannot be distributed like a commodity, as required by property (3). But social recognition makes it possible to produce goods that can be commodities and be appropriated, as required by property (4).

Similarly, synergies of interaction result from the fact that we need one another. I can have more or less of it, depending on how intensely I am cooperating and on what kind of interaction I am involved in. For instance, I can be engaged in a tennis match more or less intensely, and both the joy and the fret I have when I play can be more or less great and can make me more or less active both in the tennis match and outside it. In general, the more interaction with other people we have and the more intense it is, the more we get of the synergies of interaction: energy and high motivation to do whatever we want to do. Such energy and motivation cannot be distributed and appropriated like a commodity, as little as social recognition can. In fact, social recognition and love are special sources of the synergies of interaction. All sources of the synergies of interaction share with social recognition and love the property that they are no longer what we want them to be when we buy or exchange them for an exchange value.

Again, both the things we produce with the help of the synergies of interaction, and the things we produce with the help of the social recognition we get, can be appropriated and distributed like commodities. They also can be produced as commodities or for a market. In fact, all human action and production depends on the social recognition and the synergies of interaction that we get or do not get in society.

What does this mean for the individualist approach to justice? It does not rule out, if you work longer or have a nastier work than I do, that you get more salary. On the contrary, as people often appreciate other people doing long work, you can expect to get more recognition than me for your longer work and more reward from other people. But it does rule out that you consider your product something that is only your product. It is always the product of both you and the society or societies you live in. So the distribution of anything distributable has to take into account the social conditions on which anything individually produced is dependent.

In a way, this is trivial; no one will deny that individuals wouldn't even exist without favorable social conditions, not to mention that any virtue or productive quality of an individual is codetermined by their society. In another way, it's not trivial, as individualists insist on the priority of individuals. If by priority they mean that individuals must be respected in their will to decide for themselves on issues pertinent to their life, they are perfectly right. But if they mean that they have an unconditional or natural right to appropriate what they have produced, they are wrong, for no one can produce anything without help from other people. So no one can claim to be the exclusive producer of a good and deduce that he has a natural right to the product.

Yet just as we can consistently assume there is a natural right to punish those who deliberately destroy or harm other people, we can consistently assume there is a natural right to liberty and to being adequately rewarded or honored for one's contributions to the flourishing of society. Hence, if you work more than I do, you have a right to get more pay, but not because you have produced something whose natural proprietor you are but because you have contributed more to the flourishing of society than I did.

In effect, that is Rawls' claim too, though not in principle, as he relies on the psychological rather than moral argument that those who contribute more should have more because otherwise they would stop contributing. But instead of focusing on differences between a conception of justice that bases societal claims on irreducibly social values rather than on Rawls' social values, let us stay with the topic of irreducibly social goods. Are there more examples of them, and what are the consequences we have to draw from their existence for the conception of justice?

We may add trust, the mutual, more or less strong, trust of individuals in one another, but also in their institutions, as another irreducibly social good; as well as the security people feel that their lives and actions are protected against force and fraud. Whatever in our social conditions favors our life but is not brought about for exchange is an irreducibly social good.

Such goods, however, cannot be equally distributed. If everyone got the same amount of social recognition, the distributed thing wouldn't be recognition any more. Nor can the synergy of interaction, or trust or security, be the same for everyone in a population. Equality for irreducibly social goods can consist only in equal access to them, or even just in non-exclusion from them.

Again, in effect, Rawls has taken account of this fact. For his second principle of justice reads:

> Social and economic inequalities are to be arranged so that they are both (a) reasonably expected to be to everyone's advantage, and (b) attached to positions and offices open to all.

Although Rawls understands this principle as "a special case" of the "more general conception of justice" that requires "all social values ... to be distributed equally unless an unequal distribution of any, or all, of these values is to everyone's advantage", in fact his second principle of justice requires the social values of "positions and offices" to be accessible for everyone rather than to be equally distributed. Now, not only are "positions and offices" the goods that Rawls lists as social values, but also "liberty and opportunity, income and wealth, and the bases of self-respect". Positions and offices belong only to opportunities; so there are but few social values left for equal distribution rather than for equal access. However, liberty cannot be equally distributed either; rather, equal liberty is to be understood as equal access for everyone to the laws and institutions that protect individual liberty. The basis of self-respect, to which belongs parental care, cannot be equally distributed either, as parents and their care are indelibly different. It's only income and wealth that can be equally distributed. Yet, that justice requires their equal distribution (unless inequality benefits everyone) is counterintuitive. Wealth and income are the Rawlsian social goods that most obviously are not irreducibly social goods.

Let's draw some rough conclusions from the existence of irreducibly social goods in the sense provisionally defined. Here is not the place to formulate them with sufficient prudence and precision; I only sketch them to show what kind of consequences we might expect from the recognition of irreducibly social goods.

5 Some conclusions

The existence of irreducibly social goods is enough to refute the kind of political individualism that, like Locke's and Nozick's, claims a natural right for individuals to appropriate the product of their labor, but not to refute what I'll call minimal political individualism. Minimal individualism is necessary to maintain if we don't want to deny humans the moral quality that distinguishes them from animals. It assumes that individuals have the liberty to choose between deliberated actions, including the choice between doing more or less for society, and that having the liberty to choose between deliberated actions provides creatures with a quality that requires their actions meet the conditions of morality and justice.

As to justice, this requirement implies that I must respect everyone's actions, as long as they too respect the actions of other humans. The requirement bestows on everyone the right to be protected against harm and the duty to harm no one. Recognizing this right to protection implies the recognition of universal human rights. It also implies the idea that everyone ought to be blamed or punished for their harmful actions. Correspondingly, for morality, the requirement implies that everyone should help anyone in need of help, and that everyone ought to be honored or applauded for actions that help other people or society. So, minimal individualism claims a right for individuals to get a reward in proportion to their contribution to the well-being of society. Yet it does not imply a right to receive a proportional reward in money or another specific form. Reward may be in money or medals, in prize or privilege.

Aristotle's notorious thesis that the polis is prior to the individual (*Pol.* I 2, 1253a18f.) can be and has often been understood to imply that individuals exist for states rather than the other way round. Yet if we understand the priority of the polis as the irreducibility of social values to goods individuals can produce alone, we can both insist that societies exist for individuals and conceive of justice as a system protecting not only individuals against harm, but also social goods. In this conception, justice includes not only "negative liberty", consistent with the value pluralism of the more radical individualist Isaiah Berlin; rather, justice also includes "positive liberty" (Berlin 1958).

Negative liberty is the liberty to be free of any prescriptions that do not maximize everyone's liberty; positive liberty is the liberty that can coerce us to protect certain social conditions without which, according to the defenders of positive liberty, individuals cannot enjoy their individual liberties. If justice is conceived as negative liberty only, the laws of justice, to use Nozick's term, are side-constraints to our actions that prevent harming the rights of other people. But if justice includes positive liberty, the laws of justice include signposts that coerce us to go in a certain direction. In fact, if there are irreducibly social values that every human depends on, it would risk harming everyone if they were not protected by the laws of justice too.

What does protection of irreducibly social goods more concretely mean? It means no one must be excluded or hindered from access to such goods. People are hindered from access to social recognition when they are systematically discriminated against. Discrimination is recognized as an injustice in many societies; therefore, systematic discrimination is prohibited in many states. Unemployment is another obvious case of hindered access to social recognition, but there are no laws to prevent unemployment from being a hindrance to social recognition. Considering the prospect that technology makes more and more traditional occupations economically superfluous and that machines do much of human labor better than humans, societies should use the chance of getting rid of labor and find ways to turn the status of unemployment from something despicable into something honorable. The institution of a basic income may help in achieving such a change (cf. Steinvorth 2014). Introducing basic income can be justified not only as a means to compensate the individuals who are excluded from actively using natural resource, but also as a means to prevent exclusion from the sources of social recognition.

Similarly, lack of a basic education and health care (not caused by one's own negligence) hinders people from access to social recognition. Therefore, provision of such basics is a requirement of justice, not of benevolence or charity, and can justly be imposed on a society.

Rawls understood that justice forbids exclusion. As mentioned, by his second justice principle he required inequalities to be arranged so that they are not only "reasonably expected to be to everyone's advantage" but also are "attached to positions and offices open to all" (Rawls 1971, p. 60). This condition does not conform to his general conception of justice that forbids "inequalities ... not to the benefit of all". If positions and offices are open to all, they must be neither equally distributed nor distributed to everyone's advantage. Nor is this condition deducible from the harm principle or the prohibition of inequality. Rather, it conforms to our moral intuition that everyone has a right to participate in the interactions that provide irreducibly social goods.

Recognizing positive liberty does not imply, as is often assumed, that the state should not be minimal. Libertarians are right to warn against state power. The enforcement of justice that today is assigned to the state, along with many other tasks that are difficult to combine with the enforcement of justice, should better be assigned to a public office that pursues the enforcement of justice, or even better to a branch that enforces justice as its only task. Political philosophy faces the task of developing a theory that replaces the state's traditional role as enforcer of justice with separate institutions tasked with realizing justice. The task is not utopian. As political theorists have observed, in international affairs state institutions are already "disaggregating" (Slaughter 2005) into task-oriented international institutions that administer what nation states cannot provide. For reasons I have pointed to elsewhere (Steinvorth 2013, Ch. 6 and 7), we should dismiss the idea that the modern state is the most adequate institution to implement justice and the many other tasks it has arrogated, such as the provision of economic superstructure and of the basics of education and health care.

Dismissing this idea will also help answer the question of which society has to institute the principles of justice, the global society or the regional societies, which today are most often ruled by national states. Rawls, in his *Law of Peoples*, has argued against applying the difference principle to international relations (Rawls 1999). If we replace the difference principle with the principle that no one must be excluded from the sources of social recognition and other irreducibly social goods, should we still follow Rawls, claiming that the prevention of such exclusion is not the task of the global society, the system of regional societies, but of regional societies and their states?

Rawls argued that a society should not bear the consequences of deliberated actions that another society has decided on. Indeed, it is not plausible that if a society opts for using its resources for having many (or few) children, other societies are under a duty of justice to help them overcome the bad results that may follow. However, does this imply that the children in a society that has opted for ways that led to disaster may be excluded from the sources of recognition and other irreducibly social goods? This is not plausible either.

The solution to this dilemma should be to further restrict the sovereign rights of states, divesting them of their right to demographic decisions and other options whose consequences affect the whole world. The sovereign rights of the states, however, should not go to a world government, but to a democratically controlled global institution whose authority is restricted to issuing rules for a specific topic, such as demography, to be valid all over the world. If the rules are violated by a regional state or another institution, then, in accordance with the idea of replacing traditional justice enforcement institutions with separate institutions of justice realization, it should be the task of another democratically controlled global institution to decide on sanctions to deter the violation.

The consequences of recognizing irreducibly social goods may seem rather utopian. Still, they do show that the difference between Nozick and Rawls, and more general that between political individualism and political commonalism, does not witness to Berlin's value pluralism. We have become skeptical about the skeptical claim that there is not just one truth, and we should become equally skeptical about the skeptical claim that there is not just one justice.

6 The Thrasymachean kind of irreconcilability of a justice conception

Nonetheless, Berlin may shrug off any effort to rationally arbitrate between Nozick and Rawls, pointing to the difference between conceptions of justice such as that of Plato and Thrasymachus.

Yet we should see that there is a categorical difference between incompatibilities of the sort that exist between Rawls and Nozick, and incompatibilities of the sort that exist between Plato and Thrasymachus. The former type is a difference between *interpretations* of the concept or idea of justice that we find in all societies; the latter is a difference between *upholding* the idea of justice, however interpreted, and *denying* the idea of justice. Thrasymachus, as represented in the first book of Plato's *Republic*, does not really propose a conception of justice, even though in the beginning of his argument he presents a thesis on what justice is. Rather, he denies that the commonly held, naïve, as he says, views on justice, explicated by Socrates, can be taken seriously.

Thrasymachus does claim that "justice is nothing other than the advantage of the stronger" (*Resp.* I 338c), that justice is "the advantage of the established rule" (339a), that justice is the advantage of the ruler and stronger "in the most precise sense" of a craftsman whose craft "never errs" (340e, 341b). But after being shown by Socrates that these claims entangle him in contradictions, he falls back on the ordinary use of the terms *justice* and *injustice*, claiming that "injustice ... is stronger, freer, and more masterly than justice" (344c). By this remark he implies that the actions ordinarily blamed by describing them as *unjust* should not be avoided by the few who are clever enough to see the uncomfortable consequences of being just, but on the contrary should be followed, and that correspondingly the actions ordinarily praised by calling them *just* should be avoided. Thus, he does not develop a theory of *justice* but a defense of *injustice*.

A defense of injustice is certainly a challenge to any theory of justice, more difficult to refute than any competing theory of justice. But it does not provide an "end equally ultimate, equally sacred" as the end of justice. There can be no end or value of injustice if there was not an end or value of justice, but there can be a value of justice without there being a value of injustice. In this sense, the value of injustice, attractive as it is presented by Thrasymachus and later by Nietzsche (in his *Genealogy of Morals*, though this is probably only one aspect of his views on justice), cannot be "equally ultimate, equally sacred" as the end of justice.

Therefore, Berlin cannot point to the incompatibility between Plato and Thrasymachus as evidence for his claim that "So long as only one ideal is the true goal, it will always seem to men that no means can be too difficult, no price too high, to do whatever is required to realize the ultimate goal". As the ideal defended by Thrasymachus and Nietzsche's *Genealogy* is a defense of injustice, it is not only incompatible with justice; it is the entire rejection of justice. It cannot be understood as a possibly "true goal" beside the goal of justice, but only as the excluding alternative to justice. If we decide for it, we decide against justice in any understanding, exclude toleration of justice and are excluded from toleration by any understanding of justice. Obviously, although Berlin implies this consequence, it is not what he wanted to defend.

Therefore, reference to the irreconcilability between Thrasymachus and Plato cannot support Berlin. Rather, the reference confirms our skepticism about the skeptical claim that there is not just one justice, just as we have become skeptical about the skeptical claim that there is not just one truth.

Bibliography

Berlin, Isaiah (1958): *Two Concepts of Liberty*. Oxford: Clarendon.
Berlin, Isaiah (2013): "The Question of Machiavelli". In: *New York Review of Books*, 4 November 1971; shortened reprint 7 March 2013; www.nybooks.com/50/Machiavelli, accessed March 9, 2013.
Herwig, Dagmar (1984): *Gleichbehandlung und Egalisierung als konkurrierende Modelle von Gerechtigkeit*. Munich: Fink.
Marx, Karl (1987): *A Contribution to the Critique of Political Economy*. In: Marx, Karl/Engels, Friedrich: Collected Works. Vol. 29, Moscow: Progress Publishers.
Marx, Karl/Engels, Frederick (1970): *Manifesto of the Communist Party*. Samuel Moore (Trans.). Peking: Foreign Languages Press.
Nozick, Robert (1974): *State, Anarchy, and Utopia*. New York: Basic Books.
Plato (1992): *Republic*. G.M.A. Grube/C.D.C. Reeve (Trans.). Indianapolis: Hackett.
Rawls, John (1971): *A Theory of Justice*. Cambridge, MA: Harvard University Press.
Rawls, John (1999): *The Law of Peoples*. Cambridge, MA: Harvard University Press.
Slaughter, Anne-Marie (2005): *A New World Order*. Princeton: Princeton University Press.
Steinvorth, Ulrich (2013): *The Metaphysics of Modernity*. Milwaukee: Marquette University Press.
Steinvorth, Ulrich (2014): "Capitalism, Unemployment, and Basic Income". In: *Homo Oeconomicus* 31. Nos. 1–2, pp. 125–143.

Michael Haus
Equality beyond Liberal Egalitarianism: Walzer's Contribution to the Theory of Justice[1]

Abstract: This contribution develops a particular perspective on the value of equality and the claims of egalitarianism. It suggests an alternative to the egalitarian theories of John Rawls and other liberal egalitarians. The alternative presented would not give up the commitment to egalitarianism; renouncing the commitment to equality as a normative ideal would violate a deep consensus within modern political theory. It would also disrupt the consensus shared in liberal democratic societies that hierarchical ways of thinking are inappropriate and the normative demand that all human beings should be equally capable of leading an autonomous life. At the same time, the commitment to equality and egalitarianism should transcend the liberal egalitarians' focus on compensating individuals for the relative disadvantages they have in comparison with other individuals. This is possible by interpreting the idea of equal autonomy in a different, more political way. To do this, Michael Walzer's understanding of social justice is used to elaborate on the value of equality, demonstrating its usefulness by applying it to the field of educational justice. This application shows that a political understanding of egalitarianism, focussing on the abolition of domination may avoid certain shortcomings and paradoxes the liberal egalitarian discourse runs into.

1 Introduction

In the following, I will propose a perspective on social justice which aims to go beyond that of John Rawls and other liberal egalitarians which does not give up the commitment to egalitarianism. My thesis is that instead of criticising this commitment in the name of non-egalitarianism we should understand equality in a non-Rawlsian way, but take it even more seriously. I make the point that

---

[1] This paper was first presented at the conference "Pluralism and Conflict: Distributive Justice Beyond Rawls and Consensus", held 6–8 June 2013 in Istanbul. I am thankful to Manuel Knoll, who was the organiser of this conference and is now the co-editor of this volume, for his valuable comments. I am also deeply grateful to Stephen Snyder, Dirk Jörke and Basil Bornemann for commenting on the manuscript.

https://doi.org/10.1515/9783110537369-005

to give up the commitment to equality as a normative ideal would mean to revert to thinking about justice in terms of social hierarchy, i.e. giving human persons different overall normative ranks in society and attributing to them unequal value as persons. I suggest that there is indeed what can be called a *deep consensus*, not only within political theory, but also shared in liberal democratic societies regarding the inappropriateness of such hierarchical ways of thinking. At the same time, the commitment to equality and egalitarianism as an attempt to honour this consensus has to transcend the liberal egalitarians' focus on compensating individuals for the relative disadvantages they have in comparison with other individuals.

This deep consensus, I suppose, reflects a basic way of socially imagining the world we live in: we imagine ourselves as living in societies as individual members with what Charles Taylor has called "direct" or "unmediated access" (Taylor 1998, pp. 196–200), and this means, among other things, that our development and social position are structured by common institutions and practices. Ironically, though, "deep" with respect to the consensus does not mean "substantial" or "elaborated" (although the reference to "autonomy" is a central normative idea, see below). It rather means "latent" or "fundamental" and it points to a question, not a solution. We are in permanent disagreement about equality *because* we all believe in equality as a basic status of persons. Borrowing a term from Laclau and Mouffe (1985), *because* equality is an "empty signifier" the idea can form a common point of reference in societal discourse without ever being conceptualised in one "reasonable" manner and without ever being institutionalised in a definite way.

The impossibility of definite institutionalisation does not simply originate in the fact that equality can be understood differently; its impossibility is also related to the circumstance that equality is never the only idea with normative relevance. The consensus also affirms (the "empty signifiers" of) liberty or freedom or as I will say in the following, the idea of *autonomy* (see Bornemann/Haus 2014). With Honneth, I am convinced that it is the idea of *equal autonomy* which lies behind the relevant conceptions of justice in modern political theory (Honneth 2011, p. 122). It is never equality *per se* that is affirmed, but always equality in connection with autonomy, i.e. to lead one's life by relying on one's own capabilities, in accordance with one's own needs, desires and commitments etc. Thus, it is not a value in itself that two persons have the same goods – it is only a value insofar as this expresses their moral status as having the same claim to leading an autonomous life. Again, autonomy can be understood in different ways. No doubt, Rawls has contributed to a remarkably powerful view on how to understand autonomy in connection with equality. But this is only one view and its success comes at a certain price.

How then, can we go beyond Rawls? The answer I will give in the following will, informed by Walzer's theory of justice,[2] interpret the commitment to equality and autonomy in a different way. It aims to show that because different interpretations are possible, the role of a theory of justice cannot be to overcome disagreement; rather, it is firstly, to provide for the strong and imaginative articulation of equality and autonomy and secondly, to make possible critical observations about the prevailing discourse on social justice in a society. I believe that we can learn much from Walzer's contribution to thinking about social justice here. In the following, I will first recapitulate how Rawls and liberal egalitarians in general perceive equality, consensus, and autonomy and I will discuss how convincing alternatives to this could look arguing that non-egalitarianism is not convincing. I will then bring in Walzer's perspective on social justice and show how it can help us to go beyond Rawls.

2 The ideal of equality and its connection to autonomy

2.1 The Rawlsian perspective on social justice

Rawls and his followers perceive the linkage between consensus, equality and autonomy in a manner characteristic for the contractarian tradition: valid principles of justice must receive reasoned support from all members of a society (consensus), and such support will be possible if all members are treated as moral equals (equality), rooted in the intuition that morally equal persons have a claim to equal freedom (autonomy). The consensus to be reached is thus a consensus of moral and rational agents and its content is a conception of justice that treats them as equals with respect to being autonomous in the same basic way. Political theorists who can be considered Rawlsians in a broad manner support the idea that the basic regulatory mechanisms, material means, and cultural preconditions which enable being individually autonomous are what social justice demands in order to be shaped in an egalitarian manner. I would call this the egalitarianism of an individualist conception of autonomy.

If we accept this as the broad frame of Rawlsian approaches to social justice, against the background of what has been argued above two sets of questions arise: (i) How is (dis)agreement about equality and autonomy *within* these ap-

---

[2] For my earlier interpretation of Walzer's conception of social justice see Haus 2000, 2012, 2014.

proaches structured, and how does the liberal egalitarian political discourse cope with this internal kind of disagreement? (ii) Is there "reasonable" room for *other* perspectives beyond this restricted space of disagreement occupied by the liberal egalitarian discourse? If yes, what happens to equality and autonomy in the context of these other perspectives of social justice?

Concerning the first question, it is worth having a quick look at the so called "equality-of-what?" controversy (see Dworkin 1981, Cohen 1993, Sen 1993). On the one hand this debate reflects what basic liberal egalitarians take as the central moral intuition of social justice, namely that important goods have to be distributed "endowment-insensitive" and "ambition-sensitive" (Dworkin 1981, p. 311; see Kymlicka 2002, pp. 75–87), in other words: that (brute) luck, undeserved (dis)advantages due to the natural and social "lottery", has to be compensated by society, whereas autonomous actions by individuals constitute self-responsibility for distributive consequences. On the other hand, this debate demonstrates that even on the basis of a common intuition (which Rawls regards as an intuition shared by us all), the concrete meaning of this intuition remains controversial. More concretely, what remain controversial are the implications of individual *autonomy*, i.e. in how far autonomy shall be taken to constitute a compensatory claim towards the state or to refute such claims. This is because there is no objective way to demonstrate that a certain act or even thought has been done autonomously or that a person is really autonomous. For example, is the interest and effort to be successful in the educational system a lucky package of socialisation and the right genes? Or is it a singular individual choice? Is individual autonomy a plausible idea at all in the light of scientific claims to explain the cerebral mechanisms that cause thoughts and actions and produce the illusion these are "ours"?[3]

Leaving the last point aside, it seems that what is needed for promoting *political* agreement among liberals is some *unquestioned* assumption about what would *normally* happen, if individuals *behaved* really autonomously and *had* the resources to realise their autonomous life-plans. For example, if we presuppose that attractive positions in a society are distributed by competition, it would be rational to assume that individuals normally undertake efforts to be successful in that competition (at least if they know they have a real chance). If it were otherwise, why should we consider these goods as attractive? Thus, if certain groups are in average less successful in this competition, this means they are dis-

---

[3] Korsgaard makes the interesting point that "[j]udgements about whether others have freely chosen their conceptions of the good are not only ones we cannot very easily make, they are ones we ought not to make. Such judgements are disrespectful" (Korsgaard 1993, p. 61). Compensatory claims, however, inevitably do make such judgements.

advantaged and compensation is demanded. Liberal egalitarian claims become particularly "fit for consensus" and thus discursively strong, when "overlapping consensus" is connected with such views of what would normally happen and, put in Foucauldian terms, with respective ways of knowledge-production. What is interesting in the end is not the single individual and the autonomy of her action or ambitions, but attributes of specific social groups (income, race, education of parents etc.) that can be correlated with "success" in society. The causality we cannot observe "within" the concrete individual is made visible at the level of statistics in large numbers. As will be discussed below, educational justice is a topic in which liberal egalitarianism gains this strength, even if with considerable costs.

2.2 Is "non-egalitarianism" an alternative?

Some have argued that egalitarians and non-egalitarians should be clearly distinguished in contemporary political theory; the latter should be considered as the better alternative to first (see the anthology edited and introduced by Angelika Krebs [2000] referring to authors like Elizabeth Anderson, Harry Frankfurt and others and, notably, also to Walzer). It has even been suggested that the struggle of egalitarianism and non- or even anti-egalitarianism is a dualism that reaches out far back into the history of political thought (Knoll in this volume). On the contrary, my opinion is that whatever the illuminating implications of these accounts may be, a more convincing theory is one that sees egalitarianism as the driving force of Western political thought. In this sense equality can be understood as the deep consensus that generates conflicts of conceptualisation and interpretation (see e.g. Kymlicka 2002, Miller 1989). I do not doubt that the idea of equality has been and is still criticised. My main point is that there is no convincing way of philosophically conceptualising non-egalitarianism as a coherent normative perspective within the imaginative frame of modern societies.

How can one conceptualise non-egalitarianism? I first refer to Manuel Knoll's Aristotelian conceptualisation because it seems to me a most "principled" one (see Knoll 2009). According to the Aristotelian position, it is just to allot equal shares only to equals, not to everyone. I do not want to dwell on the fact that Aristotle used the notion of proportional *equality* to label just distributions, because indeed *proportional* equality sees distributive justice as a function of the moral worth of persons and this worth, according to Aristotle, was an unequal one. My point is that this definition ("equal shares only to equals") *by itself* does not constitute a distinction between egalitarians and non-egalitarians because firstly it could be that *everyone is equal* in the respects crucial for distributing goods, and secondly, egalitarians also agree that allotting equal shares simply "to everyone" is just only *under certain circumstances* (namely, when there are no good reasons to distribute goods unequally). What is necessary in order to make the distinction between egalitarianism/non-egalitarianism is a premise, namely that *we are not equals* in these crucial respects, that it is impossible that "everyone" is "equal". But what does it mean then, to be *an* equal or *an* unequal in this crucial sense?

Consider a basic egalitarian commitment of modern constitutionalism like "we believe that all men are created equal". It is *not* a denial of this commitment to say that "all men are created different", since equality does not mean uniformity. Being diverse could be just what we have in common as human beings. Only to say that "all men are created *unequal*" would indeed directly deny the commitment. Would anybody say so and what does it mean to say so? The main implication, it seems to me, is that "crucial inequality of persons" has to rely on a negation of autonomy and on a naturalisation of social order. (Actually, the formulation of the commitment ("all men [...]") is itself an expression of naturalising the social order, namely as a gendered order.) To say that "men [persons] are created unequally" means to claim that there is a kind of inequality that is outside the scope of *autonomy*, an inequality which has its origins in nothing we could shape (individually or collectively) by our efforts, i.e. in "nature". For if the inequality would be the result of our autonomy, we (i) would have something fundamentally important (autonomy) in common (i.e. would be equals in a fundamental sense) and (ii) would have to care about the way we use the capacity to shape our lives, i.e. inequality would become a topic of human will and the subject of reasoning.

As even strong supporters of the Aristotelian tradition concede, today it is not possible to refer to "natural ends" derived from a metaphysical biology as in Aristotle (see MacIntyre 1981, ch. 12). Thus, what the good means is open to interpretation, and there can be no natural privileges of persons having the attributes necessary for achieving natural ends. There can also be no "slaves by nature". Factually, there might appear "slave natures" in the sense of servile personalities (Nietzsche), but any notion of justice that would be taken seriously today would have to claim that it would be unjust to categorise individuals as having slave natures before they had a chance to prove the opposite. If there are "slave natures", then these are not "slave natures by nature". Furthermore, all persons are equally part of the community which discusses and decides controversial normative questions.

If it is the concept of "slaves by nature" which divides Aristotle's "classical" non-egalitarianism from any kind of egalitarianism, in modern discourse two

other ways of reasoning for non-egalitarianism have become obsolete as well, namely *functional* and *heteronomous* arguments:
- "Functional" arguments would claim the functional necessity of some obeying others and doing all kinds of work in order to make possible free agency for those others who can then strive for perfection (a model practised in the Greek city-states). If the critical point, according to this "excellence" discourse, is that in the name of equality the many mediocre ones constrain the few excellent ones, this condition would be exacerbated in a society where individuals are arbitrarily organised in ranks of unequal worth. In order to avoid such arbitrariness at least some kind of *meritocratic* criteria would have to be implemented, and meritocracy is far from being the opposite to egalitarian conceptions of justice; on the contrary, it is the egalitarian notions which take meritocratic principle most seriously (and maybe too seriously, see below).
- By "heteronomous" arguments I mean that a hierarchical order is justified by referring to some transcendent source (God, the spiritual world, the etc.). In some cases such heteronomous justifications might rest on the assumption that by birth individuals have an unequal moral value, as e.g. in the caste hierarchy. Here the heteronomous argument approximates the "slave by nature" argument, although the reference is not to some "natural" potential for virtue, but to individual deeds in a preceding life (i.e. to meritocratic principles which are, however, linked to a mechanism of multiple lives which transcends what we can immanently experience). In other cases the heteronomous argument might come closer to the functional argument in that a certain hierarchical *order* is considered the mirror of God's will and that it is in itself good or promoting the public good if individuals get a place in this order and stick to what is "their own", even if this does not mean that those in the higher ranks are necessarily of higher moral value.

Accordingly, Will Kymlicka has presented the recognition of the moral equality of all individuals as the basic value on which *all* contemporary conceptions of social justice are based (i.e. those which in some way are taken seriously in a most minimal way by the discourse of political theory, Kymlicka 2002, pp. 3–4). Miller gives this view a political twist when he argues that equality is to be understood as "equality of status", "social equality" or "equality as citizens" (Miller 1989, Miller 1997).[4] If we assume that an egalitarian theory de-

---

[4] Equality of status refers to "the ideal of a society in which people regard and treat one another

mands that all citizens as citizens count as equal and rightfully claim equal respect, it seems adequate to call all contemporary theories of justice (from liberal over libertarian, utilitarian, communitarian and marxist) "egalitarian" and thus to talk of a deep consensus concerning equality.[5]

Against this background, it becomes plausible why perspectives considered as "anti-" or "non-egalitarian" in contemporary political theory are not and cannot be based upon principled arguments against equality as such, but actually share the commitment to equality as highlighted by Kymlicka. What they claim is that equality of membership in society or citizenship in a liberal state does not demand, or even allow, the equalisation of resources in the name of compensating those who are in a weaker position (thus, the egalitarianism of the Rawlsian approaches).

That equalisation is *not allowed* is argued most radically by theories of absolute property rights like Nozick's (Nozick 1974). His position can be taken as a prominent example of what Kymlicka has called the "bifurcation of liberalism" (Kymlicka 2002, p. 91).[6] The origins of this bifurcation lie in the controversial nature of the compensatory claims which are seen by libertarians and "old liberals" as an arbitrary intrusion into individual choices. Libertarians, who are less dogmatic about the absoluteness of property rights, and embrace utilitarian notions of the good, also affirm principles that are compensatory in character (Friedman 1955). Quite true, what is compensated here is only the failure of the market to provide equal opportunities – not the failure of the "lottery of nature" to provide everyone with exactly the same resources in terms of individual capacities and social conditions. However, if we support the idea of equal opportunities, why should we refrain from compensating individuals in a more comprehensive way?

It is regularly argued, by referring to the concept of "sufficiency", that there is *no demand* for equalisation (e. g. Frankfurt 2015). If everybody has enough, so the argument goes, we need not be concerned with relative inequality, because equality is not a value in itself. The basic conceptual problem of sufficiency theories is, in my view, that they present sufficiency as some kind of basic or minimal justice, but they do not say much about justice beyond that minimal stage.

---

as equals, in other words a society that is not marked by status divisions such that one can place different people in hierarchically ranked categories" (Miller 1997, p. 224).

5 Albert Camus has made a similar point in *L'Homme revolté* when he remarked upon the discoursive shift from "grace" to "justice: "A partir du moment, en effet, où la pensée libertine met Dieu en question, elle pousse le problème de la justice au premier plan. Simplement, la justice d'alors se confond avec l'égalité" (Camus 1983, p. 141).

6 Kymlicka refers to Conolly 1984, p. 234. Conolly, however, does not refer to the juxtaposition between social liberals and libertarians in his account of the "bifurcation of liberalism".

I agree that sufficiency is a core concept when it comes to the just distribution of goods; however, sufficiency is not a free-standing criterion, and it does not make obsolete the aspect of comparing individuals and their position in society. Enough is not enough. I will come back to this point when I discuss Walzer's conception of social justice and its implications for educational justice.

For now, let me sum up that all modern political theories can be regarded as "egalitarian" in a specific sense. They all claim equal membership and the right to lead an autonomous life. Whereas "equal basic rights for all members" is a normative demand shared by all relevant perspectives of social justice today, demands for compensation by redistribution are controversial. Liberal theories, broadly understood, converge in relation to the value of equality to an individualist notion of autonomy, but disagree in regard to compensatory claims to be made in the name of individualist autonomy. Strong liberal egalitarian claims of compensating individuals for disadvantages need the social construction of "normal" choices to identify the whole range of compensatory claims. This leads to the paradox that in the name of autonomy they must deny that people act autonomously. Still, in some principled way, non-egalitarianism is not an alternative. It is not convincing to dogmatically refute compensation as such or to restrict justice to sufficiency. As I will argue in the following section, however, it is worthwhile to question compensatory individualism and confront it with another egalitarian perspective.

3 Going beyond Rawls with Walzer

In *Spheres of Justice* and other writings Walzer defends a vision of "political egalitarianism" which suggests an alternative to Rawls' individualist egalitarianism. I will first give a general account of Walzer's perspective on justice. Second, I will try to demonstrate the potential of Walzer's perspective by illustrating its implications using a practical example, i.e. the debate on educational justice.

3.1 Consensus, equality, and autonomy in Walzer

Walzer's conception of justice is informed by an interpretative approach to political theory. It is often claimed that Walzer's theory presupposes a high level of consensus – because he refers to "shared understandings", "social meanings", "a common way of life" etc. This, as is argued, presumes there is a comprehensive agreement on ethical questions that simply needs to be uncovered. In the light of actual disagreement or uncertainty, Walzer's liberal critics claim that he misses the task of political theory which is to give orientation when our shared understandings "break down" (Rawls 1993, p. 44). However, Walzer stresses that interpreting shared understandings always means to generate agreement as well as disagreement (for a similar view see Taylor 1985, pp. 36–37). In fact, Walzer's understanding of an interpretative political theory is in fact close to Laclau's and Mouffe's poststructuralist perspective on political discourse,[7] although it does not stress the agonistic aspects to the same degree and has a more benevolent attitude towards normative arguments.

As Walzer recognises, *equality* is one of the basic ideas of modern societies. It is part of an established set of legitimatory practices available to social critics (see Walzer 1987, p. 43). No doubt, leftists have always put equality at the centre of their demands. As Walzer stressed (in order to avoid non-egalitarian readings of his conception) citizenship as such entails equality, and justice is violated whenever persons are driven to the margins (Walzer 1986, p. 149; 1993, p. 63). The central question for Walzer is how to interpret equality in an attractive way – not least because neo-conservatives have profited much from unattractive interpretations (see Walzer 1980, originally published in 1973). His attractive interpretation of the idea of equality is "complex equality". As a political ideal, complex equality implies the criticism of inequality in the form of dominating distributions, i.e. distributions systematically overriding the social meaning intrinsic to the goods in question. The idea of autonomy comes in here: to be faithful to the meaning of citizenship and to the intrinsic meanings that different goods have for social life can be regarded as the "autonomous distribution" of goods (Walzer 1983, p. 20), because it respects the imaginative frames, social practices and participatory opportunities of a shared way of life.

The conceptual link between autonomy and equality in Walzer is thus the promotion of a certain quality of equality through the autonomous distribution of social goods. Autonomous distribution demands consideration of the specific meaning of the goods within a sphere of distribution. In a certain sense, complex equality is thus a by-product of autonomous distribution. At the same time, complex equality is not just a coincidence of autonomous distribution, but an intended goal of distributive justice as such. Thus, Walzer asks: "how many goods must be autonomously conceived before the relations they mediate can become the relations of equal men and women?" (Walzer 1983, p. 28). Complex equality thus is an emergent quality of social practices in which goods are produced and distributed. As such a quality, it is a good in itself, a *telos* of social justice. Only in a just

---

[7] In a dialogue between Walzer and Mouffe, published in French and German, this becomes astonishingly clear (see Mouffe/Walzer 1992 for the German version).

society of this type can persons experience themselves as equals in an enriching way. The egalitarianism connected with complex equality is a *political egalitarianism*. The following quotation illustrates what political egalitarianism means:

> The aim of political egalitarianism is a society free from domination. This is the lively hope named by the word *equality:* no more bowing and scraping, fawning and toadying; no more fearful trembling; no more high-and-mightiness; no more masters, no more slaves. [...] Men and women are one another's equals (for all important moral and political purposes) when no one possesses or controls the means of domination (Walzer 1983, xiii).

Against this background, we can locate the potential of using Walzer to go beyond Rawls in the following three ways:

- Walzer discusses social justice on the basis of a theory of goods that stresses not only the social character of goods, but also the constitutive role of goods for collective and individual identities. Whenever we make up our minds about what is just or not, we should consider the ways in which distributions, but also discourses about the meaning of goods and how they should be distributed, are interwoven with the construction of identities, social positions, questions of habitus, in Bourdieu's sense, etc. To go beyond Rawls using Walzer would mean to reflect oneself as part of social practices by which identities are articulated and inclusions/exclusions enacted.
- Domination is not equivalent to inequality, because shared practices of distributing social goods may lead to unequal results that are in accordance with the meaning of the social good. For example, if we consider "money and commodities" as a distributive sphere, it is in accordance with the distributive logic of this sphere that those who are particularly good in producing commodities that fit the demand of others get the rewards offered by the respective sphere (here: that they become "wealthy"). Inequality is connected with dominance in two cases: (i) if the way these inequalities are generated are not inclusive, so that not all members of a society can substantially participate in a way faithful to equal citizenship and the normativity incorporated in the sphere (which in the case at hand becomes virulent when economic relationships are transformed by power relationships); (ii) if gains within this sphere (here: money, wealth) are exchangeable for advantages in other spheres (money is used to get political influence, better education and health services, social recognition etc.). To use Walzer to move beyond Rawls would mean to see inequality as a question of power and its effect on the social practices relevant for our self-understanding.
- The focus on different spheres with goods of distinct social meaning and the distortive role of certain goods like money, political power, formal education and career positions makes it possible to bring together and articulate *expe-*

riences instead of relying on an abstract procedure (like the original position) and resources. Articulating such experiences can be seen as the part of political theory within larger social practices which constitute political discourses characterised by certain political demands. By articulating identities, aspirations and criticisms of prevailing practices the deep consensus of modern political communities is reproduced without ever reaching a kind of overlapping consensus in the Rawlsian meaning. Indeed, a Walzerian account of social justice can help us to question far reaching agreement in societies on particular questions, and not only go beyond Rawlsian notions of justice, but beyond established hegemonies in Laclau's and Mouffe's sense as well.

In the following final section, I am going to illustrate how a Rawlsian and a Walzerian perspective shape our perspective on one hotly debated issue, often referred to as "educational justice".

3.2 Illustration: Perspectives on educational justice

Within Rawls' conception of "justice as fairness", questions of educational justice are addressed by the second principle, especially "fair equality of opportunity" (where "fair" means the compensation of social background conditions) – and to a lesser degree the "difference principle" (inequalities must work to the best advantage of the worst-off).[8] Reference to this principle would be seen as the basis for a rational consensus, because it takes equally into consideration the vital interests of all members of society. It is based on individual autonomy since the crucial question is what one wants to do with one's life and what decisions and efforts one takes. Brighouse and Swift nicely summarise the broader liberal egalitarian view on educational justice, which is obviously in agreement with Rawls:

> The fundamental reason for caring about educational equality is closely related to the reason for caring about equality of opportunity in general. Modern industrial societies are structured so that socially produced rewards – income, wealth, status, positions in the occupational structure and the opportunities for self-exploration and fulfilment that come

---

[8] It is irritating how Rawls' actual views of educational justice are regularly fallen short of. Many commentators assume that the difference principle and not the principle of fair equality of opportunity would be Rawls' favoured principle with respect to educational justice (e.g. Nathanson 1998, pp. 28–30; Gale 2000, p. 254).

with them – are distributed unequally. Education is a crucial gateway to these rewards; a person's level and kind of educational achievement typically has a major influence on where she will end up in the distribution of those potentially life-enhancing goods. It is unfair, then, if some get a worse education than others, because, through no fault of their own, this puts them at a disadvantage in the competition for these unequally distributed goods (Brighouse/Swift 2014, pp. 14–15).

When Brighouse and Swift call this "the meritocratic conception of educational equality" they do not only point to the link between egalitarianism and meritocracy mentioned above, but they also make clear the centrality of the idea of compensation of what happens to individuals "through no fault of their own" in liberal egalitarianism.

The current philosophical debate on educational justice is often said to be shaped by the opposition between an "egalitarian perspective" (i.e. the one just described, represented by Brighouse and Swift) and an "adequacy account" (represented by Amy Gutmann, Elizabeth Anderson, and Debra Satz). According to this description, egalitarian perspectives share a comparative view ("equally good educational opportunities") whereas their opponents think that justice is done when all individuals get an adequate education, where adequacy is defined by the competences needed for participating fully in politics and society or some other "absolute" standard (Meyer 2014, p. 3). Conceptions of adequacy can thus be considered as a variant of "sufficiency" theories (see above, section 2). In a Walzerian perspective, however, this opposition is not satisfying. On the one hand, Walzer shares many assumptions with the adequacy account. He stresses that the good of education is above all to be distributed in a way that every individual can effectively practice the role of a citizen and act as a competent member of contemporary society. This is because only under this condition can equal membership be realised and participation in the political community be achieved. In this respect, education is a "need" that has to be fulfilled according to the requirements of individuals (Walzer 1983, p. 203) and that can be conceptualised as referring to an individual's functioning or capability as citizen. Beyond the basic function of education as enabling citizens, education should not be considered a "need" and should be distributed on the basis of individual capacity, interest, and coherent financial schemes (i.e. if education is publicly financed for some, then it must be for all citizens). On the other hand, political egalitarianism demands much more than just enabling individuals to become competent citizens. It requires reflection on education as a particular practice in itself as well as on the role educational goods play in society. From a Walzerian point of view, distributive arrangements founded on a singular normative idea always have to be regarded with suspicion. They are neither capable of articulating the autonomy of the social practices in question, nor of forcefully addressing patterns of dominance.

Concerning the liberal egalitarian perspective of educational justice, a Walzerian suspicion would target the idea of "meritocracy". In the meritocratic perspective, educational goods are understood as exclusively instrumental, and thus from an external perspective. At a closer look, the apparent evidence of meritocratic principles is fuelled by patterns of dominance. Education is a "gateway" in Brighouse's and Swift's words (see above), a gateway in the competition for "rewards" which everybody is supposed to find attractive (because these rewards represent "basic goods" as Rawls would say) and even the place where one will "end up" in society. In turn, education from a liberal meritocratic perspective can be regarded as practised in the right way, when it prepares students in the best way to participate in the competition for rewards in the form of external goods. The best way then means: it compensates best for the "lottery of nature" (disadvantages in the capability and willingness to cultivate one's talents due to social background, but also to physical endowments) and it comprises contents that are actually needed for getting positions that are connected with rewards. Without being able to give a comprehensive empirical proof here, it seems fair to say that this view has become mainstream in public discourse (e.g. for the German case see Stojanov 2011, ch. 7) – interestingly without necessarily leading to the kind of egalitarian policies favoured by Rawlsians.

Walzer for his part stresses the internal logic of education as a social practice producing and distributing specific goods. According to him, education is foremost a practice located in a social space in between the family and broader society. It is of ultimate importance that the boundaries are defended – against parents who want to "take care" of their children "in their own best interest", but also against pressures coming from strong groups in society who want to "take care" that children function in a way they want them to. The autonomy of the sphere is thus intrinsically connected with individual autonomy. Whether educational practice is making sense or not has to be answered foremost by those involved in it – but that means that the students also have to *learn* how to make autonomous judgements. This is why *teachers* are so important in Walzer's account (this becomes visible in his discussion of the Japanese teachers' union defending school autonomy versus both economic and political pressures (see Walzer 1983, pp. 204–206)). It is teachers who share the ethos of educational practice. At this point, it becomes again clear, that Walzer's account is not just an "objective" description or empirical analysis of the educational system or the functioning of specific educational institutions. It is an interpretation of what is constitutive for education and the appropriate role of specific actors. As an interpretation, it is open for debate and the criticisms of competing interpretations. As would be any account of the meaning of education, schools and teachers.

Whereas the liberal discourse focuses on the question how to distribute educational opportunities for individuals, Walzer's focus on the dominance of goods raises the question of education as a dominant good itself. If specialised education is a legitimate monopoly of the talented, the distribution of status, power and wealth need not be connected to specialised education (Walzer 1983, p. 211). If we problematise the monopoly, we will heat the competition and that means – produce more over-all losers. We then need still more compensatory efforts and more places for specialised education and that means educational practice will be dominated even more by the perspective of competitive success and less by internal standards.

Walzer's approach can thus help to critically reflect on the prevailing discourse. Whereas the dominance of the good is not put into question, the question of how far this good can be legitimately monopolised or whether it has to be distributed equally is hotly debated. The apologetics of monopoly can rightfully claim that parents have the freedom to make their children familiar with cultural goods and educate them to their advantage, and that redistributing the dominant good would require comprehensive state intervention (above all in family life, but also in other social communities), which in the end results in a kind of socialising childhood. The egalitarian side rightfully demands an equal share of the crucial good, since nobody "deserves" a greater share. In the perspective of autonomous distribution/complex equality, however, it is the dominance of the respective good that should be analysed and questioned. Individuals cannot live as free and equal if they predominantly regard each other as competitors in the race to gain crucial goods; and the educational system cannot function as a practice focused on internal goods if it carries the burden or exercises the power of exclusively distributing to persons the track to a specific opportunity. Teachers may well share an *ethos* committed to the educational practice, but as long as their judgements mitigate access to other goods (higher education, good jobs, social status) their role is characterised by "schizophrenia" (see Stojanov 2011, p. 169).

How can we overcome this power nexus and the "schizophrenia" produced by it? There clearly is no once-and-for-all solution. But it is certainly *not* enough to establish thresholds, as proposed by the "non-egalitarian" "adequacy" approach, i.e. to define an "adequate" level of education to be reached by all children. We need a different perspective on how schools can unfold the internal good of education.⁹ The perspective I have sketched here would demand going beyond the meritocratic vision of arranging success according to individual merit and beyond the discourse of how and whether to compensate or avoid disadvantage in the competition for the attractive positions. It would demand an educational system that is foremost a place to experience a good that cannot be experienced elsewhere. It would demand a society in which educational success is primarily an internal good, whereas there are lots of other goods that are distributed in accordance with their own meaning. Finally, it would demand a society where the better-educated and the lesser-educated (problematic terms, if we think that experience is the best teacher!) live together as equals because education does not dominate social relations. A utopian vision? Maybe, but with MacIntyre, one may say that "Utopianism rightly understood is no bad thing" (MacIntyre 2006, p. 63). We need radically critical accounts of contemporary society, and the truth is these do not come from Rawlsians.

Going beyond Rawls does not mean, of course, to deny every demand supported by Rawlsians. Of course, there are complementarities and overlaps. For example, if we stress the autonomy of education vis-à-vis the sphere of money and commodities, it is clear that setting education free from the dominance of wealth implies what egalitarian liberals would support as a compensation of the lottery of nature. Nevertheless, both perspectives – individualist egalitarianism and political egalitarianism – constitute distinct ways of coming to judgements about the educational system and its role in society. In the real world, theories of social justice are connected to broader discourses and to political "storytelling". Discourses legitimise specific ways of knowledge-production and in turn are then fuelled by the knowledge produced. I agree with Wesselingh's account of the predominant discourse on educational justice when he writes that "predominantly economic considerations have prompted the rapid expansion of equal-opportunities research" (Wesselingh 1997, p. 183). It is within the package together with economic imperatives that the just provision of educational oppor-

---

9 Stojanov suggests that the most important aspect is to relieve schools from the task of selection. For example, tests for entering colleges and universities could be made on-site and not at secondary schools (this is actually practised in a lot of countries, including, e.g. the US). This proposal, however, ignores that under these conditions secondary schools still function in the shadow of competition and as a consequence private wealth becomes enormously important with respect to test preparation (see e.g. Dawson 2010). We should thus not only reform the educational systems as taking explicit selection functions away from schools, but we should also struggle to making education less important for overall life success. In other words, we should struggle against education as a dominant good or, to use Brighouse's and Swift's expression, against education as the "gateway" for one's place in society.

tunities has raised awareness in public discourse. Although it would be unfair to make liberals responsible for everything that comes along with the package, it does not come without their own fault that they have become part of the package. We cannot develop alternatives to the predominant discourse and knowledge-production by relying on liberal egalitarianism. We need other kinds of theoretical perspectives for this. Walzer's would be one, but only if we do not get stuck in categorical debates about equality, consensus and autonomy, but begin to interpret them in different ways.

Bibliography

Bornemann, Basil/Haus, Michael (2014): "Politische Autonomie. Semantiken, Entwicklungslinien, Theoriekontexte". In: Franzen, Martina/Jung, Arlena/Kaldewey, David/Korte, Jasper (Eds.): *Autonomie revisited. Beiträge zu einem umstrittenen Grundbegriff in Wissenschaft, Kunst und Politik*. Weinheim: Beltz Juventa, pp. 260–283.

Brighouse, Harry/Swift, Adam (2014): "The Place of Educational Equality in Educational Justice". In: Meyer, Kirsten (Ed.): *Education, Justice and the Human Good. Fairness and Equality in the Education System*. Routledge International Studies in the Philosophy of Education 33. London, New York: Routledge, pp. 14–33.

Camus, Albert (1983): *L'Homme revolté*. In: Camus, Albert: *Œvres complètes*. Vol. 3. Paris: Gallimard/Club de l'Honnête Homme.

Cohen, Gerald Allan (1993): "Equality of What? On Welfare, Goods, and Capabilities". In: Nussbaum, Martha C./Sen, Amartya (Eds.): *The Quality of Life*. New York: Clarendon Press/Oxford, pp. 9–29.

Dawson, Walter (2010): "Private Tutoring and Mass Schooling in East Asia: Reflections on Inequality in Japan, South Korea, and Cambodia". In: *Asia Pacific Educational Review* 11, pp. 14–24.

Dworkin, Ronald (1981): "What Is Equality? II. Equality of Resources". In: *Philosophy & Public Affairs* 10, pp. 283–345.

Frankfurt, Harry G. (2015): *On Inequality*. Princeton, Oxford: Princeton University Press.

Friedman, Milton (1955): "The Role of Government in Education". In: Solo, R.A. (Ed.): *Economics of Public Interest*. New Brunswick: Rutgers University Press, pp. 123–144.

Gale, Trevor (2000): "Rethinking Social Justice in Schools: How Will We Recognize It when We See It?". In: *International Journal of Inclusive Education* 4. No. 3, pp. 253–269.

Haus, Michael (2000): *Die politische Philosophie Michael Walzers. Kritik, Gemeinschaft, Gerechtigkeit*. Wiesbaden: Westdeutscher Verlag.

Haus, Michael (2012): "Blockierter Tausch – befreite Gerechtigkeit? Walzer und die Tyrannei des Geldes". In: Nusser, Karl-Heinz (Ed.): *Freiheit, soziale Güter und Gerechtigkeit. Michael Walzers Staats- und Gesellschaftsverständnis*. Baden-Baden: Nomos, pp. 59–88.

Haus, Michael (2014): "Komplexe Gleichheit – Wie egalitär ist Walzers Gerechtigkeitstheorie?". In: Knoll, Manuel/Spieker, Michael (Eds.): *Michael Walzer.*

Sphären der Gerechtigkeit. Ein kooperativer Kommentar. Staatsdiskurse 29. Stuttgart: Steiner, pp. 27–50.

Honneth, Axel (2011): *Das Recht der Freiheit.* Frankfurt a.M.: Suhrkamp.

Knoll, Manuel (2009): *Aristokratische oder demokratische Gerechtigkeit? Die politische Philosophie des Aristoteles und Martha Nussbaums egalitaristische Rezeption.* Munich, Paderborn: Fink.

Korsgaard, Christine Marion (1993): "G. A. Cohen: Equality of What? On Welfare, Goods, and Capabilities. Amatya Sen: Capability and Well-Being". Commentary by Christine M. Korsgaard. In: Nussbaum, Martha C./Sen, Amartya (Eds.): *The Quality of Life.* New York: Clarendon Press/Oxford, pp. 54–66.

Krebs, Angelika (2000): *Gleichheit oder Gerechtigkeit. Texte der neuen Egalitarismuskritik.* Frankfurt a.M.: Suhrkamp.

Kymlicka, Will (2002): *Contemporary Political Philosophy. An Introduction.* Second edition. Oxford, New York: Oxford University Press.

Laclau, Ernesto/Mouffe, Chantal (1985): *Hegemony and Socialist Strategy. Towards a Radical Democratic Politics.* London: Verso.

MacIntyre, Alasdair (1981): *After Virtue. A Study in Moral Theory.* South Bend, IN: University of Notre Dame Press.

MacIntyre, Alasdair (2006): "Natural Law as Subversive. The Case of Aquinas". In: MacIntyre, Alasdair (Ed.): *Ethics and Politics.* Cambridge, pp. 41–63.

Meyer, Kirsten (2014): "Introduction". In: Meyer, Kirsten (Ed.): *Education, Justice and the Human Good. Fairness and Equality in the Education System.* London, New York: Routledge, pp. 1–13.

Miller, David (1989): "Equality". In: *Royal Institute of Philosophy Supplement* 26, pp. 77–98.

Miller, David (1997): "Equality and Justice". In: *Ratio* 10. No. 3, pp. 222–237.

Mouffe, Chantal/Walzer, Michael (1992): "Man muß nicht nur tolerant sein, sondern auch demütig. Chantal Mouffe im Gespräch mit Michael Walzer". In: *Prokla* 22. No. 87.2, pp. 286–297.

Nathanson, Stephen (1998): "Are Special Education Programs Unjust to Nondisabled Children? Justice, Equality, and the Distribution of Education". In: *Journal of Education* 180. No. 2, pp. 17–40.

Nozick, Robert (1974): *Anarchy, State, and Utopia.* New York: Basic Books.

Rawls, John (1993): *Political Liberalism.* New York: Columbia University Press.

Sen, Amartya Kumar (1993): "Capability and Well-Being". In: Nussbaum, Martha C./Sen, Amartya (Eds.): *The Quality of Life.* New York: Clarendon Press/Oxford, pp. 30–53.

Stojanov, Krassimir (2011): *Bildungsgerechtigkeit. Rekonstruktionen eines umkämpften Begriffs.* Wiesbaden: VS Verlag für Sozialwissenschaften.

Taylor, Charles (1985): "Interpretation and the Sciences of Man". In: Taylor, Charles (Ed.): *Philosophy and the Human Sciences.* Philosophical Papers 2. Cambridge: Cambridge University Press, pp. 15–57.

Taylor, Charles (1998): "Nationalism and Modernity". In: Hall, John A. (Ed.): *The State of the Nation.* Cambridge: Cambridge University Press, pp. 191–218.

Walzer, Michael (1980): "In Defense of Equality". In: Walzer, Michael (Ed.): *Radical Principles. Reflections of an Unreconstructed Democrat.* New York: Basic Books, pp. 237–256.

Walzer, Michael (1983): *Spheres of Justice. A Defense of Pluralism and Equality.* New York: Basic Books.

Walzer, Michael (1986): "Justice Here and Now". In: Lucash, Frank (Ed.): *Justice and Equality Here and Now*. Ithaca: Cornell University Press, pp. 136–150.

Walzer, Michael (1987): *Interpretation and Social Criticism*. Cambridge, MA: Harvard University Press.

Walzer, Michael (1993): "Exclusion, Injustice, and the Democratic State". In: *Dissent* 40, pp. 55–64.

Wesselingh, Anton (1997): "Spheres of Justice: The Case of Education". In: *International Studies in Sociology of Education* 7. No. 2, pp. 181–194.

Giovanni Giorgini
Stuart Hampshire and the Case for Procedural Justice

Tout homme est libre de se choisir une patrie
Voltaire, *Dictionnaire philosophique*, entry "Patrie"

Abstract: This essay examines the notion of procedural justice elaborated by the British philosopher Stuart Hampshire. It reviews Hampshire's intellectual biography, showing the influence of Aristotle and Spinoza on the development of his thought. From Aristotle Hampshire derived the idea that moral theory should focus on the problems of moral agents and their view of the good life; from Spinoza he derived the importance of passions in politics and the view that human freedom depends on the knowledge of the reasons for our actions. Through an intellectual path in which the notion of freedom plays a fundamental role (freedom of mind, freedom of the individual, freedom and imagination), Hampshire arrived at the conclusion that moral and political conflict will always be inevitable because it results from the faculty of imagination, which enables human beings to elaborate a personal image of the good life. However, the faculty of reason unites human beings in the recognition of the great evils of mankind (starvation, imprisonment, death) and paves the way to a view of procedural justice as adversarial argument: when conflict arises, the reasonable solution is to find an umpire who listens to the opposed, conflicting arguments according to the maxim *audi alteram partem*.

Prologue

Among the many widely-debated topics in political philosophy of the past three decades, the debate on liberal justice and pluralism, and more generally on how to construct a just society, characterized by distributive justice, in a multicultural context is undoubtedly one of the most interesting. Although many voices entered this debate, I find particularly promising two approaches, characterized by their completely different view of human nature. There is, on the one hand, the proposal to find a common identity of the human being *qua* human being in the shared characteristics of freedom and rationality, a proposal perfectly exemplified by John Rawls' *A Theory of Justice* (1971), perhaps the foundational text of modern liberal universalism. There is, on the other hand, the proposal to go back to Aristotle and his view of human nature, conceived as inevitably situated inside a specific society. On the former view, all human beings share the features of being free, reasonable and rational; once challenged to create a just society, they would all come to the same conclusion simply through a reasoning based on rational choice. Through a refined mental experiment that situates them in an "original position" mainly characterized by a "veil of ignorance", which should warrant that their judgement is not influenced by their contingent circumstances (age, race, gender, capabilities, social status and so on), all free and rational human beings would eventually choose two principles of justice, to be conceived as fairness, which would be the foundation of a just society and which can be thus summarized: all citizens should have the broadest system of equal fundamental liberties compatible with a similar system of liberties for everybody; social inequalities should be acceptable only if they arise from social positions to which everybody has equal access and if they are oriented towards the most disadvantaged members of society. Rawls' attempt to single out the basic principles of a just society by eliciting an "overlapping consensus", i.e. areas and themes of consensus, from people who still retain diverse visions of the good and different life projects, is founded on the assumption of the existence of a common human nature characterized by freedom, reason and reasonableness. It is this assumption, this image of the human Self, that allows Rawls to maintain that his vision of a just society could be accepted by all human beings, for it is independent from, or rather prior to, their different visions of the good. I do not need to dwell on the merits of Rawls' theory: suffice it to say that not only did it shape the debate on the just society for the next three decades, but it was also instrumental in the revival of the discipline of political philosophy itself. However, as some critics have sharply pointed out, and as is confirmed by Rawls' own theoretical development,[1] its fundamental limit lies in the tacit assumption that all individuals share, or accept, some liberal presuppositions: the vision of the human being as a free and rational agent, to begin with (most political and religious conservative authors would challenge this presupposition); the notion that the "right" is prior to the "good", and law to morality; the persuasion that the "overlapping consensus" could lead individuals to identify morally neutral laws which would enable them to follow their personal image of the good life; the connected persuasion that everyone would accept "reasonable pluralism", namely rationally argued contrasting values; the very clear dichotomy between the public and the private, in the wake of the sharp Kantian distinction between *Legalität* and *Moralität*. Another debatable feature is Rawls' defence of this vision of the Self and politics in the name of their pur-

---

[1] I am especially thinking of Rawls 1980; Rawls 1987; Rawls 1993.

ported "thinness" and "neutrality"; in fact, they appear to have a 'thick' liberal connotation, with an idiosyncratic emphasis on the importance of reasonableness and consensus in founding a really just society.[2] Finally, Rawls neglects the fact that some individuals are not free and rational because of disabilities and other circumstances and that all human beings have periods of their life, notably infancy and old age, when they are dependent on other members of society.[3] This cursory account surely does not render justice to Rawls' complex and refined theory of justice (which is a sad irony), but I hope it gives at least a glimpse of the reasons why his ambitious attempt still lies in the background of most subsequent political theories; the most conspicuous reason is, in my view, its plea to universality, to universal acceptance in the name of a universal, shared human nature.

It is interesting to compare Rawls' vision of human nature, and his connected theory of justice, with the revival of Aristotelian ethical and political theory put forth by a number of contemporary authors, such as Stuart Hampshire, Alasdair MacIntyre and Martha Nussbaum. All of these thinkers argue that Aristotelian philosophy is central to our Western cultural heritage but they 'use' Aristotle to arrive at very different conclusions: Hampshire's revival of Aristotle enables him to overcome the abstractness of analytic moral philosophy; MacIntyre presses Aristotle's view of the virtues in order to use it as the foundation for a shared cultural identity for specific communities; in Nussbaum's case, a moderate Aristotelian essentialism enables her to identify a notion of human nature which can serve even as the foundation of a cosmopolitan identity. To be sure, the revival of Aristotle's ethical and political theory is not peculiar to Hampshire, Nussbaum and MacIntyre. Just to mention a few important authors of the recent past, we range from Jacques Maritain's already classic humanistic liberal approach to John Finnis' and Robert P. George's conservative natural law theories; from T.H. Green's and Ernest Barker's liberal perfectionism to the humanistic Marxism of the founding authors of the journal *Praxis*, Mihailo Markovic and Svetozar Stojanovic.[4] Not to mention the many authors influenced by Aristotle's ethical and political thought such as Joachim Ritter (together with other theorists participating in the general enterprise of the *Rehabilitierung der praktischen Philosophie*), and Joseph Raz, who, however, do not put forth a specifically Aristo-

---

[2] Among the vast literature on Rawls' theory of justice, I find especially interesting the criticism put forth by these authors: Hampshire 1993; Raz 1986; and, obviously, Martha Nussbaum; in this respect, see her Presidential Address in Nussbaum 2000.
[3] This fact has been aptly pointed out by MacIntyre 1999.
[4] See Maritain 1936 and Maritain 1954; Finnis 1980; George 1993 and George 1999; Green 1883; Barker 1906; Markovic 1982.

telian political vision.⁵ For reasons of space, I will confine my analysis to Hampshire's work, whose main merit is to present a theory of justice which is merely procedural, based on history and experience instead of a theoretical image of the Self and of society.

Stuart Hampshire, the reluctant Aristotelian

Aristotle's thought, together with Spinoza's, has undeniably been one of the main influences on the intellectual development of the British philosopher Stuart Hampshire. Educated at Oxford, a contemporary of Isaiah Berlin, A.J. Ayer and Gilbert Ryle, Hampshire started his career very young in the tradition of analytic philosophy and the Oxford ordinary language philosophy. Like many of these authors, he believed that by analysing ordinary language it was possible to dispel the confusion which is the origin of most philosophical problems: by investigating current linguistic uses we can elaborate a "cartography" of knowledge and "rectify the logical geography" of our knowledge – to borrow Ryle's words (Ryle 1949, p. 1). Two powerful influences can be clearly detected in this approach. On the one hand, the researches of the 'second' Wittgenstein, intent on reviewing his own thought while teaching at Cambridge at the end of the 1920s': these researches were mostly known in Oxford through oral reports and showed Wittgenstein interested in the analysis of ordinary, non-scientific and non-formalized language. On the other hand, there is the influence of logical positivism, which Ayer inserted in the British tradition of empiricism and made known to the English audience through his very successful *Language, Truth, and Logic* (1936). Hampshire's early works are thus in the tradition of analytic philosophy and the philosophy of mind: they are subtle analyses of the peculiarities of propositions and statements containing modal and evaluative words, indicating dispositions, intents, judgements and mental states. Broadly speaking, these works belong to the tradition of analytic moral theory and it is perhaps worthwhile recalling the contemporary situation in moral theory.

After the publication, at the turn of the 20ᵗʰ century, of G.E. Moore's *Principia Ethica* (1903) which labelled as "naturalistic fallacy" the attempt to found ethics on nature, deriving value-judgements from judgements of fact, and to try to arrive at some definition of the word 'good', there ensued a debate on the foundation of ethics which saw the participation of a number of authors, known as "the Oxford moralists" (which included J. Cook Wilson and H.A. Prichard) who main-

---

5 See Ritter 1969; Raz 1986; Riedel 1972–74.

tained the impossibility of founding ethics on scientific knowledge. There also appeared intuitionist theories, such as David Ross' *The Right and the Good* (1930), which maintained the possibility of having an intuition of prima facie duties and of founding one's decision in practical situations upon the perception of one's duties in the specific circumstances. In the background there were the traditional utilitarian theories, tracing back to Jeremy Bentham and John Stuart Mill and revived by Bertrand Russell, which were very influential in social life up to the outbreak of World War Two through such authors as John Maynard Keynes and Leonard Woolf. The publication of Alfred Ayer's *Language, Truth, and Logic* marked a turning point: in the first chapter, significantly titled "The Elimination of Metaphysics", Ayer distinguished between statements that are true by definition (tautologies); statements that can be verified by direct experience; and metaphysical statements, whose truth-content cannot be verified and are thus, properly speaking, 'senseless': these included statements about God, ethics and aesthetics. Another landmark work in this tradition was C.L. Stevenson's *Ethics and Language* (1945): it made 'emotivism', which argued that moral values are the mere expression of moral feelings, of personal preferences and emotions, the dominant ethical theory. Moral theory entered the so-called 'meta-ethical phase', focussing primarily on the examination of the peculiarities of value judgements as opposed to statements of fact; 'Hume's law', which affirmed the impossibility of deriving statements about what *ought* to be from statements about what *is*, ruled apparently unassailable.

Hampshire launched his onslaught on emotivism and 'Hume's law' in his *Fallacies in Moral Philosophy* (1949), where he argued for the existence of a connection between increase in knowledge and widening of the possibilities of free action.[6] This essay marks a turning point in Hampshire's intellectual development: moral theory had always been his main interest, in conjunction with the philosophy of mind. From now on, however, he abandons the investigation of linguistic usages and of statements containing modal and evaluative words to focus on the problems concerning human beings' actual conduct, and especially on what will become the main topic of his subsequent works: the problem of human freedom. 'Hume's law' is erroneous, in Hampshire's opinion, because arguments on practical conclusions are arguments about facts and we experience every day that our moral judgements are rectified and modified by experience and observation of facts. Forty years later Hampshire will address again "the amiable ghost of Hume" in *Innocence and Experience* (1989) to argue that Hume's "trick" consisted in a kind of "false isolation", namely isolating state-

---

6 Hampshire 1949, pp. 466–482.

ments from the normal presuppositions which regulate human life: a *ceteris paribus* clause is always implied, even if not stated, in any human transaction; and nobody in making an arrangement for the following day really thinks that tomorrow the sun might not rise.[7] In turning his back to the analytic examination of morality, Hampshire deliberately drew on Aristotle's approach to moral problems. As is testified also by the subsequent *Ethics: A Defence of Aristotle* (1967), Hampshire praises Aristotle for looking at human morality from the point of view of the moral agent and not that of the moral observer or judge; this fact confers an immediacy and relevancy to moral theory which is absent from contemporary theories of morality.[8] Aristotle examined the processes of thought, or types of argument, which lead up to the *choice* of one course of action, whilst contemporary philosophers describe the arguments which lead up to the acceptance or rejection of a moral *judgement* about actions (Hampshire 1949, p. 43): the defining characteristic of a moral problem – Hampshire contends – is that it requires the choice of an action.

In 1959 Hampshire publishes what is arguably his philosophical masterpiece, *Thought and Action*. In this book he finely intertwines his ideas in the philosophy of mind with his conclusions about practical agency. Hampshire investigates our perception of external objects as well as of our internal mental states and notices a peculiarity in the causal explanation of the latter: our knowledge of the reasons for our actions influences those very actions; there is thus a kind of feedback effect on the percipient subject, who has evidently an active role in the explanation of this kind of phenomenon as contrasted to what happens in the natural sciences. Moreover, the emotions and feelings I can experience are, in a certain measure, circumscribed by the vocabulary I have learnt in my intercourse with other people.[9] Hampshire also points out that individuals often have a different perception of the reasons for their beliefs and desires from that of a detached observer; and coming to know the 'objective' explanation alters such beliefs and desires and therefore modifies the very phenomena to be explained. This fact reverberates on practical conduct for it shows that the perception of the 'terms of the question' that moral agents have in any actual practical situation is not a neutral assessment but is influenced by their background of feelings, beliefs and intentions.[10] This conclusion explains the peculiar complexity we encounter when we want to provide a causal explanation of human behaviour but at the same time it represents the source of human

---

[7] Hampshire 1989, pp. 83–88; see in general chapter 3.
[8] See Hampshire 1967a, pp. 23–38.
[9] This point will be central in Hampshire 1966.
[10] Hampshire 1959, pp. 177–181.

freedom; this is clearly shown by the familiar observation that no detached observer can ever exactly foretell from their knowledge of the situation how the agent involved will behave. This observation has a further important consequence for moral theory: human beings are truly free to the extent that they know the reasons for their actions, and this knowledge modifies their actions. Hampshire credits Aristotle's notion of the *phronimos*, the perfectly virtuous man who perceives correctly the terms of the practical situation facing him, for leading him to this important insight.[11]

As it is further evident from *Two Theories of Morality* (1977), Aristotle and Spinoza had a persisting influence on Hampshire's thought.[12] What Hampshire finds still valid in Aristotle at this stage is the notion of right balance between two extremes, which can be invoked to solve conflicts between contrasting moral assertions, together with Aristotle's common-sensical examination of the predications of the word 'good'. This persuasion leads Hampshire to maintain that politics needs Aristotelian prudence, the capacity for practical wisdom.[13] From Spinoza who, in his opinion, came closer to truth in the philosophy of mind than any other author, Hampshire derives the idea that adequate knowledge promotes freedom: by giving us an objective view of the causes of our negative and destructive passions, knowledge makes possible the functioning of our mind without illusions. By combining this Spinozian intuition with Freud's hypotheses about the subconscious, Hampshire adds that every new discovery of the limits of our free will, along with the discovery of our possibility to alter our perceptions and be aware of it, in fact increase our freedom because they contribute to our freedom of mind: knowledge of the reasons for our actions promotes our freedom of mind and therefore our ability to be really free in making our practical decisions. A theory of knowledge, and of self-knowledge, should thus be the foundation of all ethical investigation. However, Hampshire remarks, neither Spinoza nor Freud were optimists: they believed that freedom can only be partial and intermittent and they had a very realistic view of the role of passions in human morality.[14] Furthermore Spinoza, differently from Aristotle, had identified the pivotal role of the notion of individuality when we wish to grasp the essence of what a human being is; Hampshire criticizes Aristotle for presenting us the vision of the existence of a single *ergon* for all human beings and for his notion of the perfect human being. Aristotle's mistake consisted in trying to extrapolate from natural functioning a determinate end for all human beings;

---

11 Hampshire 1959, pp. 212–213. For a careful examination of this work see Hacker 2005.
12 See Hampshire 1977, passim.
13 See also Hampshire 1978, p. 52.
14 See Hampshire 1968, p. 68.

and then, of inferring from propositions about human nature what is universally the best way of life. More specifically, Aristotle's mistake originates from his conception of the soul, which emphasizes man's distinct capacity to think and the fixity of typically human potentialities. Hampshire objects that this is a simplistic view, which does not take into account the variety existing among human beings nor the specialization typical of men nor, finally, the power of human imagination. What characterizes human beings is their singularity; and individuality, which emerges from the exercise of imagination in the original search for the good life, is an absolute value. For, if the entire humanity could be united in its reaction to Euclid's demonstrations, it is inevitably and irreparably divided in its reaction to a musical performance or the reading of a novel, events which call for our imagination. It is thus a mistake to found morality on the vision of the perfect human being, looking for a single and clear foundation in a vision of the complete virtues present in a single individual (like Aristotle's *phronimos*): there is no univocal image of the good life nor, as a consequence, completeness and perfection in morality. In *Morality and Pessimism* (1972), the Leslie Stephen lecture held at Cambridge on 24 February 1972, Hampshire makes his stance on morality clearer: after paying tribute to the role of Utilitarianism in the past – a bold and innovative doctrine which was very influential in social life – he shows how the utilitarian mental attitude brought a new abstract cruelty into politics because of its mechanical and quantitative reasoning. Against Utilitarianism, Hampshire defends absolute moral prohibitions and the idea that human nature has a unique value, maintaining that morality sets the conditions for the survival of the species. "A morality" – he concluded – "with its ordering of virtues and its prohibitions, provides a particular ideal of humanity in an ideal way of life" (Hampshire 1972, p. 34).

Hampshire shows an acute awareness of the fact that the work of the moral philosopher should not be disjoined from the actual historical circumstances and the political forces of the age. In a paper read at a conference in Jerusalem in December 1974 and appropriately titled *Making Morality Effective*, Hampshire emphasizes how ethical discussions lead nowhere if they are not shared by social groups who can transform theory into practice. Political philosophers should not simply focus on what is ultimately desirable or possible, while neglecting the social, political and institutional forces which can make their diagnosis effective.[15]

Morality and Conflict (1983) marks the conclusion of Hampshire's analysis of the foundation of morality and paves the way for his subsequent political, pro-

---

15 Hampshire 1980, pp. 201–202.

cedural solution of conflict. In this work Hampshire argues that morality and conflict are inseparable for one is the precondition of the other. He adds that conflict should be interpreted as conflict between different admirable ways of life and different, equally sustainable, moral ideals; conflict of allegiances and fundamental but incompatible interests – which makes impossible an Aristotelian-style conclusion of any moral investigation with the univocal picture of the ideal human life and the possible harmony between conflicting elements. It is impossible – he argues – to infer what is universally the best way of life from human nature; also, there can be no harmony among the essential virtues in a complete life and there cannot therefore be any complete human good. In the span of a human being's lifetime there can occur situations in which they face contrasting claims having identical plausibility and in case of conflict between moral principles we must choose between two ways of life: it is in this commitment, in the deliberate choice of a way of life, that morality consists. Chance and choice both play a part in human morality for it is chance that decides whether the agent will ever face dramatic alternatives, but choice is the prerogative of each human being. Moreover, when the choice is to be taken, there exist limitations due to circumstances: in actual decisions, the peculiarities of the historical situation come into play, so that one must always decide between imperfect alternatives. Hampshire sees this conflict between competing ways of life as everlasting and, at this stage of his intellectual development, does not believe that there is a constant method for solving conflicts. This vision of a choice between alternative ways of life is the core of Hampshire's moral theory, and it is once more striking how Aristotelian echoes are here still clearly perceivable. Hampshire asserts the necessity of setting before one's eyes the ideal of a right balance between extremes in order to decide between contrasting moral claims; furthermore, the very perception of any moral dilemma varies according to the agent's instruction and education – two notions strikingly reminiscent of Aristotle's *phronesis* and *aisthesis*. In addition, Hampshire's analysis reveals the existence of two distinct aspects of morality: the universal, rational aspect, that of general moral theories; and the particular, historically conditioned aspect, that of the single agent's individual choice. In a very Aristotelian tone, Hampshire maintains that we learn to recognize normal conduct in our society in the same way that we learn our native language, namely by imitation (Hampshire 1983, p. 148). Following Aristotle, Hampshire even maintains that beyond the apparent diversity there exist evident uniformities in the virtues recognized by different societies in different times and places, just like in love and friendship. Individuality and uniformity can coexist when we look at human morality *sub specie aeternitatis*, from the standpoint of human history and human nature.

Overcoming Aristotle: Hampshire on the role of procedural justice

The new phase and the final overcoming of Aristotle takes place in Hampshire's last great work, *Innocence and Experience* (1989).[16] Here he deliberately starts on a Platonic/Aristotelian note, with a provocatively outmoded first chapter titled "Parts of the Soul". Hampshire questions the Platonic image of the tripartite soul arguing that it is a political construction in which the soul is seen as healthy and harmonious when the aristocratic element – reason – is in charge and passions and feelings are subjugated and follow along as a "dumb proletariat". At the same time, he challenges Aristotle's picture of the perfectly virtuous man, arguing that certain virtues are inevitably opposed to others in a complete life and therefore the image of the perfectly rounded human being is an unattainable ideal. Hampshire now realizes that what drove him to philosophy in the first place was exactly his interest for the complexities of human nature: a nature capable of treachery and treason, experiencing conflicts of allegiance, sometimes driven by tortuous calculations in making decisions sometimes by unexpected idealism, distinguished by an unexhausted imagination in searching for a characteristic, unique, even idiosyncratic way of a life. In his literary essays Hampshire had maintained that he always sought in philosophy, as well as in fiction and in poetry, "a particular kind of confusion", which originates from the attempt at exploring conflicting possibilities of description and from postponing a decision between them.[17] Here Hampshire states clearly that conflict is unavoidable in society as well as in individual life because it is the consequence of one of the characteristic faculties of the human mind: imagination.[18] Imagination makes everyone of us unique and explains the difference we exhibit in our taste for music and food, for literature and clothing and so on; more importantly, our imagination makes us conceive of an image of the good life and of happiness which is uniquely ours. On the other hand, humanity is united across barriers by the faculty of intellect, which makes us all agree on a mathematical demonstration or a geometrical theorem: even though Pythagoras' theorem was invented by a Greek, it applies, and its validity is recognized worldwide. Human beings are

---

[16] On this phase of Hampshire's moral and political thought see Lassman 2009.
[17] See Hampshire 1969, p. xiv.
[18] The fundamental role of imagination in morality and politics was already identified in Hampshire 1967b, where we read: "It is of the nature of imagination that it generally deals in conflicts and contradictions, in dubious meanings, and not in definite conclusions and in unambiguous assertions" (p. 44).

thus separated by the response to Caruso's singing but united by their acknowledgement of Newton's gravitational theory. This is the reality of life as well as the reality of the human mind, or soul – if we wish to preserve Hampshire's metaphor. It is from this reality of unavoidable conflict, a conflict experienced both individually and as a group, in private and in collective choices, inside the soul and on the public square, that Hampshire derives his notion of procedural justice, conceived as the basic indispensable virtue for a tolerable human life. It consists, in its minimal aspect, in listening to and weighing, equally and without prejudices, contrasting arguments for or against a certain position or course of action and in concluding with a decision which is obviously not independent from the specific arguments produced. Hampshire believes that this basic and minimal procedural notion of justice, conceived to avoid or to solve conflict, is a universal constant in human history: it can be traced back to the earliest documents of human civilization – we may think of the war-council in Homer's *Iliad* – and could be accepted by any person regardless of their political, moral and religious beliefs for it appeals merely to our rationality. This procedural notion represents the minimum level of justice, it is entirely negative because it does not include any substantial vision of the good, and it is the necessary foundation of every particular morality.

It is at this level that we encounter Hampshire's reply to the moral relativist, embodied by "the amiable ghost of Hume", who maintains that good and evil are not perceivable features of the external world and justice is consequently an artificial virtue. Hampshire's objection to the relativist is that there exists an immediate and observable feeling about fairness and justice, and justice is therefore a natural virtue, because all human beings, regardless of their notion of good and bad, could agree that certain events and situations – imprisonment, starvation, death – are evils to be avoided. Reducing to a bare minimum and thus overthrowing the Enlightenment universalistic ideal, Hampshire maintains that mankind is united in recognizing the great evils that make life almost intolerable while the glory of mankind consists in devising and pursuing different images of the good life. Procedural justice should be conceived as a tool to enable people to coexist without reconciling or standardizing their different visions of the good; it is therefore the indispensable precondition of any morality and for any substantial vision of the good.

The notion of conflict is connected to the singularity of every individual, to the obvious consideration that every human being is unique, which leads to the notion of identity. All human beings have a unique story and through their unique experiences they mould a peculiar vision of the good, develop a style and characteristic manners and pursue a way of life that is uniquely theirs: all these peculiarities constitute personal identity. Since every human being is unique, their death inevitably provokes an impoverishment of the world: it is an absolute loss, even if the individual in question was not an admirable human being. We have thus arrived at Hampshire's notion of the Self, which is rich in Proustian and Freudian suggestions. The uniqueness and originality of every individual and memory, which confers unity to their existence in time, are the foundations of personal identity and the Self. The actual history of a person may be conceived as a path running between two borders, which represent the unrealized possibilities, what could have been but never was, discarded alternatives and options: in the retrospective memory, actual events and decisions are always accompanied by the unrealized possibilities and all human beings elaborate a selective interpretation of their past, which moulds their imagination in a specific way. From the attachment to one's past there may descend particular obligations and duties that a person may feel to have as a consequence of encounters or influences, personal debts to repay that are difficult to defend through a clear practical argument: for their personal origin, private and accidental, these represent a fatal objection to any universalistic or utilitarian morality.[19]

A powerful challenge to this vision of morality and politics comes from Machiavelli. Machiavelli showed in the clearest possible manner how great political accomplishments are often accompanied by great crimes; how the imperative of political effectiveness and the overarching task of saving the State lead to commit unjust acts which are morally reprehensible; how statesmen must necessarily have a guilty conscience, for they have to know "how to enter evil, if necessitated". Machiavelli's vision, far from being immoral, is founded on a specific notion of human good that identifies it with earthly glory, recognized in history, which confers to the agent a sort of transcendence and immortality. Machiavelli was the first thinker who clearly showed the inevitable contrast between innocence and experience, between the hope to realize a pure and perfect vision of the good and the knowledge, acquired through disillusions, of the inevitable squalor and imperfection of human life and of the necessity to choose, in actual circumstances, the lesser evil. Hampshire thus offers an interpretation of Machiavelli that is not banal and grasps the fundamental seriousness of his thought, which is the reason for its everlasting charm. The response to Machiavelli draws on the notion of basic procedural justice, without which human life loses its most typical human features; at the same time, Hampshire suggests that conflict is not only unavoidable but also useful for human morality, and compro-

---

[19] Hampshire admits that this is the case with his long-lasting attachment to socialist ideals, which he describes as "far from unreasonable"; see Hampshire 1974, 1989 and 2000.

mise and precariousness are typical of every human society as well as characterizing the entire human life.

Hampshire further examines these themes in his final work, *Justice is Conflict* (2000). The evocative title, taken after Heraclitus, encapsulates the main argument of the book: moral and political philosophers, starting with Plato, have always considered passions and conflict as negative features in political communities as well as in individuals; they have accordingly elaborated theories that inevitably end with an image of peaceful agreement. These conclusions collide with the actualities of history and of human life, where conflict, at a personal or political level, is the norm, and this fact confers a fairy-tale aspect to those theories. Hampshire traces back to Plato the discovery of inner conflict and the elaboration of an epoch-making solution which he bequeathed to subsequent political thinkers.[20] Plato believed that inner conflict is to be explained through the existence of different parts in the soul which have different, and conflicting, desires and pursuits. For him, the human soul is in harmony when reason rules and the appetitive part is tamed by it, with the support of the spirited element. Plato bequeathed to Western political thought the belief in the power of reason to dominate passions and impulses and to devise a regime where rationality rules and is therefore just – a belief we find in most authors from Plato, through Marx, up to John Rawls.[21] However, Hampshire contends, this approach which ends in the presentation of a rationally defendable vision of the good fails to consider the divisive role of passions and feelings, stirred by our power of imagination. Moreover, "parts of the soul, unlike arms and legs, are a philosophical invention" (Hampshire 2000, pp. 29–30). In his opinion, there is no substantial vision of the good which can appeal to all human beings regardless of its purported rationality. Our rationality, on the other side, enables us to identify certain events as perennial evils for mankind: imprisonment, starvation, tyranny and death (when not self-inflicted) have always been considered evils, in all societies and at all times. They elude relativism because all human beings, at all latitudes and in any age, have considered them evils. Mankind can therefore be united in the recognition of the great evils and this can be construed as the ethical foundation for a notion of justice which concerns only procedures: it does not require agreement on any substantial vision of the good; it simply requires fairness in the procedure, namely that both parties should be heard according to the maxim *audi alteram partem*, the principle of adversary argu-

---

20 Hampshire refers to the episode of Leontius in *Republic* IV, 439e–440a.
21 See Hampshire 1993.

ment.[22] Fairness in procedures can be construed as a constant in human nature whereas justice in substantial matters will always vary with varying conceptions of the good.

Hampshire persuasively contends that "in private deliberation, the adversary principle of hearing both sides is imposed by the individual on himself as the principle of rationality" (Hampshire 2000, p. 22): evaluating all options is simply the rational way to arrive at making a choice. At the public level, the principle of adversary argument implies that neither side should have an unfair advantage, an idea embodied even in primitive practices such as the duel: everyone realizes its superiority in fairness to an ambush or a mere affray as a way to resolve a dispute (p. 28). Throughout his argument, Hampshire emphasizes how human life and institutions are precarious, conflict is unavoidable and fairness in procedures is the only solution: a solution that can be accepted by everyone merely by reasoning on the consequences of its unacceptance. This is what Hampshire describes as "the superior power of the negative" (p. 41). This is also his final answer to the objection that some people's conception of the good might have no place for procedural justice: these people may reject the idea that fairness in the settlement of disputes is a virtue since they can rely on their superior strength. However, one may point out that even such people balance the pros and cons in their minds when they make a decision, because this constitutes simple, common prudence in the pursuit of one's interests. Everyone employs adversarial reasoning in the ordinary run of affairs, balancing different alternatives, and it is therefore not far-fetched to ask them to also be rational in the public sphere, to abide by common everyday rationality. Refusing to do so would amount to abandoning thought altogether and this alternative is contrary to all historical experience.

An Aristotelian conclusion and a modest proposal

I think it is possible to build on Hampshire's work and use some Aristotelian suggestions to elaborate a notion of justice and education which has interesting consequences for contemporary liberal-democratic societies.[23] Our starting point

---

[22] Hampshire credits the Oxford legal philosopher Herbert Hart for drawing his attention to the centrality of this phrase when justice is to be done: Hampshire 2000, p. 21.
[23] I already explored some of these suggestions in Giorgini 1989, my first encounter with Hampshire's ideas.

can be the Aristotelian notion of "habituation through education", that is, the creation of character through education (*paideia*). In a passage in the *Nicomachean Ethics* on which Hampshire drew our attention half a century ago, Aristotle maintains that the perfectly virtuous man *perceives* in a different, and better, manner the details of the practical situation he faces as compared to the ordinary man and especially as contrasted to the base man.[24] Aristotle famously states that the *spoudaios* is *kanon kai metron*, "the standard and measure" of what is good in practical situations. This is because practical situations are unique due to their singular circumstances; and with respect to particulars

> Judgement resides in perception (*en te aisthesei he krisis*).[25]

What Aristotle means is that the way we interpret the data of a practical situation influences our course of action. And our interpretation depends on our character, on our *hexis*, which results from education: the virtuous man, who is identified with the "reasonable" man, judges correctly (*orthos*) the practical situation and therefore chooses the right course of action.[26] If I am persuaded that theft and appropriating what is not mine are always morally wrong, I will not hesitate to give back the purse fallen from the bag of the lady standing in front of me on the bus. If I believe that every human being is a centre of absolute value, and not "Nature's wholesale merchandise" (Schopenhauer), I will reject any racist policy, and, in addition, I will be able to understand and sympathize with someone's grieving a beloved person. Aristotle thinks that this does not happen naturally; rather, that this "second nature" is brought about by education, in the broadest meaning of the word.

Another Aristotelian passage is of central importance for my argument. In *Politics* V 9, 1310a12–19, Aristotle comments:

> But the greatest of all the means spoken of to secure the stability of constitutions is one that at present all people despise: it is a system of education suited to the constitutions. For there is no use in the most valuable laws, ratified by the unanimous judgment of the whole body of citizens, if these are not trained and educated in the constitution, popularly if the laws are popular, oligarchically if they are oligarchical.

---

[24] See Hampshire 1959, pp. 212–213, who arrives at different conclusions from mine in Hampshire 1983, pp. 152–153.
[25] Aristotle, *Nicomachean Ethics* II 9, 1109b24. All translations from Aristotle's *Nicomachean Ethics* and *Politics* are mine.
[26] Aristotle, *Nicomachean Ethics* III 6, 1113a.

Two observations are here in place. What Aristotle recognizes here is, on the one hand, the central importance of education in supporting a form of government, a tool that he considered neglected by legislators already in his age; it is, on the other hand, important that this education aim at creating good citizens in relation to the specific form of government in which they live. There is not, in his view, a universally applicable perfect education. This surely does not mean that citizens should be indoctrinated into acceptance of the regime in which they happen to live, for there is no education to tyranny, for instance. What Aristotle means is that there are many good or acceptable regimes and that education in the values embodied in the constitution contributes both to the flourishing of the citizens and to the stability and goodness of the political community in which they live.

Finally, Aristotle has another fine observation we should always bear in mind. He identified and clearly stated the fact that the notions of "good citizen" and of "good human being" do not overlap; or rather, they do only in the best form of government. Being a good citizen means obeying the laws of one's country and pursuing the country's ideal of justice; being a good human being means displaying and exercising the virtues which promote humanity. This fact is apparent in a very bad form of government and is well caught in novels and movies, such as Milan Kundera's *The Unbearable Lightness of Being* (1984), Florian Henckel von Donnersmarck's *The Lives of Others* (2006) or Quentin Tarantino's *Inglourious Basterds* (2009): in 1941 occupied France, when asked whether there are Jews hiding in the farm, the good human being's answer to the Nazi officer is to lie. The good citizen would report them instead. Aristotle thus enables us to identify a serious problem typical of liberal societies: Liberalism draws a hard-and-fast distinction between the public and the private realm. Born out of the necessity to pacify conflict during the civil and religious wars of the 16th and 17th centuries, Liberalism found the solution in this distinction, placing religion in the private sphere and maintaining that the State is concerned only with the laws and what happens in the public sphere. This leaves the door open to the possibility of committing murderous acts (not crimes, properly speaking) according to the laws of the country.

We should be aware of the limitations pointed out by Aristotle. We should not attempt to bring about a historical transformation of "human nature" – the way utilitarian or Marxist authors hoped – because no such transformation can be expected. Instead, Liberal societies should emphasize the importance of supporting a liberal education aimed a creating autonomous and complete individuals, endowed with critical reasoning: the kind of individuals who are able to discern that, although certain acts may be allowed by the laws of the State, they are against the very notion of humanity: they may not be illegal, but they are certainly immoral. Moreover, our view of liberal education recognizes that it pursues the ideal of creating a "liberal" human being, in the old-fashioned and most elevated meaning of the word. This education aims at creating a "liberal", not a neutral identity, in the citizens: extolling critical reasoning and rationality, respect for the individual as an absolute centre of value, the consequent defence of personal freedom and of toleration of diversity are all liberal values. But this does not mean that they cannot be made universal or universally acceptable: again, Pythagoras' theorem was discovered by a Greek but does not apply only in Greece. The recognition of the historicity and 'situatedness' of these values and the consequent rejection of the illusion – and the hypocrisy – of "liberal neutrality" do not diminish at all the value of liberal education. On the contrary, it enables us to see in it a *value* and not a 'fact' or a neutral entity.

Bibliography

Ayer, Alfred Jules (1936): *Language, Truth & Logic*. London: Victor Gollancz.
Barker, Ernest (1906): *The Political Thought of Plato and Aristotle*. London: Routledge.
Finnis, John (1980): *Natural Law and Natural Rights*. Oxford: Clarendon.
George, Robert P. (1993): *Making Men Moral: Civil Liberties and Public Morality*. Oxford: Clarendon.
George, Robert P. (1999): *In Defense of Natural Law*. Oxford: Oxford University Press.
Giorgini, Giovanni (1989): "Crick, Hampshire and MacIntyre, or Does an English Speaking Neo-Aristotelianism Exist?" In: *Praxis International* 9, pp. 249–272.
Green, Thomas Hill (1883): *Prolegomena to Ethics*. Cambridge: Cambridge University Press.
Hacker, P.M.S. (2005): "Thought and Action: A Tribute to Stuart Hampshire". In: *Philosophy* 80, pp. 175–197.
Hampshire, Stuart (1949): "Fallacies in Moral Philosophy". In: *Mind* 58, pp. 466–482; reprinted in Hampshire 1971, pp. 42–62.
Hampshire, Stuart (1959): *Thought and Action*. London: Chatto & Windus.
Hampshire, Stuart (Ed.) (1966): *Philosophy of Mind*. New York, London: Harper & Row.
Hampshire, Stuart (1967a): "Ethics: A Defence of Aristotle". In: *University of Colorado Studies* 3, pp. 23–38; reprinted in Hampshire 1971, pp. 63–86.
Hampshire, Stuart (1967b): "Commitment and Imagination". In: Black, Max (Ed.): *The Morality of Scholarship*. Ithaca, Cornell University Press, pp. 29–55.
Hampshire, Stuart (1968): "Spinoza and the Idea of Freedom". In: Strawson, P.F. (Ed.): *Studies in the Philosophy of Thought and Action*. Oxford: Oxford University Press, pp. 48–70.
Hampshire, Stuart (1969): *Modern Writers and Other Essays*. London: Chatto & Windus.
Hampshire, Stuart (1971): *Freedom of Mind and Other Essays*. Princeton: Princeton University Press.
Hampshire, Stuart (1972): *Morality and Pessimism*. Cambridge: Cambridge University Press.

Hampshire, Stuart (1974): "Unity of Civil and Political Society". In: Kolakowski L./ Hampshire, S. (Eds.): *The Socialist Idea: A Reappraisal*. London: Weidenfeld and Nicolson, pp. 36–44.
Hampshire, Stuart (1977): *Two Theories of Morality*. Oxford: Oxford University Press.
Hampshire, Stuart (Ed.) (1978): *Public and Private Morality*. Cambridge: Cambridge University Press.
Hampshire, Stuart (1980): "Making Morality Effective". In: Kranzberg, Melvin (Ed.): *Ethics in an Age of Pervasive Technology*. Boulder: Westview, pp. 201–202.
Hampshire, Stuart (1983): *Morality and Conflict*. Oxford: Blackwell.
Hampshire, Stuart (1989): *Innocence and Experience*. London: Penguin.
Hampshire, Stuart (1993): "Liberalism: The New Twist" [review of John Rawls, *Political Liberalism*]. In: *The New York Review of Books*, 12 August 1993.
Hampshire, Stuart (2000): *Justice is Conflict*. London: Duckworth.
Lassman, Peter (2009): "Pluralism and Pessimism: A Central Theme in the Political Thought of Stuart Hampshire". In: *History of Political Thought* 30, pp. 315–335.
MacIntyre, Alasdair (1999): *Dependent Rational Animals*. Chicago, Lasalle: Open Court.
Marcovic, Mihailo (1982): *Democratic Socialism: Theory and Practice*, Brighton: Harvester.
Maritain, Jacques (1936): *Humanisme Integral*. Paris: Aubier.
Maritain, Jacques (1954): *Man and the State*. London: Hollis & Carter.
Moore, George Edward (1903): *Principia Ethica*. Cambridge: Cambridge University Press.
Nussbaum, Martha (2000): "The Future of Feminist Liberalism". In: *Proceedings and Addresses of the American Philosophical Association* 74, pp. 47–79.
Rawls, John (1971): *A Theory of Justice*. Cambridge, MA: Harvard University Press.
Rawls, John (1980): "Kantian Constructivism in Moral Theory". In: *Journal of Philosophy* 9, pp. 515–572.
Rawls, John (1987): "The Idea of an Overlapping Consensus". In: *Oxford Journal of Legal Studies* 7, pp. 1–25.
Rawls, John (1993): *Political Liberalism*. New York: Columbia University Press.
Raz, Joseph (1986): *The Morality of Freedom*. Oxford: Clarendon.
Riedel, Manfred (Ed.) (1972–74): *Rehabilitierung der praktischen Philosophie*. 2 Vols. Freiburg: Rombach.
Ritter, Joachim (1969): *Metaphysik und Politik*. Frankfurt a. M.: Suhrkamp.
Ross, William David (1930): *The Right and the Good*. Oxford: Clarendon.
Ryle, Gilbert (1949): *The Concept of Mind*. Chicago: University of Chicago Press.
Stevenson, Charles Leslie (1945): *Ethics and Language*. Yale: Yale University Press.

Bertjan Wolthuis
Public Reason in Circumstances of Pluralism

Abstract: Recently, several theorists have argued that John Rawls's political liberalism, with its notion of public reason, is based on presuppositions so idealistic and moralistic, that it cannot provide a relevant standard of argumentation in real political circumstances, where disagreements concerning matters of justice may run deep. The question raised in this contribution is: which notion of reasonableness, if any, could be used as a standard with which to distinguish between reasonable and unreasonable political positions in such circumstances of radical pluralism? I examine here whether contemporary realists may find helpful Jürgen Habermas's notion of public opinion or Aristotle's idea of reputable things or *ta endoxa*. It is argued here that realists may find the latter particularly useful in developing a realist notion of public reason.

Political liberals claim that politicians have a moral duty to refer only to reasons that all reasonable citizens can reasonably be expected to accept (Rawls 1993, p. 217). This notion of public reason or the reasonably acceptable reflects the moral core of any Kantian political theory: the equal freedom of moral persons. The content of public reason is given by a political liberal conception of distributive justice, in John Rawls's version of political liberalism (1993, p. 223).

Critics have argued that this political liberal notion of public reason conflicts with everyday political experience in which decisions are taken in circumstances of disagreement about the justice of a certain course of action or law (Hampshire 1999; Waldron 1999). Political liberalism's notion of public reason misunderstands therefore the radical nature of genuine political disagreement, these critics claim, which is problematic for a political theory (Galston 2010, pp. 385–411; Horton 2010, pp. 431–448; Williams 2005).

Of course, for Rawls "the crucial fact is not the fact of pluralism as such, but of reasonable pluralism", which is "the long-run result of the powers of human reason within an enduring background of free institutions" (Rawls 1993, p. 144). Reasonable persons are thought to "desire for its own sake a social world in which they, as free and equal, can cooperate with others on terms all can accept" (Rawls 1993, p. 50). However, this is dismissed by realists as "harmony within the liberal stockade" (Hampshire 1999, p. 32). The realist adopts the point of view of "the real world of necessary politics" (Hampshire 1999, p. 36) or "the circumstances of politics" (Waldron 1999, p. 160) instead.

The issue whether the realist criticisms have a point, has been widely discussed. This article takes up another issue thus far ignored. It addresses the question of whether there is – and, if so, what could be – an alternative, realist, non-liberal, notion of public reasonableness, which is consistent with the adoption of such a realist perspective of politics. This question need not involve exploring the incomprehensible; contemporary political realists[1] do not simply accept wholeheartedly the world of Realpolitik. Political power is also, in their view, not just a form of domination (Williams 2005, Chapter 1); it comes with a notion of legitimacy (Williams 2005, Chapter 1; Sleat 2014). Since the issue of a realist notion of the reasonable still awaits exploration (Wolthuis 2016a), this contribution aims to gain insight into both sides of the debate by asking: What notion of public reason may be adopted by the realist who views radical disagreement[2] concerning distributive justice as one of the circumstances of politics?

There are many reasons for reflecting on the question of public reason in these circumstances of politics. Let me distinguish here two. The first is: how is it even possible, or how can it ever be effective, to reason with others in circumstances of radical disagreement? In the liberal view it is precisely agreement that makes public reasoning intelligible. Of course, citizens will disagree about how to interpret or weigh liberal principles, liberal theorists claim, but they will be able to discuss political matters rather comfortably because they share a liberal vocabulary and a consensus on basic, distributive justice. If the assumption of this deep liberal consensus is dropped, however, understanding the possibility of public reasoning becomes problematic.

The second reason for reflecting on public reason in circumstances of politics is related to the point of the liberal duty to use public reason. The rationale of this duty is that all citizens are in this way free, in the sense that ideally they will be subjected only to laws based on reasons they can reasonably accept. The assumption is that the reasonable citizens of liberal democratic societies share a

---

[1] See for an overview and some characteristics of contemporary "political realism", as it is commonly referred to: Galston 2010.

[2] In this contribution the term disagreement in the discussion of political realism equals what Rawls refers to as disagreement or pluralism "as such" (Rawls 1993, p. 144). The question in this contribution is what notion of public reason may be consistent with the "circumstances of politics" (Waldron 1999) which I take to be characterised by "pluralism as such", which must be distinguished from reasonable disagreement or reasonable pluralism. The latter idea is part of the political liberal notion of a political conception of justice.

commitment to the basic norm of free and equal citizenship. Since radical realist critics do not (want to) make this assumption, the question becomes upon what idea of reasonableness an alternative notion of political liberty, an alternative understanding of acceptability, can be based. Can a law be viewed as acceptable (or inacceptable) in circumstances of disagreement about distributive justice, and if so, according to which notion of reasonableness?

It is already clear, I hope, that the question touches upon several major issues. It is impossible to do justice to them all within the scope of this contribution. I have therefore limited the contribution in three important ways. First, since the issue of political reason is by itself already quite a handful, I will not take sides in the discussion between liberals and realists. This means that I do not examine here the issue whether the realist criticism has a point. That question has already been dealt with elsewhere (Thomas 2017; Jubb 2015; Wolthuis 2016b). My question is confined to this: which notion of reasonableness may the realist critics referred to above – right or wrong – themselves want to adopt? Second, this contribution is limited in the sense that I examine here no more than two alternative approaches to Rawls's political liberal understanding of public reason (Habermas's notion of public opinion and Aristotle's idea of *ta endoxa*) as possible candidates for a realist understanding of public reason. Third, since these two highly complex alternatives simply cannot be thoroughly discussed within the confines of this contribution, I examine these theories exclusively from the rather sceptical point of view of the contemporary political realist (see section 2), who is assumed to look for inspiration for a notion of public reason compatible with radical disagreement about political justice. Jürgen Habermas's notion of public opinion is in the end dismissed by this realist, I conjecture here (section 3), because Habermas frames this idea of public reasonableness in liberal, democratic terms. I then turn to a pre-liberal theory of politics in which argumentation in circumstances of disagreement about distributive justice turns out to play a central role: Aristotle's. I show why Aristotle's notion of "acceptable things" may inspire the realist to develop a notion of reasonableness which takes the "circumstances of politics" seriously (section 4). First, I recapitulate briefly those features of liberalism (section 1) which, realist critics claim, culminate in a misunderstanding of politics (section 2).

1 From distributive justice to politics

The opening sentence of section 1 of Rawls's *A Theory of Justice* reads: "Justice is the first virtue of social institutions, as truth is of systems of thought" (Rawls 1999, p. 3). The status of first virtue is reflected, for instance, in the four stage structure of Rawls's theory. From an "original position" of artificial impartiality equal and free parties are to choose the principles of justice which in turn direct the choices concerning the implementation of these principles in later stages, for instance the stage in which a political constitution is selected (Rawls 1999, p. 174). Rawls treats justice as a first virtue here in the sense that it comes first in order (in the theory) and therefore occupies the highest rank (in the liberal moral outlook). It is important to keep in mind that Rawls does not just argue from distributive justice to politics in general. Rather, the choice of a political constitution depends on the choice of a specific view of justice, i.e., the two principles of distributive justice that Rawls thinks would be chosen in the original position. (The two principles amount to a social kind of liberalism.)

In *Political Liberalism* Rawls remains true to this line of reasoning from distributive justice to politics. Political power is legitimate only if it is justifiable in terms of public reason, the content of which is given by a political liberal conception of justice. The collection of arguments that all reasonable citizens can reasonably be expected to accept, are given by "the values expressed by the principles and guidelines that would be agreed to in the original position" (Rawls 1993, p. 227). Rawls's theory is interpreted by realists as a form of "political moralism" (Williams 2005, p. 2).

Rawls develops his theory of justice for what he calls a "well-ordered" society, i.e., a society "in which everyone accepts and knows that the others accept the same principles of justice" (Rawls 1999, p. 4). Rawls understands his theory as "ideal theory" in this respect (Rawls 1999, p. 8). Of course, Rawls's choice to abstract from disagreement about justice indicates that he thinks this kind of idealisation does not obstruct its application to political practice. Rawls presupposes that reasonable disagreement about justice is limited and therefore need not be (or can be) overcome, especially if we bracket our private interests and beliefs. This presupposition is further reflected in Rawls's method of attaining a reflective equilibrium between "our shared considered convictions about justice" (Rawls 1999, p. 18), the design of the original position and the principles of justice but also, of course, in the entire project of producing principles of justice by means of social contract theory.

It is also made perfectly clear by Rawls why reasonable agreement about justice must occupy a place right in the centre of liberal thought. Freedom is for Rawls intimately connected to reasonable agreement. Political freedom is understood as being able to accept the laws that govern you. You are unfree, Rawls argues, if you are subjected to laws that you cannot reasonably accept. You are oppressed in this situation. This notion of freedom/oppression requires that there is agreement between reasonable citizens about what counts as reasonably acceptable (Rawls 1993, p. 37). Rawls argues that only liberalism, of a social kind, specifies a notion of justice that is reasonably acceptable to reasonable persons, in their capacity as citizens, and, consequently, is able to make everyone free in the above sense.

To round up the picture of public reason presented in *Political Liberalism*, let me briefly answer two questions: first, what exactly is the content of public reason and second, what is its domain of application? In *Political Liberalism* Rawls argues that liberalisms other than "justice as fairness" could function as sources of public argumentation. These liberalisms need to meet certain criteria (Rawls 1993, p. 223) and fall within the range of, broadly speaking, social or emancipatory forms of liberalism.

Concerning the domain of public reason, citizens and politicians have a duty to use public reason only in official political forums. Citizens are allowed to refer to non-public reasons in background forums. There is one exception: citizens and politicians may refer to their "comprehensive doctrines", i.e., their ethical, religious or philosophical views in the official political sphere, "provided they do this in ways that strengthen the ideal of public reason itself" (Rawls 1993, p. 247).

2 "Pluralism as such" –The circumstances of politics

In this contribution I discuss the criticism that Rawls, by reasoning from distributive justice to politics in both *A Theory of Justice* and *Political Liberalism* as indicated above, cannot but misunderstand politics, because politics or political decision making is about selecting a policy, taking a course of action, or giving a law, in a situation where citizens disagree about what policy, course of action or law is just (because of the divergent conceptions of distributive justice prevailing in society). Disagreement about justice is in this view one of the "circumstances of politics" (Waldron 1999, p. 160). The need for a common decision is the other, according to Waldron. Rawls's subordination of politics to distributive justice therefore begs the question that legislators must face, the question which conception of justice to follow. Citizens disagree about justice and need to decide what to do in this situation of disagreement. Abstracting from this disagreement from the start, by ignoring "pluralism as such" and focusing on "reasonable pluralism" instead, misses the point of what politics is all about, Waldron claims. In this section I want to discuss briefly this critique as it is brought forward in particular by Stuart Hampshire and Jeremy Waldron.[3] I draw attention to two ele-

---

[3] I cannot do justice to the theories of Hampshire and Waldron in this contribution. For a dis-

ments: (1) the realistic character of these critics' theories (as opposed to Rawls's ideal theory) and (2) these realists' idea that disagreement about justice is a circumstance of politics as we know it (and the claim that Rawls errs in what they view as subordinating politics to justice). (3) At the end of the section I return to the two questions distinguished in the introduction.

(1) While Rawls's theory is an example of ideal theory because of its assumption that everyone accepts the same principles of justice, the theories developed by Hampshire and Waldron can be called realistic by comparison. The starting point of these authors is not the well-ordered society in which basic agreement regarding justice is assumed. Instead, the point of departure is "the real world of necessary politics" (Hampshire 1999, p. 36), which is characterised by disagreement about distributive justice (Hampshire 1999, p. 18).

(2) From within this point of view the basic *direction* of Rawls's reasoning, from agreement about distributive justice to a theory of (legitimate) politics, is problematic. While in Rawls's theory the principles of justice are prior to and higher in rank than the principles regulating political decision making processes, Waldron and Hampshire explain that this misses the point that there is a difference in *level* between justice (in substantial matters), on the one hand, and procedural, technical norms and values regulating decision making processes, on the other. There are many conceptions of distributive justice that gain support in a society and these may conflict with one another at the decision making level. Both Waldron and Hampshire take their theoretical stance at this level of decision making. In these circumstances of politics there is disagreement ("pluralism as such"); thus, technical decision making rules are needed. "To say that in such a case justice is being subordinated to procedural values in political decision making would be to beg the question of which of the positions competing for political support is to be counted as just" (Waldron 1999, p. 161). Waldron describes this point in terms of logical error. One commits "something of a 'category-mistake' in treating justice and fairness as co-ordinate principles, competing on the same level" (Waldron 1999, pp. 195–196).

(3) Hampshire and Waldron do not reflect upon the issue of public reason in the circumstance of disagreement. (Which is the *raison d'être* of this contribution.) Is it possible to be reasonable or unreasonable in these circumstances of politics, and if so, according to which notion of reason? These issues are not sys-

---

cussion of Hampshire's thought, see G. Giorgini, "Stuart Hampshire and the Case for Procedural Justice", in this volume. Giorgini focuses on the influence of Aristotle's philosophy on Hampshire's work. I show in section 4 why Aristotle's notion of acceptable things may help contemporary realists, influenced by Hampshire's work, construct a realist notion of public reasonableness. I believe the two contributions reinforce each other.

tematically dealt with by Waldron or Hampshire. Hampshire pays some attention, however, to the question of how freedom – acceptance of laws in circumstances of politics – is possible. Since the outcome of the political process in such circumstances may be highly controversial, the quality of political *procedure* becomes the key variable. What is required, Hampshire argues, is that minorities are properly heard (Hampshire 1999, pp. 50–51). Hampshire insists in this regard on the value of a "smart compromise, one where the tension between contrary forces and impulses, pulling against each other, is perceptible and vivid" (Hampshire 1999, p. 39). What this kind of compromise exactly entails, is not spelled out by Hampshire, but evidently the influence of minorities must be somehow recognisable in the procedure's outcome. In the penultimate paragraph I return to the realist's notion of compromise.

3 Habermas's government by public opinion

I now explore two possible answers to the question raised in the introduction: Habermas's notion of public opinion (this section) and Aristotle's idea of "*ta endoxa*" (next section). I lay out Habermas's theory of deliberative politics in two parts: (1) a part about argumentation and (2) a part about the role of argumentation in a democratic society. (3) I end this section with Habermas's view of the content of public reason.

(1) To confront our question – what view of public reason may be consistent with argumentation in circumstances of disagreement about distributive justice – adequately, it seems that Habermas's work cannot be bypassed, since its characteristic feature is that it starts with real argumentation. One of the basic questions raised in Habermas's work is what standards or rules participants to real practices of argumentation must accept, simply by participating in these practices. This question indeed is a promising start.

The answer is provided in two steps. First Habermas defines argumentation, then he formulates the rules that constitute this practice or game. Argumentation is a reflexive kind of communicative action. Communicative action is action coordinated by reaching agreement or understanding ("Verständigung"). "Verständigung" means that two or more speakers share the same reasons or convictions ("Überzeugungen") (Habermas 1981, p. 387). It is the "telos" of human language; speech directed at agreement is the "original mode" of speech (Habermas 1981, pp. 387–388). By understanding argumentation as a reflexive kind of communicative action, the attention is drawn to the disagreement solving capacity of argumentation and Habermas also defines an argumentation as a collection of speech acts aimed at reaching understanding/agreement by advancing arguments (Habermas 2007, p. 413).

Everyone who engages in argumentation must accept the following rules of this game (Habermas 2008, p. 150; Wolthuis 2013): (a) no contribution to the discussion is excluded, (b) all participants are given an equal opportunity to participate in the discussion, (c) every participant is sincere and (d) the discussion is free from domination, so that opinions are motivated by nothing but better reasons (Habermas 1996, p. 62). These rules constitute the practice of argumentation in the sense that it is impossible to play the game of argumentation and break these rules at the same time. When a participant makes a threat, for instance, he is simply no longer arguing, no longer committed to the game's goal of reaching shared understanding by rational means. Habermas claims that argumentation is a universal practice and has no alternative when participants genuinely strive to reach an agreement (Habermas 1996, pp. 60–61). The rules or standards of argumentation inherent in this universal practice are understood as objective (Wolthuis 2013, p. 118); Habermas claims they are the ultimate foundation of a morality of impartiality (Habermas 1996, pp. 60–61).

The above outline of Habermas's view of argumentation is not necessarily incompatible with the realist's recognition of fundamental disagreement about social and political justice. The fact that agreement, the goal of argumentation in his reconstruction of the practice, is quite rare in actual politics, for instance, is in itself insufficient to conclude that Habermas's reconstruction of the game is simply inapplicable in circumstances of disagreement. (Of course, it is reasonable to conclude, then, that it is an incredibly *difficult* game to play well, i.e., to reach a genuine consensus by rational means in politics – but that is something quite different.)

It is the explanation of argumentation's disagreement solving potential, however, which makes Habermas's approach of argumentation in the end unsuitable in circumstances of politics, if we adopt the sceptical realist's point of view. Argumentation, Habermas explains, can solve disagreement because of its "triadic" structure (Habermas 2007, p. 415). Participants are able to reach agreement by referring to a collection of fundamental or higher reasons, a third authority they can appeal to.

Realists need not deny that it may be meaningful to say, from a participant's point of view, that argumentation has a triadic structure. Players of the game of argumentation may adopt this metaphor of a hierarchy of reasons to make sense of what they do when they advance reasons. Confronted by disagreement, a participant may describe what he or she does as reaching for higher (or deeper) reasons, reaching out to find common ground, etc., in order to attain consensus. However, if we leave the participant's point of view and move to the level of political decision making, as Waldron and Hampshire do, where the realist assumes and expects genuine disagreement concerning distributive justice, there is no assurance that each participant regards the same reasons as higher, deeper or shared. Indeed, Waldron's idea of the circumstances of politics is that an overlap in higher reasons cannot be assumed in politics. The question is: does Habermas really assume such an overlap? Realists can find in his work support for an affirmative answer.[4] Let me explain.

(2) The support can be found in his political theory, in which argumentation in the public sphere is interpreted as the way in which political decision making in representative and governmental bodies is to be rationalised and legitimised. The public sphere ("Öffentlichkeit") is a communication network in which opinions are circulated and filtered and eventually public opinion ("öffentliche Meinung"), the result of argumentation, is created. Political officials have the duty to translate public opinion into political decisions.

Argumentation can only create public opinion, however, if the public sphere is fostered by a liberal, rational civil society. Civil society is the collection of (non-governmental and non-economical) free associations between citizens. The anarchical character of this sphere is protected by constitutional liberties such as freedom of association and of opinion. But this reference to a liberal civil society is also meant to convey the idea that civil society is characterised by a liberal culture:

> A robust civil society can develop only in the context of a liberal political culture and the corresponding patterns of socialization, and on the basis of an integral private sphere; it can blossom only in an already rationalized lifeworld. Otherwise, populist movements arise [...]. These movements are as modern as they are anti-democratic (Habermas 1997, p. 371).

Habermas expects citizens, if they are left in civil society's anarchical peace, to socialise themselves into a liberal culture and in this way socialise themselves as rational citizens, i.e., as citizens who are able to play their part in creating a truly rational public opinion, a public opinion that is able to legitimise and rationalise politics (Habermas 1997, p. 382).

---

[4] As indicated in the introduction: within the confines of this contribution it is not possible to discuss Habermas's theory thoroughly or objectively. The line of argument presented here, circling around the contemporary realist's point of view and its notion of circumstances of politics, should not be read as addressing the question whether Habermas's work is, all things considered, a realistic theory of law and politics. That question requires a much more thorough examination.

But this view of the public sphere as liberal and democratic in this sense – also in terms of public opinion as output – means that Habermas's approach will need to be rejected in the end, if we adopt the realist's point of view discussed earlier. The reason is that the realist will see a view of politics and reason analogous to the picture drawn before by Rawls. Where Rawls confronted politics with the outcome of an artificial, impartial choice situation, Habermas will be understood by these realists to subordinate politics to a rational process of public opinion formation, to the free discussion in the contained anarchy of civil society. In Habermas's view politics can be said to be *also* in need of legitimation by pure and liberal reason, outside politics, in this case by free, rational agreement in the public sphere where a liberal culture reigns. Habermas expects civil society to foster this sphere and that agreement, on the condition that its anarchical character is guaranteed.

(3) The discussion of Habermas's view of public reason remains incomplete if we do not attempt to determine its content. The content of public reason can be deduced rather straightforwardly, I propose, from Habermas's support for Rawls's position that politicians have a moral duty to refer to reasons that all reasonable citizens can freely accept:

> Majority rule turns into repression if the majority deploys religious arguments in the process of political opinion and will formation and refuses to offer those publicly accessible justifications which the losing minority, be it secular or of a different faith, is able to follow and to evaluate in the light of shared standards (Habermas 2006, p. 12).

This position assumes that there are such shared standards. Indeed, Habermas claims in this article on religion and public reason that only substantial agreement is able to prevent a political community from "disintegrating":

> the conflict on existential values between communities of faith cannot be solved by compromise. They can be contained, however, by losing any political edge against the background of a presupposed consensus on constitutional principles (Habermas 2006, p. 12).

By taking this position, Habermas must have meant with the agreement embodied in public opinion (the result of argumentation in the public sphere) a view consistent with liberal justice.

While it has become clear, on the one hand, in what respect Habermas's theory of deliberative government differs from Rawls's political liberalism, I hope to have shown, on the other hand, why it will be rejected if one adopts the realist's perspective in which the idea of the circumstances of politics or pluralism as such plays such a central role. (1) Argumentation has a triadic structure, in Habermas's view. The participants of a discussion are able to reach agreement by referring to a collection of higher reasons, a third authority. (2) This is problematic in so far as Habermas expects reasonable participants to refer to the *same* reasons as higher in this respect, culminating in a "public opinion" rationalising and legitimising political decision making processes. (3) From a realist's perspective the conclusion is that politics is evidently in need of rationalisation or legitimisation by a public reason *external* to politics, in the form of public opinion developed within the anarchy of a liberal civil society.

4 Aristotle's "reputable things"[5]

The analysis of Habermas's notion of public reason suggests that the specification of the notion of political reason that can be part of a realist picture of politics may require inspiration from a non-liberal or pre-modern understanding of political reasoning. I will argue in this paragraph why Aristotle's notion of "*ta endoxa*", "acceptable" or "reputable things" (*Top.*, 100 a 30), is a promising candidate to function as such a source of inspiration.[6] This notion was understood as compatible with Greek politics, which was characterised by deep disagreements about distributive justice. I will discuss here, based on a reading of Aristotle's works on argumentation and rhetoric, (1) Aristotle's view of public reason,[7] and (2) how it may help explain argumentation in circumstances of disagreement, and also (3) how acceptance of political decisions is possible in the face of disagreement about the distribution of the rights of citizenship in the polis.

(1) To understand what acceptable means in the context of political argumentation, we need to appreciate first what reasoning or argumentation in public amounts to, in Aristotle's view. Important for our purposes is that Aristotle distinguishes deliberation from demonstration. Where the scientist demonstrates the truth of a conclusion through logical deduction from true premises, the politician works from premises that are acceptable instead. There is a crucial difference, Aristotle explains, between the sphere of necessary relations with which a

---

5 An analysis similar to the first two parts of this section is incorporated in Wolthuis 2016a.
6 See the bibliography for the translations of Aristotle's works referred to in this section.
7 Again, as indicated in the introduction, the point here is *not* that Aristotle is a realist *avant la lettre* or that his philosophy as a whole is realist. Rather, the argument here is limited in the following sense: the notion of reasonableness inherent in ancient Greek *rhetoric* (to which Aristotle has made an important contribution) is interesting for the realist hoping to find an alternative to *liberal* public reason.

scientist is occupied and the sphere of freedom (from necessity) which characterises human affairs, and with which the politician is concerned. Aristotle concludes that the politician would make a serious mistake if he would deliberate about necessary relations: "everything which of necessity either is or will be, or which cannot possibly be or come to pass, is outside the scope of deliberation" (*Rhet.*, 1359a2–3). Political speech and discussion is "limited to those subjects about which we take counsel; and such are all those which can naturally be referred to ourselves and the first cause of whose origination is in our power" (*Rhet.*, 1359a3).

Aristotle claims that the activity or practice(s) of politics can in this sense not be reduced to a science. Notice that Aristotle's *Politics* is primarily concerned with the *stage* of politics: the constitution of the polis, not political *activity* itself – which is the domain covered by the arts of rhetoric and dialectic, which deal with producing/doing something: making/holding a speech (rhetoric) or preparing/having a discussion (dialectic). "In proportion as anyone endeavours to make of dialectic or rhetoric, not what they are, faculties, but sciences, to that extent he will, without knowing it, destroy their real nature, in thus altering their character, by crossing over into the domain of sciences" (*Rhet.*, 1359b6).

It is important to clarify as precisely as possible the difference between scientific truth and political acceptability. Aristotle gives a clue when he distinguishes truth from acceptability:

> Those things are true and primary which get their trustworthiness through themselves rather than through other things [...]. Those are acceptable, on the other hand, which seem so to everyone, or to most people, or to the wise – to all of them, or to most, or to the most famous and esteemed (*Top.*, 100b18–23).

The difference is instructive. Where sciences deal with necessary relations between things that "get their trustworthiness through themselves", arts of argumentation deal with "things" that get their trustworthiness through people (everyone or most people, etc.). The things that play a role in human affairs are valuable or recommendable or acceptable not because of a quality in those things themselves, but because people *attach value* to them, *think* they are right, *believe* they are true (Höffe 2006, p. 57). This has important corollaries for Aristotle's view of political argumentation or deliberation, because, since people attach trustworthiness to the things people are concerned with (war and peace, for instance) and a polis consists of people of "different kinds" (*Pol.*, 1261a 23), there can also be disagreement about these things (war or peace with Sparta?). And indeed, Aristotle explains that argumentation deals with problems "about which people either have no opinion, or the public think the opposite of the wise, or the wise think the opposite of the public, or each of these groups has opposed opinions within itself" (*Top.*, 104b4–6).

What is "acceptable" in this regard? Aristotle explains the character of τα ενδοξα, "the reputable things", in the definition in *Topics* referred to earlier: "those [things, BW] are acceptable [reputable, translated in Barnes 1980, p. 500, BW], which seem so [i.e., true, trustworthy, BW] to everyone, or to most people, or to the wise – to all of them, or to most, or to the most famous and esteemed". Barnes (1980, p. 500) concludes that this does not "explain" what the term τα ενδοξα "means", but the fragment nevertheless teaches us something very important: that acceptability or reputability is a relative concept (Smith in Aristotle 1997, p. 42). "That which is persuasive is persuasive in reference to some one" (*Rhet.*, 1356 b 11). In the *Eudemian Ethics* Aristotle confirms this view of opinions as *endoxa* in the sense of "prevalent", but he adds there a second characteristic: those views are *endoxa* that "seem to have some reason" (Barnes 1980, p. 503). This evidently needs to be taken in the literal sense as: accompanied by reasons, thought through (Barnes 1980, p. 504). Höffe (2006, p. 56) agrees and translates this component as "wohlbegründet", well-considered. So, *ta endoxa* refers to opinions or views that are prevalent and based on reasons. Nothing in this understanding of the reputable things contradicts the realist idea of the circumstances of politics. On the contrary: this conception of public reason may be viewed by the realist as highly attractive, it seems, since Aristotle presupposes sharp disagreement in matters concerning human affairs; these are affairs about which the public and the wise may have "opposite" opinions, "or each of these groups has opposed opinions within itself" (*Top.*, 104b4–6).

(2) However, this account of disagreement and public reason raises questions, for instance: how is meaningful political argumentation in such circumstances possible? Of course, an orator must use acceptable reasons, but some of the acceptable reasons may only be acceptable or even intelligible to the wise while others may only be acceptable to the many. A politician can never be certain that his particular audience considers the particular reasons he refers to as acceptable or not. This is precisely the reason why the audience needs to play a part in these public processes of political argumentation. Political argumentation can only be effective if the audience accepts the premises from which the conclusions are drawn. In a dialectical discussion (illustrated by Plato's dialogues) this is done by questions. The speaker asks his opponent (an audience of one) to accept the premises, from which he eventually hopes to deduce his position. In a speech before a large audience the orator cannot ask for acceptance; he simply needs to estimate what his audience will accept (*Rhet.*, 1356b11). What rhetoric and dialectic share is that it is this cooperation between speaker

and audience, in both oratory and discussion, which explains how political argumentation is *possible*.

It is the competition between speakers, or to be more precise, the competitive setting of political speech and political discussion, which is designed to make argumentation in circumstances of politics *effective*. In circumstances of disagreement multiple speeches are always to be expected. These speeches are not aimed at agreement, as in Habermas's model, but victory. The orators aim to win the discussion, i.e., get the support of the majority of the assembly. With dialectical discussion the case is a little more complicated. In a political context such a discussion is highly competitive. The questioner's aim may be to refute the thesis of the answerer, i.e., "to lead the argument so as to make the answerer state the most unacceptable of the consequences made necessary as a result of the thesis" (*Top.*, 159a18–25). The answerer is only forced (by logic) to give up his thesis when he accepts premises from which the questioner can deduce the opposite of (or something else than) the answerer's initial position. Therefore, as long as the answerer avoids inconsistency in his reasoning, he is not logically compelled to give up his position. This makes it very difficult for participants with more or less equal capacities to force the other to give up his position. And this explains why in the competitive variant it is anticipated that such a clear victory is usually unattainable. This variant's goal is therefore formulated by Aristotle as follows: "The questioner must at all costs appear to be inflicting something on the answerer, while the answerer must appear not to be affected" (*Top.*, 159a31–32). The stress on appearance suggests the presence of an audience, picking the winner (Smith in Aristotle 1997, pp. 128ff.). This competitive variant of dialectical argumentation seems not all that different from competitive political discussion as we know it (Wolthuis 2013).

I conclude that Aristotle's view of argumentation in speech and discussion explains both how argumentation is possible in circumstances of politics (through cooperation between speaker and audience) and how in these circumstances of politics disagreement can be made productive (through competition before a judging audience or public). Let me stress, before moving on, that this setting of political speech and argumentation also explains why the views or opinions on which the politician bases his conclusions need to be *both* prevalent (in order to gain support from a majority in speeches) and rational (in order to survive rational criticism in discussions with rivals). In sum: it is clear why the views need to be *endoxa*.

(3) The remaining question is how is it possible to attain acceptance of political decisions concerning "constitutional essentials and questions of basic justice", as Rawls (2001, p. 91) refers to these issues, in circumstances of fundamental disagreement about distributive justice. A key insight is provided by Ar-

istotle's discussion of "politeia" or the constitutional type of government. This is a "mixture of oligarchy and democracy"; in an oligarchy the wealthy rule, in a democracy the free (the poor). In this polity, however, the wealthy, the poor and "those in between these" (*Pol.*, 1295b2) are all included in the government of the city. This "middle constitution" is stable but not because these groups agree. On the contrary, oligarchs and democrats disagree about how to distribute political offices justly – indeed how to constitute the city. "For one lot thinks that if they are unequal in one respect (wealth, say) they are wholly unequal, whereas the other lot thinks that if they are equal in one respect (freedom, say) they are wholly equal" (*Pol.*, 1280a22).

How can groups with so different views live peacefully together? One of Aristotle's answers is: build a constitution that combines and mixes elements of both types of constitution. There are three ways to do that: "to take legislation from both constitutions", "to take the mean between the organisations of each" and "to take elements from both organisations" (*Pol.*, 1294a35 – 1294b7). A good mix is the result of true political craftmanship.

> In a constitution that is well-mixed, [...] both elements [democracy and oligarchy, BW] should be held to be present – and neither; and it should survive because of itself and not because of external factors, and because of itself, not because a majority wishes it (since that could happen in a bad constitution too), but because none of the parts of a city-state as a whole would even want another constitution (*Pol.*, 1294b34 – 39).

So acceptance is, in this approach to politics, not based on agreement in the sense of consensus, as in the liberal case, but on agreement in the sense of compromise: compromise between groups who disagree sharply about what the right constitution is. These groups all get something (not everything) out of the deal. It may not be the constitution of their first choice. They may not "want another constitution", however, once they realise that all groups play their part in this constitution and that it is stable precisely because of this. Freedom as acceptance can be attained in this mixed constitution, because citizens can accept the laws they live under, not because they agree with the laws but because the laws are the result of a "smart compromise", using Hampshire's words, a compromise that is stable because there is something to gain for all political groups.

I briefly recapitulate this discussion of Aristotle's *reputable things*. Recall that the question was: which notion of public reasonableness could be adopted in what the realist critics of political liberalism referred to as the "circumstances of politics". The conclusion of this section is that realists may be able to learn valuable insights from Aristotle's notion of reputable things (*ta endoxa*). Reputable things are opinions or views that are prevalent and defensible. The ideas of prevalence and rationality inherent in this notion are not inconsistent with deep disagreement about distributive justice, with the idea of the "circumstances of politics". *Ta endoxa* does not imply agreement and Aristotle explains in his *Rhetoric* and *Topics* how oratory and dialectical discussion can proceed and yield results in circumstances of disagreement and how freedom as acceptance is possible even in circumstances of radical disagreement about basic distributive justice.

5 Conclusion

Aristotle's account of public reasoning could inspire the contemporary political realist struggling to find a standard of public reasonableness. Aristotle's rhetorical understanding of the reasonable is able to set aside views that are not prevalent or simply cannot be defended against rational criticism. This is no external, independent standard of the reasonable with which to assess political positions and argumentations. What is reasonable can only be concluded *in* politics, by political argumentation itself. Inspired by Aristotle, political realists may propose, in other words, oratorical and dialectical forms of politics as a means to filter out views that turn out to be not rational or not prevalent. And it is clear that realists need to rely in this respect on political procedures and on politicians participating with all their vigour in public and political discussions, exposing the lack of consistency or prevalence in their opponent's views.

The discussion so far has also made clear that there is a wide divide between the views of political liberals or deliberative democrats such as Rawls and Habermas on the one hand and those of their most radical realist critics on the other. While the first outlook takes a substantial idea of public reasonableness as its point of departure and unrelentingly affirms the Kantian norm of equal freedom for all persons, a standard which may under no circumstance be compromised, the second strand of thought views political compromise in circumstances of disagreement about distributive justice as a political aim worthy of admiration. The search for a realist notion of public reason in this contribution supports the hypothesis that a combination of truly liberal and radical realist theories of politics is just not possible.

Bibliography

Aristotle (1926): *'Art' of Rhetoric*. J.H. Freese (Trans.). Cambridge, London: Harvard University Press.

Aristotle (1982): *Eudemian Ethics. Books I, II, and VIII*. Translated with a commentary by Michael Woods. Clarendon Aristotle Series. Oxford: Clarendon Press.

Aristotle (1997): *Topics. Books I and VIII*. Translated with a commentary by Robin Smith. Clarendon Aristotle Series, Oxford: Clarendon Press.
Aristotle (1998): *Politics*. C.D.C. Reeve (Trans.). Indianapolis, Cambridge: Hackett.
Barnes, Jonathan (1980): "Aristotle and the Method of Ethics". In: *Revue Internationale de Philosophie* 131–132, pp. 490–511.
Galston, William (2010): "Realism in Political Theory". In: *European Journal of Political Theory* 9, pp. 385–411.
Habermas, Jürgen (1981): *Theorie des kommunikativen Handelns*. Vol. 1. Frankfurt a. M.: Suhrkamp.
Habermas, Jürgen (1996): *Die Einbeziehung des Anderen*. Frankfurt a. M.: Suhrkamp.
Habermas, Jürgen (1997): *Between Facts and Norms. Contributions to a Discourse Theory of Law and Democracy*. William Rehg (Trans.). Cambridge, UK: Polity Press.
Habermas, Jürgen (1998): *Faktizität und Geltung*. Frankfurt a. M.: Suhrkamp.
Habermas, Jürgen (2006): "Religion in the Public Sphere". In: *European Journal of Philosophy* 14, pp. 1–25.
Habermas, Jürgen (2007): "Kommunikative Rationalität und grenzüberschreitende Politik: eine Replik". In: Niesen, Peter/Herborth, Benjamin (Eds.): *Anarchie der kommunikativen Freiheit*. Frankfurt a. M.: Suhrkamp.
Habermas, Jürgen (2008): *Ach, Europa*. Frankfurt a.M.: Suhrkamp.
Hampshire, Stuart (1999): *Justice is Conflict*. London: Duckworth.
Höffe, Otfried (2006): *Aristoteles*. Munich: C.H. Beck.
Horton, John (2010): "Realism, Liberal Moralism and a Political Theory of Modus Vivendi". In: *European Journal of Political Theory* 9, pp. 431–448.
Jubb, Robert (2015): "Playing Kant at the Court of King Arthur". In: *Political Studies* 63, pp. 919–934.
Plato (1987): *Politeia*. London: Penguin.
Rawls, John (1993): *Political Liberalism*. New York: Columbia University Press.
Rawls, John (1999): *A Theory of Justice*. Revised edition. Cambridge: Belknap Press of Harvard University Press.
Rawls, John (2001): *Justice as Fairness. A Restatement*. Erin Kelly (Ed.). Cambridge: Belknap Press of Harvard University Press.
Sleat, Matt (2012): "Legitimacy in a Non-Ideal Key. A Critical Response to Andrew Mason". In: *Political Theory* 40, pp. 650–656.
Sleat, Matt (2014): "Legitimacy in Realist Thought. Between Moralism and Realpolitik". In: *Political Theory* 42, pp. 314–337.
Thomas, Alan (2017): "Rawls and Political Realism: Realistic Utopianism or Judgment in Bad Faith?" In: *European Journal of Political Theory* 16, pp. 304–324.
Tully, James (1999): "The Agonic Freedom of Citizens". In: *Economy and Society* 28, pp. 161–182.
Waldron, Jeremy (1999): *Law and Disagreement*. Oxford, New York: Oxford University Press.
Williams, Bernard (2005): *In the Beginning Was the Deed: Realism and Moralism in Political Argument*. Selected, edited, and with an introduction by Geoffrey Hawthorn. Princeton: Princeton University Press.
Wolthuis, Bertjan (2013): "Objective Rules of Argumentation". In: Husa, Jaakko/Van Hoecke, Mark (Eds.): *Objectivity in Law and Legal Reasoning*. Oxford, Portland: Hart.

Wolthuis, Bertjan (2014): "Do EU Citizens Have a Duty to Use Public Reason?" In: *Rechtstheorie* 45, pp. 487–506.

Wolthuis, Bertjan (2016a): "A Political Realist Notion of Public Reason". In: *Netherlands Journal of Legal Philosophy* 45, pp. 42–59.

Wolthuis, Bertjan (2016b): "The Realism of Political Liberalism". In: *Theoria. A Journal of Social and Political Theory* 63, pp. 1–17.

Manuel Knoll/Nurdane Şimşek
Does Rawls's First Principle of Justice Allow for Consensus? A Note

In his later writings, Rawls narrows down his theory to a "strictly political conception of justice" in order to ensure both the stability of a "well-ordered society", and an "overlapping consensus" on his own and other liberal principles of justice in a pluralist society.[1] He opposes this political conception to "a comprehensive philosophical and moral doctrine" (2005, p. XV). However, this move cannot ensure agreement on his principles. A libertarian like Nozick, of course, continues to disagree with Rawls's difference principle (see Knoll in this volume, p. 37f.). Likewise, critics of democracy persist in their disagreement with the part of Rawls's first principle that demands "an equal right" to political liberties such as the right to vote and to be eligible for public office (1971, §§ 11, 36f., 46; pp. 61, 221–234, 302). What follows is a short note to point out a serious problem in Rawls's "consensus approach" to political justice.[2]

After *A Theory of Justice*[3] was published in 1971, Rawls was misunderstood by some scholars, such as Axel Honneth, to be trying to justify the timeless validity of his two principles of justice (Honneth 1995, p. 11). As a response, Rawls stated that his conception of justice as fairness does not depend on "claims to universal truth" and was framed to apply to the basic structure "of a *modern constitutional democracy*" (1985, p. 223f.; our italics). A thorough reading of *Theory* shows, however, that the book doesn't claim that the principles of justice are "necessary truths or derivable from such truths" (1971, § 4, p. 21). Rather, Rawls asserted that of the "traditional views" his conception of justice "consti-

---

[1] For a more detailed and innovative account of Rawls's approach in *Political Liberalism*, see Siani in this volume.
[2] Rawls's first principle of justice doesn't only declare that the political liberties are a command of justice but also the classical civil liberties and human rights. This article does not discuss the latter part of Rawls's first principle. In order to give a negative answer to the question in its title, it is enough to demonstrate that the former part does not allow for consensus. However, the general arguments of this note also apply to the civil liberties. In order to present a cogent argument for such liberties, Rawls would need to refute their critics. One of them is Rousseau, a defender of direct democracy. In *On the Social Contract*, Rousseau does not concede to individual citizens the freedom of assembly and the right to found political parties since such associations would be inimical to the sovereignty of the general will (II 3).
[3] Henceforth referred to as *Theory*.

tutes the most appropriate moral basis for a *democratic society*" (1971, Preface, p. VIII; our italics).

In *Theory*, Rawls argues for his two principles of justice by combing a "contractarian method", integrating elements of "the theory of rational choice", with a method that attempts to produce coherence among principles of justice and "considered convictions of justice" aiming at a "reflective equilibrium" (1971, §§ 3 f.; pp. 16 f., 19 f.). Central premises of his argument are a democratic social and political framework, the value of equality, and "considered judgments" about justice of a democratic culture such as "religious intolerance and racial discrimination are unjust" (1971, §§ 4, 9; pp. 19, 46–53). Rawls concludes that in the "original position" free, equal, and rational people would *agree* on choosing equal political liberties.[4] However, this conclusion was already assumed in the premises. Rawls's "consensus approach" to political justice commits a *petitio principii*. This becomes even clearer when the later Rawls abandons the theory of rational choice and relies more on his coherence method (1985, p. 237, n. 20). The coherence theorist extracts "settled convictions" about justice and "recognized basic ideas and principles" from his "public political culture" and "its main institutions" and seeks to combine them "into a coherent conception of justice" (1985, p. 228). Rawls extracts a conception of democratic political justice from his account of democratic political culture and concludes that it is just. In order to present an interesting and convincing argument for democratic political justice, however, Rawls would rather need to refute the arguments of the critics of democracy.

Modern theoreticians of democracy disagree on the definition of their subject. However, the main problem of democracy is linked to its core principle "one citizen/one vote" through which the sovereignty of the people is implemented. With Plato we can criticize the low capability of the people to adequately judge political matters and to select truly apt representatives. The ancient philosopher also argues that people are rather irrational and easily manipulated by politicians and demagogues (*Resp.* VI 488a/b, 492b–496e). It is hard to deny that the 2016 British referendum to leave the European Union and the presidential elections of Georg W. Bush (2000 and 2004) and Donald Trump (2016) support Plato's criticism. Also, if Adolf Hitler's party hadn't achieved 37.2 percent of the votes of the German citizens in July 1932, he would have likely never ascended to power. From Plato's perspective, elections and referenda are unjust because of their egalitarian character. Because of their different intellectual capabilities

---

[4] Likewise, in *Political Liberalism* Rawls "*supposes* that a reasonable comprehensive doctrine does not reject the essentials of a *democratic* regime" (2005, p. XIV; our italics).

and education, not all men and women should have the same vote. Similarly, the liberalist John Stewart Mill claimed that people's votes should have unequal weight because people have unequal intelligence and knowledge (2001, chap. 8).

It is quite surprising that after Rawls discussed Mill's proposal for unequal voting rights he states: "I do not wish to criticize Mill's proposal" (1971, § 37, p. 233). In order to claim agreement or consensus for his principle of equal political liberty and for democratic political justice, Rawls would need to critically engage with Mill and Plato and show that equal voting rights are better or more just than unequal ones. In order to do this, he would also need to reject Mill's and Plato's anthropological premise that people have unequal "value" and that the "worth" of their opinions is unequal (2001, chap. 8, pp. 163, 169 f.). Such views as Plato's and Mill's are by no means just historical but are still shared by numerous citizens in democratic political cultures. To sum up, it is more relevant to focus on debating and analyzing actual disagreements in our political culture than to pretend the possibility of a consensus that cannot be reached.

Bibliography

Honneth, Axel (1995): "Einleitung". In: Honneth, Axel (Ed.): *Kommunitarismus. Eine Debatte über die moralischen Grundlagen moderner Gesellschaften*. Third edition. Frankfurt a. M.: Campus.

Mill, John Stuart (2001): *On Representative Government*. London: Electric Book Company.

Rawls, John (1971): *A Theory of Justice*. Cambridge: Belknap Press of Harvard University Press.

Rawls, John (1985): "Justice as Fairness: Political Not Metaphysical". In: *Philosophy & Public Affairs* 14, pp. 223–251.

Rawls, John (2005): *Political Liberalism*. Expanded edition. New York: Columbia University Press.

Part II: Ancient Perspectives and Critiques of the Centrality of Justice

Francisco L. Lisi
Aristotle on Natural Right*

Abstract: This paper argues against the existence of a notion of natural law in Aristotle. Contrary to Plato, Aristotle limits the scope of justice to what is strictly human and, continuing a trend begun in the Sophistic movement of the fifth century B. C., breaks with its cosmic foundation. One of the most striking features of his writings of practical philosophy is the scant reference they make to the divine realm. When they do refer to it, it is primarily to emphasize the difference and not the connection between the two the human and the divine spheres.

The theory of natural right has a great significance in the fields of law, ethics, and political theory, especially in recent times. For centuries, legal theory has considered Aristotle to be the initiator of the doctrine of natural law. It is not surprising, therefore, that one of the most controversial chapters of the book devoted to justice in the *Nicomachean Ethics* has been the one analysing the difference between conventional and natural right. My exposition will include a short analysis of the *status quæstionis* in order to identify the main problems in the interpretation of Aristotle's conception of natural law. I shall illustrate the main significations of the word *physis* in Aristotle's work in order to understand its possible meaning in the corresponding passage. Finally, I shall consider the ethical-political implications of his theory of the just by nature.

1 Current state of research

In the last forty years, Aristotelian practical philosophy has undergone a revival that focused substantially on the discussion of Aristotle's supposed theory of natural law (for an overview see Volpi 1988). The exegesis of the 7th chapter of the 5th Book of the *Nicomachean Ethics* can be divided into two clear positions, the supporters of the traditional view who considers Aristotle as the initiator of the theory of natural law, influenced by his teacher Plato, and those who

---

* This paper has been written within the framework of a project financed by the Spanish Secretaría de Estado de Investigación, Desarrollo e Innovación of the Ministerio de Economía y Competitividad (FFI2016–76547-P). Translations without indication of author's name are mine.

https://doi.org/10.1515/9783110537369-009

deem him a supporter of a legal positivism very near to the sophist Protagoras. The first group (cf. Lapié 1902; Joachim 1951, p. 155; Trude 1955, pp. 150–173; Moraux 1957, p. 132; Gadamer 1999, pp. 324–329; Faulkner 1972, p. 89; Aubenque 1995; Miller 1995, pp. 41, 74–80; Roberts 2000, pp. 345–350, Burns 2011) operates with an undefined concept of natural law that corresponds more to vague beliefs about its character than to the actual historical doctrine. Nevertheless, they agree on some basic points:
- the existence of a set of invariable rules that have a not always clearly defined relationship with the positive laws, but are independent of them,
- the higher and founding character of these rules, either as the goal of any political organization or as its source and foundation, and
- the existing tension, and to a certain point, contradiction between the positive and the natural law, where the latter becomes the evaluative criterion of the former.

There is no concrete specification of the supposed rules that the natural right should have beyond these general characteristics. Even if some sections of the Aristotelian text could be interpreted in this sense, it is obvious that this reading reflects the modern approximation of the problem, which contradicts the literal sense of the whole chapter referred to in the *Nicomachean Ethics*.

The second interpretative approach (Salomon 1937a, 1937b; Yack 1990; Zanetti 1993, pp. 50–80; Bodéüs 1996) won more influence in the second part of the past century on the basis of the evident difficulties of the traditional readings. However, a mere conventionalist understanding of Aristotle's position cannot explain the relationship between the conventional and the natural just, because, in a Protagorean way, they deny the existence of an objective justice independent of the positive laws. Therefore, they cannot clearly explain what the difference is between the natural and the conventional just and what the political just really is. A different attitude is shown by Michelakis (1968), who combines the evolutionary approach of Jaeger and tries to delineate a progression from a perspective influenced by Plato to a more positivistic view present in the *EN* and the *Politics*. Finally, there are some scholars who do not believe that it is possible to reconstruct any theory of the just by nature in Aristotle in the present state of the textual evidence (e.g. Girardet 1989, p. 5).

It would be impossible to illustrate the relationship between the just (*dikaion*) and nature (*physis*) in the *Nicomachean Ethics* or in Aristotle in general without specifying what needs to be understood by 'nature', since much of the dispute lies in the different meanings given to the term and the vagueness with which the concepts are applied. Since its origin among the sophists, a certain tension between the positive laws of the states and the existence of supposed natural rules is implicit in the conception of natural law. The positive laws can be conceived as an imperfect realization of the natural norms or the natural laws can be considered as having a separate existence and as standing in opposition to the positive laws. While the validity of the positive laws is based on the authority of the legislator, and the community's broader acceptance of the legislator's guidance, the legitimacy of the natural law stems from a higher principle, i.e. nature, abstract human reason or god. Tradition has established three main characteristics of natural law defined in this way: it has universal application, it is immutable and everlasting (cf. Cicero, *Rep.* III, 22, 33).[1] In the following part of my exposition I shall consider Aristotle's approach taking these criteria into account as a guideline. There are two main points that should be noted: (1) Apparently Aristotle asserts that the just by nature is valid everywhere (EN V 7 1134b18–20).[2] (2) He also states that the best constitution is by nature and, therefore, valid "in all places" (1135a4–5; trans. Rackham, Aristotle 1934).[3] In other words, the just by nature apparently has universal validity.

2 Nature

Lately the debate has focused on the meaning of *physis* (nature) and *physikon* (natural). For some scholars, Aristotle here uses the word *physis* in a negative sense, i.e. he employs it only to underline that these rules are not influenced by human beings and have no relation to the Aristotelian doctrine on nature. Other researchers, taking a contrary position claim that the word has the same meaning as in the *Physics* and the biological writings (Miller, 1995, pp. 75f.; Keyt 1996). The conception of a natural law originates in the extreme opposition between law and nature from the second part of the 5th century B. C. on.[4] Both terms designated realities with contradictory principles, which were usually opposed in a particularly negative way, but without attributing any specific order to nature. We can here observe the combination of two different and partially con-

---

[1] The classical version of the interpretation of natural law can be found in Christian Wolff's (1738–1739) Philosophia practica universalis. Ritter (1969, pp. 133–140) has presented a detailed exposition of the contents of Wolff's opus.
[2] The parallel passage of the *Rhetorics* (I 13, 1373b4–24) clearly shows that it is impossible to overlook this fact.
[3] For a more detailed analysis of this passage, cf. below section 3.
[4] The well-known work by Heinimann (1945) continues to be the book of reference on the subject.

tradictory traditions. If we consider that already Plato attributes the expression to the Sophists, we cannot exclude the sophistic origin of this idea.

Plato made the reflexion on *physis*, especially the relationship between nature and the world of human conventions, one of the central issues of his philosophy. His main dialogues show that he tried to overcome the relativism originated from some Sophistic positions, which considered the social norm as something arbitrary, the expression of the will of power of those who hold the political rule. According to Plato, society and universe are built on the same structural principles.[5]

In this context, nature has the position that corresponds to the material cause in the Aristotelian philosophy: the legislator finds a collective of idiosyncrasies, which refer roughly to two basic groups, the temperate and the courageous. At the end of the *Statesman* (308a – 311c), Plato defines the fundamental task of the political art as that of leading these two extreme types of human natures to a just middle term by means of two expedients. First, the development of a eugenic policy that encourages marriage between opposed temperaments in order to naturally produce a middle character. Second, he proposes the use of education, putting it under the tutelage of the state. This was a revolutionary innovation for all poleis except Sparta, at least in the extension and intensity in which Plato proposes it. The scheme of the *Statesman* is outlined in more detail in the *Republic*, where the selection of the appropriate natures plays a substantial role. Only those characters who combine the characteristics of both extreme natures are selected to become guardians. When the selection is done, the education begins. The task, on the other hand, is ongoing, since it is performed not only when the state is created, but continues throughout its entire existence by means of exclusions, expulsions and even through the elimination of unsuitable elements.

Now, Plato also gives to the word *physis* another meaning in his political thought. It can also mean what Aristotle would call the final cause, the goal of political organisation, i.e. the product of the combination of inborn characteristics and legislation. Plato uses this connotation in the case of the philosophical natures when they have completed their formation (*Resp.* VI 485a – 487a; cf. *Leg.* XI 918c – d). The philosopher is so 'by nature' in the sense that he has succeeded in imposing order in his soul, he is virtuous, the goal of the whole human development. The ordered soul is also called *nomos* (*Gorg.* 504d) and it is the expression of health, in opposition to the vicious disordered soul, which is supposed to be sick. In these passages, *physis* has a normative value, which has the purpose

---

[5] In Lisi (1985, pp. 173 – 193 and 1987), I have offered a more detailed analysis of this issue.

of determining the degree of correction or sanity of the other psychic states (cf. *Resp.* IV 444a–e). Human nature defined in this way functions as norm, which coincides with the *nomos* and makes justice beneficial by nature (*Resp.* III 392c).

In so far as legislation must embed justice in man and society, and justice consists in a hierarchical order that Plato calls natural in which the immortal principle rules over the mortal one, the institution of justice becomes the natural goal of legislative action and of social development. This is the way in which politics according to nature turns into the foundation of Plato's political thought. Natural justice coincides with political justice and the contradiction defended by some sophistic groups is confuted. It is the strong normative character of this goal which allows Plato to speak of right or wrong laws according to nature (*Leg.* I 627d). Besides, just law is able to determine what is naturally just and beautiful. For that reason, the Callipolis is considered a natural state or a state according to nature, in an especially illuminating passage for understanding Aristotle's position on the natural just (*Resp.* IV 428e–429a). In the *Republic* (III 395b–d) itself, Plato explains the way in which the norm acts over the individual through education. According to this passage, the norm, which has to become the content and the essence of the person, must be a prized model, since its imitation transmits a form to the psychic and corporeal nature of the citizen.[6] Nature here takes on a double valence. On the one hand, it is the stuff that will acquire the form and, on the other, it represents the rule, which is the result that is expressed in the norm, which will become reality through the determination of the not yet educated character. In this way, the relationship nature-law/just is referred to the ontological couple model-copy and analysed from the perspective of Platonic philosophy. This conception clearly emerges in the treatment of the guardians' education in gymnastics and music in the *Republic* (III 410a–412b). Education has the specific task of modifying the natures of the future guardians, for them to achieve the golden mean. Too much musical education in a tempered nature, for instance, produces its degeneration into the corresponding extreme, pusillanimity. In the description given by Socrates, it can be seen that natures can be lead even to their opposite characteristics by education. This shows a radical belief in the formative power of social rules and customs. This belief can be found again in Plato's last dialogue, the *Laws*. On it, the philosopher rested the stability of the whole structure of education in general and of children's games in particular (*Resp.* VII 796e–798b). Through games,

---

[6] Cf. especially *Resp.* III 395d1–3. About the ideological and cosmological implication of this conception cf. Lisi (1985, p. 183 and 2004).

the youngest members of society must learn and internalize the existing rules in society.[7]

In general, the meaning of Plato's criticism of law in the well-known passage of the *Statesman* (294c–295b) has not been completely understood. Indeed, Plato points there to a real weakness of the law: its scarce adaptability to human variety, complexity and change, aspects that are present in the chapter of the *Nicomachean Ethics* under analysis. For Plato, the philosopher ruler has the advantage of adaptation to temporal changes, even if the ruler must still use a general norm instead of indications focused on every particular case. One of the conditions, which determines the philosopher ruler's action, is the nature of the people who build up his community. The constitutions of the different peoples are the result of these natures (cf. *Menx.* 238e–239a; *Leg.* III 681a–b) and the philosopher has to take them into account when he establishes the political systems and their laws, as well as other natural conditions like geography and the historical context. For Plato, therefore, the variety of human beings and of the specific situations calls for different laws and political systems. Hence, it would be wrong to speak of natural law in the sense that this term has acquired later. Therefore, norms change people's natures, but they have to change according to the change generated in human nature.

Aristotle discusses the different significations of the term *physis*, both in the *Metaphysics* (V 4) and in the *Physics* (II 1). As Ross (Aristotle 1924, I, p. 296) has already pointed out, both chapters are closely parallel. In the *Metaphysics*, Aristotle distinguishes between the following meanings:

(a) The process generation of growing things (*Met.* V 4 1014b16–17),
(b) the thing out of which something grows and which has an existence previous to the being that emerges from it (*Met.* V 4 1014b17–18),
(c) the principle of movement in every natural being (*Met.* V 4 1014b18–26),
(d) the primary stuff, shapeless, which does not have the capacity of changing on its own and from which any natural object is built up or generated (*Met.* V 4 1014 b26–35),
(e) the union of form and matter, i.e. the category of substance (*Met.* V 4 1014b35–1015a19), and
(f) essence in general (*Met.* V 4 1015a11–19).

---

[7] Similar examples of the influence of *nomos* on the *physis* can be found in *Leg.* V 747b; VII 794d–795d (example taken up again by Aristotle in the chapter I am dealing with), 804e–806c, etc. Cf. Lisi (1985, pp. 186f. and 2004).

While meanings (b) and (d) correspond to the material cause, (c) gives 'nature' the sense of efficient cause, (e) takes it as final cause, and (f) as formal cause. (a) alludes to the process that begins the development which leads to the final cause. Aristotle repeats this multiple approach to the problem in the first chapter of the second book of the *Physics*, where he points out that natural beings have in themselves as a characteristic the principle of movement and rest (*Phys.* II 1 192b13–14), i.e., they have in themselves the efficient cause, unlike artificial beings (cf. *Phys.* II 1 192b28–29). In this passage, also the notion of 'nature' as material cause (*Phys.* II 1 193a9–28) appears, and it is linked to the sophist Antiphon. Further, 'nature' is defined as the formal cause as well (*Phys.* II 1 193a30–31, b4), and as final cause (*Phys.* II 1 193b13). Aristotle's consideration of the notion of nature reveals that he stays within the academic tradition, which focuses on the link between matter and form and on the teleological character of the natural process (*Phys.* II 1 193a30–3 l).[8] In accordance with Plato, Aristotle uses two meanings of the word 'nature' that will be important for politics: (a) as the material cause and (b) as the final cause, i.e. the form, which the natural being tends towards. The union of both elements is considered 'natural', i.e. when the potentiality of the object becomes its actuality in its highest expression. *Physis* in a strict sense is, as it was for Plato, the form, the essence of a fully developed natural being (cf. *Phys.* II 1 193b, 6–7). Aristotle here adopts the terminological inversion made by his teachers, as his remarks show that nature is the form and the species of the beings that have in them the principle of movement, which is one of their essential qualities. Aristotle is conscious about the difference between his notion of nature and the Platonic one: i.e. the problem of the separate existence of the essence of objects. The following chapter, which engages in the criticism of the academic theories, supports this interpretation. Nevertheless, like Plato, Aristotle also uses the word *physis* in both the Sophistic and the traditional sense of material substrate and in the specific Platonic-academic sense of 'form' (cf. *Phys.* II 2 194a12–13). Although the *eidos* is not separated from the object, it continues to perform the same function of formal and final cause which it had in the Platonic ontology.

One of the most discussed issues in later times is whether it is possible to apply this specific meaning of 'nature' to Aristotle's practical philosophy. This is just the case in a central passage of the second chapter in the first book of the *Politics*. Here, the emergence of the polis is described as the product of a natural impulse (*Pol.* I 2 1253a20). What is specifically natural in human beings and

---

8 The illustration with fire mentioned at *Physics* II 1 192b36 also appears in the *Nicomachean Ethics* in the distinction between the natural and the legal just (*EN* V 7 1134b26).

what differentiates them from animals is the possession of reason and language,[9] as well as their ability to distinguish between just and unjust (a9–18). In human beings also the use of practical intelligence is natural, as well as learning in a social medium in order to make appropriate decisions that carry them to virtue. The practice of justice is, in the terms of the *Politics*, the way in which human beings attain their goal and, therefore, their nature.

3 The natural just

When analysing the issue of the natural right, we should not forget that Aristotle is very conscious of the sophistic approach and that precisely this represents one of the main concerns in his ethics:

> The beautiful and the just, which are the subjects studied by political science, involve much difference and variability, so that they seem only to be conventional (*nomôi*), but not natural (*physei*). The goods have a similar variability, because often occurs that from them derive harmful consequences for the common people (*EN* I 2 1094b14–18).

This passage designates the three main research fields of practical philosophy: the just, the beautiful, and the external goods. It also objectively states the diversity and variability (*planên*, b16) existing in each. This must be the starting point for the interpretation of the meaning of 'just by nature' in the seventh chapter of the fifth book.

Paraphrase of the passage

This chapter has four sections. (A) In the first (1134b18–24), Aristotle introduces the basic difference: the political just is divided into the natural just and the conventional just. Further, he states that the natural just has the same power/capacity everywhere and that it does not depend on opinion or decision, while for the conventional just it is, in principle, indifferent if it is settled in one way or the other, but once settled, it ceases to be indifferent. Aristotle gives three examples of this conventional just: the price of a ransom, the sacrifice of a kind and a number of animals in religious ceremonies, and the special decrees. (B) In the second section (1134b24–34), the philosopher analyses and confutes the position of

---

[9] '*Logos*' in this passage has the double meaning of reason and word, as Miller (1995, p. 445) has pointed out.

those who claim that there is no natural just, because what is natural is unchangeable and has the same power everywhere, while the just changes. Even though it is true that the just changes, among human beings everything changes. Nevertheless, there is an objective natural justice and another kind of the just that is not natural. Both kinds are mutable and can also be otherwise. The same situation exists in other fields of human life. (C) The third part (b35–1135a5) states that the conventional just and the useful just are not always the same, since not even the constitutions are the same, but only one is the best by nature everywhere. (D) Finally, he establishes a relationship from general to particular between the rule defined by law and the specific actions (a5–15). He distinguishes, therefore, the just act from the unjust one and the just from the unjust. Objective injustice, he insists, can exist by nature or by convention (a10).

Interpretation

The chapter cannot be fully understood if we do not clearly establish the context in which it occurs. It lies between the distinction of the unjust act from the vice of injustice, which was treated at the beginning of the sixth chapter, and the following theory of the unjust act. After clarifying that committing an unjust act does not imply subjective injustice (6 1134a17–24), Aristotle ascertains that the political just can occur only among those who have a life in common, in order to attain an independent government, and are free and equal according to proportional or arithmetical equality. The political just, therefore, can only be realised among those who are under the rule of one law. The function of the law and of the ruler is to maintain the kind of equality that characterises a particular regime. This equality is known as objective justice (a26–1134b8). Discarding other areas where distribution also takes place, but not among equals (b8–12), he concludes that objective justice or injustice exists necessarily according to law and among those for whom the existence of a law is natural (b14). These people are those among whom there is equality in governing and being governed (b15).

Before beginning with the analysis of the political just, Aristotle establishes that:
- The political just occurs in the field of law (1134b13–14; cf. 1134a30–31).
- Law is a way of natural organization among equals (1134b14).
- This equality implies a natural equality among the participants of the community, since the community is the only basis that allows equality in governing and being governed (cf. *Pol.* I 2 1252a30–b9). The possibility of a political community exists only with the emergence of this kind of equality. This rad-

ically distinguishes the political just from the other kinds of objective justice. According to the principles established in *Politics* I 2, political justice is more natural than the other kinds of objective justice, and hence there is a relation of likeness between the different kinds of justice (*EN* V 6 1134a29–30).

It is clear that with these assumptions the solution of the seventh chapter cannot be found in the traditional opposition between nature and law. Kuypers (1937, p. 296) has rightly indicated that the relationship between the natural just (*physikon dikaion*) and the legal just (*nomikon dikaion*) cannot be reduced to the dichotomy natural law/positive law. The natural just is such because it has its foundation in the nature of things, while conventional right is based on the agreement of the community. Nevertheless, both are *social norms* (*nomima*), i.e. part of the positive law of the city, since they are part of political justice.

However, we should now proceed very carefully, since we could risk putting the Aristotelian doctrine into an interpretative Procrustean bed forcing it to be coherent, when coherence simply does not exist. At the beginning of his analysis of the political just, Aristotle's first distinction establishes that one part of the political just is natural, i.e., that the law, which regulates the political life of the city contains some natural prescriptions (cf. Salomon 1937b, pp. 122–123; Aubenque 1980, p. 154). There are two terms which persistently occur in the passage and could perhaps disclose its actual sense: *dynamis* (1134b19, 25) and *pantachou* (1134b19, 25; 1135a1, 4). Salomon (1937b, p. 123) translates the first one with *validité*, a match generally accepted, but hardly applicable to the realm of nature and natural phenomena on which the comparison is based. Neither does it seem possible to speak of validity in the case of the best constitution mentioned later (1135a5). In the *Metaphysics* (V 12, 1019a15–32), Aristotle distinguishes between five meanings of the word *dynamis*:

(a) source of movement or change, which is not in the changing being or is in it qua other,
(b) the source of a thing's being moved or changed by another thing, or by itself qua other,
(c) the power of performing a change for the better or according to intention,
(d) the power of undergoing a change for the better or according to intention, and
(e) all states in virtue of which things are unaffected generally, or are unchangeable, or cannot readily deteriorate.

If we take into account that the just is the objective rule that organises society, the only meaning which can be applied with any likelihood is the first one in the sense of final cause and form to which society changes. Therefore, *dynamis* must be understood as the capacity or power, which every norm dictated according the conditions of the community has of helping the individual as well as society to reach its own aim. Accordingly, the just by nature does not indicate an unchanging constant validity for any situation and everywhere, but rather refers to the capacity that the right norms have of determining what is most useful in each specific situation, i.e. the goal that a society can long for in a specific moment in time. In Aristotelian terms, this means the ability of performing the highest degree of happiness a community can attain according to its possibilities.

As the analysis of the second chapter of the *Physics* has made manifest, every natural object has, together with its essential features, a set of contingent characteristics. If we apply this schema to the chapter we are analysing, it means *that the just by nature is the set of essential rules that a society must have in order to achieve its specific form*. Nevertheless, this form is determined in turn by the nature of the stuff that makes up the social body. In so far as the social body is diverse and changes in time, the characteristic of the just by nature changes and varies according to the conditions in which a specific society lives.

This interpretation can be supported by several passages in the text. First, Aristotle clearly states that the just by nature in the human realm belongs to what can also be different (1134b31). Secondly, he likewise claims that the just by nature and the mere conventional just are both variable in a similar way (1134b30 – 33). Finally, when he proceeds in his criticism of the rigid interpretations of the just by nature, Aristotle bluntly states that the just by nature and the conventional just are not the same everywhere (1134b35). In this phrase, the natural just is represented by the useful, convenient or fitting (*to sympheron*), the essential characteristic of the political just.

The interpretation I have developed until now finds a significant obstacle in the use of the adverb *pantachou*, which is one of the key words in the text. Its first three occurrences do not apparently cause major problems as far as their meaning is concerned. However, Mulhern (1972), Aubenque (1980, p. 154 and 1995, p. 44) and Knoll (2009, pp. 174 – 179) have proposed to give a distributive value to the fourth occurrence of the adverb. According to this interpretation, only one constitution is natural and the best in every situation.[10] *Pantachou* is one of the main terms of the passage, if not the most important. It has no distributive value in any of the other occurrences. It would be very odd if Aristotle had radically changed its meaning just in this phrase, as Mulhern pretends (Eng-

---

10 Aubenque bases his interpretation on H.-G. Gadamer (1999, p. 325). Personally, I think that the German philosopher defends an interpretation opposed to Aubenque's and I do not see on the quoted page any reference to the adverb in question.

berg-Pedersen 1995, pp. 56–57). In this sentence, the philosopher first uses an implicit opposition between the just by nature and the human just, which, if it is understood in its strict literality, contradicts all preceding statements. In it he asserts the existence of a natural just coincident everywhere and opposed to the world of human conventions in the same sophistic sense which he was criticising. Hence, either we eliminate the negative adverb (*mê*) at *EN* 1135a3 or we understand the sentence as stating that the just is not something natural in the sense of the theories rejected by him. The latter interpretation could find some backing in the sentence, which denies that there can be any kind of identity in the objective justice or in the "political systems" (*politeiai EN* 1135a4), in which certainly there are norms that are just by nature, if we stick to the definition provided at the beginning of the chapter and concede Aristotle a minimum amount of coherence. Nevertheless, the best constitution distinguishes itself from the others. As a system of social organization, it has a validity that allows it to be used as a yardstick for all other political regimes. In other words, the subject of the sentence is not the existence of the natural just in a sophistic sense, but the statement of superiority of the best city as aim of all social order.

If this interpretation is correct, Aristotle's thought is different not only from the traditional sophistic school, but also from the Socratic, non-academic currents, which antithetically denied the interpretations of thinkers like Antiphon or even Critias. Xenophon's Socrates, for instance, appears defending the existence of unwritten laws of divine origin with a universal validity, whose infraction implies severe punishment (*Memorabilia* IV, 4, 19–25). These laws are in tension with the positive legislation and have a higher value. In the pseudo-Platonic *Minos*, Socrates also argues that just and unjust are the same everywhere like heavy, light, beautiful and harmful (*Min.* 316b). In the present Aristotelian text, a more complex relationship between nature and social rule, in which there is no contradiction, is perceptible. The social norm expresses a specific form, which corresponds to the state in which society is at this moment. However, Aristotle also assumes the existence of a political system that is the best and appears as the aim of every social organization. Yet it cannot be established in all circumstances nor are all people able to attain it.

Since it is an essential determination of a natural being, the just by nature is necessarily identified with a specific society and is thus independent of the decision or will of the legislator or of the part that exercises the power. Its righteousness does not depend on the fact that human beings accept it or not. In the eighth book of the *Nicomachean Ethics*, when he considers the different kinds of friendship, Aristotle distinguishes between two kinds of the just, the unwritten and the legal. He equates both to two kinds of friendship, the ethical and the legal (*EN* VIII 13 1162b21–23). The two forms of objective justice mentioned there cannot be connected to the binomial natural/conventional.[11]

Another passage differentiates the first just from the written just (*EN* V 9, 1136b32–33). This passage seems to point to the existence to a notion of justice superior and previous to the justice that regulates political life. However, I think this is not the case for the following reasons:

- *Nomikon dikaion* in this passage has a different meaning than in the seventh chapter of the fifth book. In fact, the examples given there were not of written, but of unwritten laws, and of specific minor norms. Here *nomikon* refers not to conventional right, but to the written dispositions.
- Even if we identify the first just (*to prôton díkaion*) with natural right, it is not necessarily true that this kind of right does not belong to the political just. Moreover, the given illustration concerns a judgment given by a judge. This is possible only among citizens.

This interpretation is perhaps supported by another passage in the eighth book of the *Nicomachean Ethics*, where Aristotle states that every human being believes in the existence of some kind of objective justice for everyone able to participate in law and convention (*EN* VIII 11, 1161b4–5). It is not necessary to identify this kind of the just with the natural law. In point of fact, the indefinite pronoun points to the circumstance that it is not objective justice in a proper sense. The slave has the capacity of participating in a political system, but he does not. The sense of justice of the virtuous man in relation to a slave is in his quality as human being, in so far as he could be capable of participating in a polis.

As the analysis has made clear, Aristotle is stressing the fact that the natural law/the just can change, against the sophistic interpretation. There is a passage in the *Rhetorics* (I 11, 1370a3–9), which shows that also in this issue Aristotle has a very Platonic approach. In it, the philosopher assumes the proximity between habit and nature, since "what is habitually done becomes in some sense natural, because the habit is something similar to nature" (a6–7). Like his teacher, Aristotle tries to overcome the sophistic and Socratic contradiction affirming the interdependence of both spheres.

---

11 However, at *Rhetorics* I 13 1373b2–9, there is a division of the just by nature, which usually is put into relation with the written and the unwritten law, but that does not correspond exactly to this passage.

4 Natural right, the best state and the best man

The analysis of this difficult chapter has confirmed that there is no Aristotelian theory of natural just or of natural right similar to what later gave rise to the doctrine of natural law. His thought points in the opposite direction. It is based as much on equality as on difference. Equality in the case of political justice among the members of the community, but inequality to the members of other communities, either Greeks or Barbarians. Each of these societies accounts for a different idea of justice, which implies a hierarchical structure according to variable criteria. There are also forms of justice beyond the political order, in the household, the village, in the marriage. These forms are not justice in a proper sense; they have only a vague similarity to political justice, which, strange as it may seem to our way of thinking, is the most natural and the only actual form of justice. Political justice thus acquires a normative character with respect to the other forms existing within the state. The best state also appears as the best expression of social organization and the *telos* of human evolution. This idea also shows some trace of the Platonic participation, because the different forms of justice of the actual existing political regimes are nothing but "similar" to the form par excellence.

A look at some texts of the *Politics* could perhaps help to confirm some of the theses about the relationship between nature and convention. On this matter it will also be useful to look at the relationship of the Aristotelian approach to Plato's thought. Aristotle had a very practical view of historical change. For him, regimes are overthrown for various reasons. In some cases, internal dissent leads to destruction. In others, the reason is the intervention of external powers that want to establish an opposed political regime (*Pol.* V 8, 1307b20–25). Since he considers that change is a negative principle for the state, Aristotle's work tries to provide a solution to preserve the ruling constitution as long as possible. In the fifth book, he dedicates the ninth chapter to a general analysis of the causes due to which regimes are destroyed. In it, he states that there are three fields on which the legislator must place special attention: magistrates, laws and education. The main magistrates must show a strong adhesion to the political system, the highest ability in the exercise of their magistracies, and possess the virtue and justice corresponding to each kind of constitution (1309a32–1309b8). Secondly, the laws must try to foster the part of the state that supports the regime against those who disagree. Another essential element is the preservation of the mean, i.e. the kind of mixture which Aristotle as well as Plato consider fundamental for the right running of the state. One of the most important functions of the legal system is to prevent the deviation of the regime to an extreme. That means the preservation of an order that maintains the balance between the different parts of society in the distribution of power and goods.

Another passage of the fifth book (7, 1307a5–10), in which Aristotle analyses the *polity* and the aristocracy, shows the significance of the notion of *dikê* as order in a specific political system. Both regimes are overthrown because of their deviation from the concept of justice, which they originally had. According to Aristotle, this change is caused by a fault in the mixture of democracy and oligarchy. Anyway, the most important factor is education in the laws of the political system in a way that allows oligarchs and democrats to preserve their respective systems (1310a12–22). Beyond the obvious significance of education in safeguarding a political system, and considering our previous analysis, we will see that the internalisation of the norm by the soul of the individual produces the virtue of justice, a subjective state, which becomes a reflection of the objective order imposed on society by the constitution. Individual and society thus attain an analogous order. This interpretative hypothesis could explain the importance that Aristotle attributes to education. Subjective and objective justice must be related and shape a unity that serves as a foundation for the conservation of the corresponding regime.

The demand of legislation according to nature presupposes the need of different political systems and laws for different peoples. The basic requirement of any political order is its agreement with nature. This can be summed up in the principle: "equality among equals and inequality among unequal people". This principle also determines that among equals there should be an alternation in ruling (cf. *Pol.* VII 3 1325b8–10). However, natural legislation implies something more than a natural principle, even if it has a general value. It is also related to the various kinds of people to which the legislator must give his laws. The factors that determine a person's character are three: temperament, law, and reason. The legislator has to consider if the different temperaments require specific kinds of legislation. Aristotle pondered this issue in the seventh chapter of book seven of the *Politics*. Here, he distinguishes between three kinds of people. First, nations that live in the cold regions of northern Europe have a temperament in which the courageous part of the soul predominates (*Pol.* VII 7 1327b24). They lack discursive intelligence and art. Though they live in freedom, they do not have a political organization and are unable to rule their neighbours. On the opposite end are the Asian peoples with a soul in which the highest part of the soul predominates and, therefore, they are more intelligent, but they lack nerve. The consequence is that they are persistently dominated and enslaved. Finally, the temperament of the Greeks partakes in both characteristics "just as it occupies the middle position geographically" (*Pol.* VII 7 1327b29–30, trans. Rackham, Aristotle 1944). The localization of the different nations and the link that he establishes with their geographic position and their temperament are similar to the Platonic theory (cf. Lisi 1985, pp. 318–345, esp. pp. 331ff.). Moreover, like Plato, he believes that the same situation can be observed among Greeks. The different Greek populations also have a different quality of the mixture of both temperaments (*Pol.* VII 7 1327b34–36). Like the Socrates of the *Republic*, Aristotle affirms that those who will be lead with ease towards virtue have to combine both qualities in their temperament, courage and intelligence (*Pol.* VII 7 1328a36–38).[12] The natural characteristic of a population also determines the intensity of the legislative action in order to attain the highest possible degree of happiness and to exercise its full capacity of virtue. The aid of the legislative art must be more intense when the natural ability is less (cf. *Pol.* VII 13 1331b37–1332a7).

Nature/temperament is one of the decisive factors, together with the law, in order to become a virtuous man (*Pol.* VII 13 1332a39–b11). Law and reason can influence nature even in its natural tendency. Hence, the legislator must have a very profound knowledge of the people to whom he will give his laws. For Aristotle, as for Plato, the temperament corresponds to the political system, and the better the character, the better can a political system become (*Pol.* VIII 1 1337a14–16). The legislator has to accompany and lead this natural disposition through his legislation. In other words, when the temperament of a people tends towards freedom, the legislator should try to keep their tendency in a correct mean, but he may not legislate in an utterly contrary direction. Consequently, the composition of a state's population is crucial for the constitution the legislator must establish (cf. *Pol.* IV 12 1296b24–34), "because it is quite possible that although one form of constitution is preferable it may often be more advantageous for certain people to have another form" (*Pol.* IV 11 1296b10–12, trans. Rackham, Aristotle 1944). The relationship between the nature of a population and its political system also determines that what is just or useful by nature is also different according to the regime (*Pol.* III 17 1287b37–39). Therefore, the deviations from the right constitutional forms are, for Aristotle, against nature (*Pol.* III 17 1287b39–41). For Aristotle, as well as for Plato, natural right requires precisely the differentiation of laws according to the stuff that the legislator has to order. It is plainly clear that this view is diametrically opposed to our concept of natural law.

---

[12] The following reference to the *Republic* (*Pol.* VII 7 1328a38–41) shows that Aristotle was very conscious of the relationship of his theory to Platonic thought.

Bibliography

Aristotle (1966): *Aristotle's Metaphysics*. A Revised Text with Introduction and Commentary by William D. Ross. Oxford: Clarendon Press.
Aristotle (1934): *The Nicomachean Ethics*. In: *Aristotle in 23 Volumes*. H.R. Rackham (Trans.). Vol. 19. Cambridge, MA, London: Harvard University Press/William Heiniman.
Aristotle (1936): *Aristotle's Physic*. A Revised Text with Introduction and Commentary by William D. Ross. Oxford 1979.
Aristotle (1944): *The Politics*. In: *Aristotle in 23 Volumes*. H.R. Rackham (Trans.). Vol. 21. Cambridge, MA, London: Harvard University Press/William Heiniman.
Aubenque, Pierre (1980): "La loi selon Aristote". In: *Archives de Philosophie du Droit* 23, pp. 147–158.
Aubenque, Pierre (1995): "The Twofold Natural Foundation of Justice According to Aristotle". In: Heinaman, Robert (Ed.): *Aristotle and Moral Realism*. London: Routledge, pp. 35–47.
Bodéüs, Richard (1996): *Aristote: la justice et la cité*. Paris: Presses Universitaires de France.
Burns, Tony (2011): *Aristotle and Natural Law*. Continuum Studies in Ancient Philosophy: London, New York: Continuum
Engberg-Pedersen, Troels (1995): "Justice at a Distance: Less Foundational, More Naturalistic: A Reply to Pierre Aubenque. Aristotle and Moral Realism". In: Heinaman, Robert (Ed.): *Aristotle and Moral Realism*. London: Routledge, pp. 48–60.
Faulkner, Robert K. (1972): "Spontaneity, Justice and Coercion: On *Nicomachean Ethics*. Books III and V". In: Pennock, J. Ronald/Chapman, John W. (Eds.): *Coercion*. Chicago: Aldine/Atherton, pp. 81–106.
Gadamer, Hans-Georg 1999 : *Gesammelte Werke*. Vol. 1: *Wahrheit und Methode. Grundzüge einer philosophischen Hermeneutik*. Tübingen: Mohr Siebeck.
Gaiser, Konrad (1961): *Platon und die Geschichte*, Stuttgart-Bad Cannstatt: Fromman-Holzboog.
Gaiser Konrad (^{2}1968): *Platons Ungeschriebene Lehre. Studien zur systematischen und geschichtlichen Begründung der Wissenschaften in der platonischen Schule*. Stuttgart: Klett.
Gaiser, Konrad (1988): *La metafisica della storia in Platone*. Milan: Vita e Pensiero.
Girardet, Klaus M. (1989): "'Naturrecht' bei Aristoteles und bei Cicero: ein Vergleich". In: Fortenbaugh, William W./Steinmetz, Peter (Eds.): *Cicero's Knowledge of the Peripatos*. New Brunswick, NJ: Rutger, pp. 114–132.
Heinimann, Felix (1945): *Nomos und Physis. Herkunft und Bedeutung einer Antithese im griechischen Denken des 5. Jahrhunderts*. Basel: Friedrich Reinhardt.
Joachim, H.H. (1951): *The Nicomachean Ethics*. A Commentary by the Late H.H.J. Ed. by D.A. Rees. Oxford: Clarendon Press.
Keyt, David: (1996): "Fred Miller on Aristotle's Political Naturalism". In: *Ancient Philosophy* 16, pp. 425–430.
Knoll, Manuel (2009): *Aristokratische oder demokratische Gerechtigkeit? Die politische Philosophie des Aristoteles und Martha Nussbaums egalitaristische Rezeption*. Munich: Fink.
Kuypers, Karel (1937): "Recht und Billigkeit bei Aristoteles". In: *Mnemosyne* 5, pp. 289–301.
Lapié, Paul (1902): *De iustitia apud Aristotelem*. Paris: F. Alcan.

Lisi, Francisco L. (1985): *Einheit und Vielheit des platonischen Nomosbegriffes. Eine Untersuchung zur Beziehung zwischen Philosophie und Politik bei Platon*. Königstein, Taunus: Anton Hain.

Lisi, Francisco L. (1987): "Nomos y physis en el pensamiento político de Platón". In: *Actas del VII congreso Nacional de la Asociación Española de Estudios Clásicos* 2, Madrid: Ediciones Clásicas, pp. 239–243.

Lisi, Francisco L. (2004): "Arte, legge e dialogo nelle *Leggi* di Platone". In: *Studi Italiani di Filologia Classica* 11. No. 1, pp. 42–61.

Miller, Fred D., Jr. (1995): *Nature, Justice, and Rights in Aristotle's Politics*. Oxford: Clarendon Press.

Michelakis, Emmanuel M. (1968): "Das Naturrecht bei Aristoteles". In: Berneker, E. (Ed.): *Zur Griechischen Rechtsgeschichte*. Darmstadt: Wissenschaftliche Buchgesellschaft, pp. 146–171.

Moraux, Paul (1957): *À la recherche de l'Aristote perdu. Le dialogue "Sur la Justice"*. Louvain: Publications Universitaires.

Mulhern, John J. (1972): "ΜΙΑ ΜΟΝΟΝ ΠΑΝΤΑΧΟΥ ΚΑΤΑ ΦΥΣΙΝ Η ΑΡΙΣΤΗ". *Phronesis* 17, pp. 260–268.

Ritter, Joachim: (1969): "Naturrecht bei Aristoteles. Zum Problem einer Erneuerung des Naturrechts". In: Ritter, Joachim: *Metaphysik und Politik*. Frankfurt a. M.: Kohlhammer, pp. 133–179.

Roberts, Jean (2000): "Justice and the Polis". In: Rowe, Christopher/Schofield, Malcolm (Eds.): *The Cambridge History of Greek and Roman Political Thought*. Cambridge: Cambridge University Press, pp. 344–365.

Salomon, Max (1937a): *Der Begriff der Gerechtigkeit bei Aristoteles*. Leiden: A.W. Sijthoff.

Salomon, Max (1937b): "Le droit naturel chez Aristote". In: *Archives de Philosophie du Droit* 7, pp. 120–127.

Salomon, Max (1954–55): "Der Begriff des Naturrechts in der 'Grossen Ethik'". In: *Archiv für Rechts und Sozialphilosophie* 42, pp. 422–435.

Trude, Peter (1955): *Der Begriff der Gerechtigkeit in der aristotelischen Rechts- und Staatsphilosophie*. Berlin: De Gruyter.

Volpi, F. (1988): "Che cosa significa neoaristotelismo? La riabilitazione della filosofia pratica e il suo senso nella crisi della modernità". In: Berti, Enrico (Ed.): *Tradizione e attualità della filosofia pratica*. Genoa: Marietti, pp. 111–135.

Wolff, Christian (1744–1750): *Philosophia practica universalis methodo scientifica pertractata* Halae Magdeburgicae: Oficina Libraria Rengeriana.

Yack, B. (1990): "Natural Right and Aristotle's Understanding of Justice". In: *Political Theory* 18, pp. 216–237. Reprinted in: Murkherjee, Subrata/Ramaswamy, Sushila: *Aristotle (384BC–322BC)*. New Delhi 1993: Deep & Deep, pp. 249–272.

Zanetti, G. (1993): *La nozione di giustizia in Aristotele: un percorso interpretativo*. Bologna: Il Mulino.

Eckart Schütrumpf

What Is "Just in Distribution" in Aristotle's *Nicomachean Ethics* and *Politics* – Too Much Justice, Too Little Right

Abstract: This paper argues that in Aristotle's *Nicomachean Ethics* and *Politics* there is no "distributive justice" (which would be the ethical attitude of the person who distributes things in a just manner), but a norm of just distribution. However, in *Nicomachean Ethics* Aristotle reveals only that the norm of just distribution does not demand the allocation of the good in question to every citizen in the same amount, but to make distinctions according to merit. In *Politics*, Aristotle refers explicitly to this principle only twice (3.9 and 5.1), and then, in regard to marginal issues. Here, his recommendations for a distribution of power among groups that compete for it do not follow a principle of what is just. Rather, Aristotle is guided by the expectation that a stable constitution will be created if it takes into account the ambitions and different strengths of competing groups as well as the behavior of the powers that be in a manner which does not harm the subjects.

1 The hyperbolic modern account of justice in Aristotle

Can there be too much justice as the subtitle of this paper suggests? The common experience is rather the opposite, namely that there is not enough justice, and the ancient Greeks did not have a different experience, nor did their political theory assume an abundance of justice. Plato in *Resp.*, whose subtitle is *On Justice* (cf. Schütrumpf 1997, p. 29), views the politics of his day as characterized by injustice (*Resp.* 6 496d,e). In Aristotle's *Nicomachean Ethics* (*EN*), justice retains a prominent role, this is evident because of all the ethical virtues, justice is the only virtue to which an entire book, book 5, is dedicated. Aristotle's concepts have had considerable influence. Thomas of Aquinas coined the terms *iustitia distributiva* and *iustitia regulativa sive corrective*, referring to concepts described by Aristotle in *EN* 5 which have become an important part of later legal thought, in English as "distributive" or "corrective justice" respectively, and they appear prominently in scholarly literature and in translations (Kraut 2002, p. 107).[1]

In the opinion of most scholars, in Aristotle's political philosophy "distributive justice" regulates how honors should be allocated among members of the political community who compete for them. In "Aristotle's Theory of Distributive Justice,"[2] D. Keyt had tried to untangle Aristotle's political theory from this perspective, and this concept of distributive justice is a staple in almost every account of Aristotle's teaching on politics (Miller 1995, pp. 70–73; Roberts 2000, pp. 360–365; Kraut 2002, pp. 145–148; Young 2009, pp. 461f.; recently Pangle 2013, pp. 134–138). However, in the very brief explanations of distribution in *EN* 5 Aristotle does not describe "distributive *justice*" (Aristotle 1954, p. 114)[3] but what is "*just* in distribution."[4] The same is true for Aristotle's *Politics*. This work is a study on constitutions (*EN* 10.10 1181b12–23), and here the difference between constitutions is traced back to the fact that different social groups wield the supreme power (*to kyrion*) in the *polis* (*Pol*. 3.6 1278b8–15; 7 1279a26f.; 10 1281a4; 13 1283b5f.; 4.2 1289a15–17). Thus the main topic of *Politics* is the distribution of political power, however, "distributive justice" is never used in the *Politics*.

I am not aware that the secondary literature on Aristotle addresses the problematic nature of this aspect of Aristotle's political philosophy; the legitimacy of the use of the term "justice," is ignored. Since "justice" is a concern of philosophers of classical antiquity its use by modern scholars is not objectionable *per se*, but as I see it, its overuse – "too much justice" – is irritating. Take, for example, the following translations by Lord and Irwin: "if justice is not the same in all regimes, [the virtue of] justice must also necessarily have varieties" (Lord in Aristotle 1984a, p. 165, trans. of *Pol*. 5.9 1309a37f.), and "Justice is the state ... that makes us do justice" (Irwin in Aristotle 1999, p. 67, trans. of *EN* 5.1 1129a7f.) These translations illustrate my case most clearly – Aristotle would not understand

---

[1] "Justice as equality is further divided into distributive and corrective justice." For other representatives of this view see Schütrumpf 2016, p. 245, cf. below n. 5; 6.
[2] Revised version in Keyt/Miller 1991, pp. 238–278.
[3] Translation of 5.7 1131b27 *to dianemêtikon dikaion*: "the justice which distributes ...," cf. p. 112: "Distributive justice"; Aristotle 1999, p. 74: "reciprocity suits neither distributive nor rectificatory justice," translation of 8 1132b24. However, the issue is not "justice" but "what is just in the distribution," Ostwald in Aristotle 1962, p. 120. Ostwald is the notable exception in English who observes the distinction between "justice" and "what is just," cf. his translation p. 118 of *to dikaion en tais nomais EN* 5.6 1131a25f.: "in distributions the just share must be given."
[4] *To dikaion en tais nomais* (*EN* 5.6 1131a25, see previous n.); *to en dianomêi dikaion* (7 1131b10); *to dianemêtikon dikaion* (1131b27–32); *to nemêtikon dikaion* (8 1132b24).

what the modern author means by "to do justice." We observe here an almost universal tendency to project modern notions of "justice" onto Aristotle.

I must be very brief on Aristotle's concept of justice in *EN* 5. He distinguishes two kinds: first *complete* justice that covers all virtues or praiseworthy qualities as required by laws and comprises all expectations we place in an ethically good man (3 1129a35–1130a16), and second justice as *part* of virtue, in short: "particular justice," which secures that everybody possesses what is his – the corresponding vice is wanting to have more (*pleonektein*, 4 1130a14–b1). Both kinds of justice are virtues (*EN* 5.3 1129b23–4.1130a14), *hexeis* (*EN* 5.1 1129a6–23; 3 1130a13; *Rhet*. 1.10 1369a16f.; *Top*. 6.5 143a15), that is: "stable states (of the irrational part) of the soul," (2.2 1104b19)[5] ethical attitudes of an individual that are acquired through habituation. In Aristotle's *EN* "distributive justice" – if we dare to use the term – is one subcategory of particular justice.

"That justice be done" is the title of a short 1946 American Anti-Nazi propaganda movie. "That justice be done" is perfectly good English, but phrasing it so annihilates the distinction clearly expressed in the Greek in *EN* 5.1 between "just" or "right things one does" (*EN* 6.13 1144a13f.; 10.8 1178a10f (*ta*) *dikaia*) and "justice that makes one do them,"[6] that is: "justice makes one do just things." However, in the text of Aristotle one does not "do justice" – one needs to be equally stingy in the use of "injustice": some commit murder, an act, but Aristotle cannot say that someone commits injustice (Aristotle 1999, p. 77),[7] an attitude. In this case, I prefer the translation "do wrong."

The implied imperative in "that justice be done," namely that the principles of what we consider justice and the pertinent requirements like due process are carried through, cannot be reconciled with the Greek term "justice." Nouns with the suffix -*osynê*, like *dikaiosynê*, "indicate the character, often the outstanding character, of the person who possesses the quality of the adjective,"[8] and this is Aristotle's understanding of justice as a stable condition of the soul. "Justice for x" who is perceived to be treated unfairly is a popular slogan, but the implied expectation of a fair trial or verdict is not justice in the Aristotelian sense. Neither the title of the movie "That justice be done" nor protest signs with the writ-

---

5 "established states of the soul," (2.4 1105b20–1106a13).
6 "Right" is something one does, administers (5.9 1134a2f.), whereas justice is the quality that causes one to do these right things (1 1129a7f.; 9 1134a1). "*Fiat iustitia, et pereat mundus*" is not a translation of a classical Greek adage, but a 16th-century motto.
7 Irwin translates *adikei* 5.10 1134a21 "does injustice," where Aristotle refers to someone who "is not unjust" (*adikos ouk estin*)!
8 "-(o)σύνη bezeichnet ... die Art, oft auch die hervorragende Art ... des Trägers eines Adjektivbegriffes" (Schwyzer 1959, I, p. 529, III. 33).

ing "Justice for x" nor "meting out justice" nor "poetic justice" for that matter could be translated into Greek by using the word *dikaiosynê* according to classical Greek and Aristotle's usage, and conversely: using "justice" when dealing with Aristotle's political philosophy is most of the time without basis, therefore, confusing and misleading.

There is one widespread un-Aristotelian use of justice found in studies on Aristotle, namely the notion of a general principle that is applied in regulating specific relationships or situations as in the following quotes: "The principal question of justice ... is: who should have power?" (Kraut 2002, p. 147); or "Distributive justice requires that equal persons receive equal shares" (Young 2006, p. 461). Here justice is a principle that determines the solution of certain politically important issues or requires certain actions or regulations. Whereas justice is for Aristotle a condition of the soul, the special quality of people who act with intention and possess a firm habit, justice becomes in the lingo of interpreters of Aristotle a general norm.[9] By contrast, the correct understanding of distributive justice as virtue can be found already in Thomas of Aquinas who explains *iustitia distributiva* as moderation which directs the process of distribution (*Summa Theologiae* II–II qu. 61).[10]

In this paper I want to deal with two issues: first I want to correct the misunderstanding in the reading of Aristotle that results from the use of "justice" where it does not belong; and second, I want to show that even the correct notion of the concept of just in its political application as "what is just in distribution" is all but absent from Aristotle's political theory. It follows from both arguments that one cannot ascribe to Aristotle the position of virtuism which sees in the justice, a virtue, of the leaders or citizens to whom political power has been allocated the solution to all problems in the *polis*. In the first sections the paper will be deconstructive. However, I will at the end identify Aristotelian suggestions for stability of a *polis* guaranteed by a specific distribution of power which is based on other criteria than "what is just in distribution."

---

9 See below pp. 156, 158 for *to dikaion* as norm or principle.
10 Contra ad 1: *in distributione communium bonorum est moderatio servanda, in quo dirigit iustitia distributiva.*

2 "What is just" as correct alternative to "justice"

Morphologically, the noun "justice" (*dikaiosynê*) is derived from the adjective "just" (*dikaios*) to which the suffix -*osynê* is added (see below p. 156). The ancient Greek language can add the article to an adjective in order to create a noun (Kühner/Gerth 1966, II 1 p. 594, § 461.4.). In our context two alternatives occur: first, mostly in the plural, referring to things that are just, as in the initial sentence of *EN* 5, Aristotle's comprehensive treatment of justice:

> We observe that all men want to call that attitude justice (*dikaiosynê*) based on which they are capable of doing just things (*praktikoi tôn dikaiôn*) ... and want the things that are just (*ta dikaia, EN* 5.1 1129a6 – 9).

The distinction between justice, *dikaiosynê*, and just things, *ta dikaia*, made here is straightforward,[11] with the former being the personal condition or state that impresses its quality on the actions performed: they qualify to be called just if and only if justice is the cause that the actions are performed in that specific way (cf. *EN* 5.9 1134a1f.; 2.3 1105a28 – 33).[12] The terms "just" or "right," which will be used here indiscriminately, express a judgment regarding things such as actions (*EN* 10.8 1178b10f; *Rhet.* 1.9 1367a22, cf. 12 1373a25; a27), people (*Pol.* 7.9 1328b38), or laws (*Pol.* 3.12 1282b8 – 13).

Little attention has been paid to the second alternative, the noun formed by the article in the neuter singular (to) added to the adjective *dikaion*. When introducing the two kinds (*eidê*) related to distribution and correction Aristotle starts with the remark:

> Of particular justice (*dikaiosynês*) and of what is just in accordance with it (*tou dikaiou kat' autên*), one kind is ... (5.5 1130b30f.) (Schütrumpf 2016, p. 254f.).

"What is just" does not refer in the plural to specific just acts performed by someone who possess justice, and the relationship between "justice" (*dikaiosynê*) and what is just (*to dikaion*), used in the singular, is not one of cause and effect, but of *correlation* or *classification* that clarifies through additional

---

[11] Befuddling the tautology of Irwin in Aristotle 1999, p. 67: "Justice is the state ... that makes us do justice," see above p. 152.
[12] Actions are performed in a just and self-controlled manner "if the person who acts performs them in a certain state (*pôs echôn*)." As one of the three conditions "being in a firm and unshakeable state" (*bebaiôs kai ametakinêtôs echôn*) is mentioned, see above p. 153 with n. 5.

qualifiers in which sense what is just is used (cf. *EN* 5.5 1130b18–22),[13] and as such it has an existence in its own right: the status of "what is just" is elevated since it possesses different forms (*eidê*) which will be distinguished in the same way as those of the related form of justice. Actually, the distinction between "justice" and "what is just" marks at *EN* 5.5 the structure of the discussion of the subject matter that is to follow after that of justice as the complete virtue has been concluded:

> One has to discuss particular justice (*dikaiosynês*) and particular injustice, and in the same way what is just (*tou dikaiou*) and unjust (*EN* 5.5 1130b16–18).[14]

Here "what is just" or "right" (*to dikaion*) is, again in the singular, a norm (see below p. 158) which Aristotle announces to treat independently of "justice" (*dikaiosynê*), and the implication is clearly that the results will differ from those on justice because otherwise the separate analysis would be unnecessary. Aristotle's treatment of distribution (*to dianemêtikon dikaion*), correction (*to diorthôtikon dikaion*), relations among citizens (*to politikon dikaion*), and reciprocity (*to antipeponthos dikaion*) in *EN* 5 is conducted in terms of the concept of "what is just" (*to dikaion*), but not that of "justice" as almost everybody writes, and the restoration of the original concept of "what is just" or "right" (*to dikaion*) and the rejection of justice where it does not belong and is cause of misunderstanding is the purpose of this paper.

In the treatment of all these kinds of "what is just" Aristotle does not expect that the people involved, e.g. in "mutual exchange" or "reciprocity"[15] which deals with the business relations of shoemakers, builders, farmers possess justice. Their business transactions are described in the pertinent passage (*EN* 5.8 1132b21–1133b28) as being governed by "what is just" (*to*) *dikaion*, and not "justice" (*dikaiosynê*).[16] However, what is just (*dikaion*) must be maintained or restored in interactions where one of the participants who do not meet the requirements of justice takes an advantage. If disputes of the people mentioned here cannot be settled among themselves they can turn to a judge, and here justice comes in. Aristotle lists in *Politics* 4.4 the professions every *polis* needs,[17] and

---

[13] "It is evident how that what is just or unjust according to the respective kinds of justice and injustice (*to dikaion de kai to adikon to kata tautas*) must be defined."
[14] Summarized at 9 1134a14–16. cf. already 5.1 1129a4f., cf. 10.8 1178a10f.; *Pol.* 5.9 1309a37–39.
[15] dikaion to antipeponthos, *EN* 5.8 1132b22; b32; 1133a11.
[16] For acting according to the norm of what is just without possessing justice see Schütrumpf 2015, pp. 164–167.
[17] E.g. for the best state *Pol.* 7.8–9. The most detailed account is *Pol.* 4.4 1291a10–33 where Aristotle criticizes Plato's insufficient blueprint of the first state in *Resp.* since it leaves out indis-

among these "necessary parts" he names one "which has a share in justice as it pertains to courts" (1291a27). And later (1291a39f.) when he mentions the group "which makes decisions on things which are just (*tôn dikaiôn*) for those who have a dispute" he adds that this needs to be done in a just way (*dikaiôs*), and concludes that for this reason "some citizens must share *aretê*" (1291a39–b2). The individual or the body that decides on what is just, the court, possesses *aretê*. The quality *aretê*, more specifically: justice, is required from some members of the community; justice enables men to decide, as judges, on what is just (*Pol.* 4.4 1291a39–b2; cf. 1.2 1253a38f)[18] for people who do not need to possess justice, e.g. certain business partners.

The issue is: whose justice does Aristotle talk about in the rare cases when he uses this term in the section on particular justice? He is not the first to raise the question. At the end of the myth in Plato's *Protagoras*, Hermes asks Zeus how respect and right, *aidôs* and *dikê*, should be distributed among men: like professional skills, as medicine, are distributed (*nenemêntai*) where one expert meets the needs of the rest of the population, or whether each should possess them? "Distribute them among all, and all should have a part in them" is Zeus' answer (322c3–d5; trans. by E. Sch.). This is not Aristotle's response. Being a judge is a special role for which only few have the appropriate qualification, justice. Justice comes in short supply. Aristotle says explicitly that one cannot expect that each citizen is a good man (*Pol.* 3.4 1276b37–39)[19] – except in the best state (*Pol.* 4.7 1293b1–6; 7.9 1328b38f.; 13 1332a34). Justice is a quality a small number of people possess[20] while ordinary citizens who do not possess justice need to follow established principles of what is just (*dikaion*) in their dealings with one another, and, if necessary, they have legal disputes about what is just decided by a judge or someone else who possesses justice (*dikaiosynê*).

The same scenario is envisioned at *EN* 5.9 (*EN* 5.9 1134a1–6)[21] for distribution. Here justice is first described as the quality of the person "who is regarded

---

pensable higher functions like the military or institutions that make political and judicial decisions.
18 Justice (*dikaiosynê*) determines the decision on what is just (*tou dikaou*).
19 "the best are few": 3.11 1281a40f., cf. 5.1 1302a1f. The best state is an exception, since in it all citizens are good men: 7.13 1332a33–36.
20 See below p. 162 on *Pol.* 5.1. In 3.13 1283a38–40 *aretê* and *justice* are the qualities of only *one* of the groups that compete for power.
21 "justice is the quality according to which a just man is called capable of doing what is just based on a decision and capable of making a distribution both to himself in dealing with another man and to another in his dealing with another, not in such a way that he allocates more of the desired good to himself but less to the other ... but allocates the proportionally equal, and in the same way to another man in his dealing with another."

to be capable of doing deliberately what is just (*tou dikaiou*) and of *distributing* (*dianemētikos*) ... what is equal in terms of proportion." However, Aristotle goes beyond the interaction of two men when he adds the quality of "distributing what is equal ... to another man in his dealings with a third party."[22] As the person in charge of distribution or as judge or arbitrator in disputes he allocates by virtue of his justice what is just (cf. *Rhet.* 1.13 1376b19 f.; 1.1 1354b4) in relationships between two parties without being himself part of the deal. Again Aristotle distinguishes here the *personal quality* "justice," in accordance with which a judge or arbitrator acts, from the *quality of the result* he accomplishes[23] and the disputing parties receive, and this is "what is just" (*to dikaion*, 5.6 1132a21–32).

Both in *EN* 5 and *Politics* Aristotle looks beyond the small circle of ethically good and just men and includes in his analysis society at large where one finds "nowhere one hundred good men" (*Pol.* 5.1 1302a1 f.). When most of the citizens are expected to possess an ethical quality, this is not justice but can only be the one needed in battle by hoplites (3.7 1279a39 ff.). And in *EN* 3.11 Aristotle distinguishes from true courage which is practiced because such a behavior is noble (1117b9) the one found in citizens (*politikē*) which makes them endure dangers because of the threat of punishments and the disgrace awaiting cowards (1116a17–26). There is, however, no lower level form of justice, no "economy class justice,"[24] and this awareness of the reality affects the concepts Aristotle developed and the terminology he used: the emphasis is on "what is just" or right, in specific contexts without reference to justice. All those who do not belong to the less than "one hundred good men" who live in the *polis* are involved in most diverse interactions, and they need a standard to live by. Aristotle makes up for the absence of justice in ordinary men by having them act in accordance with what is just – formulating not just *one* standard, but *different forms* of what is just which are valid in the different types of interactions he distinguishes (see above p. 156).

"Distributive justice" is the quality of the lawgiver or legislator who distributes power in a just way because of his just character. Otherwise, given the strict standards Aristotle maintains, one should not expect too much justice in the

---

[22] *heterôi pros heteron*, *EN* 5.9 1134a3; *allôi pros allon*, a6.
[23] This is consistent with his ethics where he puts *activity* over possessing a quality: *EN* 1.8 1098b31 ff.
[24] Nor should one assume an inferior form of justice comparable to the natural form of *aretê* Aristotle discusses at *EN* 6.13 where being just is included in these natural qualities (1144b5). However, in book 5 this category is ignored, obviously because there was no need to deal with an immature state.

polis, that is not justice in many citizens, and one should not expect that solutions to political problems involve justice of citizens; however, observance of what is just in the various interactions by those involved is something a society can count on. The whole-sale use of justice for the account of various interactions of people Aristotle describes in *EN* 5 ignores his realistic insight into the limited ethical potential within society, fosters an illusion about the possibility of ethical actions by the citizens, and ignores the categories of "what is just" he introduces to regulate the main forms of interactions of citizens.

The result of the vague and amorphous use of "justice" found in scholarship and translations (Ross in Aristotle 1954, p. 122)[25] covering the notions of the ethical attitude of being a just man, a general principle, or an arrangement of things (see above p. 152), is that there is no *specific* term reserved for Aristotelian justice (*dikaiosynê*), the quality of a person. Modern interpreters should show greater awareness of Aristotelian ethical terminology, and the need to give an accurate equivalent of the Greek term. They could do this by creating a term such as, perhaps, "justitude," in analogy to fortitude, or use existing "justness"; even "fairness" would be less ambiguous. However, evoking justice in multiple contexts, or condemning injustice, as has been done for so long in publications on Aristotle, has something of a rhetorical exaggeration with undertones of claiming for its conception an unassailable principle – who would dare to argue against justice?[26] These undertones, which carry with them expressions of righteous indignation, are applied broadly to other matters as examples of what could be Aristotelian injustice. But Aristotle, who so consciously strives to employ correct terminology in his writings and condemns the incorrect usage for terms in the writings of others, is more restrained and does not evoke the highest moral and social norm in justice. The use of "justice" for certain sorts of interactions he considers as conforming to "what is just" elevates them to a rank they do not have in Aristotle. Or the other way round: when Aristotle discusses a transaction on a market e.g. between two farmers who swap eggs against olives, he

---

25 "Political justice"; Irwin in Aristotle 1999, see above nn. 3; 11; below 18, and virtually everybody else translated Greek (*to*) *dikaion* as "justice," although H. Joachim in his commentary on *EN* insisted on "right" (Joachim 1951, p. 136, n. on 1130b30–1134a16, used "rights" and rejected n. 1 the common assumption that Aristotle deals with *dikaiosynê*. cf. p. 138: "τὸ διανεμητικὸν δίκαιον – dianemetic rights." F. Dirlmeier, also a commentator of the *EN*, described these forms of right as "vom handelnden Subjekt ablösbare äußere Tatbestände des Rechts," that is: "external conditions of right that can be viewed in isolation from the acting subject," Aristotle 1974, p. 406 n. 100, 5, cf. 404 n. 100, 2.

26 Not even Callicles rejected the notion of justice but replaced traditional *law* with that of nature, *Gorg.* 483d–484c.

deals with it as an issue of proportional value determined by the skills of the producers and the resulting value of their products. Since he insists that equality in the services rendered (cf. *Pol.* 2.2 1261a30f.: *to ison to antipeponthos*) has to be established according to a notion of what is just he focuses on the worth of the merchandise they exchange, keeps the *character* of the merchants out of the picture, spares us the deep dimension of justice, and prevents justice from becoming vulgarized or trivialized, by being used in a context for which it was not meant.

Making these distinctions is not philological hairsplitting, but is an attempt to cut down on the justice-inflation translators and interpreters of Aristotle are guilty of, leading a reader to believe that Aristotle speaks of an ethical attitude when he does not. Insisting on these distinctions is an attempt at determining more clearly in which different ways Aristotle speaks about these issues and which categories he introduces and how they differ from one another. It is important as well not to lose sight of how he sees the personal conditions of citizens in the *polis*, and this includes how little justice he expects, which in turn affects the options left for the distribution of honors.

3 The concept of what is "just in distribution" in the *Politics* – without virtue (*aretê*)

It was pointed out that in *EN* 5.6 Aristotle does not deal with distributive *justice* but with what is *just* applied in distribution, among other things, of honor.[27] We now turn to this concept. Right practiced in distribution is based on merit (*axia*). Aristotle assumes a dispute between advocates of democracy and oligarchy over the merit of their claims, and this controversy reflects the fact that in Aristotle's time the debate about which constitution should be established was still undecided. Different groups base their claim to participate in government on different qualities: supporters of democracy on freedom, that is to be born free, oligarchs on wealth, and aristocrats on virtue (*aretê*, 1131a26–29).

The relevant section of *EN* 5.5/6 deals more with the difference between the two concepts of what is just in distribution and correction in terms of the mathematical formulae to be used in establishing the correct form of equality (cf. Schütrumpf 2011, pp. 227–229) than with helping to clarify the specifics, in particular how to implement what is just in distribution. Its explanation is rather

---

[27] *En tais dianomais timês* ..., *EN* 5.5 1130b31. For honor see *Pol.* 3.10 1281a31: "we state that political offices are honors."

anemic and offers hardly more than the lemma (5.5 1130b30–34) while the account of what "mathematicians call geometric proportion" (6 1131b12f.) is disproportionately expanded (1131a14–22; a29–b17). Aristotle does not reveal here which of the qualities, with which the different groups justify their claims for power, should count most and in which way the other qualities could be recognized or which weight they carry, and thus he does not inform how their dispute could be decided. We do not learn much more than that "what is just in distribution of honor" must apply proportional equality, equality according to merit, but there is no guidance here on how to fill in the blanks.

The one and only chapter in *Politics*, 3.9, that refers to this concept with the remark "as has been stated earlier in the *Ethics*" (1280a18f.), repeats from *EN* 5.6 the positions on what is claimed as just and equal by supporters of oligarchy and democracy and explains their dispute by pointing out the narrowness of the view of each party which makes the all too human mistake of overstating its own importance when its interests are at stake. However, only here Aristotle corrects their views and determines the relative value of their claims: he transcends their position by the new category of "what is just in the decisive sense" (*to kuriôs dikaion*, 1280a10) which is based on virtue (*aretê*) and the contribution to the goal of the *polis*, the good life, while he acknowledged that the claims for equality or superiority made by oligarchs and democrats are "sort of what is just" (1280a22) or "part of what is just" (1281a9).[28] Here different degrees of participation in the polis are assigned to different groups commensurate with their contribution to the goal of the polis, and the superior contribution to the well-being of the polis is the one and only correct standard to be used, it is "what is just in absolute terms" (*dikaion haplôs*, 1280a22), justifying participation in the affairs of the polis to a higher degree (3.9 1281a4f., see Schütrumpf in Aristotle 1991, p. 269, n. 31, 11 on 2.8 1268a16). The result reached here, the relative ranking of the claims, meets the standard of what is just in distribution. However, it is only provisional and invalidated by subsequent challenges in the two following chapters – actually, Aristotle offers in 3.11 a different solution as an answer to the objections raised (Schütrumpf [1976] 2009, pp. 111f.; Schütrumpf 2015, pp. 169–174).

In *Politics* 5, the book on change of constitutions and on revolutions, Aristotle again explains political strife from the mistaken views held by groups that compete in the *polis* for political influence, and he mentions two: those who possess equality in one quality, free birth, demand to receive all things in an equal

---

28 *dikaion ti*, *Pol.* 3.9 1280a9; a22; 1281a9, wrongly translated as "justice" by Jowett in Aristotle 1984b, p. 73; (for Jowett see Schütrumpf 2016, p. 239f.); Irwin 1988, p. 432.

amount, and those who are unequal, that is: superior,[29] in another quality, wealth, believe to be absolutely superior (1301a25–39). In these comments he explicitly refers to previous remarks on the wrong views on (in)equality, and this reference can only go to 3.9. (See Schütrumpf in Aristotle 1996, p. 428, n. 49, 14 on 5.1 1301a28.) When Aristotle makes this disagreement responsible for the outbreak of civil wars in cities where the respective expectations are not fulfilled, he echoes a view expressed in *EN* 5.6. (*Pol.* 5.1 1301a25ff., cf. as well *EN* 5.6 1131a22–24) This does, however, not mean that we have one consistent concept of what is just in distribution.

As in *Politics* 3.9 Aristotle had transcended the claims of democrats and oligarchs, who can muster only a "part of what is just" by the category of what is "just in the decisive sense" (*to kuriôs dikaion*, 1280a10), based on *aretê*, so in 5.1, after having reported the claims of democrats and oligarchs, he moves to those "who excel in *aretê*." He views them from the same perspective as he looked before at democrats and oligarchs: the readiness for civil war (1301a37–39). Those "who excel in *aretê* ... might have *the best right* (*dikaiotata*) of all to start a rebellion ... for ... they alone are absolutely *unequal*" (1301a39f.). The concept of what is just in distribution might well be alluded to here both in "*the best right* (*dikaiotata*)" and "absolutely *unequal*," however, Aristotle adds – maybe with some disappointment or resignation: "but they do this the least." In the political reality these men do not get politically involved (cf. 4 1304b4f.). While he did not throw out the basic assumption about what is just in distribution, he points out that in the real world those who meet this standard to the highest degree according to 3.9 refuse to shoulder what would be their "moral" responsibility, as one might be tempted to say – strictly speaking the use of "moral" blurs the line between ethics (*dikaiosynê*) and the obligation to do what is just (*dikaion*). Those "who excel in *aretê*", who "might have *the best right*" (*dikaiotata*, 5.1 1301a39) are the same men as those who meet what is "just in the decisive sense" (*to kuriôs dikaion*) in 3.9 (1280a10) based on *aretê*. Thus by not seizing the role they are entitled to most, those "who excel in *aretê* ..." do not live up to what is just in distribution, and this principle, while not being refuted, is for all practical purposes eroded by the lack of commitment on the part of those who meet its standard.

There is another aspect in which Aristotle departs from "what is just in distribution" in *EN* 5. There the equality to be applied in distribution is one of proportion (*EN* 5.7 1131b26ff., see above p. 161) whereas arithmetic equality is to be

---

[29] Proportional equality is in truth inequality, cf. *Pol.* 5.1 1301a29–39, and inequality is superiority: 3.12 1283a6–9; 1282b21–27: *hyperochê*; 5.1 1301a39: "those who *excel in aretê* are with good reason alone absolutely *unequal*."

used in correction – arithmetic is the form of equality which considers only the numbers or size (as 3 differs from 2 by the same amount as 2 from 1) without recognizing any distinctions in terms of quality whereas geometric equality according to merit takes qualities into account; it is expressed by a proportion (4 differs from 2 by the same ratio as 2 from 1). (See Schütrumpf in Aristotle 1991, pp. 478–480, n. 62, 40 on 3.9 1280a9.) In *Pol.* 5.1 Aristotle argues:

> It is bad that (a constitution) is arranged absolutely in every way according to one of the two forms of equality. Events demonstrate this since no constitution of this kind is stable (*Pol.* 5.1 1302a2–5).

Aristotle demands here that in the allocation of political prerogatives both forms of equality be applied whereas "what is just in distribution" of *EN* 5 which was based solely on geometric equality.

Three passages agree that the false assessment of their status by both those who are free as being equal and by the wealthy as being superior is the cause of civil war, however, the answers given could not be more different. In 3.9 Aristotle transcended the claims of democrats and oligarchs by introducing a *third quality*, *aretê*. In 5.1 those who possess *aretê* were mentioned but discarded as unreliable; now Aristotle seeks a solution by suggesting that that the *relationship* of those who are free and the wealthy *towards one another* be arranged differently, by adopting *the principles of both*.

The discrepancy between the instruction in *Politics* 5.1 to combine the two forms of equality and the concept of what is just in distribution of *EN* 5 which was based solely on geometric equality seems to have one simple explanation: Aristotle presented in *EN* 5 the various categories of what is just in their textbook simplicity. Therefore, *EN* 5 displays a rigidity and inflexibility of the concepts introduced when Aristotle must have known better: in *EN* 5 he did not show the wisdom Plato had revealed in the *Laws* where he, after extolling the natural form of equality which secures a higher position to the better man, advised in the same breath to take off the edge of this concept by allowing at times numerical equality or equality created by lot to be introduced in order to spare a polis civil war from one part (*Leg.* 6 757d,e), and this recommendation Aristotle follows in *Politics* 5.1. When Aristotle introduced in *EN* 5 the principle that proportional equality be applied in distributions he did not add immediately that it is unworkable since it leads to civil wars. Here his account is still "unbroken" and does not compromise on what is "perfect and exact" as Plato (*Leg.* 6 757e) described the rigid approach whose effects he mitigated by the compromise recommended. Only in *Politics* 5.1 does Aristotle adopt the conciliatory stance of Plato by demanding that the two forms of equality must be combined. This means that the principles developed in *EN* 5 for what is just in distribution, the sort of equality demanded there, does not guide Aristotle in his recommendations in *Politics* 5.1 for stable political constitutions. Just the opposite is true, the remarks in *EN* 5 on what is just in distribution help to illustrate how much Aristotle deviated in *Politics* 5.1 from the true principle of equality according to merit and how little it matters in reality.

In *Politics* 5.1 Aristotle does not consider *aretê* as a quality that is to be counted under geometrical equality as he did in 3.9, rather, geometric equality is established by granting to the *wealthy* their share of political power. As Aristotle had started in *Politics* 5.1 with the establishment of the two predominant constitutions, democracy and oligarchy (1301a28–39), so the focus remains in the following remarks on these two constitutions, on the qualities and expectations of their advocates, (cf. *Pol.* 5.1 1301a38: "each of the two" (*hekateroi*)) and an assessment of their respective stability. Far from being the crucial element for the stability of the *polis*, a role of *aretê* is not mentioned at all in this context, and its noted absence – one finds "nowhere one hundred good men," 1302a1f. – has no destabilizing effect on the *polis*. On that score, democracy is actually more stable than oligarchy (1302a11–13).

This reading pulls the rug from under the virtuism interpretation of the *Politics* which is proposed, among others, by Irwin who writes: "Aristotle recommends the virtues as sources of stability and of other benefits for a state. When he stresses the importance of justice and the common advantage (1320a11–17), resulting in concord (1306a9–12; 1310a2–12), he recommends the virtues to common belief" (1988, p. 460). The texts cited do not appeal to justice or virtue – Irwin's reading is not supported by Aristotle's fundamental statements on the issue: the introduction to the book on revolutions and civil war, *Politics* 5.1–4, which outlines in general terms the causes for these disruptive events, does not once refer to justice (*dikaiosynê*) – it is not before 5.9 that this concept comes up, as a qualification for office, not as a quality required to have a stable constitution. *Politics* 5.1 tells a different story: those who have a mistaken view about the qualities that can claim an equal or superior status, democrats and oligarchs respectively, engage in civil wars and one of them prevails so that mostly either democracies or oligarchies exist – with democracies being more stable – while those "who excel in *aretê*" remain on the sidelines and stay out of the nasty and dangerous involvement in civil wars. They are not a political force to be taken seriously, let alone as a source of stability.[30]

---

[30] Against Irwin's view that Aristotle's analysis of change of constitutions and revolutions in

Add Miller 1995, p. 80: "The close connection between justice and the constitution is a central theme in book iii, and indeed throughout the *Politics*." Too much justice indeed,[31] a mere phantasmagoria.[32] Justice understood as the ethical quality of men is not Aristotle's panacea for the political woes Greek *poleis* were afflicted with.

4 Aristotle's approach to the distribution of power in the *Politics*

This negative result concerning Aristotle's reliance in *Politics* on a general concept outlined in *EN* 5 is confirmed by his general approach to the distribution of power in the Politics. If *EN* provided the theoretical basis for the political enquiry in *Politics* and both works formed a unity as the transition to the *Politics* at the end of *EN* 10.10 1181b12ff. suggests, one could expect Aristotle as a systematic thinker and writer to refer to the pertinent category of "what is just in distribution" according to *EN* at the first opportunity in *Politics* when the topic of allocation of political power came up and use it ever after, no later than in *Politics* 2. However, the extensive criticism of the political structure proposed in Plato's *Resp.* (2.5 1264a18–b15) or *Laws* (2.6 1265b26–1266a28) or by Hippodamus (2.8 1268a14–b4) never refers to "what is just in distribution" – actually in the whole book 2 which deals extensively with misconceptions on political participation, both in theoretical works on the best states and in actual states, the noun justice (*dikaiosynê*) is never used and the adjective just (*dikaios*) only once in that context.[33] When Aristotle objects to the arrangement in Plato's *Resp.* that the same men rule all the time by pointing out that even men with "no claim of worth" (*mêden axiôma*) do not accept this arrangement (2.5 1264b6–10) he reveals that he does not consider the hierarchy of claims developed in 3.9 as a recipe for a stable constitution. In fact not one criticism of ex-

---

Pol. 5 is based on his ethics, see Schütrumpf in Aristotle 1996, pp. 110f. I differ *toto coelo* from Irwin 1988, e.g. p. 451f. "Vice and conflict."

[31] In *Pol.* 3, justice, *dikaiosynê*, is used four times, in 4 1277b17; b19; 12 1283a20 and 13 1283a39, all for the virtue of the citizen; there is no "close connection between justice and the constitution ... in Book III," let alone as "a central theme."

[32] It is difficult to resist the suspicion that Aristotle is sought as an authority to give support to a morally elitist and ultraconservative ideology.

[33] *Pol.* 2.2 1261a39–b2: "among whom it is impossible (that the same men rule all the time) since they are all equal in their nature, it is at the same time just ... that all share in it," a context which virtually cries for a reference to the concept of "what is just in distribution."

isting constitutions or a single proposal for constitutional arrangements in the whole of *Politics* is based on the "right of distribution," let alone on justice (*dikaiosynē*). Much ado about nothing.

The same absence of what is just in distribution must be noted when Aristotle gives a blueprint of a constitution. One example must suffice. In 6.4 he deals with the best democracy; he first addresses the source of income of its dominant group, the peasants, turns then to its preference for work ("more pleasant") over holding offices, and expresses the view that this segment of the *demos* strives more after gain than political influence (1318b16f.). He supports this assessment by reference to experiences made under previous tyrannies and oligarchies. This very general statement about the political interest of the *demos* is then made more specific when Aristotle explains which political prerogatives its members insist on exercising and which others they are happy to concede to those who are wealthy or powerful (b20/26). The arrangement outlined here leads to marvelous harmony between the best men among the citizens and the demos (1318b32–1319a4).

None of these arguments owes its origin to the concept of "what is just in distribution." In *EN* 5.6 1131a25–29 disagreements among democrats, oligarchs, the well-born, and aristocrats about which qualities constitute equality or inequality were mentioned, and struggles and accusations described as the consequence of a discrepancy between the actual status of groups and the sort of equality or superiority they claim (1131a22–29). The key term of this concept, equality, is missing in *Politics* 6.4, and with it the whole adversarial scenario of struggle for equality or superiority according to *EN* 5.5 1131a23 (cf. *Pol.* 3.9 1280a19). The view of society in *Politics* 6.4 is on the contrary not one of power-grabbing at all costs and even with questionable legitimacy, but of conceding to the best, who are not described as political enemies, the highest offices. This passage breathes the spirit of political agreement and cooperation between different groups. Admirable is the faith Aristotle puts in *Politics* in the success of constitutional reforms which can be devised in such a way that its citizens "will be convinced" to adopt them (4.1 1289a1–3). This political stance he did not get from what is "just in distribution" in *EN* 5.

Viewing this issue in more general terms, we could not confirm that it was Aristotle's method and his interest as a theorist of political philosophy to first establish somewhere a general principle like "what is just in distribution" to be applied then in the appropriate contexts in *Politics* – this would be virtually everywhere – as the compass for decisions on who should rule. The irrelevance of "what is just in distribution" for his constitutional theory demonstrates that Aristotle did not want his political theory to be understood as derived from such "first principles."³⁴ Aristotle's method is rather that of providing to the legislator in every situation the answer to the task in front of him, e.g. the best democracy, without referring to the general principle that determines elsewhere, e.g. in *EN*, the solution to the distribution of power. In *Politics* he does not even reveal that there exists a general principle that could be used. His approach is rather to explain for every specific condition the pertinent principle that serves as basis for the solution offered; the arguments are custom-designed according to the specific point of departure, as in *Politics* 6.4/5 and passim. Far from developing the norms to be followed in *Politics*, the brief explanations in *EN* offer at best a first glance at an issue that needs to be addressed and provide a cursory, simple version of something which belongs to politics and needs to be dealt with in detail, elaborated, expanded, or altered in the work that specializes on politics according to standards developed there.³⁵ The *Politics* provides the detailed study the subject matter requires without accepting and implementing the narrow specifications the *EN* offers.

5 Conclusion

In the whole *Politics* two references to aspects of the concept of what is "just in distribution" can be found, in 3.9 and 5.1, however they deal only with a subordinate aspect, the mistaken assessment by democrats and oligarchs of their own equality or superiority respectively. In neither case does "what is just in distribution" provide assistance for devising the blueprint of a constitution: in 3.9 because the result reached there, a relative ranking of the claims, is only provisional and invalidated by subsequent challenges in the two following chapters – actually, Aristotle offers in 3.11 a different solution as an answer to the objections raised (Schütrumpf [1976] 2009, p. 111 f.; Schütrumpf 2015, pp. 167–174). And geometric equality required in *EN* 5.5 for what is "just in distribution" proves in *Politics* 5.1 too rigid, or unworkable, to satisfy the political ambitions of the two predominant groups within the *polis*. In 5.1 Aristotle responds to the views of both advocates of democracy and oligarchy on (in)equality, mistaken as they are, by demanding to apply both forms of equality, contradicting *EN* 5 – in *Politics* 5.1

---

34 I am alluding to the title of Irwin 1988. I have given a very critical assessment of Irwin's reading of Aristotle's *Pol.* in Schütrumpf 2015, pp. 174–181.

35 Even in the treatment of the best state Aristotle does not take over from his ethics the results on what the best life is, but develops it from scratch, from the beginning under the aspect of what it means for the *polis*: *Pol.* 7.1–3.

the requirement of the exclusive implementation of geometric equality is given up, following the conciliatory stance of Plato's *Laws* 6.

The problem with an influential tendency of scholarship on Aristotle's *Politics* seems its focus on general concepts Aristotle outlines somewhere, mostly in *EN*, which are then extolled to be the core of his political thinking and passed on as such. Distributive justice is such a concept to which a significance for Aristotle's *Politics* has been ascribed which finds no support whatsoever in this work. Furthermore, the discussion about "distributive justice" suffers from the indifference to Aristotle's philosophical terminology, in particular it suffers from the failure to distinguish between *"justice"* (*dikaiosynê*) and "what is just" (*to dikaion*). The claim of the existence of a concept of "distributive *justice*" by interpreters that explains the allocation of political power in Aristotle's *Politics* blurs a crucial Aristotelian distinction, suggests the notion of justice as *aretê*, and invites those so inclined to draw up a morally loaded theory of distribution.[36] The correct name for this concept as dealt with in *EN* 5 is "what is *just* in distribution." It is the universal paradigm of what is just (see above p. 156) in the allocation of certain goods to at least two parties according to their respective merit. This concept, and not "justice," deserved a more detailed analysis than could be given here. Our examination has shown that, as applied to the distribution "of honors," it is all but absent from Aristotle's *Politics*.

And last but not least: a reading of Aristotle's *Politics* that does not recognize that in some contexts he gives a new answer to a topic discussed elsewhere, as in 5.1 compared with 3.9, and an approach that fails to analyze the reason for the new solution misses the distinctions Aristotle makes, passes in silence over the curiosity with which he pursues many specific aspects of the complex area of human affairs, and politics in particular, misses the openness he shows for considering refreshingly new options, and reduces his political theory to a rather narrow and simplistic system of thought, a dumbed down version of his political philosophy. One needs to analyze the *Politics* for what this work conveys, register everything Aristotle actually writes, and uncover the strategy of his arguments and their internal connection. Such an approach will offer a more differentiated and multi-faceted, and I dare to say: a more interesting and more relevant political theory.

---

[36] Lamont/Favor 2013: "While Aristotle proposed virtue, or moral character, to be the best desert-basis for economic distribution ....". See above p. 164 on virtuism.

Bibliography

Anagnostopoulos, Georgios (Ed.) (2009): *A Companion to Aristotle*. Malden, MA: Wiley-Blackwell.
Aristotle (1954): The *Nicomachean Ethics*. William D. Ross (Reprint of the 1925 edition). The World's Classics. London: Oxford University Press.
Aristotle (1962): *Nicomachean Ethics*. Translated, with Introduction and Notes by Martin Ostwald. Indianapolis: Bobbs-Merrill Educational Publishing.
Aristotle (⁶1974): *Nikomachische Ethik*. Franz Dirlmeier (Trans.). In: *Aristoteles Werke in Deutscher Übersetzung*. Vol. 6. Berlin, Darmstadt: Wissenschaftliche Buchgesellschaft.
Aristotle (1984a): *The Politics*. Translated with an Introduction, Notes and Glossary by Carnes Lord. Chicago: The University of Chicago Press.
Aristotle (1984b): *The Politics and the Constitution of Athens*. Stephen Everson (Ed.). Cambridge Texts in the History of Political Thought. Cambridge: Cambridge University Press.
Aristotle (1991): *Politik: Buch II – III. Übersetzt und erläutert*. Eckart Schütrumpf (Trans.). In: *Aristoteles Werke in Deutscher Übersetzung*. Vol. 9.2. Berlin, Darmstadt: Wissenschaftliche Buchgesellschaft.
Aristotle (1996): *Politik: Buch VI – VI. Übersetzt und erläutert*. Eckart Schütrumpf (Trans.). In: *Aristoteles Werke in Deutscher Übersetzung*. Vol. 9.3. Berlin, Darmstadt: Wissenschaftliche Buchgesellschaft.
Aristotle (²1999): *Nicomachean Ethics*. Terence Irwin (Trans.). Indianapolis: Hackett Publishing.
Höffe, Otfried (Ed.) (1997): *Platon: Politeia*. Klassiker Auslegen 7. Berlin: Akademie Verlag.
Irwin, Terence (1988): Aristotle's First Principles. Oxford: Clarendon Press.
Joachim, Harold H. (1951): *Aristotle. The Nicomachean Ethics*. D.A. Rees (Ed.). Cambridge, MA: Clarendon Press.
Keyt, David (1991): "Aristotle's Theory of Distributive Justice". In: Keyt/Miller (1991), pp. 238–278.
Keyt, David/Miller, Fred D., Jr. (Eds.) (1991): *A Companion to Aristotle's "Politics"*. Oxford: Blackwell.
Kraut, Richard (2002): *Aristotle: Political Philosophy*. Oxford: University Press.
Kühner, Raphael/Gerth, Bernhard (³1966): *Ausführliche Grammatik der griechischen Sprache*. Part II: *Satzlehre* (repr. of edition of 1898). Darmstadt: Wissenschaftliche Buchgesellschaft.
Lamont, Julian/Favor, Christi (2013): "Distributive Justice". https://plato.stanford.edu/entries/justice-distributive/ June 27 2018.
Liddell, Henry G./Scott, Robert/Jones, Henry S. (⁹1940): *A Greek-English Lexicon* (with a revised supplement 1996). Oxford: Clarendon Press.
Lockwood, Thornton/Samaras, Thanassis (Eds.) (2015): *Aristotle's Politics. A Critical Guide*. Cambridge: Cambridge University Press.
Miller, Fred D. Jr. (1995): *Nature, Justice, and Rights in Aristotle's Politics*. Oxford: Oxford Clarendon Press.
Pangle, Thomas L. (2013): *Aristotle's Teaching in the "Politics"*. Chicago: The University of Chicago Press.

Rapp, Christof/Corcilius, Klaus (Eds.) (2011): *Aristoteles-Handbuch: Leben – Werk – Wirkung*. Stuttgart: Verlag J.B. Metzler.
Roberts, Jean (2000): "Justice and the Polis". In: Rowe, Christopher/Schofield, Malcolm (Eds.): *The Cambridge History of Greek and Roman Political Thought*. Cambridge, pp. 344–365. Cambridge University Press.
Schütrumpf, Eckart ([1976] 2009): "Probleme der Aristotelischen Verfassungstheorie in Politik Γ". In: Schütrumpf (2009), pp. 92–113.
Schütrumpf, Eckart (1980): *Die Analyse der Polis durch Aristoteles*. Studien zur Antiken Philosophie 10, Amsterdam: B.R. Grüner.
Schütrumpf, Eckart (1996): "Nature, Justice, and Rights in Aristotle's Politics". In: *Ancient Philosophy* 16, pp. 514–521.
Schütrumpf, Eckart (1997): *Konventionelle Vorstellungen über Gerechtigkeit. Die Perspektive des Thrasymachos und die Erwartungen an eine philosophische Entgegnung*. In: Höffe, Otfried (Ed.): *Platon: Politeia*. Klassiker Auslegen 7. Berlin, pp. 29–53: Akademie Verlag.
Schütrumpf, Eckart (2009): *Praxis und Lexis. Ausgewählte Schriften zur Philosophie von Handeln und Reden in der klassischen Antike*. Palingenesia 95. Stuttgart. Franz Steiner Verlag.
Schütrumpf, Eckart (2011): "Gerechtigkeit". In: Rapp, Christof/Corcilius, Klaus (Eds.): *Aristoteles-Handbuch: Leben – Werk – Wirkung*. Stuttgart, pp. 226–231. J.B. Metzler.
Schütrumpf, Eckart (2015): "Little to Do with Justice. Aristotle on Distributing Political Power". In: Lockwood, Thornton/Samaras, Thanassis (Eds.): *A Critical Guide to Aristotle's Politics*. Cambridge, pp. 163–183: Cambridge University Press.
Schütrumpf, Eckart (2016): "An Overdose of Justice or The Chimera of alleged 'Distributive Justice' in Aristotle's Politics". In: Havlíček, A./Horn, Ch./Jinek, J. (Eds.): *Nous, Polis, Nomos. Festschrift für Francisco Lisi*. St. Augustin, pp. 239–255. Academia Verlag.
Schwyzer, Eduard (1959): *Griechische Grammatik*. In: *Handbuch der Altertumswissenschaften*. Div. II, Part I, Munich: Beck.
Young, Charles M. (2009): "Justice". In: Anagnostopoulos (2009), pp. 457–470.

Christoph Horn
Justice in Ethics and Political Philosophy: A Fundamental Critique

Abstract: In many contemporary accounts of justice, both in moral and political philosophy, there is a tendency to give too much weight to the concept of justice. 'Justice', we often read, is at the center of our normative intuitions. I call this the 'primacy thesis', which, for the most part, seems to be inspired by J.S. Mill and by J. Rawls. I challenge the primacy thesis and its four basic convictions: (1) Cases of essential moral importance are always simultaneously questions of justice. (2) Cases of justice are always at the same time questions of essential moral importance. (3) Cases of justice have basically to do with aspects of the legal or political order. (4) Cases of justice are never morally neutral or indifferent.

Many contemporary philosophers consider 'justice' to be the crucial normative concept in ethics and political philosophy. The theoretical foundation for ascribing such a key function to our idea of justice has, as far as I can see, two different origins. It can be traced back, in the case of moral philosophy, to J.S. Mill's little treatise *Utilitarianism* (1969; ch. 5), and of course, in political philosophy, to J. Rawls' *A Theory of Justice* (1971). Roughly speaking, Mill's idea is that the expression 'justice' signifies the innermost core of moral duties; and, again very broadly, the Rawlsian approach presupposes that 'justice' should be taken to signify a basic social order in its normatively desirable state. In this paper, I wish to challenge both of these views by raising a series of objections against those current ethical and political theories which give justice a dominant role. To my mind, the pride of place broadly given the idea of justice is exaggerated. We should neither maintain that justice expresses the core of our normative convictions (in ethics as well as in political thought) nor defend the claim that we are faced with questions of justice whenever our central normative convictions are involved. As I will try to show, our idea of justice is a much more specific one. It turns out to be an important, but nevertheless subordinate normative concept. Instead of justice, I think, one should reserve the role of the dominant normative concept for 'good' and 'evil' (in the moral sense); but I cannot argue for this in the present context (cf. Horn 2014).

In order to achieve my purpose, I provide a series of philosophical considerations about the meaning of 'justice' and 'injustice', based on examples of how we use the expression in everyday life. In the vast philosophical literature on justice from the last four decades I found astonishingly few reflections on these semantic fundaments; in contrast, numerous philosophers and political theorists simply repeat the shared conviction which I would like to label ‚the 'primacy thesis'.

1 Preliminary remarks on the primacy thesis

To formulate my thesis in a somewhat provocative way: in my view, justice is one of the most misconceived and overrated concepts in contemporary philosophy. Let me start with two preliminary remarks. (1) As I just mentioned, it is certainly a somewhat surprising fact that this concept has rarely been the object of close semantic scrutiny.[1] Especially within the debate on Rawls, the expression 'justice' has started a career as a semi-technical concept more or less independent of our ordinary use of it. Given that the criterion for correct use is our common everyday application of the term, interpreting justice along these lines is, to my mind, grossly incorrect. Compared with what we normally think of as the importance of justice, it is strongly overrated by philosophers, lawyers, and political theorists. I am well aware of the fact that not everybody using the concept of justice as a basic normative concept in his/her moral and political philosophy wants to give a semantic reconstruction of what the expression ordinarily means. And, of course, every theorist in this field is free to use 'justice' as a purely technical term. One might go as far as to define 'justice' e.g. as 'what is normatively crucial in ethics (or political philosophy)' – regardless of which content might turn out to be crucial. But this should clearly be indicated; most authors, however, suggest that their philosophical considerations are closer to how we ordinarily think about justice.

(2) By pointing out that the emphatic interpretation of 'justice' in moral philosophy can be traced back to J.S. Mill I don't want to claim that it was he who brought up this way of employing this concept. As a historian of philosophy, I know very well that a similar use of justice can already be found in Adam Smith who, for his part, received it as a coinage from the Protestant line of the early modern natural law tradition.[2] Also in Kant's *Metaphysics of Morals*

---

[1] An exception is an essay written by Koller 2001; Koller to some extent undertakes a semantical analysis. Cf. also Krebs 2000 and Horn/Scarano 2002.

[2] We find a distinction quite similar to the one provided by Mill in Smith's *Theory of Moral Sentiments* (1759) where he contrasts justice and beneficence and parallels this distinction with an antithesis between enforceable and voluntary moral duties (Part II, Sect. II).

(1797), we find the distinction between 'duties of justice' (*Rechtspflichten*) and 'duties of virtue' (*Tugendpflichten*), echoing the dichotomy of 'perfect obligations' and 'imperfect obligations' in the *Groundwork* (1785). This usage has roots in the medieval natural law tradition, and its roots can ultimately be identified in Cicero's distinction between the *iustum*, the *honestum* and the *utile* in his *De officiis* (II.10). But the decisive impact on modern debates is that of Mill's wide-spread and influential little treatise.

One can easily see the enormous impact of Mill's primacy thesis on the Anglo-American contemporary debate on justice. The same holds true for the discussion of this issue in German-speaking countries: We find the idea expressed in the primacy thesis in authors such as Otfried Höffe (2001), Stefan Gosepath (2004), or Rainer Forst (2007). The well-known philosopher Ernst Tugendhat explicitly invokes Mill's treatise as the best text ever written on the fundamental signification of justice (1993, pp. 364–391).

2 Mill's idea of the primacy of justice

In order to get an impression of Mill's use of the term, let us look at a famous quotation found in *Utilitarianism*, ch. 5:

> When we think that a person is bound in justice to do a thing, it is an ordinary form of language to say, that he ought to be compelled to do it. We should be gratified to see the obligation enforced by anybody who had the power. If we see that its enforcement by law would be inexpedient, we lament the impossibility, we consider the impunity given to injustice as an evil, and strive to make amends for it by bringing a strong expression of our own and the public disapprobation to bear upon the offender. Thus the idea of legal constraint is still the generating idea of the notion of justice, though undergoing several transformations before that notion, as it exists in an advanced state of society, becomes complete (Mill 1969, pp. 245–246).

In the quoted passage, Mill tries to identify the core idea behind our notion of justice. For him, justice is basically a highly specific moral sentiment, namely an emotion which contains the desire for revenge or retaliation towards the perpetrator thought to have broken a moral or juridical law. Mill's fundamental intention in ch. 5 is to reconcile our justice-based moral intuitions with utilitarianism (since the latter seems to leave no room for justice). According to him, utilitarianism is compatible with justice, if correctly understood. In Mill's view, justice always has to do with the desire for compulsion and enforcement; obligations of justice are those the compliance with which we want to see enforced. Therefore, he contends, claims of justice constitute a normative class of their own, namely the so-called 'duties of perfect obligation'. This is expressed in a second passage from the same chapter:

> Now it is known that ethical writers divide moral duties into two classes, denoted by the ill-chosen expressions, duties of perfect and of imperfect obligation; the latter being those in which, though the act is obligatory, the particular occasions of performing it are left to our choice, as in the case of charity or beneficence, which we are indeed bound to practise, but not towards any definite person, nor at any prescribed time. In the more precise language of philosophic jurists, duties of perfect obligation are those duties in virtue of which a correlative right resides in some person or persons; duties of imperfect obligation are those moral obligations which do not give birth to any right. I think it will be found that this distinction exactly coincides with that which exists between justice and the other obligations of morality (Mill 1969, p. 247).

Following Mill, the distinctive feature of a duty of justice is that it must be strictly fulfilled by the bearer of the obligation (the bearer has to do some precisely defined actions); this implies the existence of a corresponding right on the part of the addressee. Cases of justice are what we would call negative duties: i.e. obligations to omit violations of some basic moral or legal rights. Furthermore, while we react on violations of duties of charity and beneficence with disappointment, we are touched by cases of injustice in a much deeper form; we are outraged and feel the desire for revenge, sanctions, and punishment. As this emotional reaction shows, we regard the unjust person as someone who acts against absolutely crucial rules of conduct. Let me add a third passage from ch. 5 of *Utilitarianism*:

> To recapitulate: the idea of justice supposes two things; a rule of conduct, and a sentiment which sanctions the rule. The first must be supposed common to all mankind, and intended for their good. The other (the sentiment) is a desire that punishment may be suffered by those who infringe the rule. There is involved, in addition, the conception of some definite person who suffers by the infringement; whose rights (to use the expression appropriated to the case) are violated by it. And the sentiment of justice appears to me to be, the animal desire to repel or retaliate a hurt or damage to oneself, or to those with whom one sympathises, widened so as to include all persons, by the human capacity of enlarged sympathy, and the human conception of intelligent self-interest. From the latter elements, the feeling derives its morality; from the former, its peculiar impressiveness, and energy of self-assertion (Mill 1969, pp. 249–250).

In this third quotation, we get a specific idea of how Mill tries to reconcile our common concept of justice with utilitarianism, namely by interpreting justice as an expression of a fundamental anthropological capacity to expand our sympathy to all of humankind and to include other people in our well-considered rational interest. This seems attractive, but is ultimately a doubtful strategy since justice as described by Mill need not imply the aspect of universalism which is crucial for utilitarianism. Be that as it may, what we found in Mill's text is the idea of the primacy of justice as a moral concept. Questions of justice are identified with the core of what is morally relevant.

3 Rawls' version of the primacy thesis

As is well known, we find quite a different idea of what is constitutive for the primacy of justice in the ground-breaking early monograph of John Rawls. In *A Theory of Justice* (1971), Rawls is not concerned with individual cases of morality (although the later Rawls shows some interest in justice as a personal feature of individuals), but considers 'justice' as the most fundamental normative concept within a theory of social institutions. Rawls thinks that a society is adequately organized in a normative sense if its basic structure is 'just'. In order to be just, it must consist of institutions which establish a lexical priority for rights and liberties with regard to all other political goods, especially socioeconomic ones. What he has in mind are the rights and liberties of the early modern liberal tradition – and in this respect Rawls is not that far from Mill. In a famous passage from the beginning of *A Theory of Justice*, Rawls compares justice as the first, and decisive, virtue of social institutions with truth as the crucial virtue of epistemic systems such as theories. He then explains what he means by justice, and by the analogy between justice and truth (TJ, ch. 1.1):

> Each person possesses an inviolability founded on justice that even the welfare of society as a whole cannot override. For this reason, justice denies that the loss of freedom for some is made right by a greater good shared by others. It does not allow that the sacrifices imposed on a few are outweighed by the larger sum of advantages enjoyed by many. Therefore in a just society the liberties of equal citizenship are taken as settled; the rights secured by justice are not subject to political bargaining or to the calculus of social interests. The only thing that permits us to acquiesce in an erroneous theory is the lack of a better one; analogously, an injustice is tolerable only when it is necessary to avoid an even greater injustice. Being first virtues of human activities, truth and justice are uncompromising (Rawls 1971, pp. 3–4).

According to the quoted passage, justice signifies the idea that certain basic liberties should categorically override other interests. For Rawls, the restriction of individual rights to freedom cannot be compensated by a higher degree of socioeconomic welfare or any other advantage; liberties must be distributed equally (and in the largest possible 'packages') among the citizens of a legitimate society. If this idea is taken seriously, the society has met the most important criterion of a just society. Following Rawls, the concept of justice resembles, the idea of truth, in that both are absolute and uncompromising.

Both Mill and Rawls defend a conception of justice with a strong normative primacy, even if there are considerable differences between their views. Whereas Mill thinks that justice basically is a moral sentiment connected with a desire for retaliation – a sentiment directed to cases in which someone infringes the rights of some other person (and thereby contravenes his or her perfect duties), Rawls, emphasizing the overridingness of a set of basic liberties, believes that justice adequately designates the normatively optimal state of a basic order of social institutions. And while Mill speaks of justice in a moral sense, Rawls uses the term in a socio-political context. The common point shared by Mill and Rawls is the idea of the primacy or privileged normative function connected with the concept of justice. And both philosophers clearly want to remain close to our everyday usage of the term (Mill more explicitly than Rawls, but I think it can also be said of the latter). Both philosophers exerted and exert an enormous influence on the following discussion and especially on the current debate.

4 Some fundamental semantic considerations about justice

Justice is certainly one of the most important evaluative concepts in everyday life as well as in ethics and political philosophy. If we consider a person as just (or fair), then we believe to have identified a deeply valuable feature of this person; and if we regard a given social institution as deeply unjust, we find ourselves in a state of outrage and demand for a change. As these examples imply, we use the term 'justice' and its cognates both for individuals (*grosso modo* in the sense of a personal virtue) and for the conditions of social institutions (the organization of economy, the tax system, the education system etc.). The oldest use in the Western conceptual history seems to be that of 'cosmic justice' meaning the distribution of natural goods and evils among persons – and meaning the 'moral order of the world', i.e. the principle of divine reward for the just individuals and of divine punishment for the unjust ones. Both the idea of personal justice and that of cosmic justice are not strongly present in contemporary philosophical debates, except in the sense that the former is discussed in the context of virtue ethics (including the topic of desirable personal features of citizens and politicians in our societies), whereas the latter appears in discussions of the welfare state in terms of when the natural handicaps of a person should be considered as reasons for support and when they should simply be seen as someone's personal fate. Although these two aspects are still important they alone would not justify the enormous role played by the idea of justice in contemporary philosophy.

To be more precise, we have to acknowledge that the concept of justice has a very complicated usage. Let me illustrate this in more detail in terms of the various objects which can be characterized as just or unjust. As far as I can see, one can distinguish between ten different sorts of objects: (1) persons and social groups (*personal use*), (2) characters, attitudes, motives of individuals (*virtue ethics use*), (3) judgments, ideas, values of persons (*ethical use*), (4) procedures, social principles, guiding lines (*procedural use*), (5) social institutions (*institutional use*), (6) abstract principles, theories, and arguments (*theoretical use*), (7) distributions of goods and evils (*distributive use*), (8) relation between a gift and a result or an investment and the benefit (*relational use*), (9) result of a procedure, e. g. a competition (*resultative use*), and (10) the state (of the world or of a particular social situation) in which goods and evils are allocated in a certain way (*situative use*, also *cosmic use*). I have argued in some length for the thesis that (10) is our primordial idea of justice while the other variants are derivation of it (see Horn/Scarano 2002).

A further observation of some importance for an appropriate philosophical analysis is that 'justice' can mirror at least eight different basic ideas: (i) justice as equality in the distribution of goods and evils (*distributive justice*), (ii) justice as impartiality of the application of rules (*impartial justice*), (iii) justice as equivalence of goods in exchange (*commutative justice*), (iv) justice as compensation of disadvantages and handicaps (*corrective justice*), (v) justice as gratification of merits and achievements (*meritorious justice*), (vi) justice as equivalence of criminal action and punishment (*retributive justice*), (vii) justice as equivalence of investments and results (*connective justice*), (viii) justice as adequate distribution of natural goods and evils (*natural or cosmic justice*).

A point of even greater systematic importance is the distinction between the Platonic and the Aristotelian ideas of justice. ('Platonic' and 'Aristotelian' are used here as quite rough labels.) Both of them are still of major importance for our understanding of justice in general – in everday life and in philosophical contexts. The Platonic concept can be rendered by the famous Latin formula *suum cuique tribuere* – to give everybody his own, whereas the Aristotelian idea is 'equal cases should be treated equally and unequal cases unequally'.[3]

---

[3] Plato, *Republic* IV.433a8 ff.; IX.586e and Aristotle, *Politics* III 12, 1282b14–22. Note that M. Knoll 2010 has challenged this simple opposition. Nevertheless I think that *grosso modo* it is correct.

Justice in the first, Platonic, sense is based on the idea that persons merit to gain something regardless of what the others get; they have a 'right' to it or deserve it. Justice in the second, Aristotelian, sense is founded on the idea of interpersonal comparisons: some person A gets x *since* B gets y; what A and B are receiving, is always interelated. One can easily see that justice in the Platonic sense is quite different from the Aristotelian idea: the first signifies an *absolute* or *personal* understanding of justice while the second is based on a *relational* or *interpersonal* concept.

5 Objections against the primacy thesis

Whatever the precise conceptual content of 'justice' may be, Mill and Rawls defend the primacy thesis – even if they do it in quite different senses. Since the impact of both philosophers on the current debate is deep and thoroughgoing, I would like to raise several objections against it. To clarify my basic intention, it should be said that I wish to reject the following four claims:
(1) Cases of essential moral importance are always simultaneously questions of justice.
(2) Cases of justice are always at the same time questions of essential moral importance.
(3) Cases of justice have basically to do with aspects of the legal or political order.
(4) Cases of justice are never morally neutral or indifferent.

Now, let me try to provide some intuitive support for these rejections. One of the most serious cases in which we see a violation of moral norms is that of committing a murder. We clearly consider cases of murder to be instantiations of what Mill calls perfect duties, and having strong sentiments, we wish the murderer to be punished by the legal order. Yet we would not call these incidents cases of injustice – in none of the Western languages (as far as I know). The same holds true for many other cases in which crucial moral rights or interests of persons are violated: I am thinking of torture, mutilation, rape, robbery, or deprivation of personal liberty. It seems true for all of these crimes that they aren't regarded as cases of injustice while they are unambiguously seen as hard moral cases, i.e., as violations of essential moral rights.

The point I have in mind is quite clearly expressed by a passage one finds in H.L.A. Hart:

> There are indeed very good reasons why justice should have a most prominent place in the criticism of law arrangements; yet it is important to see that it is a distinct segment of morality, and that laws and the administration of laws may have or lack excellences of different kinds. [...] A man guilty of gross cruelty to his child would often be judged to have done something morally *wrong*, *bad*, or even *wicked* or to have disregarded his moral *obligation* or duty to his child. But it would be strange to criticize his conduct as *unjust*. [...] "Unjust" would become appropriate if the man had arbitrarily selected one of his children for severer punishment than those given to others guilty of the same fault, or if he had punished the child for some offence without taking steps to see that he really was the wrongdoer (Hart 1961, p. 154).

I think that Hart is right in claiming that cruelty is normally not seen as an injustice. While nobody would classify one of the crimes mentioned above under the category of injustice, the issues which are in fact discussed in the debates on justice are mainly the following seven: (i) political justice (in the sense of basic rights and liberties), (ii) social and economic justice (questions of the distribution of goods within a society), (iii) justice between men and women, (iv) justice with regard to social minorities, (v) intergenerational justice, (vi) juridical aspects of justice (especially just und unjust punishment) and (vii) international justice.

In our common language, nobody characterizes crimes like murder as cases of injustice, and even in contemporary philosophical debates, we would hardly find anybody who would actually do this. Seen in this way, it seems even difficult to figure out examples for which it might be true to maintain that they are simultaneously cases of hard moral cases and injustice. In fact, no one uses murder as an example for injustice. Within the philosophical literature on issues of justice, we find instead examples such as a child's birthday party. It serves as a typical paradigm for injustice that, *ceteris paribus*, one child receives a smaller piece of cake than the others.

Let me now give two somewhat elaborate examples which show how injustice can be clearly distinguished, more or less, from the aspect of moral importance. (a) Think of two situations in a bakery shop. In the first, the customers are waiting in a queue, and Muhammed, a guy from Nigeria, is part of his line; but for reasons of racism and xenophobia, he is at first neglected by the shopkeeper. In the second case, Sandra, a girl from the neighborhood, waiting in the same queue, is at first neglected by the shopkeeper; but in her case, the reason for postponing her is simply that a close friend of the shopkeeper enters the bakery. Suppose that both persons, Muhammed and Sandra, are treated in the same unjust way: they are not served when it is their turn. Nevertheless, the two different motives of the shopkeeper make the cases very different. In Muhammed's case, the injustice is done from a genuinely immoral attitude, racism; in Sandra's case, it is done from a (more or less acceptable) attitude of privileging friends. (b) Suppose that a military instructor treats young recruits differently, privileging those of his own ethnic origin while afflicting the young soldiers belonging to a certain minority with great distress. In this case, we are confronted with a violation of basic moral rights which we wish to see legally punished and an instantiation of an injustice which 'cries out to heaven'.

So far, I think we have formulated considerable challenges to Mill's view: the moral primacy of 'justice' is certainly not a highly convincing claim. Let us now have a look at the Rawlsian view. A first point to be made is that Rawls neglects all topics of justice except those of the 'basic order'. Consider this minor criticism of Rawls: it seems quite artificial to say that normatively virtuous, perfect, choiceworthy, or desirable institutions can simultaneously be called 'just' in the same sense in which we say that normatively ideal scientific theories are those that turn out to be true. We wish institutions to be, e.g., efficient, lean, non-bureaucratic, open-minded, easily accessible, inexpensive, or flexible (these attributes are different from being just, and I see no precise equivalent for them in scientific truth). Second, not every perfect social institution is a justice one, and, *vice versa*, not every just social institution is at the same time of essential normative importance.

A stronger criticism of the Rawlsian view is exhibited by the fact that the moral implications of agents acting with institutional authority cannot always be classified as cases of justice or injustice. Take the case of a protester beaten up by some policemen in a dark alley at night. To my mind, we should distinguish here between two possibilities. (i) The violation of the protester's bodily and psychic integrity and civil rights is simultaneously a case of injustice if there exists, e.g., an order given by a local politician who instructed the officers to do so. (ii) Imagine the policemen are frustrated from their hard working conditions, drunken, and feel underprivileged compared with the academic protesters they are facing; then their aggressive act of beating up a protester would still be morally intolerable, but we should not classify the case under the heading of injustice.

If I am right, what we gather from these considerations is the following: the examples of the queue in the bakery shop and the military instructor make plausible that the perspective of justice (at least in many cases, perhaps even always) presupposes the element of interpersonal comparisons. What is unjust about the shopkeeper's and the instructor's behavior is that they are treating the customers/recruits unequally. In the case of the aggressive policemen we are confronted with an example of injustice only if they are following a rule or a decree that allows or orders them to behave like that. But seen from this perspective, the decree is what is really unjust. If the policemen acted out of some spontaneous frustration or hatred, they would not behave unjustly, they would simply be criminals who should be punished and should quit their service. If this distinction is correct, then cases of injustice have two constitutive features which have to do with unequal treatment in relevant respects (which implies interpersonal comparisons), or presuppose rules of conduct, decrees, or guiding principles which are unlawful.

In many contexts, justice can be understood in terms of lawfulness. An example illustrating this intuition is, to my mind, that of a referee involved in a soccer game: if the referee privileges one of the teams while disadvantaging the other, he commits the paradigmatic case of an injustice. He neglects the principle of impartiality which is one of the ideas constitutive for lawfulness. Now note that we would count an unfair soccer match neither among the cases of violating a perfect moral duty (in the Millian sense) nor among the cases of injustice (according to the Rawlsian understanding). But clearly we would speak here of a basic instantiation of unfair conduct.

6 Further objections

I think we have so far considered a number of examples sufficient to come to the crucial point of my argument. We can clearly see that it is not due to the component of being just or unjust that a given case of misbehavior can be characterized as morally essential or marginal. There are numerous cases in which perfect duties and moral rights are violated that aren't simultaneously cases of injustice: murder, torture, rape, robbery, and so on, and there are lots of cases in which justice is involved without a strong element of morality being present. For the latter, only think of the standard example of a child's birthday party where the underprivileged child receives a minor piece of cake, but is thereby not really damaged. If we might speak, in such a case, of 'damage' at all, we would certainly say that the detriment is confined to the *surplus zone* of the child's goods. Even if the child might feel deeply outraged and believes to be strongly disrespected, it is not mistreated in a moral sense. As Mill correctly points out, our sense of injustice gives us a strong feeling, but this feeling is no reliable indicator for substantial moral violation. Often it simply indicates a case of being discriminated in a peripheral way. Only imagine the following possibility: the father who wanted to prepare a cake for the birthday party fails and has to put the cake ultimately into the rubbish bin; in this case, no child is 'damaged' at all by the fact that no one receives a piece of cake at all.

At least I should try to give a rough idea (even if an extremely brief and necessarily insufficient one) which provides an answer to the question of what is the moral element – the fact of being moral or immoral – within our actions. I think that this answer should be founded on the concept of *basic human goods* which can either be respected and supported in our interpersonal relations or disrespected and destroyed. It would list a number of goods which I take as morally central and among which I count: life (survival), physical health, bodily integrity, psychic health, social and political autonomy etc. Goods such as spare time interests, travel habits, musical or artistic taste etc., on the contrary, are not in the center of our moral concerns and can be deemed as peripheral. It is not the aspect of justice or injustice that decides on the moral value of an action, but the respect for or violation of of the crucial goods.

I want to go one step further with my observation that justice is not the constitutive aspect for the morality or immorality of an action since there are both cases of injustice which are morally marginal and cases of morality which have nothing to do with justice. This step goes as follows: cases of justice and injustice are not only sometimes morally marginal; they can also be morally neutral or even deeply immoral. Take the elementary example of a band of robbers that discusses the problem how to distribute the haul: they can allocate goods, e.g., according to the rank of a robber or according to his achievement or according to his neediness or health state or whatever else. If they are discussing their standards, they might finally arrive at a solution which is regarded by them as just. Here then we are confronted with a just distribution of goods (let us assume: with a *perfectly just* distribution), but it is a case of immoral behavior from the outset, since the goods under consideration have been robbed from their legitimate owners. Compare the following four examples:

(1) *Just and unjust distribution*
   (a) A mafia gang is discussing how to distribute the illegally earned fortune: according to the rank of a member or according to his achievement or according to his neediness or according to his health or age etc. Depending on how they decide we might be willing to concede that their distribution is just. But this just distribution does not legitimize the entire situation *in a moral sense*. On the contrary, we would say that there is an overriding aspect that determines our moral judgment, namely that the fortune to be distributed have been gained before in an immoral way, by all sorts of crime. Note the remarkable fact that a just distribution does not outweigh the situation's immorality; from the moral point of view, it does not count to the slightest extent.
   (b) A group of nuns living in a monastery prepare lunch for homeless people. They do it every day, seven days a week, and it is a demanding and expensive element in the life of the monastery. Among the homeless coming to the meals is Carl, a funny and good-humored guy who is

the favorite guest of the nuns. They always prefer him and give him a better share of the lunch (without giving less than a normal share to all others). Carl is privileged, but all other homeless are not in danger of malnutrition or starvation. In this case, again, the injustice committed by the nuns does not modify the fact that they are doing a morally admirable job. Again, the aspect of justice does not morally count.

(2) *Murder*
   (a) Take again the example of a band of robbers. After having distributed the haul, one robber, Jim, out of avarice, brutally kills another robber, Tom. Suppose that it is a clear case of murder. Assume additionally that the distribution which preceded the murder was unjust, and this injustice was part of the motivation of Jim to kill Tom. Even then the only thing that counts for our moral judgment is the murder. Note the fact of an unjust distribution which immediately preceded the murder may explain, but not justify the conduct of Jim. In our moral judgment, Jim is guilty of having participated in a robbery and of having committed a murder. The additional injustice is without any relevance.
   (b) A group of nuns again, on a regular basis, serves lunch for homeless people. They are distributing the meals in exactly equal portions. But one day Herbert, one of the homeless, wants to have a double portion. He accuses the nuns of committing serious injustices, which is a completely unjustified allegation. Bernadette (one of the nuns) thereby becomes so angry that, finally, she murders Herbert by beating him with a fry pan on his head. In this case again, the unjust allegation might explain the murder, but not justify it. And the fact the Bernadette is usually doing a morally admirable job does not justify her conduct. Nevertheless, we have to take it into account when we try to give a moral judgment on her. But note that the fact that Bernadette always distributed the meals equally does not count at all for our moral judgment on this situation. Even if she might have been inadequately accused of unfairness, this would be an irrelevant part of the story.

We can conclude from this that justice is not only morality-neutral (in the sense that is does not constitute morality), but even morality-insensitive (in the sense that it is perfectly compatible with deeply immoral background conditions).

Take a very classical example to see this point even clearer. In the Homeric *Iliad*, the hero Achilles is angry and outraged since he has been deprived of his concubine named Briseis. The young female has been given as a present to king Agamemnon because of his higher rank, although Achilles has been the most courageous and efficient warrior so far. We are clearly confronted here with a case of injustice, and this explains the extreme anger (*mênis*) of Achilles. But obviously, we are at the same time confronted with a case of serious immorality – namely the practice of giving young females captured during war to merited warriors as their awards. If somone regards his slave as legitimate property gained by his enormous efforts, he is clearly justified in feeling outraged when he is treated in an unjust manner. But slavery is immoral in itself. As this shows, justice is nothing but a secondary normative idea, an idea which can even be applied when we are facing cases of serious immorality.

I think that immorality should be described as an interpersonal violation of the realm of someones 'moral goods' (in the sense characterized above). Cases of injustice can then in fact be morally relevant, but *not due to the aspect of injustice*. Instead, immorality is ascribed to an action or a situation on the basis of the moral goods that are involved. And questions of the institutional design of a society are neither *eo ipso* questions of justice nor of morality. They can be, but need not.

7 The Aristotelian and the Platonic idea of justice

I have now discussed all of my four theses. Let me add one final remark. One might object that so far I only considered the Aristotelian concept of justice and neglected the Platonic one. This is certainly correct, and I want to catch up this now in a very brief form. I take both classical theories – the Platonic and the Aristotelian one – as genuine paradigms of our ordinary way of thinking about justice. Justice is always about the distribution of benefits and burdens, of goods and evils, of advantages and disadvantages. Whether one interprets justice in an interpersonal and relational way (the Aristotelian version) or according to a personal and absolute paradigm (the Platonic version) it is indifferent from my point of view. What really matters is the question of whether or not the goods and evils that are distributed are moral goods (and evils) or peripheral goods (and evils respectively).

Bibliography

Forst, R. (2007): *Das Recht auf Rechtfertigung. Elemente einer konstruktivistischen Theorie der Gerechtigkeit.* Frankfurt a. M.: Suhrkamp.
Gosepath, S. (2004): *Gleiche Gerechtigkeit. Grundlagen eines liberalen Egalitarismus.* Frankfurt a. M.: Suhrkamp.

Hart, H.L.A. (1961): *The Concept of Law*. Oxford: Clarendon Press.
Höffe, O. (2001): *Gerechtigkeit. Eine philosophische Einführung*. Munich: Beck.
Horn, Ch. (2014): "Kritische Bemerkungen zum aktuellen Gerechtigkeitsdiskurs". In: *Jahrbuch für Angewandte Ethik* 1, pp. 121–147.
Horn, Ch./Scarano, N. (Eds.) (2002): *Philosophie der Gerechtigkeit. Texte von der Antike bis zur Gegenwart*. Frankfurt a.M.: Suhrkamp.
Kant, I. (1996): *Metaphysics of Morals*. Mary Gregor (Trans. and Ed.). Cambridge: Cambridge University Press.
Kant, I. (1998): *Groundwork of the Metaphysics of Morals*. Mary Gregor (Trans. and Ed.). Cambridge: Cambridge University Press.
Knoll, M. (2010): "Die distributive Gerechtigkeit bei Platon und Aristoteles". In: *Zeitschrift für Politik* (ZfP) 1, pp. 3–30.
Koller, P. (2001): "Zur Semantik der Gerechtigkeit". In: Koller, P (Ed.): *Gerechtigkeit im politischen Diskurs der Gegenwart*. Vienna: Passagen, pp. 19–46.
Krebs, A. (Ed.) (2000): *Gleichheit oder Gerechtigkeit. Texte der neuen Egalitarismuskritik*. Frankfurt a.M.: Suhrkamp.
Mill, J. S. (1969): *Utilitarianism*. In: Collected Works, vol. 10. J.M. Robson (Ed.). Toronto: Toronto University Press.
Rawls, John (1971): *A Theory of Justice*. Cambridge, MA: Belknap Press of Harvard University Press.
Rinderle, P. (2006): "John Stuart Mills Theorie der Gerechtigkeit". In: Assländer M./Ulrich, P. (Eds.): *John Stuart Mill – der vergessene politische Ökonom und Philosoph*. Bern: Haupt, pp. 79–123.
Smith, A. (2002): *The Theory of Moral Sentiments*. Knud Haakonssen (Ed.). Cambridge: Cambridge University Press. Another solution would be to put the bibliography in alphabetical order.
Tugendhat, E. (1984): "Bemerkungen zu einigen methodischen Aspekten von Rawls' *Eine Theorie der Gerechtigkeit*". In: Tugendhat, E. (Ed.)., *Probleme der Ethik*. Stuttgart: Reclam, pp. 10–32.
Tugendhat, E. (1993): *Vorlesungen über Ethik*. Frankfurt a.M.: Suhrkamp.
Tugendhat, E. (1997): *Dialog in Leticia*. Frankfurt a.M.: Suhrkamp.

Chandran Kukathas
Justicitis

Abstract: This contribution argues that, despite its undeniable importance, the topic of justice has become an oversold theoretical and normative commodity. Theories of justice abound covering what seems to be nearly every aspect of human existence. Without criticizing the aim of improving these disparate aspects of human existence, a problem arises insofar as justice as a concept is overburdened; rather than resolving the problems it seeks to better, its conceptual proliferation seems to do little to improve actual human existence. The essay's main contention is that if justice is seen a la Rawls as the keystone of moral and political thinking, and given its primacy among the virtues, any injustice found within our social institutions will not be tolerated. The result is that matters very basic to our lives, such as choosing whether to send one's child to a private or public school, can be seen as a matter of justice or injustice, when, in fact, it is not. Hence, our conception of justice is sick and it needs a cure.

> *In medical parlance, the suffix "-it is" is used to indicate the presence of inflammation in that part of the body subject to the particular disorder or disease. Tonsillitis is the inflammation of the tonsils, gingivitis the inflammation of the gums, pancreatitis the inflammation of the pancreas, and so on. Inflammation is not always easy to treat, and medical professionals understand this, even as they recognize the importance of bringing it under control if the patient is to be restored to good health.*

> ... a theory of justice defends a particular view of what is owed to whom. In other words, it delineates both the content and the scope of those obligations.
> (Cécile Fabre 2007, p. 162)

However much we might decry the lack of justice in the world, there is no shortage of books and papers on the subject. In academia, and particularly in political philosophy, justice is booming. After a bear market that lasted decades – perhaps even centuries – the bull is back. We can say with some confidence that we have now had nearly four decades of bull, and there is no sign that justice is about to go out of fashion. Today, particularly among analytical philosophers, political theory is fundamentally about justice.

We should take a moment to review the evidence for this claim. Since the purpose of this essay is to lament the triumph of justice in the academy, it should begin by offering some account of the state of things. The most obvious piece of evidence of the spread of the discourse of justice is the success of Michael Sandel's Harvard lecture course on Justice. So popular was this course that the Fall 2005 version was recorded and offered online to students through the Harvard Extension School. A TV series and accompanying book, *Justice: What's the Right Thing to Do?* (Sandel 2010), soon followed, supplemented by a sourcebook, *Justice: A Reader* (Sandel 2007). In Japan, the broadcast rights were acquired by NHK (the Japan Broadcasting Corporation), and the course became a popular pay-per-view download. A book tour in 2010 saw Professor Sandel lecture to packed auditoriums, with tickets reportedly available from scalpers for as much as $500. In 2011 the BBC broadcast an eight-part TV series drawn from these lectures.[1] In his very first book, *Liberalism and the Limits of Justice*, published nearly 30 years earlier, Sandel famously criticized John Rawls, and liberalism more broadly, for exaggerating the importance of justice. Now he has his own book on justice, which prompts one to wonder whether the critic has gone native, and succumbed to the temptation to make justice the measure of all things political.

Michael Sandel's success is undoubtedly due in good measure to his own talents as a teacher and public speaker, but the issue here is not his bringing political philosophy to a larger audience (which is all to the good). The point is that the introduction to reflection on politics offered by these lectures is precisely the introduction offered by academic political theory: justice. Since Rawls's first book on justice, we have had a succession of treatises on the subject: *Spheres of Justice, Principles of Justice, Elements of Justice, Contexts of Justice, Bounds of Justice, Theories of Justice*, and even *Justice for Hedgehogs*; not to mention a variety of conceptions of justice offered for our consideration, including *Justice as Impartiality*, justice as even-handedness, *Justice as Fairness*, justice as utility maximizing; and works explaining *Why Social Justice Matters* or aimed at *Rescuing Justice and Equality*. Yet it's not simply that, woken by these human voices, we are drowning in treatises and academic articles on the subject. If one thinks of each work as a contribution to or an intervention in an ongoing conversation, the volume of work is not troubling in itself. One might even think of it as a reflection of the vitality of the profession that so many voices enter the discussion and so many thoughts are given expression. My complaint is *not* like that of the Emperor to Mozart: that the music has too many notes. The worry is the framing of the discourse in such a way as to make justice the fundamental problem of political order, and to see many aspects of social life matters of justice.

Consider, for example, Adam Swift's book, *How Not to Be a Hypocrite* (2003), which purports to offer some guidance to the morally perplexed parent struggling with the question of whether to send the children to a private school rather

---

[1] Sandel had earlier presented the 2009 Reith Lectures: *A New Citizenship*, which took up many of the same themes in his lectures on justice, but on this occasion *not* under the rubric of justice.

than the local state-run institution. The question with which it grapples is what parents may justly do for their children, given that all kinds of acts that benefit their offspring also give them an advantage over the young from other families that are unable or unwilling to do more for them. Can a father committed to social justice in good conscience read his daughter bedtime stories, buy her music lessons, move house so she can go to a better comprehensive school, or *in extremis* send her to a private school? Swift comes to the very moderate conclusion that the father can justifiably (and without hypocrisy) do any and all of these things (although he himself is convinced that private schools ought to be abolished). What is striking, however, is that these decisions are considered to be matters of justice.[2] The blurb at the back of the book illustrates the point especially well. "Many of us," it says "believe in social justice and equality of opportunity – but we also want the best for our kids. How can we square our political principles with our special concern for our own children?" The blurb goes on to say that this book takes us "through the moral minefield that is school choice today." Without wishing to deny for a moment that Adam Swift has written an engaging and interesting book, I nevertheless wonder whether there really is a minefield out there. Should choosing a school be considered a matter of justice? (Whatever is the reverse of preaching to the choir, I suspect I am doing it here!)

If there is a tension between the idea of doing the best for one's children and one's political principles it seems more obvious that the political principles are the things that are in danger of blowing up. At this point all I have to offer is this counter-intuition, which in itself does not establish very much. One point to note, however: Swift says quite correctly that there are things one cannot justify on the grounds that one is helping one's children (Swift 2003, pp. 9–10). Committing murder, for example; or stealing. Yet these things are wrong regardless of one's motives, and few would deny that it is wrong to cheat or assault or bully someone for the sake of one's children – because it is always wrong to cheat or assault or bully anyone. What is notable about the issue raised in the book is that it considers that some actions might be wrong – unjust – *because* they help one's children.

There are many other things that have been presented in the literature of political theory as matters of justice. Oral health is a matter of justice, if we are to believe the editor of a collection of papers, *Justice in Oral Health Care*, which includes a contribution on "Just Dentistry" (Welie 2006; also see Winslow

---

[2] I should stress that Swift comes very quickly to the conclusion that it is fine to read bedtime stories to your children. The book is primarily about the ethics of school choice. Those looking for a good excuse *not* to read to their children will be as disappointed as I was.

2006, pp. 81–96). So is access to playgrounds, if we read such works as *The Right to the City: Social Justice and the Fight for Public Space* (Mitchell 2003). What we eat is a matter of justice, as is the issue who provides the food (Meislik 2004, pp. 781–813). The use of cognitive enhancement technologies is a matter of justice (Caldera 2008 pp. 116–123). There is health justice, climate justice, climate change justice, sex-selection justice, genome justice, brewing justice (coffee trading justice), justice in childcare provision, language justice, and of course, intergenerational justice, inter-cultural justice, and global justice. The pursuit of women's literacy is a matter of justice, as is water policy, the provision of public toilets (Gershenshon/Penner 2009), and access to the internet (Deloney 2011).

Now, I don't wish for a moment to suggest that any of these issues is unimportant. Dental health is a good, and it is vital that we take proper care of the planet. I applaud the work of Jack Sim and his founding in 2001 of the World Toilet Organization, dedicated to improving sanitation and giving more people access to a facility most of us in the prosperous parts of the world take for granted.[3] These, and many other things, matter. But I wonder whether they are matters of justice.

The thesis I wish to defend is that we have erred in putting justice at the centre of moral and political reflection, for justice is neither the first virtue of social and political institutions nor even a virtue we should rate very highly in our, or possibly any, society. We have greatly exaggerated the value of justice, and this has led us to misunderstand the nature of political society as well as tempted us to overreach ourselves in the pursuit of goals that are chimerical – and even dangerous.

To see the nature of the problem we might turn to the famous passage in the opening chapter of Rawls's *A Theory of Justice*. Rawls writes:

> Justice is the first virtue of social institutions, as truth is of systems of thought. A theory however elegant and economical must be rejected or revised if it is untrue; likewise laws and institutions no matter how efficient and well-arranged must be reformed and abolished if they are unjust (1999a, p. 3).

The unyielding character of this contention is worth noting. Institutions, *no matter how efficient or well-arranged*, must be reformed, and indeed *abolished* if unjust. Justice is *infinitely* weighty; injustice *absolutely* intolerable. There can be no

---

[3] November 19 is World Toilet Day. In Malaysia the 2010 World Toilet Day was celebrated with cash prizes for the 7% of public toilets earning 5-star ratings – though, sadly, more than half the toilets inspected by the Ministry for Housing and Local Government were awarded two stars or fewer. For a discussion of this other WTO (Mahbubani 2008, pp. 15–16).

compromise with injustice, for "injustice is tolerable only when it is necessary to avoid an even greater injustice" (Rawls 1999a, p. 4). As first virtues, "justice and truth are uncompromising" (Rawls 1999a, p. 4). I wish to suggest that this is not the lens through which we should view human society, nor the attitude we should adopt in thinking about how we should live together. We have made too many things matters of justice; and made justice something that matters too much. Indeed we have, on occasion, expanded the concept itself so that it encompasses so much of our moral life that we have lost any sense that it is only one among a number of virtues and values – one that exists in tension, and even in conflict, with others. Explaining why this is a problem is the purpose of this paper.

The origins of justice

This is not an easy matter to explain since to attempt to do so is to go against the spirit of the age. But one useful starting point would be to consider justice anthropologically, and ask a question about the origins of justice, and its place in human society. The most comprehensive answer we have to this question is David Hume's, and this is as good a place as any to begin.

Justice arises, Hume reasons, because of certain features of our nature and of our environment. We are, by nature, even if not entirely selfish, creatures of "confined generosity," who are most inclined to look out for their own interests and the interests of those closest to them. The world we inhabit is one in which the goods we desire, for ourselves and those most important to us, are moderately scarce and also sought by others. In this condition our hold on any of the goods we might obtain is insecure. A dim awareness of this problem is enough to bring us to settle upon conventions that establish stability of possession. With the (wholly unintentional) development of norms of property, as people learn to abstain from the possessions of others, emerges human society, which arises spontaneously in much the same way as money and language do – without explicit agreement (Hume 1976, pp. III, ii, 489–490). With the emergence of this convention of abstaining from others' possessions immediately also arise the idea of justice and injustice, as well as the ideas of property, right, and obligation (Hume 1976, pp. III, ii, 490–491).

What Hume suggests is that society cannot be understood except as a form of association among human beings which embodies relations of property, which in turn can only be understood as relations that depend for their existence on people acquiring and deploying notions of *justice*, *right*, and *obligation*. In other words, society is human association under the aspect of moral norms embraced or internalized by each individual. Now, this social condition, in Hume's analysis, is the original condition of mankind – for it is inconceivable that humans could survive for long outside of society (Hume 1976, pp. III, ii, 493). Only in a realm in which there was some kind of stability of possession could society arise, so only in a condition in which norms of justice exist could there be society. Only in such a condition could there be peace (Hume 1976, pp. III, ii, 493).

Hume offers us in this analysis a moral anthropology. He explains how morality is a practice that is wholly consistent with our nature given our condition. At the core of that practice is the idea of justice, understood as a norm of respect for the possessions of others or, more simply, respect for property. The importance of the norm of justice lies in the crucial nature of its role in making society possible. However, the content of this norm is never specified by Hume. The reason is that the content is of little consequence. It is quite possible for societies to evolve very different norms of justice and ideas of property – as indeed they have. All that is necessary is that there exist norms of justice and that people embrace and abide by them.

In fact, Hume thinks, we come quickly to embrace these norms. In the first instance our self-interest leads us to do so, as we see that it is impossible to live in society without restraining ourselves by rules. Then, practice makes us take pleasure in the actions we view as tending to the peace of society, and this gives rise to the idea of the *morality* of such conduct. The sense of morality in the observance of rules follows quite naturally; but is augmented by new forms of artifice, as the public instruction of politicians and the private education of parents inculcate notions of honour and duty in the strict regulation of our actions (Hume 1976, pp. III, vi, 533–534).

What Hume does not suggest, however, is that norms of justice need to be just. There is a fairly straightforward reason for this: there is no need for norms of justice to be just in order for them to serve their purpose: to make human society possible. This does not mean that we cannot coherently ask questions about the norms of justice that govern society, or criticize them, or say that some of them are unjust in some higher sense. We can do any and all of these things. Indeed we might criticize a society's rules of justice from the perspective of any number of values. We might think its rules do not sufficiently value liberty, or tend to promote inequality, or are inefficient, or discourage innovation or enterprise, or unfairly favour the elderly, or are unstable and likely to foment discord or even revolution. There can be better and worse norms of justice. But human society depends for its existence upon having norms of justice, and not upon the justice of its norms.

Hume himself had quite a bit to say about what kinds of norms of justice, and social norms more generally were desirable. But in his view these were highly variable, being dependent upon social circumstances, political conditions, and cultural attitudes. He does not think there can be a perfectly just society; nor does he try to imagine what one would look like. I suspect he thinks the idea does not make much sense since justice is, by its very nature, a response to imperfect circumstances: a world of moderate scarcity inhabited by beings of limited benevolence.[4]

Contemporary approaches to justice, taking their cue not from Hume but from John Rawls, adopt a very different view. It is not only possible but also vital to ask whether norms of justice are just, and it is not a mistake to conduct such an inquiry by trying to imagine a perfectly just society.

The Rawlsian turn

John Rawls is the modern theorist who insists that we try to imagine what a perfectly just society looks like. Though he accepts Hume's contention that it is our circumstances that give justice its purpose, he thinks we need to ask whether or not our institutions are just, and that we should try to answer this question by examining them against a standard of perfection. "Though justice may be, as Hume remarked, the cautious, jealous virtue, we can still ask what a perfectly just society would be like" (Rawls 1999a, p. 8). We should begin with "ideal theory," Rawls says, because it provides "the only basis for the systematic grasp of these more pressing problems" we need to address. A "deeper understanding can be gained in no other way, ... the nature and aims of a perfectly just society is the fundamental part of the theory of justice." In the end, the point is to establish a conception of social justice, which "is to be regarded as providing in the first instance a standard whereby the distributive aspects of the basic structure of society are to be assessed" (Rawls 1999a, p. 8).

Though in his early writings[5] Rawls had approached the analysis of justice by thinking about it in the way Hume did, as an indeterminate solution to a coordination problem, by the time he came to write *A Theory of Justice* he was no

---

4 "Let us suppose, that nature has bestowed on the human race such profuse *abundance* of all *external* conveniencies.... It seems evident, that, in such a happy state, every other social virtue would flourish, and receive tenfold increase; but the cautious, jealous virtue of justice would never once have been dreamed of" (Hume 2010, p. 13).
5 See in particular the papers "Outline of a Decision Procedure for Ethics," "Justice as Fairness," and "Distributive Justice," all in John Rawls, *Collected Papers*.

longer able to abide the indeterminacy. More particularly, he thought that for the solution to a coordination problem to qualify as a conception of justice it had to be *just*. The idea of justice as *fairness* expresses this concern that just arrangements had to be just not merely in Hume's limited sense but in some deeper ethical sense. Justice might well arise because circumstances give it its purpose; nonetheless, it is only justice if it has a moral quality to it. If so, it is important that we ask what kind of moral conception is best. Rawls's famous answer was that only one conception of justice was worthy, for only one was capable of being endorsed by people in society: *justice as fairness*. This was the only idea of justice that respected individual freedom and equality while at the same time giving appropriate weight to other considerations such as economic efficiency, and social stability.

Robert Nozick observed in the preface to his critical remarks on *A Theory of Justice* in chapter 7 of *Anarchy, State and Utopia* that from now on political philosophers "must either work within Rawls's theory or explain why not" (1974, p. 183). Much of political philosophy since then has chosen to work within the Rawlsian perspective on the question of justice. Philosophers have departed from Rawls, however, to the extent that they have come up with different principles or conceptions of justice, or have argued for particular interpretations of Rawls's own principles.

Inspired (or provoked!) by Rawls, contemporary political theory is now replete with conceptions of justice. Ronald Dworkin has advanced a theory advocating *equality of resources* as the core of a theory of justice (Dworkin 2002 and 2013). Martha Nussbaum has developed a theory emphasizing the need to equalize and promote human capabilities (2006). Philippe Van Parjis has a theory of justice that requires a redistribution of freedom so that there is "real freedom for all" (1998 and 2011). Others still, including Joseph Carens, Kai Nielsen, and G.A. Cohen, have developed stricter egalitarian conceptions of justice according to which justice requires a more radical redistribution of the social product (Carens 1981; Nielsen 1979; Cohen 2008). Libertarians such as Nozick offer conceptions of justice that deny that justice requires redistribution rather than the protection of individual rights (Nozick 1974, ch. 7 in particular; also see Steiner 1994).

Even those who criticized the contemporary literature for an excessive preoccupation with *distributive* justice have themselves taken justice as the focus of their concern. When, in *Justice and the Politics of Difference*, Iris Marion Young lamented the emphasis on issues of distribution she did not call for the deploying of other normative concepts to replace justice, but for an expansion of our understanding of justice to combine distributive concerns with an appreciation of the importance of questions of group recognition (Young 1990; also see Fraser 1997, ch. 8).

The centrality of justice in contemporary theorizing is evident not only in the numerous conceptions of justice on offer, but also in the conviction that runs through much of political theory that justice supplies the foundation of political society. This is expressed with great force and clarity by Rainer Forst, who asserts that the most important normative concept that applies to the political order is justice (2011). Political society, he explains, is an order of justification – an order consisting of norms and institutions that are to govern how people live together in a justified or justifiable way (Forst 2011, p. 1). 'Overarching' every form of political community is justice, which demands reasons why some have rights, and asks how it is determined who may make what claims, and how persons stand in relation to one another as authors and addressees of justifications. Everyone has a right to justification – as a matter of justice. This is not to say that there are no other important ethical concerns in a political society; but all other ethical concerns are either subordinate to or dependent upon justice.

The thesis advanced in this paper denies that justice is really so important, and rejects the idea that it is in fact the concept that lies at the foundation of a proper understanding of political order. It may be the case, as Hume suggests, that every society is governed by norms of justice, for the ideas of justice, property, and right are a part of the very idea of a society. But this does not mean that justice is the only – or even the proper – normative concept by which we judge a social order. To suggest that it is requires an exaggeration or an inflammation of the concept of justice that is unwarranted. To see why we should look more closely at the question of the place of justice as an ethical value in society requires us to return once more to Hume.

Justicitis

Justice is not a fundamental value but one ethical concern among many. It is not the foundation of society but one of the values whose pursuit society makes possible. Justice is not something to be disparaged; but neither should it be overrated.

Establishing society is not itself an ethical or normative act. While society is itself a system of moral relations, its founding cannot be of a normative character because without it there are no agents capable of taking actions that have any normative quality. Individuals become moral or ethical agents – persons – as a result of entering and growing up in society. Yet how is it that society comes into being? Hume's analysis is instructive.

Hume suggests that society comes into existence simultaneously with the emergence of property, justice, obligation and right. At first blush, it looks as though Hume is placing justice at the foundation of society. But his account bears closer examination. Society in his explanation does not come about as the result of any kind of agreement among persons to form such a thing but simply as a matter of convention. It is a product of spontaneous cooperation among individuals. Yet at the outset it is not even *cooperation* if we take cooperation to be a form of action in which one recognizes another as a *co*-operator. There is an even more basic starting point. Cooperation begins when one party decides to abstain from the possessions of another. At this point there is, of course, no notion of property, only a dim awareness that some people have particular things in their possession – perhaps merely in their grasp. Cooperation is underway not only when one person is inclined to abstain from the possessions of others, but those others are also so inclined to abstain from possessions that are not their 'own'. Not to so abstain would mean to ignore the wishes of other possessors and, in effect (assuming they protest or resist) to use force. To abstain from the possessions of others is to forsake the exercise of force and, in effect, to pursue peace. To the extent that others behave in the same way, society comes into existence. Society emerges at the moment there is mutual forbearance.

This is fundamentally a Humean story, but Hume's analysis skates quickly over the crucial step and so does not make as clear as necessary the place of justice in a proper understanding of the nature of society. Hume wants to explain that justice, right, and obligation all come into existence with the emergence of society, but the condition that makes possible the normative relations that give these notions their point is the condition of peace. Morality has its beginnings in an act of abstinence: when someone decides to abstain from the exercise of violence or force. It starts to take root when others imitate this act; and when imitation becomes mutual, cooperation begins. When cooperation is stable enough to be predictable there is a convention – and so, property, society, and all the notions that enable the participants to make sense of their activity: justice, right, and obligation.

While the terminology might suggest that justice is the foundation of society in Hume's account, the truth is that the foundation is peace, for the idea of justice at work here is little more than that condition of mutual recognition of individuals that each has a claim on the forbearance of the other. Now this is not to say that this understanding cannot develop into something more sophisticated. To the contrary, Hume insists that it will. But everything begins with mutual forbearance, or peace, or what we might call, in the broadest sense of the term (though here departing from Hume's language), toleration.[6]

Now Hume does not generally invoke the importance of peace, and it may look as though the argument here could draw more helpfully on Hobbes, for whom peace is, if not the first virtue, at least the first and preeminent goal, and one that all are obliged (by the laws of nature) to pursue. But there are two aspects to the Hobbesian story that make it a problematic starting point. The first is that the pursuit of peace is, for Hobbes, a moral demand, written in the laws of nature. The second is that peace is established by *agreement*, as all individuals agree with one another to give up their right to all things and authorize a third party – the sovereign – to govern them and to embody their person. However this story is told, the subjects involved are ethical agents who either recognize the binding force of the laws of nature, or at least accept the idea that contracts and covenants obligate. Peace is therefore an ethical construction that is the product of the interaction and agreement of ethical agents. Peace, for Hobbes, is a normative ideal; one that we are obliged to pursue. His is, to be sure, a very thin conception of peace, understood as the absence of war or any tendency to war; but it is a normative conception all the same.

In the Humean story, however, peace is not a normative ideal. It is a condition that makes society possible, but it is not the product of agreement or the result of ethically motivated action. Peace is what we have when the practice of refraining or forbearing or abstaining from taking from others what they have in their possession. It is *as if* individuals acted as though there was no right of nature – no right of each to do as he pleased. Peace is the outcome that emerges with the spontaneous practice of restraint. Peace does not result because people see the morality, or even the rationality, of pursuing it. It arises by accident.

Once we are in the social condition, however, and relate to one another as moral agents or persons, other questions can and will arise. These will include questions about the very conventions that have arisen and developed, about the terms of cooperation that exist, and about whether those terms are desirable, or good, or fair, or efficient, or likely to be followed in the future, or a threat to some interests, or just according to some proposed understanding of justice.

Now one question that might well arise in this condition is a very general question about no particular aspect of the conventions that have emerged or adopted but about the entire structure of relations among human beings in

---

[6] I have developed this line of argument for fully in my book, *The Liberal Archipelago: A Theory of Diversity and Freedom* (2003).

this order. What should be the terms of cooperation, or the terms of association? More pointedly, someone might ask: is the whole arrangement *just*? The person asking this particular question might well put it more forcefully still by prefacing it with the observation: this is, after all, the most important question we should consider. Is there any reason to think this is indeed the most important question confronting people in society?

I think there is no compelling external reason to believe it is. Clearly some people might think it is. Others might not. It is, after all, only one possible question. Although mutual forbearance has established society and the minimal peace that characterizes it, values remain plural. The thought that one particular issue (or value) is of supreme importance is a possible thought, but only one possible thought – even if the issue is justice.

From the perspective of the inhabitants of society it is difficult to see what reasons might be offered for saying that the question of justice is the most pressing, or that justice in social relations is the most important consideration when judging social arrangements. Any reason that appealed to some particular value would be of no great significance to anyone who did not accept that value. And it can't be claimed that justice is the very thing that makes society possible because it's clearly not true – indeed the very reverse is true: only the existence of society makes it possible to consider the question of its justice.

If someone were to come along and assert that justice is the first virtue of social institutions, and insist that unjust institutions must be reformed or abolished, it's hard to see why the rest of society should regard this as anything more than another point of view.

Yet there may be other reasons to look even more skeptically at assertions of the centrality of justice to the assessment of social arrangements. First, if we think of society as the result of spontaneous settlements on conventions among people who fall into practices of cooperation, we have no basis for drawing boundaries delineating any particular subset of people as forming a society that might readily be distinguished from any other. Civil society, or human society more generally, has no natural borders and any assertion that some part of it must be isolated and assessed to determine whether or not it conforms to particular strictures will be arbitrary to some degree. In reality, the movement of peoples for reasons of commerce or religion or friendship means that there will be relations among people who live in different jurisdictions and some rules of justice will have to operate across legal and political boundaries. If the thought is that within particular jurisdictions there must be rules of justice that uphold the integrity of that particular entity, say the nation or the state, then the important value in question is the integrity of the political community rather than the conception of justice.

Second, even if we accept that there is a determinate set of boundaries identifying a *closed society*[7], we will probably still have to recognize that there are many understandings or theories of justice. If we wish to remain in society the priority has to be abstaining from any act of violence or aggression so that we might actually be able to figure out what justice requires. Establishing a conception of justice cannot be achieved without the exercise of force for as long as there is dispute about what justice requires, and justice cannot settle such disagreements. The starting point under these circumstances has to be some kind of agreement to refrain from violence while issues such as justice are addressed. Justice cannot be our guide here.

Third, even if upon reflection or after deliberation and extensive inquiry there is a general consensus that existing arrangements are unjust, there will remain the question of what should be done. That existing arrangements are unjust and that better, more just arrangements can be conceived tell us little about what we ought to do. We still need to consider the opportunity cost: what would we have to give up to ensure that justice is served? Let justice be done though the heavens fall is a good slogan, but an implausible principle. Yet even a more modest principle, such as 'let justice be done even if it's quite expensive' is not obviously compelling. How expensive? Who will bear the heaviest burden? Can the burden of bringing about justice be shared – and shared equitably or without causing resentment among some – or must we trade off some injustice now for the sake of greater justice in the future? (And if so, what is the discount rate, if any?) Social institutions may need to be reformed – or even abolished. Justice is one possible reason why. But it is neither necessary nor sufficient.

Even if we think justice is especially important, however, this does not mean that we need to search for a general theory of justice. We can certainly examine particular institutions or practices or laws and criticize or seek to reform them if they are unjust, but we don't need to devote much attention to the question of what a just society looks like overall. It is neither necessary nor especially likely to be helpful. Amartya Sen makes this point very clearly in his critique of what he calls transcendental theories of justice which, he thinks, assume that having an ideal standard in view makes it easier or just possible to make comparative judgments among existing and other likely social arrangements. If we know what is ideally just, the thought goes, we will be able to compare different arrangements for their justness by referring to the ideal. Yet there is no reason

---

[7] I am using this term following Rawls, who builds his theory of justice on the basis of an assumption that the society he has in mind is fixed in character and not open to the changes that come from the movement of population or changes in boundaries. There is a fixed entity with a particular history.

to think the ideal is likely to help. As Sen points out, if comparing two mountains to try to determine which is higher it makes no difference whether we have knowledge of the height of the highest of all mountains. If we can tell that B is higher than C, we can tell this whether or not we know anything about A, which is higher than either B or C, and is indeed the highest of them all (Sen 2009).[8]

Thus far I have tried to suggest that justice is not a foundational value since it is not the basis of human society, and that even to the extent that we wish to look critically at social institutions and assess their worth we do not need to appeal to a theory of justice since a general theory is not necessary for making normative assessments. There is no reason to think that justice is the only possible standard of judgment. It might be objected, however, that the whole point of developing a theory of justice is precisely to enable us to make an assessment of a complex world of competing values. The best theory of justice is one that incorporates a range of other ethical considerations. A theory of justice is only worthy of the name if it is properly cognizant of such considerations as the value of liberty, the need to uphold and respect individual equality, the desirability of preserving standards of economic efficiency so that overall welfare is not lost in the pursuit of other ends, and the importance of community. Moreover it must have other qualities such as the capacity to command allegiance so that it will be a stable conception inasmuch as it will be one that people will accept for the right reasons and not simply because current circumstances warrant it.

Unfortunately, this will not do. The problem with the focus on the simple theory of justice is that justice is inflamed at the cost of attention to other serious ethical concerns. The problem with solving this problem by building these other concerns into the idea of justice is that justice is inflamed by making it subsume (or consume) all other values. When justice includes all the possible values of a social order it is a notion that has grown fat to the point of uselessness.

We are in a condition in political theory in which justice has grown fat. It has either consumed other ethical notions, or edged out of the picture. It's time to put justice on a diet.

Why worry?

I have so far offered conceptual and theoretical reasons for giving justice less weight in our philosophical reflections and inquiries. But even if my skepticism

---

[8] For a critique see my "On Sen on Comparative Justice" (2013).

is warranted, it might be objected, why worry. What's the harm after all in raising the question of what justice requires. After all, we should at least think about the justice of some of our institutional arrangements, even if that isn't all we should think about.

A part of my concern here is simply conceptual and theoretical. Justice loses its usefulness when it becomes a theory of everything, and justice becomes insufferable when it is presented as the value that always trumps all others. But there is a further, more practical concern.

There is, I think, lurking behind the discourse of justice, an attitude or outlooks that we need to bring some kind of order or regularity into our moral life. It's not simply that it is important that we, as individuals, be reflective, and ask ourselves how we should live. It is important that we ask how *we* should live. The ethical life is not something, in this conception, that emerges out of our disparate efforts to make sense of the world and each other – the consequence of our intricate negotiations and compromises as we try to make our way through life. It is, rather, something that needs to be interrogated more rigorously, regularized, standardized, made more consistent, and then called upon to govern and, ultimately, transform us. What this process is doing is making us into beings who see themselves not so much as individuals or as members of groups and communities but as parts of a greater whole. It is making us into beings who feel guilty about where we sent our children to school, and guilty if someone living in a neighbouring county has bad teeth.

Perhaps there is nothing wrong with this. It is difficult to present an argument as to why this is a bad thing since the appeal I am making here rests on the assertion of the importance of a particular sensibility rather than on anything more determinate. I can only suggest that this worry is not new. It is a worry Tocqueville expressed in *Democracy in America* when he began to reflect, at the end of that work, on the kind of society he saw emerging in the United States – a form of social organization he thought would eventually make its way to, and transform Europe as well. Here are some of the observations he made.

> Above this race of men stands an immense and tutelary power, which takes upon itself alone to secure their gratifications and to watch over their fate. That power is absolute, minute, regular, provident, and mild. It would be like the authority of a parent if, like that authority, its object was to prepare men for manhood; but it seeks, on the contrary, to keep them in perpetual childhood: it is well content that the people should rejoice, provided they think of nothing but rejoicing. For their happiness such a government willingly labors, but it chooses to be the sole agent and the only arbiter of that happiness; it provides for their security, foresees and supplies their necessities, facilitates their pleasures, manages their principal concerns, directs their industry, regulates the descent of property,

and subdivides their inheritances: what remains, but to spare them all the care of thinking and all the trouble of living? (Tocqueville 2010, p. 1250).

Tocqueville was not, of course, writing about academic discourses of justice but about a cast of mind he thought had enveloped a society. The worry I have is that our discourse of justice is a reflection of the transformation history has wrought. Our preoccupation with justice is not the activity of free beings reflecting in Socratic question on how they should live but a mark of the triumph of a way of thinking that regards our individuality not as the source of the social life but as gift of a collective that hovers above us like a great alien power.

If there is anything to this worry, political theory would do well to spend less time dwelling on the intricacies of various theories of justice on offer, or constructing theories anew. Perhaps we should be reading less of Rawls and more of Tocqueville and, among more recent thinkers, Hayek.

Bibliography

Caldera, E. O. (2008): "Cognitive Enhancement and Theories of Justice: Contemplating the Malleability of Nature and Self". In: *Journal of Evolution and Technology* 18. No. 1, pp. 116–123.

Carens, Joseph (1981): *Equality, Moral Incentives and the Market*. Chicago: Chicago University Press.

Cohen, G.A. (2008): *Rescuing Justice and Equality*. Cambridge, MA: Harvard University Press.

Deloney, Amalia (2011): "Internet Access is a Human Right." http://centerformediajustice.org/2011/06/10/internet-access-is-a-human-right/, visited on 6 March 2018.

Dworkin, Ronald (2002): *Sovereign Virtue: The Theory and Practice of Equality*. Cambridge, MA: Harvard University Press.

Dworkin, Ronald (2013): *Justice for Hedgehogs*. Cambridge, MA: Harvard University Press.

Fabre, Cecile (2007): *Justice in a Changing World*. Cambridge: Polity Press.

Forst, Rainer (2011): *The Right to Justification: Elements of a Constructivist Theory of Justice*. New York: Columbia University Press.

Fraser, Nancy (1997): *Justice Interruptus: Critical Reflections on the "Postsocialist" Condition*. London: Routledge.

Gershenshon, Olga/Penner, Barbara (Eds.) (2009): *Ladies and Gents: Public Toilets and Gender*. Philadelphia: Temple University Press.

Hume, David (1976): *Treatise of Human Nature*. L.A. Selby-Bigge (Ed.) with an introduction and notes by P.H. Nidditch. Oxford: Oxford University Press.

Hume, David (2010): *Enquiry Concerning the Principles of Morals*. Oxford: Oxford University Press.

Kukathas, Chandran (2003): *The Liberal Archipelago: Theory of Diversity and Freedom*. Oxford: Oxford University Press.

Kukathas, Chandran (2013): "On Sen on Comparative Justice". In: *Critical Review of International Social and Political Philosophy* 16. No. 2, pp. 196–204.
Mahbubani, Kishore (2008): *The New Asian Hemisphere: The Irresistible Shift of Global Power to the East*. New York: Public Affairs.
Meislik, Alyse (2004): "Weighing in on the Scales of Justice: The Obesity Epidemic and Litigation Against the Food Industry". In: *Arizona Law Review* Vol. 46, pp. 781–813.
Mitchell, Don (2003): *The Right to the City: Social Justice and the Fight for Public Space*. New York: Guildford Press.
Nielsen, Kai (1979): "Radical Egalitarian Justice: Justice as Equality". In: *Social Theory and Practice* 5, pp. 209–226.
Nozick, Robert (1974): *Anarchy, State and Utopia*. Oxford: Blackwell.
Nussbaum, Martha (2006): *Sex and Social Justice; Frontiers of Justice: Disability, Nationality, and Species Membership*. Cambridge, MA: Harvard University Press.
Rawls, John (1999a): *A Theory of Justice*. Revised edition. Cambridge, MA: Harvard University Press.
Rawls, John (1999b): *Collected Papers*. Cambridge: Harvard University Press.
Sandel, Michael J. (2007): *Justice: A Reader*. Oxford: Oxford University Press.
Sandel, Michael J. (2010): *Justice: What's the Right Thing to Do*. London: Penguin.
Sen, Amartya (2009): *The Idea of Justice*. Cambridge: Harvard University Press.
Steiner, Hillel (1994): *An Essay on Rights*. Oxford: Blackwell.
Swift, Adam (2003): *How Not to Be a Hypocrite: School Choice for the Morally Perplexed Parent*. London: Routledge.
Tocqueville, Alexis de (2010): *Democracy in America (Vols 1–4)*. A Bilingual French-English edition. Translated by James T. Schleifer. Indianapolis: Liberty Fund.
Van Parijs, Philippe (1998): *Real Freedom for All: What (if Anything) Can Justify Capitalism?* Oxford: Clarendon Press.
Van Parijs, Philippe (2011): *Just Democracy: The Rawls-Machiavelli Programme*. London: ECPR Press.
Welie, Jos V.M. (2006): *Justice in Oral Health Care: Ethical and Educational Perspectives*. Milwaukee: Marquette University Press.
Young, I. Marion (1990): *Justice and the Politics of Difference*. Princeton: Princeton University Press.

Part III: **The Problem of Consensus**

Alberto L. Siani
Rawls on Overlapping Disagreement and the Problem of Reconciliation[1]

Abstract: This paper claims that Rawls's idea of a political liberalism has a radical innovative potential for political philosophy that still needs to be fully appreciated. To this aim, the paper works between the poles of overlapping disagreement and reconciliation. Political liberalism relinquishes once and for all the idea that an adequate philosophical account of rationality is capable of establishing political consensus even among reasonable individuals. Accordingly, political agreement, if possible at all, has to be achieved on the basis of existing political ideas, whereby political liberalism delimits the domain of public reason, i.e., the space of the public discussion on the most reasonable political conception, which, according to Rawls, is "justice as fairness". Hence, the task of political liberalism and that of justice as fairness constitute the two complementary yet distinct aspects of a project of philosophical reconciliation, the limits of which this paper discusses in order to consolidate the thesis that overlapping disagreement can never be fully dissolved through philosophical means.

While it might seem that a perspective on justice beyond consensus (the main topic of the present volume) should also go beyond Rawls, I maintain that it is both possible and rewarding to read Rawls himself, and more specifically the political liberalism project, in terms that go beyond consensus. The crucial point of the "dissident" reading I propose in this article (section 1) is this: it is not really important whether or not we can come to rational agreement on Rawls's design of the original position, or even on his formulation of the principles of justice. Rather, the "dissident" reading asks whether political liberalism provides the right conceptual tools to inquire into the possibility, the critical and progressive character, and limits of a political agreement not conceived as the unanimous result of rational argumentations by reasonable citizens. While I do not enter into the debate over the two Rawlsian principles or on the original position, I claim that political liberalism has a radical innovative potential for

---

[1] I presented a first draft of this paper in a seminar at Istanbul Technical University in October 2015. I want to thank my audience for the many precious suggestions, and in particular Jan Kandiyali, Manuel Andreas Knoll, Giovanni Mion and Barry Stocker. My gratitude goes to Manuel Andreas Knoll and Stephen Snyder as well for their comprehensive reviews.

https://doi.org/10.1515/9783110537369-014

political philosophy that still needs to be fully appreciated. This potential lies in the non-philosophical conception of the elements of political agreement and disagreement, and in their philosophical articulation for political purposes. To the aim of a fuller appropriation of this potential, I work between the poles of overlapping disagreement and reconciliation.

To the notion of "overlapping consensus" (explicitly central in political liberalism), I juxtapose the idea of "overlapping disagreement", which, though not explicitly thematized as such, is arguably equally central to the project of political liberalism (section 2). By introducing this notion, my main intention is to rebut the reading of Rawls according to which he attempts an explanation of consensus on the principles of justice based on a philosophical theory of rationality yielding univocal and ahistorically valid results. Against this reading, I place Rawls's understanding of political consensus within his idea of the task of political philosophy and show that he employs a minimalistic and flexible version of consensus. Political liberalism relinquishes once and for all the idea that an adequate philosophical account of rationality is capable of establishing political consensus among reasonable individuals, let alone among unreasonable ones. On the contrary, political liberalism aims at showing that political agreement, if possible at all, has to be achieved on the basis of existing political ideas, which constitute the groundwork of the philosophical construction, but are not themselves philosophically deduced. In other terms, political liberalism delimits the space of the public discussion on the political conception (section 3). Within this space, the domain of public reason, Rawls then proposes "justice as fairness" as the most reasonable candidate for a political conception, whereas it is fundamental to stress that he never claims that justice as fairness is the univocal philosophical answer to the task delineated by political liberalism, nor, for that matter, that there is such a univocal philosophical answer. The task of political liberalism and that of justice as fairness are hence to be kept distinct (something Rawls himself is not always consistent in doing).

I then argue that both tasks constitute the two steps of a project of philosophical reconciliation, a project whose centrality emerges in the Rawlsian works especially after *Political Liberalism* (section 4). Finally, I discuss the limits of reconciliation through philosophy in order to consolidate the thesis that overlapping disagreement can never be fully dissolved through philosophical means, and that political liberalism, in virtue of its realistic yet not resigned understanding of the task of political philosophy, is a formidable contender within the debate on justice and pluralism (section 5).

1 Introduction: For a "dissident" reading of Rawls

In his 2003 review essay, Anthony Simon Laden identifies "two blueprints that guide much of the literature" on Rawls (Laden 2003, p. 370). The first one, which is the mainstream or standard one, includes the following features:

> (1) Rawls is engaged in a grand philosophical project; (2) in particular, he is developing a theory in the traditional sense of that word; (3) that theory is Hobbesian in that it starts from an account of human rationality; and (4) it aims to show the rationality of justice via its centerpiece, the argument from the original position in favor of the choice of the two principles of justice (Laden 2003, p. 371).

The second one, referred to as "alternative" or "dissident" (Laden 2003, p. 370), is summarized as follows:

> (1) Rawls's projects are focused and narrower than is generally thought; (2) he is engaged in philosophy as defense rather than philosophical theorizing; (3) his arguments are meant to serve as public justifications rather than as deductions from premises about human nature or rationality; and (4) the central idea and high point of his achievement is the idea of public reason and its accompanying picture of political deliberation, and the importance of the original position argument is that it is one possible route by which to justify principles of justice publicly (Laden 2003, p. 379).

The present article follows the second blueprint in claiming that the Rawlsian conception of consensus is not grounded in a philosophical account of human rationality, but is rather characterized by the acknowledgment of deep and permanent moral and political conflicts that cannot be solved by the philosophical appeal to a common rationality. In fact, the Rawlsian conception of rationality draws attention to the existence of irreconcilably opposed conceptions of the good, rather than to the possibility of a universal consensus. In political liberalism, rationality refers to the non-public level of individual or communitarian conceptions of the good. The public dimension is grounded in the "reasonable", which however is not a philosophical construct, but rather a political-cultural trait expressing the collective recognition of a restricted pool of shared ideas or values. As a matter of fact, the consensus on the principles of justice is established through the reference to a notion Rawls explicitly refuses to define and explain in a rigorous philosophical manner.[2] Within the framework of political

---

2 See Rawls 2005, p. 48. Rawls 1999b, p. 86, footnote 33, acknowledges that *Political Liberalism*

liberalism, this is an expedient or even necessary move. If Rawls offered a systematic, philosophically articulated definition of the "reasonable", he would have to face the objection of operating from within a comprehensive doctrine.[3]

Thus, at the very philosophical core of political liberalism we find two ideas whose radical implications possibly do not emerge from Rawls's detached style, but which nonetheless should not be underestimated: 1) rationality belongs to the private dimension and 2) reasonableness, while applying to the public realm, is not the product of a philosophical elaboration, but rather its historically and culturally given starting point. Rationality alone, under the condition of lasting free and democratic institutions, necessarily leads to deep and persisting disagreement, while reasonableness can be used as a basis to work out some measure of agreement, but it is not sufficient to establish consensus on any single political conception. In short, what we have in *Political Liberalism* "is really an attack on the traditional view of reason: an attack on the idea that reasonable people can all (or at least sufficient numbers of them) be brought to agree solely through the use of reason on the same philosophical doctrine" (Dreben 2003, p. 319).

2 Overlapping: Consensus or disagreement?

The work of political philosophy, starting with the acknowledgment of the existence of irreconcilable moral and political conflicts in society, aims at finding the answer to the central problem of political liberalism: "How is it possible for there to exist over time a just and stable society of free and equal citizens, who remain profoundly divided by reasonable religious, philosophical, and moral doctrines?" (Rawls 2005, p. 4). The work of political philosophy hence starts with the recognition of what I will refer to as "overlapping disagreement" as the result of the free use of reason and autonomy by citizens under free institutions, and thus as a permanent and ineliminable fact of democratic societies, and proceeds to look for a basis to narrow it so that the principles of justice can be freely accepted by citizens without impairment to their overlapping-disagreement-producing autonomy.

I insist that the kind of consensus put forward by Rawls is remarkably limited as to its scope, subject, context and philosophical presuppositions. The phil-

---

is misleading from this point of view since in many places it gives "the impression that the content of the reasonable and the rational is derived from the principles of practical reason", and at the same time takes some distance from a strictly Kantian interpretation of the two terms.
3 See Dreben 2003, p. 322.

osophical work on consensus is limited to a political construction aiming at establishing coherence among our existing fundamental political ideas in order to narrow our disagreement as to what principles should regulate the basic structure of society. Furthermore, this understanding of consensus does not claim to be universally valid, but it is limited to societies (and within societies, to doctrines) aiming at establishing and preserving a view of the associate living as a fair system of cooperation between free and equal citizens. Political liberalism has nothing to say to individuals or societies who do not accept these premises. Finally, consensus does not require agreement on any metaphysical (philosophical, religious, moral) doctrine or conception of the truth or the good. Political liberalism is definitely not a "grand philosophical project" in this sense.

It might be objected that, even if we accept this minimalistic reading of consensus, it is still true that both in *Political Liberalism* and in other writings we find substantial discussions of an undoubtedly central idea: that of "overlapping consensus". How is this compatible with the "overlapping disagreement" interpretation I suggest? I argue that the notion of overlapping consensus not only does not contradict my reading, but is an integral part of it. To elaborate, political philosophy only moves and only makes sense as a practically oriented enterprise taking place in the space between overlapping disagreement and overlapping consensus. To discuss this point, I refer to a significant passage in which Rawls clarifies depth, breadth and application of overlapping consensus. Overlapping consensus

> supposes agreement deep enough to reach such ideas as those of society as a fair system of cooperation and of citizens as reasonable and rational, and free and equal. As for its breadth, [overlapping consensus] covers the principles and values of a political conception (*in this case* those of justice as fairness) and it applies to the basic structure as a whole (Rawls 2005, p. 149, emphases by A.L.S.).[4]

To begin with, there needs to be a given common ground of agreement from which the justification process begins, and this common ground is constituted by the two "public and shared" ideas of society as a fair system of cooperation and of citizens as free and equal (in the following I will simply refer to them as "the two fundamental ideas").[5] This is the necessary groundwork for the con-

---

4 Rawls's terminology here and on pp. 164–168 is a bit confusing. On p. 149 he speaks of "specificity", but does not further define it, while he clarifies the "application", which seems however to be a part of the "breadth". For the sake of simplicity, I will only refer to the quoted passage, which clarifies depth, breadth, and application.
5 See also Rawls 2005, pp. 90 and 107–110. The two fundamental ideas also constitute the necessary complement to, or the groundwork of, the use of the principles of practical reason in po-

struction of any reasonable political conception: based on this, the consensus aimed for is as broad as, or covers the principles and values of, a political conception, and justice as fairness is a particular instance of political conception. Finally, the application is to the basic structure, or in other terms the required consensus applies to, and only to, the basic structure as a whole. Thus a bridge can be drawn between the two fundamental political ideas and a political conception of justice applying to the basic structure.

Now the point to be emphasized here is the asymmetry between depth, breadth and application. Depth and application respectively describe the starting and the arrival point of the overlapping consensus. We start with an agreement on the two fundamental ideas, and we want to go from there to the characterization of the basic structure. Both depth and application are thus fixed: there needs to be exactly that starting point, and we move exactly toward that destination. The breadth, on the other hand, describes the path between the starting and the arrival point, that is, it gives expression to the question asked in the conclusion of the passage: "Consistent with plausibly realistic assumptions, what is the deepest and widest feasible conception of political justice?" (Rawls 2005, p. 149). This undercuts the thesis of a direct correlation between the characterization of depth, breadth and application on the one hand and *one* particular political conception on the other hand.[6]

Rawls does not claim that, given the starting agreement on the two fundamental ideas and the aim of describing the principles applying to the basic structure, it necessarily follows that justice as fairness is *the* political conception on which all citizens need to reach an overlapping consensus.[7] More precisely, *Political Liberalism* does not make the case that, starting with its own premises, it is possible to philosophically establish that justice as fairness is the logical answer to the main question formulated in the passage just quoted.[8] The theory support-

---

litical constructivism. It is crucial to stress that within the latter the two fundamental ideas are not themselves constructed, but assumed as the starting point of the construction: this clearly imposes a contextualist limitation on the idea of political constructivism and sets it apart from Kantian moral constructivism. For a discussion of these points see my Siani 2016.

[6] Here I draw in part on the alternative view of overlapping consensus recently proposed by Quong 2011 and itself based on Laden's alternative blueprint.

[7] In this respect, Rawls's conception of consensus is plainly anti-perfectionist and anti-teleological, though there is some element of empirical and very cautious teleology in his thesis that stability of reasonable institutions over generations will gradually lead to the broadening of their own support basis (see Rawls 2005, pp. 163–164).

[8] Or in a straightforward formula: "Political liberalism, then, does not try to fix public reason once and for all in the form of one favored political conception of justice" (Rawls 1999b, p. 142).

ing political liberalism does not also claim to undergird justice as fairness, and vice versa.

The content of the breadth is not fixed: we know that we need a political conception, but its formulation is not among the tasks of political liberalism, but rather of a separate domain, namely the domain of public reason. *A Theory of Justice* and the related reformulations and restatements propose, within the domain of public reason, that that political conception should be presented in the terms of justice as fairness. Thus even the harshest critique of justice as fairness, of the original position and of the two principles of justice does not, by itself, affect the argument and the structure of political liberalism, and vice versa: one can endorse the framework provided by political liberalism while rejecting the choice of justice as fairness as the most adequate or most reasonable political conception, or one can agree with the principles and values of justice as fairness without committing to the political liberalism framework. The scope of *A Theory of Justice* and of its later restatements is the elaboration and defense of a particular political conception,[9] whereas *Political Liberalism* deals with the place, the role, the aim and the general limits of *any* philosophically elaborated political conception. To anticipate what I will argue in more detail in the fourth section, *Political Liberalism* is a metapolitical work, while *A Theory of Justice* is a work of moral and political philosophy in the strict sense, and together they constitute the two steps of a political philosophy whose central task is political reconciliation.

To sum up this point: the idea of overlapping consensus is not meant to provide an empirical or sociological confirmation of principles of justice that are elsewhere deduced philosophically, in which case it would be superfluous or unrealistic or even detrimental to the whole idea of political liberalism. Overlapping consensus represents the minimal, non-philosophical basis from which the justification process can start – that is, the basis on which we can claim that political consensus is possible despite the irreconcilable character of the opposition between comprehensive doctrines. Briefly, if there were no overlapping disagreement, no philosophical justification process would be needed, and if there were no overlapping consensus, no philosophical justification process would be possible. Only the coexistence of these two facts, which are both

---

9 Clearly this is true only from the point of view of *Political Liberalism*, as *A Theory of Justice* had not yet elaborated the notion of a political conception in political liberalism's terms.

"goods" of any truly democratic society, makes the whole work of political philosophy both necessary and possible.[10]

3 The space of public reason

One substantial implication is that the theory expounded in *Political Liberalism* is not self-sufficient. Its necessary counterpart is the public confrontation on the political contents, or, in Rawlsian terms, public reason. While political liberalism as a philosophical theory sets the limits of public reason, the contest between political conceptions and thus between different descriptions of the basic structure is ultimately settled not by political liberalism itself, but by public reason. The latter is, namely,

> in a democratic society [...] the reason of equal citizens who, as a collective body, exercise final political and coercive power over one another in enacting laws and in amending their constitution. [...] The limits imposed by public reason do not apply to all political questions but only to those involving what we may call 'constitutional essentials' and questions of basic justice (Rawls 2005, p. 214).

Thus, the very existence of public reason as an always ongoing but always inclusive contest between (reasonable) peers is an inescapable mark of democratic societies, as it embodies the idea that citizens are to rule themselves based on the principle of reciprocity, and in parallel it rejects the idea that politics has to be inspired by a necessarily exclusive struggle for the whole truth.[11]

It is important to stress that the idea of public reason is a component of political liberalism, and in this capacity a piece of philosophical elaboration whose limits are set by the latter. Nonetheless, the contents of public reason are not and

---

10 The basis of the justification process is not only minimal but also – as I will stress in the next section – continuously reinterpreted and reshaped. Severing the philosophical ties between the given political basis and *one* necessary outcome in terms of a political conception also implies that justification proceeds in a nonfoundationalist manner, and its task can never be concluded: "The idea of justification paired with full reflective equilibrium is nonfoundationalist in this way: no specified kind of considered judgment of political justice or particular level of generality is thought to carry the whole weight of public justification. [...] The most reasonable political conception for us is the one that best fits all our considered convictions on reflection and organizes them into a coherent view. At any given time, we cannot do better than that" (Rawls 2001, p. 31). The groundbreaking article (Selg 2012), following the "dissident" blueprint identified by Laden, stresses these points in order to claim a proximity between political liberalism and the radical democracy of Ernesto Laclau and Chantal Mouffe.
11 See Rawls 1999b, p. 132.

cannot be philosophically determined once and for all, not even in the freestanding form of a political conception. Rawls is very clear about this:

> It is crucial that public reason is not specified by any one political conception of justice, certainly not by justice as fairness alone. Rather, its content – the principles, ideals, and standards that may be appealed to – are those of a family of reasonable political conceptions of justice and this family changes over time. These political conceptions are not of course compatible and they may be revised as a result of their debates with one another. Social changes over generations also give rise to new groups with different political problems. Views raising new questions related to ethnicity, gender, and race are obvious examples, and the political conceptions that result from these views will debate the current conceptions. The content of public reason is not fixed, any more than it is defined by any one reasonable political conception (Rawls 2005, pp. l–li).[12]

So, what is the relationship between political liberalism and public reason? Political liberalism "is a kind of view. It has many forms, [which] have in common substantive principles of justice that are liberal and an idea of public reason. Content and idea may vary within these limits" (Rawls 2005, p. 226). In other terms, political liberalism sets the limits of the inquiry (the liberal principles of justice and the idea of public reason), but does not claim to present a philosophical argument to give a univocal answer to the inquiry itself. One can accept political liberalism while disagreeing with justice as fairness: "The view I have called "justice as fairness" is but one example of a liberal political conception; its specific content is not definitive of such a view" (Rawls 2005, p. 226). These passages very clearly demonstrate that political liberalism argues for the possibility of an overlapping consensus reaching as deep as the two fundamental ideas, covering the breadth of a political conception and applying to the basic structure, but not for the necessity that justice as fairness be exactly the focus of the overlapping consensus. Much to the contrary,

> it is inevitable and *often desirable* that citizens have different views as to the most appropriate political conception; for the public political culture is bound to contain different fundamental ideas that can be developed in different ways. An orderly contest between them over time is a reliable way to find which one, *if any*, is most reasonable (Rawls 2005, p. 227, emphases by A.L.S.).

---

[12] Notice the Wittgensteinian use of the term "family". Political liberalism does not specify a single conception of justice as the right one to be accepted by public reason, but rather establishes a "resemblance" criterion (namely, the criterion of reciprocity) allowing to "recognize" political conceptions belonging to the liberal family, all of them being possible candidates to "win" at any given time the public reason debate. See also the strikingly clear formulation in Rawls 1999b, pp. 140–141.

Political liberalism provides the indication of the necessary depth, breadth and application of the framework for this orderly contest, in which, at the level of public reason, justice as fairness is one of the contestants.[13] Once again, Rawls takes overlapping disagreement very seriously:[14] he maintains that no permanent overlapping consensus is to be expected even on his own favored political conception (justice as fairness). In other words, there is no way to philosophically settle once and for all the disagreement on the best (most reasonable) political conception to adopt for the basic structure, even if all citizens and parties are sincerely committed to the two fundamental ideas. Even more, there might be no single doctrine to define as the most reasonable! The contest is for the most reasonable political conception and it is simply not possible to offer a philosophical deduction of the reasonable from a rationality theory. It follows that the contest between different political conceptions cannot be settled once and for all through philosophical means, or in other terms, it cannot be equated with a contest between philosophical theories to be univocally decided with philosophical means (in this case we would have to refer to the winning theory as absolutely "true", not as more or most "reasonable"). Public reason is the space in which the philosophical work becomes practical, but it is at the same time the space in which the citizens' different views and interests inevitably clash. This clash is not philosophically eliminable, just as the very physical existence of citizens with opposed views and interests who are struggling for recognition cannot be eliminated in a democratic society.[15]

4 Political philosophy as reconciliation

One upshot of the previous step of my argument is that in political liberalism the domain of overlapping disagreement seems to be broader and better guarded than the domain of overlapping consensus. There needs to be agreement on the

---

[13] It is hence clear why public reason does not play a prominent role in *A Theory of Justice*: "The two books are asymmetrical, though both have an idea of public reason. In [*A Theory of Justice*], public reason is given by a comprehensive liberal doctrine, while in [*Political Liberalism*], public reason is a way of reasoning about political values shared by free and equal citizens that does not trespass on citizens' comprehensive doctrines so long as those doctrines are consistent with a democratic polity" (Rawls 1999b, pp. 179–180).
[14] See Dreben 2003, p. 321.
[15] See the illuminating remarks by Larmore 2003, pp. 390–391, which also touch upon the proximity between the idea of public reason in the later Rawls and the German Idealist tradition (and Hegel in particular), a theme that will be in the background of my next section.

two fundamental ideas (depth), on the necessity to work out *a* political conception (breadth) and to apply it to the basic structure (application). On pretty much everything else, preserving the possibility of disagreement seems to be not only inevitable, but even often desirable, including the disagreement over *which* political conception is the most reasonable one, and even over the question of *whether* there is such a thing.

This raises a number of questions. In particular, I want to focus on this: since political philosophy is no longer charged with the task of providing truth about moral and politics (which was its central task at least since Plato), what is its actual role? In line with my argument up to this point, I suggest that political philosophy has two major roles. On the one hand, it sets the framework, the presuppositions, the limits, and the aim of *any* theory dealing with the principles of justice (metapolitical task). On the other hand, it attempts to work out *the* theory best fit to provide the basis and criteria to deal with disagreements in our shared political understanding (practical task).[16] As argued, political liberalism is charged with the metapolitical task, while justice as fairness is, in Rawls's eyes, the most reasonable theory to deal with the practical task. Even though Rawls does not always pay close enough attention in distinguishing between the two tasks, they can be kept apart, insofar as the endorsement of the Rawlsian elaboration concerning one of them does not commit one to the endorsement of the other.

I now make a step further, and suggest that both tasks should be read as the philosophical components of a broader project, which can be characterized as a project of reconciliation through philosophy.[17] Compared to other concepts, reconciliation does not seem to be a central one for Rawls, if nothing else because he does not particularly care to define it with the same level of detail as other concepts, at least in his major works. However, as some scholars have recently pointed out, the notion of reconciliation occupies a prominent place both in Rawls's later works (e.g. in *The Law of Peoples* and in *Justice as Fairness: A Restatement*) and in the later formulation of his lectures on the history of moral

---

16 Both the former and the latter task are, to be sure, practical tasks. The latter could be referred to as "practical in the strict (or direct) sense", but for the sake of brevity I will only speak of "practical".
17 I may add that just a reading focusing on reconciliation might, if not reconcile, at least form a bridge between the traditional and the dissident reading of Rawls, insofar as it becomes clear that each of them tackles specific aspects of the Rawlsian project, which by itself often gives rise to (productive) misunderstandings.

philosophy.[18] In both cases, Rawls relates his own understanding of reconciliation to Hegel's one.[19]

The central tenet of the idea of reconciliation is that the general task of political philosophy is not to rationally deduce ahistorical moral and political contents and principles to be endorsed by all citizens, but rather to point out the reasons why free and equal citizens divided by reasonable comprehensive doctrines can reconcile with, criticize and amend the democratic political principles and institutions of their given, but constantly changing, social world. In other words, the idea of reconciliation focuses on why and how the coercive force of those principles and institutions can be legitimately exercised on citizens with irreconcilable comprehensive doctrines.

As conflict in political understanding in democratic societies is not only interpersonal but also intrapersonal,[20] so the idea of reconciliation applies not only to the question of conflict and consensus between citizens divided by reasonable comprehensive doctrines, but also to the (moral-psychological) question of citizens being torn between their comprehensive conceptions of the good and their allegiance to the political values of a democratic society.[21] The question of how political liberalism is possible can also be reformulated in these terms:

> How can the values of the special domain of the political – the values of a subdomain of all values – normally outweigh whatever values may conflict with them? Put another way, how can we affirm our comprehensive doctrine and yet hold that it would not be reasonable to use state power to gain everyone's allegiance to it? (Rawls 2005, p. 139).

It is clear that, as Rawls insists, this is not an epistemological or metaphysical problem, but a thoroughly practical (and very pressing) one in our world. The dramatic character of this reconciliation problem, its conflict-ladenness, is apparent even from Rawls's terminology, which for once abandons its emotionless tones:

> Throughout, I have been concerned with a torturing question in the contemporary world, namely: Can democracy and comprehensive doctrines, religious or nonreligious, be com-

---

18 Most notably Schaub 2009.
19 The later Rawlsian turn away from Kant and toward Hegel is another important piece of my overall reading that I cannot address here.
20 "We turn to political philosophy when our shared understandings, as Walzer might say, break down, and equally when we are torn within ourselves" (Rawls 2005, p. 44).
21 The issue of reconciliation also applies to the international level, where it takes a different form and is subject to different conditions. I cannot enter into the topic here (but see at least Rawls 1999a, pp. 124–128).

patible? And if so, how? At the moment a number of conflicts between religion and democracy raise this question. To answer it political liberalism makes the distinction between a self-standing political conception of justice and a comprehensive doctrine (Rawls 1999b, p. 175).

In order to address the Rawlsian turn to a reconciliation theory as an attempt to answer this "torturing question", I will focus on a passage from the first paragraph of *Justice as Fairness: a Restatement*, dealing with the four roles of political philosophy. The first two are 1) to attempt to uncover a basis of "philosophical and moral agreement", or at least to narrow "the divergence of philosophical and moral opinion at the root of divisive political differences" and 2) of orientation in the Kantian sense (Rawls 2001, pp. 1–3). The third is that of reconciliation and the fourth, of bringing forth a realistic utopia, "is a variation of the previous one" (Rawls 2001, pp. 3–4). Thus, in two of its four roles political philosophy aims at reconciliation.[22] Rawls presents reconciliation as follows:

> A third role, stressed by Hegel in his *Philosophy of Right* (1821), is that of reconciliation: political philosophy may try to calm our *frustration and rage* against our society and its history by showing us the way in which its institutions, when properly understood from a philosophical point of view, are rational, and developed over time as they did to attain their present, rational form (Rawls 2001, p. 3, emphasis by A.L.S.).

Vis-à-vis the frustration and rage ensuing from overlapping disagreement, political philosophy attempts to calm us and to reconcile us with the society we live in:

> I believe that a democratic society is not and cannot be a community, where by a community I mean a body of persons united in affirming the same comprehensive, or partially comprehensive, doctrine. The fact of reasonable pluralism which characterizes a society with free institutions makes this impossible. [...] But this fact is not always easy to accept, and political philosophy may try to reconcile us to it by showing us the reason and indeed the political good and benefits of it (Rawls 2001, pp. 3–4).[23]

Since there is irreconcilable disagreement in our comprehensive doctrines, we are forced to live according to coercive rules that do not depend on the moral values and conception of society we endorse and might therefore look unacceptable to us, thus leading to a feeling of lacking autonomy and freedom, and con-

---

[22] According to Schaub 2009, p. 13, footnote 6, the reconciliation role is the fundamental one, and the other three can be understood as different aspects of it.
[23] Interestingly, in the quoted passage the fact of reasonable pluralism is said to concern not only moral, but also aesthetic values.

sequently of frustration and rage. Rawls's insistence on this point clarifies once again how deep-going and inevitable overlapping disagreement is:

> We do not enter [the political society] voluntarily. Rather we simply find ourselves in a particular political society at a certain moment of historical time. We might think our presence in it, our being here, is not free. In what sense, then, can citizens of a democracy be free? Or as we shall ask eventually, what is the outer limit of our freedom [...]? (Rawls 2001, p. 4).

In confronting this question, political philosophy tries to offer an alternative perspective on how we can nonetheless feel free and autonomous, and thus be reconciled to our society and its history:

> One can try to deal with this question by viewing political society in a certain way, namely, as a fair system of cooperation over time from one generation to the next, where those engaged in cooperation are viewed as free and equal citizens and normal cooperating members of society over a complete life. We then try to formulate principles of political justice such that if the basic structure of society – the main political and social institutions and the way they fit together as one scheme of cooperation – satisfies those principles, then we can say without pretense and fakery that citizens are indeed free and equal (Rawls 2001, p. 4).

I maintain that the two sentences constituting this passage each tackle one step of the process of reconciliation. The first step is the metapolitical clarification of the proper domain of political philosophy once we agree on some minimal political values, i.e. the clarification of the basis of reconciliation (political liberalism's task). The second step is the practical formulation of a political conception that bridges the gap between the basis of reconciliation and the actual principles aiming at reconciliation (justice as fairness's task). Both here and in the lectures on the history of moral philosophy Rawls is adamant that reconciliation with our society does not mean reactionary acquiescence to the existent reality, and, in parallel, that the Hegelian concept of reconciliation can and must stand the test of Marx's critique (see Rawls 2001, p. 4, footnote 4).[24]

Here as in other Rawlsian passages it is important to stress the element of time as fundamental in countering the ideology critique and in clarifying the relationship between political liberalism and public reason. Public reason is not an ahistorical philosophical construct, but the living and changing social reality of free and equal citizens accepting to conduct the political practice within limits

---

[24] Thus, for Rawls, showing that we *can* be reconciled to our social world does not mean showing that we *should* be happy with our present society as it is, but only that justice might be inhabiting our social world even if at the present time it does not, and that we have a reason to strive to this aim through our actions: see also Rawls 2001, pp. 37–38.

that will enable them to continue being free and equal under mutating external circumstances and moral-political beliefs and under shifting power balances. If political philosophy takes the side of a single political conception to be enforced over time no matter what, then it becomes ideological in that it legitimizes the oppressive use of state power.[25] Of course it is not to exclude that the very limits set by political liberalism and the related acceptance of the necessary limits of public reason are put in question, or even violated in the adjustment of the political contents. But in that case the very framework of political liberalism provides a basis to evaluate the society in which we live as no longer democratic and liberal. This brings me to the last point I want to touch upon, namely the issue of the limits of reconciliation.

5 The limits of reconciliation

Rawls directly deals with the limits of reconciliation in the conclusion of his discussion of public reason:

> There are limits, however, to reconciliation by public reason. Three main kinds of conflicts set citizens at odds: those deriving from irreconcilable comprehensive doctrines; those deriving from differences in status, class position, or occupation, or from differences in ethnicity, gender, or race; and finally, those deriving from the burdens of judgment (Rawls 1999b, p. 177).

The distinction between the first two kinds of conflicts clarifies also the distinction of roles between political liberalism and justice as fairness:

> Political liberalism concerns primarily the first kind of conflict. It holds that even though our comprehensive doctrines are irreconcilable and cannot be compromised, nevertheless citizens who affirm reasonable doctrines may share reasons of another kind, namely, public reasons given in terms of political conceptions of justice. [...] Political liberalism does not explicitly consider [...] conflicts [of the second kind] but leaves them to be considered by justice as fairness, or by some other reasonable conception of political justice (Rawls 1999b, p. 177).

The genuine field of concern for political liberalism is the first kind of conflicts: how to reconcile citizens holding irreconcilable (yet reasonable) comprehensive

---

[25] This is the counterpart to the fact of reasonable pluralism, namely "the fact of oppression", meaning "that a continuing shared understanding on one comprehensive religious, philosophical, or moral doctrine can be maintained only by the oppressive use of state power" (Rawls 2005, p. 37).

doctrines with themselves, with each other and with the society they live in. This is the "metapolitical" task of delimiting the space of reconciliation between citizens whose beliefs and ways of life are irreconcilable. This space, as we saw, is where different political conceptions compete with each other, or the space of public reason. Conflicts of fundamental interests, on the other hand, are left to be considered by "justice as fairness, or by some other reasonable conception of political justice". This is the "practical" task of attempting to provide the most suitable (that is, the most reasonable) political conception (which can be justice as fairness or any other conception), a task which is explicitly disentangled from the first one, and on which, more in general, political liberalism does not raise claims.

As for the third kind of conflicts, they fall under the "jurisdiction" of neither political liberalism nor justice as fairness: "Finally, conflicts arising from the burdens of judgment always exist and limit the extent of possible agreement" (Rawls 1999b, p. 177). Conflicts of this kind cannot be overcome, and accepting this as well as the ensuing limitation on "the extent of possible agreement" is an integral part of reasonableness.[26] This very idea, together with the ideas of public reason and democracy itself, will be rejected by "fundamentalist religious doctrines and autocratic and dictatorial rulers" who cannot tolerate moral and political disagreement. However, the existence of such unreasonable doctrines or beliefs, something normal in any society, does not constitute a philosophical problem: "We simply say that such a doctrine is politically unreasonable. Within political liberalism nothing more need be said" (Rawls 1999b, p. 178). Besides, unreasonable doctrines do not, with their existence, contradict the idea of public reason, they only show that there are limits to its actual operation. We can still be reconciled with our social world, even in the face of the presence of doctrines which completely reject the very basis of reconciliation (see Rawls 1999b, p. 179).

To conclude, I will recapitulate the most salient points of my argument, which at the same time constitute serious reasons why it would be unwise to dismiss political liberalism as yet another out-dated rationalistic political theory, and why, on the contrary, it is fruitful to continue dealing with it as a highly productive and stimulating reflection on justice and pluralism. In the transition from *A Theory of Justice* to *Political Liberalism*, the task of philosophy is shifted to showing that the elements of reconciliation are already there, and, since they are political elements, they do not need to be philosophically produced, but rather made explicit together with their consequences through a procedure of construction. This is the central meaning of Rawls's later turn to Hegel's understand-

---

26 See Rawls 2005, pp. 54–58.

ing of (political) philosophy as reconciliation. Political philosophy does not result in the creation of an ahistorical conception of justice on which all components of society are then called to agree in virtue of their shared rationality, but rather in showing us that we can, to some extent, be reconciled to our society, since in the latter our strongest political values are at least in part already embodied and expressed and we find that it is possible to work at deepening this embodiment. Since political values and institutions are not fixed, but develop over time, so does the nature of conflict concerning them. Political philosophy is called to adapt to these changes, and to attempt to bridge the gap between what is already shared and what is not yet shared, or, from the reverse perspective, between overlapping disagreement and overlapping consensus.

The space between overlapping disagreement and overlapping consensus can be interpreted as the space of a possible, but always limited reconciliation, a reconciliation which is one of the primary tasks, or possibly the primary task, of political philosophy. In extending and guarding this space, political philosophy shapes what Rawls fittingly calls a realistic utopia. The reconciliation task of political philosophy has two aspects: the metapolitical one, carried out by political liberalism, and the practical one, carried out by justice as fairness. Each of these two aspects is charged with dealing with a kind of conflict arising in a democratic pluralistic society. Political liberalism handles conflicts arising from citizens' irreconcilable comprehensive doctrines, while justice as fairness handles conflicts between citizens' fundamental interests. In the first case, the reconciliation is with the very society we live in, with its history, and in particular with the fact of reasonable pluralism. In the second case, the reconciliation is, broadly, between the two central values of liberty and equality,[27] and more particularly, on what is a fair distribution principle (with the difference principle being one of the possible candidates).[28] Last but not least there are conflicts that simply cannot be dealt with by philosophy, namely those deriving from our burdens of judgment. Here reconciliation has its limits, as this kind of overlapping disagreement cannot be bridged. These limits bring us back to the groundwork of the justification process, namely the two fundamental ideas, as the endurance of the democratic character of society depends on their rootedness and their capacity to resist their "other", namely the unreasonable, possibly in a constructive peaceful way (through education, moral suasion, etc.) or, if needed, through forcible containment. But whether a given democratic society

---

27 See Rawls 2005, pp. 4 ff.
28 See Rawls 2001, p. 76.

at a given moment of time can preserve itself is ultimately a matter of its moral and political strength, not a philosophical one.

Bibliography

Dreben, Burton (2003): "On Rawls and Political Liberalism". In: Freeman, Samuel (Ed.): *The Cambridge Companion to Rawls*. Cambridge: Cambridge University Press, pp. 316–346.

Laden, Anthony Simon (2003): "The House that Jack Built: Thirty Years of Reading Rawls". In: *Ethics* 113, pp. 367–390.

Larmore, Charles (2003): "Public Reason". In: Freeman, Samuel (Ed.): *The Cambridge Companion to Rawls*. Cambridge: Cambridge University Press, pp. 368–393.

Quong, Jonathan (2011): "The Role of an Overlapping Consensus". In: Quong, Jonathan: *Liberalism without Perfection*. Oxford: Oxford University Press, pp. 161–191.

Rawls, John (1999a): *The Law of Peoples*, with *The Idea of Public Reason Revisited*. Cambridge, MA: Harvard University Press.

Rawls, John (1999b): *The Idea of Public Reason Revisited*. In: Rawls 1999a.

Rawls, John (2001): *Justice as Fairness: A Restatement*. Cambridge, MA: Belknap Press.

Rawls, John (2005): *Political Liberalism*. Expanded edition. New York: Columbia University Press.

Schaub, Jörg (2009): *Gerechtigkeit als Versöhnung. John Rawls' politischer Liberalismus*, Frankfurt a.M., New York: Campus.

Selg, Peeter (2012): "Justice and Liberal Strategy: Towards a Radical Democratic Reading of Rawls". In: *Social Theory and Practice* 38, pp. 83–114.

Siani, Alberto L. (2016): "Political Constructivism". In: Babür, Saffet (Ed.): *Method in Philosophy/Felsefede Yöntem*. Istanbul: Yeditepe University Press, pp. 85–108.

Chong-Ming Lim
Public Reason, Compromise within Consensus, and Legitimacy

Abstract: A central idea of public reason liberalism is that the exercise of political power is legitimate when supported only by reasons which all citizens accept. Public reason serves as a necessary standard for evaluating the legitimacy of political decisions. In this paper, I examine the directive to employ public reason from the citizens' perspective. I suggest that employing public reason potentially involves them engaging in different types of compromise. I consider how acknowledging these compromises sheds light on public reason liberalism. Public reason may not offer a necessary standard for evaluating the legitimacy of decisions, and the evaluation it offers may not have great weight relative to other moral and political considerations.

Introduction

How should we organise our political institutions, and thus common life with others, given pervasive and deep disagreements about the nature of the truth, the good, and justice? As a common story goes: since John Rawls, there has been a renewed and deeper recognition of how citizens' cooperative relationships (through these institutions) with each other profoundly shape their life prospects, in terms of what they can expect to be and how well they can hope to do (Rawls 1999a, pp. 6–7). Citizens, however, disagree about how these relationships are specified and organised – partly due to their different comprehensive views. Comprehensive views cover most, if not all, aspects of human life. Some of these views are religious in nature; others are not. Crucially, they contain ideals "of what is of value in human life", including human beings' relationships with their families, associates, environment, and their place in the universe writ large (Rawls 2005, p. 13). They inform people's political values and conceptions, which come into conflict in a pluralistic world. Yet collective decisions have to be made. The challenge is to create a common life together in a way that respects these disagreements without the unacceptable use of state power by some over others.

Consider the following, broad-stroke presentation of public reason liberalism, which is sometimes regarded as one of the "standard" responses to these disagreements. It requires that political decisions (or cooperative relations more generally) are supported by reasons which are acceptable to all citizens from the perspectives of their plural comprehensive views (Rawls 1997, p. 766). Their disagreements are to be negotiated by restricting themselves to using only such public reasons.[1] The considerations from their comprehensive views are to be bracketed – set aside, and not to be invoked.

Rawls describes the source of public reasons as the "shared fundamental ideas implicit in the public political culture" (Rawls 2005, p. 100). This culture comprises their existing political institutions, how they have been understood, and even historical texts and documents that are common knowledge (Rawls 2005, pp. 13–14). The content of public reason is filled in by a family of liberal political conceptions of justice. These conceptions are liberal in that they affirm certain key features of liberalism. They specify certain basic rights, liberties and opportunities, accord them a special priority relative to other values, and include measures ensuring that citizens have adequate means to intelligently and effective make use of them (Rawls 1999a, pp. 581–582; 2005, p. 223). They are political in that they apply only to a society's basic social and political institutions, are independent of any particular comprehensive view, and must draw from ideas implicit in the public political culture (1999a, p. 584). These political conceptions – along with the public reasons they contain – are (to be) embedded in each citizen's comprehensive views (2005, p. 387). This occurs when citizens find deeper non-public considerations within their own views to support and justify a political conception of justice and its reasons. Such affirmation is moral. It is not supported by pragmatic reasons of self- or group-interests, and does not hinge on the mere balance of forces or political power (Rawls 1999a, p. 573; 1999b, pp. 426–432). When all citizens manage to fit any one member of a family of liberal political conceptions of justice into their comprehensive views, an overlapping consensus is constituted (2005, p. 388).

According to public reason liberalism, political decisions are legitimate when supported only by public reasons. When decisions are supported by non-public considerations – which are *not regarded as reasons from plural comprehensive views* – they violate the requirement of public reason, and are illegit-

---

[1] This is one of two dominant interpretations of Rawls' political liberalism, known as the consensus model of public reason. Its main competitor is the convergence model, according to which public reason requires only that the decisions or relations themselves are acceptable to all citizens, without any accompanying restrictions on what reasons citizens regard as supporting them. For further discussions, see (D'Agostino 1996; Vallier 2011, pp. 262–264; Lister 2011). In this paper, I focus on the consensus account of public reason. I leave open the questions of whether and how my discussions apply to the convergence account, and also about their implications for the choice between the two accounts.

imate. Understood this way, public reason may be taken as a necessary standard for evaluating the legitimacy of political decisions (Enoch 2015, p. 115).[2]

Public reason liberalism is set against the background of the disagreements between reasonable citizens in a well-ordered society. Reasonable citizens are described as "not moved by the general good as such but desire for its own sake a social world in which they, as free and equal, can cooperate with others on terms all can accept" (Rawls 2005, p. 50). Further, they accept the "burdens of judgement" which are the "hazards involved in the correct (and conscientious) exercise of our powers of reason and judgment in the ordinary course of political life" (2005, pp. 55 – 56). When citizens accept the burdens of judgement, they accept that people may – because of the free exercise of reason – reasonably come to different and conflicting answers about what is true and good. They do not regard such reasonable pluralism as an "unfortunate condition of human life" (2005, p. 37). This lends motivation for pursuing public reason as a way of organising their common lives together – since doing so is a way of ensuring that the decisions reached are acceptable to all. Of course, these citizens have comprehensive views which may conflict with the values underlying, and within, public reason. However, for these citizens, the political values which justify the employment of public reason are "very great values and not easily overridden" (Rawls 2005, p. 139), relative to the considerations within their comprehensive views. Because of this, they may put aside the considerations from their comprehensive views, for those of public reason.

This stands in stark contrast with what we know about actual citizens. Actual citizens have a whole range of comprehensive views – not just those narrowly described as reasonable. A formulation of public reason which allows it to serve its function, would be one which allows its conclusions to be relevant, and contribute, to adjudicating these actual citizens' disagreements. Suppose it were otherwise – that public reason applies only to disagreements between ideally-described "reasonable citizens". In such a case, the conclusions of public reason may well be regarded as irrelevant to how actual citizens regard and negotiate their disagreements. Additionally, when the considerations within their comprehensive views conflict with those of public reason, actual citizens neither

---

2 Here, I understand public reason as an expression of the principle of legitimacy, concerning the exercise of political power (Rawls 1997, p. 767; 2005, p. 217; Peter 2007). I set aside Rawls' second understanding of public reason, as an ideal regulating how public officials and citizens should speak deliberate in public fora (Rawls 1997, pp. 767, 798; 2005, p. 215).

necessarily nor automatically judge that the latter conclusively outweigh the former.³

Many justifications have been given for employing public reason. Perhaps testament to the reality of pluralism, various answers have been given. For example, Joshua Cohen argues that employing public reason is justified by the value of democratic inclusion (Cohen 2011); James Boettcher and Charles Larmore argue that it is justified by that of respect (Boettcher 2007; Larmore 1999); Jonathan Quong argues that it is justified by the value of justice (Quong 2014); Andrew Lister argues that it is justified by civic friendship (Lister 2013), Chad Van Schoelandt, by "moral community" (Van Schoelandt 2015), and so on. These public reason philosophers disagree with each other about which value actually justifies the employment of public reason. Less attention, however, has been given to *how citizens regard* employing public reason as a way of addressing their disagreements, from the perspective of their comprehensive views.

I undertake this examination in this paper – specifically, of the directive to employ public reason, from the perspectives of citizens' comprehensive views. I suggest that they have to engage in several potential compromises in employing public reason. I consider how acknowledging these compromises sheds light on the status of the standard of legitimacy offered by public reason liberalism. Specifically, public reason may not be a necessary standard for evaluating the legitimacy of political decisions, and moreover, its evaluation may not have great weight relative to other moral and political considerations.

---

3 The situation is not easily ameliorated by positing the above conception of reasonable citizens as an *ideal* for actual citizens. Here and again, the relevant question is: for whom? In posing the question, we see that the ideal will again be subject to disagreements stemming from individuals' plural views. Positing the conception as an ideal does not make it immediately shared or shareable by individuals with plural views. Additionally, recall that public reason is invoked to adjudicate the problem of disagreements stemming from citizens' comprehensive views. It presents a way through which people who disagree morally may nevertheless find ways of living together. It may be a surprising turn of events if what is needed to solve the problem turns on moral education – of emulating a specifically-described ideal citizen for whom employing public reason is the accepted conflict-resolution strategy. Moreover, if some form of moral education is the answer, why may we not simply begin with it in our attempt to adjudicate disagreements? Why should we go along with public reason philosophers, down a circuitous route, only to reach what seems to be a similar conclusion?

1 Public reason and compromise

Recall that citizens have different comprehensive views about the truth and good, and disagree with each other because of these views. From their perspectives, the ideal situation would be one in which their comprehensive view determines (or significantly influences) the political decisions that are made. How would they judge the political values that have been given as justifications for employing public reason?[4]

A note before proceeding. My discussion of the employment of public reason is not held at a very general level. Instead, I am concerned with specific issues or political decisions. That is, I take it that citizens deliberate, on each issue, about whether to adjudicate their disagreements by employing public reason, by other means, or even by refusing to have a decision. Their commitment to employing public reason for a specific issue does (and need) not carry over to other issues. This level of specificity also allows us to be clearer about the stakes involved, at each point, in asking citizens to employ public reason.

First, citizens may not judge any (or all) of the political values as *actually* justifying the employment of public reason in a particular case. The acceptability of reasons as it features in the lives of individuals is intimately tied to their comprehensive views. Since there is a plurality of such views, there will be different

---

[4] Here, I am side-stepping some complications. In modern democracies, and certainly in Rawls' well-ordered society, political decisions are made by politicians (in their role as legislators) or public officials more generally, rather than directly by citizens. As with others within the debates within public reason, I take it that such public officials accurately and unproblematically represent the views of their constituencies – that is, the views of citizens. This picture makes a number of simplifying assumptions. First, that any constituency to be represented is homogenous in terms of their comprehensive views, such that no further input is required on behalf of those who represent them, and which may subsequently be a source of disagreement. Second, that the public officials do not have comprehensive views in tension, or outright conflict, with those of their constituencies. Third, that public officials do not have any other aims beyond representation – importantly, not even common-good or other perfectionist aims, when their constituencies do not regard them as important. In sum, representation is not a simple relationship. Jane Mansbridge (2003) provides a detailed account of the different forms of representation of citizens (and their claims and interests) in modern democracies. These are constituted by different relationships between citizens' claims and interests, and those of the officials who represent them. This means, also, that there are complications with asking citizens to ideally model the deliberations of legislators (Rawls 2005, pp. 444–445).

While I think that public reason liberalism should acknowledge these complications, and explain how the weight of the available justifications for employing public reason may change in view of them, doing so is beyond the scope of this paper.

judgements about whether any value actually justifies the employment of public reason. A value which has been offered as a justification for employing public reason may be accepted by one individual, but rejected by another. We may not have to go far to find evidence for this. As we have seen above, public reason philosophers disagree among themselves about which of the values actually justifies employing public reason.

Second, and supposing that all citizens judge that a particular value actually justifies public reason in a particular case, there is still the question of the weight of that value relative to the considerations from within their comprehensive views. Very likely, the latter are accorded greater weight. This is because they are regarded as expressing the "full light of reason and truth" (Raz 1990, p. 31), in contrast to the more contained scope of the political values. More generally, citizens with different views will judge the weight of any given value differently. Some may regard the candidate values as sufficiently weighty, and conclusively in favour of employing public reason, whereas others may judge the same values to be trivial.

Given this, we may say that any value offered as a justification for employing public reason is at best only *pro tanto* in nature. In effect, it is a consideration in favour of employing public reason, but is not necessarily conclusive. The claim that such values are *pro tanto* in nature, is arrived at by taking citizens' plural comprehensive views seriously. Different views will give rise to different evaluations of whether any value actually *pro tanto* justifies employing public reason, and their weight relative to other considerations (within the views). These considerations may also be regarded as either *pro tanto* justifying (or rejecting) the employment of public reason. Citizens employ public reason when they judge that the available *pro tanto* justifications for doing so are undefeated by the considerations from their comprehensive views.

Importantly, the force of *pro tanto* justifications persists even after their defeat by other considerations. They stand in contrast to *prima facie* justifications. When a *prima facie* justification is defeated, the supporting consideration either no longer applies, or loses its justificatory force, or both. However, when a *pro tanto* justification is defeated, its consideration still applies (despite being defeated) and retains its force.[5] Framing the values and considerations this way shows that *even when* citizens judge that the political values conclusively justify employing public reason, the considerations within their comprehensive views still have force – and vice versa. That they remain in force, contributes to citi-

---

5 Andrew Reisner (2013) provides a detailed discussion of the distinction, as applied to 'oughts'.

zens' thoughts that the employment of public reason is less than ideal – they cannot or do not (entirely) fulfil the demands of their comprehensive views.

Because of this, we may say that citizens engage in a kind of compromise when they employ public reason. Here, their compromise consists in their refraining from appealing to the considerations in their comprehensive views, to determine how the political decision at hand is to be settled (Lister 2007, p. 16). I adopt a basic conception of compromise.[6] A compromise occurs when individuals settle for choices that they regard as less-than-ideal. A compromise may be made with other people, or it may not. Because this is a minimal conception of compromise, it allows more room for a wider range of phenomena to be understood as compromise. In the rest of this section, I briefly enumerate several more compromises that citizens may engage in, when employing public reason.

Another potential compromise when citizens employ public reason lies in their recognition of each other as people with whom they can converse and cooperate, and to whom justification is to be given. They cease seeing each other as people over whom they must thoroughly triumph, or over whom their comprehensive views may be implemented without acceptance. For them to even enter (constructive) conversation requires them to set aside their beliefs that their opponents are fundamentally misguided and *thus* need not (or do not deserve to) be conversed with. This kind of compromise should not be downplayed. In many conflicts, the disputants are unwilling to make this crucial move (Margalit 2010, p. 42). Yet these views do not disappear. From each's perspective, entering into conversation involves a compromise – they do something which is less-than-ideal, and moreover deviates from their firmly-held beliefs. This explains why these decisions are often accompanied by accusations of "selling-out" on one's beliefs, made by those who refuse to bracket their beliefs and who are not motivated to begin conversation. A clarification: the disputants need not supplement their recognition of each other as being owed justification, with the further thought that they are moral equals – though doing so is probably helpful for establishing fruitful conversation and stable cooperation. Their recognition of each other as being owed justification, even if purely in pragmatic terms, is sufficient for us to characterise it as involving a compromise.

Yet another compromise may consist in citizen's refraining from appealing to their comprehensive views in their discussions about the weight of the various public reasons. One aspect of comprehensive views is that they cover "all recognized values and virtues within one rather precisely articulated system" (Rawls

---

[6] See (Fumurescu 2013) for a political and philosophical survey of the idea of compromise, and the discussions surrounding it.

2005, p. 13). Within different systems, the available public reasons are accorded different weight. Citizens compromise when they refrain from relying on their views' ranking or prioritisation of reasons in their discussions. Even if one judges that a certain reason should outweigh another, the supporting considerations they invoke cannot be taken simply from their comprehensive views without consideration of their acceptability to others. Consider one interpretation of the *Imago Dei* doctrine, according to which human freedom trumps all other considerations in virtue of it being that which reflects human beings' special relationship with God. A believer may hence regard all limits on human freedom with great suspicion, if not reject them outright. Yet she cannot publicly invoke the *Imago Dei* doctrine to support her prioritisation of human freedom, if it is not also acceptable to others.

Citizens may also compromise on how a particular issue is framed. Some disagreements, for example, seem to reduce to discrete, yes or no, questions. For example, in the disputes about abortion, "the most crucial point of contention is a discrete question: either a woman has the right to abort a pregnancy in her first trimester simply because she does not wish to carry it to term, or she does not" (May 2005, p. 347). Here, the compromise may consist in how the issue is framed. For example, rather than have the decision be about women's absolute right to abortion, it can be framed as one concerning the *circumstances* in which women have the right to abortion, or what circumstances in which women are *legally permitted* to abort.[7] Changing the framing of the disagreement will involve a compromise because both parties are likely to regard it as far from ideal or even fundamentally misguided. At its roots, altering the framing of a disagreement is a form of attending to its content. Both parties are likely to think that the new framing does not accurately reflect what the issue *is truly about*. For those who believe that women have the right to abort a pregnancy, this is regarded as erroneously introducing qualifications to something which they regard as being absolute. For their opponents, this may involve a sell-out on their belief that human life in any form is sacred. But whereas the issue of possessing an absolute right admits of little or no compromise, altering how the disagreement is framed – no matter how reluctantly – opens up space to locate a middle ground and overcomes decisional paralysis.[8]

---

[7] Avishai Margalit suggests that there is a radical element to reframing contentious issues: when he argues that Jews and Muslims may reframe their disagreements concerning the *sovereignty* of Temple Mount in Jerusalem to one concerning its *use* (2010, p. 50).

[8] I am not endorsing a compromise of this sort. My point is only that even seemingly intractable disagreements may admit of some compromise of this sort.

Throughout these potential compromises, the parties involved do not forsake the view that their comprehensive views are correct, and offer the ideal response to the issue in concern. Their compromises do not commit them to the falsity or triviality of their views. Nor do they adopt a new position on how things should ideally be done. If they did, there would not be a compromise – they would have just changed their minds (Weinstock 2013, p. 540). Rather, they set aside the considerations within their comprehensive views, seeking terms of cooperation acceptable to all. From each's perspective, concessions are made which constitute their cooperation.

This sampling of different potential compromises, while brief, shows how compromises may well be involved in the employment of public reason, from citizens' perspectives, informed by their comprehensive views.[9] This aspect of citizens' relationships with each other appears to be largely unaccounted for by public reason liberalism (or Rawlsian accounts of political liberalism more generally). This has prompted political theorists to seriously contemplate moving beyond them (Wendt 2013, 2016).

---

[9] An unexpected payoff of rendering citizens' employment of public reasons as involving compromise, is in identifying a new kind of compromise in addition to the "integrative" and "substitutive" compromises commonly cited in the discussions concerning the general categorisation of different kinds of compromise. Integrative compromises are those in which the eventual decision contains elements of the initially conflicting positions. This may be done via drawing from and balancing elements of their different views which both sides deem most crucial to their interests. Substitutive compromises replace the conflicting positions with a different position regarded as less-than-ideal for both parties, but nevertheless acceptable (Weinstock 2013, pp. 539–540). The compromise involved in settling on public reasons does not involve the parties directly settling on, or being committed to, intermediate positions. Instead, the analyses here about public reason reveal the possibility of compromising by settling on the reasons which enter as appropriate for formulating their future collective decisions and cooperation. This kind of compromise allows for the possibility that the eventual decision may be either integrative or substitutive, or both, depending on the issue. In our context, this foregrounds the relative priority or fundamental nature of the common reasons which the parties are committed to for future decisions. This allows us, when intermediate decisions are rejected, to have a clearer picture of the source of disagreement – as lying in reasons deemed unacceptable to serve as the bases of cooperation. There may yet be additional kinds of compromise, as we look closer at real cases. This claim learns from the insight that "different types of conflict will generate different sorts of compromise" (Bellamy/Hollis 1999, p. 65).

2 Compromise and legitimacy

Recall that public reason is intended to be a necessary standard for evaluating the legitimacy of political decisions. Decisions are legitimate when they are supported only by public reasons. Citizens are asked to aim at decisions that are legitimate in this sense, and avoid those which are not. As we have seen, employing public reason may involve citizens' engaging in several compromises. These potential compromises occur at two broad stages – when entering into cooperation (as when they refrain from employing considerations from their comprehensive views, and use only public reasons), and during the course of specifying the terms of cooperation (as when they refrain from using their comprehensive views' prioritisation of reasons, and when they frame the issue in a way different from what their views require). The acknowledgement of the potential compromises that citizens have to engage in, when employing public reason, has implications for how we understand public reason liberalism's idea of political legitimacy. Specifically, we see that public reason may not offer a necessary standard for evaluating the legitimacy of decisions, and moreover that its evaluation may not have great weight relative to other moral and political considerations.

Consider, first, citizens' entering into cooperation. As discussed earlier, citizens employ public reason to adjudicate their disagreements when they judge that the available justifications for doing so defeat the considerations within their comprehensive views. Such judgements, however, should be understood as being made against the background of their willingness to cooperate to reach a common political decision in a particular case. That is, in other cases, they may think that no political decision is needed, desirable, or even possible. For instance, they may regard it as unnecessary for decisions regulating the internal dynamics of private organisations such as businesses or religious institutions, that it is undesirable to have decisions regulating family dynamics such as how spouses and their children relate to each other, or that it is impossible to have decisions about how disputed territories are shared. The issue is left open concerning the extent and shape of their cooperation. We need not posit that the issues for which they are willing to cooperate takes the exact form of the basic institutions of society. Their cooperation may concern only a few issues, and thus constitute a minimally shared life. Or it may be thick, comprising many cooperative decisions constituting a richly shared life. In these situations, it is unnecessary to employ public reason. Citizens do not regard there as being any common political decision which needs to be made – and much less one that has to be supported by reasons acceptable to all. In effect, they leave that issue open and unregulated by a common decision.[10]

I leave open what considerations undergird their willingness to cooperate in any particular case. What is important is simply that they are willing to do so. In this case, the pressure to provide a further explanation for their willingness may not yield fruitful answers. If we are to respect the different, and often mixed, reasons that people have for cooperation, this general claim may be as specific as we can get. Moreover, providing such an explanation runs the risk of speaking about their motivations presumptively – which may not sit well with our wanting to take the pluralism in their views seriously.

Our discussions of the compromises that citizens have to engage in, when employing public reason, highlights the stakes that are involved in their doing so. From their perspectives, employing public reason is not always easy. Frequently, it may be very difficult for them to side-line and refrain from using the considerations from their comprehensive views, just to reach a common political decision using public reason. The proffered justifications for employing public reason may sometimes not be weighty enough for them, to (decide to) employ public reason. They may judge it more important to appeal to and employ the considerations from their comprehensive views. This, however, does not mean that they give up on pursuing cooperation through a common political decision. That the justifications for employing public reason are insufficiently weighty, simply means that citizens will not adjudicate their disagreements through public reason. They may yet reach decisions by other means.

One way they may reach such decisions is by appealing to considerations within their comprehensive views, but they may also compromise by incorporating and accommodating such considerations within the political decision itself. For instance, in discussing the United States of America's Tax Reform Act of 1986, Amy Gutmann and Dennis Thompson observe that

> All supporters of the [Tax Reform Act] gained something they desired, but all also made concessions that flew in the face of their most principled reasons for supporting comprehensive tax reform in the first place. Democrats wanted to end loopholes for special interests and the wealthy, but they also agreed to radically lower the top tax rate (from 50 percent to 28 percent). Republicans wanted to lower marginal tax rates, but they also agreed to eliminate $30 billion annually in tax deductions, which resulted in the wealthy contribu-

---

10 When decisions are not made in modern societies, there is often a status quo – of a pre-existing decision – to fall back upon. This, however, is not always true. My formulation, being more general, accommodates citizens' potential unwillingness to reach common political decisions for novel cases not covered by pre-existing decisions.

ting a higher percentage of income-tax revenues than they previously had done (Gutmann/Thompson 2010, p. 1126).

In this case, the disputants compromise by allowing the final decision to contain clauses that they do not regard as being supported by reasons from their perspectives. This means that there are (different) portions of the decision that are not supported by shared reasons. Here, we may say that they are compromising on the content of the decision directly. They do not employ public reason, but nevertheless reach a decision. We may see them as motivated by a willingness to reach a decision, because they think that "tax reform was long overdue" (Gutmann/Thompson 2010, p. 1126), and that they would rather have marginal improvements on some fronts (while conceding on others), than no decision at all. More generally, and for other cases, disputants may judge that a lack of, or prolonged delay in reaching, decisions is costly – as it may unduly prolong an undesirable status quo, or lead to unpalatable long-term consequences.[11]

Are such decisions illegitimate? According to public reason, they are. This is because they are not supported *only* by considerations which all parties involved regard as reasons. This means that there are points at which some may regard themselves as being unacceptably – without reason – subject to state power.

However, these decisions may still be legitimate in a different, more minimal sense. That is, they are legitimate insofar as citizens accept a decision for whatever reason – even if (part of) the decision is supported by considerations they do not regard as reasons. The parties' acceptance of the decision is, in such cases, stripped of the strong endorsement which public reason liberalism requires. Specifically, the parties need not integrate the considerations supporting the decision into their comprehensive views. This way, decisions may be regarded as legitimate despite their sustained disagreements with (portions of) them.

This more minimal sense of legitimacy helps us to better understand some kinds of fundamental disagreements fuelled by comprehensive views. Consider the example of the Quakers. Rawls describes them as endorsing the principles (including the accompanying organisation and incorporation of public reasons) of the political conceptions of justice which shape the society's institutions and laws through political decisions. However, they nevertheless have fundamental disagreements – informed by their comprehensive views – with existing institutions, policies, or enacted legislation. In expressing their disagreement, they engage in what Rawls describes as "witnessing" (Rawls 1999a, pp. 594–595, foot-

---

[11] As is the case of the delay in introducing legislation, in many countries, aimed at curbing carbon emissions to slow down, and mitigate the effects of, climate change, among others.

note 57). Rawls does not say very much about what is exactly involved, except to note that it does not involve civil disobedience or conscientious refusal. Presumably, it involves engaging other citizens through established channels of communication and debate, or voting against existing institutions and legislation.

The question arises as to why the Quakers would endorse, in the first place, a political conception and all its constituent reasons, some of which are opposed to what they stand for. On Rawls' account, such endorsement has to be fit into their comprehensive views. Yet in this case, they regard there to be some unacceptable reasons, which cannot be fit into their views. For them, the mere fact that they are born into a society where these reasons and conceptions are operative for others, may not count towards, and may be no guarantee of, the kind of endorsement Rawls requires. How do we square their purported endorsement, and their commitment to their comprehensive views, without positing a deep inconsistency in their beliefs, or split in their personalities?[12]

Understanding decisions as legitimate in this sense, helps us to better understand this situation. Such citizens can regard these decisions as legitimate, merely because the decisions are acceptable in light of their willingness to cooperate with others. They do not need to endorse all the content of the decisions, or the considerations supporting them. Thus, they do not commit themselves to any deep inconsistency in accepting political decisions as legitimate, the contents of which they disagree. Moreover, they would not, in "witnessing" their disagreement, be open to accusations of inconsistency arising from their simultaneous affirmation of the very considerations which lead to decisions with which they disagree. They are also freed from the charge of hypocrisy, in their recognition that the existing institutions may be required, in a deep way, to support their survival and flourishing.[13] Importantly, they are not committed to any future decisions on the basis of allegiance (which they may lack) to any particular consid-

---

[12] Here, it is inadequate to point to the fact that for most people, their views may not be regarded as fully comprehensive. There is sufficient slippage, such that a given political conception may "cohere loosely" with the commitments of their incompletely comprehensive views. Consequently, "many if not most citizens come to affirm their common political conception without seeing any particular connection, one way or the other, between it and their other views" (Rawls 1999b, p. 441). While this may be accurate, what it does is to solve the problem here by appealing to citizens' hastiness or ignorance. Moreover, we may rightly be less optimistic than Rawls, when he writes that citizens "might very well adjust or revise these [comprehensive] doctrines rather than reject the political conception" (Rawls 1999b, p. 441) after coming to notice the deep tensions upon careful reflections about their commitments. And most importantly, it leaves unanswered the issue of parties who disagree in light of their fully comprehensive views and thoroughly thought-out commitments.

[13] Many thanks to Stephen Snyder for urging me to clarify this.

erations which support those (portions of) decisions with which they disagree. This leaves room for them to advance different conceptions for future issues.

If this more minimal sense of legitimacy is genuine, then public reason may not be a necessary standard for evaluating the legitimacy of political decisions. That is, citizens may judge decisions to be legitimate even if they violate the standard set by public reason liberalism. This is not all – a further worry arises when we think about the potential compromises that citizens make over the course of specifying the terms of their cooperation.

Recall that citizens also compromise by refraining from using their comprehensive views' ranking or prioritisation of values or reasons in their deliberations. That is, a political decision may be settled, which relies on according great weight to a particular value that does not have very much weight in some citizens' comprehensive views. For instance, a particular decision – say, concerning a country's membership in a particular union – may be primarily supported by the consideration of political community or sovereignty, understood in a specific sense. Many citizens may agree that political community or sovereignty understood in that sense are valuable, but reject that it has sufficient weight to determine the decision in the way that they did. That is, they may judge *both* that the considerations employed have little weight in relation to other public reasons, as well as to considerations within their comprehensive views. They may think that the considerations of economic prosperity, of protecting the vulnerable, of even regional community, each (or all) outweigh the considerations currently supporting the decision. In such a case, what is achieved by telling these dissenting citizens that the decision is legitimate because it is supported by considerations that they (all) regard as reasons? It does little to rehabilitate their view that the decision is wrong – because it relies too heavily on trivial values, and too little on important ones.[14]

That is to say, the evaluation that a particular decision is legitimate, may, in some cases, count for very little. If the reasons supporting a particular decision are regarded as trivial, the evaluation may not count for much. To illustrate further, suppose that all parties involved in a decision regard the consideration of 'being presented using beautiful prose' as indeed a reason for any political de-

---

14 Rawls appears to acknowledge this, when he writes that while citizens may disagree about which particular conception of justice (or its accompanying public reasons) is most reasonable, "they will agree that all are reasonable, even if barely so" (Rawls 1999a, p. 578). My point here is that their judgements that a particular political conception of justice (or its accompanying public reasons) are barely reasonable or acceptable, may count for very little. And echoing an earlier point, we must not assume that the citizens involved will automatically or easily accord the available public reasons great weight within their views.

cision. Suppose further that this consideration is primarily (or even solely) relied upon, to deliver a particular political decision. This decision, on public reason terms, would be legitimate. Now, unless we can show that the consideration is accorded great weight by all citizens from the perspectives of their comprehensive views, it will be of little consolation to them that this decision is in fact legitimate in this way. Their judgements that the decision is wrong, and their rejection of it, are unlikely to be rehabilitated by the evaluation of that decision as legitimate. This worry is even starker when we consider compromises concerning how decisions are framed – which are often regarded as even more profound than those about the weight of the available reasons.

Put together, we see that public reason may not be a necessary standard for evaluating the legitimacy of political decisions. Decisions may be legitimate even though they fail to meet the requirement of public reason to be supported only by reasons acceptable to all. Additionally, the evaluation of political decisions as legitimate on public reason terms, may, in some cases, count for very little from the perspectives of some citizens – who disagree with how the decisions rely on the available reasons, or how the decision is framed. Public reason offers us but one way, among many others, of evaluating political decisions (Enoch 2015, pp. 138–139).

3 Concluding thoughts

In this paper, I have considered the directive to employ public reason from the perspectives of citizens with plural comprehensive views. I observed that in employing public reason, they may engage in several types of compromises. The compromises occur at two broad stages – when entering into cooperation (as when they refrain from employing considerations from their comprehensive view, and use only public reasons), and compromises during the course of specifying the terms of cooperation (as when they refrain from using their comprehensive views' prioritisation of reasons, and when they frame the issue in a way different from what their views require). I then considered how acknowledging these compromises sheds light on public reason liberalism. Public reason may not offer a necessary standard for evaluating the legitimacy of decisions, and its evaluation of decisions may not have great weight relative to other moral and political considerations.

What can public reason philosophers do, in response to this gloomy discussion? It is open for them to argue that the legitimacy offered by public reason liberalism is the appropriate standard to aim for, in any given specific case. That is, they may argue that the fact (or possibility) that the decision in concern is legitimate in the way public reason requires, is *more important* than the plural values and considerations that citizens may bring to the table – including those that move them to cooperate on different terms, or forsake cooperation altogether. If so, citizens should neither settle for a more minimal sense of legitimacy, nor regard as trivial the evaluation that the decision is illegitimate on public reason terms. However, and depending on the issue for which a decision is required, such a position may not be easily taken. In disputes such as same-sex marriage, sex education, climate change, or animal rights, among others, it is not clear that it is more important to have decisions which are supported by reasons which all citizens can accept, than any of the other available non-public considerations. In such cases, we might think that imposing state power in a way that may be regarded as unacceptable by some, may be an evil we are willing to incur in order to do what is right. Public reason liberalism has to say more if it is to convince us otherwise.

Bibliography

Bellamy, Richard/Hollis, Martin (1999): "Consensus, Neutrality and Compromise". In: Bellamy, Richard/Hollis, Martin (Eds.): *Pluralism and Liberal Neutrality*. Portland: Frank Cass.

Boettcher, James W. (2007): "Respect, Recognition, and Public Reason". In: *Social Theory and Practice* 33. No. 2, pp. 223–249.

Cohen, Joshua (2011): "Establishment, Exclusion, and Democracy's Public Reason". In: Wallace, R. Jay/Kumar, Rahul/Freeman, Samuel (Eds.): *Reasons and Recognition: Essays on the Philosophy of T.M. Scanlon*. Oxford: Oxford University Press, pp. 256–275.

D'Agostino, Fred (1996): *Free Public Reason: Making It Up As We Go*. New York: Oxford University Press.

Enoch, David (2015): "Against Public Reason". In Sobel, David/Vallentyne, Peter/Wall, Steven (Eds.): *Oxford Studies in Political Philosophy*. Vol. 1. Oxford: Oxford University Press, pp. 112–142.

Fumurescu, Alin (2013): *Compromise: A Political and Philosophical History*. New York: Cambridge University Press.

Gutmann, Amy/Thompson, Dennis (2010): "The Mindsets of Political Compromise". In: *Perspectives on Politics* 8. No. 4, pp. 1125–1143.

Larmore, Charles (1999): "The Moral Basis of Political Liberalism". In: *The Journal of Philosophy* 96. No. 12, pp. 599–625.

Lister, Andrew (2007): "Public Reason and Moral Compromise". In: *Canadian Journal of Philosophy* 37. No. 1, pp. 1–34.

Lister, Andrew (2011): "Public Justification of What? Coercion vs Decision as Competing Frames for the Basic Principle of Justificatory Liberalism". In: *Public Affairs Quarterly* 25. No. 4, pp. 349–367.

Lister, Andrew (2013): *Public Reason and Political Community*. London: Bloomsbury Academic.

Mansbridge, Jane (2003): "Rethinking Representation". In: *American Political Science Review* 97. No. 4, pp. 515–528.
Margalit, Avishai (2010): *On Compromise and Rotten Compromises*. New Jersey: Princeton University Press.
May, Simon (2005): "Principled Compromise and the Abortion Controversy". In: *Philosophy & Public Affairs* 33. No. 4, pp. 317–348.
Peter, Fabienne (2007): "Rawls' Idea of Public Reason and Democratic Legitimacy". In: *Politics and Ethics Review* 3. No. 1, pp. 129–143.
Quong, Jonathan (2014). "On the Idea of Public Reason". In: Mandle, Jon/Reidy, David (Eds.): *A Companion to Rawls*. First edition. Oxford: Blackwell, pp. 265–280.
Rawls, John (1997): *A Theory of Justice*. Revised edition. Cambridge: Belknap Press.
Rawls, John (1999a): "The Idea of Public Reason Revisited". In: Rawls, John: *Collected Papers*. Samuel Freeman (Ed.). Cambridge: Harvard University Press, pp. 573–615.
Rawls, John (1999b): "The Idea of an Overlapping Consensus". In: Rawls, John: *Collected Papers*. Samuel Freeman (Ed.). Cambridge: Harvard University Press, pp. 421–448.
Rawls, John (2005): *Political Liberalism*. Expanded edition. New York: Columbia University Press.
Raz, Joseph (1990): "Facing Diversity: The Case of Epistemic Abstinence". In: *Philosophy and Public Affairs* 19. No. 1, pp. 3–46.
Reisner, Andrew E (2013): "*Prima Facie* and *Pro Tanto* Oughts". In: LaFollette, Hugh (Ed.): *The International Encyclopedia of Ethics*. Chichester: Blackwell, pp. 4082–4086.
Vallier, Kevin (2011): "Convergence and Consensus in Public Reason". In: *Public Affairs Quarterly* 25. No. 4, pp. 261–279.
Van Schoelandt, Chad (2015): "Justification, Coercion, and the Place of Public Reason". In: *Philosophical Studies* 172, pp. 1031–1050.
Weinstock, Daniel (2013): "On the Possibility of Principled Moral Compromise". In: *Critical Review of International Social and Political Philosophy* 16. No. 4, pp. 537–556.
Wendt, Fabian (2013): "Introduction: Compromising on Justice". In: *Critical Review of International Social and Political Philosophy* 16. No. 4, pp. 475–480.
Wendt, Fabian (2016): *Compromise, Peace, and Public Justification*. London: Palgrave Macmillan.

Ulrike Spohn
From Consensus to Modus Vivendi? Pluralistic Approaches to the Challenge of Moral Diversity and Conflict

Abstract: This essay considers two critiques of Rawls' overlapping consensus that move beyond the Kantian paradigm, investigating instead solutions to problems of value pluralism in terms of a modus vivendi. Specifically, it examines the models of Charles Taylor and John Gray, presented respectively as dialogical and agonistic variants of modus vivendi. It is argued that Taylor, though accepting a form of overlapping consensus, is nonetheless critical of Rawls' claim that it is justified through a freestanding and independent notion of political liberalism. For Taylor, there is no neutral conception of justification beyond the overlapping consensus itself. Gray also rejects Rawls' notion of a freestanding justification for overlapping consensus, seeing in it the privileging of a single comprehensive view. However, he also rejects Taylor's dialogical account which results in a consensus on something like liberal values. While Gray cannot accept Taylor's optimistic notion that humans want to understand each other, it is argued that Gray's "neo-Hobbesian" account of modus vivendi is likely inadequate to explain the notions of civic virtue which are an essential part of democracies today.

Introduction

One of the most pressing issues for Western countries today concerns the question of how to deal with the growing religious, cultural and moral diversity of their populace. In the face of increasingly different and partly conflicting visions of the good life and corresponding social practices, questions of justice arise as various groups struggle to defend their religious and/or cultural rights. In mainland Western Europe, the general situation is characterized by a field of tension, competition and changing coalitions between three major (but internally heterogeneous) groups: adherents to Christianity, areligious or even antireligious secularists and a substantial number of people of Muslim belief and an immigrant background. The struggles among these groups reflect a profound diversity of existential understandings of world and man, each with different implications for the shaping of society. In recent decades, this has become recognizable in conflicts over moral issues ranging from bio-political topics, such as abortion, assisted suicide, or male circumcision, to questions concerning diet, clothing or gender segregation in public spaces inside or even outside the doors of state-run institutions. These issues stir controversy over the basic values of the polity or their proper interpretation because they touch on core aspects of the political community's collective identity. This means that moral issues are often also public political issues, and moral disagreements are often tantamount to political conflict.

While much of the literature in normative political theory dealing with moral diversity and corresponding questions of justice draws on a liberal, Kantian paradigm – Rawls is the towering figure here – this essay discusses the approaches of two political philosophers who can be located in a *pluralistic* paradigm: Charles Taylor and John Gray. Taylor and Gray are concerned not only with how to deal adequately with the challenge of diversity in the political realm but also seek to elucidate on a deeper philosophical level *the causes* of the factual diversity of moral-political standpoints. While Taylor and Gray invoke the same concept to *explain* the existence of moral-political diversity and conflict – namely value pluralism – they reach different conclusions with regard to how it should be *dealt with*. This essay gives an account of Taylor's and Gray's preferred models of tackling moral-political diversity and conflict: "overlapping consensus" and "modus vivendi", respectively. I point out commonalities and differences in their models and elaborate on value pluralism as the shared philosophical foundation of their divergent trajectories of political thought. As the term "overlapping consensus" has been coined by Rawls, one might get the impression that Taylor advocates some variant of a liberal, Rawlsian theory of consensus. Against this view, this essay argues that Taylor's and Gray's models should both be understood as variants of a pluralistic modus vivendi approach that is generally critical of Rawlsian notions of consensus. Their models are presented as a *dialogical* (Taylor) and an *agonistic* (Gray) variant of modus vivendi. The conclusion takes a critical look at both models. By placing them in juxtaposition, their respective weaknesses are pointed out, which is meant as a starting point for further developing both models.

Charles Taylor: Overlapping consensus *as* modus vivendi

The phenomenon of a diversity of worldviews and conceptions of the good life, or rather, the question of how to deal with this phenomenon in the political realm, can be said to be the original problem of liberalism as a paradigm in political theory. In an influential contemporary variant, the problem is stated like this: "How is it possible that there may exist over time a stable and just society of free and equal citizens profoundly divided by reasonable religious, philosophical, and moral doctrines?" (Rawls 2005, p. xxv). In his later writings, John Rawls has developed a new concept, the "overlapping consensus", which is supposed to reconcile the "fact of reasonable pluralism" (Rawls 2005, p. xvii) with the (assumed) need of a general consensus on a "political conception of justice" (Rawls 2005, p. 11). The political conception of justice, often just called "political conception" in Rawlsian terminology, is meant to provide a generally binding moral basis for society that is believed to be acceptable to everyone. In the first place, a political conception specifies "certain basic rights, liberties, and opportunities" and "assigns a special priority to these [...] especially with respect to claims of the general good and of perfectionist values" (Rawls 2005, p. 223). Rawls takes the political conception to be the source of public reason, which means that its contents provide individuals with moral-political arguments that are believed to be generally acceptable. Rawls thinks that the values enshrined in a political conception "give a reasonable public answer to all, or nearly all, questions involving [...] basic questions of justice" (Rawls 2005, p. 225). There can be (small) variations in these answers in so far as Rawls grants that there is not only his own conception, "justice as fairness", but "a family of reasonable political conceptions" (Rawls 2005, p. 450). But he takes all such conceptions to be "broadly liberal in character" (Rawls 2005, p. 223) and allows only for a minimum of variation.

Rawls deems the liberal conception to be "freestanding", which means that it is comprehensible and acceptable in and of itself, without reference to any "comprehensive doctrine" that formulates a distinct worldview and conception of the good life (cf. Rawls 2005, pp. 10f., 12f.). He thinks, though, that the political conception does not stand in opposition to such doctrines but fits into a wide range of them like a "module", at least as long as they are "reasonable" (cf. Rawls 2005, p. 12). This is what creates an "overlapping consensus". The main idea of this concept is that the political conception can be affirmed from the different standpoints of a broad range of comprehensive conceptions of the good life, "religious, philosophical, and moral" (Rawls 1997, p. 766): "In such a consensus, the reasonable doctrines endorse the political conception, each from its own point of view" (cf. Rawls 2005, p. 134).

Charles Taylor gives Rawls credit for this novel way of conceiving the notion of consensus and puts it at the center of his own reflections about dealing with diversity. He expounds the workings of the overlapping consensus as follows:

> A Kantian will justify the rights to life and freedom by pointing to the dignity of rational agency; a Utilitarian will speak of the necessity to treat beings who can experience joy

and suffering in such a way as to maximize the first and minimize the second. A Christian will speak of humans as made in the image of God. They concur on the principles, but differ on the deeper reasons for holding to this ethic (Taylor 2011a, p. 311).

Or instead of that typically Jewish or Christian perspective, a Buddhist may draw strong reasons to uphold rights of this kind from a certain reading of the ethical demand of non-violence (Taylor 1998, p. 49).

There is, however, a crucial difference between Taylor and Rawls with regard to the role the overlapping consensus plays in their political thought. As explained above, Rawls wants to see the political conception as a "freestanding" conception of justice that is comprehensible and acceptable in and of itself and to which the overlapping consensus just lends further stability: "[T]o see how a well-ordered society can be unified and stable, we introduce [...] the idea of an overlapping consensus of reasonable comprehensive doctrines" (Rawls 2005, p. 134). Rawls asks "that we must distinguish between how a political conception is presented and its being part of, or as derivable within, a comprehensive doctrine" (Rawls 2005, p. 12). He stresses that "a distinguishing feature of a political conception is that it is presented as freestanding and expounded apart from, or without reference to, any such wider background" (Rawls 2005, p. 12). This means that, for Rawls, the affirmation of the political conception from the different standpoints of diverse comprehensive doctrines in the form of an overlapping consensus is intended to enhance the *stability* of the polity but is not substantially required for the *justification* of the political conception as the polity's moral basis.[1] Taylor makes clear that he sees great potential in the concept of the overlapping consensus as a mode of dealing with diversity but at the same time has "some difficulties with its detailed working out in Rawls' theory" (Taylor 1998, p. 37). Taylor rejects the notion of a "freestanding" conception of justice because he views it as a successor of the (in his view erroneous) Enlightenment idea of an "independent political ethic". This idea was based on the belief that certain universal norms could be derived from the study of supposedly perennial features of the human condition, leaving aside all religious, cultural and other particular features in the search for an independent moral basis for living together justified by "neutral" or "generally acceptable" reasons (cf. Taylor 1998, pp. 33 f.). Taylor's criticism is that Rawls clings to the idea that the political conception can have a "neutral" justification independent from any comprehensive doctrine and thus acceptable to all. Rawls tries to arrive at this justification by means of a thought experiment: the "original position" (see in more detail: Rawls 2005, pp. 304 ff.). Taylor thinks that this is not a

---

[1] This aspect is stressed by Gutmann (2012, pp. 297 f.).

"neutral" method but rather a particular "doctrine of political constructivism" (Taylor 1998, p. 51), which means that the political conception is not really "freestanding" but in fact rooted in a specific comprehensive doctrine that is given priority over all others by Rawls. Against this, Taylor argues that

> [t]he whole point of the overlapping consensus – better put, its superiority as a basis for society over the old post-Enlightenment independent ethic – was just that it doesn't prescribe any underlying justification. These are left to the different families whose members make up the society (Taylor 1998, p. 51f.).

According to Taylor, there is no way of justifying the political conception completely independent or apart from all comprehensive conceptions of the good life. There is no "neutral" justification *beyond* the overlapping consensus.

This has important implications for the practice of politics, because as soon as the unity of the justification is eclipsed, the range of possible interpretations of the political conception widens considerably. For instance, to take up again Taylor's example, it can make a significant difference whether one affirms the freedom, equality and dignity of persons and the derived right to life from a secular Kantian standpoint or from a Christian standpoint. When it comes to designing political regulations for moral issues such as abortion or assisted suicide, the different comprehensive backgrounds of reasoning and justification might yield different preferred policy options that stand in conflict with each other:

> [A] political ethic doesn't interpret itself, any more than a charter of rights does. As it extends to further cases, it will be interpreted in the light of the entire background of justification from which it springs. When there are several such backgrounds, the interpretations are going to diverge, often seriously. We already see this with our abortion debates in some Western societies, where generally accepted 'right to life' is given a very different meaning by people with a different basic understanding of human agency, and its place in the universe, or in God's plan. In a society conceived as an overlapping consensus, this kind of dissensus will ineluctably become more common (Taylor 1998, pp. 49f.).

Even though Taylor resorts to the language of (overlapping) consensus, it must be acknowledged that in his thinking, the notion of consensus only applies to an overall unifying framework of broadly liberal values in a very wide, general sense that remains largely unspecified. On the level of concrete moral-political questions, the relevant parameters Taylor refers to are disagreement, conflict and compromise (as against consensus):

> [I]n the political arena, we have to operate on the assumption that disagreement will continue, that there will be no agreement on the authoritative canon for adjudication. And this means that we will have to live with compromises between two or more such views. That is,

this will have to be understood as not an abnormal, scandalous, and hopefully temporary shift, but as the normal state of affairs for the indefinite future (Taylor 1998, p. 51).

With the rejection of the notion of "independent" justification, the resulting weak or thin notion of consensus, and the emphasis on the inevitability of perpetual moral-political disagreement which yields a need for building compromises, Taylor's political theory significantly differs from the Rawlsian framework. In fact, these features make Taylor's approach a candidate for classification as an instance of modus vivendi theory. It is true that Taylor at one point affirms that "Rawls rightly distinguishes the overlapping consensus from a mere 'modus vivendi'" (Taylor 1998, p. 51; cf. also Rawls 2005, p. 147), but both Taylor and Rawls think of modus vivendi as a (temporary) arrangement which settles a conflict of interest between parties who are basically ready to impose their will upon the others but (momentarily) just lack the power to do so (cf. Taylor 1998, p. 51; Rawls 2005, p. 147). One need not reduce the concept of modus vivendi to a matter of calculation of pure interest in this way, though. Alternatively, it can be conceived as an arrangement that is grounded in the mixed motives of the parties involved, which "includes, contra Rawls, whatever moral values and ethical commitments the parties bring to the conflict that can be constructively utilized in the forging of a workable settlement" (Horton 2009, p. 7). In addition, it can be understood as "carr[ying] with it the sense that the arrangements are to some extent accepted as legitimate by the various parties to it, even if that acceptance is, as it often will be, to varying degrees reluctant, grudging and qualified" (Horton 2010, p. 443). Forging workable settlements of this kind seems to be what Taylor means by saying that "we will have to live with compromises" (see above). Thus, instead of accepting Rawls's opposition of overlapping consensus and modus vivendi, we can read Taylor's approach as a model of overlapping consensus *as* modus vivendi.

John Gray: Modus vivendi beyond consensus

While Taylor presents his position as a modification or further development of Rawls's theory of overlapping consensus, John Gray places himself openly in opposition to Rawls and criticizes the notion of consensus straightforwardly. In his 2000 book, *Two Faces of Liberalism*, Gray explicitly distances himself from Rawlsian liberalism, rejecting it as a way of prescribing one particular form of life for society as a whole. Against this, he promotes a version of (pluralistic) liberalism that is intended to enable the peaceful coexistence of different and possibly conflicting forms of life in the same society (cf. Gray 2000, p. 2). The main point of criticism Gray levels against Rawls is the same as Taylor's: it concerns Rawls's claim that his conception of justice is independent of and neutral against any conception of the good life. Gray, like Taylor, rejects the notion of a "freestanding" conception of justice and emphasizes the inevitable rootedness of all conceptions of rights and justice in particular conceptions of the good: "in all theories of rights and justice, differing views of rights spring from different views of the good" (Gray 2000, p. 17). Gray and Taylor both oppose the idea of a neat separability between "the right" and "the good" that Rawls and other proponents of political liberalism maintain.

Gray's theory of modus vivendi is meant as a counterpart to any liberal consensus ideals that focus on some set of "freestanding" norms. In Gray's view, the justification of the moral basis of Western liberal society, with its emphasis on individual freedom and equality, flows from the particular conception of the good life the West has come to embrace in the course of history (cf. Willems 2012, pp. 284, 286). As we have seen, Taylor does not believe in the concept of independent justification either. But in contrast to Gray, he tends to regard the liberal values of Western society as potentially universal, provided that they are left open to various "comprehensive" groundings and interpretations. Gray rejects Taylor's hope for a worldwide overlapping consensus on liberal values that shall arise from a dialogical encounter of different traditions.[2] Gray does not preclude the possibility that hermeneutic dialogue can eventually yield a contingent consensus or shared perspective among parties with different "comprehensive" commitments. What he opposes, however, is a teleological expectation that the emerging consensus will be about *liberal* values: "A hermeneutic method may well lead to a more universal moral perspective, but there is no reason why it must be liberal in content. [...] It is only where the hermeneutic method has been rigged to deliver liberal values that it can be relied upon to do so" (Gray 2006, p. 331).

It was explained above that Taylor expects that in a diverse and pluralistic society, perpetual disagreement and conflict will be the normal state of affairs and that thus the readiness to compromise will have to be an important civic virtue. This testifies to a somewhat agonistic view on morality and politics. This agonistic side of Taylor's thinking is balanced by a reconciliatory, harmonistic side, however. His reasoning proceeds on the assumption that in principle, there is a chance in any given moral-political conflict that different positions might be reconciled, and he implies that this is what conflicting parties should always aspire to:

---

2 See Taylor's essay "Conditions of an Unforced Consensus on Human Rights" (Taylor 2011b).

> We can be virtually certain that [...] there will always be some conflict and bad feeling between different groups of human beings [...]. But that doesn't mean that the opposition is fated in any given case, either between goods or between groups. It always makes sense to work toward a condition in which two cherished goods can be combined, or at least traded off at a higher level, just as it does to work for peace between any pair of combatants (Taylor 2001, p. 117 f.).

This points to a second level of (overlapping) consensus in Taylor's thinking. It seems that besides a general commitment to liberal values broadly understood, it is even more important to Taylor that there be an overlapping consensus on *the manner of approaching difference*. This second-order consensus revolves around a "civic philosophy of openness to fellow citizens" (Gagnon 2014, p. 115). This civic philosophy or civic ethos proceeds on the assumption that the different comprehensive conceptions of the good life can "experience a form of sharing in complementarity with other ontological views", and it suggests that this complementarity "provides a way not only to escape the narrow-mindedness of our own views, but also to be enriched by the views of others and to form a unity with them, while respecting differences" (Gagnon 2014, p. 115). While Taylor views an overlapping consensus on such a civic philosophy of openness as a precondition for pluralism to flourish and unfold, others argue that it in fact curtails pluralism because it is built on one particular conception of the good itself.[3] This idea will be expounded in some more detail in the next section (see below: "Taylor and Gray – Shared Foundations, Diverging Pathways").

Gray stays true to his general rejection of consensus and his commitment to "deep" pluralism in that he declines any aspiration to build a shared civic ethos that could bind all parties together in unity on some higher level. The only consensual element in his political theory is a commitment of all parties to peaceful coexistence, but even this is not meant as a moral imperative which "must" be embraced by all, as will be further explained below. Gray defends an approach that starts from a fundamental initial acceptance of an (assumed) reality of deep, irreconcilable differences between human conceptions of the good. In differentiation to Taylor's model of dealing with moral-political conflict – the "overlapping consensus *as* modus vivendi" –, Gray's model can be described as "modus vivendi beyond consensus" because it really does away with consensus as a meaningful category in the process of handling disagreements in the realm of morality and politics. It is aimed at "forging a workable settlement", as Horton says (see above), in situations where different conceptions of the good life just

---

[3] For this line of argument see Curtis (2007). See also Jones (2006, p. 196).

clash. Accordingly, Gray himself describes his approach as a "neo-Hobbesian philosophy of modus vivendi" (Gray 2000, p. 139).

Up to this point, two pluralistic approaches to dealing with moral-political conflict have been presented as alternatives to liberal, Rawlsian theories of consensus: Taylor's "overlapping consensus *as* modus vivendi" and Gray's "modus vivendi beyond consensus". Both these modes start from a rejection of the idea of a neat separability of "the right" and "the good" and concomitant notions of independent justification. But it has also become clear that there are significant differences between the Taylorian and the Grayian variants of modus vivendi. In order to better understand the commonalities and differences between Taylor's and Gray's models, the following section explores the wider philosophical background of their political thought.

Taylor and Gray – Shared foundations, diverging pathways

In their effort to understand and explain the existence of moral-political diversity and conflict, Taylor and Gray refer to the same philosophical concept: value pluralism. Both thinkers are influenced by Isaiah Berlin who conceives disagreement and conflict in the realm of morality and politics as the expression of an ontological reality of a plurality of partly incommensurable and incompatible human values (cf. Berlin 1991 as cited in Curtis 2007, p. 89).[4] The incompatibility of values implies that the combination of such values within the same individual life or moral tradition is (in terms of consistence or coherence) impossible. Incommensurability means that there is no higher measure available to compare the values at stake with each other for the sake of establishing a hierarchy among them (cf. Curtis 2007, p. 89; Willems 2012, p. 273f.; Cherniss/Hardy 2010, section 4.1; Pavel 2007, p. 201; Gray 2000, pp. 35f.; Horton 2006, p. 158). From the viewpoint of value pluralism, moral-political conflict, that is, conflict between competing conceptions of the good and concomitant ways of life, must be understood in terms of conflict between the incommensurable and incompatible human values enshrined and realized in these conceptions and life forms (cf. Willems 2012, pp. 273, 276). An example given by Gray can help to get a clearer idea of what this entails concretely. Gray points to the fundamentally different ideals and connected virtues that are conveyed by a range of literary,

---

[4] This notion is developed in Max Weber's thesis of a "polytheism of values" which was influenced by Nietzsche (cf. Turner 1996, p. xxix).

cultural and religious traditions, such as the Iliad (warrior ethos), Christianity (ethos of love, *agape*), the practice of Socratic self-inquiry, the Buddhist teaching of detachment, or the ideal of self-creation as articulated e.g. by Proust. These different ideals and virtues are *incommensurable:* they cannot be set off against each other. None of them can be distinguished as a right or wrong, better or worse realization of "the" (unified) human good. Rather, they must be viewed as disparate paths of realizing a variety of human *goods* in the plural which, moreover, are not unlikely to turn out as *incompatible* with one another (cf. Gray 2000, pp. 38f.).

While value pluralism is not indifferent with regard to making a distinction between moral and immoral actions, its particular focus is to emphasize that "[t]he most difficult political choices are not between good and bad but between good and good" (Galston 1999, p. 771; cf. also Ivison 2002, p. 174, endnote 9). Value pluralism departs from the monistic assumption that there is *one* unified morality valid for all humankind and the concomitant belief that, in any given value conflict, the *one* right answer exists (cf. Cherniss/Hardy 2010, section 4.1). The monistic position, in the view of value pluralism, overlooks the ontological fact of the plurality, incommensurability and incompatibility of genuine human goods (cf. Gray 2000, p. 6; 2006, pp. 325f.). The understanding of the human good conveyed by value pluralism implies that the moral existence of human beings is inevitably marked by the experience of loss and tragedy because any decision in favor of particular goods always is, at the same time, a decision *against* other goods (cf. Berlin 2002, p. 213f.; Cherniss/Hardy 2010, section 4.1; Curtis 2007, p. 89; Joas 2005, p. 55; Gray 2006, p. 331; Pavel 2007, p. 210; Jones 2006, pp. 193f.). Berlin regards such value conflicts as "an intrinsic, irremovable element in human life" (Berlin 2002, p. 213; cf. also Cherniss/Hardy 2010, section 4.1). Monism, by contrast, does not know such inescapable dilemmas. It is committed to the idea that human values can be measured on the scale of one super-value or be judged against some higher standard and can thus be brought into a coherent, harmonious order (cf. Pavel 2007, p. 209; Taylor 2001, p. 116).

Value pluralism advances a truth claim about the ontological structure of the human good and the moral life of human beings. This claim is founded empirically by reference to the common life experience that humans are sometimes faced with the challenge of making a (radical) choice between equally absolute goods which can neither be compared nor combined or reconciled in any way (cf. Berlin 2002, pp. 213f.; Cherniss/Hardy 2010, section 4). Galston illustrates this experience by recalling an example given by Sartre, where a young man is torn by the challenge of choosing between "his mother and the French Resistance" (Galston 1999, p. 771). Galston (1999, p. 771) argues that "it is concrete experience that provides the most compelling reasons for accepting some form of value pluralism", stressing that "[n]ot infrequently, our lives present conflicts of goods or values that seem fundamental but heterogeneous, with no evident basis for comparison and choice". Monism, in the view of value pluralists, denies the complex and often aporetic character of moral life. A major charge against monist theories is that they are basically out of touch with important experiences of humans in moral life (cf. Gray 2000, pp. 45 ff.).

A commitment to value pluralism does not imply a commitment to any particular political theory regarding modes of dealing with moral-political conflict. Berlin himself arrived at the conclusion that liberalism, with a focus on negative liberty, is the adequate answer to the problems that arise from the plural nature of the human good on the political plane. By contrast, Taylor and, even more, Gray reject the view that (mainstream, individualistic) liberalism must take precedence in any given case. Instead of resorting to a particular liberal conception of justice as the final authority whenever moral-political conflicts occur, they suggest trying to negotiate the diverse, conflicting conceptions of justice involved in the conflict so as to build a compromise in the form of a workable modus vivendi. The political settlement of the issue of abortion in Germany can serve as an example of such modus vivendi politics where liberalism has not taken unconditional precedence over other views of justice.[5] The settlement consists in a regulation that abortion is generally prohibited (§ 218 of German criminal code) but goes unpunished if conducted within the first three months of the pregnancy at the will of the mother (§ 218a). In order to obtain an abortion, however, women have to undergo a compulsory pregnancy counseling and prove their participation by a certificate (§ 218a). Moreover, this counseling is explicitly directed towards the protection of the life of the unborn child (§ 219). Once they have undergone the counseling, though, women are free to decide to have an abortion without any further explanation. This settlement can be regarded as a compromise that accommodates different conceptions of justice arising from different "comprehensive" views of the human good in that the legislation acknowledges the moral concerns of both the "pro-choice" faction and the "pro-life" position. This compromise can be said to have defused the abortion conflict in Germany since the late 1970s. In the USA, by contrast, the situation is different. There, the conflict still appears much more acute and vigorous. Some scholars argue that the militancy of the "pro-life" faction in the USA can be attributed to some degree to a political marginalization of positions other than individual-

---

5 I thank Ulrich Willems for drawing my attention to this example and to how it constitutes an instance of modus vivendi politics.

istic liberalism (cf. Willems 2003, p. 103, referring to Wolterstorff 1997; cf. also Gray 2000, p. 116).

Taylor's and Gray's models of modus vivendi, which both aim at building compromises between different conceptions of justice and the good, spring from their shared belief in the plural and complex nature of the human good. But they are animated by different ideals. As has already been noted above, for Gray, modus vivendi politics is supposed to be at the service of guaranteeing peaceful coexistence. He does not conceive this goal as some kind of transcendent super-value, however, because this would amount to a fallback into monism. He declares that "[p]eaceful coexistence is worth pursuing only insofar as it advances human interests" (Gray 2000, p. 135). Furthermore, he stresses that "[l]ike any political ideal, it is a contingent good" (Gray 2000, p. 135). With its limited focus on peaceful coexistence, Gray's neo-Hobbesian model of modus vivendi is quite minimalistic in terms of its normative ambitions. The advantage of this is seen as lying in its broad compatibility and good chances of acceptance, because most communities most of the time have an interest in peaceful coexistence (cf. Gray 2000, p. 136). This minimalism encompasses little demanding standards concerning the civic virtues citizens are asked to develop and cultivate in a regime based on modus vivendi politics of the Grayian kind. They can be captured in terms like "gritting teeth tolerance" or "agonistic respect" (Bader 2007, p. 78) which contain the idea that citizens are not expected to affirm or accept different ways of life as genuine and valid expressions of the human good (cf. Willems 2012, p. 294). This also means that Gray does not expect everyone to accept value pluralism as an explanation for the fact of diversity (cf. Jones 2006, p. 200), because as was explained above, value pluralism tends to view different ways of life as a range of different practices that reflect different human goods. The reason for the parties of a modus vivendi to tolerate each other, then, does not necessarily lie in a shared belief in value pluralism but rather in "people's overlapping interests in peace" (Jones 2006, p. 201).

Taylor's model of modus vivendi politics is very different in this regard. As has already been mentioned earlier, Taylor's thought is directed towards a second-order consensus on a "civic philosophy of openness": i.e., a particular manner of approaching difference that is welcoming towards it. In comparison to the rather basic ideal of ensuring peaceful coexistence which animates Gray's model, Taylor's variant of modus vivendi politics is linked to much more ambitious and specific normative notions. Inspired by Romanticism and particularly Herder, Taylor nurtures a vision of humanity as "the orchestra, in which all the differences between human beings could ultimately sound together in harmony" (Taylor 2010a, p. 320). This background implies that the search for compromises in this model is meant to be inspired by a will of mutual understanding and reciprocal appreciation by the parties involved. For Taylor, "gritting teeth tolerance" is not enough; he seeks to establish "friendship" and foster "the kind of understanding where each can come to be moved by what moves the other" (Taylor 2010a, p. 320). This, however, implies civic virtues that are much less minimalistic than the ones connected to Gray's model. These virtues revolve around notions such as openness and curiosity towards unfamiliar moral horizons and the readiness to view diversity and difference as *enrichment* for oneself and society. Moreover, the notion of being "moved by what moves the other" implies an acknowledgment that "the other" is on to some genuine and valid human good. This in fact presupposes the acceptance of some comprehensive doctrine or philosophy akin to value pluralism. So a problem of Taylor's variant of modus vivendi politics seems to be that it is based on a civic ethos that is itself so specific or "comprehensive" that it eventually enters into rivalry with the various conceptions of the good life it was actually meant to reconcile. Gray's variant, on the other hand, might be more hospitable to a broad range of conceptions of the good life due to its minimalistic normative demands, but it raises the question of social cohesion: Do notions of "gritting teeth tolerance" and an interest in peace provide a sufficient basis to forge workable and lasting settlements between parties who hold deeply conflicting conceptions of the good?

Conclusion – Modus vivendi and its discontents

This essay has drawn attention to modus vivendi as an alternative, pluralistic, approach to the challenge of moral diversity and conflict beyond liberal theories of consensus. It has distinguished two different variants of modus vivendi politics: a *dialogical variant*, which is directed at reconciliation and mutual understanding (Taylor), and an *agonistic, neo-Hobbesian variant*, which is animated by "gritting teeth tolerance" and the will to peaceful coexistence (Gray). Both models have particular weaknesses that become apparent when regarded from the respective viewpoint of the other model.

From the agonistic viewpoint, the dialogical model misses central dimensions of politics by overemphasizing aspects like dialogue and mutual understanding while neglecting the area of power struggles and competition. Taylor suggests that "we're in the business of friendship" (Taylor 2010a, p. 320). But is politics really (mainly) about *friendship*? John Horton, another proponent of the agonistic modus vivendi variant, is skeptical with regard to such harmonistic visions of politics: "much of politics is about contesting, pursuing, preserving or enhancing power" (Horton 2010, p. 433 f.). Horton stresses that "it is necessary to have political power to achieve almost anything at all in politics" (Horton 2010,

p. 433f.). While Taylor does not avoid the notion of conflict, he maintains the hope of final harmony in the form of an overlapping consensus that shall arise from hermeneutic dialogical practice, reconciling different conceptions of the good without erasing their differences. Gray generally criticizes political philosophies that focus on harmony as an ideal. He thinks that "an ideal of harmony is not the best starting-point for thinking about ethics or government" (Gray 2000, p. 5). So we are faced with the principled question of how to properly conceive moral diversity and conflict in the realm of politics. As the critical look from the stance of the agonistic model suggests, it is inadequate to let our political imagination and expectations be formed exclusively by ideas such as friendly dialogue and mutual understanding; the dimension of power and competition needs to be taken into account as well.

From the viewpoint of the dialogical model, on the other hand, the agonistic modus vivendi variant seems to neglect unity and cohesion as crucial aspects related to the functioning of democracy. The vision of a "neo-Hobbesian" politics raises concerns whether it can adequately capture the notion of equal respect as a crucial concept of modern democracy. Moreover, the stability of modern democracies is not supposed to be guaranteed by a *Leviathan*-like superior power but is expected to arise from within the political community itself. This points to particular requirements concerning the relationship between the citizens of a democratic polity. Gray (2000, p. 126) admits that "democracy needs trust", but it remains open whether or how his preferred model of a neo-Hobbesian modus vivendi can meet this requirement. Taylor argues that modern democracy "requires a high degree of common commitment, a sense of common identification" and that difference and conflict need to be balanced by some "feeling of common belonging" (Taylor 2010b, p. 30 f.). This is why Taylor clings to the second-order consensus of a potentially unifying civic ethos of openness. The agonistic position rejects the requirement of such a consensus on a welcoming stance towards difference as potentially homogenizing and eventually repressing plurality. Agonistic modus vivendi can be described as a political mode where citizens are not expected to necessarily acknowledge different ways of life as legitimate alternatives of human flourishing worthy of respect (cf. Willems 2012, p. 294). It is an approach to politics that explicitly seeks to avoid "demanding notions such as openness, curiosity, enthusiastic endorsement of difference, or harmonious respect" (Bader 2007, p. 78). The crucial question is what resources this model can provide to generate the kind of trust Gray himself deems necessary for the functioning of democracy.

Neither of these two models of modus vivendi provides a wholly satisfactory solution to the challenge of diversity so far. While the issue with Taylor's model is that its insistence on a second-order consensus on a civic ethos of openness fails to take the real depth of diversity seriously enough and does not properly acknowledge struggles for power as an integral part of politics, Gray's model eventually lacks the sources of trust and cohesion that are important to the stability of a democracy. Nevertheless, both variants of modus vivendi provide us with promising alternative approaches to the challenge of diversity beyond the Rawlsian "dream of consensus politics" (Wolterstorff 2012, p. 286). Thus, to point out their weaknesses is not to dismiss them. Rather it is meant as an impulse to think further and improve the concept of modus vivendi as a mode of dealing with moral-political diversity and conflict in modern democracies.

Bibliography

Bader, Veit (2007): *Secularism or Democracy? Associational Governance of Religious Diversity*. Amsterdam: Amsterdam University Press.
Berlin, Isaiah (1991): *The Crooked Timber of Humanity: Chapters in the History of Ideas*. Henry Hardy (Ed.). New York: Alfred A. Knopf.
Berlin, Isaiah (2002): *Liberty*. Henry Hardy (Ed.). Oxford: Oxford University Press.
Cherniss, Joshua/Hardy, Henry (2010): "Isaiah Berlin". In: Zalta, Edward N. (Ed.): *The Stanford Encyclopedia of Philosophy* (Fall 2010 Edition), http://plato.stanford.edu/archives/fall2010/entries/berlin/, visited on 18 September 2015.
Curtis, William M. (2007): "Liberals and Pluralists: Charles Taylor and John Gray". In: *Contemporary Political Theory* 6. No. 1, pp. 86–107.
Gagnon, Bernard (2014): "Reconciling Diversity and Solidarity? A Critical Look at Charles Taylor's Conception of Secularism". In: Ferran Requejo/Camil Ungureanu (Eds.): *Democracy, Law and Religious Pluralism in Europe: Secularism and Post-Secularism*. London: Routledge, pp. 106–120.
Galston, William A. (1999): "Value Pluralism and Liberal Political Theory". In: *The American Political Science Review* 93. No. 4, pp. 769–778.
Gray, John (2000): *Two Faces of Liberalism*. Cambridge: Polity Press.
Gray, John (2006): "Reply to Critics". In: *Critical Review of International Social and Political Philosophy* 9. No. 2, pp. 323–347.
Gutmann, Thomas (2012): "Religiöser Pluralismus und liberaler Verfassungsstaat". In: Gabriel, Karl/Spieß, Christian/Winkler, Katja (Eds.): *Modelle des religiösen Pluralismus. Historische, religionssoziologische und religionspolitische Perspektiven*. Paderborn: Schöningh, pp. 291–315.
Horton, John (2009): *Towards a Political Theory of Modus Vivendi*. Keele. Paper in the Political Theory Seminar Series (Winter 2009/10, 2 December) at University College London.
Horton, John (2010): "Realism, Liberal Moralism and a Political Theory of Modus Vivendi". In: *European Journal of Political Theory* 9. No. 4, pp. 431–448.
Ivison, Duncan (2002): *Postcolonial Liberalism*. Cambridge: Cambridge University Press.

Joas, Hans (2005): "Glaube und Moral im Zeitalter der Kontingenz". In: Hermann Fechtrup/Friedbert Schulze/Thomas Sternberg (Eds.): *Wissen und Weisheit. Zwei Symposien zu Ehren von Josef Pieper (1904–1997)*, Münster: LIT, pp. 49–65.

Jones, Peter (2006): "Toleration, Value-Pluralism, and the Fact of Pluralism". In: *Critical Review of International Social and Political Philosophy* 9. No. 2, pp. 189–210.

Pavel, Carmen (2007): "Pluralism and the Moral Grounds of Liberal Theory". In: *Social Theory and Practice* 33. No. 2, pp. 199–221.

Rawls, John (1997): "The Idea of Public Reason Revisited". In: *University of Chicago Law Review* 64. No. 3, pp. 765–807.

Rawls, John (2005): *Political Liberalism*. New York: Columbia University Press.

Taylor, Charles (1998): "Modes of Secularism". In: Bhargava, Rajeev (Ed.): *Secularism and Its Critics*. New Delhi: Oxford University Press, pp. 31–58.

Taylor, Charles (2001): "Plurality of Goods". In: Dworkin, Richard/Lilla, Mark/Silvers, Robert B. (Eds.): *The Legacy of Isaiah Berlin*. New York: The New York Review of Books, pp. 113–119.

Taylor, Charles (2010a): "Afterword. Apologia pro Libro Suo". In: Warner, Michael/VanAntwerpen, Jonathan/Calhoun, Craig (Eds.): *Varieties of Secularism in A Secular Age*, Cambridge, MA: Harvard University Press, pp. 300–321.

Taylor, Charles (2010b): "The Meaning of Secularism". In: *The Hedgehog Review* 12. No. 3, pp. 23–34.

Taylor, Charles (2011a): "What Does Secularism Mean?". In: Taylor, Charles: *Dilemmas and Connections*. Cambridge, MA: Belknap Press of Harvard University Press, pp. 303–325.

Taylor, Charles (2011b): "Conditions of an Unforced Consensus on Human Rights". In: Taylor, Charles: *Dilemmas and Connections*. Cambridge, MA: Belknap Press of Harvard University Press, pp. 105–123.

Turner, Brian S. (1996): *For Weber. Essays on the Sociology of Fate*. London: Sage.

Willems, Ulrich (2003): "Religion als Privatsache? Eine Kritische Auseinandersetzung mit dem liberalen Prinzip einer strikten Trennung von Politik und Religion". In: Minkenberg, Michael/Willems, Ulrich (Eds.): *Politik und Religion*. Wiesbaden: Westdeutscher Verlag, pp. 88–112.

Willems, Ulrich (2012): "Normative Pluralität und Kontingenz als Herausforderungen politischer Theorie. Prolegomena zur Theorie eines Politischen Pluralismus". In: Willems, Ulrich/Toens, Katrin (Eds.): *Politik und Kontingenz*. Wiesbaden: Springer VS, pp. 265–301.

Wolterstorff, Nicholas (1997). "The Role of Religion in Decision and Discussion of Political Issues". In: Audi, Robert/Wolterstorff, Nicholas: *Religion in the Public Square: The Place of Religious Convictions in Political Debate*. Lanham: Rowman & Littlefield, pp. 67–120.

Wolterstorff, Nicholas (2012): "Why Can't We All Just Get Along With Each Other?". In: Wolterstorff, Nicholas: *Understanding Liberal Democracy. Essays in Political Philosophy*. Terence Cuneo (Ed.). Oxford: Oxford University Press, pp. 277–297.

Manon Westphal
What Bonds Citizens in a Pluralistic Democracy? Probing Mouffe's Notion of a *Conflictual* Consensus[1]

Abstract: One crucial challenge resulting from today's conditions of pluralism is to grasp a suitable understanding of democratic commonality. I argue that John Rawls's *overlapping consensus* is insufficiently sensitive to the depth of disagreement inherent within pluralism, and that Chantal Mouffe's *conflictual consensus* offers an alternative that may be better equipped to capture democracy's agonistic state. The key feature of conflictual consensus is its negative nature: citizens agree on the need to exclude certain positions that negate freedom and equality but continuously dispute the positive meaning of these values. However, we have to go 'beyond Mouffe' at least in two respects. First, a clearer understanding of the content of the consensus, the range of excluded positions, is needed. Second, under conditions of power asymmetries a tamed struggle for hegemony should not be the exclusive model for a political process in which citizens give expression to the conflictual nature of their consensus.

1 Introduction

This chapter addresses the task of theorising political commonality under conditions of pluralism. Without a doubt, pluralism has become one of western societies' most prominent features and as such, it poses a crucial challenge for liberal democracy. Even if liberal democracies have long been familiar with diversity and disagreement and the task of conflict management, processes of social differentiation and migration have increased the number of cultural, religious and moral identities. What is more, technical progress has extended the options for human action in ethically sensitive domains and, as a result, forced deeply contested issues onto the political agenda, as can be seen in conflicts over issues like stem cell research or physician-assisted suicide. Against this background, specifying the communal aspect of a democratic society poses a

---

[1] An earlier version of this paper was presented at the conference "Pluralism and Conflict: Distributive Justice beyond Rawls and Consensus" at Fatih University, Istanbul, 6–8 June 2013. I thank all participants for the helpful discussion. Also, my thanks are due to John Horton, Manuel Knoll and Stephen Snyder for helpful comments on the draft.

https://doi.org/10.1515/9783110537369-017

challenging task. In the face of the range and depth of disagreements, it has become more and more difficult to identify agreed-upon values or norms. However, some shared commitments seem needed in order to bind citizens to their shared project of political cooperation. What might the nature of such commitments under conditions of contemporary pluralism be?

One of the most notable answers to this question was given by John Rawls. In *Political Liberalism*, Rawls argues that a pluralism of "religious, philosophical, and moral doctrines" (Rawls 2005, p. 4) requires the basic institutions of society to be in line with a political conception of justice. The crucial feature of a political conception is that it does not depend on a particular conception of the good and therefore can become the subject of an *overlapping consensus* among citizens holding different worldviews (Rawls 2005, p. 15). Building on this idea, Rawls argues that citizens should deal with their moral disagreements by restricting themselves to public reason whenever basic institutions are concerned. As a result, nobody will be forced to live under rules that he or she cannot reasonably accept. The central idea of this proposal indeed seems indispensable for democratic politics in pluralist societies: if citizens' conceptions of the good diverge, the political bond that unites them must consist in something that abstracts from the differences among their conceptions of the good. However, Rawls's account insufficiently takes into account the depth of disagreement that is implied in the wide range of worldviews in contemporary societies. In this chapter, I argue that Chantal Mouffe's theory of agonistic pluralism and its notion of a "conflictual consensus" (Mouffe 2000, p. 103) invites us to rethink democratic commonality 'beyond Rawls' in a way that is sensitive to deep disagreement.

The argument develops in three steps. First, I refer to specific political conflicts extant in liberal democracies in order to justify the view that the capacity of Rawls' overlapping consensus to acknowledge the depth of disagreement is limited. I then present Mouffe's discourse theory as an explicitly conflict-focused conception of pluralism. Second, I introduce Mouffe's notion of a conflictual consensus and show that it differs from overlapping consensus because it abandons the idea of agreement concerning the positive meaning of political norms. Third, I argue that it is necessary to theorise this concept 'beyond Mouffe'. I show how it may be possible to specify the (negative) content of the conflictual consensus and argue that political conflicts, which are welcomed by the conflictual consensus, sometimes require more cooperative political responses than tamed hegemonic struggles.

2 Rawls's *overlapping consensus* and the need to reach beyond

In *Political Liberalism*, Rawls famously asks: "How is it possible for there to exist over time a just and stable society of free and equal citizens, who remain profoundly divided by reasonable religious, philosophical, and moral doctrines?" (Rawls 2005, p. 4). Rawls explicitly acknowledges that today's pluralism implies disagreements which are deep, in the sense that they result from people's diverging ideas of what a valuable life means or morality requires. Likewise, his proposal that society's basic institutions should be organised in accordance with reasons that are independent of any particular worldview is driven by the intention to accept the persistence of differences among worldviews. In the light of these observations, it is not obvious why Rawls's theory is vulnerable to the objection that it neglects the depth of disagreement. In his essay *The Idea of Public Reason Revisited*, Rawls stresses that political liberalism does not even expect citizens to agree on the exact shape of political justice. He considers *justice as fairness* to be the most preferable conception, but it is only one possible manifestation of political justice (Rawls 1997, pp. 774–775).

However, even though political liberalism allows for disagreements about political justice, it expects the core of political justice to be exempt from disagreement. Citizens are legitimately divided on, say, the status of the difference principle, but they are meant to agree on the principles that constitute the fundamentals of political justice. This becomes clear when Rawls specifies the features which *every* conception, in order to belong to the family of political conceptions of justice, must exhibit. "First, a list of certain basic rights, liberties, and opportunities [...]; Second, an assignment of special priority to those rights, liberties, and opportunities [...]; and Third, measures ensuring for all citizens adequate all-purpose means to make effective use of their freedoms" (Rawls 1997, p. 774). Rawls thus seems to distinguish between a reasonably disputed periphery and a core of political justice that cannot be reasonably challenged. The latter is meant to provide the stable substance of an overlapping consensus that can function as the uniting bond among citizens.

The most important challenge to this way of thinking about democratic commonality is that liberal democracies are witnessing a discrepancy between the idea of a robust basis for consensus and the reality of political disagreement (Waldron 1999). The societies we live in face conflicts that result from disagreements on basic rights and liberties in the first place. Consider two examples. The first is the debate on abortion. The main arguments put forward by the conflicting parties are the need to protect human life ('pro-life') and the need to protect women's right to self-determination ('pro-choice'). Both principles are widely accepted and certainly belong to the core of political justice. Yet, the legal status of abortion is the object of one of the most fiercely disputed and most persistent conflicts in liberal democracies. What renders this case illuminating for our discussion is that the persistence of the conflict cannot be explained in terms of one party's or both parties' political unreasonableness. Neither do 'pro-choice' activists negate the necessity to protect human life, nor do 'pro-life' activists reject the idea that women have a right to self-determination. Rather, the conflict is rooted in citizens' diverging understandings of the stage in the development of human life beyond which there exists a person with a right to life (e.g. Waldron 2007, p. 118). Definitions of this moment, however, are bound to convictions linked to particular worldviews, and therefore remain matters of dispute. As a consequence, those who are involved in the conflict find themselves thrust back on their deep moral disagreements. Public reason does not offer a solution to the conflict; instead it presents itself as the very mode through which the conflict is carried out.

The second example is the controversy on caricatures offending religious sensibilities. Even though this controversy was fuelled by the murderous attacks on the editors of the satirical magazine *Charlie Hebdo*, its main lines of dispute were established earlier. In his critical engagement with Rawls's theory, John Horton refers to the debate which arose from the publication of Salman Rushdie's novel *The Satanic Verses* and points out that both defenders and critics of the publication referred to core values of political justice. This is obvious on the part of the defenders. Rushdie's right to publish the book, they contended, was a matter of freedom of speech (Horton 2003, p. 17). But also the critics justified their view by reference to public reasons like "respect for persons, civility, incitement to religious hatred, group defamation, offence and such like, all of which could be reasonably accepted by anyone" (Horton 2003, p. 17) and clearly belong to the core of political justice. The more recent controversy around the caricatures of the prophet Mohammed reflects the same lines of argument. Again, there is an opposition between defenders who uphold freedom of speech and critics who refer to public principles, like those identified by Horton, rather than to the specific norms of their religion. This means that we encounter a situation similar to the abortion case: once again, public reasons are at the centre of political conflict and do not serve as a means to solve it.

What cases like these demonstrate is that citizens' disagreements also affect political justice at the core. A political theory that aims to reflect the fact that political justice is a possible source of division rather than a reliable basis for unification cannot rely on overlapping consensus and must find a different way of conceptualising political commonality. In addition, the re-conceptualisation of political commonality must go hand in hand with a re-conceptualisation of politics. If there is disagreement on the content of political justice, citizens will often be unable to identify solutions that each can consider reasonable. Therefore, what is required is a political rationale that shows how conflicts can be processed in the absence of a shared understanding of what political justice requires. In the following, I discuss Chantal Mouffe's *agonistic pluralism* as a fruitful basis for dealing with these tasks.

In her early work co-authored with Ernesto Laclau, *Hegemony and Socialist Strategy*,[2] Mouffe develops a discourse theory of the social that describes disagreement and conflict as constitutive features of pluralism. Central to this theory is the idea of the "'negative essence' of the existing" (Laclau/Mouffe 2001, p. 97) – the notion that exclusion, not similarity or even sameness, is constitutive of identity formation. An identity only comes into existence by distinguishing itself from an 'other', something that is outside itself (Laclau/Mouffe 2001, pp. 105 ff.). A practical example helps to illustrate this rather abstract idea. Take the difference between male and female. The crucial factor that generates the identity of a female is her being different from males or, more concisely, from certain images of masculinity and social roles generally attributed to males. We would be unable to give a description of a female, or even think of it as a social category, if there was not the notion of a male, and vice versa. While this consideration may appear trivial at first glance, the crux of Mouffe and Laclau's argument is that the 'negative essence' of the social grounds a conflictual understanding of politics. If the difference to an 'other' is a constitutive feature of identity, the political views of a particular identity cannot merge with those of other identities. Every consensus reached would dissolve the difference among the identities and, as a consequence, reduce social pluralism as such. On the basis of these considerations, Mouffe and Laclau paint the picture of society as "a field criss-crossed by antagonisms" (Laclau/Mouffe 2001, p. 135) – a field in which even basic norms and principles cannot assume to be protected from disagreement because every interpretation of these norms and principles depends on the existence of other interpretations.

I do not claim that Laclau and Mouffe's discourse theory delivers an indisputable description of social relations. For instance, one could object that, at least from time to time, we are able to agree on things thought to be rooted in deeply entrenched disagreements. However, even if the theory does not deliver a sufficiently complex picture of the social, the fact that Mouffe and Laclau pro-

---

2 The book was first published in 1985. In the following, I cite the second edition published in 2001.

pose that antagonisms be understood as natural features of the social means that the theory provides a promising basis for a discussion of how democratic commonality may be theorised such that it is able to include deep and persistent conflicts on political justice.

3 Mouffe's *conflictual consensus* – re-conceptualising democratic commonality

Mouffe's democratic theory, the *agonistic pluralism*, contains two central themes. The first is directly taken from discourse theory: the notion of an ever present potential for *antagonism* in politics. "[T]he political in its dimension of conflict/decision" (Mouffe 2005, p. 2) becomes visible whenever the existing ordering of social relations is opposed and, through the articulation of alternatives, possibilities of installing new orders open up. Mouffe distinguishes the *political* from *politics* in order to emphasise the crucial role of antagonism.

> 'The political' refers to this dimension of antagonism which can take many forms and can emerge in diverse social relations. It is a dimension that can never be eradicated. 'Politics', on the other hand, refers to the ensemble of practices, discourses and institutions that seeks to establish a certain order and to organize human coexistence in conditions which are always potentially conflicting, since they are affected by the dimension of 'the political' (Mouffe 2013, pp. 2–3).

The second theme of agonistic pluralism concerns the features of a liberal-democratic political order. Mouffe assumes that such an order requires a common bond among its citizens, "a form of commonality strong enough to institute a 'demos' but nevertheless compatible with [...] religious, moral and cultural pluralism" (Mouffe 2000, p. 55). A liberal democracy thus cannot embrace every kind of disagreement; there must be limits to legitimate pluralism (Mouffe 2005, p. 227). In her description of this common bond, Mouffe in fact comes close to the Rawlsian vocabulary. In a liberal democracy, she maintains, citizens are bound together through their shared "adhesion to the ethico-political principles of liberal democracy: liberty and equality" (Mouffe 2000, p. 102). This does not preclude citizens thinking that other values are also important for democracy. However, Mouffe focuses on these two, and the reason for this seems to be that she considers them the most important and broadly supported ones – since the democratic revolution liberty and equality are the general identifiers of democracy (Laclau/Mouffe 2001, pp. 154–155). According to Mouffe, it is a never-ending dispute on the *meaning* of liberty and equality which provides for the conflictual nature of this agreement. "[T]here will always be disagreement concerning the meaning of those values and the way they should be implemented. This consensus will therefore always be a 'conflictual consensus'" (Mouffe 2013, p. 8).

The question that arises at this point is whether the two themes of agonistic pluralism contradict each other. How is it possible to acknowledge the ineradicable potential for antagonism and, at the same time, maintain the need for citizens to hold a consensus on certain values? At first sight, there seem to be two options. Either Mouffe has to bite the bullet and accept as an implication of the political that the notion of consensus is not feasible, or she has to give up on her account of the political in order to defend the notion of consensus. In the first case, it would be unclear how agonistic pluralism could provide insights about ways to conceptualise political commonality at all. In the latter case, the line between agonistic pluralism and political liberalism would become more than blurred. If the only difference between an overlapping consensus and a conflictual consensus were that the former assumes agreement on a list of basic rights and liberties whilst the latter refers to liberty and equality more generally, the concepts would offer very similar descriptions of the kind of bond that may unite citizens in a pluralist society.

However, I suggest that it is possible to connect the two themes of Mouffe's theory such that the apparent dilemma dissolves. The key to this solution is an interpretation of conflictual consensus that explores what the socio-ontological framework that grounds Mouffe's political theory implies regarding the nature of consensus. Such an analysis starts from the insight that the agreement on liberty and equality is nothing but one concrete instance of the social phenomenon which Laclau and Mouffe deal with in their discourse theory on a more general and abstract level: political identity. If the conflictual consensus of agonistic pluralism is an instance of political identity – the identity of liberal democratic communities – and, as defined by the notion of constitutive difference, it is the fact of being different from something else that brings identities into being, the nature of the consensus can only be understood through a clarification of its particular mode of differentiation. But this is still a very general approach. In order to give flesh to this idea, it is required to look deeper into Laclau and Mouffe's theory and consider the processes through which identities come into being. As these processes are entwined with the notion of antagonism, this step of the analysis requires us to investigate the first theme of Mouffe's political theory more thoroughly.

Laclau and Mouffe use the term "antagonism" in an ontological and in a phenomenological sense. The ontological sense was sketched in the previous section: politics necessarily faces a potential for conflict. It is the notion of antagonism as phenomenon that we need to address now. Antagonisms so understood are the moments in which the potential for conflict realises itself and, at the same time, political identities emerge. This interrelation between conflict formation and identity construction becomes apparent once we take a closer look at how the opposition to a social order's status quo effects changes within existing relations. Laclau and Mouffe describe this change as a "subversion" that dissolves the established meaning of identities through creating a new identity (Laclau/Mouffe 2001, p. 127). The source of this newly created identity is the antagonism itself: the joint opposition, a shared negation of the respectively challenged aspect of the social order, generates a basis for identification. Laclau and Mouffe coin the term *equivalence* to signify the relation between elements that become bound along the lines of their involvement in an antagonism (Laclau/Mouffe 2001, p. 127). This choice of terminology stresses how the understanding of political identity as being created through antagonism differs from understandings of political identity as being grounded by the sameness of its sub-identities. Those elements that jointly take sides in an antagonistic opposition constitute an *assemblage of identities* whose parts remain different from each other. They are equivalent in the sense that they have something in common without being identical with each other. The critical consequence of this account is that the *only* substantial characteristic of political identities is to be found in their exterior – in the respective positions they negate. "[I]f *all* the differential features of an object have become equivalent, it is impossible to express anything *positive* concerning that object; this can only imply that through the equivalence something is expressed which the object is *not*" (Laclau/Mouffe 2001, p. 128; italics in original).

If we read Mouffe's concept of conflictual consensus against the background of this theory of identity formation, we learn something crucial about its nature. The agreement on liberty and equality must have a purely negative character. What citizens who commit themselves to liberty and equality share is an opposition against a political 'other'. The positive side of the agreement, though, remains undetermined and is open to interminable disagreement. In other words, the content of the conflictual consensus runs out in something that citizens reject: in positions they conceive of as being *incompatible* with liberty and equality. On the one hand, there will be situations in which the members of the polity jointly identify certain political projects – be it hypothetical scenarios or projects put forward by real political actors – as threats to their political community. On the other hand, they do not share an understanding of what realising liberty and equality in a positive sense requires. It is at this point that the conflictual consensus reveals its conceptual distinctiveness. The indeterminacy of its positive side implies that it does not assume a core meaning of liberty and equality unaffected by disagreements. The agreement on the need to hinder certain positions sets limits to the range of accepted interpretations of these values, which implies that not *every* political position may count as an interpretation of liberty and equality. However, within these boundaries, no specification of the shared principles is taken to be beyond dispute. Thus, Mouffe's notion of consensus is conflictual in the sense of assuming even the fundamentals of political justice to be objects of citizens' disagreements.

Against the background of these clarifications, the two themes of Mouffe's political theory can be related such that they do not contradict each other. The suggestion is that to understand the conflictual consensus as an agreement on the need for political exclusion is compatible with ineradicable antagonism. If the agreement on liberty and equality ends in the rejection of certain political positions and projects, positive interpretations of these values, like any other element of the social order, still belong to the realm in which oppositions to potentially every aspect of established interpretations may emerge. The consensus only sets limits to the range of interpretations that may legitimately take the place of what has previously become a matter of dispute. We can draw a picture of *two levels of antagonism* in order to illustrate this interpretation. The first level concerns the limits of political legitimacy. On this level, citizens of a liberal democracy find themselves allied in one large chain of equivalence that opposes political projects striving to realise orderings of social relations which citizens jointly consider threats to liberty and equality. On the second level, citizens find themselves building opposing chains of equivalence, fighting for divergent and possibly incompatible interpretations of liberty and equality, which might have nothing more in common than their non-reliance on those positions that are rejected on the first level. This two-level-picture of antagonisms shows that Mouffe does not need to decide between either staying true to her claim about the ever present potential for antagonism in politics, or, defending a notion of political agreement. Due to the fact that it locates the substance of agreement in negative interpretations of the values in question and not, like the overlapping consensus, in their fundamentals, the conflictual consensus shows how it is possible to understand antagonism and agreement not as contradictions but as complementary.

Given the suggested specifications of the concept, Mouffe's notion of a conflictual consensus presents a viable alternative to the overlapping consensus. First, by accepting conflicts about the core meaning of shared values, it offers a description of democratic commonality that is sensitive towards deep disagreements. Thus, unlike political liberalism, a political theory that is based on the notion of conflictual consensus is capable of assessing conflicts like those discussed in the previous section not as defective but as normal phenomena that need to be recognised through political theorising. Second, while leaving room for disagreement even about the core meaning of basic values, the concept does not slide into an anything-goes-perspective. Through binding citizens to a negation of positions that violate central normative commitments of liberal democracy, the conflictual consensus offers a meaningful description of what belonging to the political project of democracy implies. Because of this second feature, it is not at the price of giving away any basis for identification among citizens that the conflictual consensus arrives at its greater potential to embrace deep disagreements. This advantage is reason enough to value Mouffe's concept as a worthwhile starting point for the endeavour to rethink democratic commonality beyond Rawls. However, in order to further pursue this project, it is important to tackle challenges that are left unanswered by Mouffe. The next section addresses two of them. Rather than offering ready solutions, I make explicit what the challenges are and sketch preliminary ideas for fruitful ways of dealing with them.

4 Building on the conflictual consensus 'beyond Mouffe'

The first challenge that should be addressed is the question of the content of the conflictual consensus. So far, it has only been established that there must be something – some political positions or projects – that citizens jointly regard as negations of liberty and equality. But what is this 'something'? Which positions or projects, given the conditions of pluralism within democratic societies, can be considered elements of a wide agreement on what is beyond the range of acceptable interpretations?

To begin with, it seems that the advantage of the conflictual consensus hinges on the fact that it involves a rather modest set of components. If the consensus about what negates liberty and equality were to embrace an extensive set of political positions and projects, the argument that the conflictual consensus proves superior to the overlapping consensus in terms of conflict-inclusiveness would lose its persuasiveness. A political theory that focuses on the need to acknowledge the depth of disagreements cannot take judgements about the incompatibility of political positions with shared values to be beyond dispute. In many cases citizens will disagree on whether a particular position actually contradicts liberty and equality. Hence, the thicker the content, the less likely it is that the conflictual consensus will be able to unlock its potential of offering a realistic description of political commonality in today's pluralistic democracies. In light of this consideration, rich definitions of the range of jointly negated positions run the risk of too significantly downsizing the realm for disagreements whose potentially extensive scope I presented as the major achievement of Mouffe's concept. Theorists who want to build on the notion of a conflictual consensus should thus be careful not to undermine the strength of its conceptual distinctiveness through overloading its (negative) content.

Having said this, it is necessary to become more concrete as regards possible components of the conflictual consensus. Mouffe herself remains very vague at this point. A rare passage in which she gives examples for what, according to her view, the consensus among citizens in liberal democracies must imply is to be found in *The Return of the Political*. Here, Mouffe argues that the "distinction between the public and the private" as well as "the separation of Church and State" must not be called "into question in the name of pluralism" (Mouffe 2005, pp. 131–132). It is necessary to shed some critical light on these examples. On the one hand, there is a serious objection to be raised against them. Recent history of liberal democracies shows that ideas of what poses a threat to the distinction between public and private, as well as that between state and church, are among the most disputed issues. A good example of this is the feminist movement whose very goal was to unsettle established institutions and role models previously considered to set the limits between the public and the private. Also, to hint at a very recent example, public security concerns, which have been increasing in the aftermath of terrorist attacks, and evidence of the extensive collection of personal communication data by intelligence services have unleashed controversies on whether liberal societies are facing circumstances that legitimise measures transgressing established limits of citizens' private sphere. As to the distinction between state and church, it seems at least worth noting that liberal democracies have institutionalised significantly divergent understandings of what this distinction requires. France, for example, is known for its laicism, implying a strict separation between state institutions and religious institutions. The situation in Germany, in contrast, is characterised by more cooperative relations between the two spheres. And in England there is an established church, even if its political powers are highly circumscribed. Consequently, what appears as a violation to the principle of the distinction between state and church will differ from case to case.

These examples demonstrate that, far from sketching firmly agreed upon limits of acceptable political positions, the distinctions mentioned by Mouffe are regularly contested and settled in ways that not only differ from society to society but also change over time. On the other hand, though, it seems implausible to deny that within a particular societal context and for a certain period of time concrete visions of what is incompatible with the respective distinctions are in fact agreed upon by the vast majority of citizens. The feminist movement, to refer back to an earlier example, would not have had to engage in such hard and long-lasting struggles if there had not been a widely shared understanding of its demands being in contradiction with existing norms regarding the private and the public. Today, in turn, political proposals which, for instance, demand the (re-)introduction of a legal duty for wives to consult their husbands before entering a profession would widely be judged illegitimate. Thus, it is on the basis of a critical awareness for contextual and historical contingency that Mouffe's examples present plausible specifications of the conflictual consensus: in a specific context and for a certain period of time citizens may understand oppositions to certain positions they jointly consider as threats to the public-private-distinction or the separation of Church and State as important implications of their commitment to liberty and equality. However, this cannot mean, as Mouffe puts it, that the public-private-distinction and the separation of Church and State must not be called "into question in the name of pluralism". First, due to the fact that the agreement on the need to defend these norms does not go beyond a shared commitment to fend off certain positions, positive interpretations will remain subject to disagreement and potential conflict. Second, like the different interpretations of the separation of Church and State indicate, even those positions that are widely considered threats to these norms at a given point of time will not necessarily remain the same. As a result, it is vital for agonistic pluralism to recognise that the distinctions highlighted by Mouffe may regularly be questioned 'in the name of pluralism'.

A possible consequence of this could be that it is entirely up to contingent developments to define the content of the conflictual consensus. But this would be a premature conclusion given that the conflictual consensus is meant to bind citizens not just to *any* political regime but to a democratic one. It seems that certain exclusions from the game of legitimate contestation must not be up for grabs because there are political positions and projects whose realisation would go beyond the scope of democratic politics and which have been conceived as threats throughout the history of liberal democracies – for example, the implementation of a one party regime that suppresses any dissenting voice by violence. A plausible conceptualisation of the conflictual consensus thus faces the challenge to take into account both considerations: neither is it possible to give a comprehensive definition of what the conflictual consensus requires citizens to oppose, nor is it cogent to refrain from substantial determinations altogether. This challenge may be met with the help of a distinction between a *variable* and a *stable* part of the consensus. According to this suggestion, the conflictual consensus contains a variable part that includes rather specific interpretations of what poses a threat to liberty and equality. Negations of this sort may regularly become subject to political disagreements and re-negotiations. The stable part of the conflictual consensus, however, embraces positions which citizens jointly consider beyond the pale independently of their specific societal circumstances. In consideration of the depth of disagreements in today's societies, this part should be limited to a thin set of scenarios. Value pluralist John Gray develops an argument that may point towards a plausible specification of such a set's components. Gray argues that, notwithstanding the condition of pluralism and deep disagreement, it is possible to determine certain moral evils, which can be called universal, because they impede the realisation not only of distinctly liberal ways of life but of any vision of a good life. Political regimes, Gray argues,

> in which genocide is practised, or torture institutionalized, that depend for their continuing existence on the suppression of minorities, or of the majority, which humiliate their citizens or those who coexist with them in society, which destroy the common environment, which sanction religious persecution, which fail to meet basic human needs in circumstances where that is practically feasible or which render impossible the search for peace among different ways of life – such regimes are obstacles to the well-being of those whom they govern (Gray 2000, p. 107).

It seems conclusive that the perception of such scenarios as political threats is not bound to support of specific interpretations of political justice. The notion of moral evils captures a set of positions that democratic citizens can be expected to constantly oppose and thus offers a plausible interpretation of what the stable part of the conflictual consensus may contain. Above the threshold set by such moral evils, a citizenry regularly builds (and argues about) more specific understandings of what they expect their political community to achieve. Without doubt, these ideas remain sketchy and in need of further elaboration. Nevertheless, they demonstrate that the distinction between variable and stable parts of what citizens of a liberal democracy jointly consider incompatible with their political community enables political theorists to draw a picture of democratic commonality that takes into account both contextual variety and limits of what any such variations may encompass.

The second challenge I want to explore concerns the account of politics that complements the notion of democratic commonality as suggested by the conflictual consensus. The crucial consequence of the concept's defining the substance of shared ideas in a negative way lies in the fact that accounts of public reasoning are deprived of a reliable basis. Citizens who are united by a conflictual consensus are capable of identifying scenarios they jointly intend to *prevent*. But as soon as the task of political decision making requires the specification of positive interpretations, these shared identifications do not provide any guidance.

In principle, Mouffe's own account of politics does justice to this fact. Her agonistic pluralism leaves behind the notion of a joint search for generally acceptable reasons and introduces an account of conflict processing that is compatible with persisting disagreements on the fundamentals of political justice. Instead of referring to or longing for consensus, Mouffe suggests, the aim of democratic politics should be "to transform an 'antagonism' into an 'agonism'" (Mouffe 1999, p. 755). An agonism, like an antagonism, constitutes an oppositional relation. But it differs from the latter in the sense that it is deprived of its violent character. Parties who confront each other in antagonistic oppositions are *enemies*; parties who are involved in agonistic oppositions identify the other as an *adversary* – as "somebody with whose ideas we are going to struggle but whose right to defend those ideas we will not put into question" (Mouffe 1999, p. 755). This description implies two things. First, the kind of transformation that the political process is expected to achieve has the form of a 'mere' taming of conflicts. Second, and as a consequence of this, political actors owe each other nothing more than refraining from the use of violence. The political process thus is an ongoing struggle for hegemony (Mouffe 2000, pp. 98–105). Consequently, Mouffe clearly succeeds in developing an alternative to consensus-oriented public reasoning.

But, how powerful is this alternative? On the one hand, the principle of taming will often serve as a valuable orientation for political conflict processing. As the case of the abortion controversy in the United States demonstrates, it is far from unrealistic that the deep moral disagreements liberal democracies are facing may turn into violent conflicts. The political achievement of effectively taming processes must therefore not be underestimated. On the other hand, though, Mouffe's exclusive focus on taming transformations of conflicts has an important downside, which comes to the fore once we clarify the (inarticulate) preconditions of her account of politics. If parties can expect nothing more than that they will not be hindered from taking part in the struggle for hegemony, the goal of agonistic pluralism, which is to enable a lively and never-ending contestation on the rules for all, requires competing groups to be on a roughly equal footing. As long as groups do not differ significantly in terms of power-related categories like size and resources, or at least have roughly equal prospects of overcoming temporary disadvantages, the question for winners and losers is likely to find different answers from case to case. But the problem is that today's societies are not like that. The effect of ongoing pluralising processes is that liberal democracies are increasingly constituted by a wide range of smaller groups – William Connolly coins the term "minoritization" (Connolly 2010, p. 230) for this phenomenon – who will not have a realistic chance of gaining political hegemony in the long run. This means that in order to prevent the advantage of the account's ethical modesty, which consists in its large inclusiveness, turning into a hindrance to the realisation of its own political vision, political theorists who draw on the agonistic pluralism seem well advised to consider possibilities of broadening the theory's view of potential forms of conflict processing. This means that it is desirable to consider principles other than taming which may complement Mouffe's favoured principle and make agonistic pluralism operate with a set of principles instead of just a single one.

The criteria that such complementary principles would have to meet are twofold. First, the nature of the conflictual consensus requires that they, just like taming, do not presuppose the availability of generally acceptable reasons with the force to make citizens agree on political goals that go beyond the need to fend off certain violations of shared norms. Second, in order to function as a counterweight to the identified weakness of a tamed but still hegemonic politics, additional principles would have to differ from Mouffe's favoured principle in the sense that they indicate the desirability of cooperation across differences and a balancing of diverging views. In this regard, a candidate worthy of scrutiny is *compromising*. Building compromises is a mode of politics that can be more sensitive to asymmetries of power than a tamed struggle for hegemony because it rejects the dichotomy of winning and losing by aiming at solutions that accommodate conflicting views through mutual concession making (see, e.g., Wendt 2013). There is a likely counter-argument to be raised against this suggestion. That is, if parties are supposed to compromise, they are left with less room to play out contestation and give expression to the incompatibility of their political projects. In comparison to political struggles that are driven by the sole intention to tame, this is certainly the case. However, it is crucial to note that a compromise differs significantly from a consensus. A compromise allows for conflict parties to maintain their disagreements as it may take, for instance, the shape of a composite agreement which those who are involved in the conflict may accept for very different reasons. Hence, the suggestion that agonistic pluralism could benefit from considering compromise as an additional political principle does not undermine its valuable achievement in offering a deeply pluralistic notion of democratic commonality. To the contrary, it may be an opportunity to advance the conceptual resources of agonistic pluralism such that it is better equipped to identify ways of realising its ideal of a vibrant pluralistic democracy in the face of the asymmetries of power that characterise the plurality of groups in today's societies.

Bibliography

Connolly, William E. (2010): "A World of Becoming". In: Finlayson, Alan (Ed.): *Democracy and Pluralism. The Political Thought of William E. Connolly*. Abingdon, New York: Routledge, pp. 222–235.

Gray, John (2000): *Two Faces of Liberalism*. New York: New Press.

Horton, John (2003): "Rawls, Public Reason and the Limits of Liberal Justification". In: *Contemporary Political Theory* 2. No. 1, pp. 5–23.

Laclau, Ernesto/Mouffe, Chantal (2001): *Hegemony and Socialist Strategy. Towards a Radical Democratic Politics*. Second edition. London, New York: Verso.

Mouffe, Chantal (1999): "Deliberative Democracy or Agonistic Pluralism?" In: *Social Research* 66. No. 3, pp. 745–758.

Mouffe, Chantal (2000): *The Democratic Paradox*. London, New York: Verso.

Mouffe, Chantal (2005): *The Return of the Political*. Second edition. London, New York: Verso.

Mouffe, Chantal (2013): *Agonistics. Thinking the World Politically*. London, New York: Verso.

Rawls, John (1997): "The Idea of Public Reason Revisited". In: *The University of Chicago Law Review* 64. No. 3, pp. 765–807.

Rawls, John (2005): *Political Liberalism*. Expanded edition. New York: Columbia University Press.

Waldron, Jeremy (1999): *Law and Disagreement*. Oxford: Clarendon Press.

Waldron, Jeremy (2007): "Public Reason and 'Justification' in the Courtroom". In: *Journal of Law, Philosophy and Culture* 1. No. 1, pp. 107–134.

Wendt, Fabian (2013): "Introduction: Compromising on Justice". In: *Critical Review of International Social and Political Philosophy* 16. No. 4, pp. 475–480.

Michał Rupniewski
Citizenship, Community, and the Rule of Law: With or Without Consensus?[1]

Abstract: The primary questions addressed in this paper examine equal citizenship: its strength and depth, as well as its relation to the other commitments (of philosophical or religious nature, for example) that play a role in people's lives. The underlying focus is the problem of finding sources of civility, legality and social stability such that one's autonomy would be fully respected when forming a conception of the good and a general worldview. To develop an answer to these questions, I examine Rawls's doctrine of an overlapping consensus. However, I proceed from a somewhat different perspective. I consider the ideal of the rule of law as at least partially realised in contemporary democracies and ask what kind of civic community it requires. This paper is composed of three sections. The first two focus specifically on Rawls – in the first section I provide the essential points of Rawls's account of social stability; in the second section I discuss the idea of an overlapping consensus in theory, and from the perspective of its realisation in political practice. In the final section I explain the reasons why I consider Rawls's project unsuccessful, and provide my own reinterpretation of the idea of an overlapping consensus arguing that Rawls's theory should be modified. My main proposal is to replace the idea of an overlapping consensus with the idea of a thinner, less specific, but still prospectively stable, solution: the rule of law consensus.

Introduction

The vast majority of people enjoy state citizenship that makes them members of their national legal communities. Given this, statelessness is generally uncommon today, and we often take citizenship for granted. When subject to common jurisdiction citizens share basic civil rights and duties. In the same legally relevant circumstances, they may make the same claims, and like sanctions are im-

---

[1] This paper presents a part of the results of the project financed by the National Science Centre (Poland) granted in the decision DEC-2012/07/N/HS5/01017. I am also grateful to Manuel Knoll who persuaded me to highlight my disagreements with Rawls on some matters discussed here. While I was working on the paper, I also benefited from discussions with Thom Brooks who received me in Durham, and for which I am indebted.

https://doi.org/10.1515/9783110537369-018

posed on like infringements. This is the way political and legal institutions make citizens equal, or more precisely they provide the institutional basis for treating all *as equals*.² This has been acknowledged widely in democratic societies to the extent that it makes it trivial to be reminded of it. What is less obvious, however, is the relation between civic and other social ties, as they may very easily enter into conflict. The main reason for this is the fact that we differ and disagree. A democratic society is supposed to be a relatively united community of equal citizens, but at the same time must be able to sustain a diversity of religious, cultural, or philosophical commitments which are to be freely formed. Moral and metaphysical views underlying these commitments are very often irreconcilable, and sources of our disagreement very often lie at the heart of our identity as moral or religious persons. This requires us to ask the following set of questions. How strong should the bond of citizenship be? What is its normative basis? In what sense do citizens constitute 'a community' sharing not simply a commitment to the rule of law, but to the rule of *their law*, even though in a particular case they would vote against it? The problem underlying all these questions could be called "the problem of oppression", that is, the problem of finding sources of civility, legality and social stability such that one's autonomy would be fully respected when forming a conception of the good and a general worldview.

One of the most insightful contributions to the topic comes from John Rawls. Introducing the idea of an overlapping consensus, he insists that a democratic polity should respect pluralism. With regards to public reason, Rawls argues that there are paths to reconciliation and to rendering society stable, which do not necessitate the violation of fundamental freedoms or the equality of citizens. These are the main tenets of Rawlsian political liberalism. In my paper I examine Rawls's doctrine from a somewhat different perspective. Namely, I'm going to consider the ideal of the rule of law as at least partially realised in contemporary democracies and ask what kind of civic community it requires.³ In other words, I'm going to ask if the Rawlsian idea of an overlapping consensus, in the form Rawls wanted it, is plausible enough from a contemporary lawyer's perspective. If it turns out that it is not, I'm going to ask how far beyond Rawls could and should we go. The rule of law has its own substantive theory, and can be understood in a variety of competing ways.⁴ For our purposes, I assume the following:

---

2 The distinction between treating people equally and treating them as equals comes from Dworkin (1981, p. 186). As he argued, contemporary political institutions aim at treating every individual with equal concern, i.e. as equals. This is the perspective I take in this essay.
3 As a matter of fact, Rawls discussed the rule of law in TJ (Rawls 1971, pp. 235–243). However, the rule of law was never a central idea of his thought, at least explicitly.
4 For a general discussion, see Krygier (2012). For historical background, see Sellers (2010).

first, rule of law obtains when a society is governed by law, i.e. the law is the final instance to which people appeal when a conflict occurs; second, the content of law meets some standards of decency (if not morality) – equality before the law and basic liberties among others; and third, the public authority is subject to law, especially in the sense that the government cannot determine the legal situation of a citizen without the legal basis at hand. The third feature has been discussed the most, because the rule of law has been conceptualised chiefly as opposed to arbitrary power. In my view, however, only these three conditions taken together constitute the rule of law, which means that the idea also has some relevance with respect to relations among citizens as being subject to the same jurisdiction. The rule of law constrains not only the discretion of my government, but also my own discretion. And the boundaries of the rule of law are not obvious in the latter case. If this is true, the rule of law faces a problem similar to that of contemporary political philosophy. That is, the problem of the right conceptualisation of civility in the circumstances of modern democracy. Therefore, we can (and should) investigate civic community from both perspectives – that of political philosophy and that of law.

This paper is composed of three sections. The first two focus specifically on Rawls – in the first section I will provide the essential points of Rawls's account of social stability; in the second section I will discuss the idea of an overlapping consensus, in theory, and from the perspective of its realisation in political practice. In the final section I will explain the reasons why I consider Rawls's project unsuccessful and provide my own reinterpretation of the idea of an overlapping consensus. I will argue that Rawls's theory, particularly when one fully recognises the burdens of judgement (this term, introduced by Rawls himself, shall be defined later), should be modified. My main proposal is to replace the idea of an overlapping consensus with the idea of a thinner, less specific, but still prospectively stable, solution: the rule of law consensus.

Consensus and stability in the late Rawls: An overview

Recall that Rawls rejected the ideal of political community in the strong sense, i.e. the ideal of a society unified by endorsing one "collective" conception of the good (Rawls 1996, p. 146). Rather, in his well ordered society individuals would be free to form and revise conceptions of the good on their own. Saying this, Rawls acknowledges the fact of pluralism which is an inevitable mark of contemporary democratic societies. It is important to emphasise that Rawls discusses neither the pluralism of value nor any other moral-theoretic standpoint claiming pluralism in the realm of moral truth. What he is concerned with is a sociological observation that contemporary people have different and irreconcilable comprehensive doctrines or hold only partially comprehensive views that nonetheless differ deeply. To Rawls, this is not an unfortunate condition. Rather, it is one of the key features of a democratic society, so pluralism is both persistent and desirable. Thus, a political conception of justice which is to regulate such a society must take pluralism into consideration. Justice shouldn't overcome or sublate this fact but adjust to it.

On the other hand, Rawls is not a radical individualist, and he does not reject the idea of community altogether[5] He believes that despite the disagreement, individuals can accept and endorse some reciprocal rules which are justified publicly and are supposed to regulate the basic structure of society; in other words, they can share civic commitment despite the lack of full reconciliation in other spheres of social life. And they can really consider belonging to a civic community of intrinsic value. In *Theory of Justice* he expresses this with an idea taken from Humboldt, which is the idea of a social union of social unions. The opposing model, rejected by Rawls, would be that of private society (close to Hegel's *bürgerliche Gesellschaft*). As Rawls writes:

> [i]ts chief features are first that the persons comprising it, whether they are human individuals or associations, have their own private ends which are either competing or independent, but not in any case complementary. And second, institutions are not thought to have any value in themselves, the activity of engaging in them not being counted as a good but if anything as burden (Rawls 1971, p. 521).

For Rawls, such a model is inadequate to what society really is. He proposes a model in which social cooperation possesses an intrinsic good, and it is not merely a means to an end of subsistence or prosperity. This is the model of a social union of social unions.[6] Cooperation under publicly recognised rules is cru-

---

5 An insightful account on the 'social' dimension of Rawls's thought may be found in Proudfoot (1974).
6 It is not clear to what extent the idea of society as social union of social unions remains topical also in *Political Liberalism*. In *Reply to Habermas* (i.e. Lecture IX of the 1996 edition), in a footnote, Rawls explicitly says that it "is no longer viable as a political ideal" because it "depends [...] on everyone's holding the same comprehensive doctrine" (Rawls 1996, p. 288, footnote 21). As a reaction to this, Paul Weithman proposes a less demanding ideal, i.e. the Ideal of Democratic Governance (Weithman 2015, p. 92) which obtains when "citizens follow the guidelines of public reason and govern themselves in accordance with a just constitution" (Weithman 2015, p. 93). However, the late Rawls too says that ideally the citizens should share the same conception of justice, and it is the justice of basic structure which allows us

cial in this model because "successes and enjoyments of others are necessary for and complementary to our own good", and thus we need to regard society as a bond through which "each person can participate in the total sum of the realized natural assets of the others" (Rawls 1971, p. 523). Society may be then pictured as an orchestra – each member plays his instrument, performing his part, but he's doing it not only for his career, but also for the sake of the whole, the symphony as such. The aims of all musicians are different (everyone wants to play his part the best he can) but complementary.

Now, if we reconsider this idea, we will find ourselves surprised that apparently, there is a prima facie tension between pluralism (which is a fact Rawls takes for granted) and the idea of social union of social unions, especially in a form of a well-ordered society.[7] I emphasise here that the idea of the social union of social unions makes us assume a situation in which the individual aims are *complementary*, which means something far different from their simply being in accordance with the common aims, not to mention the idea that the latter should overcome the former. This merges uneasily with the idea of a well-ordered society. But why? To answer that, we must take a look at the sources of pluralism.

Pluralism is a long-term outcome of two very important factors – free exercise of human reason and the so called "burdens of judgement". The former assures that the worldviews emerge and develop spontaneously. The latter means that even a reasonable person faces "many obstacles to the correct (and conscientious) exercise of [...] powers of reason and judgment in the ordinary course of political life" (Rawls 2001, p. 35), and thus disagreement is very likely even among reasonable persons. When those two factors are granted, we must end up with divergent worldviews. As emphasised earlier, Rawls does not take any firm position concerning the nature of morals,[8] and he abstains from metaphysics generally. However, the burdens of judgement are one epistemological assumption underlying his political liberalism. According to the doctrine of the

---

to say that the good of political society is "the good that citizens realize both as persons and as a corporate body in maintaining a just constitutional regime and in conducting their affairs" (Rawls 1996, p. 201). So certainly, also in the project of *Political Liberalism* the society itself is a part of each citizen's good, and the well-ordered society of *Political Liberalism* is something more than Hegelian "private society". It seems, therefore, that the difference between the social union of social unions and Democratic Governance is not very sharp.

[7] It is important to remember that this idea is also found in the late Rawls (Rawls 2001, pp. 8–10).

[8] His strong inclination is constructivism, but the project of political liberalism was aimed at developing a theory which would be neutral, and possible to be endorsed both by constructivists and moral realists as a political conception.

burdens of judgement, we will disagree when it comes to questions of the good life, the existence of God, the nature and content of morals simply because our human reason is limited. In each such case we face conflicting and complex evidence, assessed with vague concepts open to interpretation and judgement about interpretation.[9] What is more, our life situations differ, and if the reasoning of each of us is inevitably rooted in our own particular experience, such that we do not always share the same prerequisites as relevant in a case; and even if we do share, we do not weigh them alike. Those are the main obstacles preventing us from grasping the whole truth, and if this is combined with liberal freedoms assured over time, we have no other possible outcome but pluralism of comprehensive doctrines.[10]

The tension between social unity and pluralism (which has an individualistic foundation) is now becoming clear. Recall that the idea of a well-ordered society consists of three elements, in other words, in a well-ordered society the three following conditions are met: (1) everyone accepts the same political conception of justice as a publicly recognised conception, (2) the main political and social institutions satisfy and realise the principles constituting this conception, and (3) citizens' understanding and application of the conception of justice is supported by their effective sense of justice (see Rawls 2001, p. 8). If this requires social unity (all citizens have one and the same conception of justice), how could it be reconciled with the fact of social diversity in terms of irreconcilable general worldviews people hold? Rawls (the later Rawls in particular) shows he is well aware of this problem when he writes that "[f]inding a stable conception is not simply a matter of avoiding futility. Rather, what counts is the kind of stability, the nature of forces that secure it" (Rawls 1996, p. 142).[11] This is the problem of right reasons for stability, which I have called the problem of oppression.[12] In

---

[9] Here I paraphrase Rawls, who gives the full list of burdens of judgement in Rawls (2001, pp. 35–36).
[10] It may seem that Rawls adopts some form of value pluralism, as Raz or Berlin do, but this is not the case. For this argument see Nussbaum (2011).
[11] George Klosko distinguishes between the purely sociological dimension of stability, and the normative one. The sociological component means simply the lack of revolts or frequent constitutional change. The normative aspect requires the spontaneous acceptance of the political system by the majority of citizens, with respect for the basic liberties granted. See Klosko 1993, pp. 349–351.
[12] Of course, the primary concern of Rawls's *Political Liberalism* is the problem of stability (Rawls 1996, p. xxvii). However, Rawls wants not mere stability, but stability for the right reasons, and he explicitly admitted that the original project of TJ failed to conceptualise such a stability. Given this, plus the fact that *Political Liberalism*'s solution seems problematic as well, I introduce the notion of the oppression problem as the key issue to deal with in this paper.

his early work Rawls wanted to show that his conception of justice reflects an adequate ethical conception of the autonomous person and thus avoids the oppression problem. In his later works, Rawls looks for a conception of stability which would show respect not only for autonomy understood as an abstract philosophical ideal coming from a particular moral theory, but also for actual self-determination, i.e. free formation of one's conception of the good which could come from any reasonable philosophical idea or values of religious ancestry.

What is particularly striking in this context is a possibility that the stability of a well-ordered society could be realised through oppressive state power. Rawls draws attention to that possibility, although it seems underestimated by the commentators. Of course, a strictly authoritative or totalitarian state is not compatible with liberal freedoms. But even in a democracy, if the political system was dependent on nothing but public institutions shaping social circumstances, chiefly through legislation and enforcement, and at the same time the society was lacking strong civil society, the system would be oppressive. If we want to maintain both things – the fact of pluralism and the idea of a well-ordered society, we must come up with an ideal which allows citizens to differ reasonably when it comes to their worldview, but at the same enables a free endorsement of the political conception of justice. The Rawlsian solution is that his conception of justice – understood as a political conception – can be the subject of an overlapping consensus. In this new view, justice is not supported by any particular, general and comprehensive worldview, but everyone may accept its content from within his or her own doctrine. As Rawls writes:

> While in a well-ordered society all citizens affirm the same political conception of justice, we do not assume they do so for all the same reasons, all the way down. Citizens have conflicting religious, philosophical, and moral views and so they affirm the political conception from within different and opposing comprehensive doctrines, and so, in part at least, for different reasons (Rawls 2001, p. 32).

It's worth recalling that the conception Rawls writes about – justice as fairness – even in his late works has chiefly the same contractual justification as before.[13]

---

[13] There are some minor changes. For instance, the parties to the original position are aware of the fact that they represent free and equal citizens having the moral powers of rationality and reasonableness. So the parties are now trustees of rational and reasonable citizens. While choosing the principles of justice the parties strive to protect the higher-order interest of citizens they represent, i.e. assure their developing and maintaining the moral powers. In *Theory of Justice* the parties were depicted as rational (and free and equal too) agents, but it was not clear if the parties are moral agents or merely rational agents. The change I talk about clearly incorporates moral prerequisites regarding the moral nature of citizenship. However, the idea of the

This could simply entail a constructivist position in meta-ethical questions, but according to the doctrine of the overlapping consensus this justification should no more be read as a part of a comprehensive moral theory. For Rawls, we should be able to accept justice as fairness being a moral realist as well as an evolutionary moral theorist, because what underlies justice as fairness is not a moral theory, but political reasonableness. This does not mean, however, that being a political liberal one is indifferent about morality, and says that politics is about nothing but "avoiding conflict".[14] Rawls emphasises that "[j]ustice as fairness is not procedurally neutral. Clearly its principles of justice are substantive and express far more than procedural values" (Rawls 1996, p. 268). He believes, however, that the substantive values he draws on are not divisive, because they originate from our common, democratic tradition. Thus, Rawlsian political philosophy becomes now a sort of hermeneutics of democracy, revealing "fundamental intuitive ideas implicit in the public political culture" (Rawls 1996, p. 268). Forming an overlapping consensus, Rawls hopes, we maintain both values – social stability and pluralism. In this sense an overlapping consensus is introduced in order to resolve the oppression problem.

Justice as the basis of social unity? The depth, breadth and specificity of an overlapping consensus

It is still unclear, however, how an overlapping consensus resolves the oppression problem. If justice as fairness is not merely procedural, how strong is its influence on the comprehensive doctrines forming the society? How can citizens come into an agreement and still remain so different that we call their worldviews *irreconcilable*? Does it really sustain both the freedom to form and revise one's conception of the good and the social unity required for stability? All these questions evoke a well-justified doubt: is the project of an overlapping consensus – the project of a society in which the citizens are unified by endorsing one and the same conception of justice – realisable and desirable? After all, it may be deemed merely a utopian ideal. While even reasonable persons differ, how can real people, who are perhaps not so often reasonable, come to an overlapping

---

original position (with the veil of ignorance) remains one of foundational ideals also in *Political Liberalism*.

14 This is the way some see it, though. See Sellers (2003).

consensus? And even if they could, why should they declare only one conception of justice as the most reasonable? By insisting on justice as fairness as the prevailing political conception, Rawls is vulnerable to critiques as strong as Bhikhu Parekh's, who says that political liberalism "is largely only the old comprehensive liberalism restricted to the political realm" (Parekh 2006, p. 86), and "is, or could be seen by some as, not a principled and self-limiting moral position but a political device with a large hidden agenda" (Parekh 2006, p. 88). Any compelling response to such a critique, must show a sketch of a social mechanism which can be reasonably expected to lead to an overlapping consensus, while at the same time preserving the deep, spontaneous commitments of citizens.[15]

Indeed, Rawls does take pains to provide such sketch, for an overlapping consensus is not an interpretation of any actual democratic society; rather, it is a philosophical project aiming at improving one, and that is why Rawls shows the "steps to overlapping consensus" (Rawls 1996, pp. 158–168). The idea of an overlapping consensus is determined with respect to the three most important features: the depth, breadth, and specificity. In order to see how an overlapping consensus could emerge, we must first briefly see what those features mean.

The depth shows how far the political conception goes into the comprehensive doctrines participating in the consensus. In other words it specifies the extent to which the conception of justice (together with its contractual justification!) becomes a part of a reasonable comprehensive doctrine. Rawls thinks that stability requires a deep consensus. The principles are substantive and they must become an essential part of citizen's worldview, or at least there must be some kind of congruence between the comprehensive doctrine and the political conception. It entails that the particular (i.e. Rawlsian) interpretation of the conception of citizens as free and equal persons as well as that of society as a system of fair cooperation also becomes a part of consensus (Rawls 1996, p. 149). Those conceptions, however, stay political and refer to the civic life only.

The breadth of the consensus determines the range of matters regulated by the conception of justice. A thin consensus covers only the sphere of political procedures in the strict sense, i.e. the basic liberties and general principles of government. A broad consensus, and that's what Rawls argues for, covers the

---

[15] Traditionally, liberal theory thinks of individual commitment as chosen. This is for the most part untrue – people do not 'choose' their comprehensive doctrine as simply as they choose products on the market. It is rather upbringing or conversion, or persuasion that forms an individual conception of the good. But political liberalism, from its inner perspective, does treat them as subject of rational choice.

whole "basic structure of society" – not only the most fundamental constitutional rules but also their more specific interpretation, as well as all other major social and political institutions.[16] Citizens agree that the political conception should be a common point of reference when it comes to resolving conflicts regarding issues of public education, healthcare system, or the general legal boundaries of entrepreneurship.

As far the specificity is concerned, the consensus may or may not consist of one conception only. If there is some wider range of competing conceptions of justice, the consensus is not specific to one. An overlapping consensus assumes pluralism only in the sphere of comprehensive doctrines, and at the same time unanimity as to the conception of justice is required. Rawls admits that this (i.e. an exclusively specific consensus) may be seen more like an ideal than the real outcome of a realistic hope – it is much more likely that the consensus would be less specific and cover not the exclusive one, but a family or "a focal class" of liberal conceptions of justice. Even in this case, however, justice as fairness would be the leading one, constituting the centre of the consensus (Rawls 1996, p. 166).

Having defined an overlapping consensus with respect to its depth, breadth and specificity, we may now roughly understand how Rawls sees its emergence in a democratic society. He argues that the public rules, (e.g. freedom of conscience) at first, are accepted merely as a modus vivendi. In this case (and that has happened, Rawls believes, in Europe after the Reformation and the religious wars) there is a fragile peace, but there is no genuine agreement in the society. The modus vivendi will be broken immediately when the circumstances change. The reason for this is that modus vivendi is neither deep nor broad. The liberal principles are seen as a "truce" and thus are completely alien to the comprehensive doctrines of those who make it. The first step to an overlapping consensus is constitutional consensus, which is much deeper than modus vivendi. Citizens see that liberal principles have intrinsic value, thereby including them in their own general views. Rawls believes that political practice leads the state of public affairs into deeper, broader and more specific agreement of which an overlapping consensus is the final stage. This final stage assures the long-term stability of a just basic structure.

---

[16] There is a huge disagreement among commentators regarding what the basic structure specifically is. For the purpose of this essay, we can stay at the intuitive level presented above. For deeper discussions, see Cohen (1997).

Rule of law: Community without consensus?

I maintain that the Rawlsian project, although impressive and inspiring, remains unsuccessful in many crucial respects, especially if it is interpreted as a solution to the problem of oppression. Although Rawls briefly shows a mechanism laying out the "steps to overlapping consensus", the picture remains blurry, especially as far as a full (i.e. exclusively specific) overlapping consensus is concerned. He considers the possibility of a weaker version of overlapping consensus, where citizens do not affirm one and the same conception of justice, but "a class of liberal conceptions". Nonetheless, it is only a step to the final end, which is a full overlapping consensus with only one conception of justice being accepted and endorsed.[17]

Rawls emphasises that this perhaps will never be achieved, but he has an inclination to blame the contingencies of political life rather than deep philosophical obstacles. I think this is problematic, and the Rawlsian justification of an overlapping consensus contains a gap. Who, after all, decides if the political conception of justice is really accepted by all and the process of formation of the consensus has been accomplished? Can we really think of this process as fully spontaneous? If the steps to overlapping consensus were taken without a proper self-limitation in mind, and with no vivid civic participation, they could simply become just another "road to serfdom". Surprisingly, the main reason for which the idea of an overlapping consensus in the original formulation seems misconceived can be found among the crucial premises of Rawlsian philosophy itself. What I have in mind here is the abovementioned foundation of political liberalism, namely, the burdens of judgement.[18] As I wrote at the beginning of the paper, Rawls acknowledges the possibility that even reasonable persons, working in good faith, still may disagree when they discuss crucial philosophical issues. In other words, there is a possibility of reasonable disagreement – a disagreement not resulting from bias or underlying self-interest, but simply

---

[17] It should be noted that Rawls's planned (but not fully completed) revisions of *Political Liberalism* shed new light on this matter. Martha Nussbaum cites a letter to the editor, written in 1998, in which Rawls seems to have resigned from the centrality of his conception of justice, writing: "[j]ustice as fairness itself now has a minor role as one such political conception among others" (Nussbaum 2015, p. 21). But even if this means that Rawls did no longer believe that his conception had an elevated status in an overlapping consensus, but instead were merely one of many equally reasonable conceptions, he still would restrain the family of reasonable political conceptions to the liberal conceptions of justice, with quite rigid criteria for the term "liberal" (the criteria may be found in Rawls 1999, p. 582).

[18] For the full list of the burdens of judgement see Rawls 2001, p. 35.

from the obstacles of human reasoning. At the same time, Rawls seems to assert that this is possible (and permissible) only in case of a clash between comprehensive doctrines, and he does not take it into consideration when it comes to the controversies over political justice. If he hopes for a full overlapping consensus, he must believe that reasonable persons *will not differ* when it comes to the political conception of justice.[19] It remains completely unclear why burdens of judgement were not to work in discussions on justice, and Rawls does not take pains to explain why he thinks they don't.[20] The evidence, however, obviously shows they do. No significant books on justice would have been written if the differences were simply an outcome of bias and self-interest. Quite to the contrary, the continuous scholarly interest in justice is a genuine effort. The intended outcome, however, i.e. the most reasonable conception of justice, seems to be out of its range. Surprisingly, the Rawlsian description of burdens of judgement is a very good explanation why.

If the burdens of judgement were taken seriously (which is not the case in Rawls, as I have been trying to argue) justice would not make a good basis for the political community. If we are not likely come to a specific agreement on the principles of justice, we cannot say that the commitment to a widely shared political conception of justice really underlies our civic bonds. On the other hand, contemporary democratic societies are relatively peaceful and stable. They would not be so if there was no consensus whatsoever. Thus, it seems prudent to look for some other, less specific form of consensus which could explain how we actually work together (despite our deep differences, which extend to the domain of justice) while providing some normative conception of how we should improve our cooperation.

In *Political Liberalism* Rawls presents a model in which a constitutional consensus is followed by an overlapping consensus. In constitutional consensus, citizens agree only on a thin set of political rules. In this the latter case, the subject of an overlapping consensus is a conception of justice or at least a family of

---

19 This has been pointed out and criticised by Sandel (1994, p. 1783). The problematic nature of an "uncogenial conclusion" was pointed out also by Jeremy Waldron (See Waldron 1999, p. 153).
20 One could argue, however, that the disagreement about justice is perhaps less fundamental than disagreement about comprehensive worldview. I think it is so because in the domain of the political we (i.e. almost all citizens and political thinkers) share most of the ideals. In the domain of comprehensive doctrines there is no such common ground – if a theistic, dignity-based ethics meets a utilitarian, hedonistic standpoint, there is hardly anything in common. In the domain of justice, even if we consider the Rawls-Nozick debate, there is some stock of shared ideals (that of freedom and equality for instance). It doesn't change the fact that even the widely shared ideals are interpreted differently, as is their overall importance if they come into conflict with one another.

conceptions. In my view making this the transition from the constitutional consensus directly to the consensus on the principles of justice is too rushed. On the other hand, the actual civic cooperation in democratic societies seems to have broader foundations than merely a constitutional consensus, which is restricted to political procedures only. Therefore, the original model of consensus evolution should be expanded to include one more form of consensus, which can be called the idea of 'the rule of law consensus' and can be presented as an intermediate step between constitutional and overlapping consensus. The rule of law, a subject of consensus in this step, can serve the purpose of explaining our civic commitment. At the same time, it can escape the problems of the original Rawlsian doctrine I have been pointing out throughout the paper.

In contrast to an overlapping consensus, the rule of law in a democratic society is a fact. In all democratic societies, although we constantly discuss, and sometimes even fight about what is politically just, we somehow do this as members of one civic community. Although we do not always obey perfectly, we all respect the law – not only as a modus vivendi, but as something of intrinsic value. In this sense the law stands for the common good of our pluralistic societies. It is one of the achievements of democratic judicial culture that regardless of the particulars of the political system, we respect basic liberties, and we require the public authority to "function on the basis of, and within the limits of law"[21]. So despite the vivid diversity that exists among people enjoying democratic citizenship – diversity going deeper than Rawls had an inclination to acknowledge – something really overlaps, and in the vast majority of the cases citizens agree to reciprocally limit themselves by law. This is not only about the constitution, so the constitutional consensus Rawls writes about seems insufficient. The rule of law covers the whole basic structure, but only a few interpret it as a mere coercion. The rule of law consensus, then, is not only a normative idea helping to reshape our life together as citizens, but also a part of our everyday life, taking different forms in different societies.

I think that the main reason for this is that the rule of law consensus fully acknowledges the burdens of judgement. A brief explanation of how the consensus on the rule of law is possible with the burdens of judgement taken for granted would go as follows. If the citizens are supposed to reciprocally limit themselves by law, they have to acknowledge that law always has reasonable justification. Justification consists in giving reasons, drawing either on justice or on the good. As the doctrine of the burdens of judgement assumes, we do not always share reasons with our fellow citizens, or we assign different mean-

---

[21] This is a quotation from Article 7 of the Polish Constitution.

ings or different weight to different reasons. As a result, we will perhaps never fully agree on the justification of law. But it does not mean that some form of consensus is not possible. Even if I do not share a reason, I still recognise it as a reason. So even if I do not consider a law perfectly good or just, I recognise it as *justified*. If the shortcomings of law are not extreme, I obey the law, even when I consider it defective. And it is not a mere modus vivendi – I obey because I owe respect to my fellow citizens and as a reasonable citizen I prefer to compromise on some matters concerning the justification in order to maintain social cooperation of the free and equal. As a result, we all can agree on the rule of law even though our conceptions of the good, and conceptions of justice, differ. This renders the consensus more loose, allowing citizens differ reasonably also when it comes to justice, but at the same time gives a solid normative basis of social cooperation.

The abovementioned gives us reasons to look into the actual consensus on the rule of law rather than a potential (and potentially oppressive) overlapping consensus in the form Rawls argued for. The price we were to pay, however, would be that of specificity and depth of the consensus. With the rule of law consensus, we assume that social and political unity does not consist in affirming one and the same conception of justice. Rather, it affirms in a continual discourse on justice, constantly reshaping the content of law. The threat of the problem of oppression is much weaker here, as everyone is entitled to propose as a justification for the law, a new conception of justice.[22] The commitment to the rule of law can be inferred from many irreconcilable views, so the rule of law consensus does not require as much depth as Rawls does for his overlapping consensus. On the other hand, the rule of law consensus is relatively broad, as it focuses on standards and principles for the whole legal system, not only the political procedures. It seems, then, that we cannot escape some form of consensus if we think of society as a social union of social unions. It does not have to be very specific and fixed, in order to constitute a stable community of citizens. In-

---

22 Some (and perhaps Rawls among them) might find such a solution too fragile. Perhaps, one might argue, this solution escapes the problem of oppression, but at the same it time falls short of resolving the fundamental question of stability as such. As Thom Brooks shows, however, even in the original doctrine of political liberalism, the consensus on justice is not the only source of political stability, and we can speak of "political stability by other means" (Brooks 2015, pp. 150–154). As Brooks argues, these other political values, like shared endorsement of constitutional essentials, reciprocal recognition of one another as free and equal, or a social minimum, secure stability together with an overlapping consensus. If this is true, one can reasonably hope for social stability even if there is some other form of consensus, like the rule of law consensus, for example.

deed, the legal discourse is often shown as freestanding, i.e. not derived from any particular comprehensive doctrine. And at the same time it is subject to constant redefinition in the public discourse. Improving the legal institutions is then also improving, or redefining, the consensus.

Bibliography

Brooks, Thom (2015): "The Capabilities Approach and Political Liberalism". In: Brooks, Thom/Nussbaum, Martha C. (Eds.): *Rawls's Political Liberalism*. New York: Columbia University Press, pp. 139–173.
Cohen, G.A. (1997): "Where the Action Is: On the Site of Distributive Justice". In: *Philosophy & Public Affairs* 26. No. 3, pp. 3–30.
Dworkin, Ronald (1981): "What is Equality? Part 1: Equality of Welfare". In: *Philosophy & Public Affairs* 10. No. 3, pp. 185–246.
Klosko, George (1993): "Rawls's 'Political' Philosophy and American Democracy". In: *The American Political Science Review* 87. No. 2, pp. 348–359.
Krygier, Martin (2012): "Rule of Law". In: Rosenfeld, Michael/Sajó, András (Eds.): *The Oxford Handbook of Comparative Constitutional Law*. Oxford: Oxford University Press, pp. 233–240.
Nussbaum, Martha C. (2011): "Perfectionist Liberalism and Political Liberalism". In: *Philosophy & Public Affairs* 39. No. 1, pp. 4–45.
Nussbaum, Martha C. (2015): "Introduction". In: Brooks, Thom/Nussbaum, Martha C. (Eds.): *Rawls's Political Liberalism*. New York: Columbia University Press, pp. 1–56.
Parekh, Bhikhu (2006): *Rethinking Multiculturalism. Cultural Diversity and Political Theory*. New York: Palgrave Macmillan.
Proudfoot, Wayne (1974): "Rawls on the Individual and the Social". In: *The Journal of Religious Ethics* 2. No. 2, pp. 107–128.
Rawls, John (1971): *A Theory of Justice*. Cambridge, MA: Belknap Press of Harvard University Press.
Rawls, John (1996): *Political Liberalism*. New York: Columbia University Press.
Rawls, John (1999): "The Idea of Public Reason Revisited". In: Rawls, John: *Collected Papers*. Samuel Freeman (Ed.). Cambridge, London: Harvard University Press, pp. 573–615.
Rawls, John (2001): *Justice as Fairness: A Restatement*. Cambridge, MA: Belknap Press of Harvard University Press.
Sandel, Michael (1994): "Political Liberalism" [book review]. In: *Harvard Law Review* 107, pp. 1765–1794.
Sellers, Mortimer (2003): *Republican Legal Theories*. New York: Palgrave MacMillan.
Sellers, Mortimer (2010): "An Introduction to the Rule of Law in Comparative Perspective". In: Seller, Mortimer/Tomaszewski, Tadeusz (Eds.): *The Rule of Law in Comparative Perspective*. Dordrecht, Heidelberg: Springer, pp. 1–9.
Waldron, Jeremy (1999): *Law and Disagreement*. Oxford, New York: Clarendon Press.
Weithman, Paul (2015): "Legitimacy and the Project of Political Liberalism". In: Brooks, Thom/Nussbaum, Martha C. (Eds.): *Rawls's Political Liberalism*. New York: Columbia University Press, pp. 73–112.

Peter Caven
Political Liberalism: The Burdens of Judgement and Moral Psychology

Abstract: John Rawls' political liberalism holds that an overlapping consensus on a liberal political conception of justice is possible, in spite of deep and intractable moral disagreement. This, he argues, is partly because reasonable people recognise that moral disagreement sometimes stems from the 'burdens of judgement' rather than moral or epistemic failure on the part of others, and so accept that imposing one's own conception of the good on another on the political level is unjustified. However, Rawls does not provide an account of the burdens of judgement which will persuade all those he counts as reasonable, and thus a stronger case for them must be made if they are to serve their place in his overall argument. I draw on empirical evidence to support an affect-based account of moral psychology, whereby much moral disagreement stems from differences in affective dispositions between individuals. This account helps vindicate the burdens of judgement, and thereby improves Rawls' case for the possibility of political liberalism.

If we take moral disagreement to be an intractable feature of human life, then how are we ever to reach a consensus on substantive political principles? In *Political Liberalism* John Rawls recognises that fundamental moral disagreement is inevitable, as an element of what he calls 'reasonable pluralism'. This is the notion that under conditions of freedom of thought, reasonable people (i.e. those who are willing to cooperate with others on terms that are mutually agreeable) will forever be committed to a plurality of conflicting worldviews. Reasonable pluralism is a consequence of the 'burdens of judgement': aspects of human reasoning which preclude substantive agreement on what makes for a good life among all reasonable people. Nonetheless, Rawls is optimistic about the prospect of a liberal society regulated by a conception of justice which everyone can agree upon. He claims that recognition of the aforementioned burdens of judgement plays an important role in convincing citizens that any political arrangement justified purely in light of one's own worldview would be illegitimate, and so we must restrict ourselves to drawing on shared political values when proposing terms of cooperation. In this way we can reach an overlapping consensus on a liberal political conception of justice, despite fundamentally disagreeing on matters of value.

In this essay I will argue that Rawls is right that recognition of the burdens of judgement promotes toleration, and is a vital criterion of reasonableness. However, the burdens of judgement are a controversial supposition regarding the nature of reasoning which Rawls fails to properly substantiate. Given this, it is important to make a stronger case than Rawls provides for the proposition that those whom one morally disagrees with are not necessarily exhibiting irrationality, wilful ignorance or selfishness in their disagreement. To this end, I suggest that Rawls's account of the burdens of judgement can be reinforced and rendered more persuasive through reference to a psychologised account of moral disagreement.

My argument will take the following structure. Section 1 will discuss how moral disagreement poses a problem for liberalism and outlines Rawls's basic project. Section 2 explicates the burdens of judgement and their role in *Political Liberalism* in more detail. Finally, section 3 will demonstrate how an affect based-account of moral psychology can buttress Rawls's case for the burdens of judgement and consequent reasonable pluralism. I conclude with some remarks on how moral psychology can influence political theory more generally.

1 The problem of disagreement and Rawlsian political liberalism

What unites the various articulations of liberalism is a fundamental concern for protecting the individual freedom of citizens, combined with the recognition of the necessity of endowing a central political authority with coercive power. In doing so, all forms of liberalism must offer a means by which individual freedom can remain unthreatened by the prospect of state coercion. The vast majority of contemporary liberal theorists do so by drawing on the consent-based notion of legitimacy from the social contract tradition.[1] The basic idea is that the laws of the state are legitimate, binding and do not violate freedom just so long as all those subject to them can be taken to have consented to them in some form. Liberal theorists typically recognise that attaining the actual consent of all citizens is impossible, and so too stringent a requirement for legitimacy. Instead, they suggest that it is enough that citizens can be said to *hypothetically* consent to

---

[1] This is not to say that all forms of liberalism share these moral foundations. For instance, on one plausible reading of Mill's liberalism, the ultimate justification for privileging liberty is in its instrumental role in terms of maximising utility. More recently, Joseph Raz notably avoids grounding legitimacy upon consent (Raz 1986).

the state which governs their society.² That is, coercive power is legitimate if agents would consent to the political authority under certain idealising conditions, such as being fully informed, consistent and instrumentally rational.

However, some question the feasibility of a state which all citizens would willingly consent to the authority of, given the moral disagreement which we routinely encounter. As Matthew Sleat puts it in his book on political realism:

> The persistence of disagreement is one of the fundamental and 'stubborn facts' of political life which ensures that there is rarely any natural harmony or order in human affairs. The most basic political question, what I shall call '*the* political question', is how we are to live together in the face of such deep and persistent disagreement (Sleat 2013, p. 47).

For political realists like Sleat, liberalism's ambition of reaching a universal consensus on political principles that we can all consent to is hopelessly utopian. We can never attain what Bernard Williams described as the "insatiable ideal of many a political theoretician: universal consent" (Williams 2005, p. 6). This train of thought leads realists to emphasise the importance of negotiation and compromise in reaching a *modus vivendi*; a political settlement the content of which is determined by the particular balance of power within a society, and which all citizens can accept in the name of attaining the universal goods of peace and stability.

The liberal theorist might respond that the moral disagreement that we observe is only apparent; although people may profess to hold fundamentally different ethical beliefs, this is only due to contingent factors, such as self-interest, disagreement over the relevant non-moral facts or due to the differing contexts of disputants. If this is true, then moral disagreement is something we can overcome, given time, and the liberal ideal of hypothetical consent lives on. Nonetheless, recent empirical studies have cast doubt on the extent to which such so called 'defusing explanations' of moral disagreement are in fact applicable (Doris/Plakias 2008). In fact, it seems that although some cases of moral disagreement may be only apparent, in many cases it is genuinely fundamental, stemming from different understandings of how values are properly weighed when they conflict, rather than anything else.

Insofar as most contemporary accounts of liberalism are grounded on a consent-based account of legitimacy, the problem posed by the prospect of such fundamental moral disagreement is clear. Not only does it imply that no political authority can become an object of actual consensus amongst citizens, but it

---

2 Another strategy involves following the Lockean tradition of grounding legitimacy upon tacit consent, an approach which I will not discuss here.

also suggests that none could even hypothetically enjoy universal endorsement. For the principles which justify any political system are ultimately based on particular conceptions of value. Thus, fundamental disagreement over the relative weight of values implies that for any and each proposed political system, some individuals will reject it as incongruent with their value system. Since this disagreement is fundamental rather than merely apparent, liberal theorists cannot sidestep the issue by insisting that all would ultimately consent to a particular authority under certain hypothetical conditions. For even if we make idealising assumptions which abstract away citizen's constraints on knowledge, rationality and consistency, we can still expect there to be disagreement about which principles should regulate how society is organised.

Nonetheless, Rawls's account of political liberalism is expressly supposed to make room for moral disagreement, whilst retaining the liberal ideal of consensus as necessary for legitimacy. Rawlsian political liberalism, then, offers liberals the best hope of addressing the political problem of moral disagreement without jettisoning a consent-based account of legitimacy. Rawls's transition of thought from his seminal work of *A Theory of Justice* to his second book *Political Liberalism* was largely shaped by his recognition of the fact of 'reasonable pluralism' and how this presents a problem for his earlier position. Reasonable pluralism is manifest when reasonable people, who regard themselves as free and equal citizens and are willing to cooperate under fair terms of cooperation when assured that others will do so, are committed to a diversity of incompatible comprehensive doctrines. A comprehensive doctrine is an exercise in both theoretical and practical reason and roughly translates to a 'worldview'. Examples of which include moral doctrines such as Utilitarianism and Kantianism, as well as religious doctrines such as Catholicism and Buddhism. Each doctrine typically entails an associated conception of the good: a view on what is of final value in human life and how values are to be weighed against each other when they conflict.

One important aspect of reasonable pluralism is moral disagreement, insofar as it involves diversity in people's conceptions of the good. For instance, some individuals will reason to the conclusion that consequentialist considerations are paramount and may typically resolve moral conflicts by appealing to something like the principle of utility. Others will be led to endorse a more deontological moral worldview, leading them to conceive a different account of what is of most value in life. Still others will refer to a traditional religious doctrine with its own set of prescriptions and values to determine their conception of the good. Yet Rawls admits that as it is presented in *A Theory of Justice*, 'justice as fairness' represents a partially comprehensive doctrine of its own, and thus will not be endorsed by all reasonable citizens (Rawls 1993, p. xvi). This,

Rawls suggests, entails that his earlier project is not fully publicly justifiable, and presents difficulties in terms of both liberal legitimacy and, relatedly, stability.

According to Rawls's liberal principle of legitimacy:

> Our exercise of political power is fully proper only when it is exercised in accordance with a constitution the essentials of which all citizens as free and equal may reasonably be expected to endorse in the light of principles and ideals acceptable to their common human reason (Rawls 1993, p. 137).

This principle is one of Rawls's chief normative assumptions and is derived from the idea inherent in the political culture of liberal democratic constitutional regimes that only the collective body of the public, conceived of as free and equal citizens, can justify the enforcement of state statutes. Yet reasonable pluralism necessarily implies that no single comprehensive doctrine can be the object of consensus amongst reasonable people exercising freedom of thought. Thus, if we accept the liberal principle of legitimacy, then a society which is governed according to any particular comprehensive doctrine cannot legitimate the coercive power of the state.

Rawls thereby admits that a universal consensus on moral principles, even amongst those he classes as 'reasonable', is impossible. However, he is not willing to give up on the liberal principle of legitimacy, and denigrates the *modus vivendi* settlements favoured by political realists as "political in the wrong way" (Rawls 2001, p. 188). Not only do such solutions infringe on the liberal principle of legitimacy, but Rawls deems them fundamentally unstable due to them being ultimately hostage to the particular balance of power within a society (Rawls 1993, p. xli).

Moreover, reasonable pluralism entails that any society which is governed according to any particular comprehensive doctrine will fail to win the support of each and every reasonable citizen by addressing their freely exercised reason. And if some reasonable individuals within such a society do not have *internal reasons* as to why they should obey the laws as they are specified by the state, it remains fundamentally unstable. Internal reasons are those reasons which one identifies with as normatively significant in light of one's own set of values. Without such internal reasons, an individuals' compliance with the state will always be contingent on externally imposed sanctions. Now of course a state may attain a high level of a kind of stability without meeting the demand that all reasonable citizens freely support its governance. Nonetheless, for Rawls the problem of stability is not merely the practical matter of how to ensure that citizens comply with the statutes of the state, willingly or not. Instead, he wants to attain stability *for the right reasons*, whereby reasonable citizens are motivated to comply for internal reasons. So a society governed according to any particular comprehensive doctrine cannot be stable in the sense which Rawls regards as essential. Thus, Rawls sums up his project in *Political Liberalism* as addressing the following problem: "How is it possible that there may exist over time a stable and just society of free and equal citizens profoundly divided by reasonable though incompatible religious, philosophical and moral doctrines?" (Rawls 1993, p. xviii).

Rawls's solution to this problem is to propose a 'freestanding' liberal political conception of justice which is not derived from any particular comprehensive doctrine. Rather, it aims to be as neutral as possible between controversial philosophical, religious and moral positions. It can thus act as the subject of an 'overlapping consensus' on the most appropriate conception by which to regulate society. This does not represent a mere *modus vivendi*, as those who live under the political conception endorse it for internal reasons rather than grudgingly accepting it out of pragmatic considerations. For although it is a moral conception, it is one which is compatible with any reasonable comprehensive doctrine, and thus reasonable pluralism does not preclude reasonable citizens from endorsing it. This is because its fundamental ideas are derived from the widely accepted values implicit within the public political culture of liberal democratic states. Moreover, a political conception of justice need only be endorsed by citizens as appropriately regulating the political sphere. It does not strive to provide answers to questions which go beyond this distinct subject matter, such as whether God exists, or what a flourishing life consists in; citizens are left to freely answer such questions on their own. Adherents of such diverse comprehensive doctrines as Catholicism, Utilitarianism and Kantian Liberalism can find moral reasons to affirm the liberal political conception from their own internal perspectives. It thus acts as a 'module' which can slot into any reasonable system of values and widely be regarded as the proper basis of societal governance.

2 The burdens of judgement

To take a step back: why does Rawls conceive of reasonable pluralism as an inevitable consequence of maintaining freedom of thought? Because, he suggests, the theoretical, and more significantly, the practical reasoning of all reasonable individuals is subject to the 'burdens of judgement'. These burdens represent constraints on our reasoning and lead us to reach different conclusions on matters relating to our comprehensive doctrines.

Rawls proposes six burdens which I briefly name and summarise below, although he admits that this list is not exhaustive:

Assessment of Evidence: The relevant evidence is often hard to assess.
Difference in Weighing: Different people give different weight to different considerations.
Conceptual Vagueness: Concepts are vague and in need of interpretation.
Different Experiences: We are subject to different life experiences.
Normative Conflict: Normative considerations sometimes conflict.
Range of Values: There are multiple values, and societies must choose which to prioritise.
(Rawls 1993, pp. 54–58)

To illustrate how Rawls most plausible conceives of the burdens as leading to a reasonable diversity of both general comprehensive doctrines and more particular conceptions of the good, I will demonstrate how the burdens can lead to reasonable disagreement over a particular moral issue – namely, whether or not it is morally permissible to consume meat and other animal products.

When we are assessing the moral permissibility of consuming animal products, the first thing which we might notice is that there are many distinct normative considerations which we might take into account. On the one hand, there is the appreciation of the distinct gastronomic experiences which can only be achieved from eating meat and dairy products and the supposed nutritional advantages of a balanced omnivorous diet. On the other hand, we might conceive of animal rearing agricultural practices as involving the suffering of sentient beings, causing environmental damage and cultivating vicious character traits. Assuming that we accept that these are all legitimate candidates for normative considerations relevant to the issue, we can see that the two sets of competing concerns come into conflict. Whilst there may indeed be means of minimising such conflicts, in some cases trade-offs must be made. Hence, *Normative Conflict* applies in this and many other cases.

However this burden isn't in itself a direct cause of disagreement. For although we might all recognise that normative considerations sometimes conflict, we could nonetheless agree on what trade-offs should be made between them when they do. Rather, *Normative Conflict* represents a background factor concerning the ways in which normative considerations can interact with one another, setting the scene for reasonable moral disagreement. This is also the case with regard to *Range of Values*. As some scholars have noted, the fact that societies are limited in the range of values which they can simultaneously realise presents reasonable people with the occasion for disagreement rather than causing it directly (Wenar 1995, pp. 41–42).

Yet when we take burdens of *Assessment of Evidence*, *Difference in Weighing* and *Conceptual Vagueness* into account, reasonable disagreement is to be expected over the issue under consideration. *Assessment of Evidence* entails that given the difficulty in assessing evidence reasonable individuals will often come to different conclusions regarding, for instance, how much negative environmental impact animal husbandry has, how much animals suffer from contemporary farming practices and the extent to which an omnivorous vs. a vegan diet is beneficial to one's health.

Moreover, as *Difference in Weighing* makes clear, reasonable individuals also come to different conclusions regarding the relative importance of the relevant considerations, even when there is agreement on the facts which are relevant to the issue at hand. For instance, some might take animal suffering to be an extremely important normative consideration. They might take it to easily outweigh what is in their eyes the relatively negligible concern that minimising it diminishes our capacity to enjoy the full range of eating experiences available to us. Yet others might take the opposite view. There is also the further difficulty that some will not even recognise the same sorts of considerations as being pertinent. For instance, one might come to the conclusion that animal suffering is not a legitimate normative consideration, lacking as they do certain psychological characteristics which they take to be morally salient.

Conceptual Vagueness meanwhile highlights the further complicating factor that the concepts which we refer to when taking the considerations into account might themselves be subject to differing interpretations. For example, two individuals who are independently attempting to determine the extent to which raising animals necessitates animal suffering might come to very different conclusions because they are relying on different notions of what 'suffering' entails. One might take a thin conception of suffering which is constituted by directly painful experience, whilst another could employ a thicker conception which also includes being deprived of autonomy, companionship and access to a certain environment which promotes flourishing.

Finally, *Different Experiences* suggests that people's individual life experiences also contribute to reasonable disagreement. To take a charitable interpretation, it makes sense to suppose that Rawls appeals to *Different Experiences* in order to help provide a partial explanation for *Assessment of Evidence*, *Difference in Weighing* and *Conceptual Vagueness*. The implicit claim seems to be that the reason people assess evidence differently, attribute different weight to different considerations and interpret concepts differently is partly due to their unique life experiences. To illustrate, one who has been brought up on a cattle ranch is likely to have different views concerning the permissibility of eating animal products than another who grew up in a counterculture commune. This is in virtue of the fact that they are subject to different life experiences which mould their values, concepts and the ways in which they interpret evidence relevant to the case.

For Rawls, recognition of the burdens of judgement plays a crucial role in political liberalism, in terms of cultivating principled mutual political restraint between those with very different conceptions of the good. To count as reasonable, citizens must maintain a commitment to abide by fair terms of cooperation and recognise the burdens of judgement, along with some other moral and epistemic requirements. Reasonable citizens take proposing terms of co-operation which are grounded entirely on their own particular conception of the good as illegitimate, and are thereby willing to limit themselves to appealing to widely shared political values when engaging in public political discourse. This ensures their commitment to the political conception of justice.

Without recognition of the burdens, there is always the possibility that citizens will take themselves to be justified in proposing terms of cooperation which others reasonably reject. Reasonable individuals will refrain from proposing terms of cooperation which they take others to be reasonable in rejecting: this is ensured by the commitment to abide by fair terms of cooperation. Given the background values of liberal democratic societies, people typically recognise that it would be wrong to impose political terms on those who disagree with them yet are nonetheless reasonable. However, on its own this is not enough for people to refrain from proposing terms drawn from their own particular conception of the good which others reject.[3] On the contrary, if someone takes another to be *necessarily* unreasonable by virtue of them rejecting the terms that one favours, then it is entirely consistent for an otherwise reasonable person to refuse to see the need to publicly justify such terms. If one is convinced that those who reject one's favoured terms of cooperation could only possibly do so because they are irrational, wilfully ignorant or motivated by the distorting influence of self or group interest, then one generally does not see the need to attain public endorsement for their terms. Insofar as people perceive their opponents as morally and/or epistemically unjustified in their disagreement, citizens generally do take themselves to be justified in riding roughshod over them. For individuals will take such a failure to endorse the terms drawn from their own comprehensive doctrine to be an indication that their opponents are unreasonable. This will, in their eyes, nullify the requirement to publicly justify themselves to such opponents.

To elaborate, when we morally disagree with one another it is often tempting to ascribe to our opponents morally dubious motivations, wilful ignorance or irrationality. For instance those who endorse left wing economic policies, such as market regulation and the redistribution of wealth, will sometimes accuse those

---

[3] Leif Wenar argues that not only is recognition of the burdens of judgement on the part of citizens an unnecessary requirement to get political liberalism off the ground, but that it is inimical to the project since it is too demanding (Wenar 1995, pp. 32–62). Although I agree that recognition of the burdens is more demanding a requirement of reasonableness than Rawls takes it to be, I deny that it is unnecessary, for the reasons spelt out above.

who oppose them of doing so because they are either selfish, or in the grip of false consciousness. They may insist that their opponent's typical appeal to economic theories which insist on the efficiency of free market practices is purely borne out of a desire to maintain a status quo which is favourable to their class interests. Meanwhile, those on the political right will often claim that left wingers are motivated by envy rather than social justice, and that the economic arguments against *laissez faire* capitalism are only made by those who are either irrational or have been blinded by socialist ideology.

The burdens of judgement suggest a more charitable potential interpretation of one's opponent's reasoning. Insofar as individuals are receptive to the possibility of this alternative explanation of their disagreements, they are less likely to feel publicly justified in riding roughshod over their opponent's conception of the good when it comes to political decision making. Note that this is not on the grounds that they come to see that they are unjustified in remaining firmly committed to their own conception of the good. As Rawls makes clear, reasonable persons can be convinced that they are unquestionably correct with regards to their comprehensive doctrine and conception of the good, even in the face of their recognition of the burdens of judgement (Rawls 1993, p. 63).[4] Although it is inevitable that individuals will typically take their opponents to be mistaken in coming to different conclusions, what is important is that they do not regard them as necessarily unreasonable. Individuals within democratic societies implicitly do take fair terms of cooperation to be publicly justifiable, due to the widely shared background values and practices in the public political culture. But people are typically only apt to feel the need to provide a public justification to those whom they take to be reasonable, even if misguided. So, the path from the burdens of judgement to a commitment to the political conception runs through recognition that those who hold contrary comprehensive doctrines and associated conceptions of the good potentially do so for reasons which, from their own internal perspective, are genuinely moral and rationally justifiable.

Nonetheless, the insistence that all reasonable citizens accept the burdens of judgement threatens to undermine Rawls's case for the possibility of an overlapping consensus. For despite recognition of the burdens of judgement being cru-

---

[4] This may seem like an odd claim – one might suppose that recognising that our own reasoning capacities are hindered by the burdens of judgement provides grounds to be wary of being too confident in our conclusions. Nonetheless, Rawls claims that it is not necessarily unreasonable to remain stalwart in one's beliefs even in the face of recognition of the burdens of judgement, and that to insist otherwise would be to rule out many otherwise reasonable comprehensive doctrines.

cial for Rawls's project to be feasible, in the real world many people do not always recognise the extent of their influence. Many who share liberal values and would otherwise meet the criteria of reasonableness steadfastly hold those whom they disagree with on certain issues must necessarily be doing so out of irrationality or self-interest. They might not actually reject the burdens wholesale – they could concede that in some instances they apply, but nevertheless hold that they do not allow for as much reasonable disagreement in certain areas as Rawls takes them to. For instance, whilst many individuals today would accept that general religious disagreement might stem from the burdens of judgement, people are typically less inclined to give a similar explanation for disagreement over particular moral issues, such as abortion or euthanasia. Given that people are so strongly invested in the moral judgements which they favour, it should not come as a shock that they are reluctant to attribute reasonableness to those who come to different conclusions. They will thus be motivated to reject the influence of the burdens in such cases.

In Rawls's presentation the burdens of judgement are not especially well established, leaving us with little to say to such people. For the most part he simply asserts them as facts concerning the nature of reason that plausibly account for the pluralism which he takes to be inevitable under liberal institutions, as evidenced by its growth since the European reformation of the church. But as Leif Wenar points out, many Catholics reasonably favour a very different interpretation of this historical story which does without the burdens as a factor in shaping pluralism, and instead emphasise human immorality or wilful ignorance in explaining it (Wenar 1995, pp. 43–45). Indeed, it is not only religious believers who have a conception of reasoning which is incompatible with Rawls's account of reasonable pluralism. Many, if not most, agnostic and atheistic believers similarly account for the extent of the moral disagreement by citing the moral blindness or viciousness of those with whom they disagree rather than appealing to something like the burdens of judgement. If people continue to conceive of pluralism in this sort of way, then they will take public justifiability to have a relatively narrow scope, and thus remain unreasonable in Rawls' terms.

An implication of this is that if we want Rawls's project to be practically realisable, then we need to present the burdens of judgement in a more convincing manner. Now one might argue that since Rawls is working within the remit of ideal theory, it still remains the case that nothing hinges on people actually recognising the burdens of judgement in his presentation of political liberalism. One might contend that what is or is not practically conducive to the establishment of an overlapping consensus on the political conception of justice is beside the point: all that matters is that it is realisable under certain idealised assumptions. Nonetheless, Rawls himself is perfectly clear that the relative feasibility of his project actually being realised is of great importance to him. He suggests that although he need not guarantee that we will, in fact, eventually achieve the sort of society legitimately and stably governed by the political conception of justice he imagines, it is not enough that he describes a mere conceptual possibility. Rather, it is incumbent on him to provide the grounds for a "reasonable faith in the possibility of a just constitutional regime" (Rawls 1993, p. 172). Insofar as this is the case, and widespread recognition of the burdens of judgement is a precondition for such a hope, it is vital for the Rawlsian project to provide as compelling a case for them as possible.

3 The import of moral psychology

I now want to suggest that the case for the burdens of judgement as some of the major sources of moral disagreement can be improved by appealing to an affect-based account of moral psychology. If such a psychologised account of the burdens of judgement can be made, then this buttresses Rawls's claims regarding the reasonableness of pluralism: it provides an empirical basis for what I have argued is a crucial element of his central thesis. Moreover, if this presentation of the burdens of judgement is more amenable to the wider population than Rawls's rather abstract and contestable account, it has the potential to help persuade a wider range of individuals of reasonable pluralism. This, in turn, improves the chances of realising the conditions under which an overlapping consensus could develop and vindicates Rawls's reasonable faith in his project being practicable.

In the last few decades, advancements in moral psychology have highlighted the extent to which much of our moral judgement is a product of automatic, affective processes as opposed to deliberative reasoning. This focus on the emotional basis of moral judgement has been substantiated by various independent experimental findings, which I will now briefly review.

Firstly, in psychopathology it has been found that psychopaths cannot distinguish between prototypical moral rule violations and conventional rule violations, whereas those with many other mental disorders (notably autism) retain the ability to draw a moral/conventional distinction (Blair 1995, pp. 1–29). The primary symptom of psychopathy is widely recognised to be an inability to experience certain affective responses – most importantly, psychopaths have been shown to exhibit no physiological response to the distress of others (Blair, 1997, pp. 192–198). On the other hand, they do retain their ability to reason perfectly well, and this therefore suggests that affect is an important component in facilitating moral judgement.

Meanwhile, in social psychology, a plethora of recent studies have shown that manipulating the affective responses of individuals heavily influences their answers in moral judgement surveys. Furthermore, particular emotional states are shown to have differential influences upon different domains of moral judgement (Horberg et al. 2011, pp. 239–240). For instance, participants primed for disgust were found to be especially likely to make more severe moral judgements towards purity-based transgressions (such as drug consumption and sexual promiscuity) (Schnall et al. 2008, pp. 1096–1109), whereas those primed for anger tended to make stronger moral judgements in favour of retribution (DeSteno et al. 2004, pp. 43–56).

Finally, there is also evidence that the particular emotional dispositions of individuals can reliably predict their moral judgements in particular areas. In a study by Inbar et al., it was found that participants who ranked highly on a measure of general sensitivity to bodily disgust were more likely to make judgements which indicated an intuitive moral disapproval of gay men kissing in public. This effect did not occur when participants were asked about public kissing between heterosexual couples. The more disgust sensitive participants were, the stronger the effect was, despite most participants not offering explicit moral condemnation of homosexuality (Inbar 2009, pp. 435–439). This suggests that one's particular affective dispositions have the capacity to influence one's moral judgements, at least on the implicit level.

In summary, then, the available empirical evidence strongly implicates our affective responses in both facilitating moral judgement in general, and also in shaping our particular judgements across distinct moral domains.[5] An implication of this is that one way of accounting for moral disagreement is through disputants possessing different affective dispositions. To elaborate, on my view values and norms gain their perceived normative force from affective dispositions, and the extent to which we take a particular value or norm to be morally salient is dependent on our particular set of affective dispositions. That is, the particular moral weight which we assign to a moral concept, such as a value (and the norms underpinned by that value), will depend upon how strongly disposed we are to experience an affective response towards the stimuli which the value relates to. Within any particular culture, there will be a plurality of values which draw their normative force from distinct affective bases. When conflicts

---

[5] For a more detailed account of the distinct moral domains and their relation to our affective dispositions, see Graham et al. 2012, pp. 1–64.

occur between these values, one resolves them by weighing their relative importance against each other. This process, I hold, is heavily influenced by one's particular set of affective dispositions. Thus, in a conflict between compassion and equality, one who has a stronger disposition towards harm aversion is more likely to weigh compassion over equality, whereas one who has a stronger inequity aversion is more likely to weigh equality over compassion.

Moreover, our affective dispositions will further influence our interpretation of moral concepts. For instance, those who possess a stronger disposition towards disgust are likely to interpret the concept of 'moral purity' as involving refraining from certain sexual practices, as well as placing greater normative weight on values relating to sexual purity than those with a weaker disgust response. Meanwhile, those with a stronger disposition towards harm aversion are more likely to interpret justice as involving provisions for the weak and sick, along with weighing compassion higher than those without such a strong affective disposition. Our particular set of affective dispositions are thus liable to be strong determinants of our particular conceptions of the good.

Furthermore, evidence from behavioural genetics suggests that differences between the affective dispositions of individuals stem from both variations in non-shared environmental influences that individuals have been exposed to, but also from innate factors. Studies which measured the relative similarity between adopted and non-adopted siblings, twins and identical twins raised in both similar and non-similar cultural environments have consistently found that, roughly speaking, our genetic makeup accounts for about 50% of the overall influence upon our temperament (Turkheimer 2000, pp. 160–164). It thereby does seem to be the case that some are genetically predisposed to develop, for instance, stronger dispositions to experience disgust or anger than others.[6]

What is the upshot of all this for Rawls's account of the burdens of judgement? For one it vindicates his claim that people's conception of the good will inevitably differ as a consequence of the uniqueness of their life experiences. Recall that I earlier suggested that, on my interpretation of Rawls, this burden is to be conceived as fundamental insofar as he intends it to explain the other burdens. One of the major reasons we will always differ over the proper weight of values, our interpretations of concepts and assessments of the evidence is be-

---

[6] In further support of my position, some recent twin studies have also found that one's political leanings are to a large extent inheritable (Funk et al. 2013, pp. 805–819). This is not, of course, because genes directly encode for the development of specific political ideologies. Rather, it is far more plausibly the case that more general psychological tendencies which influence an individual's political views, such as our affective dispositions, are partly determined by our genetic endowment.

cause the different influences that we've been exposed to lead us to do so. I have argued that non-shared environmental influences not only shape our concept interpretation, but also the affective dispositions which indirectly make some concepts more psychologically appealing to us than others. Rawls's contention that our unique life experiences contribute to moral disagreement thereby gains some credence. Environmental influences upon us do indeed play a strong role in determining our conception of the good, especially our interpretation of value concepts and the degree of normative weight that we assign to them.

However the evidence which indicates the importance of genetic influences on our affective dispositions also suggests an additional way in which the burdens of judgement can be reinforced. It implicates another major factor which contributes to moral disagreement and which is both inevitable and does not stem from either irrationality or the distorting influence of self-interest on the part of agents, for it is simply the case that individuals who possess different genetic dispositions will tend to come to endorse different conceptions of the good. This is because the affective mechanisms that are partly shaped by such dispositions influence which values most strongly resonate with us.

Insofar as this is the case, an affect-based account of moral psychology lends extra weight to Rawls's account. This model of moral psychology provides another reason to suppose that the conceptions of the good of those that one morally disagrees with can sometimes be interpreted as both reasonable and internally rational, rather than necessarily stemming from either wilful ignorance or selfishness. It further vindicates the notion that enforcing a society-wide adherence to a particular conception of the good necessarily involves reneging on the liberal principle of legitimacy. Given the evidence, it is fair to suppose that the only kind of society wherein one could conceivably reach full consensus on a conception of the good whilst maintaining freedom of conscience would involve ensuring that the life experiences and genetic makeup of individuals would be utterly identical. Even if such a society were ever to be realisable in practice, it would necessitate such overwhelming control of the lives of individuals that only those with a complete disregard for liberal values would be willing to implement it.

This reinforced, psychological account of the burdens of judgement thereby helps to show that Rawls is right to highlight the possibility of reasonable disagreement with regard to conceptions of the good. Given that the burdens of judgement are a crucial element of Rawls's scheme, this represents a bolstering of the overall argument for political liberalism. Moreover, a psychologised account of the burdens has the advantage that it is not reliant on any abstract claims regarding the nature of reasoning itself, but is rather based upon empirical evidence regarding how our moral psychology operates. Rawls claims that one epistemic requirement of reasonable citizens is that they recognise the five essential elements of a conception of objectivity, and one of these involves drawing inferences and making judgements "on the basis of mutually recognised criteria and evidence" (Rawls 1993, p. 111). This being the case, an account of the source of reasonable disagreement backed up by empirical findings is less likely to prove controversial amongst those who might otherwise reject the current presentation of the burdens of judgement.

Hence, public awareness of moral psychology could play an important role in fostering the conditions under which an overlapping consensus is possible. It has the potential to persuade the wider population that moral disagreement can be, and often is, the result of affective variation rather than it being the case that those they disagree with are necessarily unreasonable. Once people are convinced of this, they might realise that their own comprehensive doctrine is not necessarily publicly justifiable, and therefore cannot legitimately ground a political conception of justice.[7]

4 Conclusion

In this paper, I have attempted to apply the implications of affect-based moral psychology to liberal political theory. In doing so, I have moved from a descriptive endeavour towards normative enquiry. At first, this might appear controversial, for the recent development of empirically informed moral psychology has ignited fierce debate within ethical theory. Whilst some have contended that this new understanding of moral psychology should help shape our values, others have remained stalwart in their resistance to the influence of this research program on our normative principles. The latter camp often cite Hume's claim that we cannot directly derive an 'ought' from an 'is', and this equally holds with regard to those facts concerning the psychological mechanisms which facilitate moral judgement itself.

---

[7] Of course, an affect-based account of moral psychology may also have a more problematic implication for Rawlsian political liberalism; that in Rawlsian terms, a significant proportion of individuals within any society will always be unreasonable. For meeting the criteria of reasonableness requires that one accept the normative priority of liberal political values such as equality and liberty within the political sphere, and as many have argued, the burdens of judgement may preclude many from accepting this. (See, for instance, Freyenhagen 2011, pp. 327–334.) Insofar as an affect-based account of moral psychology reinforces the case for the burdens of judgement, it may equally cement this worry. Nonetheless, addressing this issue is beyond the scope of this paper.

However, descriptive truths always influence our normative practices – our knowledge of them is crucial when we consider how to instrumentally realise those moral values which we already hold dear. This in no way offends against Hume's claim, which specifically states that only *direct* moves from an 'is' premise to an 'ought' premise are fallacious. Moving from an 'is' to an 'ought' indirectly via an intermediate ethical principle which the 'is' pertains to is not debarred.

When it comes to deciding how we should live together, moreover, facts regarding the motivations and behaviour of humans, and the extent to which they can be directed, become particularly salient. Determining whether or not a society run according to any proposed set of terms of cooperation will in actuality instantiate the values we desire to bring about depends upon what we think about how humans are, or have the potential to be. It is for this reason that some psychologists and biologists who have studied human nature from an ostensibly descriptive standpoint have unwittingly provoked intense ideological controversy. Given that our moral values are such an important component in shaping our motivation and behaviour, then, facts concerning how people come to have these values, and the extent to which we can come to share them or not, become extremely relevant.

Here, I have demonstrated one way in which affect-based moral psychology can have important implications for a particular type of political theory. I have argued that recognition of the burdens of judgement is in fact a necessary criterion for signing up to an overlapping consensus on a liberal political conception of justice. Furthermore, affect-based moral psychology can help buttress Rawls's case for the burdens of judgement as an explanation of moral disagreement as reasonable. Since Rawls's current account of the burdens is inadequate, persuading individuals of this model of moral psychology is a fruitful path towards creating the sort of conditions under which political liberalism could be realisable. This is, I hope, illustrative of how an area of enquiry which some claim can only possibly be descriptive can indeed have indirect normative implications on the political level. As moral psychology develops as a sub-discipline, we can expect the impact upon political philosophy to be of far wider ranging significance.

Bibliography

Blair, R. (1995): "A Cognitive Developmental Approach to Morality: Investigating the Psychopath". In: *Cognition* 57, pp. 1–29.
Blair, R. (1997): "The Psychopathic Individual: A Lack of Responsiveness to Distress Cues?" In: *Psychophysiology* 34, pp. 192–98.

DeSteno, D., Petty, RE., Rucker, DD., Wegener, DT., & Braverman, J. (2004): "Discrete Emotions and Persuasion: The Role of Emotion-Induced Expectancies". In: *Journal of Personality and Social Psychology* Vol. 86, No. 1, pp. 43–56.

Freyenhagen, F. (2011): "Taking Reasonable Pluralism Seriously". In: *Philosophy, Politics and Economics* Vol. 10, No. 3, pp. 327–334.

Funk, C. et al. (2013): "Genetic and Environmental Transmission of Political Orientations". In: *Political Psychology* 34. No. 6, pp. 805–819.

Graham, J., Haidt, J., Koleva, S., Motyl, M., Iyer, R., Wojcik, S., & Ditto, P. H. (2012): "Moral Foundations Theory: The Pragmatic Validity of Moral Pluralism". In: *Advances in Experimental Social Psychology* 47, pp. 1–64.

Horberg, E.J., Oveis, C., & Keltner, D. (2011): "Emotions as Moral Amplifiers: An Appraisal Tendency Approach to the Influences of Distinct Emotions upon Moral Judgment". In: *Emotion Review* 3. No. 3, pp. 239–240.

Inbar, Y., Pizarro, DA., Knobe, J., & Bloom, P. (2009): "Disgust Sensitivity Predicts Intuitive Disapproval of Gays". In: *Emotion* 9. No. 3, pp. 435–439.

Rawls, J. (1993): *Political Liberalism*, New York: Columbia University Press.

Rawls, J. (2001): *Justice as Fairness: A Restatement*, Harvard: Harvard University Press.

Raz, J. (1986): *The Morality of Freedom*. Oxford: Oxford University Press.

Schnall, S., Haidt, J., Clore, GL., & Jordan, AH. (2008): "Disgust as Embodied Moral Judgment". In: *Personality and Social Psychology Bulletin* 34, No. 8, pp. 1096–1109.

Sleat, M. (2013): *Liberal Realism: A Realist Theory of Liberal Politics*. Manchester: Manchester University Press.

Sinnott-Armstrong, W. (Ed.) (2008): *Moral Psychology. Vol. 2: The Cognitive Science of Morality: Intuition and Diversity*. Cambridge, MA: MIT Press.

Turkheimer, E. (2000): "The Three Laws of Behavioural Genetics and What They Mean". In: *Psychological Science* 9, No. 5, p. 160–164.

Wenar, L. (1995): "Political Liberalism: An Internal Critique". In: *Ethics*, Vol. 106, No. 1., pp. 32–62.

Williams, B. (2005): *In The Beginning Was The Deed: Realism and Moralism in Political Argument*. Princeton: Princeton University Press.

Part IV: **Expanding the Perspective on Obligations**

Angela Kallhoff
John Rawls and Claims of Climate Justice: Tensions and Prospects

Abstract: John Rawls has never addressed natural goods as "primary goods", nor has he paid attention to environmental justice. Rather than speculating on the reasons for this omission and elaborating on a proposal for how Rawls's approach to justice could be expanded to integrate issues of environmental justice, this paper defends another claim. It argues that John Rawls's theory of justice still provides a groundbreaking approach to environmental justice. The paper starts with challenges that this field of research presents to Rawls's theory of justice. In order to illustrate these claims, the paper includes a short sketch of climate justice as an emerging field of environmental justice. The contribution then draws attention to several of Rawls' very basic insights which are critical to the discussion of environmental justice. In particular, his insights regarding the political nature of fairness are still particularly important.

Introduction

In the context of political philosophy, "fairness in distribution" has been a leading paradigm in discussing social justice. Following Rawls's approach in *A Theory of Justice*, principles of fairness serve two goals. *Firstly*, they guide patterns of distribution of primary goods and of joint burdens in order to safeguard a fair distribution of both. Therefore, they should be implemented in institutions of a basically well-ordered society (Rawls 1996, pp. 11–15; 2005, pp. 60–65). Following the crucial demand of respecting the factum of a "reasonable pluralism" (Rawls 1996, p. 64), not only does Rawls acknowledge that personal viewpoints differ, and are therefore difficult to accommodate in the public arena, he also thinks that people share religious and philosophical doctrines that cannot be reconciled. "Our individual and associative points of view, intellectual affinities, and affective attachments, are too diverse, especially in a free society, to enable those doctrines to serve as the basis of lasting and reasoned agreement" (Rawls 1996, p. 58). In particular, they cannot serve as legitimation of principles of fairness. Instead, the defense of principles of justice results from processes of public reasoning.[1] *Secondly*, principles of justice contribute to stability by safeguarding

---

1 The concept and the objects of "public reasoning" have been emphasized in *Political Liberal-*

a fair distribution of goods that citizens generate by means of cooperation (Rawls 1996, p. 16).

The fair distribution of a range of basic goods supports citizens in order to realize two moral capacities: the sense of justice and the capacity to develop a concept of the good life (Rawls 1996, pp. 187–189). The primary goods Rawls proposes include basic rights and liberties, freedom of movement and free choice of occupation, powers and prerogatives of offices and positions of responsibility, income and wealth, and self-respect (Rawls 1996, p. 181). Yet, do the concepts of justice that Rawls proposes also apply to environmental goods? These are a particularly endangered set of goods; simultaneously they serve the most basic needs of persons. Persons need water, fresh air and food in order to survive and to accommodate most basic needs.

This contribution attempts to provide an answer to that question. My answer proceeds in three steps. *Firstly*, I shall argue that Rawls's approach to justice is not particularly well equipped to address natural goods. This is in line with the critiques of other authors who argue that the debate on environmental justice needs to transcend and even correct Rawls's ideas of distributive justice in several critical respects (Schlossberg 2007; Walker 2012). *Secondly*, the first statement does not mean that Rawls's path-breaking proposals in addressing social justice should be discarded when addressing issues of environmental and climate justice. Quite to the contrary, some of Rawls's insights in distributive justice remain central, especially in the field of environmental justice. Even though natural goods do *not* fit into the scheme of distributive justice proposed by John Rawls, I shall argue that nevertheless many of his core insights are important in the context of environmental justice. *Thirdly*, I shall argue that even though the debate needs to move beyond Rawls on several points, some of his theoretical insights are still quite relevant to the debate on environmental justice.

1 Confronting Rawls with the claims of environmental justice

In discussing Rawls's approach to justice, it is not difficult to acknowledge the fact that he more or less omits natural goods and issues of environmental justice. In particular, a tension results from a misfit between key assumptions in his theory of justice and the theoretical tools that are needed to address environmen-

---

ism in order to highlight the prospect of getting the principles of justice implemented, see Rawls 1996, pp. 212–254.

tal goods accordingly. In particular, Rawls shows some interest in environmental change.

In *A Theory of Justice*, Rawls comments on his approach to the environment in the context of a theory of justice. Instead of ignoring issues of environmental justice, Rawls even contextualizes it as necessarily included in an approach to the natural order. In part three, which is dedicated to institutional arrangements that support an incorporation of principles of justice, Rawls states at the very end of the chapter on "the sense of justice":

> A correct conception of our relations to animals and to nature would seem to depend upon a theory of the natural order and our place in it. One of the tasks of metaphysics is to work out a view of the world which is suited for this purpose; it should identify and systematize the truths decisive for these questions. How far justice as fairness will have to be revised to fit into this larger theory it is impossible to say (Rawls 1971, p. 512).

From these brief remarks, two things are apparent: *Firstly*, Rawls does not deliver a theory of justice which is prepared to address the relationship of humankind to animals and nature. He acknowledges though that this would be a demanding enterprise, one that would even include a metaphysics explaining the relationship among persons and animals. *Secondly*, fulfilling this task would involve fundamental revisions to his general approach to justice.

Followers and subsequent philosophers have demonstrated that Rawls's claims regarding the revisions necessary to include environmental concerns might be somewhat overstated – most prominently Thomas Pogge (Pogge 1998, pp. 501–536). In my view, the undesirable theoretical consequence is that – even if Rawls's theory of justice would be broadened – it would not suffice to get the role of principles of justice into the right place. In this respect, Rawls' speculations regarding the major systematic revisions his theory would require were right: he must integrate a normative perspective on animal life and environmental resources. In particular, three obstacles need to be addressed: the limited view of "objective circumstances of justice", the "distributive paradigm" and "value pluralism". I shall discuss these in turn.

1.1 Objective circumstances of justice

Following Rawls in elaborating a theory of justice, it must be presupposed that the idea of a society which is regulated by an effective public conception of justice is "suitably realistic" (Rawls 1996, p. 66). Therefore, circumstances of two kinds of justice need to be given and respected: objective circumstances of moderate scarcity, and subjective circumstances expressing the fact of pluralism

(Rawls 1996, p. 66). In *A Theory of Justice*, Rawls gives a lengthy explanation of what "circumstances of justice" include: these are "normal conditions under which human cooperation is both possible and necessary" (Rawls 2005, p. 126). Whereas the latter contributes to persons making "conflicting claims on the natural and social resources available" (Rawls 2005, p. 127), both contribute to persons being interested in "how the greater benefits produced by their collaborations are distributed" (Rawls 2005, p. 126). Moreover, the circumstances of justice are not simply there. Following Rawls, persons and parties in the original position also need to know that these circumstances will apply (Rawls 2005, p. 128). This means that not only in practice, but on the most fundamental theoretical level of his theory, these circumstances need to be presupposed. They are part of the design of the original position which is the most basic justificatory tool in selecting principles of justice that each person is willing to subscribe to in terms of a reasonable agreement.

A first point in discussing whether or not Rawls's theory of justice is applicable to the distribution of natural goods is the following: It is doubtful whether or not the objective circumstances of justice are a helpful and realistic expectation regarding natural resources. Not only water (Feldman 2007, pp. 1–33), but various natural goods are endangered by over-exploitation. Following the report of the Intergovernmental Panel on Climate Change (IPCC), climate instability and an overall rising temperature do not only result from high emission rates in greenhouse gases. The IPCC states: "Anthropogenic GHG emissions are mainly driven by population size, economic activity, lifestyle, energy use, land use patterns, technology and climate policy" (IPCC 2014, p. 8). Instead of lowering emission rates, the atmosphere has been used as a waste dump for greenhouse gases without respecting reasonable limits. Therefore today the space for additional emissions has become particularly scarce. Instead of "moderate scarcity", a sort of "radical scarcity" has emerged – at least when severe consequences are to be avoided.

1.2 The distributive paradigm

In explaining the underlying ideas of the "original position", Rawls explains that the "veil of ignorance" is not only a strategic device used to prevent persons from adopting principles of distribution from a partial position. Moreover, he states:

> The reason the original position must abstract from and not be affected by the contingencies of the social world is that the conditions for a fair agreement on the principles of political justice between free and equal persons must eliminate the bargaining advantages

that inevitably arise within the background institutions of any society from cumulative social, historical, and natural tendencies (Rawls 1996, p. 23).

Instead of reiterating rules which give advantage to some while disadvantaging others, "contingent advantages" need to be eliminated. In light of this, Rawls's theory of justice is discussed as a theory of distributive justice with the goal to distribute basic goods according to principles of non-discrimination. It also argues for egalitarianism in regard to the most basic goods, including freedoms. According to Rawls, both principles "express an egalitarian form of liberalism" (Rawls 1996, p. 6).

In particular, in arguing for principles of fair distribution, Rawls refers to a list of "primary goods" which underlies the discussion of principles of fairness. This list includes basic rights and liberties, freedoms, powers and prerogatives of offices and positions, income and wealth, and the social bases of self-respect (Rawls 1996, p. 181). One of the challenges in applying Rawls's approach to distributive justice in real scenarios is the question of how this list of basic goods resonates with goods that people need in order to realize their life-plans. It is also difficult to agree with Rawls in another respect: He is rather confident in just stating that these goods and related burdens are the outcome of cooperation in modern societies. Societies will produce these goods; the only thing that really is at stake is fairness in distribution (Rawls 1996, pp. 15–21). Yet, neither the joint production of good nor the need to really distribute them is self-explanatory.

As applied to issues in environmental justice, two problems prevail. *First*, natural goods are not *outcomes of cooperation* in any reasonable sense. Even though authors in the field of sustainability studies lay emphasis on the need of management systems that indeed are the outcome of cooperation, the adequate frameworks do not primarily imply rules of cooperation. In addressing natural goods, systems of governance and of management, which, contribute to sustainable management of water or other goods, need to be flexible and need to cohere with the exigencies presented by those goods (Norton 2005).

Second, natural goods might figure as resources whose distribution accords to principles of fairness that in turn relate to justified claims of persons as citizens. In Rawls's view, citizens regard each other as "self-authenticating sources of valid claims" (Rawls 1996, p. 32), which will be addressed rightly to political institutions. Rights to fair access conditions in terms of water rights, for example, are today part of the range of basic human rights (Kallhoff 2014, pp. 416–426). Yet, regarding natural goods, *distribution* of these resources is not actually the primary need addressed in replying to claims of justice. Instead, claims of justice can best be expressed as fair access conditions to natural goods (Brown/Schmidt 2010). The justification of fair access conditions could in part resonate with principles of fairness by distributing eco-services derived from natural goods. In elaborating on fair access conditions, the burdens of establishing and supporting eco-system management systems prevail. In both respects, egalitarianism is not particularly helpful. Instead, a fine-grained approach to justice is needed – one that also includes special obligations and special rights of profiteers from a natural resource (Kallhoff 2012).

1.3 Value pluralism

A further tension arises when theories of environmental justice are contrasted with Rawls's ideas concerning the "factum of pluralism" (Rawls 1996, p. 64). Rawls draws a line between value commitments which – in his view – are best explained as being part of the "comprehensive doctrines" of people and the reasons that persons present in the public sphere of a political society. In Rawls's view, persons do not just develop a rational idea of their own good lives; instead, they also cling to worldviews which are both coherent with rational requirements and with the major traditions of thought (Rawls 1996, p. 58). Independently of whether or not persons adhere to a moral theory or to a religious worldview, they subscribe to value commitments which, following Rawls's proposal, should not guide the justification of political claims. An approach to social justice needs to cohere with claims of fairness that are political, not metaphysical (Rawls 1996, pp. 10, 97). Personal values need to be distinguished neatly from political values. And, in entering the public arena, persons need to abstract from these commitments and transcend their individual value commitments. Principles of fairness are legitimated by procedures of rational consent, not by value commitments of individuals (Rawls 1996, pp. 212–219).

The commitments to value pluralism on the one hand, and neutrality in the public sphere on the other, are severe obstacles to justifying claims of environmental justice. One important resource for defending claims of environmental protection is an analysis of values in nature – either in an emphatic sense of "life's intrinsic value" (Agar 2001) or in a more pragmatic interpretation of "value" in terms of "eco-systemic services". These services are valuable in that they respond to basic needs of persons (Costanza et al. 1997). In particular, environmental values cannot be chosen or rejected; instead, they are part of nature. They respond to "the good" of living beings (Attfield 1991); at least they correspond to a range of values with different significance, including instrumental values (Muraca 2011). Some authors argue that the values in nature need to be answered by a set of virtues (Sandler 2007). When it comes to most basic needs, it might be right to claim access to some natural goods, including water and clean air, as more or less "neutral" regarding further value commitments. Yet, beyond that threshold of basic human needs, one of the difficulties in addressing environmental goods in the context of claims of justice is the idea of "values in nature".[2]

Overall, it appears to be difficult to translate claims for environmental justice into value-neutral statements in the Rawlsian sense. For sure, some claims for sustainability might rest on prudential reasons which all persons are likely to share. But these claims are limited to existing communities; which means they do not usually include a trans-generational perspective. This does not imply that justice is not at stake here. But the debate on value pluralism needs to be taken into account when addressing the value of nature within a debate on justice.

To sum up this first assessment of how Rawls's approach to justice relates to the debate on environmental justice, the following needs to be said: Obviously, the current situation of several very basic natural resources, including water and the atmosphere, does not match the condition of "moderate scarcity". Therefore, the conditions which provide the background for reasonable discussion of principles of fairness in Rawls's approach to justice are threatened. Moreover, fair access conditions to natural goods do not fit particularly well into the distributive paradigm. In particular, Rawls's respect for value pluralism does not pave the way to a straightforward application of his proposals to environmental justice. Therefore, authors in the field of environmental justice side-step Rawls and instead indulge in different types of justification – at least it seems so on first glance. The next section presents some of these proposals in the field of climate justice that point in new directions, yet still remain within the framework of elaborations on justice.

2 Climate justice as a new approach to justice

To focus the claims of this paper, I shall discuss a number of recent proposals made in regard to climate justice to provide the background needed to contrast Rawls' theory with theories advocating environmental justice. I wish to highlight that environmental justice, and climate justice in particular, are particularly challenging to reason. Natural goods are becoming scarce in a world in which

---

2 It should also be noted that authors in political philosophy have attempted to resolve this problem by developing principles of environmental justice in the context of a liberal state (Dobson/Bell 2006; Wissenburg 2006).

the world population still grows. Moreover, they differ from other goods in that they cannot be generated by means of cooperation, but need to be protected from over-exploitation. In addressing issues of justice that relate to the climate, it is helpful to start with an insight that Peter Singer introduced into the debate on climate justice, in which he defines the main problem as an unfair depletion of a shared natural resource. Singer (2002) argues that in discussing climate justice, it is helpful to frame the scenario in the following way: For centuries, the atmosphere has served as a sink for greenhouse gases; yet, this space has become dramatically limited. Therefore, one of the main issues from the perspective of justice is a fair distribution of the remaining space.

In order to address climate justice, an even more complex scenario must be addressed (Gardiner/Caney/Jamison 2010; Shue 2010, 2013). In particular, it is not only physical space that needs to be distributed according to principles of fairness. Instead, a list of secondary goods, including profits from emitting greenhouse gases in terms of welfare goods, but also in terms of a high level of economic performances, are also at stake. It includes the costs for remedies that become necessary regarding damages and harm that people suffer from climate change. In the context of climate change, a fair distribution of its burdens includes a fair scheme of international contributions to a climate fund that restores living conditions in the most badly hit spaces of the world. Therefore, it has been argued that a "hybrid account", combining various principles of justice and human rights-claims are needed in order to develop an approach to justice that fits claims of climate justice (Caney 2005a). One urgent issue in climate justice is a suitable interpretation of "fairness" in the first place. Overall, three different interpretations have been proposed: one in terms of "green democracy", one in terms of a rather complex distributive paradigm, and one in terms of a priority view. I shall introduce these in turn.

Firstly, authors in the field of green democracy defend a view, according to which "fairness" is not restricted to a distributive claim. Instead, fairness is outlined in terms of procedural rights which guarantee a due process of political decision-making. In particular, these proposals say that environmental fairness comprises rights which guarantee access to information, rights that help persons to articulate their opinions, for instance: the rights to assemble, to form private associations and to protest in the public, and rights that guarantee participation in political processes. Much of the literature is dedicated to overhauling a theory of liberal democracy such that it incorporates environmental goals.[3] Unlike

---

[3] The debate on political institutions that are ready to include environmental agendas is vast, in

Rawls's proposal, a fair procedure is regarded as the main scope of justice in the liberal state.

The *second* interpretation in discussing principles of fairness is indeed a debate of *distributive justice*. Here, it is important to distinguish two issues in addressing natural goods: The first issue is the distribution of a life-sustaining natural good so that each person receives a fair share. As for this claim, an approach to justice must work on two issues simultaneously. First, it is necessary to demonstrate that claiming a fair share is justified. Second, the question of how a fair share can best be determined also needs to be answered. This raises the question of whether there are general criteria, or only meta-criteria which indicate how a distinction of a fair share and undue claims can be distinguished. Most authors agree that principles of fairness can be argued, yet they depend on the specific good of which distribution is at stake. In particular, within a distributive framework, secondary burdens also need to be discussed. They include costs that are caused by climate change and by developing procedures and instruments to cope with the effects of climate change. This includes costs for *mitigation*, which is the reduction of emission rates, and costs of *adaptation*, which means new buildings and instruments needed to cope with severe weather events. In addition, support and relief efforts for persons who flee regions which are severely hit by weather events that result from climate change also need to be included.[4] Finally, there are also direct costs of extreme weather events. In sum, there are many different items that need to be distributed once fairness is called upon.

As for the principles, distributive justice also implies a discussion of issues of *compensatory justice* or even *restorative justice*. Compensatory justice claims that victims of climate change need to be compensated for their suffering; this includes the naming of a person or a group of persons who is responsible for doing so. Restorative justice, instead, goes one step further. It also claims that a situation of justice has been forfeited by an act of harm. Whether or not the application of these concepts it is justified is a matter of debate in theories of climate justice (Gosseries/Meyer 2009).

Since the inception of the debate on justice, a *third* interpretation has been put on the table. This resonates with another particularly pressing question: Because justice does not necessarily mean that each person receives exactly the same share of a good or needs to shoulder the same burden, criteria for unequal

---

particular their approaches to democracy. For important contributions, see (Eckersley 2004; Hayward 2004; Scerri 2012).

4 For a debate on current approaches to climate victims in the EU and the debate on the political implications of the term "victim" in this context, see Ammer (2015).

distributions of benefits and burdens are pivotal. When framed in a theory of joint action, this problem received new weight. For groups focusing on some natural good, the issue of *justified priorities*, regarding both relief efforts as well as gains from climate policy, need to be discussed anew (Shue 1999).

To conclude, in addition to the diversity of principles of justice that results from different types of fairness, principles also need to be adjusted according to various types of burdens and gains that in turn resonate with specific features of natural goods. Different from Rawls's approach, the debate is not about a single list of primary goods. Instead, it is about principles of fairness that accrue to a variety of distributive scenarios, including secondary goods and burdens resulting from climate change. In addition, it is not preset that fairness is spelled out in terms of principles of a fair distribution. Instead, climate justice is also about fair procedures in the liberal state and beyond.

3 Paying tribute to Rawls

As noted in section 1, environmental justice provides a range of challenges for Rawls's approach to justice. Yet, even though there are challenging issues included, it is also important to highlight some very basic insights in Rawls's thoughts on justice that are helpful and perhaps even necessary when considering climate justice. I shall now focus on the elements that Rawls's theory includes and that are important to any discussion of climate justice at a very basic level and present the second half of my argument: Even though Rawls's theory is far from perfect in the context of environmental justice, it nevertheless includes some elements that are helpful to a successful consideration of environmental justice. My modest goal in this section is to demonstrate that Rawls's theory of justice, even though confronting environmental justice with significant challenges, is helpful in developing a framework that transcends individual value judgments and comes to grip with principles of fairness.

3.1 Establishing reasonable goals

The latest IPCC report states:

> Continued emission of greenhouse gases will cause further warming and long-lasting changes in all components of the climate system, increasing the likelihood of severe, pervasive and irreversible impacts for people and ecosystems. Limiting climate change would

require substantial and sustained reductions in greenhouse gas emissions which, together with adaptation, can limit climate change risks (IPCC 2014, p. 8).

Following this assessment, greenhouse gas emissions need to be cut dramatically. Accordingly, principles of justice were primarily designed as principles which contribute to a fair distribution of costs which result from reducing climate gases. More recently, the discussion has made a major shift to principles of adaptation. "These are the costs to persons of adopting measures that enable them and/or others to cope with the ill effects of climate change" (Caney 2010, p. 124), including costs to minimize cholera and malaria, costs for strengthening coastal regions against rising sea levels etc. (Caney 2010, p. 125).

As for theorizing justice, this shift of opinions includes the following: There has been an ongoing reassessment of what the reasonable goals are. Yet, a theory of climate justice does not only have to defend reasonable goals that each actor can subscribe to. They also need to be combined with other global agendas. Some claim that climate goals need to be compatible, perhaps even correlated with the goal to reduce poverty (Posner 2008). Overall, the challenge to define "reasonable goals" remains a big issue.

Following Rawls, reasonable goals of justice need to resonate with a set of claims that are basic in addressing cooperation in modern societies. One important insight of Rawls is that social justice is supportive regarding stability, yet stability needs to be chosen for the right reasons (Rawls 1996, p. 390). In particular, stability is not a political goal per se. Instead, it is supposed to be the effect of an established order that accords with basic principles of fairness. This is an important argument in the international arena, too. Not establishing fair principles of distribution of environmental goods threatens stability in a very fundamental way. Some even address "resource wars" and the collapse of societies as the anticipated scenarios, unless environmental justice is addressed successfully in the international arena (Diamond 2005). Yet, reasonable goals in Rawls are also tied to a concept of citizenship: citizens regard themselves for good reasons as "self-authenticating sources of valid claims" (Rawls 1996, p. 32). Even though Rawls limits his theory of justice to nation states, the underlying ideas also provide a very basic backdrop for developing goals of justice as related to environmental goods. Though the concept of citizenship needs to be tested in terms of cosmopolitanism (see e.g. Caney 2005b), the insight that persons as citizens have justified claims is important. What if anything is a valid claim if not the claim for water, air and food and for stable environmental living conditions?

3.2 Priority to the worst off

Henry Shue argues that in discussing climate justice principles of fairness need to address the discrepancy between the rich nations and the poor nations. In order to prevent further severe injustices, the rich nations are obliged to compensate the poor for harm which was primarily caused by the richer nations (Shue 1993, 2010). Even though the nations are divided into rich and poor nations, this does not say that only part of the world needs to act. Instead, Shue has recently acknowledged that each actor is obliged to contribute to a radical shift both in means of carbon-free energy resources and in means of a global effort to compensate the poor (Shue 2013, pp. 381–402). Simon Caney also develops a theory of international justice which draws heavily on the basic rights of persons – and correlative duties which relate to human rights (Caney 2005b). In particular, he argues that international obligations do not result only from former incidents of harm. Instead, he discusses "beneficiary pays principles" which argue that

> where A has been made better off by a policy pursued by others, and the pursuit by others of that policy has contributed to the imposition of adverse effects on third parties, then A has an obligation not to pursue that policy itself (mitigation) and/or an obligation to address the harmful effects suffered by the third parties (adaptation) (Caney 2010, p. 128).

This principle goes back to the gains from greenhouse gas emission. Caney argues that persons have been made better off by a higher standard of living which is correlated with greenhouse gas emission. Therefore, they should now give back to those who do not have gains, but instead suffer from the emissions.

This claim resonates with John Rawls's distinction between two principles of justice that respond to different claims. Basic goods, including freedoms and liberties, need to be distributed according to principles of justice. In Rawls's approach, this egalitarianism is part of what constitutions should guarantee to each single citizen (Rawls 1996, pp. 227–230). Obviously, this claim is restricted to citizens of a single nation. Yet, the second principle is reasoned against an economic insight, the maximin principle (Rawls 2005, pp. 75–82). Even though the extension of Rawls towards an international approach to justice or a cosmopolitan principle focuses on primary goods and their distribution, it is reasonable to rethink a difference principle in the international arena, too. Actually, economic and utilitarian approaches take into account that marginal expenses can lead to very good outcomes in poorer regions of the world (Posner 2008). Even though a great deal of work would have to be invested in adapting Rawls's concept to an international theory of justice, it is not just a moral argument for prioritization of the worst off, but also Rawls's economically based proposal for supporting the poor that at least to some degree is still important.

3.3 Moral concepts underlying justice

Even if it is granted that climate change is – to some degree – due to manmade causes, the relationship between climate change and moral demands needs to be made explicit. It appears as if claiming justice also includes the claim of responsibility or at least liability at some point. The normative claim is that if someone caused climate change, this very actor needs to take responsibility for the harmful effects. Moreover, the question of why persons need to assist other persons in order to cope with climate change is close to debates on international obligations to the poorer nations. Yet, the situation is particularly complex, because climate change is not an event which takes place suddenly. Instead, it will affect coming generations; and it was caused by generations in the last century.

Overall, climate change correlates to deep moral claims and with issues of justice. Yet, neither the relationship to morality, nor the underlying claims are self-explanatory. Therefore, it is part of the theoretical endeavor when discussing environmental justice to develop a thorough picture and a clear-cut understanding of the underlying moral claims involved in the climate debate. As already noted, John Rawls is far from arguing principles of environmental fairness as an important ingredient in theories of justice. But he is aware of the need to address moral concepts at a very basic level of theoretical reasoning. Even his concept of a person is a deeply moral one. He argues that persons are equipped with two *moral* powers – including a sense of justice and a capacity to develop a life-plan for a good life (Rawls 1996, p. 19). Possibly, Rawls is far too optimistic here. Yet, he is certainly right in addressing a moral backdrop of theories of justice. In applying this insight to the climate debate, two options prevail: Either persons are regarded as equipped with basic rights, including rights to access to basic environmental resources; or normative claims are defended with respect to justice as itself a normative notion. Rawls also reminds us of a third important option. Persons are equipped with moral capacities. Therefore, it is obligatory to theorize and finally also to realize principles of fairness that resonate with these capacities. Even in a global world, persons can be regarded as being equipped with a sense of justice that somehow needs to be responded to in readjusting and building institutions that care for environmental goods.

3.4 Political, not metaphysical

John Rawls did not just address justice anew. He also contributed to a theory of justice that he himself interprets as "justice as fairness". This has many different implications. An easily overlooked, yet for climate justice central, aspect is that the methods he chooses are "political" and not "metaphysical" (Rawls 1996, pp. 12–15). Rawls does not wish to go beyond the public arena; nor does he provide a foundation of justice that goes back to metaphysical claims. This backdrop has several implications. One implication has already been mentioned: Rawls regards it as obligatory to cope with the factum of reasonable pluralism in a constructive way. He does not reject the idea that persons have values, even values contextualized in reasonable doctrines. But he rejects the idea that these doctrines also frame political decisions in the public arena. Another implication is his concern for a basically well-ordered society, guided by principles that citizens can agree upon (Rawls 1996, pp. 12–15). Rawls does not start with a theory of well-ordered institutions, nor does he wish to present a comprehensive account of justice in societies. Instead, he argues that a political conception needs to argue principles of justice that each citizen can subscribe to.

As for environmental justice and climate justice in particular, this claim cannot be underrated. In particular, it forestalls two options to discuss justice that have also been put on the table. This forecloses a primarily economic approach to climate justice (Stern 2007); and it forestalls a normative approach that resonates with distinct values. In particular, Rawls's approach supports a view of justice in terms of fairness resulting from networks of cooperation that already exist. As for environmental justice, it is important to understand that – even though the goods are not man-made as discussed in section 1 – the patterns of cooperation are there. Persons are not free to choose environmental surroundings, but are confronted with them. And the outlook of these surroundings is to a high degree shaped not only by institutions, but also by various patterns of exploitation. Those patterns are often unfair and need to be corrected in the context of politics (Walker 2012).

Conclusion

It is possible that John Rawls could not foresee the rapid degradation of natural resources and the already dramatic weather events resulting from climate change. In particular, he never provided a background for discussing a fair distribution of environmental resources. Instead of concluding that these facts forestall a debate about "John Rawls and environmental justice", I have argued two claims. *Firstly*, the tensions that result from confronting Rawls with claims of environmental justice can be specified. In particular, they transcend the usual reservations against Rawls's theoretical approach as not confronting global issues of justice accordingly. Instead, they include the normative presuppositions of the necessary background conditions for justice, a particular interpretation of "distribution" that is at stake here, and respect for value pluralism. These aspects of Rawls's theory provide particular challenges in addressing environmental justice.

Secondly, I have argued that even though Rawls is not prepared to address environmental justice accordingly, he makes a number of important points. As well, some of his insights are crucial when considering climate justice. Besides ideas about the moral powers of persons and concern for stability and cooperation, Rawls also highlights that his theory of justice is a political, not a metaphysical theory. This is an important aspect to arguments addressing environmental justice and more specifically climate justice: Instead of focusing on "values in nature", it is helpful to focus on patterns of cooperation that are forward-looking in two respects. They should pay tribute to the needs of the worst-off regarding environmental resources as basic as water supply and stable environmental living conditions. And they should resonate with the validity claims of persons.

Bibliography

Agar, Nicholas (2001): *Life's Intrinsic Value. Science, Ethics, and Nature.* New York: Columbia University Press.

Ammer, Margit (2015): "Klimawandel und Migration/Flucht: Welche Rechte für die Betroffenen in Europa?" In: Kallhoff, Angela (Ed.): *Klimagerechtigkeit und Klimaethik.* Berlin, Boston: De Gruyter, pp. 81–103.

Attfield, Robin (1991): *The Ethics of Environmental Concern.* Athens, London: University of Georgia Press.

Barry, J./Wissenburg, M.L.J. (Eds.) (2001): *Sustaining Liberal Democracy: Ecological Challenges and Opportunities.* Houndmills, Basingstoke, Hampshire, New York: Palgrave.

Bell, Derek (2004): "Environmental Justice and Rawls' Difference Principle". In: *Environmental Ethics* 26. No. 3, pp. 287–306.

Brown, Peter G./Schmidt, Jeremy J. (Eds.) (2010): *Water Ethics. Foundational Readings for Students and Professionals.* Washington, DC: Island Press.

Caney, Simon (2005a): "Cosmopolitan Justice, Responsibility, and Global Climate Change". In: *Leiden Journal of International Law* 18, pp. 747–775.

Caney, Simon (2005b): *Justice beyond Borders: A Global Political Theory.* Oxford, New York: Oxford University Press.

Caney, Simon (2010): "Cosmopolitan Justice, Responsibility, and Global Climate Change". In: Gardiner, Stephen M./Caney, Simon/Jamieson, Dale/Shue, Henry (Eds.): *Climate Ethics. Essential Readings*. Oxford, New York: Oxford University Press, pp. 122–145.

Costanza, R. et al. (1997): "The Value of the World's Ecosystem Services and Natural Capital". In: *Nature* 387, pp. 253–260.

Diamond, Jared M. (2005): *Collapse: How Societies Choose to Fail or Succeed*. New York: Penguin.

Dobson, Andrew/Bell, Derek (Eds.) (2006): *Environmental Citizenship*. Cambridge, MA.: MIT Press.

Eckersley, R. (2004): *The Green State: Rethinking Democracy and Sovereignty*. Cambridge, MA: MIT Press.

Feldman, David Lewis (2007): *Water Policy for Sustainable Development*. Baltirmore, MD: Johns Hopkins University Press.

Gardiner, Stephen M. (2001): "The Real Tragedy of the Commons". In: *Philosophy and Public Affairs* 30, pp. 387–416.

Gardiner, Stephen M. (2011): *A Perfect Moral Storm. The Ethical Tragedy of Climate Change*. Oxford, New York: Oxford University Press.

Gardiner, Stephen M./Caney, Simon/Jamieson, Dale et al. (Eds.) (2010): *Climate Ethics. Essential Readings*. Oxford, New York: Oxford University Press.

Gosseries, Axel/Meyer, Lukas H. (Eds.) (2009): *Intergenerational Justice*. Oxford, New York: Oxford University Press.

Hayward, Tim (2004): *Constitutional Environmental Rights*. Oxford, New York: Oxford University Press.

IPCC (2014): Climate Change 2014: "Synthesis Report. Contribution of Working Groups I, II and III to the Fifth Assessment Report of the Intergovernmental Panel on Climate Change" [Core Writing Team, R.K. Pachauri and L.A. Meyer (eds.)]. IPCC, Geneva, Switzerland. https://www.ipcc.ch/pdf/assessment-report/ar5/syr/AR5_SYR_FINAL_SPM.pdf, visited on 25 October 2016.

Kallhoff, Angela (2012): "Addressing the Commons: Normative Approaches to Common Pool Resources". In: Potthast, Thomas/Meisch, Simon (Eds.): *Climate Change and Sustainable Development. Ethical Perspectives on Land Use and Food Production*. Wageningen: Wageningen Press, pp. 63–68.

Kallhoff, Angela (2014): "Water Ethics". In: Thompson, Allen/Gardiner, Stephen (Eds.): *Oxford Handbook of Environmental Ethics*. Oxford, New York: Oxford University Press, pp. 416–426.

Locke, John (1980): *Second Treatise on Civil Government*. C.B. MacPherson (Ed.). Indianapolis: Hacket.

Muraca, Barbara (2011): "The Map of Moral Significance: A New Axiological Matrix for Environmental Ethics". In: *Environmental Values* 20. No. 3, pp. 375–396.

Norton, Bryan G. (2005): *Sustainability: A Philosophy of Adaptative Ecosystem Management*. Chicago: University of Chicago Press.

Pogge, T. (1998): "A Global Resources Dividend". In: Crocker, David/Linden, Toby (Eds.): *Ethics of Consumption. The Good Life, Justice, and Global Stewardship*. New York: Rowman and Littlefield, pp. 501–536.

Posner, E. (2008): "Climate Change Justice". In: *Georgetown Law Journal* 96, pp. 1565–1612.

Rawls, John (1971): *A Theory of Justice*. Cambridge, MA: Belknap Press of Harvard University Press.
Rawls, J. (1996): *Political Liberalism*. New York: Columbia University Press.
Rawls, J. (2005): *A Theory of Justice*. Cambridge, MA: Belknap Press.
Sandler, R.L. (2007): *Character and Environment. A Virtue-Oriented Approach to Environmental Ethics*. New York: Columbia University Press.
Scerri, Andy (2012): *Greening Citizenship. Sustainable Development, the State and Ideology*. Basingstoke: Palgrave Macmillan.
Schlossberg, David. (2007): *Defining Environmental Justice. Theories, Movements, and Nature*. Oxford, New York: Oxford University Press.
Shue, Henry (1993): "Subsistence Emissions and Luxury Emissions". In: *Law and Politics* 15. No. 1, pp. 39–59.
Shue, Henry (1999): "Global Environment and International Inequality". In: *International Affairs* 75. No. 3, pp. 531–545.
Shue, Henry (2010): "Deadly Delays, Saving Opportunities. Creating a More Dangerous World?" In: Shue, Henry/Gardiner, Stephen M./Jamieson, Dale (Eds.): *Climate Ethics. Essential Readings*. Oxford: Oxford University Press, pp. 146–162.
Shue, Henry (2013): "Climate Hope: Implementing the Exit Strategy". In: *Chicago Journal of International Law* 13. No. 2, pp. 381–402.
Singer, Brent A. (1988): "An Extension of Rawls' Theory of Justice to Environmental Ethics". In: *Environmental Ethics* 10. No. 3, pp. 217–231.
Singer, Peter (2002): "One Atmosphere". In: *One World. The Ethics of Globalization:* New Haven, CT: Yale University Press pp. 14–50.
Stern, Nicholas (2007): *The Economics of Climate Change. The Stern Review*. Cambridge: Cambridge University Press.
Walker, G.P. (2012): *Environmental Justice. Concepts, Evidence, and Politics*. London, New York: Routledge.
Wissenburg, Marcel (2006): "Global and Ecological Justice: Prioritising Conflicting Demands". In: *Environmental Values* 15, pp. 425–39.

Annette Förster
Assistance, Emergency Relief and the Duty Not to Harm – Rawls' and Cosmopolitan Approaches to Distributive Justice Combined

Abstract: There are diverse ideas and conceptions of distributive justice with regard to the principles on the basis of which goods should be distributed as well as the methods to identify them. Whereas John Rawls in his domestic theory favours the difference principle as an element of the two principles of justice, in *The Law of Peoples*, he argues in favour of a duty of assistance when it comes to the international justice. Cosmopolitans have challenged Rawls' reasoning. In this context, I substantiate two claims: 1. The duty of assistance is a suitable principle of international distributive justice. 2. Nevertheless, it is insufficient to regulate international distributive justice fairly and in need of augmentation. I introduce the duty of assistance, defend it against its critics, and argue that competing claims could reasonably substantiate each other.

1 Introduction

What are the fundamental principles on which a fair distribution of goods shall be organized in the international sphere? When it comes to the question of international distributive justice, there are diverse egalitarian and non-egalitarian conceptions exploring which distribution of goods is to be considered just, e.g. on the basis of which principles goods should be distributed, as well as different methods of identifying those principles. John Rawls' conception, as presented in *A Theory of Justice* (TJ, 1971), has been among the most influential. But even within Rawls' writing, there seem to be two conceptions of distributive justice – one for the domestic realm, the difference principle in combination with fair equality of opportunity,[1] and one for the international realm, presented in

---

[1] The difference principle and conditions of fair equality of opportunity constitute the second of the two principles of justice introduced in *A Theory of Justice*, the first principle being a right to equal basic liberties.

The Law of Peoples (LP, 1999), the duty of assistance.[2] The application of different norms to the national and international realm, and within that the rejection of the application of the difference principle when it comes to the relation between states have been called into question by cosmopolitan thinkers such as Thomas Pogge or Charles Beitz, who presented their own conceptions of distributive justice in the international arena.

In this context, I will substantiate two claims: 1. The duty of assistance is a suitable principle of international distributive justice. 2. However, it is not sufficient to regulate international distributive justice fairly and the principle is in need of additions. The paper thus first explores the content, scope and foundation of the duty of assistance and discusses it against the background of its critics. Alternative conceptions are analysed from a Rawlsian perspective. This paper shows why the duty of assistance is a suitable principle, but not a sufficient one, and claims that the negative duties not to harm and not to profit from injustices, introduced by Thomas Pogge (2004, p. 278), are necessary amendments to Rawls' principles of the Law of Peoples,[3] as well as a principle of emergency relief. Such additions seem in line with *The Law of Peoples*, as the list of principles possibly covered by the Law of Peoples is left open and as Rawls deliberates on principles of (fair) trade, the effect of which has to be considered when it comes to the duty of assistance (LP, pp. 42–43).

2 The duty of assistance

"Well-ordered peoples have a duty to assist burdened societies" (LP, p. 106). Burdened societies are regimes burdened by unfavourable conditions such as a lack of cultural, civic, material and/or technological resources, a too large or undersized population, historical, economic or social deficits (LP, pp. 5, 90, 106). They are willing to but not capable of establishing a well-ordered basic structure on their own due to their specific burden. "The Law of Peoples establishes, as a long-term goal of liberal foreign policy, the elevation of burdened societies to

---

[2] The duty of assistance is one of the eight principles of the Law of Peoples on the basis of which liberal democracies ideally should organize their foreign relations.
[3] The 'Law of Peoples' following Rawls refers to the eight principles of fair international cooperation introduced in his eponymous monograph *The Law of Peoples*: the duties 1. to respect a people's freedom and independence, 2. to observe treaties, 3. to consider the equality between peoples, 4. the principle of non-intervention, 5. the right to self-defence, 6. the duty to honour human rights, 7. the duty to observe restrictions in the conduct of war and 8. the duty to assist burdened societies (LP, p. 37).

a point at which they can sustain liberal or decent institutions for themselves" (Beitz 2000, p. 688). The duty of assistance aims to provide burdened societies with the means necessary to manage their affairs in a reasonable manner (LP, p. 111). To reach that aim, members of society need to participate in the social and political life of the community and their basic needs[4] have to be met (Freeman 2007, p. 454).

How can these objectives be accomplished? Assistance implies concrete and suitable advice and support to alleviate specific burdens. Rawls formulates three guidelines: First, the purpose of the duty of assistance is to establish and preserve "just basic institutions […] and to secure a social world that makes possible a worthwhile life for all its citizens" (LP, p. 10). Second, the political and social culture needs to be changed and human rights need to be respected (LP, pp. 108–110). Third, burdened societies must be enabled to "manage their own affairs reasonably and rationally" (LP, p. 111). Therefore, corruption should be eradicated, and the rule of law established. It is crucial not to simply throw funds at them. Rather, it is necessary to provide adequate economic resources and the capacity to use them in order to establish and maintain well-ordered institutions. Assistance in areas such as education, infrastructure, agriculture or technology might be needed (Freeman 2007, pp. 440–441). If a well-ordered basic structure can be maintained over time, no further assistance is necessary. The duty of assistance is, thus, not a principle of mitigating inequalities but rather one of transition (LP, p. 119). Furthermore, it is a complex and demanding concept, the implementation of which would take decades of case-specific assistance for each burdened society.

But how is the duty of assistance justified? Why should well-ordered societies take on such extensive commitments? One might argue that the "the chances for peace would be greater in a world in which all societies had been lifted out of burdening conditions" (Beitz 2000, p. 689) and that, therefore, liberal democracies have an interest in increasing the number of well-ordered societies for the sake of their own security. Whereas the peace-argument is central in Rawls' reflections, it does not cover the whole ground. The duty of assistance is also a humanitarian duty of aid and a duty of justice, acknowledging that individuals need goods, such as food or medicine, to make values such as health or self-respect social reality, and that it is a moral wrong to withhold such goods from them (Hinsch 2001, pp. 66–67). Both the interest in a peaceful international

---

[4] "By basic needs I mean roughly those that must be met if citizens are to be in a position to take advantage of the rights, liberties, and opportunities of their society. These needs include economic means as well as institutional rights and freedoms" (LP, p. 38).

realm and a concern for the well-being of individuals around the globe explain the duty of assistance. Still, the question remains: why opt for a duty of assistance rather than for a global difference principle?

2.1 The duty of assistance vs. the difference principle

How do the duty of assistance and the difference principle differ and how can the apparent incoherence be explained? To put it very simply, while the difference principle demands one to 'give to the least privileged', the duty of assistance raises the claim to 'give to those who are in need of help' (Hinsch 2001, p. 66). If one looks for a concept similar to the duty of assistance in Rawls' earlier work, the basic needs conception comes to mind. Whereas on the domestic level, the basic needs of citizens have to be met in order to enable them to practice their rights and liberties, on the international level regimes need to possess the means necessary to establish and maintain a well-ordered basic structure that guarantees both the satisfaction of basic needs and the respect for core human rights (LP, p. 114). Two arguments might explain Rawls' shift from the difference principle to assistance: first, a development within his thinking towards considering pluralism and real world conditions even further and second, the formulation of a different problem or question for the international realm.

In *A Theory of Justice*, Rawls focuses on the question of what the most appropriate conception of justice for a liberal democratic society should look like, and does so on the basis of which fair terms of cooperation between free and equal citizens can be established. He introduces his method of the original position in which representatives of all members of society select – behind a veil of ignorance[5] – a set of principles according to which they want to organize the basic structure of society (TJ, p. 138). He then, as a result of that procedure, introduces two principles of justice:

1. "Each person is to have an equal right to the most extensive total system of equal basic liberties compatible with a similar system of liberty for all" and 2. "Social and economic inequalities are to be arranged so that they are both:
   (a) to the greatest benefit of the least advantaged, [...] and

---

5 The veil of ignorance hides the knowledge of the specific characteristics of the person or in the international realm the state represented in the original position such as the respective age, gender or conception of the good or the size or economic resources of the country. In this way, the veil shall guarantee impartiality and thus a fair set of principles resulting from the original position (Barry 1975, p. 13).

(b) attached to offices and positions open to all under conditions of fair equality of opportunity" (TJ, p. 302).

The second principle guarantees the basic needs essential to pursue one's interests and to preserve one's self-respect (Freeman 2009). The satisfaction of basic needs, however, is also covered by the first principle as this is a necessary condition for exercising the rights granted under the first principle (PL, p. 7).

In *A Theory of Justice* Rawls overestimated the possible homogeneity of a democratic society (Rawls 2005c, p. 489; see also Audard 2007, p. 186). In *Political Liberalism* (PL), he therefore becomes more concerned with real world conditions, especially with pluralism. In a modern democratic society, citizens hold different comprehensive moral or religious views that may be considered reasonable but are incompatible with one another as a result of the free exercise of reason (PL, p. xvi). Whereas in *A Theory of Justice*, the citizens of a well-ordered society adopt the principles of justice on the basis of a shared comprehensive doctrine, in *Political Liberalism*, Rawls argues that citizens can hold differing reasonable doctrines, but need to share a *political conception* founded on and supported by an overlapping consensus between those pluralistic doctrines; this conception must remain freestanding, meaning without a link to any specific comprehensive doctrine (PL, pp. xviii–xx, 36–41).

The development towards considering real world conditions and pluralism continues in *The Law of Peoples*.[6] Here, Rawls puts representatives of well-ordered societies behind a veil of ignorance and claims they would choose a set of principles, the principles of the Law of Peoples, as a guideline for their foreign policy; instead of containing an international difference principle, this set includes the duty of assistance. At a first glance, this seems incoherent considering that *The Law of Peoples* is an extension of Rawls' domestic theory; at a second glance, it becomes comprehensible considering the developments in Rawls' thinking. In *The Law of Peoples*, Rawls transfers the principle of reasonable pluralism from the interpersonal to the international level. There is not only a reasonable pluralism between comprehensive doctrines, but also between political conceptions. In the same way in which citizens can support a diversity of reasonable opinions and still share a political conception, well-ordered regimes can maintain a diversity of reasonable political conceptions, but agree on shared principles of fair international cooperation. Here, Rawls is not just searching

---

6 Accordingly, Rawls constructs his theory within a realistic utopian framework: A realistic utopian conception goes beyond the limits of what is ordinarily understood as possible by staying within the framework of an achievable social world. Rawls, thus, does not sketch the best of all worlds but rather the "best we can realistically – and coherently – hope for" (LP, p. 78).

for principles of international justice. Instead, he aims for principles on which a peaceful, stable and just international system of cooperation between reasonable, well-ordered societies can be based. At the same time he leaves room for self-determination and on how this system can be enlarged to potentially cover all the regimes in the world, the duty of assistance being one of the proposed principles (Kreide 2002). A mitigating principle, i.e. redistributing from one society to another, would cause interdependence for Rawls; the worst-off regimes would rely on a redistribution whose amount depends on the economic well-being of the better-off regimes. This would limit their autonomy and self-determination. Also, for Rawls, self-determination covers self-responsibility.

The rejection of an international difference principle has led to extensive critique from those thinkers who built on Rawls' earlier work. The critique and alternative conceptions are discussed in what follows to substantiate the first claim: that the duty of assistance, despite the critique, is a suitable principle of international distributive justice.

2.2 The duty of assistance, its critics and alternative conceptions

Diverse authors have argued in favour of a global difference principle rather than a duty of assistance. Brian Barry, in reaction to Rawls' elaborations on international justice in *A Theory of Justice*, argues that the representatives in an international original position would, for the same reasons as individuals within liberal societies, opt for "maximizing the wealth of the worst-off", arguing that "what this minimum is should not depend capriciously upon the good luck of being born into a rich society or the ill luck of being born into a poor one" (Barry 1975, p. 129).

With a focus on the arbitrary distribution of natural resources around the globe, Beitz argues for a scheme of global redistribution of resources: "Citizens of a nation that finds itself on top of a gold mine do not gain a right to the wealth that might be derived from it simply because their nation is self-sufficient" (Beitz 1999, p. 140). In an international original position, representatives would know that resources are unequally distributed, that they are scarce and necessary for a functioning domestic cooperative scheme. They would select a principle that provides them with the resources necessary to have a fair chance to establish a well-ordered basic structure and to satisfy the needs of the members of their society: an international resource redistribution principle (Beitz 1999, pp. 141–143). Similarly, Pogge suggests a system of global resource taxation (GRT).

The basic idea is that, while each people owns and fully controls all resources within its national territory, it must pay a tax on any resources it chooses to extract. [...] The burdens of the GRT would not be borne by the owners of resources alone. The tax would lead to higher prices for crude oil, minerals, and so forth. [...] The GRT is then a tax on consumption. But it taxes different kinds of consumption differentially. The cost of gasoline will contain a much higher portion of GRT than the cost of a ticket to an art museum. The tax falls on goods and services roughly in proportion to their resource content: in proportion to how much value each takes from our planet (Pogge 1994, p. 200).

A different scheme of global redistribution via global taxation might be based on the national per capita income. Pogge argues that it might need only 1.13 percent tax on the incomes in high-income economies to lift those who live below the international poverty line above it. In 2001, only 0.22 percent was provided for official development assistance (Pogge 2004, p. 279).

Wilfried Hinsch argues that the duty of assistance cannot be denied, but that it does not cover the whole ground of international distributive justice. In a joint scheme of production, a more productive person deserves a higher reward and should receive a share of the total product in accordance with his or her productivity. Accordingly, the more productive person ends up with a bigger share. The incentives argument thus holds as the larger share in goods is an incentive to be more productive. This also applies to international cooperation; more productive societies have a legitimate claim to a bigger share of the fixed total product but not to the whole of it (Hinsch 2001, pp. 74–75). However, the application of this redistributive principle to Hinsch presupposes that there is a "sufficiently dense economic cooperation", and the "value of this product is largely determined by economic factors beyond the agent's control" (Hinsch 2001, p. 74).

Although the alternatives introduced seem to be in line with Rawls' domestic theory, he rejects them when it comes to the international arena. Four reasons are discussed below.

3 The duty of assistance – A suitable principle of international distributive justice

First, Rawls criticizes the notion that redistributing resources with neither a clear target nor an end leads to a dependence on these distributions. This results in states which are no longer autarkic; thus, the dependencies are perpetuated (LP, p. 116). Well-ordered regimes, however, should be self-determined and self-responsible. The duty of assistance, hence, aims at enabling burdened societies to manage their own affairs reasonably and with decency. Moreover, the reason why there is redistribution on a domestic level is due to combined effort, the cooperation that is necessary to gain those benefits. As Rawls considers states as self-sufficient and sovereign entities in *The Law of Peoples*, an international scheme of cooperation does not exist within his framework.

The claim, that whereas the duty of assistance has an aim, redistribution does not have a clear target, is not true for all approaches. The reduction of poverty and the satisfaction of basic needs are two possible examples (Kreide 2002). Nevertheless, a duty of assistance can also meet these demands, perhaps even more effectively by ensuring that basic needs are met and sustainable well-ordered structures are established.

Second, to Rawls, there are not sufficient common sympathies on the international level between societies for them to accept a mitigating principle. In Rawls' view, no people "will be willing to count the losses to itself as outweighed by gains to other peoples" (LP, p. 60). Peoples are not expected to act paternalistically (LP, p. 111). The ties between societies are weaker than within them, even more so the further they are from one another. Whereas there is a scheme of cooperation within society, where people share common sympathies, these ties are lacking on an international level. From within a realistic utopian framework, one thus has to assume that representatives of societies in an international original position would not opt for a principle of global redistribution. The difference principle relies on social cooperation and reciprocity among the members of society, neither of which exist in the international realm (Freeman 2007, p. 446).

Opposing Rawls' position, cosmopolitans hold that a shared political membership in a society is arbitrary and therefore has "no relevant role in the normative analysis of global distributive principles" (Ypi 2008, p. 443). From a cosmopolitan viewpoint, the natural resources and the wealth gained from their exploitation belong to all human beings and not those who happen to be born within a certain community and territory (Ypi 2008, pp. 447–448). Membership, however, seems to be relevant. Taking the family as an example, siblings should be cared for by their parents; this care does not equally expand to children born into other families. It likewise does make a difference to which society one belongs, as it does make a difference into which family one is born, both being arbitrary. The difference principle applies to the existent cooperative relations of a democratic society. It does not extend to the "more fluid and inchoate collaborative relations among world inhabitants" (Freeman 2007, p. 443). This argument might lose its force if international cooperation and communication increase over time; it might become adequate in a future where cooperative relations and institutions exist on a global level (Freeman 2003, p. 50). For now, within Rawls' realistic utopian framework, one could argue that a world in which peoples are ready to share the resources they have with others in order to mitigate inequalities is unrealistic, as common sympathies decrease with distance.

Third, the well-ordered character of a society, its basic institutions and political culture, but not its wealth, are central. Following Rawls, every society is generally capable of maintaining a well-ordered regime on the basis of the resources it has and, thus, does not need to be wealthy. That well-ordered societies tend to be wealthy or at least able to acquire the means necessary to uphold a well-ordered basic structure is linked to their political culture and the productivity it enhances. Instead of providing direct economic assistance, well-ordered societies need to address the burdens that keep other societies from maintaining a well-ordered basic structure (Hutchings 2010, p. 115). The existence of resource-poor, affluent societies with a well-functioning economy as well as of resource-affluent but poor societies supports this claim. A mere redistribution of natural resources from a resource-rich to a resource-poor country could even make the worst-off worse-off.

Fourth, societies hold a right to self-determination, implying that societies are also self-responsible. If equal societies by choice develop differently, why should the more industrialized, wealthier ones pay for the others? They might have approached and solved problems differently and, therefore, ended up on different economic levels. Redistribution is not necessary (LP, p. 116f.) – presupposing that the positive development is not based on unjust policies, or on the exploitation of other. If they cannot manage their own affairs in a reasonable way, but are willing to, they need to be assisted until they are able to and no further than that. In addition, following Rawls, cosmopolitanism does not consider and respect the diversity of different cultures and national identities as well as the principle of reasonable pluralism. This carries the risk of cultural imperialism (Audard 2006, p. 320f.).

All in all, Rawls rejects an international difference principle; it has neither a target, nor a cut-off point and leads to dependencies rather than autonomy and self-determination. Within a realistic utopian framework, there are not enough common sympathies to expect reasonable and rational agents to accept international redistribution. Moreover, wealth is not necessary for establishing and maintaining a well-ordered basic structure "that makes possible a worthwhile life for all its citizens" (LP, p. 10).

Interestingly, the rejection of an international difference principle in favour of a principle securing the satisfaction of basic needs and respect for core human rights overlaps with the results of Norman Frohlich and Joe Oppenheimer. Simulating an 'original position' in a laboratory, 75 percent of their test subjects opted for a mixed principle rather than a difference principle: "Subjects wanted the society to have a (legitimate) 'safety net'; but given that, they wanted producers to enjoy the benefits of their labor" (Frohlich/Oppenheimer 1990, pp. 463, 466). By establishing a well-ordered basic structure that can be maintained over time out of its own resources, a society might constitute the safety net after which the duty of assistance ends.

The duty of assistance is supported by reasonable and rational arguments: It is our normative duty, focusing on the concern for the well-being and human rights of all human beings, as well as in our rational interest in a peaceful and stable international system. Also, it is a positive-sum enterprise where both win: Burdened societies gain a well-ordered basic structure in which the basic needs of the citizens are met and well-ordered societies obtain a peaceful and stable system of cooperation, including new cooperation partners. The sympathy to people abroad may not suffice for redistribution, but for assistance based on humanitarian duties and state interest. Whereas it is not in the rational interest of liberal peoples to "maximize the wealth of the worst-off" beyond their community, they might reasonably agree to the fact that the means necessary for a decent existence should be guaranteed for everyone, no matter into which society he/she has been born. Finally, establishing well-ordered societies that effectively manage their own affairs over time might actually solve the problem of poverty within those societies.

Still, assistance might not be a sufficient means on its own; as Pogge has shown quite plainly, aspects of the international political and economic order become relevant here, leading to my second claim that the duty of assistance, despite its advantages, is not a sufficient principle of international distributive justice.

4 Why the duty of assistance is not sufficient

The unfavourable conditions under which burdened societies suffer result not only from their own actions, political decisions or the resources they have at their command, but also from external factors. Equally, if we want to reduce and eradicate the burdens, we not only require assistance on the domestic level, but must also address the negative effect of external, regional or international influences. Rawls in *The Law of Peoples* ignores that "national economic policy is shaped by international economic institutions and powerful states" (Hurrell 2001, p. 48) and that those states are co-responsible for the economic situation in poor societies (Hurrell 2001, p. 48). International economic interaction, organized by treaties and conventions about trade, can be shaped more or less favourably for poor countries. Had the economic order been friendlier to poorer countries, much of today's poverty would have been avoided (Pogge

2004, p. 263 f.). Furthermore, "by seeing the problem of poverty merely in terms of assistance, we overlook that our enormous economic advantage is deeply tainted by how it accumulated over the course of *one* historical process" (Pogge 2004, p. 262). This process was "pervaded by enslavement, colonialism, even genocide" and "devastated the societies and cultures of four continents" (Pogge 2004, p. 262). The economic advantage of rich states towards poor societies is, thus, also to be seen as a consequence of an unjust historical process (Pogge 2004, p. 262).

Pogge illustrates the argument in reference to Peter Singer's "drowning child in the pond" example.[7] However, Pogge does not consider the addressees as bystanders, who accidentally notice that a child has fallen into a pond and appears to be drowning. From Pogge's perspective, affluent societies have pushed the child into the pond and they are responsible for its life-threatening condition (Pogge 2004, pp. 261–265). Accordingly, "our failure to make a serious effort toward poverty reduction may constitute not merely a lack of beneficence, but our active impoverishing, starving, and killing of millions of innocent people by economic means" (Pogge 2001, p. 15). Therefore, in addition to the positive duty to protect persons from great harm at little cost, there also are the negative duties not to benefit from an unjust order or to take advantage of injustices at the expense of others (Pogge 2001, p. 22). From this, it follows that one may not pursue benefits that enhance poverty abroad as that would harm the poor. Governments need to not only assist, but also to reduce the unfair rules that generate unfair gains for them. Here, rational interests and demands of justice collide. However, by following Pogge's claims, on his own account, severe poverty could be eradicated "without 'sacrificing' the fulfilment of our own needs or even mildly serious interests" (Pogge 2004, p. 279).

Co-responsibility is ignored by Rawls, who sketches societies as closed, self-sufficient entities. Still, he strives to identify principles of fair international cooperation and argues that in "addition to agreeing to the principles […], the parties will formulate guidelines for setting up cooperative organizations and agree to standards of fairness for trade as well as certain provisions for mutual assis-

---

[7] Imagine you pass by a pond and recognize that a child fell in and is in danger of drowning. You can easily save the child but will get your clothes wet and dirty. All (or at least almost all) would agree that you have a duty to safe the child from drowning. Also, the fact that there are other people around who could save the child does not make a difference to your moral duty (Singer 1997). Now, imagine a child is starving far away and could be saved at very small cost, such as the cost of a CD or a shirt. This could "mean the difference between life and death to more than one person somewhere in the world" (Singer 1997). The moral duty to save a life at little cost remains (Singer 1997).

tance" (LP, p. 42). Unjustified distributive effects occurring between peoples need to be corrected (LP, p. 43). Whereas Rawls here only refers to the relations between well-ordered peoples, in principle, the rule should embrace other societies, too. Past injustices are not covered by the principles of the Law of Peoples as they are not covered by the principles of justice on the domestic level. The principles are to be freestanding, independent of historic developments, thereby claiming timeless relevance.

The duty of assistance does not cover the design of the international economic order, which is decisive for the flourishing of burdened societies. In line with Rawls, one can argue that well-ordered societies would, due to their reasonable character, support Pogge's negative duties and reform the international political and economic order into a fair system of cooperation. In addition, going back to Singer's child-in-the-pond example, one could argue for the inclusion of a further principle from within the Rawlsian framework: a principle of emergency relief. How those principles could be integrated into the principles of the Law of Peoples to add further elements of distributive justice to the duty of assistance (assistance+) is discussed in the following section.

5 Assistance+

The duty not to harm is a basic principle of social cooperation. To be integrated into the set of the principles of the Law of Peoples, it is too unspecific; it is unclear what constitutes 'harm' and in how far intention plays a role. Humanitarian interventions always cause harm; a principle 'not to harm' could thus lead to injustices in the sense that it might force them not to stop gross violations of human rights. The duty not to profit from injustices is more concrete, but still might need further specification. The negative duties as such can thus not be integrated into the principles of the Law of Peoples.

As Pogge states, international economic interaction is organized by treaties and conventions. Here, the second principle of the Law of Peoples (the duty to observe treaties) constitutes a good point to step in. The following amendment is suggested: Treaties are to be kept. *They are to be negotiated under fair conditions and may not imply injustices towards third parties. Treaties that violate any of these are invalid.* Injustices that might result from a treaty violating the principle would require compensation.

The formulation covers Pogge's two principles. Even if what injustices might cover cannot be fully explored at this point, 'injustices towards third parties' is considered to cover making burdened societies worse-off, that is to say increasing poverty abroad. This does not imply that treaties need to benefit burdened societies or the people that form them, which would bring in the difference principle, but that they should not be to their disbenefit. Economic structures that disadvantage poor societies should thus be avoided. Also, it would cover not buying resources or goods that have been produced under unjust conditions. In reference to Pogge, this would touch the resource privilege: well-ordered societies should not buy resources, such as oil from dictators that exploit the resources of the country for their own benefit (Pogge 2004, pp. 270–271). An amendment of the principles of the Law of Peoples as suggested thus seems to cover Pogge's negative duties and be in line with Rawls' theory.

In addition, a principle of emergency relief should be considered as following from the duty to honour human rights. In *The Law of Peoples*, Rawls argues that the principle of non-intervention does not hold in cases of gross violations of core human rights. Rawls' set covers the right to life and physical security. As malnutrition or, more generally, a shortage of basic supplies poses a threat to the life and physical security of people, those circumstances constitute a gross violation of those human rights and, thus, should equally trigger intervention in form of emergency relief. As is the right to war, the principle does not necessarily need to be introduced as an additional principle of the Law of Peoples, but can be deduced from the duty to honour human rights.

6 Conclusion

The duty of assistance is a suitable principle of international distributive justice as it aims at securing basic human rights and decent living conditions for all human beings as well as at securing the self-determination of societies within a just international system of cooperation. It fits into the development within Rawlsian thinking towards taking real world conditions, especially pluralism, into account. Rawls rejects a global difference principle for several good reasons: Instead of mitigating inequalities, the duty of assistance strives to enable societies to manage their own affairs in a decent way out of their own powers and with their own resources. If taken seriously, it could solve the problem of malnutrition and severe poverty and would improve "the living situation of a huge number of people" (Kreide 2009, p. 108; see also Hurrell 2001, p. 50; Wenar 2001, p. 88).

However, the duty of assistance does not suffice to regulate international distributive justice fairly and needs to be complemented (assistance+). The following amendments to the principles of the Law of Peoples are, therefore, suggested: Treaties not only need to be kept, but to be negotiated under fair terms and may not imply injustices towards third parties. A principle of emergency relief is derived from the duty to honour core human rights. As peoples are moral agents, they would not, arguing from within the Rawlsian framework, maintain an unfair global economic system that does not allow their assistance to be effective. Peoples should agree to those amendments due to their moral character.

On the one hand, Rawls' concern for a decent living standard and his duty of assistance pose a weak cosmopolitan argument, also evident in his human rights minimalism. On the other, Rawls addresses communitarian claims when ascribing a special value to communities and granting them a right to what they produce in a joint effort – after the duty of assistance has been satisfied. Moreover, he considers rational arguments in taking state interests into account, though reasonable societies pursue their rational interest only within the limits of reasonable principles. For this reason, the duty of assistance may constitute, if not an overlapping consensus, a compromise between the schools of thought connected to those concepts and, thus, a compromise between the people supporting these conceptions. The duty of assistance covers the perspective and interest of societies that understand themselves as communities with a value of their own. Equally, it presents not only reasonable, but also rational arguments for assisting burdened societies; it is a duty towards humanity, a duty of justice, but its fulfilment is also in our interest as it enhances a peaceful and stable international system.

Moreover, the suggested amendments show that the question of international distributive justice is linked to other questions and principles of international justice and, hence, needs to be analysed and discussed within the broader framework of principles that taken together lay the foundation of a fair system of international cooperation.

Bibliography

Audard, Cathrine (2006): "Peace or Justice? Some Remarks on Rawls's Law of Peoples". In: *Revue international de philosohie* 60, pp. 301–326.
Audard, Cathrine (2007): *John Rawls*. Montreal, Kingston: McGill-Queen's University Press.
Barry, Brian (1975): *The Liberal Theory of Justice: A Critical Examination of the Principal Doctrines of A Theory of Justice by John Rawls*. Oxford: Clarendon Press (first published 1973, reprinted with corrections).
Beitz, Charles R. (1999): "Social and Cosmopolitan Liberalism". In: *International Affairs* 75, pp. 515–529.
Beitz, Charles R. (2000): "Rawls's Law of Peoples". In: *Ethics* 110, pp. 669–696.
Freeman, Samuel (Ed.) (2003): *The Cambridge Companion to Rawls*. Cambridge: Cambridge University Press.
Freeman, Samuel (2007): *Rawls*. London, New York: Routledge.

Freeman, Samuel (2009): "Original Position". In: *The Stanford Encyclopedia of Philosophy (Spring 2009 Edition)*. Edward N. Zalta (Ed.). http://plato.stanford.edu/archives/spr2009/entries/original-position, visited on 28 November 2011.

Frohlich, Norman/Oppenheimer, Joe A. (1990): "Choosing Justice in Experimental Democracies with Production". In: *American Political Science Review* 84, pp. 461–477.

Hinsch, Wilfried (2001): "Global Distributive Justice". In: *Metaphilosophy* 32, pp. 58–77.

Hurrell, Andrew (2001): "Global Inequality and International Institutions". In: *Metaphilosophy* 32, pp. 34–57.

Hutchings, Kimberly (2010): *Global Ethics: An Introduction*. Cambridge: Polity Press.

Kreide, Regina (2002): "Book Review – John Rawls on International Justice". In: *German Law Journal*. www.germanlawjournal.com/ index. php?pageID=11&artID=208, visited on 11 November 2011.

Kreide, Regina (2009): "Preventing Military Humanitarian Intervention? John Rawls and Jürgen Habermas on a Just Global Order". In: *German Law Journal* 10, pp. 93–113.

Pogge, Thomas (1994): "An Egalitarian Law of Peoples". In: *Philosophy and Public Affairs* 3, pp. 195–224.

Pogge, Thomas (2001): "Priorities of Global Justice". In: *Metaphilosophy* 32, pp. 6–24.

Pogge, Thomas (2004): "'Assisting' the Global Poor". In: Chatterjee, Deen K. (Ed.): *The Ethics of Assistance. Morality and the Distant Needy*. Cambridge: Cambridge University Press, pp. 260–287.

Rawls, John (1999): *The Law of Peoples with "The Idea of Public Reason Revisited"*. Cambridge, MA: Harvard University Press.

Rawls, John (2005a): *A Theory of Justice*. Cambridge, MA: Harvard University Press (first published 1971).

Rawls, John (2005b): *Political Liberalism*. New York: Columbia University Press (first published 1993). Expanded edition with "The Idea of Public Reason Revisited" and "Reply to Habermas".

Rawls, John (2005c): "The Idea of Public Reason Revisited". In: Rawls, John (2005): *Political Liberalism*. New York: Columbia University Press.

Singer, Peter (1997): "The Drowning Child and the Expanding Circle". In: *The New Internationalist*. 5 April 1997. www.newint.org/features/ 1997/04/05/drowning, visited on 4 November 2011.

Wenar, Leif (2001): "Contractualism and Global Economic Justice". In: *Metaphilosophy* 32, pp. 79–94.

Wenar, Leif (2008): "John Rawls". In: *The Stanford Encyclopedia of Philosophy* (2008 Edition). Edward N. Zalta (Ed.). http://plato.stanford.edu/archives/fall2008/entries/rawls, visited on 11 November 2011.

Ypi, Lea (2008): "Political Membership in the Contractarian Defense of Cosmopolitanism". In: *The Review of Politics* 70, pp. 442–472.

Bill Wringe
Global Collective Obligations, Just International Institutions and Pluralism[1]

Abstract: It is natural to see political philosophy as the domain, par excellence, of collective action and collective obligation. It is therefore surprising that the notion of collective obligation rarely assumes centre-stage within the subject. Elsewhere I have argued that we have good reasons for accepting the existence of global collective obligations – in other words, collective obligations which fall on the world's population as a whole. Here I shall argue that in many situations, forward-looking global obligations give rise to an obligation on individuals to work towards bringing into existence and support an institutional system which will enable their obligations to be met. Call such an obligation the 'Obligation to Promote Satisfactory Global Institutions'. I shall also examine a significant challenge to this line of argument, which I call the 'Pluralist Challenge'.

1 Introduction

Questions about distributive justice vary in their focus along two distinct dimensions. We can look at distributive justice as something which operates on a variety of different scales: within particular local institutions, at the level of the state and perhaps also at the global level. We can also distinguish between questions about how much (if anything) each individual is owed as a matter of justice, and questions about the kinds of institution which we might put in place in order to ensure that individuals receive what they deserve and to take remedial action when they do not. Here I shall be concerned with questions at the global and institutional level: questions about the kinds of institution which we might need to ensure an equitable distribution of the world's resources, and with the duties that individuals have to support such institutions.

I shall argue that individuals have a duty to support certain kinds of institution involved in the distribution of goods. Since these duties arise out of consideration of the rights of others we should see them as duties of distributive justice. Secondly I shall be discussing how a certain kind of moral burden, which falls on all of us collectively, should be shared among the various members of the

---

[1] I am indebted to Stephen Snyder for helpful comments and to both Stephen Snyder and Manuel Knoll for their patience in awaiting a revised version of my original paper.

https://doi.org/10.1515/9783110537369-022

world's population.[2] The notion of collective obligation will play a central role in my argument.

2 Collective obligation as a key notion in political philosophy

It is natural to think that political philosophy is concerned with reflection on some of the ways in which groups of human beings come together to confront common problems: in other words, with the domain of collective action. So it seems surprising that the notion of collective obligation rarely assumes centre-stage in normative political philosophy. If there are, or can be, collective obligations, then these are constraints on the kinds of collective action in which we may permissibly engage. Beyond this, considerations about collective obligations may play a central role in demarcating the form that legitimate political organization ought to take.

One obstacle to allowing the notion of collective obligation a central role in political philosophy is that the relationship between claims about collective responsibility and any constraints or requirements that they might impose on the actions of individuals is often obscure.[3] This point is familiar in discussions of backward-looking judgments about collective responsibility. Suppose the citizens of the United Kingdom bear, collectively, some responsibility for the policies pursued by its government overseas, and in particular for its participation in illegal acts of war in Iraq. It is unclear what responsibility lies with particular individuals who might have opposed that war, actively and strenuously; those who voted for parties which did not support the war; those who reached the age of adulthood while the war was being conducted, and so on.[4] Similar points apply to forward-looking political obligation. Suppose we think the present population of the planet has a collective obligation to mitigate the effects of world-

---

[2] I am grateful to Stephen Snyder for emphasising this point to me in correspondence.
[3] Other reasons, which I shall not discuss here, might include the suspicion that the notion of collective obligation is incoherent and the idea that claims about collective obligation are in some sense reducible to claims about individual obligation. For further discussion, see Wringe 2006, 2010, 2014.
[4] On the other hand, while the relationship between collective responsibility and individual responsibility may be obscure, it is not, and is not generally thought to be, non-existent.: It would go against the judgment of many involved in such protests to say that they bore no responsibility for the actions of their government; and it would make little sense of many people's view that as citizens of a country engaged in an illegal war, they bore a special responsibility for stopping it.

wide climate change. We might disagree about what, if anything, such an obligation requires of a citizen of a historically under-developed country; an American teenager; a Norwegian Old Age Pensioner and the lone parent of a developmentally-disabled child.

One might reply that if politics is concerned with collective action, political philosophers qua political philosophers need not worry if the implications of a claim about collective responsibility for the actions of individuals are unclear. However, even if political questions typically take the form 'What should/can/must/*we* do', the question 'What should/can/must *I* do' is more fundamental. 'We' can do nothing, without some 'I' or some 'I's doing something. So if the notion of collective obligation is to play a central role within political philosophy, we must address the implications of such obligations for individuals. I shall argue, then, that some kinds of forward-looking global obligation give rise to obligations on individuals to bring into existence institutions which can enable those obligations to be met.

3 Global collective obligations: The very idea

Suppose, as many have, that the notion of a collective obligation is coherent (French 1984; May 1987; Copp 2006; Pettit 2007; Isaacs 2011).[5] We may still wonder what kinds of entities can be the subjects of collective obligations. Entities which have a formal organizational structure, such as nation-states, business corporations and smaller bodies such as committees within a larger organization are obvious candidates (Gilbert 2008; French 1984; Copp 2006). However, I have argued elsewhere that groups which do not possess a formal structure of this sort can also be the subject of collective obligations (Wringe forthcoming, 2010, 2006; cf. also Isaacs 2011, chapters 1, 2 and 5). One unstructured collective which is particularly interesting here is the collective consisting of everyone currently alive: what one might call the 'global collective'.

There are good reasons for thinking that some this collective bears significant moral obligations (Nussbaum 2006; Wringe 2006).[6] Consider a well-

---

[5] For my own views see Wringe 2006, 2010a, and forthcoming French 1984, May 1987, Copp 2006, Pettit 2007 Isaacs 2011.
[6] Not everyone would accept that the population of the world does constitute an unstructured collective of the sort I suggest here. One reason for this has been explored in detail by Pogge (Pogge 2001) who suggests that global economic interconnectedness makes the world's population part of a structured political community. Whether or not Pogge is correct, I think the argument from the nature of rights suggests that it makes sense to think of there being collective ob-

known objection to the notion of subsistence rights, conceived of as rights on the parts of individuals to have certain basic needs attended to (O'Neill [1986] 1998). It is often suggested that if such rights existed, they would necessarily give rise to obligations on agents to see to it that such needs are fulfilled (or, more plausibly to see to it that individuals acquire the capacity to meet these needs). However, it is often not plausible that this obligation falls either on some individual human being or on any salient organized collective body. Take for example the case of a starving individual in a drought-stricken region of a failed state such as Somalia. It may be quite implausible to think that any particular individual has an obligation to do something about her fate: everyone nearby who is in a position to help may be in a similar plight. It may also be true that the most obvious collective bodies are in no position to help either. Their state, for example, may lack the resources, the organizational capacity, or the territorial control which would be required to do anything about their situation.[7]

We ought not to say that individuals in such circumstances do not have the rights that more fortunately placed individuals – for example, those who are in a position to be helped by their compatriots – do have. To do so would in effect be to say that the protection that rights are supposed to afford individuals lapses in situations where they need it most.[8] An alternative is to see obligations as falling on a global collective.[9] The global collective body acts as what one might call an 'obligation-bearer of last resort'. The existence of collective obligations which fall on this body is thus something which can be taken to be a presupposition of the claim that there is a right to have certain kinds of basic needs met. We have here

---

ligations on the world's population considered in abstraction from any political structure that might fall on them (just as it might make sense to think of a group of individuals who were in fact the members of a particular club or social group having certain obligations when considered as a particular social organized group, and other obligations in virtue of some other form of social organization, or in virtue of their being placed in such a way as to enable them to act together collectively to address some pressing need. For further discussion of Pogge's view see Meckled-Garcia 2008, Wringe 2010b.

7 For useful discussion see also Griffin 2008. Sreenivasan 2012 has recently appealed to an argument along similar lines in defence of the claim that there is no human right to health.
8 Of course the protection that rights provide is only metaphorical. Rights can only protect individuals to the extent that individuals act in accordance with the obligations that those rights generate. But what would be entailed by the suggestion that people in desperate circumstances have fewer rights is not this uncontroversial claim, but that these individuals would be deprived of the protections which rights can, and should, provide.
9 See Wringe 2006 for arguments that this is the best way of avoiding the conclusion; and in particular that collective obligations falling on other bodies provide a less satisfactory solution.

what is effectively a transcendental argument for the existence of obligations falling on a relatively unstructured body – namely a global collective.

4 A Problem – The agency objection

Some authors hold that unstructured groups like the global collective cannot be the bearers of collective obligations because they are not collective agents.[10] We might express their objection as follows:

(Agency Argument)
(P1) Only groups with a certain kind of internal structure are capable of collective action.
(P2) Only groups that are capable of collective action can have collective obligations.
C   Unstructured groups cannot be the subject of collective obligation.

The first premise of this argument is questionable. The phenomenon of collective action has been analysed in different ways by different authors. Some accounts of collective action require a collective agent with a certain amount of internal structures but others, such as Christopher Kutz's 'minimalist' account do not (List/Pettit 2011; French 1984; Gilbert 1989; Kutz 2000a, 2000b). In the absence of detailed argument about the nature of collective action we cannot simply make an inference from lack of formal structure to the incapacity for agency.

The second premise is also problematic. Several authors, including Isaacs, Collins and Lawford-Smith appear to take it to be self-evident (Isaacs 2011; Lawford-Smith 2012; Collins 2013). In fact, it is highly contentious. For, as I argue elsewhere, the existence of collective obligations does not require that the collective on whom the obligation falls be an agent but only that some agent or agents be answerable for the fulfilment or non-fulfilment of the obligation (Wringe 2010a). In the case of obligations which fall on unstructured groups, the agents in question are typically some or all of those who make up the group in question (Wringe 2010a.)

Does the second premise of the argument follow from the claim that 'Ought implies Can'? It would if we accepted the claim that only agents have the capacity to carry out the actions which are necessary for a collective obligations to be fulfilled. However, if we think that some collectives are potentially agents without actually being agents, then this claim seems false. For it seems plausible that

---

10 Isaacs 2011 chapter 1, Lawford-Smith 2012 and Collins (forthcoming) all endorse the claim that only collectives which are capable of agency can be the subjects of collective obligation. For an argument against this view see Wringe 2010a.

if a collective is a potential agent, it has the capacity to do any of the things it would have the capacity to do if it were appropriately organized.[11] (The general principle involved here is that if I am capable of acquiring the capacity to do X by a certain time, then, in the only sense of can which is of interest here, I can do it. It is in this sense, for example, that one might judge that the students who are being taught by a particular teacher can pass the final exam which she devised at the beginning of the semester, and that those who are in receipt of a scholarship stand under a moral obligation to do so.)

5 Connecting individual and collective organizations

What bearing does the existence of a global obligation to satisfy subsistence needs have on questions about what particular individuals should do in particular concrete situations? Clearly it cannot give rise to an obligation on each individual to satisfy everyone's subsistence needs. No individual can do this. Indeed, the fact that no individual can do this, taken together with the claim that ought implies can, is precisely what supports the claim that there is a global collective obligation here.

However, this does not mean that global obligations cannot give rise to any obligations on individuals.[12] This would be to overlook the possibility that collec-

---

[11] Lawford Smith (2012) has argued that this is not the case: she suggests that in general an unorganised group does not have the capacity to do things which it could do if organised, simply because it may be so difficult for the group to organise itself. She cites in connection with this case the German army under Hitler which (she claims) did not have the capacity to bring Hitler down even though it could have done so if appropriately organised. Her reason for denying this is to exempt the army (considered as a collective) from blame in this context. However, it is not clear to me that Lawford-Smith draws the right lesson from this example: it seems just as plausible to hold that the army as an institution was culpable even though, perhaps, no individual serving in it was (since they were, she claims, not in a position to be reasonably sure that others would have co-operated with them). One reason that it might make sense to do so would be that one could regard the structure or character of the German army as being to blame in this case. Doing so helps to make sense of certain kinds of reactive attitude that one might have in this case: for example one might think that the army deserved contempt, while reserving judgment on whether any particular individuals did.

[12] My interest at this point is in what, in principle, individuals would have to do in order to fulfil the collective obligations which fall upon groups of which they are a member. It is a separate, and important question, and one which I have addressed as to whether they are capable of doing so, and in particular, how we ought to understand claims of collective capacity in this

tive obligations can give rise to obligations on individuals that are slightly more complex than those which we have considered so far. I have argued elsewhere that collective obligations can give rise to individual obligations without being reducible to them. In particular, I have defended the following claim:

(C to I)
If in a particular situation a collective C has an all-out obligation to Phi, then, for any member M of C, and for any set S of possible actions of members of C that, if performed together, would constitute C's Phi-ing, if S includes M's doing A, then M has a pro tanto obligation to do A.[13]

(Roughly speaking, C to I says that if there is some way for members of a collective to act which will ensure the collective of which they are a member will do the thing it is obliged to do, then each of the members has a pro tanto obligation to act in that way.)

C to I is a principle connecting all-out collective obligations with pro tanto obligations on individuals. David Copp has argued that there are no plausible principles that will enable us to derive all-out obligations on individuals from all-out obligations on collectives. But his arguments do not touch the principle which I have defended.[14]

I shall not attempt to rehearse the argument for C to I here. Instead I shall try to show that if we accept C to I, we can derive from it two further principles, which are somewhat more concrete in their implications for individuals.

(Organizational Principle 1)
OP 1: A stringent obligation which falls on a collective, and which can only be fulfilled by collective action of a sort that is unlikely to come about in a spontaneous and uncoordinated manner generates an obligation on each of the members of that collective to promote modes of organization that would enable the obligation to be carried out, to the extent that it is in their power to promote such forms of obligation.

(Organizational Principle 2)
OP 2: A stringent obligation which falls on a collective which is organized in such a way as to enable the co-ordination of collective actions that satisfy global obligations generates a pro tanto obligation on individuals who form part of that collective to act in ways which are necessary for the fulfilment of those obligations.

---

context. See in particular Wringe 2010, and for further critical discussion of the view I put forward there, Pinkert 2014, Lawford-Smith 2015.
13 I am indebted to David Copp for useful discussion of this issue (though he should not be blamed for the formulation I have settled on).
14 For further discussion see Wringe (forthcoming).

Both these principles require further explication. For example, much more needs to be said about which obligations are 'stringent obligations' and why both principles are restricted to the case of stringent obligations. The occurrence of the notion of a stringent obligation in these principles will also make a difference to the question of what counts as an adequate argument for them. Any such argument will at a minimum have to explain why it only applies to stringent obligations; ideally it should also say something about whether there are any related principles which apply to non-stringent obligations.

The intuitive case for restricting the principles in some way is fairly obvious: there would be something wrong with a principle that generated, or threatened to generate, a need for a world state out of a possible collective obligation to avoid littering sidewalks. The word stringent acts, to that extent as something of a place-holder. However, I shall take an obligation to be stringent provided that failing to meet it would result a large number of significant violations of individuals' basic rights, where I use the term basic right in Henry Shue's sense to mean a right which individuals must have in order for any further assignment of rights to them to have any point (Shue [1980] 1996).[15]

This characterization of stringency still leaves the content of OP 1 and OP 2 somewhat indeterminate. Further specification would involve discussion of which rights are basic rights; of what counts as a 'significant' violation of them; and how many such violations are required to generate a stringent obligation. These are all important issues, which I cannot pursue here. Even when these lacunae are acknowledged, it seems plausible that a good argument for OP 1 and OP 2 would go some way towards showing how claims about global obligation might give rise to relatively contentful requirements for action relating to particular individuals.[16]

OP 1 and OP 2 do not give rise to putative obligations on individuals which those individuals are unable to satisfy. Furthermore, they appear to be capable of

---

[15] Shue argues – correctly in my view – that such rights must include both rights to a basic level of subsistence and to a certain level of personal security. For further discussion, see Beitz/Goodin 2009.

[16] Although I shall be providing arguments in favour of OP 1 and OP 2, I shall not be claiming that they provide us with the full story about the ways in which global obligations might filter down to the individual level. One reason for this is that OP 2 fails to generate any obligations on individuals in situations where there is more than one way for a collective to carry out its collective obligations – as will often be the case. Nevertheless, a successful argument for them would at least show how claims about global obligation might give rise to substantive claims about the obligations of individuals.

providing some kind of guidance concerning the ways in which particular individuals should act in particular concrete circumstances.

6 Deriving OP 1 and OP 2

How do OP 1 and OP 2 follow from C to I?

OP 1 addresses situations where a collective has an obligation which is extremely unlikely to be met by spontaneous action on the part of its members. Furthermore, if collective obligations are constrained by the principle that 'ought implies can', then such obligations can be met by some combination of actions. If the obligations cannot be met by spontaneous action, yet can be met in some way, then the way they can be met is, presumably, by means of organized action. But organization of the required sort does not come out of nowhere: it needs to be put in place by the action of individuals. So if a collective can only solve a problem by acting in an organized manner, it can only solve that problem by doing what is required to organize itself in the requisite manner.

It follows that if a collective has a duty which it cannot fulfil without organized action, then the ways in which it can meet that obligation involve organizing itself in the right way.[17] If there is a duty on the part of the individuals that make up the collective to act in ways which would enable them to fulfil the obligation, and these ways involve organizing themselves in particular ways, then, according to C to I they have a pro tanto duty to organize themselves in these ways. But this is what OP 1 says.

I have said that collectives that are unlikely to be able to meet their obligations in virtue of the spontaneous actions of individuals who make up the collective may be able to meet them by organizing themselves. Is the only possibility? In principle it seems as though it might not be. A collective might acquire the sort of organization required for meeting its obligations not by organizing itself, but by having some form of organization imposed on it from outside. Suppose the citizens of a nation comprehensively defeated in war have a collective obligation to institute some form of order which will perform the basic functions of a state (as one might hold, of the people of Germany in 1945) (Wringe 2010a).[18] Sometimes the required kind of order may be likeliest to come through being externally imposed.

---

[17] Or perhaps acquiescing in having such a form of organization imposed upon it: see below.
[18] I thank my colleague Lars Vinx for suggesting this example.

This possibility is clearly irrelevant to the main kind of case that I have in mind here – that of the global collective. Here, there is *ex hypothesi* nothing outside the collective which could impose the requisite form of organization on it. However, the possibility might be thought to throw some doubt on the argument I have given for OP 2. Nonetheless, I do not think it should. In general, the chances of some external body imposing on a collective body just the forms of organization that it needs to fulfil its collective obligations (as opposed to serving the interests of those who are imposing that form of order) seems small enough to be discounted. It may be optimistic, but it does not seem to be unduly optimistic, to suppose that in general unstructured collective bodies are more likely to meet their obligations by finding their own form of organization than by having some form of organization imposed upon them from outside

OP 2 is more complicated. However, in most cases in which a collective is organized in such a way as to enable an obligation to be met, it seems likely that the way the obligation is most likely to be met will involve the individuals acting in accordance with the forms of organization that already exist and which would enable them to meet the obligations. (It need not be the only way: perhaps the institutions we have are sufficient to enable us to fulfil a certain duty, but are not the only ones which could enable us to do so.) Changing forms of organization is complicated, time-consuming and unpredictable: in most cases obligations which could be met by a changed form of organization are less likely to be met in that way. So in most cases a pro tanto duty to act in accordance with existing organizations to meet given collective obligations will not be outweighed by a competing and incompatible duty to come up with other forms of organization.

I noted in section 4 that OP 1 and OP 2 were stated in terms of 'stringent' collective obligations (and I also noticed a concomitant argumentative burden of explaining why this should be so). Nothing in the argument that I have given so far provides such an explanation. In fact, the argument seems to justify much more inclusive principles, applying to all collective obligations, and not merely to stringent ones. This might even be taken as an objection to the arguments: the objection would be that if the arguments given are correct, our collective obligations give rise to too many obligations on individuals to be plausible.

My response is that the argument does provide support for versions of OP 1 and OP 2 which are not limited to stringent obligations. However, I have also argued that the obligations on individuals which these collective obligations give rise to are only pro tanto duties, and that in some cases these pro tanto duties might have a weight that is so low as to mean that they are almost always over-ridden. The point of restricting OP 1 and OP 2 duties to situations where the obligations involved are quite stringent is that it is plausible that in these cases – and to a far lesser extent in other cases – the pro tanto duties generated by our collective obligations are likely to be strong enough not to be generally over-ridden by countervailing considerations.

7 An objection

In section 6 I argued for two principles concerning the obligations of individuals to support international arrangements. However, one might object that OP 2 is unduly conservative. For OP 2 directs us to support existing institutions insofar as they are *capable* of allowing us to satisfy our global obligations rather than, for example, devoting our energies to bringing about new forms of organisation. But it may then require us, wrongly, to support institutional arrangements which are themselves unjust.

There are three distinct questions which we might want to consider here. The first is whether OP 2 would require us to support unjust institutional structures in some possible world or other. A second is whether OP 2 would require us to support unjust institutional structures in the world as it actually is. And a third question is whether either of these two possibilities would constitute grounds for rejecting OP 2, and hence the line of argument which supports it.

I shall start by considering the last of these questions. One might think that if OP 2 would give us a duty to support unjust institutions in any circumstances whatsoever then this would give us compelling grounds for rejecting it. And it seems at least possible to imagine that there might be such grounds. Suppose we have good reasons to think that there is a global collective obligation to prevent irreversible climate change of a sort which will have catastrophic implications for unborn generations. We can certainly imagine circumstances in which the institutions which exist and which are capable of averting such a threat might be ones which engaged in practices which were obviously unjust, such as extracting forced labour from randomly chosen citizens.

Does this establish that OP 2 is unacceptable? I do not think so. There are two reasons why not. First, it is simply not clear that it is a requirement on principles of justice that they should yield intuitively acceptable results in all possible situations. Perhaps there are predicaments that are sufficiently far removed from our own circumstances that we are simply not very good at figuring out what would be the right thing to do if we found ourselves in them. If there are, then the fact that a putative principle yields intuitively unacceptable results in them should not count against the principle. Perhaps our intuitive sense of what would be right and wrong in such a situation is misleading in ways which would become apparent to us if we ever face such a situation, but which are difficult to get a sense of when we are simply imagining a sparsely described philosophical thought experiment.

The second reason why OP 2 might ground an obligation to support unjust institutions in some possible circumstances is that OP 2 only gives us prima facie reasons to support certain kinds of institutional structure. It is consistent with this that the institutions' in question being extremely unjust might conceivably give us reasons for not supporting such institutions which outweighed those prima facie reasons. If so, we would not have shown that OP 2 had any obviously unacceptable consequences even in these counterfactual circumstances.

Let us instead concentrate on whether OP 2 gives us an obligation to support unjust institutions in the actual world, and whether a positive answer to this question would provide reasons for finding OP 2 dubious. Here the news is less good. For we might think that OP 2 requires us to support unjust institutions in the actual world. If so, it is much harder to argue that the fact that OP 2 has intuitively unacceptable consequences is unimportant.

Thomas Pogge has argued that world poverty involves the violation of the human rights – including, importantly, the liberty rights of a large proportion of the world's poor. In particular, he argues that the current international economic framework, incorporating as it does such things as state sovereignty privileges, plays an important role in allowing these rights to be violated. (I focus on the passive here, rather than on Pogge's view that we are actively involved in violating these rights, because I am interested in questions about institutional frameworks.) It may still be that the existing economic system should be one which is *capable* of allowing for political action to address, say our global obligation to see that the subsistence rights of all human beings are met. If so, then OP 2 would give us reason to support an unjust institutional order in the *actual* world. This seems like a substantial and serious objection.

When considering whether OP 2 might have unacceptable consequences in some other possible world, I emphasized that OP 2 only gave rise to a prima facie duty to support certain kinds of institution; and I suggested that there might be countervailing obligations not to participate in unjust institutions which would outweigh this prima facie duty. However, this response is liable to seem somewhat thin when we are considering the implications of OP 2 for our actually existing institutions. In this context it would be good to have some idea of what this countervailing duty might be. I now turn to this issue.

8 How to develop institutions

I have argued that there are global collective obligations, that these obligations give rise to prima facie obligations on individuals to institute and promote forms of global organisation which would enable these global collective obligations to be met. If, as seems plausible, global poverty involves the violation of human rights, the institutions which are required here will include institutions which aim at preventing and rectifying distributive injustices. However, I have also argued that this prima facie obligation is likely to give us an obligation to support institutional frameworks which actually exist, even if these frameworks are ones which, in practice, enable substantial injustice. I have also argued that this unattractive aspect of my view might be mitigated to some extent if there were some kind of countervailing duty which could over-ride it.

Three things seem necessary here. The first is to say something about what this countervailing duty might be; the second is to explain why we should think that such a duty exists; and the third is to say something more detailed about the ways in which this kind of duty might interact with the problematic parts of OP 2.

As far as the content of the duty is concerned, notice that OP 2 says that we have a prima facie duty to support institutional frameworks which would enable our collective global obligations to be met. But the word 'support' is very non-specific: there are many different ways in which one can support an institution; or rather, there are many different activities that could count as forms of support. (To the extent that I pay my taxes and shop in supermarkets, I am arguably thereby supporting the existing international political and economic system. But there are other things which I could do which make my support more or less whole-hearted.) We should also notice that institutions of all sorts are not static: they are constantly subject to forces that lead them to develop in one way rather than another. Furthermore, it is arguable that in order for any existing set of institutions to actualize its capacity for meeting our collective obligations it would need to develop, and to develop in some ways rather than others.

So OP 2 is compatible with the existence of a further obligation – namely an obligation to develop institutions in ways which make them more, rather than less just. If there is such an obligation, we should probably think of it as being something like a Kantian 'imperfect duty' – one where we have a certain amount of discretion about how and to what extent we are going to fulfil it. It would surely be absurd to think that each of us should be responsible for promoting the development of all the institutions in which they participate in the direction of greater justice. However, even an imperfect duty of this sort would seem to be enough to mitigate the problematic aspects of OP 2.

But do we have such a duty? It might seem unacceptably *ad hoc* to infer from the fact that the existence of a duty of this sort would make an otherwise problematic position intuitively more acceptable. So one might hope the duty in question could be inferred from some kind of higher level principle – perhaps even from the principles connecting global and individual obligations which I appealed to in section 5. Unfortunately, it is hard to see any reason for thinking it can.

Instead, I think we should question the idea that supposing that a duty of this sort exists is *ad hoc*. Arguably, it is not less *ad hoc* than the line of thought which lay at the root of the initial objection. The idea that there would be something problematic about supporting unjust institutions, even if they were institutions which could enable us to satisfy our global obligations is not something we simply have a brute intellectual compulsion to believe. It must be based on something. If it were not, there would be no way of articulating the force of the intuition to someone who did not share it – as we are presumably inclined to think we can.

What might such a line of thought be based on? One answer is that by participating in such institutions we would be causing certain kinds of harm. If so, we might ask what kinds of obligation we have around harms that we cause. One which stands out in this context is an obligation not to cause avoidable harm. But there are certainly cases where we may cause harm, because something else we have an obligation to do cannot be achieved without it. In such cases other obligations arise: obligations to mitigate or make amends for the harms we cause. In the light of this I suggest, albeit tentatively, that we take our duty to promote just developments in the institutions in which we participate to derive from a much more general duty to mitigate harms in which we are implicated when we act in ways which are necessary for us to meet the obligations which we have.

If this is correct the upshot is that we have a duty to support institutional frameworks which would enable us to meet our collective obligations. Some of the institutions we have an obligation to support are institutions which are capable of responding to distributive injustice. But if such institutions are capable of helping us in this way, it is reasonable to expect they will have a downside: they will, in practice, often undermine our attempts to bring a more just world into existence. Alongside our duty to support such institutions, we also have a duty to be vigilant about, and to work to mitigate those injustices. To the extent that existing institutions seems to give rise – as Pogge emphasizes – to distributive injustices, we have a particularly strong reason to be attentive to these issues.

Bibliography

Beitz, Charles/Goodin, Robert (Eds.) (2011): *Global Basic Rights*. Oxford: Oxford University Press.
Collins, Stephanie (2013): "Collective Duties and Collectivization Duties". In: *Australasian Journal of Philosophy* 91, pp. 231–248.
Copp, David (2006): "On the Agency of Certain Collective Entities: An Argument from 'Normative Autonomy'". In: *Midwest Studies in Philosophy* 30, pp. 194–221.
Dancy, Jonathan (1983): "Ethical Particularism and Moral Properties". In: *Mind* 90, pp. 367–385.
Dancy, Jonathan (1993): *Moral Reasons*. Oxford: Blackwell.
Dancy, Jonathan (2004): *Ethics without Principles*. Oxford: Oxford University Press.
French, Peter (1984): *Collective and Corporate Responsibility*. New York: Columbia University Press.
Geuss, Raymond (2010): *Politics and the Imagination*. Cambridge: Cambridge University Press.
Gilbert, Margaret (1989): *On Social Facts*. London: Routledge.
Gilbert, Margaret (2002): "Collective Wrongdoing: Moral and Legal Responses". In: *Social Theory and Practice* 28, pp. 167–187.
Gilbert, Margaret (2006): "Who's to Blame: Collective Responsibility and Its Implications for Group Members". In: *Midwest Studies in Philosophy* 30, pp. 94–114.
Gilbert, Margaret (2008): *Membership, Commitment, and the Bounds of Obligation*. Oxford: Oxford University Press.
Griffin, James (2008): *On Human Rights*. Oxford: Oxford University Press.
Hooker, Brad/Little, Margaret (Eds.) (2000): *Moral Particularism*. Oxford: Oxford University Press.
Isaacs, Tracy (2011): *Moral Responsibility in Collective Contexts*. Oxford: Oxford University Press.
Kant, Immanuel ([1785] 1993): *Grounding for the Metaphysics of Morals*. James W. Ellington (Trans.). Indianapolis: Hackett.
Kutz, Christopher (2000a): *Complicity: Law and Ethics for a Collective Age*. Cambridge: Cambridge University Press.
Kutz, Christopher (2000b): "Acting Together". In: *Philosophy and Phenomenological Research* 61, pp. 1–31.
Lawford-Smith, Holly (2012): "The Feasibility of Collectives' Actions". In: *Australasian Journal of Philosophy* 90, pp. 453–467.
Lawford-Smith, Holly (forthcoming): "What 'We'?" In: *Journal of Social Ontology*.
List, Christian/Pettit, Philip (2011): *Group Agency: The Possibility, Design, and Status of Corporate Agents*. Oxford: Oxford University Press.
May, Larry (1987): *The Morality of Groups: Collective Responsibility, Group-Based Harm and Corporate Rights*. South Bend: University of Notre Dame Press.
Meckled-Garcia, Saladin (2008): "On the Very Idea of Cosmopolitan Justice: Constructivism and International Agency". In *Journal of Political Philosophy* 16, pp. 245–271.
O'Neill, Onora ([1986] 1998): "Hunger, Needs and Rights". In: Luper-Foy, Steven (Ed.): *Problems of International Ethics*. London: Westview, pp. 86–103.
Pettit, Philip (2007): "Responsibility Incorporated". In: *Ethics* 117, pp. 171–201.

Pogge, Thomas (2001): *World Poverty and Human Rights*. Cambridge: Polity Press.
Schwenkenbecher, Anne (2013): "Joint Duties and Global Moral Obligations". In: *Ratio* 26, pp. 310–328.
Shue, Henry ([1980] 1996): *Basic Rights: Subsistence, Affluence and US Foreign Policy*. Princeton: Princeton University Press.
Stilz, Anna (2011): "Collective Responsibility and the State". In: *Journal of Political Philosophy* 19, pp. 190–208.
Sreenivasan, Gopal (2012): "A Human Right to Health: Some Inconclusive Skepticism". In: *Proceedings of the Aristotelian Society. Supplementary Volume* 86, pp. 239–265.
Wiggins, David (1987): "Truth, and Truth as Predicated of Moral Judgments". In: Wiggins, David: *Needs, Values, Truth*. Oxford: Oxford University Press, pp. 139–84.
Wringe, Bill (2006): "Needs, Rights and Collective Obligations". In: Reader, Soran (Ed.): *The Philosophy of Need*. Cambridge: Cambridge University Press, pp. 156–183.
Wringe, Bill (2010a): "Global Obligations and the Agency Objection". In: *Ratio* 23, pp. 217–231.
Wringe, Bill (2010b): "War Crimes and Expressive Theories of Punishment: Communication or Denunciation?" In: *Res Publica* 16, pp. 119–133.
Wringe, Bill (forthcoming): "Collective Obligations: Their Existence; Their Explanatory Power and Their Supervenience on the Obligations of Individuals". In: *European Journal of Philosophy*.

Stephen Snyder
Intergenerational Justice in the Age of Genetic Manipulation[1]

Abstract: This article examines how conceptions of intergenerational justice could be affected by the technological capability to alter human nature. Using the argument Habermas presents in *The Future of Human Nature*, the alteration of the human genome can be connected to theories of intergenerational justice in two ways. 1) Changes to the human genome could impede the ability of our offspring to freely choose who they are, thereby lessening their motivation to act in a moral manner. Moral capacity is a fundamental tenet of contractualist theories of intergenerational justice. An alteration of this capacity could undermine these theories insofar as today we are obliged to people of future generations because we ascribe the same moral agency to them that we do to ourselves. 2) Relating to his communicative theory, Habermas argues that by denying the ability to affirm choices of past generations, we deny the world-disclosive confirmation of a notion of the good – a communicative action that spans generations. This threatens the intergenerational bond needed for trans-generational support. Contractualists developing theories of intergenerational justice, though largely agreeing with Habermas' prognosis, tend to reject his claims based on misunderstandings of Habermas' theory. The conclusion is that the critic's positions are not far from Habermas'.

This essay examines what impact the technological capability to alter human nature could have on conceptions of intergenerational justice.[2] The discussion is framed using Jürgen Habermas' *The Future of Human Nature*, examining the relation between morality, justice, and ethics in terms of our biological makeup. Habermas' account of intergenerational justice differs from most accounts, which focus on what obligations the current generation has to future generations to distribute justly potentially scarce resources, maintain the integrity of institutions we deem necessary to uphold a just democracy, and manage changes to the climate. Habermas does not refer directly to the institutions used to maintain intergenerational justice; his arguments address the underlying motivation needed to

---

[1] A shorter version of this article focusing mostly on Habermas and human nature was published in *Journal of Health & Culture*. See Snyder, 2017.
[2] I would like to thank Corey Katz and Manuel Knoll for their helpful comments on this essay.

support these, or any, institutions that maintain equity in an egalitarian society. In this sense, the arguments he raises, though rooted in the contractarian tradition, are only implicitly political. The gist of Habermas' argument, as I see it, is that elective changes to the human genome could ultimately – by perforating the line between the kingdom of ends and the kingdom of nature – level the distinction between metaphysical and moral or political will. Unintended consequences of genetic alteration could blur the line between the made and the grown, having potentially disastrous consequences for the human as a moral creature.

Habermas connects the alteration of the human genome to theories of intergenerational justice in two ways: 1) Alterations to the human genome could impede the ability of our offspring to freely choose who they are, thereby lessening their motivation to act in a moral manner. The moral capacity necessary to motivate moral action is a fundamental tenet of contractualist theories of intergenerational justice; a change to this capacity undermines these theories insofar it is assumed that today we are obliged to people of future generations because we ascribe the same moral agency to them that we do ourselves. 2) Relating more to Habermas' communicative theory, he argues that by denying the ability to say 'yes' or 'no' to choices of past generations, we deny the world-disclosive affirmation of a notion of the good. This is a communicative action which, Habermas notes, spans generations. To threaten this threatens the intergenerational bond needed for trans-generational support: the notion that we are part of something larger than ourselves. This may seem peculiar, since conversations with future or past members of society are not possible. In a strict sense this is true, but any proponent of intergenerational justice, a contractualist in particular, struggles to define what the 'real' connection among peoples past and present is, relying on some sort of presumed relation. One certain relationship is a shared language and the common transsubjective way that it forms us as individual and social beings. Thus, to limit one of the essential pillars of communicative relations – the world-disclosive discourse – could change the way that language forms us as moral beings. It is this aspect of Habermas' thought that makes the strongest contribution to intergenerational justice, and it appears also to be the most misunderstood.

This essay 1) gives a brief overview of Habermas' notion of justice and his account of the "species-ethic"; 2) examines the presuppositions that a contractualist theory of intergenerational justice needs to ground future-oriented obligations, and Habermas' concern that a diminished moral basis in a polity's future members could undermine these presuppositions; 3) discusses Habermas' claims regarding the loss of species-identity, clarifying its relevance to theories of intergenerational justice; and 4) addresses the following criticisms: a) that Habermas overstates genetic enhancement's role in determining self-understanding, b) that contrary to Habermas' claims, political systems can exist without species-reciprocity, and c) that Habermas' restriction of world-disclosive discourse to subjective application is too narrow and the universal voice of the species-ethic can broaden its scope. To conclude, I propose a reading of Habermas that circumvents the most severe criticisms of his theory by looking at Sartre's account of freedom and determination, opening the way for an account of intergenerational justice that links generations through the communicative logos of language.

Justice and the species-ethic

In *The Future of Human Nature*,[3] Habermas describes our moral precepts as the result of reciprocal concern and co-recognition of human vulnerabilities. Linked to public morality, justice is communicative and represents a shared notion of how a community ought to co-exist. "I call 'moral' such issues as deal with the just way of living together" (FH, p. 38). Morality, for Habermas, excludes aspects of the good life that cannot be applied universally to all members of a community. The good life, notions of human existence that a person or people associate with a specific sort of self-identity that may define them existentially as a member of a specific community, falls under the realm of ethics. Questions of ethics are "intuitive self-descriptions" that "guide our own identification as human beings – that is our self-understanding as a member of the species" (FH, p. 39). These realms are not necessarily separate; nonetheless, the realm of morality delimits the ethical realm of the good life. For Habermas, however, what is deemed "moral" or "just" emerges through a discourse that starts with ethical notions that ultimately are limited to what can be applied to all members of a community. Thus, unlike the neo-Kantian approach Rawls proposes with the original position, it is not a thought experiment but a process that tests the content of our notions of the good life, ultimately rendering them just through the application of publicly accepted reasons. This differentiation of the moral from the ethical places moral discourses under the realm of rational understanding, while the ethical remains closer to rhetoric and is used to foster a specific notion of human understanding.

For the ancients, justice and morality were bound together in ideas of the good life, closely tied to comprehensive worldviews and personal identity. Because of this, most contemporary theories of justice and morality have been separated from "ethical" self-understanding (FH, p. 3). This "division of labor" is

---

[3] Henceforth cited as FH.

costly, for it "dissolves the context that first linked moral judgment with the motivation toward right action. Moral insights effectively bind the will only when they are embedded in an ethical self-understanding that joins the concern about one's own well-being with the interest in justice" (FH, p. 4). For Habermas, the linguistic turn allows for an interpretation of the wholly other that goes beyond the self while still being non-transcendent. "As historical and social beings we find ourselves already in a linguistically structured lifeworld… Language is not a kind of private property. No one possesses exclusive rights over the common medium of the communicative practices we must intersubjectively share" (FH, p. 10). In this way, we inhabit an intimate part of an interconnected linguistic frame of reference. Nonetheless, no individual dictates the meanings transferred through it, and we cannot individually control the process of agreement. However, according to Habermas, we are free due to the binding force that a justifiable claim has on other speakers. The power of the logos of the language lies in bringing us to understanding. In this sense, language, when used to reach agreement, can be a "transsubjective" power that entails a binding power. This view of language as the force that glues the moral to the ethical is rooted in the notion that humans as a species share a common capacity which when used for agreement brings a form of justice rooted in freedom of self-determination.

Habermas' claim that arguments over genetic engineering, assisted reproduction, and abortion cannot be resolved at the level of morality opens the way for a transsubjective binding power that is also transgenerational. These issues force a collision of rights that find no solution in a discourse of public reason. Each side has compelling arguments that do not yield to the reasons of the other. Yet each position, as in the debate over abortion rights, is grounded in some fundamental appeal to the dignity of the species: the rights of the unborn vs. the rights of self-determination (FH, pp. 29–32). Issues such as these, which revolve around recognizing the rights of a possible member of the species vs. the dignity of existing members, point to an underlying species-ethic: a special case of ethics that holds a claim to universality. For Habermas, this class of ethical claims that holds universally is unique, but without it, the ethical drive that underlies morality would not cohere.

Though Habermas recognized from early on the role of natural capacities in human development, prior to his postulation of the species-ethic in *The Future of Human Nature*, he denied they could ever lead to universalizable claims. He saw the 'interest' of instrumentalizing nature to be a species-capacity: all humans have capacities for learning that develop an attitude essential for their interaction with the physical environment (Habermas 1972, pp. 312–314). These species-capacities are also necessary for humans in understanding social modes of action and interaction.

> Even the interest in self-preservation, natural as it seems, is represented by a social system that compensates for the lacks in man's organic equipment and secures his historical existence against the force of nature threatening from without. But society is not only a system of self-preservation. An enticing natural force, present in the individual as libido, has detached itself from the behavioral system of self-preservation and urges toward Utopian fulfillment (Habermas 1972, p. 312).

The concept of species-ethic Habermas proposes in *The Future of Human Nature* moves beyond the notion of knowledge and human interest embedded in the species-capacity. As our capacities grow, he sees a problematic dedifferentiation of the "grown" and the "made." Nature was a category to which we opposed ourselves in order to master. With the attempt to change our own nature, we cross into what Hans Jonas refers to as a "no-man's-land" (Tremmel 2009, p. 3). Habermas concurs with Jonas, citing his assessment of our ability to change our nature: "Technologically mastered nature now again includes man who (up to now) had, in technology, set himself against it as its master" (FH, p. 47). The drive for self-preservation, striving for a utopian world, ultimately leads to our own redesign. But this self-redesign brought by the manipulation of the human genome is instrumental, and for Habermas, this raises important questions that should be answered before elective choices are made that move us past the point of no return.

> The hopes entertained by certain scientists of soon being able to take evolution in their own hands ... uproot the categorical distinction between the subjective and the objective, the naturally grown and the made, as they extend to regions which, up to now, we could not dispose over. What is at stake is a dedifferentiation, through biotechnology, of deeprooted categorical distinctions which we have as yet, in the description we give of ourselves, assumed to be invariant. This dedifferentiation might change our ethical self-understanding as a species in a way that could also affect our moral consciousness – the conditions, that is, of nature-like growth which alone allow us to conceive of ourselves as the authors of our own lives and as equal members of the moral community (FH, p. 42).

Habermas surmises that knowledge of our genomes having been altered might disrupt the notion that we ourselves are our body, leading to asymmetric relations among persons, thereby fracturing the foundation of our species-based self-understanding. This could undermine the one ethical class in which he does anticipate universal consensus and disrupt the core notions of the self, which constitute the ability for free self-determination (Habermas 1972, pp. 312–315; see Bohman/Rehg 2014).

This new direction takes Habermas away from Jonas, who recognizes, as Habermas, the potential consequences genetic enhancement could have on the moral structure of human social existence. But Jonas sees the need for a "new ethics" that is able to respond to the fluid nature of the new human, *homo faber*, who now produces himself. "To 'produce,' here, means to commit something to the stream of evolution in which the producer himself is carried along" (Jonas 1985, p. 168; see FH, p. 47). In reading Habermas' *Knowledge and Human Interests*, one might predict that he would agree with Jonas, but instead he argues that the instrumentalization of the human gene could spell the end to the moral agency required to fulfill the contractualist obligation to justly govern human social interaction.

Habermas' account of the species-ethic postulates a universalizable ethical motivation that refers directly to our biological nature, albeit in a discursive manner, and at some basic level, moral behavior is underwritten by a species-based need for protection of the group as a whole.

> I conceive of moral behavior as a constructive response to the dependencies rooted in the incompleteness of our organic makeup and in the persistent frailty ... of our bodily existence. Normative regulation of interpersonal relations may be seen as a porous shell protecting a vulnerable body, and the person incorporated in this body, from the contingencies they are exposed to (FH, p. 33).

Our understanding of humanity, and human dignity, comes from an interrelation among members of a community. Through the logos of language, we affirm our value as members of the human race, which is disclosed in a self-identifying discourse.

Intergenerational justice

Habermas does not present a fully developed theory of intergenerational justice, and what he has written does not fall in the mainstream of its current debates. Still, the positions he contrasts have "common roots in the contractarian tradition and rest on the common foundation of an egalitarian universalism" (FH, p. 78). He suggests that on one side of the Atlantic, the more pragmatic American approach to liberal eugenics is understood in terms of how genetic changes should be managed in terms of market choices and freedom of choice. On the other side of the Atlantic, the approaches put more stock in a metaphysical notion of the self and protection of those most vulnerable. Because technological capability and market forces driving genetic manipulation have outstripped the discussion of whether we ought to be making such changes, Habermas sees the position of the liberal eugenicists as overhasty, calling for a discourse. Thus, his argument is a cautionary one (FH, pp. 18–19, 75–79).

Habermas' non-standard approach to intergenerational obligation intersects with the contractualist tradition in a number of ways, and it offers an alternative approach to the non-identity problem. The non-identity problem poses unique questions for theories of justice that apply to future (or past) generations insofar as they are asymmetrical: in what way are we obligated to people who do not yet, or may never, exist? This problem arises when applying contractualist theories to current generations, making the case for 'wrong' actions that leave no one wronged. If one takes a 'narrow-person-affecting' approach to contractualism, we are only morally obliged to actual people we have harmed by leaving worse off. Intergenerational justice becomes very difficult here. The 'wide-person-affecting' approach resolves the issue of the individual claim of harm by shifting the onus to people in general. In this case, we are obliged to treat others according to their autonomous humanity such that our actions are justified by reasons they could not reasonably reject. This, for some, is unsatisfactory, because when the parties harmed become hypothetical, it removes us from the obligation to do no harm to actual people. The symmetric relations that most notions of justice in some way strive to meet are impossible when dealing with persons past and future; thus, obligations to future generations generally concern questions of distributive justice concerning resources or environmental conditions. Another way to ground obligation to future persons is through membership: successive generations form what Janna Thompson calls a "transgenerational polity" (Thompson 2009b, p. 25). In this case, the obligation belongs more to a polity that takes into account the interests and needs of future and past members, much like what Walzer may have envisioned when he discussed the base meaning that underlies a political unity's notion of membership (Walzer 1983).[4]

A form of contractualism, represented here by T.M. Scanlon, takes another approach, addressing transgenerational obligation as both wide- and narrow-person affecting. This is achieved by characterizing "the basis of one set of moral norms, those concerning the obligations we owe to one another as a matter of respect for the value of one another as persons" (Kumar 2009, p. 258). The value of the person, as Kumar explains it, bridges the wide- and narrow-affecting notion of obligation because a wrong occurs when a principle or norm is violated that no one could reasonably reject. This shows how a person is wronged in the wider sense. At the same time, when deciding whether a particular type of individual in a particular situation would have grounds for rejecting the reasons for

---

4 For a discussion of membership in Walzer's *Spheres of Justice*, see Snyder 2014.

your actions, it also demands that one look to their value or humanity. Kumar argues that this conceptual bridging illustrates how the violation of the principle also harms the humanity of the potential individual, thereby addressing the non-identity issue. As Kumar sees it, Scanlon's account of contractualism can be applied to intergenerational justice because it acknowledges that not taking the future person's value into account leaves them less well off, thereby wronging an individual, and not persons in general. For Kumar this establishes an obligation to potential persons of future generations (Kumar 2009, pp. 260–261).

Habermas sees two problems relevant to the contractarian position, the problem of consent and the problem of identity. First, given the asymmetrical relation that exists between generations, what changes can be made to the biological makeup of future generations without their express consent? In the case of therapeutic changes, adjustments expected to prevent some known malady or contribute to the general well-being of our descendants, we assume consent. For the most part, an obligation not to pass on certain afflictions is assumed. Nonetheless, even these changes, which could be actualized through pre-natal care or genetic screening and are generally understood to be of benefit to those affected, are impositions of a preferred form of existence on another. Though Habermas recognizes that therapeutic changes are not in all cases of benefit, he does not view these choices as controversial.

Habermas confronts a moral question regarding whether elective genetic changes enhance or hinder autonomous self-determination of future generations. What would it mean to inscribe a purpose on the being of a member of the future generation to which they could give no assent? Many changes would be of no significance, and it can be argued that some children are indelibly stamped by the rigorous educational and developmental plans to which their parents subject them. Nonetheless, there is still a dialogical process in play, and if children will it, they have some say in altering or rejecting this attempt to form their lives (FH, p. 59). When changes are imposed at the gene level, there is no recourse; insofar as these changes could not be agreed to, a notion of human dignity is violated that Habermas understands to be inter-subjective. Future-oriented world-disclosive discourse, as Habermas defines it, brings inherited traditions to light, so they can be critiqued and subject to change (Habermas 1990, pp. 149, 319).[5] The decisions one generation makes in regard to its interpretation of cultural values can be renounced by its successors. But the power of discourse directed to these decisions is denied to a generation if elec-

---

5 Habermas foreshadows this type of discourse in *Knowledge and Human Interests* (1972), p. 313.

tive genetic changes manifest a previous generation's notion of the good (FH, pp. 2–3).

The second question posed is this: what effect might this intergenerational imposition have on the self-understanding of individuals who know that they have been designed by their forebears? Our choices in life, our understanding of who we are – up to this point – have had as their foundation the knowledge that we all come into the world with a roll of the dice. Our genetic nature is something that "we cannot dispose over" (*unverfügbar*, see FH, pp. 31–33). Habermas asks whether an individual knowing they were pre-fitted for life would lead them to give up some of the responsibility that humans share insofar as we are all 'tossed' into the world, by and large, having the same odds, the same share of fate, in terms of biological formation.

What if we were to alter our nature? Would this break the bonds of common human fellowship? H.L.A. Hart noted how species membership dictates the norms of behavior insofar as we have shared vulnerabilities: if humans were to grow hard exoskeletons, the understanding of harm in our notion of justice would drastically change.

> There are species of animals whose physical structure ... renders them virtually immune from attack by other members of their species and animals who have no organs enabling them to attack. If men were to lose their vulnerability to each other there would vanish one obvious reason for the most characteristic provision of law and morals: *Thou shalt not kill* (Hart 1994, pp. 194–195).

This perhaps extreme example underscores the challenge that genetic change might pose for a theory of justice normatively linked to co-recognition of the vulnerabilities extant within a community of one species. The non-therapeutic preferences written into the genes of future generations, for Habermas, shift the line between our nature, and the norms that have collectively emerged in response to our common nature (FH, p. 42). These changes bring about "challenges of a new order" that

> imply the license to control the physical basis which 'we are by nature'. What for Kant still belonged to the 'kingdom of necessity' had, in the perspective of evolutionary theory, changed to become a 'kingdom of contingency'. Genetic engineering is now shifting the line between the natural basis we cannot dispose over and the 'kingdom of ends' (FH, p. 28).

This shift threatens to change our self-understanding as individuals and as a species, and thereby the "structure of our moral experience" (FH, p. 28).

If we are able to shape our own being in a manner that heretofore was only possible through the instrumental attempts to dominate nature, we have dedifferentiated the moral autonomous (subjective) aspect of our being and our mechanistic (objective) aspect, what Kant would have referred to as the kingdom of ends and the kingdom of nature. By intruding upon the design of our moral self, the question arises as to how changes to our genetic design made by this generation affect the "equal" distribution of our moral basis as individuals (FH, p. 78).

The repercussions of this change in distribution threaten this contractualist prerequisite: one generation's obligation to adhere to principles that the subjects of future generations could not reasonably reject is dependent on the assumption that future subjects possess normative capacities.[6]

> The requirement that a valid principle must be justifiable to any one on grounds she could not reasonably reject in order to count as impartially justifiable rests on two ideas. First, that impartial moral justification requires that the life of each person be taken into account as intrinsically no more important than any other. Second, that the appropriate way to take a person into account is as one capable of assessing reasons and justifications, and living her life guided by her assessments and choices amongst competing reasons (Kumar 2009, p. 263).

By assuming future persons are capable moral agents having value as persons, one can theoretically address the non-identity problem of future generations; thus, the obligation not to leave them less well-off is understood in the wide- and narrow person-affecting sense.

Without addressing the validity of Kumar's case for intergenerational justice, Habermas' critique intersects with contractualism on this point: insofar as the contractualist position requires that the future affected individual has "the capacity to select among the various ways there is reason to want a life to go, and therefore to govern and live that life in an active sense" (Scanlon 1998, p. 105), the imposition of elective desires in the DNA of future humans could impact the prerequisite that humans actually have this capacity. For Habermas, the ascription of what amounts to the instrumental desires of one generation onto the heretofore untouchable genetic makeup of future generations, dedifferentiates the kingdom of nature and the kingdom of ends, or our natural being and our moral being. Though the contractualist account is not distributive insofar as it relates to goods, the attempt at the self-design of the species, *could*, so he argues, affect the equal distribution of the capacity for moral action. Seen in

---

6 Rawls presumes that persons have two moral powers: "a capacity for a sense of justice and a capacity for a conception of the good" (Rawls, 1996, p. 19; see p. 187). Rawls also holds we have a "*natural duty* to further and uphold just institutions" for the benefit of people of different generations [emphasis S.S.] (Rawls 1971, p. 293).

this manner, this is a form of distribution necessary for the contractualist model, and a redistribution of the moral basis of the species should not be taken lightly.

Loss of species-identity

Habermas' concern is that alterations made in the genetic structure of the species are going to undermine on the one hand "the reciprocity between persons of equal birth" that form the foundation of traditional social relationships, and on the other hand, will remove one of the motivators of our autonomous self-determination. It is not simply the choice of a parent at stake,

> advances of genetic engineering tend to blur the deeply rooted categorical distinctions between the subject and the object, the grown and the made. What is at stake, therefore, with the instrumentalization of prepersonal life is the ethical self-understanding of the species, which is crucial for whether or not we may go on to see ourselves as being committed to moral judgment and action. Where we lack compelling *moral* reasons, we have to let ourselves be guided by the signposts set up by the *ethics* of the species (FH, p. 71).

Inserting technical rationality into the place where only practical reason should reside would be the "colonization" of our "phenomenal" realm by instrumental reason. It is in our human interest that we *develop* in a social context and *learn* to become persons who have a place in it. If our place is seen to be destined, we may lose our moral compass, as those Puritans who deemed themselves chosen by God seemed to lose their sense of what was right in the world of man.

Habermas suggests a novel way to justify obligations to future generations through his understanding of the language/body relationship. Our identities are formed presuming we "exist as a body or ... we 'are' our body" (FH, p. 42). Yet we are social beings whose existence is mediated through language; our social actions are responses to others who also exist in this linguistic system. "What raises us out of nature is the only thing whose nature we can know: language. Through its structure, autonomy and responsibility are posited for us" (Habermas 1972, p. 314). Our human social existence has pulled us away from nature through our understanding of it; still, our bodies are grown, and the system of language we inhabit is made. The species-ethic, as I understand it, was formed over time as a defense for our bodily vulnerabilities, and the actual 'hardware' of the body has changed little since humans came to be. To change it is to change the underlying fit of language to our physical being. Habermas holds that what is right is not achieved alone but as a common endeavor: "what makes our being-ourselves possible appears more a transsubjective power than an absolute one" (FH, p. 11). If our linguistic layer no longer fits the body, instrumentalized as if to dominate, the system of norms we as a species have come to rely on may be more easily sloughed off. So the problems Habermas puts forward, regarding choice and identity, relate not so much as physical determinates, as some critics understand him, but rather as factors that disrupt the fit of our biological constitution to the linguistic framework that posits, through its structure, our "autonomy and responsibility." Habermas fears, if I may use the metaphor, that if the shoe no longer fits, we might be less likely to wear it.

One action that 'maintains the fit' is the self-understanding achieved in world-disclosive discourse, which is emancipating insofar as through it one has the opportunity to affirm or deny the presuppositions of one's cultural tradition. For Habermas, this is an individual's first-person expression articulated to others. It does not rise to the level of the universal, but as a component of communicative rationality, judgments of world-disclosure underwrite the practice of justice, or morality, in contemporary society. Though in Habermas' schema, philosophy offers no way to render universal judgments ranking one comprehensive worldview over another, the disclosive power of a culture's system of language can at least affirm to its members its future potential "In complex societies one culture can assert itself against other cultures only by convincing its succeeding generations – who can also say no – of the advantages of its world-disclosive semantic and action-orienting power" (FH, pp. 2–3). The inscription of the values of one generation, their affirmation of the good life, on the genes of future generations who have no option to affirm or deny, imposes asymmetrically the pre-determined disclosures of a different 'world'. This, in Habermas' view, could further disconnect the self-understanding of future generations from 'their' time, pushing their culture forward without self-affirmation, and hence, without the moral motivation to further the transgenerational aims of civilization.

Isolating the factors that motivate one to act in a moral manner becomes especially difficult when applied to future members of society who, as of yet, have no identity. For Habermas, the motivation that accompanies seeing oneself as part of a larger intergenerational community is threatened. Looking to the future, one must see oneself as part of a chain in which common aims and goals are shared (Birnbacher 2009, pp. 290–192). In this sense, "lifetime-transcending interests" become a factor (Thompson 2009b, pp. 34–37). Certainly, Habermas would agree, holding that future-oriented interests are fostered by the sense that one shares the random fate of their co-members. Habermas' approach also adds a linguistic dimension; our linguistic framework, which we are part of insofar as we share in its communicative structure, protects us as long as we feel our needs and meanings are communicated through it. When one type of discourse is shut out, in this case the world-disclosive, the power of language to carry forward "lifetime-transcending interests" may be disrupted. Habermas puts forward his warning as a possibility, and critics argue that his "might" is likely a not. But to be clear, the critics have no more proof of their optimism toward change than Habermas does for his warning; hence, he asks for further discussion.

Criticisms

Critics challenge Habermas' commentary on the potential downside of elective genetic enhancement insofar as a) he may have overstated his claims regarding genetic determinism, and b) that there may well be institutional forms that maintain justice in a polity without an underlying species-ethic.[7] His most vocal critics respond to *a* (Harris 2007; Agar 2004; Thompson 2009a); research indicates that a genetic predisposition, whether inborn or through design, does very little to determine an individual's actual path in life when not accompanied by appropriate environmental factors. Even if we were inscribed with certain elective attributes by our parents, a child would have to be educated and trained to actualize these attributes. A genetic disposition for excellence in math means nothing without an interest in and training in math (Agar 2004, pp. 116–117; Thompson 2009a, p. 139). Habermas recognizes that intensive training and genetic engineering appear similar, maintaining that in the latter case, if one has no way of saying yes or no, it is unilaterally mandated. Still, research shows that the line between the two is more porous than Habermas acknowledges. Habermas argues that elective selection of genetic attributes involves an 'internal' intrusion on the moral base of the individual. But the difference between internal and external alterations is also blurred. Even a mother's diet can change the DNA structure of her child (Agar 2004, pp. 119–120).

Another critic of Habermas is John Harris, who makes an ambitious case for genetically enhancing humans through a "new process of evolutionary change [that] will replace *natural selection* with *deliberate selection, Darwinian evolution* with *enhancement evolution*" (Harris 2007, p. 4). He recognizes the moral peril of changing our underlying nature. However, given the shifting landscape of human existence, he holds we have no choice but to face the change, a position which, in the end, may not fall far from Jonas' (Harris 2007, pp. 117–118). That

---

[7] Several critiques and alternatives to Habermas' position are presented in Mary V. Rorty's review of *The Future of Human Nature* (Rorty 2003).

said, for several reasons, Harris' engagement with the leading philosophical thinkers on genetic enhancement misses the mark. Though he makes a number of good points, in my reading, his mocking and somewhat abusive style – Habermas is "Bamboozled," Sandel presents a "Humpty-Dumpty" argument – indicates he has not mastered the arguments he criticizes. As well, he does not seem to realize that he represents a position that the authors he critiques explicitly address.

Habermas and Sandel aim to show how genetic enhancement could present a problem in terms of whether the basis upon which moral obligations themselves are formed would still be shared with future humans. In his discussion of Sandel, a virtue ethicist, Harris seems not to understand the nature of virtue. Harris' book starts with this scenario: what if we developed an academic model that would produce excellence and health in our students. Wouldn't we praise this? What if we could achieve this result with genetic modification? Harris argues that excellence is something we have; it is not a gift. I understand this in a Nietzschean sense that excellence simply is. But he implies there is no difference between those with lesser ability who achieve excellence with extraordinary effort and those who simply live up to talent they are born with (Harris 2007, pp. 114–115). I'm not sure that I, or the majority of thinkers, would agree: as Agar and others have noted, we put a great deal of effort into our achievements. Our society recognizes in the virtue of excellence an achievement that cannot be determined through our genes alone: we also need motivation.

Accepting that we do not choose our fate, that our natural endowments are beyond our disposition, for Sandel, is crucial to our humanity. We accept the "unbidden" when we love the children who we receive, no matter what. Harris feels we need not accept the unbidden, if there is any choice in the matter. Sandel holds we will be overwhelmed by the responsibility of living up to a talent we are aware we have by design, implying that having our attributes set through the lot of fate allows us autonomy in choosing our own path. Harris acknowledges Sandel's point, but he argues we now face inescapable choices:

> the burdens of responsibility are our fate as choosing autonomous beings. But mastery is the power to do things, not the exercise of that power. I am master of my fate if I *can* choose, not only if I *do* choose. I determine my destiny as much by declining or neglecting to exercise my mastery as by exercising it. This is a crucial point. Responsibility is a dimension of the ability to choose, not simply of a particular exercise of choice. The power of choice brings with it the burden of responsibility for the way we exercise choice, because choosing not to act is still a choice for which we are responsible. We cannot escape that burden by declining the *recognition* of our mastery of our fate or by choosing not to make decisions rather than making them in a particular way (Harris 2007, pp. 118–119).

For Harris, blinded by possible dangers, Sandel refuses to face the tough choices presented by our new technological capabilities. Agreeing with Harris on one level, the problem remains that his argument is one-dimensional; he appears not to have understood Sandel, and clearly does not understand Habermas.[8] This does not make Habermas' argument correct, but the quote above underscores what Harris, and perhaps others, are missing in Habermas' argument.

Harris' claim that "I" choose *my* "fate" indicates a problematic instrumentalizing stance for Habermas because when *he* chooses genetic autonomy, he forestalls the next generation's opportunity to affirm or deny *their* choice. This may not be a problem in the liberal world of individual choice, but Habermas understands humans to exist within a communicative framework mediated by language. Communication is not simply a desire; people *must* act communicatively.

> When parents bring up their children, when the living appropriate the transmitted wisdom of preceding generations, when individuals and groups cooperate, that is, when they work to get along with one another without the costly recourse to violence, they all have to act communicatively. There are elementary social functions that can only be satisfied by means of communicative actions. Our intersubjectively shared, overlapping lifeworlds lay down a broad background consensus without which our everyday praxis simply couldn't take place (Habermas 1994, p. 111).

Our self-understanding is something we autonomously choose, but it is within the context of the intersubjective medium of our common language. For Habermas, a genetic change "takes on the meaning of a communicative action" (FH, p. 51); when "I" choose the design of my child, in a sense, I cut them out of a dialogue. There is much, as stated above, that presumes consent; Habermas argues that basic therapeutic changes would assume this. Harris does not make this differentiation – why wouldn't we assent to being better? For Harris, the choice is self-evident. But the choice made in light of what the lot nature gives us is different, for Habermas, if we are provided something we did not ask for. Harris views his own human nature as something he can dispose over, instrumentally, and in so doing, he would instrumentalize the nature of future generations, making them in his own image with his notion of what is excellent and good. Harris affirms this in his own world-disclosive decision, but in so doing, he denies this possibility to future generations, cutting off a vital part of the discourse carried on through our language. This, for Habermas, violates the norms of communication, having a ripple effect that limits the "autonomy

---

[8] Harris indicates as much in his critique (Harris 2007, pp. 139–140).

and responsibility" of future generations. Whether or not we agree with Habermas, Harris has not understood this aspect of his argument.

Thompson and Agar also seem to have missed the linguistic orientation of Habermas' argument, while still agreeing with his call for caution. Rightly criticizing Habermas' overstatement of the power genetic changes might have on determining the life, and perhaps moral autonomy, of a child, they both acknowledge a problem with parental attempts to control their children's future; an "open future" (Feinberg 1980) is owed to the next generation. Rather than seeing it as a matter of genetic determinism, they view parental control potentially taking away the free choices of children. Combined with genetic changes, which parents would likely make their children aware of, their zealous efforts to extend themselves to their offspring could truncate their opportunity to openly choose their future (Thompson 2009b, p. 41; Thompson 2009a, pp. 131–132, 138–139; Agar 2004, pp. 123–124). They speculate that two classes could emerge, one a designed class, another a class left to fate. These groups would likely be of different socio-economic status, and this, combined with the difference they *believe* comes from their genetic makeup, could lessen the will to support democratic institutions seeking to mitigate nature's disproportionate allocation of ability and status, undermining the very presuppositions of equal membership (Thompson 2009a, pp. 139–140; Agar 2004, pp. 142–145). They also fear a more sinister scenario, in which a technologically advanced group actually engineered a genetically inferior class which would de facto violate the moral and practical norms of democracy. Agar thinks it unlikely though that parents would intentionally create a two-class society; making genetic enhancement equally available to rich and poor could prevent such a split (Agar 2004, pp. 133, 142–145). In both cases, as Thompson concedes, people could be 'created' who would not be "interested in, or capable of, maintaining the intuitions and the goods that we have reason to value" (Thompson 2009a, p. 143). This eventuality must be anticipated by a theory of intergenerational justice, and she concludes, as does Habermas, that a dialogue is needed.

On these points, Agar and Thompson come very close to Habermas, but there are differences. They speculate on the possibility of an insidious and intentional scheme that would strive, in a way that is counter to the norms of our society, to create an upper class and an underclass. Habermas does not envision an intentional scheme; parents merely wanting the best for their children, as they understand it, could inadvertently effect situations identical to those Agar and Thompson present. Oddly, though Agar and Thompson argue that genetic enhancement cannot determine change in the manner Habermas suggests; in the dystopian scenarios they hypothesize the *awareness* of the genetic changes could effect changes, loss of autonomy, or a breakdown in the presuppositions of membership which the genetic changes themselves cannot. One factor at play seems to be that Agar, Thompson, and certainly Harris, rely on the liberal model of freedom. Habermas is looking at the same future, but he follows a different path. Couching his argument in post-metaphysical terms, his critique focuses on our self-formative capacity to choose, at some base level, who we are. His critics remain within the camp of rights, freedom of choice, responsibility, and the stability of institutions that uphold the values needed to support a democratic society.

Certainly, Habermas' broader philosophy, which strives to formulate a stronger practical basis for the articulation of reason in the world, shares much with the aims of his critics. He seeks a moral theory that steps beyond the thought experiment of the categorical imperative, which is rational and universal, but socially, not transcendentally, grounded. His formulation of a broad-based species-ethic argues for a form of justice that integrates the general human respect for dignity with a culture's notion of the good life. That said, there are many empirical notions of justice that could bind a community of diverse beings which need not rely on philosophical universals.

One could ask if Kant's ratio-centric account of membership provides a better basis for cooperation among a wide plurality of life forms, binding them through practical reason and institutions supporting a diversified civil society? We can easily imagine a variety of life forms co-existing on the basis of fair trade. In such cases, ensuring the unity of the species may mean little. Indeed, proponents of intergenerational justice argue that a strong set of "transgenerational" institutions, robust enough to endure the assaults of generations bent on rolling them back, is crucial for maintaining intergenerational cooperation (Meyer/Rosser 2009, p. 238; Birnbacher 2009, pp. 295–295; Thompson 2009b, p. 33; Agar 2004, pp. 144–145).

Market-based notions of justice, nonetheless, succumb to the efficiency-oriented rationality of the technological and economic spheres, which does not recognize the core capacities of rational self-reflection. Thus, Habermas seeks motivations that go far deeper than the reciprocal self-interest of market relations. Habermas is not alone in this assessment. Walzer holds that the social contract is a "moral bond," not a relationship of mere efficiency. "It connects the strong and the weak, the lucky and the unlucky, the rich and the poor, creating a union that transcends all differences of interest, drawing its strength from history, culture, religion, language, and so on" (Walzer 1983, pp. 82–83). Nonetheless, we can speculate that the legacy of genetic engineering could be to push future notions of justice beyond the scope of our species, recognizing memberships defined along very different lines, moving closer to Jonas' position. Jonas agrees with Habermas that genetic enhancement represents a threat to human autonomy, a freedom necessary to motivate moral action, and that moral action requires a subjective and objective, personal and generalized, perspective that grounds self-identity in a transgenerational intersubjective dialogue (Morris 2013, pp. 185–186). But Jonas differs in regard to Habermas' insistence that species membership is essential to our basis as moral beings. Tinkering with our nature could bring grave danger, but in the face of humankind's ability to change our underlying nature and our planet (conceding a point to Harris), for Jonas, we are compelled to shift our traditional ethical framework: "novel powers require novel ethical rules and perhaps even a new ethics" (Jonas 1984, p. 23). This approach could lead to ways of understanding our environmental context such that our actions are bound to it as members of an ecological community, enhancing the obligating force of an intergenerational justice.

From a perspective internal to critical theory, Nicholas Kompridis frames *The Future of Human Nature* in terms of modernity's embrace of the new as something utopian and presumed to yield a solution to present problems through a break with the past. Proponents of liberal eugenics, like Harris and to some extent Agar, see in the new genetic technology a problem solving capability, and in many respects they are right. But one thing theories of intergenerational justice seem to confirm is that effecting too strong a discontinuity with the past would change the attitude toward future obligations. Kompridis lauds Habermas' use of a species-ethics, which opens members of future generations to their own slot in time; it maintains continuity with the past despite a discontinuous future. The context transcending procedurality Habermas envisions in discourse, which moves ethics to the realm of morality and justice, cuts it off from the particularity that links people to the norms of their time, much as Rawls' veil of ignorance leaves one unaware of the generation to which they belong (Rawls 1971, pp. 287–288). If modernity is cut off from its ties to tradition, utilizing a rationality cut loose from all particularities of culture, Kompridis asks how the time-sensitivities embedded in the desire to protect the human dignity of future generations can be used to motivate justice (Kompridis 2006, p. 27 n43). The species-ethic Habermas proposes allows a way to reconnect his procedural account of morality to the time-relationship need for intergenerational justice: the ethical relationship of the species becomes *our* problem. For Kompridis, this forces Habermas out of the position of neutrality toward all comprehensive worldviews. Through his notion of a species-ethic, philosophy can speak for all of humanity, for the *right cultural form of humanity in general* (Kompridis, 2006, pp. 165–166). Habermas limits world-disclosure to self-authentication and to the aesthetic sphere. Kompridis sees in Habermas' notion of species-ethic a path to grounding a stronger notion of world-disclosure which could influence all forms of rational judgment used in communicative rationality. Applied to intergenerational justice, Kompridis argues, Habermas' narrow account of world-disclosive reasoning prevents him from linking the universal motivation of a species-ethic to his procedural theory of justice precisely because the latter relies on the distinction between a generalized morality and a culturally specific ethics (Kompridis 2006, pp. 8–16, 25–28, 154–166, 294 n60).

Conclusion

A look at Arthur Danto's reading of Sartre's notion of freedom, shows a way to understand the precautions Habermas holds we should take in light of our obligations to future generations, while also acknowledging that his case of genetic determinism may be overstated. For Sartre, freedom was not release from the chain of causality, but a way of living; a choice that affected all other choices without determining them (Sartre 1992, pp. 567, 562–572). Our *original* choice is our character. It determines who we are in life; it is our being. "Our basic freedom, then, lies less in our power to choose than to choose to choose, in the respect that the primal and original choice determines a style of choosing, and the style is the man himself" (Danto 1975, p. 137).[9] The past determines the present insofar as one's past choices pervade the present, pointing to the future. "It is that in each choice I do more than choose a specific course of action; rather, I choose a style of choosing. So the original choice is made in every choice" (Danto 1975, p. 137).

Style comes from the free choice of choosing the *way* we are. Once this choice is made, we are not determined in any strong sense, but at the same time, all we do is colored by this choice. The "open future" that Habermas sees as necessary for future humans to freely 'choose their style', could be threatened by elective genetic changes inscribing the 'style' of another on their being. Jonas and Habermas agree that "human ethical self-understanding is the ground upon which reason takes root in order to shape a discourse concerning what is right. It provides significant motivating force as well, because it relates so directly to individual identity" (Morris 2013, p. 184). The choice of how to choose becomes the foundation of our future decisions. Agreeing with Kompridis, world-disclosure as a universal voice of humanity could work to safeguard the possibility of a self-identifying original choice; our species-ethic advocates for the character of the species by ensuring that no one can inscribe upon our universal style (our species-ethic) the disclosures of their own individual person. The universal,

---

9 I do not defend Danto's reading of Sartre here, I just present it.

trans-subjective, form of world-disclosure would ensure that we are able to have a world-disclosive discourse at the individual level, saying 'yes' or 'no' to who we are and the style of choices we will make for now and for the future. Habermas sounds the call to ask 'how should we be as human beings?' before we venture into questions of how we define the good life for the future, warning that inscription of the style of a past generation on future generations may make them feel as if they are not the sole authors of their lives (FH, p. 92). Jonas, despite agreeing with the gravity of that basic self-understanding, holds that we should change with our world, subsuming our entire environment under a new ethical framework, allowing for a new style of species, merging the grown and the made. If we listen to the world-disclosive voice of the species, decisions regarding the enhancement of the species will not be made based on market efficiency and individual freedom of choice alone.

Ultimately, whether we agree with Habermas' account of species-ethics or not, the advances in bio-engineering do pose questions both for the conception of and application of intergenerational justice. Enhancing our species and changing the parameters of justice is not necessarily cause for alarm. The shape of justice has changed throughout history and will continue to do so. At the same time, all Habermas asks is that we begin a dialogue over how and on what basis we should limit the changes we impose on our future species. We would be committing an injustice to those who come after us by allowing the question of 'if' we can do something to take precedence over whether we 'should' do something.

Bibliography

Agar, Nicholas (2004): *Liberal Eugenics: In Defence of Human Enhancement*. Malden, MA: Blackwell.

Bohman, James/Rehg, William (2014): "Jürgen Habermas". In: *The Stanford Encyclopedia of Philosophy* (Fall 2014 Edition). https://plato.stanford.edu/entries/habermas/, accessed 18 June 2018.

Danto, Arthur (1975): *Sartre*. Glasgow: William Collins.

Feinberg, Joel (1980): "The Child's Right to an Open Future". In: Aiken, W./Laffollet, H. (Eds.): *Whose Child? Children's Rights, Parental Authority and State Power*. Totowa, NJ: Rowman and Littlefield, pp. 124–153.

Habermas, Jürgen (1972): *Knowledge and Human Interests*. J. Shapiro (Trans.). Boston: Beacon Press.

Habermas, Jürgen (1990): *The Philosophical Discourse of Modernity: Twelve Lectures*. F.G. Lawrence (Trans.). Cambridge, MA: MIT Press.

Habermas, Jürgen (1994): *The Past as Future*. M. Pensky (Ed.). Lincoln: University of Nebraska Press.

Habermas, Jürgen (2003): *The Future of Human Nature*. H. Beister/M. Pensky/W. Rehg (Trans.). Cambridge, MA: Polity Press.
Harris, John (2007): *Enhancing Evolution: The Ethical Case for Making Better People*. Princeton: Princeton University Press.
Hart, H.L.A. (1994): *The Concept of Law*. Oxford: Clarendon Press.
Jonas, Hans (1984): *The Imperative of Responsibility: In Search of an Ethics for the Technological Age*. Chicago: University of Chicago Press.
Jonas, Hans (1985): "Laßt uns einen Menschen klonieren: Von der Eugenik zur Gentechnologie". In: Jonas, Hans: *Technik, Medizin und Eugenik. Zur Praxis des Prinzips Verantwortung*. Frankfurt a.M.: Suhrkamp, pp. 162–203.
Kompridis, Nikolas (2006): *Critique and Disclosure: Critical Theory between Past and Future*. Cambridge, MA: MIT Press.
Kumar, Rahul (2009): "Wronging Future People: A Contractualist Proposal". In: Gosseries, Axel/Meyer, Lukas H. (Eds.): *Intergenerational Justice*. Oxford: Oxford University Press, pp. 251–272.
Meyer, Lukas H./Roser, Dominic (2009): "Enough for the Future". In: Gosseries, Axel/Meyer, Lukas H. (Eds.): *Intergenerational Justice*. Oxford: Oxford University Press, pp. 219–248.
Morris, Theresa (2013): *Hans Jonas's Ethic of Responsibility: From Ontology to Ecology*. Albany: SUNY Press.
Rawls, John (1971): *Theory of Justice*. Cambridge, MA: Harvard University Press.
Rawls, John (1996): *Political Liberalism*. New York: Columbia University Press.
Rorty, Mary V. (2003): "Review of *The Future of Human Nature*". In: *Notre Dame Philosophical Reviews*, 2 December 2003. https://ndpr.nd.edu/news/the-future-of-human-nature/, accessed 1 June 2015.
Sartre, Jean-Paul (1992): *Being and Nothingness*. H. Barnes (Trans.). New York: Washington Square Press.
Scanlon, Thomas M. (1998): *What We Owe to Each Other*. Cambridge, MA: Harvard University Press.
Snyder, Stephen (2014): "Mitgliedschaft als soziales Gut und Rahmenbedingung für gerechte Verteilungen". In: Knoll, Manuel/Spieker, Michael (Eds.): *Michael Walzer. Sphären der Gerechtigkeit. Ein kooperativer Kommentar*. Stuttgart: Steiner, pp. 73–91.
Snyder, Stephen (2017): "A Problem for Intergenerational Justice: Habermas on the Ability to Alter the Future of Human Nature". In: *Journal of Health & Culture* 2. No. 1, pp. 18–26.
Thompson, Janna (2009a): *Intergenerational Justice Rights and Responsibilities in an Intergenerational Polity*. New York: Routledge.
Thompson, Janna (2009b): "Identity and Obligation in a Transgenerational Polity". In Gosseries, Axel/Meyer, Lukas H. (Eds.): *Intergenerational Justice*. Oxford: Oxford University Press, pp. 25–49.
Tremmel, Joerg Chet (2009): *A Theory of Intergenerational Justice*. London: Earthscan.
Walzer, Michael (1983): *Spheres of Justice*. New York: Basic Books.

Part V: **Diversifying the Perspective**

Kok-Chor Tan
The Contours of Toleration: A Relational Account[1]

Abstract: In this chapter, I outline a relational account of toleration. This relational account helps explain the apparent paradox of toleration, that it involves two competing moral stances, of acceptance and disapproval. It also helps clarify how toleration is a normative ideal, and not a position one is forced into out of the practical need to accommodate or accept. Specifically, toleration is recommended out of respect for that which the tolerant agent also morally disapproves of. This combination of respect entangled with disapproval results from two different evaluative perspectives of the tolerant agent. The relational account explains how an agent can hold these competing evaluative perspectives. I also discuss the scope of state toleration under this relational account.

Toleration has been variously described as an "elusive", "difficult" and "unstable" ideal (Heyd 1996; Scanlon1996; Williams 1996; Oberdiek 2001; Mendus 1989). One central reason for this perceived difficulty or the elusiveness of toleration is that it seems to be a paradoxical moral stance. Toleration calls for both an attitude of disapproval and of permissiveness on the part of the tolerant agent.[2] Since this duality lies in the attitudinal state of the tolerant agent, let us call this the *subjective paradox* of toleration.

In this paper, I propose a relational account of toleration that can make sense of this subjective paradox. This view of toleration explains the conflicting evaluative states of the tolerant agent in terms of the multiplicity of relational evaluative standpoints in which the tolerant stands to the tolerated. This rela-

---

[1] Earlier versions of this paper were presented at University College, Dublin (2010), Bryn Mawr University (Fall 2011) and Brown University (March 2012). I am grateful to members of the audience at these venues, with special thanks to Iseult Honohan, Christine Koggel, Michael Krausz, David Estlund, Jeppe Platz, and Corey Brettschneider. I benefitted also from exchanges with David Heyd, Collin Anthony, Chris Melenovsky, Daniel Halliday and Eric Boot. Finally, many thanks to the editors, Manuel Knoll and Stephen Snyder, for their very helpful substantive comments as well editorial suggestions and corrections.
[2] Samuel Scheffler, for instance, refers to this as "the paradox of suppressed disapproval". As an attitude, he notes, toleration consists "in a disposition not to interfere with beliefs and practices of which one strongly disapproves" (2010, p. 316).

https://doi.org/10.1515/9783110537369-024

tional account of toleration, I will add, is especially illustrative of the nature of liberal toleration as a political virtue.

The subjective paradox of toleration arises because it is an attitude that involves competing evaluative stances on the part of the tolerant. In situations in which an agent has no choice but to "endure" a situation or conduct, we might say that her response is more that of accommodation out of practical necessity rather than that of toleration. Likewise, we might hold that toleration is not in play when an agent withholds judgment out of moral uncertainty or out of skepticism about the existence of a right moral response. In these cases, there is no subjective evaluation to speak of, much less the presence of competing evaluations that generate the subjective paradox.

No doubt this conception of toleration is narrower than how "toleration" is ordinarily applied. But for present purposes, what is relevant is the conception of toleration under discussion, not whether it defines the entirety of the concept of toleration. If we need to distinguish it from other senses of the term, we can call this the "normative" conception of toleration. This is the kind of toleration that involves competing normative attitudes on the part of the tolerant and which presents the "difficulty" of toleration that exercises philosophers. My aim in this paper is to offer some way of elucidating the paradox that toleration so understood seems to generate. In this paper henceforth, unless otherwise qualified, toleration is understood in this normative sense.

I begin by recounting the "circumstances of toleration" in order to further highlight the subjective paradox (1). I then propose the relational account of the structure of toleration that helps explain the paradox of toleration (2). The form of the explanation offered is *not* that of dissolving the paradox or of explaining it away, but to show how the paradox arises and why the conflicting states that give rise to it do not render toleration an unstable or incoherent virtue. Following on this account of toleration, I propose that the relational approach provides an especially helpful understanding of liberal toleration as a political virtue (3).

1 The subjective circumstance of toleration

Toleration is a response to the fact of diversity; it is most poignant when it is a response to differences over values or, as Scheffler puts it, "normative diversity" (Scheffler 2010, p. 324; also Williams 1996, pp. 19–20). This fact of diversity, especially normative diversity, provides one of the circumstances of toleration; absent diversity there will be no cause for toleration. We might call the fact of diversity the *objective circumstance* of toleration since it refers to conditions external to and independent of the agent for whom toleration is to be an issue. An example of this objective circumstance is the presence of other persons holding and exercising values that stand in conflict with an agent's own.

But the fact of diversity by itself does not supply the entire circumstances of toleration. By itself, normative diversity will generate only moral disagreements. Thus, in addition to the objective circumstance of toleration provided by normative diversity, an agent must hold a particular set of evaluative responses towards the diversity that is confronting her. She must have *both* an attitude of approval and an attitude of disapproval with regard to this external condition. That is, for toleration to be a relevant moral stance for an agent, the agent must have at the same time a negative evaluative attitude and a positive one towards the object in question. The presence of both a pro- and a negative-attitude constitutes the necessary evaluative state that an agent must be in for toleration to be a salient value for her. The fact of external diversity must be matched by some kind of subjective diversity, a dualism in the agent's response to this fact. We can call this evaluative dualism on the part of the agent the *subjective circumstance* of toleration. The circumstances of toleration require the presence of both objective and subjective circumstances.

There will be no occasion for toleration if an agent fully approves of another. In this case, the person receives the agent's wholehearted approval, leaving no space for any disapproval that makes the agent's stance one of toleration. Likewise, if there is full moral disapproval of the tolerated, and the only reason for accommodation is on account of practical necessity, then we have a case of pragmatic and not normative toleration. So for toleration (in the normative sense) to be a relevant moral stance for an agent, the agent needs to hold two opposing and active evaluative judgments with respect to the tolerated.

It is the subjective circumstance that gives rise to the paradox of toleration. It requires the tolerant agent to hold simultaneously a negative and positive evaluative attitude towards another or a state of affairs. An explanation of this paradox has to explain how it is that a person can hold both a pro- and con-attitude towards the tolerated object or situation.

To complete the discussion on the circumstances of toleration, notice that the duality of evaluative states in the agent makes toleration a relevant response; but it does not guarantee that toleration will be shown. Toleration is expressed or realized only when an agent goes on to give primacy to the positive attitude. That is, her negative response has to be overridden by her positive one in order for toleration to be expressed. For example, a person may truly believe that adherents of religions other than her own are deeply mistaken; but she might also understand and accept that there are good reasons to grant them religious freedom in light of the political ideals of her society. Here there is a tension between her religious point of view and her point of view as a citizen. If she goes on to accord greater weight to the political standpoint in spite of her continuing personal objections towards other religions, then she exercises religious toleration.[3]

But even though toleration requires an agent to give priority to her pro-attitude over the negative one, the important point is this: in order for her attitude to remain that of toleration, her negative evaluation is only trumped, and not eliminated. If the negative response were to be eliminated in the above example, we would have to say that the agent fully approves of religious diversity. We can say that she "tolerates" only if she retains a certain negative stance towards the tolerated. The tolerant agent must retain her moral disapproval of the tolerated even as she accepts the tolerated on other moral grounds, if her stance towards the object is accurately to be described as a show of toleration. The duality of disapproval and permissiveness must be sustained under the normative conception of toleration. Even though the tolerant accepts in some regard the tolerated, her objection to the tolerated must remain active in the background. The negative attitude is subordinated or contained but not eliminated.

It is of course sometimes the case that, through the exercise/practice of toleration, one's negative response is eventually fully eliminated. One can come, through the exercise of toleration, for example, to recognize that there is no basis for her original negative stance. In this case, the agent ceases to tolerate, but has in fact come to fully respect and affirm the tolerated object. The elimination of the negative response results in what we may call a *moral conversion*; the agent arrives at a subjective state "beyond toleration" so to speak. We shouldn't say, I think, that she has become more tolerant (because there is nothing for her to tolerate now given her conversion); rather she has come to fully respect that which she previously had some objections to.

Thus, it is important to clarify the sense in which toleration, on the normative conception, constitutes a form of respect. It cannot mean that the agent wholly respects the tolerated, for if that were the case, we would not have the

---

[3] It is worth noting a substantive issue that I do not discuss. And this is that the subjective circumstance does not guarantee that any resulting exercise of toleration is a value or a virtue. Consider for instance, the racist who (in the normative sense) tolerates members of other races. This is an individual, who although on the one hand is personally resentful of other races, is somehow able to see and respect them as equal citizens. If this is a possible combination of attitudes, it seems nonetheless that this repressed racism is not a virtue – it would be better if the tolerant racist did not have any negative response towards other races in the first place (that she had to control by appealing to some other moral consideration). We will regard an agent's show of toleration to be a value only when both her negative and positive responses are responses that morally reasonable.

subjective condition of toleration. The respect has to co-exist with some kind of disapproval if toleration is to be a relevant response. The term "respect-toleration" that is sometimes used in the literature thus has to be properly understood – it should not be taken to imply that toleration is co-extensive with respect; rather it is meant to capture a sense of toleration that involves respect combined with disapproval without reducing toleration to just respect.[4] The subjective circumstance of normative toleration requires competing pro- and negative-responses towards the tolerated, with the positive response trumping but not eliminating the negative response. An account of the normative paradox of toleration has to thus systematize and explain this co-mingling of respect with disapproval.

To sum, the subjective circumstance of toleration obtains when an agent is committed to two opposing evaluative judgments vis-à-vis another or a state of affairs, one positive and the other negative. Absent this subjective circumstance, this duality, there will be no cause for toleration. And the agent exercises toleration when she accords primacy to the positive evaluation.

2 Relational morality and the subjective paradox

The subjective circumstance of toleration puts in sharper relief the subjective form of the paradox of toleration. The tolerant has to simultaneously hold conflicting evaluative responses – an approving attitude and a disapproving one. While toleration is expressed when the positive response is given primacy over the negative response, the negative response has to remain in play even though it is withdrawn to backstage. As noted above, actual elimination of the negative response will remove the subjective circumstance of toleration. Yet this seems paradoxical: how can a single agent coherently affirm two opposing moral evaluative stances? If there are good reasons to accept the tolerated, should this not recommend full moral conversion, that is, the elimination of any initial negative attitude? Or, conversely, if the initial negative response is warranted, should this not argue against any normative acceptance of the tolerated?

The idea of *relational morality* offers an account of people can coherently come to hold competing moral evaluations. By relational morality, I mean the family of moral views that takes our rights and responsibilities with regard to others to be dependent on the type of interpersonal relationship we stand to

---

4 See Rainer Forst's conception of "respect-toleration", which does not take toleration to be reducible to respect (Forst 2012). Also Gutmann 1994, pp. 21–22. While the normative conception involves a certain respect or at least some acceptance of the tolerated, it is a respect co-mingled with disapproval.

them.[5] Relational morality as a general position holds that what we can morally expect of each other is relationally-constituted or relationally-dependent. As I will suggest below, the idea that moral evaluative stances vis-à-vis others are relationship-dependent and the fact that we typically stand in multiple-relations to one another can result in a situation in which we have different but ineliminable evaluative standards from which to make judgments. This, I will argue, provides one basis for the subjective circumstance of toleration. To support this thesis, let me first highlight the relevant tenets of relational morality as I understand it.

First, relationships can supply unique evaluative standards that are applicable only to people in that relationship. For instance, persons in specific kinds of relationships with others have specific rights and responsibilities vis-à-vis others unique to that kind of relationship that need not apply to non-participants. The set of relation-specific rights and responsibilities people in a relationship have to each other are constituted in part by an ideal of that kind of relationship. For example, in light of background assumptions of what we might take to be the ideal of friendship, we hold that friends are expected to show special care for each other, be open and frank to another other, to take a real interest in each other's projects, and so on. These special duties and concerns apply between those in a relationship of friendship, and they do not hold among people standing outside that relationship. Because rights and responsibilities are constituted in this way by the type of relationship friendship is, friends evaluate each other's conduct *qua* friends by references to an evaluative perspective given by the ideal of friendship.

Different kinds of relationships, therefore, provide their own evaluative perspectives or standards by which persons in that relation can judge one another. But it also means that it will be inappropriate to apply an evaluative standard proper to one kind of relationship to another. By reference to the evaluative standards of friendship, a person may be morally criticized for failing to take an interest in a friend's projects; but this criticism would not apply to a stranger. Or we could be disappointed in a person qua family members, though that same disappointment would be unwarranted were she merely a friend.

The second tenet of relational morality is that different types of interpersonal relationships provide not just unique but independent evaluative standards. Because relationship-specific evaluative standards are constituted by some ideal of a given type of relationship, these standards are not reducible to some general

---

[5] Philosophers who belong to this tradition include Bernard Williams (1981), Samuel Scheffler (2001, 2010), David Miller (1988) and Thomas Nagel (1979). I rely on and adapt their ideas here.

moral principle. That is, not all the relationship specific rights and responsibilities of members in a kind of relationship can be accounted for or explained by some general and more basic principles. A simple contrast to relational morality will be utilitarianism. Utilitarianism holds that all values, even those that appear at first to be values distinctive to specific relationships, such as friendship, kinship and the like, are reducible or justifiable by reference to the principle of utility maximization. The special permissions and obligations among friends, for example, might be justified as strategies for maximizing overall social utility. In contrast, relational morality denies that all special rights and permissions specific to certain relationships, like friendship or kinship, can be analyzed wholly in terms of the principle of utility. Not only is it not possible to fully account for the values of friendship in terms of utility, but the values of friendship, as ordinary moral experience confirms, can come into conflict with the requirements of utilitarianism.

The above two tenets lead to a third, which is that there is a plurality of relational evaluative standpoints. Since morality is relationally constituted in a non-reductive way, and since there are different types of relationships that people ordinarily have with each other, it follows that there is a plurality of non-reducible moral standards and evaluative perspectives by which we assess each other. There is no one common moral point of view that can subsume and justify all other moral points of view. Thus the plurality of relationally constituted moral standpoints is in this sense ineliminable. Relational morality thus implies value pluralism, the idea that there are independent and non-reductive domains of morality, each with its own set of expectations that are not wholly reducible to some more basic moral principles.

Thus relational morality provides a particular understanding of the basis of value pluralism. It explains the different non-reducible moral domains characteristic of value pluralism in terms of the different kinds of social relationships people share with each other. That is, it holds that since morality is relationally-specified, and since there are different types of human relations, it follows that there are distinct relationally defined moral domains. How an individual is to engage morally with another in a social context in which their friendship relation is the most salient factor can be different from how she is to engage with another with whom she stands in a different kind of relationship (e. g., as a family member). Relational morality will analyze the types of moral conflicts and dilemmas that are staple examples in discussions of value pluralism in terms of the different kinds of human relationships the conflicted agent finds herself in that impose different demands on her. This last point is key to my understanding of the subjective paradox of toleration, and I will elaborate on it shortly.

The fourth tenet of relational morality is that general morality, meaning by this the morality governing interactions between persons as such regardless of their more specific relational ties, itself is basically relational as well. It is just that in this case, the relationship is the pervasive and general one that obtains between persons qua moral agents. Structurally, the kinds of obligations and rights moral agents have to each other qua moral agents is on all fours with that of some specific types of human relationships, say, friendship. The rights and duties moral agents have to each other is given by some idealized characterization of what it means to stand in relation to others qua moral beings, just as in the case of friendship it is given by some ideal of what friendship is.

That general morality, the morality of what we owe to each other *qua* moral agents, is itself relational and is compatible with value pluralism. Value pluralism does not have to deny the existence of general morality, that there are things that people owe to and can claim from each other based on their standing as moral beings. What value pluralism denies is that the principles of general morality can by themselves wholly account for all the rights and duties people have in relation to each other, including those that are given by specific kinds of human relationships. It maintains the non-reductive claim noted above, that some relationship-specific duties and rights cannot be explained by appeal to moral principles governing moral relations among moral agents in general, but by some ideal of the specific relationship.[6] But this non-reductivism is compatible with the presence of general morality, so long as it is not claimed that general morality is the basis of all rights and duties people can have. Indeed, that general morality is relational is entirely compatible with the belief that the different relationally given domains of morality can impose competing demands – expectations of friendship for instance can be in tension with expectations of strangers in a way that issues in a genuine moral tension for an agent.

Relational morality takes it that our rights and obligations are relationally-constituted. These include the rights and obligations typically known as "special", that is the rights and obligations we have with respect to others with whom we share some kind of social relationship (such as friendship). But it also includes the "general" rights and obligations we have to others qua persons. These general moral rights and obligations are relational as well in the sense that we understand what these rights and obligations are by reference to some ideal of how it is we should stand in relation to other persons qua moral agents.

---

6 Some might argue that while morality includes "relationship-dependent values", it is not relational through and through. General morality, for example, might be thought to be relationship *independent*. Regardless, what is relevant for the present is that the possibility of conflict between general morality and relational commitments remains.

That general morality is also relational does not undermine value pluralism if general morality is not taken to provide the dominant moral framework under which all other relational moral perspectives are to be subsumed. That general morality itself is relational allows for the possibility that there can be conflicts between demands of general morality (what we owe to persons at large) and what we owe specially to some others (like friends or family) unless we make the additional claim that the relational moral framework is somehow more basic. In some contexts, we might find it appropriate to give primacy to considerations of general morality over more those due to special relationships, but according primacy to one relational value does not mean that we have reduced one value to the other or analyzed that value away. The subordinated value remains operational, but it is only constrained against the primary one.

Persons morally evaluate each other by reference to the appropriate relationally-given moral evaluative standpoint. Since these relationally-constituted moral evaluative standpoints are independent and non-reducible (a point that is compatible with the acknowledgement of a general relational morality among persons qua moral agents), there is a plurality of relationally-constituted moral domains.

Relational morality not only provides one systematic account of the plurality of values; it also provides one account of the subjective circumstance of toleration. The key factor here is that each one of us typically holds more than one moral relationship with another. Basically, we stand in some general moral relationship to all other persons; but to some others, we also stand in more specific moral relations, and not just of one kind but of various kinds at once. For example, in addition to the fact that we stand in a general moral relationship to all others, we are often both friends and family members to specific others; a colleague is often also a friend; a school teacher to a student can also be her parent; and, taking an example from Plato, Euthyphro was both public official and father to the person he wanted to prosecute for murder (relational facts that when taken together, as Socrates reminded him, should at least complicate the moral matter for Euthyphro).[7] And of course we are all at the same time fellow moral agents to friends, family and countrymen, as well as to foreigners.

---

7 A famous, analagous, case from a different philosophical tradition:
 The Duke of She said to Kongzi [Confucius], "Among my people there is one we call 'Upright Gong.' When his father stole a sheep, he reported him to the authorities." Kongzi replied, "Among my people, those whom we consider 'upright' are different from this: fathers cover up for their sons, and sons cover up for their fathers. 'Uprightness' is to be found in this."
 Kongzi, *The Analects*, trans. E.G. Slingerland, in: Ivanhoe/Van Norden (2005, p. 39).

Because of this multiplicity of moral relations in which we stand to each other, we can have more than one evaluative standard by which to morally assess or comprehend another's conduct. A father may morally disapprove of her daughter's preferences (perhaps a religious preference) from the point of view of a parent; but relating to her more generally as a moral agent, he can perhaps appreciate that there is nothing objectionable about her wishes from that more general evaluative perspective. A person may find what her friend expects of her qua friend to be reasonable, but because they are also colleagues, she finds that the person's expectation, since it also trespasses onto their professional relationship, from the professional standpoint problematic. In a liberal democracy, persons may hold sincere views about the deep errors of their religious antagonists. Here they stand in regard to each other as proponents of different faiths. But because they also relate to each other as co-citizens of a liberal democracy, they occupy another evaluative perspective that recommends respect for religious differences.

Thus, that we stand in multiple moral relations to others, and that these relations can provide their own non-reducible evaluative standpoints, gives rise to the evaluative duality that is the crux of toleration. Because of the different ways an agent morally relates to another, she can arrive at competing evaluations of the other. And toleration is expressed when primacy is granted to the evaluative perspective recommending acceptance. When a father tolerates his (grown) child's behavior, he can be deferring to general moral norms (governing relations between moral agents as such) commending acceptance of the child's conduct, while retaining his specific parental disapproval of that conduct. The conflicting evaluative state that gives rise to toleration is not a logical contradiction since the different responses stem from different evaluative standpoints, and it is not a contradiction for an agent to hold different evaluative standpoints with regard to a social situation given the plurality of relations she can occupy. The parent tolerating the child's conduct retains his parental relationship to the child – obviously, he has not renounced that. What he has done is to grant primacy to some other consideration based on another moral relationship that he has to his child. A feature of toleration, I mentioned above, is that the negative evaluation, while overridden, is not eliminated. The relational morality account of toleration accommodates this requirement. The disapproval or resentment lingers, but is only overridden so long as the relationship that constitutes the evaluative framework that issues in disapproval is maintained.

We stand in a multiplicity of moral relationships to others, and to the extent that these can be relations that present their independent evaluative moral standpoints, there is the potential for conflicting evaluations towards others. Toleration is expressed when the evaluative perspective recommending acceptance or respect is given primacy over the perspective recommending rejection.

On the presumption of the irreducibility of relational moral perspectives, the trumped perspective is not necessarily eliminated. The evaluative perspective recommending rejection remains valid along with its judgment about the wrongness of the tolerated; what occurs is that the agent grants authority to the perspective urging acceptance or respect. Toleration (in the normative sense) is salient only when practical reason is in conflict with itself and the competing evaluative responses need to be ordered. Value pluralism and specifically the idea of the plurality of relational moral perspectives provide a systematic account of this subjective circumstance and the paradox of toleration. The exercise of toleration does not unify practical reason against such conflicts, if by unify we mean that it resolves the conflict. As said, toleration presumes that the tolerated remains objected to.

But the exercise of toleration is an example of how opposing judgments within practical reason can nonetheless be harmonized, that an agent need not be hobbled and be unable to respond either way just because she faces an ineliminable evaluative conflict. The conflict is resolved, though not eliminated, by according priority to one evaluative standpoint over another. On this account then, the moral justification of any practice of toleration has to make the case that the two competing standpoints are reasonable and that that the standpoint issuing in the positive evaluation should be given primacy. Thus, on this account, normative arguments for toleration have to show why certain evaluative standpoints have priority or regulative primacy over others.

In other words, the subjective paradox is not a paralyzing one: the opposing evaluations stem from different relational evaluative perspective the toleration has with respect to the tolerated. But this does not render the agent's attitude incoherent or unstable. Indeed toleration is the response that renders the duality coherent by granting priority to one evaluative standpoint. Toleration is the result of the application of a priority rule that dissolves the subjective paradox. A particular relational standpoint is given priority over another when they each offer competing evaluative standards.

3 Liberal toleration

The relational approach to toleration is especially helpful for clarifying the character of liberal toleration as a political virtue. Liberal toleration as a political ideal requires citizens to permit or respect attitudes, ways of life and pursuits that they may find distasteful, offensive or even morally mistaken. That is, while a citizen may find another citizen's conduct or conception of the good morally objectionable, she nonetheless is required to respect the conduct or conception of the good. And understood in the normative sense, this respect does not merely entail non-intervention, but requires the normative attitude that the conduct or conception of the good be respected in some sense.

The subject of liberal toleration raises important substantive questions: what are the limits or parameters of toleration? What kinds of objectionable conduct fall outside the scope of liberal toleration? My concern in this paper, however, is with the formal structure of liberal toleration. The relational account illustrates nicely the way in which a citizen can both disapprove of and yet respect the conduct or pursuits that she is required to tolerate.

A liberal citizen may find another's activity or way of life morally objectionable on account of the former's own conceptions of the good life, her religious or other value commitments, and so on. Following one common usage, we can call these a person's *ethical* ideals and commitments. From one's own ethical perspective, there can be valuable ways of life and pursuits and ideals as well as morally inferior ones. Some ways of life can be seen as offensive or even wrong on account of an observer's own conception of the good. Yet, the observer also holds the point of view of the liberal citizen in addition to that of a private individual, and here, she may be able to see that while the conduct is objectionable from the standpoint of her ideal of the good, *as a citizen* she ought not to judge another in that capacity by reference to ethical ideals that she knows is not shared by all. That is, from the standpoint of liberal political justice, a perspective that she also occupies, she can accept that this is nonetheless an activity that she ought not to compel the state to restrict.

The relational approach explains this evaluative dualism in terms of the two basic ways citizens of a liberal society stand in relation to each other.[8] Citizens stand in relation to each other *qua* citizens, and in that capacity, the main evaluative standard via which they assess one another is that of justice. But besides relating to others as citizens, each individual is also a private agent with her own special relationships, attachments, and conceptions of the good. These various attachments and relationships provide another, non-political, evaluative standpoint that can come into conflict with the standpoint of justice. Such conflicts are settled by the presumptive primacy of the standpoint of justice. Where justice demands respect for differences that an individual can personally reasonably op-

---

[8] See John Rawls: "These two kinds of commitments and attachments – political and nonpolitical – specify moral identity and give shape to a person's way of life" (1993, p. 31; see also Rawls 2001, pp. 22–23; 199–200).

pose and when primacy is given to the evaluation of justice, liberal toleration is expressed.

If we take political justice to be institutional – that is, our relationship based on justice with other citizens are largely mediated via common institutional arrangements they jointly create, support and impose on each other – then liberal political toleration is expressed by the kind of institutions we set up. For citizens to tolerate divergent practices (such as differences in religious beliefs) as a political ideal means that they support institutions respecting and permitting these practices even though qua private individuals they can have reasonable moral objections against these.

For instance, toleration of religious diversity as a political ideal is expressed when citizens are able to endorse shared institutional norms that respect religious diversity, even though it is reasonable for them at the level of personal and religious morality to sincerely believe that religious views other than their own are not just epistemically mistaken, but also morally wrong. Because they also stand in relation to other religionists as fellow citizens, and hold that shared institutions ought to show all equal respect and concern (including respecting their religious beliefs), they support and give primacy to the perspective of justice that commends respect for religious diversity. We can thus understand liberal toleration in terms of institutional respect. Liberal toleration is shown to religious minorities when they are accorded *institutional respect* in spite of the differences that persons may have at the level of personal relations. The subjective circumstance of toleration is maintained because even though individuals endorse institutional respect for the religious minority, they retain their reasonable religious objections to religions different from theirs.

This distinction between institutional rules on the one side, and inter-personal morality on the other, reveals how it is that liberal toleration is consistent with active and sincere interpersonal criticisms and arguments within the terms of just institutions. To the extent that the described duality of capacities is correct, then persons' institutional commitments need not eliminate their non-political commitments. Granting institutional respect for difference, in spite of personal objections, does not eliminate these objections when toleration is shown. Accordingly, toleration as institutional respect for other religious views is consistent with personal efforts at proselytizing and promoting one's own religious views, and even criticizing other views. On this account of liberal toleration, one can tolerate something as a matter of liberal justice while criticizing it at the personal level without being a hypocrite because one is acting on different relational capacities when doing so.

Of course some of these examples present substantive questions that need to be addressed. The relational view of liberal toleration, however, provides a focus for addressing these kinds of substantive questions about the limits of liberal toleration. Since toleration is a matter of privileging the relational perspectives of individuals qua citizens over the different relational commitments individuals also have, the limits of liberal toleration turn on how we understand the ideal of shared liberal citizenship, and what individuals owe to each other in this relational capacity.

The good of toleration as a political virtue, then, can be seen as an expression of what citizens themselves professed that they owe to each other. Liberal toleration instantiates the ideal that no particular ethical viewpoints have authority over all members of society since these are subject to reasonable disagreement – that these are matters over which reasonable persons can reasonably disagree about (e.g., Rawls 1993). What it means to stand in relationship of mutual respect with one's fellow citizens is to recognize that public institutions cannot be designed to promote some ethical values and disallow others on terms that cannot be justifiable to all. Mutual respect among citizens requires the acknowledgement that there is a certain subjectivity with respect to persons' conceptions of the good life, and respect for the subjective agency of persons requires that they be permitted to plan and organize their lives around values and commitments even when these cannot be rationally justified to all. What liberal political institutions do is to establish the parameters within which subjective agents can form, plan and pursue their personal ends in life. The ideal liberal citizen accepts the priority of the political, and respects the diversity of personal pursuits in her capacity as a citizen even though in her personal ethical capacity she disagrees with these pursuits. Liberal toleration is an expression of this public respect over personal disagreement. The priority or primacy of the political does not mean that the personal is to be eliminated. Rather it means that the personal is to be *subordinated* to the political in the following sense: one is free to pursue whatever ends one wishes so long as these ends and their pursuits fall within and do not upset the terms of just political institutions (Rawls 2001, p. 50).

What could account for this normative priority or primacy of the political over the personal? What could justify, in other words, privileging the demands of justice over the personal? This is a complicated question and there will be competing theories of the primacy of justice. But one general account is as follows: the end of justice is to allow persons with competing and incompatible ends and values to pursue and realize these on terms that all others can accept.[9] The function of justice, in short, is to serve as the ground rules endorsable by all

---

[9] I discuss this in more depth in Tan (2012), Part I.

that regulate their personal pursuits. With just institutions securely established in the background, for instance, individuals can go about fervently realizing their ends and even compete rigorously for their own goals. So long as what they do is in conformity with the rules of just institutions and do not have the effect of undermining these rules, they can seek their ends confident that they are doing this *justly*. Since there is no resolution of the conflict between personal pursuits at the personal level – since we take it for granted that disagreements at this level will remain in perpetuity on account of reasonable disagreement – the only viable option is to seek agreement on the rules of personal pursuits. The motivation for justice and the acknowledgement that it enjoys priority over the personal follow from the acceptance that pluralism and conflict at the personal level about the good are a permanent feature of the human condition. What we can aim for are common rules, not common goals.[10] On this account of justice, liberal toleration is a political virtue that affirms mutual respect for differences in the midst of irresolvable ethical conflict.

Toleration is an issue that arises from the problem of pluralism, and the question of liberal state toleration is one that, in the first instance, falls under matters of liberal political justice. For example, it primarily concerns the question how to balance the civil and political rights and responsibilities of individuals in light of their different ethical, religious or cultural commitments. But in a way, toleration engages the question of distributive justice broadly construed, if by distributive justice we mean the fair allocation of rights and responsibilities among citizens. In the case of liberal multiculturalism, moreover, debates on minority rights engage not only the question of exemptions for minorities from state laws and the accommodation of religious practices within an official state religion or secularism, but also the question of the kinds of political and material support minority groups are entitled to by way of sustaining their ways of life. Should a cultural group enjoy some state economic support for, say, its cultural activities even though this might appear to go against the ideal of equal treatment for all? The issue of toleration will come to the fore, in particular, if consideration for supporting a cultural way of life is mingled with the concern that the inner cultural life sustains values somewhat in tension with the liberal ideals of individual autonomy and equality. I leave these matters to one side here, mentioning them only to suggest that the question of toleration can be pertinent in discussions on pluralism and distributive justice.

---

10 Of course conceptions of justice can be subject to disagreement. For a statement on deep disagreements on conceptions of justice, itself a challenging issue, see Knoll in this volume.

The above account of liberal toleration as an institution ideal invites this question: If toleration is the attitude expressed by individuals when they submit to institutional requirements to respect differences that they personally (reasonably) object to, is toleration then only a stance attributable to individuals. Can the *state itself* tolerate? We after all do speak of the tolerant *state*, for example. Does this state itself exhibit this evaluative duality? I am not able to engage this question here due to space limitation, but I will briefly note the following. If toleration is expressed because of competing pro- and con-responses to a situation, then a state as such is able to express toleration if its institutional set-up is complex enough to issue in pro- and con-evaluative positions on a matter. Take for example the matter of hateful speech. In the case where a state's institutional setup supports equal protection and respect for individuals as well as the liberty of individual expression, one might imagine then a state, if it prioritizes the liberty of expression, taking a stance on hate speech that satisfies our relational criterion of toleration: the state at once disapproves but also permits the speech. But for more in this discussion, see Heyd (2008, p. 179), Brettschneider (2010), Sabl (2008), and Abrams (2008).

But to return to the main point: the ideal of liberal toleration concerns the kind of institutions persons ought to collectively support. But it remains open for individuals to engage in criticisms and objections of views they oppose so long as these are done within the terms permitted by background (just) institutions. It also shows when and in what context criticisms cannot be made. Criticisms will be inappropriate when it comes from persons in their institutional capacities. Criticisms that might be consistent with institutional respect when made in non-political contexts may be inappropriate when made from some official podium. The main point here is that a strict standard of liberal toleration does not directly limit personal freedom to engage in criticisms, arguments and challenges against normative differences.

The normative conception of toleration, as defined above, is the conception that presents the paradox-problem. However, whether this normative conception is or is not the whole of toleration, it is a conception that can clarify certain substantive debates on toleration. It particular, it vividly distinguishes the question of toleration from that of enforcement. Take the debate on international toleration: should liberal states tolerate non-liberal states? Does "tolerate" here mean "not intervening"; or is "tolerate" understood in the normative sense, and hence distinct from the question of intervention? If one takes toleration in the pragmatic sense, then one can reasonably worry that a stricter standard of international toleration will grease the way for international interventions against states that fail to meet the (strong) conditions for international toleration. But if toleration is understood in the normative sense, then not tolerating a state does not mean that intervention is right away permissible (Tan 2005). To *not* tolerate, in this case, is to take a *normative* stance. On the other hand, to intervene or not to intervene is the further and separate question of how *to enforce* or act on that stance. This allows for a stricter standard of what is tolerable without lowering the standard for when to intervene.

Bibliography

Abrams, Kathryn (2008): "Forbearance and Engaged Toleration: A Comment on David Heyd". In: Williams/Waldron (2008), pp. 195–219.
Brettschneider, Corey (2010): "When the State Speaks, What Should It Say? The Dilemmas of Free Speech and Democratic Persuasion". In: *Perspectives on Politics* 6. No. 2, pp. 1005–1019.
Darwall, Stephen (1977): "Two Kinds of Respect". In: *Ethics* 88, pp. 36–49.
Forst, Rainer (2012): "Toleration". In: *The Stanford Encyclopedia of Philosophy*. Edward N. Zalta (Ed.). http://plato.stanford.edu/archives/sum2012/entries/toleration/, visited on 10 July 2014.
Gutmann, Amy (1994): "Introduction". In: *Multiculturalism: Examining the Politics of Recognition*. Princeton: Princeton University Press.
Heyd, David (Ed.) (1996): *Toleration: An Elusive Virtue*. Princeton: Princeton University Press.
Heyd, David (2008): "Is Toleration a Virtue?" In: Williams/Waldron 2008, pp. 171–194
Ivanhoe, P.J./Van Norden, B.W. (Eds.) (2005): *Readings in Classical Chinese Philosophy*. Indianapolis: Hackett.
Kymlicka, Will (1995): *Multicultural Citizenship*. Oxford: Oxford University Press.
Mendus, Susan (1989): *Toleration and the Limits of Liberalism*. Atlantic Highlands, NJ: Humanities Press.
Miller, David (1988): "The Ethical Significance of Nationality". In: *Ethics* 98. No. 4, pp. 647–662.
Nagel, Thomas (1979): "The Fragmentation of Values". In: Nagel, Thomas: *Mortal Questions*. Cambridge: Cambridge University Press.
Oberdiek, Hans (2001): *Tolerance: Between Forbearance and Acceptance*. Lanham, MD: Rowman and Littlefield.
Rawls, John (1993): *Political Liberalism*. New York: Columbia University Press.
Rawls, John (1999): *The Law of Peoples*. Cambridge, MA: Harvard University Press.
Rawls, John (2001): *Justice as Fairness*. Cambridge, MA: Harvard University Press.
Scanlon, T.M. (1996): "The Difficulty of Tolerance". In: Heyd (1996), pp. 226–241.
Sabl, Andrew (2008): "'Virtuous to Himself': Pluralism, Democracy and the Toleration of Tolerations". In: Williams/Waldron (2008), pp. 220–242.
Scheffler, Samuel (2001): *Boundaries and Allegiances*. New York: Oxford University Press.
Scheffler, Samuel (2010): *Equality and Tradition*. New York: Oxford University Press.
Tan, Kok-Chor (2005): "International Toleration: Rawlsian vs. Cosmopolitan". In: *The Leiden Journal of International Law* 8. No. 14, pp. 685–710.
Tan, Kok-Chor (2012): *Justice, Institutions and Luck*. Oxford: Oxford University Press.
Williams, Bernard (1981): *Moral Luck*. Cambridge: Cambridge University Press.

Williams, Bernard (1996): "Toleration: An Impossible Virtue?". In: Heyd (1996), pp. 18–27.
Williams, Melissa/Waldron, Jeremy (Eds.) (2008): *Toleration and Its Limits*. New York: New York University Press.

Chad Van Schoelandt/Gerald Gaus

Constructing Public Distributive Justice: On the Method of Functionalist Moral Theory*

Abstract: Functionalism sees a conception of justice as not merely an abstract standard or value. Instead, members of society must be able to use a conception of justice for some social function. This chapter's central concern is to better understand the functionalist approach to justice through an examination of this idea in an interpretation of John Rawls's work. We seek to draw out key themes in this functionalist interpretation of Rawls's work and indicate some of the implications of a functionalist project such as the fact that functionalism may require the metrics of distributive justice to significantly differ from the metrics most relevant to personal well-being or true advantage under a moral philosophic account. The final sections highlight the potential of functionalism as a basis for a progressive research agenda, and address concerns about ideal theory.

1 A framework for a progressive research agenda

Most philosophers associate John Rawls with his work on distributive justice, in particular his "difference principle." Though some seem to think it was the last word on distributive justice, the arguments for it face serious challenges; even Rawls (2005, pp. xxxvi, xlvii) came to hold that the difference principle is only one reasonable principle among others. We do not intend to add to the vast literature defending, developing or criticizing Rawls's famous principle; instead, we seek to make some progress in thinking about the methodology for theories of distributive justice.[1] Specifically, we wish to consider the purpose of a conception of justice, highlight some of the initially counterintuitive features we should expect of such principles, and indicate the plethora of tools available to theorists.

---

* For helpful comments and discussion of earlier versions of this paper, we thank Kelly Gaus, R.J. Leland, Michael Moehler, Kevin Vallier, and audience members for presentations at Virginia Tech and Tulane University.
1 Though we focus throughout on distributive justice, particularly as regards economic institutions and the distribution of resources, our main points will also apply to issues generally not thought of as part of distributive justice.

We highlight the "functionalist" strand of Rawls's thought in contrast to a more orthodox moral philosophy. As we elaborate below, functionalism sees a conception of justice as a tool proposed to serve an important social function. Justice is not, on this understanding, merely an abstract standard or value. Instead, members of society must be able to *use* a conception of justice to *accomplish* something. Our aim here is to explore this functionalist idea via an interpretation of Rawls's work. Yet our main concern is to better understand the functionalist approach to justice – while we think it is indeed the preferred reading of Rawls's work, our aim here is not to defend this reading against other interpretations. We seek to draw out key themes in this functionalist interpretation of Rawls's work, indicating some of the implications of a functionalist project and highlighting its potential as a basis for an ongoing, progressive research agenda.

2 Functionalism

A functionalist, we shall say, is engaged in social theory and understands a conception of justice as a technology for solving a problem.[2] At the heart of Rawls's work from 1950s at least until the publication of *Theory of Justice* in 1971 was that fully cooperating members of a scheme of social cooperation press incompatible claims that are to be seen "on first sight, as meriting satisfaction" (Rawls [1951] 1999, p. 14). Institutions and social rules can settle many conflicting claims, as property rights settle whether Alf can stay on or must leave the lawn adjacent to Betty's home. Reasonable people, however, may make conflicting claims on those institutions. When told that he has to vacate, Alf may demand institutional reform. Rawls seeks a conception of justice that can adjudicate disputes about the society's most basic institutions that structure ongoing cooperation.[3] As Rawls ([1985] 1999, p. 394) puts it, we need "a public basis of political agreement."

Most important to the present analysis is that this public basis of agreement is provided by a set of principles, along with the way these principles relate to

---

[2] D'Agostino (2010, p. 4) likewise holds that "we should understand that claims about 'the right' are human constructs, in particular settings, and not discoveries of antecedently or independently existing facts about the world, whether of a natural or of some other kind." Cf. D'Agostino (1996, p. 56) on the "social role" of a conception of public justification, and his emphasis that Rawls engages in social theory rather than conceptual analysis (2003, p. 60).

[3] Rawls was concerned about adjudicating claims on existing social institutions even in his earliest publication ([1951] 1999).

each other, defining the criteria for resolving disputes.[4] Successful principles of justice serve as a basic public charter for a society (Rawls [1980] 1999, pp. 306–307; 1999, p. 114). Should such a charter be secured, there would be a fact about what conception of justice a society embraces, much as there is a fact about the society's constitution, language(s), or currency. Such a conception of justice would be not simply normatively justified, but socially embodied. The Rawlsian moral theorist assesses and proposes possibilities for an acceptable conception of justice that may be socially adopted, and aims to understand the conditions a conception must satisfy if it is to play its "expected role in human life" (Rawls [1975] 1999, p. 286).[5] A well-ordered society for Rawls (1999, p. 4) is one in which there is public acceptance of such a conception. Such a society is not merely in compliance with a conception, it is *ordered by* it insofar as the citizens recognize their mutual acceptance and use their understanding of the principles to guide their political action (Rawls 2005, p. 35).

3 Functionalist moral theory distinguished from moral philosophy

The functionalist project not only advances different answers to traditional questions of moral philosophy – it asks something different. Consider Rawls's contrast of his project – which at one pointed he dubbed "moral theory" – with that of "moral philosophy" Rawls ([1975] 1999). In essence, the latter examines philosophic questions about the good life or what is of fundamental value. Moral philosophy, we might say, aims to discover moral truth "interpreted as fixed by a prior and independent order of objects and relations," while functionalist moral theory seeks to locate "a *public basis* of political agreement" Rawls ([1985] 1999, p. 394; emphasis added). This difference means that considerations that are irrelevant for the moral philosopher are critical for the functionalist moral theorist.

---

4 For Rawls, a conception of justice would also include a justificatory basis, like the "original position" as a device of representation and the regulative ideal of society as a fair system of cooperation between free and equal people. For the present analysis we focus simply on the principles, though consideration of the other features of a conception of justice would not significantly change the analysis.

5 Rawls ([1975] 1999, p. 296) further indicates that a conception's feasibility "is settled largely by psychological and social theory...."

G.A. Cohen provides an illuminating example of a moral philosophic, non-functionalist, approach to distributive justice. Cohen's (2008, p. 7) method "investigates the shape of, and, consequently, the logical implications of, our deepest normative convictions." Convictions about distributive justice provide a standard for assessing states of affairs independent of facts about motivational, informational, physical, and sometimes even moral constraints on what we could do. Such standards are meant primarily to guide our judgment of justice: they do not need to be socially functional or action guiding (Cohen 2008, pp. 267–268; cf. Estlund 2011).

Since a functionalist account is constrained by practical considerations like stability, Cohen (2008, pp. 263ff.) would argue that a functionalist account provides us only an account of "rules of regulation," but not "justice." Rather than getting bogged down in a conceptual or semantic dispute about the meaning of "justice," we assume here that both functionalist moral theorists and moral philosophers like Cohen have a claim to be analyzing justice, but their targets are different kinds or types.[6] The key insight is that their different aims and pressing questions render different considerations relevant. The moral philosopher, in clarifying our values or discovering independent moral facts and relations, need not ensure that it is feasible for people like us to realize those values. Such an investigation could discover, for instance, that justice, virtue, or other moral concepts demand what no human can deliver. Since the functionalist seeks an answer to a social problem, she must account for the feasibility of people confronting that social problem to stably implement a proposed conception of justice. Because her question is what understanding of justice can adjudicate conflicting claims and undergird a cooperative social order, for her a conception of justice that cannot be implemented – cannot serve as the required tool – is ineligible. Imagine the philosopher told a farmer that she had designed the perfect plow but, alas, given human technology, such a plow cannot now be built, nor can she even point the way forward to learning how it might be build. Our farmer would wonder what can be prefect about a plow that cannot solve his problems.

---

6 Larmore (2013, p. 292n19) and James (2013, pp. 5 and 104) each see Cohen's conception as a form of "cosmic" justice. Cf. Mason (2012, p. 525). Anderson (2010), however, argues that Cohen's conception is not a form of justice at all because it is unsuited for grounding interpersonal demands.

4 A public political perspective

Because the moral theorist insists that an adequate conception of justice must provide for the public adjudication of our dispute, it is critical that justice serves as a public standpoint to which different private viewpoints can appeal to resolve their claims. Consistent with this, Rawls ([1985] 1999, p. 394) seeks "a public basis of political agreement." The conception of justice must be public in the sense that it can be shared and mutually recognized by the members of society. Instead of merely some special elite knowing and applying the conception of justice, all members of society, pressing their competing claims but requiring adjudication, are expected to utilize the conception.

We can understand "political" here to qualify the nature of the agreement members of society are expected to reach. The members of society take the outputs of a conception of justice to settle their dispute at least for purposes of regulating their ongoing interaction. They will not necessarily hold that public justice decides the matter in all ways.[7] For instance, with competing claims based on religious disputes, the conception of justice may provide systems of individual rights of conscience and property through which individuals can believe and practice as they see fit. This provides a public answer to what religion people should hold and practice; each should hold and practice the religion of her own choice, with the resources under her jurisdiction within the property system. The disputants can accept this as the public answer governing their ongoing cooperation without thinking it undermines the bases of their original conflicting claims. An individual may go on thinking that from her personal perspective, or the perspective of her faith, or as a matter of having true beliefs, everyone should believe and practice as she does. Perhaps if we were all as enlightened, or all had the gift of faith, we would grasp a higher, more perfect, idea of justice.

Functions give rise to necessary specifications in the tools designed to accomplish them. Thus the function of a conception of justice generates the need for the political perspective. Recall that for Rawls the essential problem is that we have conflicting claims and reasonable disagreements: the conception of justice is tasked with adjudicating them. Some might suggest that the disputes should be settled by appeal to moral truth or some similar independent standard of appropriateness for claims. After all, isn't the very point of morality to instruct us all of what we ought to do? But appeal to a controversial standard cannot

---

7 Another way in which Rawls intends his conception to be "political" is that it applies specifically to political institutions. Other conceptions of justice may be appropriate for international relations, private associations, and so on. Cf. Neufeld/Van Schoelandt (2014).

serve as a method of adjudication. As John Locke (1983, p. 23) observed of claims that we should settle religious disputes by appeal to orthodoxy, "everyone is orthodox to himself." Therefore, if the dispute is to be settled those disputants must appeal to something other than their own views of moral truth. A conception of justice can serve as a public perspective providing a point of view that each member can take up and find a common answer.

The separation of the public perspective, constituted by the conception of justice, from the personal perspective raises doubts about the feasibility of the public conception of justice. If the conception of justice is to provide a feasible answer to the problem of conflicting claims then it must be feasible that the members go along with the requirements of the conception of justice.[8] Those who do not have their claims fully honored must have sufficient devotion to the public conception to accept its verdict. This problem is particularly serious since the conception of justice may conflict with not only an individual's narrow self-interest, but also her religious and moral convictions. Moreover, the members of society are, and will continue to be, diverse in their convictions. If an individual finds the conception of justice alien and opposed to her deepest commitments, we might expect her to reject it, in whole or in part. And even if she obeys, such obedience seems to run against her own conscience, leading to alienation and dissidence. When such dissidence is widespread in society, the conception cannot be stable. And, then, of course, it cannot fulfill its expected role, and so is deficient *as* a conception of justice.

Rawls advanced a two-part reply to this challenge. First, the conception of justice must be constructed from a set of shared, yet weighty, values. If the public conception of justice is built on common commitments and values, and if each person understands these to be especially important, then appeal to the public conception will *ipso facto* be an appeal to what all care about. But then rejection and alienation should not pose a deep problem. Rawls hoped that people sharing the political culture of a democratic society would share values sufficient to generate a conception of justice and that these values were sufficiently important to provide for the stability of the conception. A conception grounded in such shared values provides for each individual at least some justification for accepting the conception insofar as the conception expresses some values that are important to that individual. Justification from shared values, however, provides only a limited, "pro tanto" justification. The possibility of instability from conflict with the deep commitments of diverse members of society remains. Because of

---

[8] Nagel (1991) discusses some of the difficulties of reconciling "partial" and "impartial" perspectives.

this, Rawls's second part of reconciliation requires showing that the conception of justice would be justified to individuals in light of their full range of values and thus the object of an overlapping consensus. When the conception is able to cohere in this way and not conflict too much with the individual's deepest commitments, then the conception might be stably realized.

It is critical, then, that a functionalist theory of justice does not hold that whatever serves cooperation and resolves conflict is just – that would not be a theory of justice at all.[9] We might use the slogan "functionality for the right reasons." An adequate functionalist conception of justice must be one that plays its expected role in human life, and part of this role is that individuals will view the resolution of their disputes as just. While the function cannot be secured if each insists on her own view and so conflicts cannot be adjudicated, neither can it be secured if the conflict is resolved, but when individuals consult their own understandings of justice, they cannot accept this resolution as adequately fair or moral. The functionalist, then, requires what might be thought of as a relation of acceptability between her overall views of what matters for justice and what the public perspective deems just such that, while the public perspective may not be perfect, it provides an adequate standard of justice.

Thus the relation between the political perspective and the perspectives of individuals, particularly as those individuals develop comprehensive views, is absolutely fundamental to the functionalist project. To understand this separation of perspectives, consider Rawls's (1955) account of justification of and within practices in his classic paper, "Two Concepts of Rules." As Rawls presents it, utilitarians may have reason to endorse a practice like retributive punishment. There may, of course, be individual cases in which were an individual to engage in utilitarian reasoning she would not comply with the practice. She might find that punishing the guilty person, or not punishing some innocent person, does not maximize utility. Be that as it may, part of the value of establishing a practice is to change the considerations relevant for an individual's decision making. Utility itself may be maximized by people reliably keeping their promises without considering the utility of doing so, rather than judging utility each time or considering utility a sufficient reason to break a promise.

On Rawls's account, we have two perspectives. On the one hand, there is the perspective from within the practice, in which promises must be kept and the guilty deserve to be punished while the innocent do not. On the other hand, there is the perspective of assessing the practice itself through a utilitarian stan-

---

9 Habermas (1995, pp. 221–222) seems to worry that Rawls's account may be functionalist in this way.

dard.[10] These perspectives are quite different, including in that they deploy totally different values. Desert, for instance, is not a consideration at all in the utilitarian perspective. The utilitarian may consider desert solely an institutional concept and deny that desert provides a standard for externally judging an institution or practice. Furthermore, the utilitarian would see punishment always to some extent an evil, rather than as something to be done for its own sake as in a retributive system. That, however, does not prevent the utilitarian from endorsing a practice in which people will be seen to deserve punishment and for that desert to be seen as an adequate reason to inflict punishment.[11] An individual is able to take up these two perspectives, reasoning within the practice in terms of crimes and deserved punishments, or about the practice in terms of aggregate utilities.

We propose that a conception of justice provides a political perspective that is essentially a practice that the diverse members of society share. It is not only a practice for promises or punishment, but is more generally a practice for adjudicating competing claims on basic social institutions.

5 Features, not bugs, of a functionalist conception

Once we grasp the nature of functionalist justice we see some traditional issues in distributive justice in a new light. Most obvious, perhaps, is the vexed question of the appropriate metric for distributive shares. If one does not appreciate the nature of functional justice, its proposals are apt to strike one as not simply erroneous, but also peculiar or even wildly misguided. Consider Rawls's (1999, sec. 15; 2005, pp. 178–183) proposal that distributive justice be thought of in terms of what he called "social primary goods." Leaving aside some complexities of Rawls's view, let's assume that the primary metric for judging in accordance with his famous Difference Principle is monetary income.

---

[10] Similar perspectival divisions can be found in P.F. Strawson's (2008) separation of the objective stance from that taken within our moral responsibility practice.

[11] In a related way, Schmidtz (2006, p. 37) writes: "We are not forced to believe in desert; neither are we forced to be skeptics. We decide. We can ask whether we treat people more respectfully when we give them credit for what they do or when we deny them credit. Or we can ask what kind of life we have when we live by one conception rather than another."

Amartya Sen (1987) argues that monetary income has serious disadvantages as a metric for distributive justice.[12] Money seems a strange metric – it appears to be a mere means for more normatively fundamental goods like subjective satisfaction, well-being, project pursuit, or the like.[13] Sen raises two important objections to income and wealth as metrics. For our purposes, what is critical to realize is that, although they prove devastating for a traditional project in moral philosophy, they have a different significance for functionalism.

5.1 Informational shortness

According to Sen (1987, pp. 215–216), Rawls's approach ignores important aspects of human diversity, particularly with respect to the fact that "people seem to have very different needs varying with health, longevity, climatic conditions, location, work conditions, temperament, and even body size (affecting food and clothing requirements)."[14] These variables affect the individual's conversion rate for money into advantage, so considering monetary income alone ignores information required to judge individual advantage. Sen (1987, p. 216) concludes that "[j]udging advantage purely in terms of primary goods leads to a partially blind morality."[15] The primary goods approach is "informationally short" (1987, p. 217).

In assessing Sen's charge of informational shortness, we must keep in mind that for the functionalist workability or feasibility is fundamental. One aspect of feasibility we must highlight here is that typical members of society must be able to learn, understand, and apply the conception of justice. A traditional moral-philosophic project need not be concerned with what typical members can understand. Perhaps the independent moral facts and relations are complex and

---

[12] Sen's (2009, p. 231) own preferred "capabilities approach" assesses individual advantage "by a person's capability to do things he or she has reason to value." For development and defense of the capability approach, see Nussbaum (2001, pp. 4–14, 59–100; 2007, chap. 3), Sen (1983; 2009, pt. III).

[13] Sen (1980, p. 216) writes: "That a person's interest should have nothing directly to do with his happiness or desire fulfillment seems difficult to justify."

[14] Marx (1970, pt. I) raises a similar point in response to a view on which justice requires that laborers be paid in proportion to their labor: "Further, one worker is married, another is not; one has more children than another, and so on and so forth. Thus, with an equal performance of labor, and hence an equal in the social consumption fund, one will in fact receive more than another, one will be richer than another, and so on."

[15] Cf. on concern about information shortness, Sen (2009, pp. 93–94).

obscure, and so require exceptional levels of intelligence and training.¹⁶ A functionalist conception of justice, on the other hand, is proposed as a device that a society can publicly adopt. A functionalist conception will only be workable if it suits its users, and so cannot depend on information that is too complex or obscure.

Despite whatever initial plausibility certain accounts of utility may have, Rawls (1999, pp. 78–81) argues that we cannot expect people to form common judgments in metrics that require interpersonal comparisons of utility.¹⁷ Principles of justice that distribute based on utility, therefore, cannot effectively order competing claims for the members of society.¹⁸ On the other hand, monetary income at least provides a "feasible way to establish a publicly recognized objective and common measure…." (Rawls 1999, p. 81; cf. Mason 2012, p. 528; D'Agostino 2003, pp. 74, 95–96). In contrast to utility, income is transparent. Functionalist justice must be publicly seen to be done. Members of society can generally agree not only in ordinal judgments about when an individual has more or less income, but also about cardinal, interpersonal, and aggregate comparisons.

We should go a step further, for a charge of informational poverty may be raised by pointing to metrics of health, leisure time, life expectancy, risks of natural disaster, or many other factors relevant to someone's well-being. Despite its availability, however, at least some of this information must be excluded from the conception of justice to avoid excessive complexity. Even if each variable, considered in isolation, could provide a feasible common measure, including all of this information would make the overall judgments of such a theory opaque. Rawls ([1974] 1999) never satisfactorily solved the "indexing problem" of taking a basket of primary goods (e. g., income, wealth, and the social bases of self-respect) and producing an index to be maximized. It is no wonder that almost all discussions of the Difference Principle take something like income or wealth as the good to be distributed. Members of society must be able to

---

16 Classically, Plato (1991, bk. III) held that knowledge of the Good was accessible only to a special elite of extraordinarily educated philosophers supported by ignorant masses. More recently, David Enoch (2013, pp. 146 and 149) compares the study of moral truths to physics. Nothing seems to require that the truths of physics be understandable to typical members of a society.
17 Of course, some argue that interpersonal comparisons and aggregation of utility are not merely obscure, but in fact impossible outside of an arbitrary selection from the infinite conflicting metrics that could be used. See, for instance, Arrow (1963, chap. IV) and Riker (1982, p. 111). Even if non-arbitrary interpersonal comparisons of utility are conceptually possible, accurately measuring the cardinal preferences of individuals is unlikely.
18 We might also wonder about the workability of Rawls's own thesis that the social bases of self-respect is a distributable primary good.

both acquire and process the information necessary for applying the principles of justice, so functional principles may exclude information out of concern for transparency and simplicity.[19]

There are candidates for better metrics than monetary income. Perhaps, for instance, health indicators or other capabilities could better represent advantage than income while remaining adequately conducive to intersubjective agreement. Even so, we anticipate that theorists will find any such metrics to lack some of the information relevant for assessing an individual's level of advantage in a moral philosophic sense. Informational inclusivity and social workability come into tension, so something must be left out. Given the role that justice is meant to play, functionalist accounts *need* to be short on information; the conception must be manageably clear and simple.

5.2 Fetishism

In addition to informational limitations, Sen (1987, sec. 3) also argues that Rawls's view is fetishistic in that "Rawls takes primary goods as the embodiment of advantage, rather than taking advantage to be a *relationship* between persons and goods."[20] Measuring advantage in terms of monetary income treats money as having a power it in fact lacks. This charge of fetishism is distinct from that of informational shortness. The latter holds that there be other aspects of advantage the standard omits, while the fetishism charge claims that the account is looking at the wrong kind of thing altogether.

If we are discussing the best moral and normative conception of "advantage" Sen is correct that income is a poor candidate. Most would admit that money is not a fundamental aspect of advantage, but is instead merely a means and matters for advantage only insofar as one can use it for something valuable.[21] This, however, is consistent with it being an appropriate metric for

---

[19] Functionalist theories of justice or morality tend to agree that complexity must be limited. See Rawls (1999, p. 114; 2005, pp. 162, 182; [1975] 1999, pp. 294–295), Baier (1958, pp. 195–200), Gaus (2011, pp. 296–297), Mason (2012, pp. 527–528), and Mackie (1977, p. 139).
[20] Sen's fetishism charge may only apply to some of the primary goods in Rawls's theory. The opportunities addressed in Rawls's principle of fair equality of opportunity seem, even if informationally short, to be looking at the kinds of relationships or capabilities that constitute advantage on Sen's own account.
[21] Ayn Rand (1996, pt. II.II) provides a perhaps surprising example when her character Francisco proclaims that "money is only a tool," and it "will not purchase happiness for the man who has no concept of what he wants: money will not give him a code of values, if he's evaded

a functionalist conception of justice. On a functionalist account, the metric is only needed for political purposes, or to adequately address the most pressing problems for which people need justice. The metric does not have to be plausible as an account of true advantage within moral philosophy, but instead need only be a viable option for application from a political perspective that tracks people's conceptions of justice in an adequate way. Participants do not have to see the metrics of the conception as morally basic or applying outside the practice any more than our utilitarian (§ 4) needs to see punishment as deserved outside of the retributive practice. The members, when in dispute about their institutions arising from conflicting values or interests, can take up the perspective of the conception of justice for the sake of giving a public resolution to that dispute. The conception of justice may still appear, from an individual's perspective, fetishistic. The same is true, of course, of the utilitarian assessment of rules. From the utilitarian perspective, the claim that someone "deserves punishment" will look wrongheaded since all that really matters are what consequences would follow from punishing the individual. The utilitarian, however, can recognize that there are good reasons even from the utilitarian perspective to adopt the practice, fetishism and all.

Since for functionalists a conception of justice is a public construction, it should not be surprising that some of its features seem artificial. Such artificiality is acceptable as long as members of society can take up the perspective of justice when needed. Even if the members see the metric as artificial, so long as they can connect their individual perspective to the public perspective in a way that endorses the latter (§ 4), their sense of justice supports it. The use of monetary income as a metric for individual advantage seems to play this role in Rawls's account.

5.3 Does endorsement of a metric require pro tanto moral justification?

It may seem from the individual perspective that, all other things being equal, it is better for a person to have more, rather than less, money since money is a valuable means to many other ends. Moreover, this way of seeing money is likely to be shared across all the individuals of society. Though members will disagree about advantage within moral philosophy, they are likely to generally agree

---

the knowledge of what to value, and it will not provide him with a purpose, if he's evaded the choice of what to seek."

that money is a good means to at least some aspects of advantage. They can see it as a proper end from the political perspective because they mutually see it as an important means from their diverse comprehensive perspectives.

There is a common explanation for each member endorsing a conception of justice using money as a metric insofar as each member sees money as at least relating to advantage. Endorsement, however, does not require such pro tanto justification. First, members of society can endorse a conception of justice containing metrics the members do not see as independently valuable even as means or as independently adequate proxies for true advantage, just as utilitarians can endorse practices with notions of desert. Second, though each member must have sufficient reason from her own perspective to endorse the conception, they do not all have to do so in the same way or for the same reason. Just as members can endorse a traffic practice despite having diverse destinations, they can endorse a common conception of justice even if they have no common grounds for doing so. The diverse members of society may converge on a functionalist conception of justice because each member sees the conception as providing an adequate means of publicly adjudicating their competing claims.[22]

6 The many tools of functionalism

We have insisted that functionalism differs from comprehensive moral philosophy in seeking a conception of justice that is a tool that helps us solve critical problems. Functionalism, then, poses a problem of settling on appropriate social technologies, and in grappling with their problem functionalists can gain insights from social science, in a way that often puzzles more orthodox approaches. Functionalists can avoid getting mired in clashes of intuition, concentrating instead on incremental improvements to their technologies. In this way, functionalism provides a progressive research agenda. Let us consider several examples drawn from diverse disciplines.

The growing literature on social norms provides an important source of insight for functionalist theories of justice.[23] For a society to establish a conception of justice it must either have a social norm about the conception or something importantly like a social norm in the way members of society internalize the conception's requirements. The members must be disposed to comply with the con-

---

[22] On convergence conceptions of public reason, see D'Agostino (1996, chap. 3), Vallier/D'Agostino (2013), Vallier (2011; 2014, chap. 4).
[23] E.g., Bicchieri (2006; 2016), Brennan et al. (2013), Fehr/Fischbacher (2004), G. Mackie et al. (2014).

ception, or more precisely to support and comply with the demands of institutions that satisfy the requirements of the conception, on the expectation that other members will do likewise.[24] The progressive functionalist draws on research on social norms to better understand the conditions for a conception of justice to be stable and workable. These insights may lead the functionalist to abandon conceptions of justice that fail to meet stability conditions for norms, such as those that cannot generate observable compliance.[25] The study of social norms may also open up possibilities for a conception of justice. For instance, initially a functionalist might be inclined to keep a conception of justice down to just a small number of principles, perhaps with a lexical ordering to minimize the need for tradeoffs. If, however, we observe that people maintain and navigate more complex systems of social norms, including systems with only implicitly understood tradeoff rates among different requirements, the functionalist may conclude that a more complex conception of justice is feasible. Understanding how systems of norms function may thus illuminate not only the limits, but also the possibilities for a functional conception of justice.

The facts of human psychology are critically important for the functionalist. If the conception is to fulfill its role, then typical members of society must be able to understand and internalize the conception. Much as we would not propose a language that typical members would not have the physical capacity to send or receive, we would not want to propose a conception of justice that typical members could not learn, apply, or stably internalize. Rawls recognized this, and discusses psychology in the (all too often overlooked) third part of *A Theory of Justice*, but psychological research is ongoing and there are further questions to be answered. Since the appropriate content for a conception of justice will depend in part upon psychological facts about what typical people can learn, internalize and find motivationally efficacious, ongoing psychological research is relevant to, and provides an important foundation for, work on justice in the functionalist tradition.[26]

Finally, of great importance to the functionalist project are the research agendas of constitutional political economy and other institutional analyses.

---

24 On Rawls's account, an individual does not directly comply with principles of justice, as by applying the Difference Principle in daily life. What an individual does, however, is obey the laws of a system satisfying those principles. It supports the maintenance of those institutions when they exist, and supports efforts to bring about such institutions where they do not exist.
25 Bicchieri/Chavez (2010); Bicchieri/Xiao (2009). Thrasher and Vallier (2013) discuss problems for a Rawlsian conception of justice relying on expressed support for stability.
26 As one recent example, Gaus and Nichols (2017) argue that psychological studies give support to a "presumption of liberty" because such a presumption is conducive to norm learning.

This includes formal work, like the economic analysis of political institutions as pioneered by theorists like James M. Buchanan and Gordon Tullock (1999), as well as interdisciplinary research drawing on extensive field work on the functioning of diverse institutions such as that of Elinor Ostrom (1990).[27] Constitutional political economy is centrally concerned with how agents respond to the incentives and restraints of public, constitutional, rules, and particularly how certain collective outcomes emerge. A conception of justice for a society's basic structure provides a framework analogous to a constitution, and could thus be helpfully modeled with the tools of political economy and institutional analysis.[28] Such tools could thereby help us understand the incentives and restraints a conception would create, how agents would respond, the kind of order that could emerge, whether the conception would discourage or be vulnerable to free-riding and exploitation, and other factors relevant to assessing competing conceptions.[29]

As the reader can see, there are many tools for advancing our understanding of conceptions of justice. This is one of the reasons that functionalism remains a vibrant and progressive research agenda – though an agenda that requires a certain kind of theorist, one willing to draw from new (and old) fields of study. Functionalism calls for an ecumenical tool kit, drawing on diverse disciplines.

7 An ideal and moral theory

Our emphasis on the constraints of an eligible conception of justice may make the functionalist project seem all too practical, insufficiently moral, and inapplicable to "ideal theory."[30] Though feasibility is important to a functionalist conception of justice, it is not the only consideration. Functionalists, at least of the Rawlsian variety, are concerned that an existing, socially-realized, conception of justice satisfy certain normative requirements, such as that it be suitable for recognizing the members of society as free and equal. Moreover, the conception must answer to the values and projects of each member in order to be the basis of a fair system of cooperation.[31] These are not mere technical considera-

---

27 Cf. Aligica (2014), and Aligica/Boettke (2009).
28 See Gaus (2013) on a "public moral constitution."
29 On the necessity of incentives for all systems of public justice, see Gaus (2016).
30 There are various ways to characterize the distinction between "ideal" and "non-ideal" theory. For an important recent collection of diverse views on the topic, see Vallier/Weber (2016).
31 The conception must also answer to the values of each if it is to be the basis for members holding each other responsible in some ways. See Van Schoelandt (2015).

tions, for authoritarian, oppressive systems may be all too feasible and stable. It is always important to keep in mind that we require functionality for the right reasons (§ 4). It is thus sensible for a functionalist to ask what sort of conception of justice and corresponding society would best realize these values. And in one sense of this ambiguous term, this is to inquire into the "ideally just society."

Of course, even when theorizing about an ideally just society the functionalist remains concerned with an ideal justice as tool for living together. The functionalist must avoid idealizing away the problem she aims to solve.[32] The functionalist will hold fixed that even the ideal society is one of cognitively limited humans facing scarcity, reasonable disagreement, or other sources of conflict that need melioration. The functionalist must be concerned with the feasibility of a proposed conception of justice given the circumstances that generate the problem, though the conception may not be feasible in every society or even the theorist's own. Though the functionalist may not tell us how to get there from here, she is concerned that a proposed conception of justice could plausibly, effectively and stably regulate some society populated by humans under conditions generating reasonable disagreement.

Bibliography

Aligica, Paul Dragoș (2014): *Institutional Diversity and Political Economy: The Ostroms and Beyond.* New York: Oxford University Press.

Aligica, Paul Dragoș/Boettke, Peter J. (2009). *Challenging Institutional Analysis and Development: The Bloomington School.* London, New York: Routledge.

Anderson, Elizabeth (2010): "The Fundamental Disagreement between Luck Egalitarians and Relational Egalitarians". In: *Canadian Journal of Philosophy* 40. (Sup. 1), pp. 1–23.

Arrow, Kenneth J. (1963): *Social Choice and Individual Values.* Revised edition. New Haven: Yale University Press.

Baier, Kurt (1958): *The Moral Point of View: A Rational Basis of Ethics.* Ithaca: Cornell University Press.

Bicchieri, Cristina (2006): *The Grammar of Society: The Nature and Dynamics of Social Norms.* Cambridge, New York: Cambridge University Press.

Bicchieri, Cristina (2016): *Norms in the Wild: How to Diagnose, Measure and Change Social Norms.* Oxford, New York: Oxford University Press.

---

32 Schmidtz (2011, p. 777) writes: "A Newtonian idealization may, for some purposes, profitably ignore wind resistance, but ignoring wind resistance when predicting the behavior of a parachute would be ignoring a 'main question' rather than a 'distracting detail.' More generally, there can be such a thing as an 'ideal solution,' but for S to be an ideal solution to problem P, it must first be a solution to problem P. *One thing we must never set aside as a distracting detail is the actual problem.*"

Bicchieri, Cristina/Chavez, Alex (2010): "Behaving as Expected: Public Information and Fairness Norms". In: *Journal of Behavioral Decision Making* 23. No. 2, pp. 161–178.

Bicchieri, Cristina/Xiao, Erte (2009): "Do the Right Thing: But Only If Others Do So". In: *Journal of Behavioral Decision Making* 22. No. 2, pp. 191–208.

Brennan, Geoffrey/Eriksson, Lina/Goodin, Robert E./Southwood, Nicholas (2013): *Explaining Norms*. New York: Oxford University Press.

Buchanan, James M./Tullock, Gordon (1999): *The Calculus of Consent: Logical Foundations of Constitutional Democracy*. In: *The Collected Works of James Buchanan*. Vol. 3. Indianapolis, IN: Liberty Fund.

Cohen, G.A. (2008): *Rescuing Justice and Equality*. Cambridge, MA: Harvard University Press.

D'Agostino, Fred (1996): *Free Public Reason: Making It Up As We Go*. New York: Oxford University Press.

D'Agostino, Fred (2003): *Incommensurability and Commensuration: The Common Denominator*. Aldershot: Ashgate.

D'Agostino, Fred (2010): *Naturalizing Epistemology: Thomas Kuhn and the "Essential Tension"*. Houndmills, Basingstoke, Hampshire, New York: Palgrave Macmillan.

Enoch, David (2013): "The Disorder of Public Reason". In: *Ethics* 124. No. 1, pp. 141–176.

Estlund, David (2011): "Human Nature and the Limits (If Any) of Political Philosophy". In: *Philosophy & Public Affairs* 39. No. 3, pp. 207–237.

Fehr, Ernst/Fischbacher, Urs. (2004): "Social Norms and Human Cooperation". In: *Trends in Cognitive Sciences* 8. No. 4, pp. 185–190.

Gaus, Gerald (2011): *The Order of Public Reason: A Theory of Freedom and Morality in a Diverse and Bounded World*. New York: Cambridge University Press.

Gaus, Gerald (2013): "On the Appropriate Mode of Justifying a Public Moral Constitution". In: *Harvard Review of Philosophy* 19, pp. 4–22.

Gaus, Gerald (2016): "The Commonwealth of Bees: On the Impossibility of Justice-through-Ethos". In: Social Philosophy & Policy 33, pp. 96–121.

Gaus, Gerald/Nichols, Shaun (2017): "Moral Learning in the Open Society: The Theory and Practice of Natural Liberty". In: *Social Philosophy & Policy* 34, pp. 79–101.

Habermas, Jürgen (1995): "Reconciliation through the Public Use of Reason: Remarks on John Rawls's Political Liberalism". In: *Journal of Philosophy* 92. No. 3, pp. 109–131.

James, Aaron (2013): *Fairness in Practice: A Social Contract for a Global Economy*. Oxford: Oxford University Press.

Larmore, Charles (2013): "What Is Political Philosophy?" In: *Journal of Moral Philosophy* 10. No. 3, pp. 276–306.

Locke, John. (1983): *A Letter Concerning Toleration*. James Tully (Ed.). Indianapolis: Hackett.

Mackie, Gerry/Moneti, Francesca/Denny, Elaine/Shakya, Holly (2014): "What Are Social Norms? How Are They Measured?" UNICEF/UCSD Center on Global Justice. https://www.unicef.org/protection/files/4_09_30_Whole_What_are_Social_Norms.pdf (accessed June 18, 2018).

Mackie, J.L. (1977): *Ethics: Inventing Right and Wrong*. New York: Penguin.

Marx, Karl (1970): "Critique of the Gotha Programme". In: Marx, Karl/Engels, Frederick: *Selected Works*. Vol. 3. Moscow: Progress Publishers, pp. 13–30.

Mason, Andrew (2012): "What Is the Point of Justice?" *Utilitas* 24. No. 4, pp. 525–547.

Nagel, Thomas (1991): *Equality and Partiality*. New York: Oxford University Press.

Neufeld, Blain/Van Schoelandt, Chad (2014): "Political Liberalism, Ethos Justice, and Gender Equality". In: *Law and Philosophy* 33. No. 1, pp. 75–104.
Nietzsche, Friedrich (1974): *The Gay Science: With a Prelude in Rhymes and an Appendix of Songs*. Walter Kaufmann (Trans.). First edition. New York: Vintage.
Nussbaum, Martha C. (2001) *Women and Human Development: The Capabilities Approach*. First edition. Cambridge, New York: Cambridge University Press.
Nussbaum, Martha C. (2007): *Frontiers of Justice: Disability, Nationality, Species Membership*. Cambridge, MA: Belknap Press.
Ostrom, Elinor (1990): *Governing the Commons: The Evolution of Institutions for Collective Action*. Cambridge, New York: Cambridge University Press.
Plato (1991): *The Republic Of Plato*. Second edition. Allan Bloom (Trans.). Second edition. New York: Basic Books.
Rand, Ayn (1996): *Atlas Shrugged*. New York: Signet.
Rawls, John ([1951] 1999): "Outline of a Decision Procedure for Ethics". In: Rawls, John: *Collected Papers*. Samuel Freeman (Ed.). Cambridge, MA: Harvard University Press, pp. 1–19.
Rawls, John ([1974] 1999): "Reply to Alexander and Musgrave". In: Rawls, John: *Collected Papers*. Samuel Freeman (Ed.). Cambridge, MA: Harvard University Press, pp. 232–253.
Rawls, John ([1975] 1999): "The Independence of Moral Theory". In: Rawls, John: *Collected Papers*. Samuel Freeman (Ed.). Cambridge, MA: Harvard University Press, pp. 286–302.
Rawls, John ([1980] 1999): "Kantian Constructivism in Moral Theory". In: Rawls, John: *Collected Papers*. Samuel Freeman (Ed.). Cambridge, MA: Harvard University Press, pp. 303–358.
Rawls, John ([1985] 1999): "Justice as Fairness: Political, Not Metaphysical". In: Rawls, John: *Collected Papers*. Samuel Freeman (Ed.). Cambridge, MA: Harvard University Press, pp. 388–414.
Rawls, John (1999): *A Theory of Justice*. Revised edition. Cambridge, MA: Belknap Press.
Rawls, John (2005): *Political Liberalism*. New York: Columbia University Press.
Riker, William (1982): *Liberalism Against Populism: A Confrontation Between the Theory of Democracy and the Theory of Social Choice*. Reissue. Long Grove, IL: Waveland Press.
Schmidtz, David (2006): *The Elements of Justice*. Cambridge: Cambridge University Press.
Schmidtz, David (2011): "Nonideal Theory: What It Is and What It Needs to Be". In: *Ethics* 121. No. 4, pp. 772–796.
Sen, Amartya (1983): "Capability and Well-Being". In: Nussbaum, Martha/Sen, Amartya (Eds.): *The Quality of Life*. Oxford University Press, pp. 30–53.
Sen, Amartya (1980): "Equality of What?" In: McMurrin, Sterling M. (Ed.), *The Tanner Lectures on Human Values, Volume I*. Cambridge: Cambridge University Press. Pp. 195–220
Sen, Amartya (2009): *The Idea of Justice*. Cambridge, MA: Harvard University Press.
Strawson, P.F. (2008): "Freedom and Resentment". In: McKenna, Michael/Russell, Paul (Eds.): *Free Will and Reactive Attitudes: Perspectives on P.F. Strawson's "Freedom and Resentment"*. Aldershot: Ashgate, pp. 19–37.
Thrasher, John/Vallier, Kevin (2013): "The Fragility of Consensus: Public Reason, Diversity and Stability". In: *European Journal of Philosophy*. Early View Online. DOI:10.1111/ejop.12020 (Accessed May 20, 2015).
Vallier, Kevin (2011): "Consensus and Convergence in Public Reason". In: *Public Affairs Quarterly* 25. No. 4, pp. 261–279.

Vallier, Kevin (2014): *Liberal Politics and Public Faith: Beyond Separation*. New York: Routledge.
Vallier, Kevin/D'Agostino, Fred (2013): "Public Justification". *The Stanford Encyclopedia of Philosophy*. http://plato.stanford.edu/archives/spr2014/entries/justification-public/ (Accessed June 18, 2018).
Vallier, Kevin/Weber, Michael (Eds.) (2016): *Political Utopias: Contemporary Debates*. Oxford, New York: Oxford University Press.
Van Schoelandt, Chad (2015): "Justification, Coercion, and the Place of Public Reason". In: *Philosophical Studies* 172. No. 4, pp. 1031–1050.

Elena Irrera
Respect as an Object of Equal Distribution? Opacity, Individual Recognition and Second-Personal Authority

Abstract: In this paper I pursue the possibility of addressing respect not only in terms of a theoretical support for the articulation of distributive policies, but also and especially as an object itself of equal distribution. I work out a specific model of "respectful treatment" of minority subjects which, if displayed by institutions and their representatives, may prove well-suited to (i) handle claims of recognition related to certain aspects of the identity of those who are issuing the request (e.g. linguistic, ethnic, religious, cultural); (ii) acknowledge the moral authority of the subjects who have advanced such claims. With a view to this, I critically engage with two normative models of equal respect for people: (1) Carter's idea of "opacity respect", which is premised on the idea that respecting people requires treating them as endowed with a minimum threshold of empirical agential capacities; (2) Galeotti's paradigm of equal respect as an individualising act of recognition.

1 Setting the issue

Over the last few decades, many attempts have been made within certain areas of political philosophy to work out conceptual patterns able to both theoretically frame and normatively respond to problematic cases of value conflict in multicultural societies. One issue of particular concern has been prominently addressed by several scholars: the need to clarify what ethical principle(s) should ultimately be invoked by political institutions and their representatives so as to accommodate specific requests of recognition advanced by individuals as belonging or adhering to minority groups (i.e. groups like those of ethnic, religious and/or cultural origin that experience certain kinds of disadvantage within a larger society). A significant number of studies have proposed to identify such a principle with the value of respect, qualifying it as one equipped with a distinctive ability to inform a wide net of human relationships within political communities (ranging from interactions of an "asymmetrical" kind between citizens and institutions to "horizontal" confrontations between citizens endorsing conflicting lifestyles, convictions and practices). Scholars have increasingly resorted to the idea of respect for persons as a particularly promising way of coping with issues of social justice (such as struggles over religion, nationality and gender), which any strategic approach based on mere appeal to principles of distribution of income, wealth and social positions would be unable to frame.[1]

In fact, redistributive policies must come to terms with the idea that the extant standards of civic participation, social success, organisation of work, and education systems are originally patterned on the needs and aims of the dominant group, as well as on the social and linguistic practices of its members.[2] This is why – as several proponents of egalitarian theories of justice have argued – a fair distribution of material resources can be implemented only in relation to the urgency of redressing the disadvantages experienced by minority members in terms of an equal recognition of their worth as persons. Elizabeth Anderson, for instance, treats recognition as a *precondition* of distributive processes.[3] Her approach to equality rests on the assumption that all human persons are equal in moral status, independently of their economic and/or social position within a given political community. Although the underlying principle of Anderson's theory appears to be widely endorsed among distributive egalitarians, she denies that inequalities can be removed by way of pure redistributions of wealth and political offices. On her theory of "democratic equality" – justice, if understood in terms of equality, requires primarily to put an end to oppressive social relationships, so as to set the basis for a community in which citizens relate to one another as equals deserving respect.[4]

In so doing, she envisions an alternative solution to issues of social justice with respect to that ideal of egalitarian distributive justice that she calls "luck egalitarianism". Despite their divergences, adherents of luck egalitarians (among whom, on Anderson's view, we find John Roemer, Erik Rakowski, Thomas Nagel, Ronald Dworkin, Gerald Cohen), agree on the idea that justice as equality ought to eliminate as far as possible the impact that bad luck exerts on people's lives (on condition that luck falls on them through no faulty conduct or voluntary choices).[5] Contrary to luck egalitarians, Anderson proposes to shift

---

[1] See Galeotti 2002, Young 1996, and Kymlicka 2007. On the conceptual distinction between specific issues of distribution and recognition see Fraser 2003, who contends that "[R]edistribution and recognition do not correspond to two substantive societal domains, economy and culture. Rather, they constitute two analytical perspectives that can be assumed with respect to any domain".
[2] See Testino 2010, p. 50.
[3] Cf. Anderson 1999, especially p. 289. Cf. Fraser (1995, 2003) and Testino 2010.
[4] Cf. Anderson 1999, pp. 312–337. Cf. Arneson's account of Anderson's position in Arneson 2000.
[5] Cf. Anderson 1999, pp. 287–288.

the priority accorded by them to private distributions of material goods towards an interplay of recognition and distribution designed to foster equal participation of each member of the political community in the social life and in the political process.

Recognition, however, can be envisaged not only as a precondition of distributive policies. When it comes to meeting the needs of minority subjects, it can also be viewed in its own way as an *object* of equal distribution among individuals.

An alternative way of thinking of recognition as free from domination by rank or status is that of qualifying it as one which individuals owe to each other simply as moral agents, independently of their desert or status as citizens. As I will suggest in this paper, respect can be regarded as an object of *equal* distribution among individuals, especially when it comes to meeting the needs of minority subjects. The need to assign equal respect to individuals as such raises a fundamental question: when it comes to according respect to people, is there a paradigm the implementation of which would prove more profitable than others in securing "non-proportional" equality of treatment? To this question I will endeavour to provide an answer by proposing a pattern of respectful treatment of minority subjects which, if displayed by institutions and their representatives, may prove well-suited to (i) handle claims of equal recognition related to specific aspects of the identity of those who are issuing the request (e.g. linguistic, ethnic, religious, cultural), and also to (ii) acknowledge the moral authority of the subjects who have advanced such claims. The pattern at stake brings together two normative models of equal respect for people. The first interpretive model, called "opacity respect", is defended by Ian Carter within an attempt to establish if there is a property which, if possessed by individuals to an equal degree, compels citizens and institutions to treat them in accordance to the principles of egalitarian justice.[6] Carter suggests that respecting persons involves treating them as endowed with a minimum threshold of empirical agential capacities, and that this occurs when the respecting subjects hold back from critically assessing the specific degrees in which such capacities are exhibited by each individual. On his view, evaluative abstinence – as an attitude that should be kept even when the varying capacities of individuals are disclosed to the observers by way of a public display of convictions, practices and lifestyles – finds its ultimate justification in the principle of recognition of the value of human dignity. Dignity is not thought of by Carter as an abstract, impersonal and uninfringeable property of human beings; it is rather conceived as an "outward" feature that is

---

6 See Carter 2011. Cf. Carter 2008.

vulnerable to inappropriate exposure and to consequent attacks by individuals and/or institutions.

The second model of respect for persons I will present is the one proposed by Anna Elisabetta Galeotti, who takes issue with respect in terms of a political value that has recently gained prominence in the struggles for recognition of the identities of oppressed, subordinated or marginalised groups.[7] Showing equal respect for persons, on her view, requires an individualising act of recognition, that is, a practice which, "looking into" each individual, takes also a rich battery of subjective habits and underlying ethical principles into account (such as those characteristic of one's original ethnic group or those proposed by religious and/or cultural groups to which one might decide to adhere more or less deliberately throughout subsequent phases of one's life). Galeotti expresses the need to work towards a politics of identity in which equal respect is exhibited by institutions through the acknowledgement of specific features of each minority group. On the basis of such a normative model of recognition, individuals and groups get respected not *apart from*, but *in virtue of* the featuring traits of their identity. My aim in this paper is to suggest that the two theoretical models can be understood as progressive steps of a possible intellectual path of equal recognition of minority members as persons.

2 The notion of "minority"

A critical enquiry on issues of respect for minority subjects and their relationships to a socially entrenched majority and/or political institutions should take its move from a preliminary conceptual clarification of the notion of "minority". Generally speaking, the word "minority" denotes a sociological category applicable to groups of individuals living in a given community, i.e. groups whose featuring traits (e.g. ethnical, religious and/or cultural) are differentiated from and, all the same, defined in relation to a given majority of people who live within the same community (we might refer to a geographical, political or, more broadly, to a moral community with no specific geographical or political boundaries). Most frequently, by "minorities" we mean groups which do not enjoy a well-grounded stability and/or public recognition within a certain context, being equipped with scant power and low social status in relation to those who, in the same context, hold the majority of positions, roles, and social power. The most prominent qualifying traits of a minority are a limited access to material and/or

---

7 See Galeotti 2008 and 2010.

non-material resources, a recent entrance in a certain society (see for instance immigrants), ethnic and/or religious specificities the maintenance of which risks to be threatened, a possible history of discrimination[8] and lack of adequate participation to the political process.

In this light, majority-minority relations (as well as minority groups taken by themselves), are not necessarily to be specified in terms of numerical proportions. An approach enabling to classify minorities in terms of emerging forms of disadvantage[9] appears to be a more promising way of setting the issue, not least because it grants special attention to individuals belonging to groups which, if considered from a purely numerical perspective, would not be regarded as minorities and, as a consequence, would risk to be excluded from those in need of special treatment (we might for instance think of "groups" like women – especially those living in developing countries or non-liberal nations – which, although being numerically outweighing, seem to be especially vulnerable and liable to various forms of discrimination under a combination of aspects, e.g. economic, social, professional, etc.).

Various cases of disadvantage are experienced when the pursuit of the cultural and/or religious practices that define someone's identity is penalised or burdened by laws and majoritarian practices. Special policies might be adopted to address specific types of demands issued by minority groups in view of the promotion of both their own welfare and a condition of equality with regard to the majority. Among such demands we might find claims for exemptions or for assistance to do those things the majority can do unassisted, requests for self-government by ethnic, cultural or national groups, and external rules restrictive of the liberty of non-members, being devised with a view to protecting the members' culture.[10]

Viewed from the perspective of a confrontation between minority groups and the relevant majority, the task of conceptualising a group as a minority can be understood as a preliminary step in the process of devising and implementing targeted policies, i.e. strategic plans designed to redress various forms of injustice. For the scope of this essay, I shall suggest that the concept of "minority group" can be ultimately framed in terms of a cluster of individuals sharing goods and values whose pursuit is at risk in societies characterised by the presence of a dominant culture. By addressing the representatives of political institutions, such individuals advance them a three-fold request: (i) a request for op-

---

[8] See Butera/Levine 2009, p. 2.
[9] Cf. Testino 2012.
[10] Examples of these different claims are provided in Levy 1997, pp. 34–36.

portunities and resources able to secure the pursuit of their life-plans within the public dimension; (ii) the request for specific forms of redress of an experienced disadvantage; (iii) a more "foundational" request, i.e. that for recognition of the individual authority of minority subjects to advance claims of equal treatment in relation to the majority.[11] To such claims, institutions are called not only to offer concrete and targeted responses, but also to implement an attitudinal model that secures an equal distribution of respect among people.

3 Carter's "opacity respect" model

Having clarified the meaning of "minority subject", I shall now attempt to work out a conceptual pattern of respectful treatment applicable to individuals who refer to such a category. My discussion will leave aside the possibility of framing minority rights as collective (or group) rights instead of rights of individuals (a possibility which, in recent years, has been the object of stark scholarly controversy[12]). I will rather assume that respect (i) should be accorded to individuals, and also that (ii) it should be accorded to them not as members of a given minority, but as moral agents who claim recognition of their possibility to pursue their chosen life-plans on an equal footing with others.

In view of this I shall critically address two models of respect for persons and/or minorities. The first model is devised by Carter and called "opacity respect" (*OR*), being designed to frame respectful actions towards individuals *qua* human, regardless of membership in minority groups that might contribute to qualify aspects of individual identity. The *OR* model is fully in keeping with the search for a suitable normative ground for the setting of an egalitarian theory of justice. The various approaches on the egalitarian ideal find substantial agreement on two basic ideas: (i) there is one (or more than one) property in the light of which persons, independently of context-related variables or empirical capacities, appear to be equal; (ii) that property justifies and binds institutions to accord people an equal treatment.

Carter's investigation is inspired by the need to provide a tentative answer to the following question: why ought any good ever to be distributed equally among people? Some have answered that people ought ultimately be "treated as equals" – that is, with equal concern and respect. Understood in these terms, respect

---

[11] The idea of authority at stake finds support in the idea of "second personal authority" devised by Darwall (2006).
[12] For an in-depth treatment of the issue and some positions adopted by scholars see Shapiro/Kymlicka 1997. Cf. Kymlicka 2007.

represents the grounding reason of an equal distribution of (material and/or immaterial) goods. On the other hand, respect appears as the object itself of a distributive process if we ask a more "foundational" question: in virtue of which property ought people to be accorded respect in an equal measure?[13]

Notably, each and every distribution must be conducted in the light of a certain rationale; the property in the light of which people deserve equal respect must not reside in empirically tested capacities (e.g. natural qualities and/or inclinations like intelligence, sensitivity etc.) that admit of various degrees, nor should it be identified with a metaphysical quality that cannot be empirically verified.[14] In the attempt to overcome such difficulties, Carter suggests to take into account a property that had already been detected by Rawls in his *A Theory of Justice* with a view to establishing the bases of equality: the one which he calls *range property*.[15] A range property is a "binary" one: it is either possessed or not possessed. If possessed, such a property ought to be singled out apart from the possibility that different people exhibit it according to a variety of degrees. On Rawls' view, equality among human beings finds its ground in the idea that each of them shares a basic level of "moral personhood". As he explains, moral persons are characterised by their 1) being able to formulate a specific conception of goodness; 2) possessing (and being able to attain) a sense of justice, that is, a desire to apply and act (at least to some extent) in compliance with principles of justice.[16] While Rawls holds the capacity for moral personhood to be a sufficient condition for equal justice,[17] Carter pushes the Rawlsian discussion a step further by asking what reason/s make(s) the range property morally relevant. Most crucially, we might wonder why a fair treatment of human beings ought to be exclusively grounded on an established range property.[18]

To answer these questions, one must identify a moral reason independent of the range property itself. Carter's investigation is premised on the idea that, in order to supply persons with an authentically respectful treatment, it is necessary to address them "as equals", and that this may happen only by abstaining from evaluation of any variable capacity that might supervene to qualify the

---

13 See Carter 2011, p. 538, footnote 1. Carter uses the expression "treating as equals" in a broad sense, i.e. as equivalent to the expression "according equal treatment". He deliberately neglects Dworkin's distinction between the two phrases, especially his use of "according equal treatment" with exclusive reference to distribution of material goods (cf. Dworkin 1977).
14 The difficulty above illustrated has been labelled as "Williams' dilemma" (Williams 1962).
15 See Rawls 1999, pp. 444–445.
16 See Rawls 1999, pp. 412–418. Cf. Carter 2011, pp. 548–550.
17 See Rawls 1999, p. 442.
18 See Carter 2011, p. 549.

bases of one's moral personhood.[19] Were it not so, the way in which external observers assess people would lead to forms of unequal treatment in terms of respect. On Carter's reading, respect is a substantive moral attitude that implies safeguarding what he calls the "external dignity" of human beings. Generally speaking, we might think of dignity as a value which, being possessed by each and every individual, implies the authority to vindicate and the mutual duty to accord it.[20] If conceived as an intrinsic and impregnable human value, dignity does not get lost, not even when the individual who possesses it undergoes extreme forms of injustice and humiliation.

On the other hand, dignity can also be observed in relation to its "outward" aspect, which can be described as an array of distinctive qualities inclusive of composure, self-control and discretion.[21] Visible expressions of human dignity are found in the public exhibition of convictions, attitudes and actions that makes individuals vulnerable to the judgement of one's fellow-humans. Outraging or deliberately rejecting a request of respect advanced by a given individual risks to produce a loss of self-esteem and a sense of distrust towards one's own distinctive life-plans.[22] Although outward dignity is the kind of dignity to which an attitude of evaluative abstinence ought to be applied, Carter's argument paves the way for the idea that the ultimate ground of the respect owed to persons to an equal degree lies in their intrinsic value as human beings and moral agents, the latter consisting in a shared minimal level of moral competence.

4 Critical remarks to the *OR* model

The pattern of respectful recognition worked out by Carter is generally addressed to cases of human interaction in which the outward dignity at risk is the one possessed by single individuals. As it has been proposed by Ceva and Zuolo,[23] such a model can be developed in terms of a promising strategy of management of "vertical" relationships, such as those occurring between an institutionalised majority and minorities in search of fairer opportunities for political participation. Ceva and Zuolo have contended that an appeal to the toleration of minoritarian practices and principles of conduct made by political institutions should

---

[19] See Carter 2011, pp. 550–551.
[20] See Darwall 2006.
[21] See Kolnai 1976, pp. 253–254, 258–259.
[22] On the relationships between lack of respect for a person and the self-respect cultivated by individuals see Taylor 1995, pp. 157–178.
[23] See Ceva/Zuolo 2013.

be backed by a model of respectful treatment that draws on the attitude to opacity.[24] In this light, minority members would be regarded as equally endowed with a minimal capacity for autonomous self-legislation, and treated as "opaque" with regard to those features that, by qualifying their outward dignity and degree of moral competence, would make them exposed to prospective negative evaluations, prejudices and/or discriminations. On their view, attitudes and practices grounded on the model of opacity respect would allow the representatives of political institutions to face two different kinds of requests. The first includes specific requests of recognition advanced by minority subjects (such as demands of preferential treatment that enable them to keep with their practices and beliefs when the pursuit of them is at risk, or requests for redress of past injustices). The second is concerned with their authority to participate as co-authors in the decisional process aimed at establishing what they are allowed or not allowed to do in relation to particular issues.[25] A mere toleration-based strategy for handling the relationships between majority and minorities, if not supported by the ideal of equal respect, is unable to frame and respond to procedural problems stemming from the unequal participation of minorities in public deliberation.[26]

The possibility of treating minority subjects as "opaque" with reference to their specific history and traditions is undoubtedly inspired by the idea that equal respect between majorities and minorities should be "vertically" allocated by institutions, and the main value of the normative model of opacity respect seems to reside in its power to avoid distortions and initial prejudices in the communicative process between the representatives of minorities and those of the political institutions to which their claims are advanced. Nevertheless, it might be suggested that Carter's model of respectful treatment, conceived by itself, does not promote a valorisation of the identities of minority groups in search of recognition. In fact, as it is reasonable to assume, the search for one's own dignity goes through and is enhanced by pursuit of the distinctive values and practices of one's culture of reference. Adopting opacity respect as an exclusive model of respectful treatment with regard to minority subjects might risk to degenerate into an attitude of institutional indifference towards them and their condition of disadvantage.

What is more, mere recognition of the equality of individuals on the basis of their shared possession of a minimum of moral properties does not by itself offer

---

24 The authors argue that the idea of toleration, taken by itself, is unable to capture the procedural problems deriving from the unequal participation of minorities in society.
25 See Ceva/Zuolo 2013.
26 See Ceva/Zuolo 2013. Cf. Jones 2007.

directions towards the implementation of strategies for the reduction of inequalities. Such strategies require an exploration of specific aspects of the minoritarian cultures at issue, and the initially adopted "opacity condition", then, ought to make room for a different outlook: one that aims at "looking into" the particular identity of minority groups.

5 Galeotti's model of equal respect

A different model of respectful treatment of minoritarian identities has been proposed by Galeotti. As she points out, an implementation of patterns of equal recognition exclusively based on an attitude of "impersonal neutrality" risks to generate a condition of "blindness to differences" which, in its turn, not only prevents the adoption of targeted measures able to foster socio-economical equalities between majority and minorities, but also jeopardises the possibility of a fair participation of minority subjects to the political process.[27] Galeotti shares Carter's idea that the members of a political community should be treated on an equal footing, given their sharing the moral condition of persons worthy of respect *qua* persons. Understanding the political principle of respect is a precondition for intervention whenever the principle at stake is not recognised.[28]

The idea of a respect equally owed to persons "*qua* persons" is compatible with the possibility of exhibiting such an attitude throughout individualising acts of recognition, i.e. actions that take their specific minority traits into account.[29] For it is through the expression and active exercise of socially entrenched practices and convictions that an abstract ideal of moral personhood finds concrete actualisation. Equal respect can be progressively exhibited throughout a series of measures that, being contextually agreed, enable minority subjects to enjoy the same range of opportunities made already available to the majority. The allocation of equal respect between majority and minorities allows the latter to coexist with their collective identities without being (and feeling themselves) discriminated, humiliated or intimidated, and puts them in the appropriate condition to develop self-esteem and self-respect.[30]

On Galeotti's view, a public recognition of specific differences represents an indispensable premise to the valorisation of the individual dignity of minority

---

[27] See Galeotti 1999, p. 26.
[28] See Galeotti 2010, p. 3.
[29] See Galeotti 1999, p. 85.
[30] See Galeotti 1999, p. 52.

members.[31] The acknowledgement of one's dignity requires a re-consideration of one's distinctive features "purified" from a range of negative meanings that might possibly be attached by external observers.[32] This suggests that, in order to accord equal respect between majority and minorities, the representatives of political institutions coping with minoritarian requests should ground their responses on an attitude opposite to that of opacity.[33] If adopted as an institutionally framed attitude, opacity as such might convey an image of respect as mere "impersonal obligation", implying a possible failure to grapple with certain socio-economic inequalities between majority and minorities. This is why Galeotti, borrowing an expression from Stephen Darwall, claims that equal respect should be "second-personally" addressed. In his *The Second Person Standpoint. Morality, Respect and Accountability*, Darwall contends that issues like moral obligation, reciprocal respect and recognition of personal identity are ultimately related to the following idea: morality is concerned with types of request that human beings are legitimately entitled to address each other *qua* beings in possession of a distinctively personal authority, especially when the latter is violated by acts of injustice or episodes which betray a lack of recognition. By advancing requests for recognition or claims of redress for past injustices, every individual pretends to be treated by her interlocutor as a "you", that is, to be recognised by the interlocutor as a "second person" deserving of consideration.[34] On Darwall's outlook, moral agency is a matter of complying with duties of justice towards an individual (i.e. the "second person") who can be regarded as a contingent example of an impersonal "other". An act of recognition of the individual's authority can be seen as an application of the universal principle of human dignity.

Although believing that the nature of equal respect is essentially second-personal, Galeotti expresses reservations towards Darwall's idea that claims for respect should be understood as requests that single individuals advance in virtue of an impersonal morality.[35] As she explains, Darwall is right in claiming that respect requires adopting a second-personal perspective, but he fails to notice that a more promising account of recognition respect should take the form of an individualising act of recognition towards a specific "you". On her account, it is throughout the acknowledgement of the equality between an "I" and a "you" – both equipped with a given identity – that an ideal of moral partnership

---

31 See Galeotti 1999, p. 38.
32 See Galeotti, 1999, p. 37.
33 See Galeotti 1999, pp. 88–89.
34 See Darwall 2006, especially pp. 3–15.
35 See Galeotti 1999, pp. 88–89.

can be reached.[36] Galeotti maintains that, when it comes to the relationships between a majority and minorities, an act of "valorisation" of "second persons" endowed with certain traits can be viewed as a valid alternative to pure "recognition as obligation" and, more specifically, as an instrument of a more equal inclusion.[37] If, on the positive side of the issue, such a model prevents the possibility of turning respect into an attitude of indifference towards people,[38] on the negative one it offers room for critical remarks. As Galeotti herself recognises, one might think that a politics of recognition based on the administering of a differential treatment risks to violate both the ideal of equal respect and the attitude of liberal neutrality,[39] endorsing social fragmentation[40] and even a stigmatisation of minority members, with negative effects on the subjects' self-esteem.[41] What is more, a recognition of the specific nature of minority subjects, even if finalised to the promotion of equal respect, might cause institutions to lose sight of those aspects which individuals ultimately share, that is, a minimum of agential capacity. In the last place, Galeotti does not seem to make room for the possibility of according respect to minority subjects even when their claims are not fully accepted. One implication of this is that equal respect is accorded only when the advanced requests are accepted and elicit a positive response by institutions. In the next section I shall suggest that Darwall's model opens the possibility of a respect as recognition of the moral authority of individual agents that can be expressed even when institutions cannot accommodate specific requests.

6 A second personal opaque recognition? Conclusive remarks

The model of recognition of minority instances proposed by Galeotti presupposes that the subjects demanding respect own a certain kind of second-personal

---

36 See Galeotti 2008, pp. 26–27.
37 See Galeotti 2008, p. 27.
38 See Galeotti 2010, p. 6.
39 As Galeotti (1999, p. 19), explains, "neutrality" means that public action should neglect personal differences, such as those related to family origin, ethnicity, religion, sex and skin colour, so as to treat everybody as equals. An attitude of neutrality can also be expressed in the activity of public justification of certain conceptions of justice. On this aspect see Bird 1996.
40 Such an objection is worked out by Galeotti herself in Galeotti 2008, p. 47.
41 This concept is underscored by Carter in Carter 2011. Cf. Anderson 1999, pp. 302–307. Wolff 1998, pp. 113–115.

authority, i.e. one substantiated by their specific ethnic, cultural or religious identity. Recognition of the authority of minority subjects *qua* members of a minority, in its turn, ought to be premised on a more "foundational" type of recognition, that is, the acknowledgement of a minoritarian subject as equal to each of the members of the majority. I suggest that Darwall's concept of "second personal authority" can be used not only to specify a pattern of recognition of identities, but also and especially to supply the *OR* model with further qualification.

Darwall defines the second person standpoint as follows:

> Call the *second-person standpoint* the perspective you and I take up when we make and acknowledge claims on one another's conduct and will.[42]

When a person acknowledges the moral requests issued by another, her act of recognition presupposes an attitude of respect for the value of the addressee of respect as a human being (i.e. respect for her dignity).[43] This value, as Darwall contends, is possessed by the respecting as well as by the respected subject, and it appears to be inseparable from the authority possessed by each of them to address and accept moral requests as legitimate. The shared authority at stake constitutes the ultimate ground of moral action, being structurally correlated to the duty of each person to recognise the authority equally possessed by others.

Darwall's argument suggests that a context-related claim of recognition addressed by a person to another presupposes a double-fold request: on the one hand, a request for the recognition of an experienced condition of disadvantage and the satisfaction of specific needs in a way suitable to the claimant's expectations; on the other, a more general request for the acknowledgement of one's own authority to advance claims, independently of their nature and quality. I believe that the pattern of "second personal recognition" devised by Darwall, although proposed with regard to cases of "symmetrical" interpersonal relationships between individuals, may suitably be applied to cases of interaction between minority subjects and the representatives of political institutions.

It is worth noting that, when it comes to the latter kind of relationship, recognising one's authority to be treated as equal to others might not be incompatible with refusing to implement strategies for the satisfaction of one's requests. In other words, one's dignity might be preserved even when the institutions do not (or not immediately) accept to meet such requests. A refusal by institutions to address specific needs and difficulties experienced by minority subjects does not imply a dismissal of the duty to recognise the moral authority of the claim-

---

[42] Darwall 2006, p. 3.
[43] See Darwall 2006, pp. 1–12 and 243–245.

ants. If this is the case, the second-personal authority of a minority subject will not reside in her substantive views of the good and chosen practices, but in the subject's dignity as a human being equal to the others – i.e. the dignity recognised through an attitude of "opacity respect".

Although the respect owed to minority subjects entails a consideration of their own identity-traits, the basis[44] of such a respect seems to reside in one's *authority* to engage in specific pursuits and life-plans, not in the pursuits and life-plans themselves. This is why I suggest that a plausible model of respectful treatment of persons belonging to minority groups ought to be premised on a "foundational" acknowledgement, that is, one in which the attitude of "opacity" towards their identity-traits is not expressed in an impersonal form, but proceeds along a path of recognition of each individual as a "you" deserving to engage in specific practices. Opacity respect may pave the way for the possibility of according individualising acts of recognition and implementing strategies for their actualisation. This second kind of recognition, when accorded by the representatives of political institutions, ought to presuppose a knowledge of the characteristics and the problems experienced by certain minority subjects. We might refer to the latter type of recognition as an "operational" phase of respect for the subjects at stake, that is, one that brings into effect the process of recognition of their second-personal authority initiated in the "opacity phase". Even when significant difficulties are encountered in the satisfaction of their requests, respect for them will be addressed by institutions by way of a public debate which takes their voices into account.

It is now time to draw some conclusions. I have tried to sketch out a pattern of respectful treatment of minority subjects aimed at the valorisation and the protection of those specific traits that, in absence of a suitable legislation, would make individuals vulnerable to the risk of emargination and even oppression. This pattern, which combines two theoretical models of equal recognition, can be viewed along two different standpoints. On the one hand, the recognition at stake provides a basis for the implementation of policies of economic and social re-distribution that aim to support the (linguistic and/or cultural) diversity of minority groups and their members. Such distributive policies, if framed within an institutional attempt to assign equal respect, do not simply point at overcoming economic disparity with the majority, but also contribute to a transformation

---

[44] The notion of "basis of respect" is developed by Cranor (1975). Cranor distinguishes between the basis of respect (e.g. a quality possessed by the addressee of respect) and "the object of respect" (e.g. persons).

of the traditional mechanisms of access to the job market and of political participation at different levels.

On the other hand, a pattern of assignment of equal respect makes respect itself an ideal object of distribution. Respect is a good accorded independently of any assessment of the distinctive features of minority cultures, and it proves "equal" just in virtue of its being an appropriate response to a certain form of authority possessed by each and every individual: the authority to be recognised as a human being equipped with the capacity to subscribe to certain convictions and lifestyles. In order to be equally distributed, respect ought not to rely on an identification of degrees of capacities and talents supposedly possessed by individuals; it ought rather be rooted on an "opaque recognition" of persons, this being a first step towards recognition of the authority that each person possesses to be treated as a "you" legitimately allowed to advance claims (and not as an "impersonal" subject).

It is worth noting that the neutral model of recognition proposed by the OR theory does not represent a competing alternative to the one centred on a recognition of cultural identities, but it is a foundational one. This implies that the OR might also pave the way for a treatment of minority subjects that, instead of focusing on the valorisation of diversity through a series of affirmative actions, prefers to abstain from offering institutional support to the cultural and/or religious background of minorities as well it does with regard to the majority.

The model of recognition I have proposed in this essay, by adopting a non-neutral recognition (at least in its final phase), appears eminently suitable to foster an idea of respect for persons who, rather than acting as "unencumbered selves",[45] develop and strengthen their identity by subscribing to specific principles and values; these are the same principles and values that enable such persons to mould a respect of themselves as specific individuals, and not as anonymous addressees of impersonal forms of institutional treatment. The pattern of respect so outlined, by grounding the acknowledgement of substantive identities on a preliminary form of recognition of persons as morally authoritative agents, conveys the idea of a human authority which dispenses with – and, all the same, prepares the way for – the individuation of the traits that structure those identities.

The existence of forms of individual standing that are accorded on the basis of specific qualities, skills and talents,[46] does not prevent the possibility of an equal recognition of persons as authoritative moral agents within other distrib-

---

45 The phrase "unencumbered self" is coined by Sandel (1998).
46 See for instance Walzer 1983, pp. 255–256.

utive justice frameworks. The authority in question does not rely on the successful establishment of specific life-plans, but in the capacity of each and every human being to create culture and to and make and inhabit meaningful worlds.[47] Such an authority is possessed even by minority subjects who dialogically forge their own identity in relation to (at least) two forms of membership: membership in the minority group itself and membership in the host community. Although minority requests are premised on a set of values elaborated within the context of a distinctive community; such values are the expression of a capacity of autonomous agency and creativity which deserves the same respect as the one which the majoritarian community tries to protect. This is why, as I believe, a model of recognition so devised can provide an ethically appropriate theoretical framework for distributive policies which, at the same time, is able to throw light on the ultimate goal in view of which such policies are set up: not a simple equal distribution of material goods, but the attempt to create a society in which individuals, at least in some respects, can be valued and treated as equals.[48]

Bibliography

Anderson, Elizabeth S. (1999): "What Is the Point of Equality?" In: *Ethics* 109, pp. 287–337.
Arneson, Richard J. (2000): "Luck Egalitarianism and Prioritarianism". In: *Ethics* 110, pp. 339–349.
Bird, Colin (1996): "Mutual Respect and Neutral Justification". In: *Ethics* 107, pp. 62–96.
Butera, Fabrizio/Levine, John M. (Eds.) (2009): *Coping with Minority Status. Responses to Exclusion and Inclusion.* Cambridge: Cambridge University Press.
Carter, Ian (2008): "Il rispetto e le basi dell'eguaglianza". In: Carter, Ian/Galeotti, Anna E./Ottonelli, Valeria (Eds.): *Eguale Rispetto.* Milan: Mondadori, pp. 54–77.
Carter, Ian (2011): "Respect and the Basis of Equality". In: *Ethics* 121, pp. 538–571.
Ceva, Emanuela/Zuolo, Federico (2013): "A Matter of Respect. On Majority-Minority Relations in a Liberal Democracy". In: *Journal of Applied Philosophy* 30, pp. 239–253.
Cranor, Carl (1975): "Toward a Theory of Respect for Persons". In: *American Philosophical Quarterly* 12, pp. 303–319.
Darwall, Stephen (2006): *The Second-Person Standpoint. Morality, Respect, and Accountability.* Cambridge, MA: Harvard University Press.
Dworkin, Ronald (1977): *Taking Rights Seriously.* London: Duckworth.
Dworkin, Ronald (1981): "What is Equality? Part 2: Equality of Resources". In: *Philosophy and Public Affairs* 10, pp. 283–345; reprinted in: Dworkin, Ronald (2000): *Sovereign Virtue. The Theory and Practice of Equality.* Cambridge: Harvard University Press, pp. 65–119.

---

47 See Walzer 1983, p. 314.
48 Cf. Wolff 1998.

Fraser, Nancy (1995): "From Redistribution to Recognition? Dilemmas of Justice in a 'Post-Socialist' Age". In: *New Left Review* 212, pp. 68–93.
Fraser, Nancy (2003): "Social Justice in the Age of Identity Politics: Redistribution, Recognition, and Participation". In: Fraser, Nancy\Honneth, Axel (Eds.): *Redistribution or Recognition? A Political-Philosophical Exchange*. J. Golb/J. Ingram/Ch. Wilke (Trans.). London, New York: Verso, pp. 7–109.
Galeotti, Anna E. (1999) *Multiculturalismo: filosofia politica e conflitto identitario*, Naples: Liguori.
Galeotti, Anna E. (2002): *Toleration as Recognition*. Cambridge: Cambridge University Press.
Galeotti, Anna E. (2008): "Rispetto come riconoscimento. Alcune riflessioni politiche". In: Carter, Ian/Galeotti, Anna E./Ottonelli, Valeria (Eds.): *Eguale Rispetto*. Milan: Mondadori, pp. 24–53.
Galeotti, Anna E. (2010): *La politica del rispetto. I fondamenti etici della democrazia*. Rome-Bari: Laterza.
Jones, Peter (2007): "Making Sense of Political Toleration". In: *British Journal of Political Science* 37, pp. 383–402.
Kolnai, Aurel (1976): "Dignity". In: *Philosophy* 51, pp. 251–271.
Kymlicka, Will (2007): *Multicultural Odysseys: Navigating the New International Politics of Diversity*. Oxford: Oxford University Press.
Levy, Jacob T. (1997): "Classifying Cultural Rights". In: Shapiro, Ian\Kymlicka, W. (Eds.): *Ethnicity and Group Rights*. New York, London: New York University Press, pp. 22–66.
Rawls, John (1999): *A Theory of Justice*. Revised edition. Oxford: Oxford University Press (first published in 1971, Cambridge, MA: Belknap Press of Harvard University Press).
Sandel, Michael (1998): *Liberalism and the Limits of Justice*. Cambridge: Cambridge University Press (first published in 1982, Cambridge: Cambridge University Press).
Shapiro, Ian/Kymlicka, Will (Eds.) (1997): *Ethnicity and Group Rights*. New York, London: New York University Press.
Taylor, Gabriele (1995): "Shame, Integrity, and Self-Respect". In: Dillon, Robin (Ed.): *Dignity, Character, and Self-Respect*. London, New York: Routledge.
Testino, Chiara (2010): "Redistribuzione vs riconoscimento". In: Biale, Enrico/Ottonelli, Valeria/ Testino, Chiara (Eds.): *Dilemmi politici*. Genoa: De Ferrari, pp. 47–68.
Testino, Chiara (2012): "Minoranze diverse, eguale rispetto". In: Ceva, Emanuela/Galeotti, Anna E. (Eds.): *Lo spazio del rispetto*. Milan: Mondadori, pp. 83–102.
Walzer, Michael (1983): *Spheres of Justice. A Defence of Pluralism and Equality*. Oxford: Martin Robertson.
Walzer, Michael (1997): *On Toleration*. New Haven: Yale University Press.
Williams, Bernard (1962): "The Idea of Equality". In: *Philosophy, Politics and Society* (Series 2). P. Laslett and W.G. Runciman (Eds.). Oxford: Blackwell, pp. 110–131.
Wolff, Jonathan (1998): "Fairness, Respect, and the Egalitarian Ethos". In: *Philosophy and Public Affairs* 27, pp. 97–122.
Young, Iris M. (1996): *Justice and the Politics of Difference*. Princeton: Princeton University Press.

Maria Dimitrova
Responsibility and Justice: Beyond Moral Egalitarianism and Rational Consensus

Abstract: John Rawls stakes the possibility of justice on the autonomy, tolerance and self-reflection of each participant in a deliberative process. The deliberation on the idea of justice behind the veil of ignorance implies a sense of indifference to the otherness of others and their life projects. However, objectivity of justice requires first and foremost a response to others' needs, protection of others' rights as well as engagement with them. The institutions are created and dedicated to this purpose instead of being committed to the fulfillment of the idea of justice as fairness. The very search for justice, without which justice is impossible, is inspired by responsibility. But responsibility and justice are unlikely to be a matter of rational consensus and moral egalitarianism.

John Rawls's theory is an attempt to legitimate "modern constitutional democracy". Rawls's intention is to avoid entanglement in metaphysical and religious debates (cf. Rawls 1985). But impartiality, or rather neutrality, manifests an unconscious backing of the *status quo* not only in politics, but in metaphysics too. Rawls's theory takes for granted many of the assumptions of modern thinking. Most of those assumptions are connected with the supposed reflectivity of modern thought that regards each individual as the autonomous center of her own decisions and acts. In postmodern times, however, many of these 'implicit' assumptions have been called into doubt.

According to Rawls, "a society is a more or less self-sufficient association of persons who in their relations to one another recognize certain rules of conduct as binding and who for the most part act in accordance with them" (Rawls 1971, p. 4). He wants to show justice to be:
1. The political conception that includes the fundamental intuitive ideas of democratic society implied by its institutions and their interpretive traditions,
2. The first virtue of social institutions and all human activities,
3. The norm or standard whereby the distributive aspects of the basic structure of society are to be assessed.

In other words, Rawls aims at a political justification of the modern constitutional regime, uniting into a consistent system three discourse levels accordingly:

1. Indicative or descriptive,
2. Evaluative or axiological,
3. Normative or regulative.

Using this approach, he wants to portray "society as a system of social cooperation".[1] But in order to view the system in its entirety, we need also a point that transcends it. The "original position" functions as a *focus imaginarius*, the point that transcends, allowing the "system of social cooperation" to be seen, assessed, and regulated *sub specie universi*. Legitimation, uniting the three above-mentioned discourse levels, not only constitutes the whole of society as a system of meanings, but goes beyond it by referring to a sort of transcendence. For John Rawls this is no longer the transcendence of power exercised on behalf of eternal entities as God, Human Nature, Reason, State, Society, etc., but the transcendence of the freely chosen ideal of Justice.

Actually, Rawls shares with the contractualists their conviction that humans are equal by their reason and moral sensitivity. This conviction is taken for granted, being a secularized version of the belief that we are all God's children. It is translated further on into an ideal of moral, social, and equal political liberty. John Rawls insists that his main idea of justice as fairness "generalizes and carries to a higher level of abstraction the traditional concept of the social contract" (Rawls 1971, p. 3). However, equality is the most artificial of all social and political relations and always depends on a comparing authority. The place of God, as an authority comparing and governing us, was taken, in secularized culture, by Reason. By the human capacity of reasoning, each of us, assuming the quality of a disinterested observer, could subsume herself under a principle (or norm). Rawls adds that by the same capacity we could deliberate on the principle (or norm) itself.

The ideal of justice that Rawls binds with moral equity and rational consensus has to be, according to him, made concrete by principles. The conversations and deliberations concerning them spring not from a clash of different positions and individual interests that are intrinsic to the totality of group – these would be only particular, conditional positions competing for universal validity (a particular interest elevated to the rank of the universal one), but from positions that are concealed behind the veil of ignorance:

---

[1] Some authors insist with good reason that Rawls is a strong supporter of the welfare state as a special form of modern constitutional democracy. He "constructs a just society as a welfare state". See Knoll 2013.

> No one knows his place in society, his class position or social status, nor does anyone know his fortune in the distribution of natural assets and abilities, his intelligence, strength and the like. I shall even assume that the parties do not know their conceptions of the good or their special psychological propensities. The principles of justice are chosen behind a veil of ignorance (Rawls 1971, p. 12).

Only then, according to Rawls, would the ideal of justice be freely recognized as universal, and, as Kant would say, "*als ob Notwendigkeit*"; it is only hypothetical, but once receiving unanimous approval, it would become apodictic; the "original position" is just simulated, but by its optics all other positions could be judged. Thanks to the veil of ignorance, Rawls believes that all real conflicts and/or agreements can be transcended by means of the original position.

We are not going to give up the idea that a conversation is capable of transcending any reality and we even are going to stress its transcending function. In a conversation, we can reject or agree with any principle, value or fact – at least hypothetically or in an imaginary fashion. However, the conversation among people begins not because of their formal equality and sameness as human beings, but because of their initial inequality and differences as collocutors. If we are the same, why should we communicate? The process of communication is a kind of transmission from one to the other of information, but also personal appeals, responses, commands, advices, requests, etc. Any speech, including one aiming at rational consensus, implies the difference of status between the addressee and the addresser of the message. While the One is speaking, the Other is listening and the words would be reduced to a vain noise, if they were not heard and understood by the collocutor, i.e. if they do not receive an answer. The conversation becomes possible not due to equal positions and mutual indifference, but, first of all, thanks to the difference between the appealing and the responding agencies, and – here we should highlight – thanks to the responsibility of the One for the Other. Any conversation begins as asymmetrical relationship by attention to the collocutor's alterity. But in Rawls' theory participants, being monologically immersed in their own life projects, are understood in advance to be symmetrically positioned around an ideal that is elevated above them; regarding Justice, each participant correlates fairly with the principles of Justice through something like auto-censorship. They make their judgments by considering themselves as particular cases of these general principles. This is the way in which everyone thinks within a reflective indicative or/and evaluative discourse. However, where responsibility and justice are concerned, we are dealing not with descriptions, narrations, judgments or, in general, designative and estimative sentences but rather with imperatives and prescriptions. The otherness of the Other can rupture any ontology, any already established principle and even the entire system of principles, as well as any already reached consensus. Prescriptions form discourse which is de-ontological as it concerns not what is present and done but what should be done.

The prescriptions or imperatives have to be fulfilled. The prescription, command or order does not ask to be thematized or commented on; the true understanding of the order is its execution. 'Close the window!' is properly understood by closing the window. The imperative form always presupposes 'you' and not the third person forms 'he', 'she' or 'they'. But someone who comments on or thematizes the order, expressed on the level of natural language, is transforming it into a descriptive sentence and meta-language – for example, via the reporting sentence, 'He said that I have to close the window'. Then, this reported sentence could be generalized as 'Everybody being in my situation has to close the window'. After these operations the prescription 'Close the window!' is transformed into a principle or norm with validity for everyone – every 'he' or 'she'. But the norm or principle neutralizes the executive force of the order. This is the case with Kant's principle of autonomy: Kant says that the moral imperative requires generalization of the maxim of my behavior as a universal norm and this is precisely a kind of neutralization achieved by declaring prescription as a principle or norm.[2] The result is that Kant's autonomous person is at the same time the prescribing agency and the executive force, the legislator and the judge – all these roles are united in each of us as citizens of modern society. Then, Kant's transcendental subject who lives in each one and is represented by "I think" supervises and controls the coincidence between one's empirical behavior and the universal principle. In this way, according to Kant's conception, the asymmetrical relations – between the appealing and the responding, the governing and the governed, the judging and the judged, and so on – are transformed into and reduced to the equality of everyone before a norm. By the principle of autonomy the difference between the One and the Other disappears; as autonomous citizens we are all made to be average, subsumed under common norm and through it connected with each other only indirectly or rather isolated from each other, deprived of a direct link between us. John Rawls follows Kant's conception of autonomy and *ipso facto* escapes from the universe of prescriptions to that of principles or norms.

The addressee of an order is in a situation quite different from the thinking or judging subject. The recipient of the order has to carry or not carry it out. If one argues about it, comments on it, or negotiates, s/he inevitably substitutes

---

[2] On this point, Jean-Francois Lyotard's excellent analysis is used from his article on Levinas' logic (Lyotard 1986).

the received order for commentary or argument. Doing so, s/he takes the order as a reference to a new speech act. The one who promotes an obligation to the status of a norm moves from the addressee of that obligation to the position of the addresser of a new speech level which declares the norm. The situation is then merely displaced: someone must not have 'taken upon her/himself' the order s/he heard, but makes this order an object of commentary, even if this commentary consists of a declaration that the order is valid as a norm for everybody starting from and including me. An expression can be considered prescriptive only from the point of view of its responder. If it is received as obligation and seizes the one who receives it, the listener becomes 'obliged'. The political and moral questions do not begin with the autonomy enjoyed by 'I think', but with obligation by which 'You' are seized. That is why, we have to speak about another kind of heteronomy – the appeal of the Other for whom I am obliged to take a responsibility. This kind of heteronomy is beyond Kant's and Rawls' horizon. Moreover, both Kant and Rawls declare war on any heteronomy.

The ideal of justice as fairness claims to outline the general institutional framework of social cooperation, but the cooperation could not even start if it were guided by the equal liberty of everyone. Institutional relationships are initially asymmetrical and non-reciprocal. They imply the need for a certain category of citizens and a response on the side of the authorized institutional officials. Institutional procedures are protocols through which the responsible individuals and groups fulfill due process in service to others. Doctors are responsible for patients, teachers – for students, the governing – for the governed, the media – for the public, and so on. The direct relation between the One and the Other is produced if the 'in order to' motives of the One become the 'because' motives of the Other.[3] This transitivity has nothing in common with autonomy, symmetry and tolerance mediated by the principles upon which Rawls' theory is based. The institutions determine not merely actions but interactions; the cooperation implies not autonomy but heteronomy. The heteronomy of others' presence and their needs, in response to which the institutions are created and to whom they are dedicated, imply not equal positions and equality with regard to an ideal of Justice. Instead, they take into consideration the otherness of others and find the resources needed to respond to them properly. The One's obligations are provoked by the primacy of the Others' difference. The objectivity of justice begins with a question about the right of the Other; it limits someone's autono-

---

3 Alfred Schutz' principle of reciprocation of motivation is founded by Schutz himself as the basis of interaction. In fact, if it is traced only in one direction and deprived of the established *post factum* reciprocity, it is rather a principle of transfer of motives. See Schutz 1967, p. 162.

mous expansionistic claims. Responsibility for others requires a protection of their rights and an engagement with them.

The major error of egalitarianism consists in its separation of institutions from responsibility and, accordingly, from care. Justice can be understood as an already institutionalized order, wherein, through formalism and codification, similar cases can be treated in a similar way – formalism is possible because of the common form and common notion by which someone is categorized. Then justice is handed out according to this common form, common rule or common law and it has validity for everyone who can be subsumed under it. In institutionalized justice the relationship between people is mediated by the law to such an extent that it is as if people are only role performers and everyone is correlated merely to the rule and not to the other person. An act is deemed a crime, because it trespasses, violates or does not abide by the law, and not because it has caused damage to the Other.

However, without the responsibility for the Other, which is inscribed even in the anonymity of social functions, institutional behavior would be inconceivable and unjustified. As truth turns into dogma when it is not re-discovered, so, in the same way, justice becomes injustice, deviates and can even involve cruelty and perversions if it is not monitored by responsibility, that is, if we are not searching for a better justice. The very search for justice, without which justice is impossible, is inspired by responsibility.[4] Injustice is already present in the act of depersonalization by bringing people under principles and classifications, substituting anonymous role performers for them. The movement for correction of existing conceptions of justice and the establishment of a better justice is provoked by the otherness of the Other. Because of it, there is an always present distance between *de jure* and *de facto* conditions of human interactions. That distance demands the change of existing policies, of the work of institutions, of the established system – all this is brought into question. The current legislation and the current ideas of rights face criticism and are shaken; they have to be justified; the search for justice is awakened by our sensitivity to that incongruence. The very transition to a better justice is a never-ending attempt to find a more appropriate response to the alterity and rights of the others. When justice falls asleep, relying on its past achievements or some immutable principles and norms, it turns into a caricature of itself. To prevent this from happening, it takes a never-ending self-critique and concern by the state in relation to guaranteeing the rights and freedoms of citizens by improving the institutional framework. But while rights are perceived as 'my rights' and their defense consists in

---

4 Levinas' entire philosophy is dedicated to this idea.

making expansionistic claims by certain groups and individuals within the whole, the state is torn apart by contradictions and struggles. In order to avoid these conflicts, John Rawls proposes his two principles of justice, relying on the honesty, self-reflection and self-control of all for compliance. He also stakes the possibility of justice on notions of autonomy and tolerance that imply a sense of indifference to the otherness of others and their life projects. But the work of institutions and social cooperation itself is inconceivable without non-indifference to each other. In the state, responsibility attaches ones to the others making them associates in justice by means of social institutions.

Bibliography

Knoll, Manuel (2013): "An Interpretation of Rawls's Difference Principle as the Principle of the Welfare State". In: *Sofia Philosophical Review* 7. No. 2, p. 5–34.

Lyotard, Jean-Francois (1986): "Levinas' Logic". In: Cohen, Richard A. (Ed.): *Face to Face with Levinas*. Albany, NY: State University of New York Press, p. 117–153

Rawls, John (1985): "Justice as Fairness: Political Not Metaphysical". In: *Philosophy and Public Affairs* 14. No. 3, pp. 223–251.

Rawls, John (1971): *Theory of Justice*. Cambridge, MA: Harvard University Press.

Schutz, Alfred (1967): *The Phenomenology of the Social World*. Evanston, IL: Northwestern University Press.

Tom Bailey
Habermas's and Rawls's Postsecular Modesty

Abstract: This essay examines neglected aspects of Jürgen Habermas's account of "translating", or "learning", from religions and John Rawls's account of religious contributions to public reasoning under the "proviso" and by "conjecture". It argues that these aspects imply that the secular grounds to which Habermas and Rawls otherwise appeal – deliberative rationality and mutual respect, respectively – have no ultimate authority over religion and, indeed, that, like religions, these grounds presuppose an unjustifiable "faith" in their own possibility. The essay also argues that Rawls pursues this postsecular "modesty" further than Habermas, insofar as, unlike Habermas, Rawls conceives of secular grounds as a contingent and dynamic achievement of citizens in elaborating their particular moral resources. It is suggested that Rawls thus expresses a novel conception of liberal politics, one that is based only on a "faith" in the possibility and value of shareable terms of political justification and is otherwise contingent in its content.

Introduction

This essay examines the resources provided by Jürgen Habermas's and John Rawls's own political theories for rethinking their senses of political conflict and its liberal, consensual and egalitarian, resolution. It does so by focusing on neglected aspects of their treatments of religion. In particular, rather than considering their much-discussed attempts to accommodate religions within a secular consensus, the essay focuses on Habermas's account of "translating", or "learning", from religions and Rawls's account of religious contributions to public reasoning under the "proviso" and by "conjecture". Both accounts concern the peculiar task of transforming religious into shareable terms of political justification. I argue that neglected aspects of these accounts imply that the secular grounds to which Habermas and Rawls otherwise appeal – deliberative rationality and mutual respect, respectively – have no ultimate authority over religion and, indeed, that, like religions, these grounds presuppose an unjustifiable "faith" in their own possibility. This "postsecular modesty" treats the secular framework concerned as merely the internal elaboration of a contingent secular commitment, with no ultimate authority over alternative, religious forms of social coordination.

While this alone sheds a novel light on Habermas's and Rawls's consensus-based frameworks for managing conflict, I also argue that Rawls pursues this modesty further than Habermas. For Rawls conceives of secular grounds not as an independent philosophical constraint that distinguishes secular from religious politics, as Habermas does, but rather as a contingent and dynamic achievement of citizens in elaborating their particular moral resources, including religious ones. By contrasting this vision of politics with the formal and overarching secular frameworks that Rawls and Habermas otherwise endorse, I argue that, at least in these moments, Rawls not only shares with Habermas a postsecular modesty towards his secular framework of consensus, but also envisions a dynamic and contingent sense of the form and content of consensus, and thus a novel conception of liberal politics.

To introduce my analysis of these neglected aspects of their theories, I begin with a brief summary of the more familiar elements of Habermas's and Rawls's secular political frameworks and their attempts to accommodate religions within them. I then consider Habermas's account of "translating", or "learning", from religions, bringing out its postsecular "modesty". I then turn to Rawls's presentation of his "proviso" and "conjecture", and show how he develops their "modest" implications further than Habermas does his own. Finally, and with reference to examples of recognitional and distributive justice, I draw out these implications for a novel conception of liberal politics.

Habermas's and Rawls's secular frameworks

I take it that in their later work, both Habermas and Rawls no longer claim that modern societies are, will be, or should be secular, and that they consequently attempt to accommodate religions in politics. Nonetheless, both continue to endorse "secular" frameworks for politics. That is, for both, political justification must be based ultimately on grounds independent of religion, since these ultimate grounds of political justification must be equally acceptable – or "shareable", or "available" – to citizens of different moral persuasions, the plurality of which precludes finding such equally acceptable grounds among them. If religions are to be accommodated in politics, then, both Habermas and Rawls insist that they must be accommodated only within, or under, such an overarching secular framework.

Thus, in response to sociological literature on the topic, Habermas (2008a, 2008b, 2008d) has replaced his earlier account of social secularization with an emphasis on the "post-secular", understood as a "return" of religions at least to the public spheres of modern societies. Yet he nonetheless continues to treat the justification of state policies as ultimately based on the shareable grounds provided by deliberative rationality, as exercised in the public sphere and parliament. For he conceives of political justification in terms of communicative reasoning, understood as a practice of coordinating social actions through reason-giving that pursues an ideal of objective rational justification – and thus supersedes "pre-modern", conventional ways of organizing social life like religions. Admittedly, Habermas insists on religious freedoms and – particularly now that he acknowledges the "postsecular" character of modern society – on an informal public sphere that is open to all arguments, including religious ones. In political contexts he also relaxes the rational justification required to what is universally acceptable, rather than a universal consensus; to procedures rather than direct participation; and to admit ethical (including religious), pragmatic, and fairly bargained arguments as well as universally "moral" ones. But, these accommodations notwithstanding, at the utmost level of political justification, that of legislative deliberations in parliament, he insists that religious arguments must be filtered out, or excluded, because the ultimate reasons for solving political problems must be equally accessible to all citizens, if the communicative ideal of objective rational justification is to be achieved. At this level, he considers religious arguments to resist the rational criticism necessary for political deliberation, and he therefore limits religions' possible contributions to the cultivation of citizens' non-rational motivation to participate in such deliberations, by developing their sense of collective self-determination, their awareness of the need to give universally accessible arguments, and even their sensitivity to injustices.

The later Rawls (2005a, 2005b) too recognizes the persistence of religions in modern societies like the U.S. – indeed, this was an important motivation for him to replace his earlier exclusion of comprehensive doctrines from political justification with a more accommodating account. Nonetheless, he too insists that religions must ultimately be excluded from political justifications. Rather than communicative reason, he conceives of political justification in terms of mutual respect, understood as a fundamental value implicit in modern liberal democratic societies and distinct from the plurality of moral worldviews, or "comprehensive doctrines", held by religious and other citizens. For him, such respect should structure our social cooperation in the form of a recognized constitution. Admittedly, like Habermas, Rawls makes certain accommodations to religions in his later work: he allows that religious arguments may be introduced into political deliberations over all but basic constitutional issues; that different moral and religious accounts may be elaborated of the mutual respect expressed in a constitution, so that the consensus over it is "overlapping"; and that religious ideas may even be introduced into deliberations over the constitutional requirements of respect, on the condition that "in due course" respectful reasons in support of them can be found (or, at least, this is the standard understanding of his "proviso", which I shall read differently below). Nonetheless, at the utmost level of political justification – for him, deliberations over basic constitutional issues by political officials and voters – Rawls too insists that religious arguments must be excluded, in order for the ultimate justification of political coercion to be equally acceptable to all citizens. For, he claims, providing each other with reasons that each other could accept is the only way for citizens to respect each other in the absence of a shared religious or other moral worldview. Rawls thus echoes Habermas in relegating religions to a supplementary role: at best, he sees them as valuable resources for cultivating consensus over a mutually respectful constitution, insofar as they offer alternative moral terms for expressing and affirming the respect involved.

Despite coming to appreciate the post- or non-secular character of modern societies, then, both Habermas and Rawls continue to endorse secular frameworks for politics, insisting that political justification must be ultimately based on grounds independent of religions, such that these grounds are equally acceptable to citizens of different moral persuasions. In other words, both respond to the moral pluralism, or moral conflict, which religions and other moral worldviews represent by appealing to further, overarching, and "liberal" grounds of ideal consensus. In Habermas's case, these grounds are to be provided by deliberative rationality, as exercised in the public sphere and parliament; in Rawls's case, the grounds are those of a mutually respectful consensus, as expressed in a constitution, government decision-making, and citizens' voting.

Now, there are lively debates under way over how inclusive and acceptable Habermas's and Rawls's secular frameworks are: some commentators welcome their attempts to accommodate religious argument within such frameworks, some propose alternative secular frameworks, and others object to such frameworks simply because, however accommodating they are, they are ultimately secular.[1] Here, though, my concern is not with these debates directly, but with the implications for Habermas's and Rawls's secular frameworks of some neglected claims which they make about the transformation of religious terms into equally acceptable terms of political justification. In particular, I will focus on Habermas's discussions of "translating", or "learning", from religions

---

[1] For representative recent examples, see Cooke 2014, Eberle 2015, Ferrara 2012, Lafont 2013, and March 2013.

and on Rawls's "proviso" about religious contributions to public reasoning and his associated notion of "conjecture". My aim is to show that these notions are distinctively "modest" in implying that the secular grounds to which Habermas and Rawls appeal – deliberative rationality and mutual respect, respectively – have no ultimate authority over religion and, furthermore, that, like religions, these grounds presuppose an unjustifiable "faith" in their own possibility. These implications show Habermas's and Rawls's secular frameworks in a different light, and, at least in Rawls's case, have novel implications for the treatment of religions in liberal politics.

Habermas on the contingency of "translation"

To begin with Habermas, it should first be noted that much of what Habermas says about "translating" or "learning" from religions treats religions merely as sources to be mined for otherwise rational "content". Like his frequent suggestion that religions might provide non-rational motivations to engage in political deliberations, then, these remarks supplement his secular framework, but do not have substantial implications for it. For he is generally careful to distinguish between the universally accessible "content" that might be translated or learned from religion, and the dogmatic "form" in which religions present that content when they appeal to a revelatory justificatory source – in other words, he carefully distinguishes "knowledge" from "faith". As he puts it in his most programmatic essay, "Religion in the Public Sphere", he considers the Western philosophical tradition to have "learned" many of its most fundamental moral concepts from religion by "freeing cognitive contents from their dogmatic encapsulation in the crucible of rational discourse", but he also insists that, "[a]t best, philosophy *circumscribes* the opaque core of religious experience ... [which] remains as profoundly alien to discursive thought as the hermetic core of aesthetic experience" (2008b, pp. 142, 143). As examples of such learning, he refers to the ideas of equality, respect, autonomy, and community (2008b, 2011; Mendieta 2010), and he appears to think that more might be fruitfully learned in this way – think, in particular, of his own appeal to the Christian notion of a given "nature", or "creation", in warning of the dangers of genetic engineering (2003, 2008c). But the neat distinction between rationally and universally accessible "content" and inaccessible justificatory "form" – between "knowledge" and "faith" – means that whatever can be learned or translated from religions is just what can be justified on rational, and not only on religious, grounds. In other words, what can be learned from religions is just what could also be learned from rational enquiry.

However, some of what Habermas claims in elaborating on this translating or learning from religions suggests that it involves much more than this mining of religions for otherwise rational "content". In particular, he claims that it reveals the contingency of his own sense of political justification itself, as well as a certain "faith" that such political justification, like religions, must have in its own possibility.

Habermas makes the first of these two claims, that regarding the contingency of his sense of political justification, most clearly in the final section of "Religion in the Public Sphere", when considering the prospects for successful learning among religious and nonreligious citizens. He begins by remarking that the development of citizens' "mentalities" in this respect is so "unpredictable" that it can hardly be considered "a cognitively steered process at all, one that may be described as a learning process", and that what he considers "learning" in this context is relative to his own sense of rational justification and the secular political framework he bases on it: "these changes in mentality count as complementary 'learning processes' only from the perspective of a specific normative self-understanding of modernity" (2008b, p. 144). This raises the question of the validity of this sense of political justification. Habermas notes that if this validity is assumed, then the problem of learning is simply one of the practical limits of theory, or what he calls the "self-limitation of political theory" – that is, it is simply the problem of the degree to which citizens actually endorse, or can be brought to endorse, the theoretically "correct" sense of political justification. But here Habermas does not insist that his is the "correct" sense of political justification. Rather, he admits that the validity of his sense of rational justification, and hence also of his secular political framework, is contingent:

> [T]his discourse concerning the correct understanding, and the correctness *tout court*, of a liberal constitution and a democratic civic ethos extends into a terrain where normative arguments do not go far enough. The controversy also extends to the epistemological question of the relationship between faith and knowledge, which itself impinges upon key elements of the background understanding of modernity. Interestingly enough, both the philosophical and the theological efforts to define the relationship between faith and knowledge in a self-reflexive manner throw up far-reaching questions concerning the genealogy of modernity (2008b, p. 145).

What is crucial here is that Habermas does not claim or suggest that his theory answers these "far-reaching" questions. That is, he does not claim or suggest that his theory establishes the "correct" distinction and relationship between "faith" and "knowledge". He thus implies that his own sense of rational justification – and thus of what counts as accessible "content", as "knowledge" rather than "faith" – is a contingent one, that the secular political framework he bases on it is therefore normatively contingent too, and, more generally, that the grounds of modern political justification are open to alternative interpretations of rational justification, and its distinction from "faith". Indeed, he confirms these implications in the final sentence of "Religion and the Public Sphere", when he emphasizes that the acceptance of his secular framework depends on "whether secular and religious citizens, from their respective points of view, are prepared to accept an interpretation of the relationship between faith and knowledge that first makes it possible to treat one another in a self-reflexive manner in the political arena" (2008b, p. 147). That is, the acceptance of his secular framework depends on the acceptance of his particular sense of rational justification, or "knowledge".

It is also notable that, as Habermas presents it, this insight into the contingency of rational justification is "learnt" not by rationality alone, but *only* through an engagement with religion. In this, it is an insight into more than the rational "content" of religions to which Habermas otherwise limits himself. In particular, he claims that this insight derives from engagements with such religious perspectives as the "radical orthodoxy" movement, and that "[c]ontroversies with such opponents must be conducted within the proper disciplinary terrain. This means that theological claims can only be met with theological counterarguments, historical and epistemological claims only with historical and epistemological counterarguments". He also proceeds to state that in a "genealogy of modernity's understanding of itself", rationality would not be reducible to scientific rationality, progressively liberated from religions, since scientific rationality itself is rather a product of religions – it is "the outcome of a history of reason of which the world religions are an integral part" (2008b, pp. 146, 147). The contingency of rational justification that is "learnt" from religion can, then, be learnt *only* from religion.

Habermas makes the second claim regarding his sense of political justification, that regarding its "faith" in its own possibility, in elaborating on how his understanding of translation or learning is exemplified by Immanuel Kant's philosophy of religion. He does this particularly extensively in another important essay, "The Boundary Between Faith and Knowledge" (2008c). Notably, there he explicitly dismisses Kant's tendency to reduce religion to a mere source of non-rational motivations or otherwise rational "content" – a tendency that, as I have mentioned, elsewhere Habermas himself shares. In particular, Habermas dismisses the "instrumental function" that Kant gives to religion insofar as "[r]evelation ... makes truths accessible in doctrinal form that human beings '*could and ought to have* arrived at ... on their own through the mere use of their reason'" (2008c, p. 223, quoting Kant 1914, p. 155). Instead, Habermas focuses on reading Kant's accounts of the "highest good" and "ethical community" as expressing a necessary "faith" that individuals' right actions will combine to improve the social world. He calls this a "faith", rather than a moral "duty" or a just political "law", because such a successful combination of actions is too complex to be pursued by individuals or enforced by a state. Yet Habermas insists that it is nonetheless necessary if we are not to "despair" of the possibility of coordinating our social actions rationally. Indeed, he presents this "faith" precisely as the orientation to pursue objective rational justification, by moving from the particular terms employed in our existing communities towards ever more universal ones. That this orientation cannot be established rationally, and yet is necessary for rational coordination, is highly significant. For it follows not only that this orientation exceeds the rational "content" of religion – as Habermas emphasizes, Kant can reveal it *only* through Christian doctrine – but also that rational justification in general, and political justification in particular, rest on a non-rational orientation towards coordinating actions in this way. In other words, for Habermas "knowledge" rests on a "faith" in its own possibility.

These claims about the contingency and the faith of Habermas's secular sense of political justification shed a significant new light on that sense.[2] In particular, they imply that, for Habermas, both rationality and religion promise shareable terms with which political action can be coordinated, and thus in this regard have the same political structure or function; but that neither rational nor religious terms possesses ultimate authority, an authority that would allow either rationality or religion to claim priority over the other – indeed, Habermas implies that each rests on a non-rational "faith" in its own possibility. If our social actions are to be coordinated in shareable terms, Habermas effectively claims, then both rationality and religion promise such terms, but – normatively, at least – the "choice" between them is simply a leap of faith. Habermas's secular framework of political justification, like his theory of rational justification generally, thus appears as merely the internal elaboration of an unjustifiable faith in the possibility of such rational justification, proposed as an alternative to other, equally unjustifiable faiths in the possibility of coordinated action, such as religions.

It is also worth emphasizing that Habermas presents these insights into the contingency and non-rational "faith" of rational justification as insights that cannot be "learnt" by rationality alone, but *only* through an engagement with religion. In this, they contravene his otherwise strict distinction between rationality and faith, by implying that religion can provide truths, or knowledge,

---

[2] These claims are perhaps expressed more pronouncedly, if not more extensively elaborated, in Habermas's more recent essays. See 2010, p. 18, and 2011, p. 28.

not accessible to rationality alone, and even the orientation to truth, or knowledge, that is presupposed but cannot be provided by rationality alone. Thus, on Habermas's account, not only do rational justification in general and political justification in particular rest on a contingent "faith" in their own possibility, but this cannot be understood or achieved without engaging with non-rational religion. To put it bluntly, in these more "modest" moments Habermas accepts that rationality, and with it political justification, cannot be fully understood or achieved without religion.

Rawls on the indeterminacy of consensus

It is this particular kind of normative modesty in the face of religions that I think Rawls develops further than Habermas. Admittedly, like much of Habermas's account of deliberative justification, much of what Rawls says about mutual respect in public reasoning – about what he variously terms "reasonableness", "fairness", "reciprocity", "civility", and "civic friendship" – suggests that he considers this concern to have overarching authority. Indeed, he first presented public reasoning as excluding religions – an infamous footnote to the first edition of *Political Liberalism*, for instance, suggests that public reasoning should exclude the articulation of religious objections to abortion (2005a, n. 32 to p. 243). But he later corrected this, emphasizing that public reasoning does not define or exclude any particular kind of reasoning, and that it requires only that reasoning be done in terms that others could accept, so as to be mutually respectful (2005a, pp. liii–lv). Furthermore, in introducing his "proviso" and the related notion of "conjecture" in his late essay, "The Idea of Public Reason Revisited", he implies that mutual respect itself is a contingent, unjustifiable commitment, analogously to Habermas's presentation of rational justification as a contingent "faith".

Rawls's proviso allows religious and other "comprehensive" ideas to be introduced into political deliberations on the condition that "in due course" supporting reasons acceptable to others can be provided. As he puts it, "reasonable comprehensive doctrines, religious or nonreligious, may be introduced in public political discussion at any time, provided that in due course proper political reasons – and not reasons given solely by comprehensive doctrines – are presented that are sufficient to support whatever the comprehensive doctrines introduced are said to support" (2005b, p. 462). On the standard reading of this, "proper political reasons" are secular ones. But Rawls emphasizes that the proviso does not require comprehensive ideas to be "rational" in any particular sense or to be expressed in any particular way, and that the specification of how, when, and by whom supporting reasons should be provided is postponed to a "due" time. These "details", he writes, "must be worked out in practice and cannot feasibly be governed by a clear family of rules given in advance" (2005b, p. 462). What, then, is the relevant "practice" in which these crucial "details" are to be worked out? It is that of searching for and affirming shared, mutually respectful terms for political justification from among the resources provided by citizens' different moral worldviews. As Rawls puts it here, it is that of recognizing and elaborating "the reasonable comprehensive doctrines that support society's reasonable political conceptions as those conceptions' vital social basis, giving them enduring strength and vigor" (2005b, p. 463). What is significant about Rawls's presentation of the proviso, then, is that, while referring to this pursuit of shared, mutually respectful terms, it leaves their nature otherwise undetermined and their discovery and affirmation to a "due" time. Indeed, Rawls emphasizes that this pursuit cannot be guided by an independent conception – or "rules" – of what mutual respect requires.

"Reasoning from conjecture" contributes to this practice by searching in citizens' worldviews for shareable, mutually respectful terms and grounds for affirming them, despite the fact that conjecturers themselves do not hold these worldviews and that citizens who do may not recognize these particular terms and grounds. As Rawls puts it, in conjecturing "we argue from what we believe, or conjecture, are other people's basic doctrines, religious or secular, and try to show them that, despite what they might think, they can still endorse a reasonable political conception that can provide a basis for public reasons" (2005b, pp. 465–466). What is significant here is that, like that of the proviso, Rawls's account of conjecturing refers to the pursuit of shared, mutually respectful terms of political justification, but leaves their nature and their possible grounds in citizens' worldviews undetermined and postpones their discovery and affirmation. Indeed, reasoning by conjecture can be taken to describe precisely the "practice" of pursuing shared, mutually respectful terms when such terms are ostensibly lacking, and indicates why no independent guidance can be provided – for this "practice" depends on contingent moral resources and their contingent elaboration.

Notably, Rawls's definition of conjecture emphasizes not only the temporal, but also the interpersonal nature of this contingency: when and whether the relevant citizens recognize a conjecturer's attempted demonstration of shareable, respectful terms cannot be known in advance; indeed, a conjecture is made precisely because currently the relevant citizens ostensibly deny that such terms can be found. (In conjecturing we "try to show" others that, "despite what they might think" currently, they "can" affirm some such terms.) Rawls's definition also emphasizes the indeterminacy and contingency of such terms themselves: rather than a single or given set of such terms, we simply pursue *some* respectful terms – in Rawls's words, we pursue "*a* reasonable conception that *can* provide *a* basis for" public reasoning (2005b, p. 466 my emphasis).

Thus, just as in some passages Habermas insists that his sense of shared justification rests on a contingent, unjustifiable orientation to, or "faith" in, its own possibility, in these passages Rawls too claims that his sense rests on a contingent, unjustifiable search for mutually respectful terms. And just as Habermas's secular framework of political justification consequently appears as merely the internal elaboration of an unjustifiable faith in the possibility of such rational justification, so too Rawls presents his own framework as having no ultimate normative authority over others – it is simply the internal elaboration of what it would mean for our shared terms of political justification to be mutually respectful.

This contingent, internal character and this faith can perhaps also be expressed in terms of the orchestra analogy that Rawls employs elsewhere, in the context of explaining his ideal of "social union" (2005a, p. 321, cf. p. 204). For a role in an orchestra gives one reasons for doing certain things *if* one takes that role, but it gives no independent reasons for wanting or having to play at all; one might, quite rationally, play a role in a different "social union", play alone, or not play at all. Pressing the analogy further, by taking a role in an orchestra one is also committing to having one's role coordinated with others' roles by a figure beyond them, the conductor – in this sense, one must have "faith" that the collective activity to which one is committed is possible.

Yet Rawls's "postsecular" modesty also goes further than Habermas's. For he does not specify the framework concerned in terms of an independent sense of rational justification, as Habermas does. He presents it simply as a contingent achievement of a contingent grouping of particular citizens in elaborating their particular worldviews. Thus, while Habermas's framework excludes religions, such that the unjustifiable choice of rational justification excludes religious alternatives – or, the unjustifiable choice of "knowledge" excludes "faith" – Rawls's framework need not, since he conceives of mutual respect as a contingent and dynamic achievement, subject to revision and recreation by means of different religious and other moral resources and different elaborations of them. That terms of political justification be "mutually respectful" is a highly indeterminate requirement, itself requiring interpretation and admitting reinterpretation in the pursuit of them.

Indeed, Rawls's accounts of the proviso and conjecture imply that what is required is merely the pursuit of "consensus" in the sense of proposing justificatory terms that others *could* accept – not that they *actually be* accepted, or that they be part of any determinate set of equally acceptable terms. If so, then for Rawls an attitude of pursuing consensus is sufficient to be "respectful" in politics, and he places no further restrictions on the kind of terms or acceptability required. This suggests that contributions to public reasoning can be "respectful" even if they are incompatible with an existing consensus or if no consensus is actually achieved.

This postsecular modesty is reflected in the "two-way" nature of the engagement with religions that Rawls envisions. Even Habermas's insights into the contingency and "faith" of rational justification are insights "for" rationality, rather than religion, and he otherwise conceives only of a "one-way" translation of religious "content" into rationally accessible terms. In contrast, Rawls conceives of transformations among shareable and unshareable, or "respectful" and un-"respectful", moral terms as going in both "directions", as it were. That is, for him, not only can prevailing mutually respectful terms be (re)articulated in religious and other moral forms, but religious and other moral resources can also provide for new mutually respectful terms. Rawls's proviso and sense of conjecture envision operations of both kinds: the proviso by provisionally admitting religious and other moral terms in view of their eventual incorporation in an existing or revised consensus; and conjecture by pursuing such incorporation either by rearticulating an existing consensus or by developing a revised one.

Modesty and justice

I have argued that in certain neglected aspects of their political theories, Habermas and Rawls recognize the contingency and unjustifiability of the religion-independent grounds on which their political frameworks are based: Habermas with his treatment of the contingent distinction of rational justification, or "knowledge", from "faith", and his understanding of the orientation towards rational justification as itself a "faith"; and Rawls with his account of our unjustifiable search for mutually respectful terms among religious and other moral resources, according to the "proviso" and by "conjecture". By comparing these aspects of their theories, I have further argued that, while Habermas's substantial and independent sense of rationality means that his faith in rational justification excludes religious justification, Rawls's faith in mutual respect avoids such a demarcation from religion, and so admits religious ideas into the elaboration of shareable political terms. In this sense, Rawls's faith in his secular framework expresses a more thoroughgoing "modesty" than Habermas's.

These strands of modesty tell against the common supposition that Habermas and Rawls attribute an ultimate authority to their respective political frameworks. In Habermas's case, this authority is standardly supposed to derive from the universality of the presuppositions of communicative reasoning, which ground his moral and political principles and their application to parliamentary legislation and informal public debate. In Rawls's case, the ultimate authority of his political principles is generally supposed to rest on the values of freedom and equality, as these prevail in modern liberal democratic societies and as he models them in the 'original position' or the requirements of "public reason". In contrast, the aspects of Habermas's and Rawls's treatments of religion that I have considered suggest that each treats his own framework as merely the internal elaboration of a contingent commitment, with no ultimate authority over competing frameworks. Understood in this way, the Habermasian pursuit of deliberative justification or the Rawlsian pursuit of consensus is merely the practice of a contingent "faith" that not all citizens need endorse. Indeed, it could be said that, at least in these moments of modesty, both Habermas and Rawls effectively share the skepticism about their frameworks' ultimate authority that many critics of their treatments of religion have expressed.

However, notwithstanding this modesty, Habermas's demarcation of rational from religious justification leaves the content of his "faith" intact, and this content is more substantial than Rawls's. That is, even while accepting its normative contingency, Habermas insists that – if and insofar as it is pursued – the pursuit of deliberative justification implies and requires the specific political framework that he derives from it. In particular, he insists that it requires that religious arguments be excluded from parliamentary deliberations, on the grounds that such arguments resist the necessary rational criticism and so cannot offer reasons which are equality accessible to all citizens. And, more generally, his framework involves a strong commitment to democratic proceduralism, according to which laws must be produced by appropriately deliberative procedures, and thus be acceptable to all citizens.[3]

In contrast, Rawls's postsecular modesty extends beyond the authority of his political framework to the content of that framework. For, unlike Habermas, Rawls avoids specifying and demarcating that content: he leaves the interpretation and expression of "mutual respect" in citizens' pursuit of shareable terms of political justification to their own contingent elaboration of their contingent moral resources. He thus accepts that other frameworks, including religious ones, may contribute to this task, and that there need not be a single determinate

---

[3] This combination of modesty about his framework's ultimate authority and insistence on its content can be seen in Habermas's recent exchange with Thomas McCarthy. See McCarthy 2013 and Habermas 2013, pp. 377–384.

set of such terms, and so a single determinate political framework, that is shareable by all.

This Rawlsian modesty of authority and content implies a novel sense of liberal politics. It acknowledges the unjustifiable "faith" expressed by the pursuit of shareable political terms, and it envisions such terms as emerging dynamically and contingently from the elaboration of prevailing moral resources, and different resources or elaborations as producing different sets of shareable terms. It thus accommodates religion more thoroughly than the secular frameworks that Rawls, Habermas and their critics standardly propose. For, rather than prioritizing and demarcating a secular political framework, it accepts that other political "faiths" are equally (un)justifiable and it admits religious terms into its pursuit of shareable political terms as much as any other moral terms. At the same time, this modesty does not reduce politics, or the place of religion in politics, to coexistence and compromise, a "modus vivendi" based merely on individuals' and groups' relative bargaining power. Of course, it acknowledges the equal (un)justifiability of other political "faiths", and that religious and other moral resources which are not, or cannot be, elaborated into shareable terms will remain "unheard" in liberal political justification. It might also appeal to the pragmatic concern for avoiding conflict in support of pursuing shareable political terms. But, ultimately, its "faith" is in the elaboration of such terms from prevailing moral resources, rather than merely in political bargaining, as the vital basis of liberal politics.

This modest sense of liberal politics can be exemplified by considering the substantial revisions it implies to Rawls's own egalitarian conception of justice. While in *A Theory of Justice* he derived substantial principles of background and distributive equality from a commitment to luck egalitarianism, in his later *Political Liberalism* he is often supposed to accept that equal basic freedoms may be sufficient for a "reasonable" commitment to freedom and equality.[4] But his postsecular modesty implies even weaker senses of freedom and equality than this. For if the pursuit of shareable terms requires some kinds of freedom of toleration and equality of consideration, Rawlsian modesty implies that the objects and means of this toleration and consideration are to be determined only in and by citizens' elaboration of shareable terms of political justification. Faced with competing conceptions of justice, then, Rawlsian modesty accepts not only that its "faith" in shareable terms has no ultimate authority, but also that the manner in which a political framework might express this "faith" depends on

---

[4] See, for instance, Freeman 2007, pp. 29–42, 324–331, and 381–415.

the contingent contents and elaborations of these competing conceptions themselves.

As an example of recognitional justice, consider how in conflicts over the place of religious symbols in public life conceptions of individual freedom and non-discrimination compete with conceptions of religious and cultural freedoms and equality. In such cases, Rawlsian modesty implies only a "faith" in the possibility and value of shareable terms of justification, without specifying or demarcating what those terms might be. In public life, these terms might concern anything from a secularist exclusion of religion to a democratic inclusion. The "mutual respect" – or the freedom tolerated and the consideration equally given – would simply be expressed in different terms.

Rawlsian modesty has similar implications for issues of material justice. For it implies that the justice of citizens' material advantages and rewards is contingent on the shareable political terms that they might elaborate – or, if these are lacking, on an alternative political "faith". From this perspective, Rawls's own early principles of background and distributive equality are only one set of possible justificatory terms, elaborated on the basis of a contingent commitment to luck egalitarianism and shared only contingently by other citizens. For instance, in conflicts over healthcare provision, such luck conceptions of equality will compete with market conceptions of free choice and fair exchange, with democratic freedoms of self-legislation, and with religious conceptions of responsibility, care, and their limits. The shareable terms that might be elaborated from these competing moral perspectives could thus justify anything from private markets to public provision. And, of course, whether and which religious and other moral resources are, or can be, elaborated into these terms is a contingent matter.

In its Rawlsian form, postsecular modesty is thus a significant challenge not only to the authority of liberal egalitarian conceptions of justice, but also to their liberal egalitarian content. It implies that in engaging competing conceptions, liberal politics can have only a "faith" in the elaboration of shareable terms of political justification, and not require or expect such terms to express any particular liberal conceptions.[5]

---

[5] For their comments on drafts of this essay, I am grateful to Alexandru Cistelecan, Pamela Harris, Manuel Knoll, Hans-Herbert Kögler, Lars Rensmann, and Manon Westphal, and especially to Stephen Snyder. I have also benefited greatly from feedback received at conferences in Bordeaux, Delhi, Florence, Istanbul, London, and Rome.

Bibliography

Cooke, Maeve (2014): "The Limits of Learning: Habermas' Social Theory and Religion". In: *European Journal of Philosophy*. DOI: 10.1111/ejop.12099, visited on 29 January 2016.

Eberle, Christopher J. (2015): "Respect and War: Against the Standard View of Religion in Politics": In: Bailey, Tom/Gentile, Valentina (Eds.): *Rawls and Religion*. New York: Columbia University Press, pp. 29–51.

Estlund, David (1996): "The Survival of Egalitarian Justice in John Rawls's Political Liberalism". In: *Journal of Political Philosophy* 4, pp. 68–78.

Ferrara, Alessandro (2012): "Hyper-Pluralism and the Multivariate Democratic Polity". In: *Philosophy and Social Criticism* 38. Nos. 4–5, pp. 435–444.

Freeman, Samuel (2007): *Rawls*. London: Routledge.

Habermas, Jürgen (2003): *The Future of Human Nature*. Hella Beister/William Rehg (Trans.). Cambridge: Polity.

Habermas, Jürgen (2008a): "Prepolitical Foundations of the Constitutional State?" In: Habermas, Jürgen: *Between Naturalism and Religion: Philosophical Essays*. Ciaran Cronin (Trans.). Cambridge: Polity, pp. 101–113.

Habermas, Jürgen (2008b): "Religion in the Public Sphere: Cognitive Presuppositions for the 'Public Use of Reason' by Religious and Secular Citizens". In: Habermas, Jürgen: *Between Naturalism and Religion: Philosophical Essays*. Ciaran Cronin (Trans.). Cambridge: Polity, pp. 114–147.

Habermas, Jürgen (2008c): "The Boundary between Faith and Knowledge: On the Reception and Contemporary Importance of Kant's Philosophy of Religion". In: Habermas, Jürgen: *Between Naturalism and Religion: Philosophical Essays*. Ciaran Cronin (Trans.). Cambridge: Polity, pp. 209–247.

Habermas, Jürgen (2008d): "Notes on Post-Secular Society". In: *New Perspectives Quarterly* 25. No. 4, pp. 17–29.

Habermas, Jürgen (2010): "An Awareness of What is Missing". In: Habermas, Jürgen: *An Awareness of What is Missing: Faith and Reason in a Post-secular Age*. Ciaran Cronin (Trans.). Cambridge: Polity, pp. 15–23.

Habermas, Jürgen (2011): "'The Political': The Rational Meaning of a Questionable Inheritance of Political Theology". In: Calhoun, Craig/Mendieta, Eduardo/VanAntwerpen, Jonathan (Eds.): *The Power of Religion in the Public Sphere*. New York: Columbia University Press, pp. 15–33.

Habermas, Jürgen (2013): "Reply to My Critics". Ciaran Cronin (Trans.). In: Calhoun, Craig/Mendieta, Eduardo/VanAntwerpen, Jonathan (Eds.): *Habermas and Religion*. Cambridge: Polity, pp. 347–390.

Kant, Immanuel (1914): *Die Religion innerhalb der Grenzen der bloßen Vernunft*. In: *Kants gesammelte Schriften*. Vol. 6. Preussische Akademie der Wissenschaften (Ed.): Berlin: Reimer, pp. 3–202.

Lafont, Cristina (2013): "Religion and the Public Sphere: What are the Deliberative Obligations of Democratic Citizenship?". In: Calhoun, Craig/Mendieta, Eduardo/VanAntwerpen, Jonathan (Eds.): *Habermas and Religion*. Cambridge: Polity, pp. 230–248.

March, Andrew (2013): "Rethinking Religious Reasons in Public Justification". In: *American Political Science Review* 107. No. 3, pp. 523–539.

McCarthy, Thomas (2013): "The Burdens of Modernized Faith and Postmetaphysical Reason in Habermas's 'Unfinished Project of Enlightenment'". In: Calhoun, Craig/Mendieta, Eduardo/VanAntwerpen, Jonathan (Eds.): *Habermas and Religion*. Cambridge: Polity, pp. 115–131.

Mendieta, Eduardo (2010): "A Postsecular World Society? On the Philosophical Significance of Postsecular Consciousness and the Multicultural World Society: An Interview with Jürgen Habermas". Matthias Fritsch (Trans.). In: *The Immanent Frame*. http://blogs.ssrc.org/tif/wp-content/uploads/2010/02/A-Postsecular-World-Society-TIF.pdf, visited on 29 January 2016.

Rawls, John (2005a): *Political Liberalism*. Exp. ed. New York: Columbia University Press.

Rawls, John (2005b): "The Idea of Public Reason Revisited". In: *Political Liberalism*. Exp. ed. New York: Columbia University Press, pp. 440–490.

Part VI: **The Difference Principle**

Peter Koller
A Defense of the Difference Principle beyond Rawls

Abstract: The Difference Principle is one of the most original and disputed components of Rawls' theory of justice. The DP, which is contained in the second of Rawls' two principles, says that social and economic inequalities are to be to the greatest benefit of the least-advantaged members of society. The aim of my paper is to defend the DP, or at least its main idea. To this end, I will first recapitulate Rawls' explication of the DP, and then give a brief review of his theory in general and of his various arguments for the DP in particular. After that, I scrutinize Rawls' justification of the DP, with the result that his arguments do not succeed. Since I nevertheless regard the DP as a sound principle of socio-economic justice, finally I attempt to defend it in a slightly modified form.

1 Rawls' Difference Principle and its main features

The Difference Principle (DP), certainly one of the most significant components of Rawls' conception of justice, has remained more or less unaffected by the revisions of this conception from its initial exposition in *A Theory of Justice* (1971, quoted as TJ) up to its final restatement in *Justice as Fairness* (2001, quoted as JF). Rawls' conception, designed to regulate and govern the institutional basic structure of a modern state-ruled society, is known to consist of two main principles: The first principle focuses on a society's *political order* and demands that every member ought to have equal basic civil rights and liberties insofar as they are compatible with the same rights and liberties for all. The second principle concerns society's *basic socio-economic system* in regard to which it aims to define the justifiable extent of social inequalities that may emerge from this system. Rawls' final formulation of the *second principle*, which contains the DP, runs as follows:

> Social and economic inequalities are to satisfy two conditions: first, they are to be attached to offices and positions open to all under conditions of fair equality of opportunity; and second, they are to be to the greatest benefit of the least-advantaged members of society (the difference principle) (JF, 42f.).

Although Rawls' two principles are closely connected and forming a unified whole, I will mainly deal with the second part of the second principle, the DP, and refer to the other demands only when this is necessary to illuminate the features of the DP under consideration. In order to simplify the matter, I will assume throughout my paper that the first principle, the principle of equal liberty, is satisfied so that there is no need to discuss Rawls' highly questionable proposition that this principle has absolute priority over the second. The aim of my following considerations is to scrutinize the DP and to defend it, though in a slightly modified form that sticks with its main idea.

Rawls' formulation of the second principle with the DP gives rise to a number of questions of interpretation, especially the following: What are the features of social and economic inequalities? What is meant by the statement that the inequalities are to be attached to offices and positions? Who are the least-advantaged members of society? And how is the relationship between the inequalities under consideration and the position of the least-advantaged members to be understood so that the former are to the greatest benefit of the latter? As for these questions, Rawls provides us with more or less definite answers, which, for the moment, I shall summarize briefly without scrutinizing them in detail.

As for the initial question concerning the nature of social and economic inequalities, Rawls defines them as the members' relative shares in certain sets of those societal resources of human well-being which he calls "primary social goods" (TJ, 90ff.; JF, 58ff.). *Primary social goods* in general are characterized by two features: first, they result from social cooperation and are distributed through the society's institutional basic structure; and, second, they are scarce goods of supreme order of which every individual reasonably wants to possess more rather than less, because "with more of these goods men can generally be assured of greater success in carrying out their intentions and in advancing their ends, whatever these ends may be" (TJ, 92).

Rawls proposes a list of such goods which contains five categories: (i) basic rights and liberties, (ii) freedom of movement and free choice of occupation, (iii) powers and prerogatives of offices and positions of authority and responsibility, (iv) income and wealth, and (v) the social bases of self-respect (JF, 58f.). While the first two kinds of primary social goods, i.e. the fundamental civil and political rights, are thought to be subject to the first principle requiring their unconditional equality, the last three kinds, that contain the most important socio-economic resources, fall in the domain of the second principle. This principle permits or even demands inequalities of their social distribution to the extent to which the inequalities are necessarily connected to a socio-economic system that improves the position of the worst-off members of society, provided that they are attached to public offices and social positions open to all under fair equality of opportunity. What is the role of these offices and positions?

Since Rawls' principles of justice apply to the *institutional basic structure* of society rather than to the interpersonal relationships among its members, they address these members not as individuals with their own personal properties and fates, but

> as representative persons holding the various social positions, or offices, or whatever, established by the basic structure. Thus in applying the second principle [...] it is possible to assign an expectation of well-being to representative individuals holding these positions. This expectation indicates their life prospects as viewed from their social station (TJ, 64).

So the DP does not demand to raise the well-being of particular individuals who, for whatever reasons, are worst-off at a certain time of their life, but it rather demands to improve the *social position*, namely the life-time prospects of well-being of the members of the least advantaged social group to the greatest possible extent in a way that meets the condition of fair equality of opportunity.

This leads to the question of how to *identify the least advantaged members* of society whose prospects of well-being could be improved to the greatest possible extent through social and economic inequalities. This question calls for a measure of people's well-being in terms of their share of the relevant primary social goods, including powers and prerogatives, income and wealth, and the social bases of self-respect. Rawls thinks it is possible to aggregate people's relative shares of the various primary goods to an appropriate index that may be used to identify the least advantaged group of society at least in an approximate way. In *A Theory of Justice* we find two suggestions for ways of defining the least fortunate group:

> One possibility is to choose a particular social position, say that of the unskilled worker, and then to count as the least advantaged all those with the average income and wealth of this group, or less. [...] Another alternative is a definition solely in terms of relative income and wealth with no reference to social position. Thus all persons with less than half of the median income and wealth may be taken as the least advantaged segment (TJ, 98).

Provided that there is a way to determine the least fortunate group, we face the following question: How is it possible that social inequalities may amount to the benefit of the least fortunate members, and under what circumstances are they to their greatest benefit? First of all, Rawls assumes that a society is a complete system of social cooperation whose overall product is not a constant sum, but variable depending on the distribution of its members' benefits and burdens.

It appears to be possible to increase the social product through schemes of division of labor including inequalities of power, influence, income and wealth. "By varying wages and salaries", Rawls notes, "more may be produced. This is because over time the greater returns to the more advantaged serve, among other things, to cover costs of training and education, to mark positions of responsibility and encourage persons to fill them, and to act as incentives" (JF, 63). Such inequalities are to the benefit of all members of society, if the benefits of the growing social product which they stimulate are "spread throughout the system and to the least advantaged" (TJ, 78). And if the social inequalities are even to the *greatest benefit* of the latter, they meet the DP and are, in Rawls' view, therefore just.

So much for Rawls' explication of his DP. On this basis, I will to take a look at his arguments for its justification.

2 Rawls' arguments for the Difference Principle

Since Rawls' reasoning in favor of the DP is deeply embedded in the highly complex architecture of his entire theory of justice, which I cannot treat here at length, I restrict myself to a rough sketch of its main points.

It is known that Rawls models the moral viewpoint, from which we are to make our judgments on matters of justice, as a fictitious initial situation, the "original position", into which all members of a society, considered as free and equal citizens, enter in order to reach a unanimous agreement on the principles of social justice which should govern their social life. In the original position, people are constructed as persons who, on the one hand, are *equally rational* in the sense that they all exclusively pursue their own well-considered interests, while, on the other hand, they are forced to *impartial reason*, since they are deprived of any particular information about their individual natural properties and social positions through a "veil of ignorance". However, they are familiar with the general facts relevant for the choice of principles of justice, such as the features of human nature, the problems of social order, and the regularities of economic systems. In view of these facts, people in the original position conceive of their respective society as a *complete system of social cooperation* whose main rules and institutions, its *basic structure*, will greatly affect their ways of life and prospects of well-being.

On the basis of these assumptions, Rawls argues that the parties in the original position will agree on the following *general conception of justice*: "All social values – liberty and opportunity, income and wealth, and the bases of self-respect – are to be distributed equally unless an unequal distribution of any, or all, of these values is to everyone's advantage" (TJ, 62). Yet, this general conception, he continues, will not be regarded as the final word by the parties, since it applies to the various categories of primary social goods in an indiscriminate way without taking their different significance and weight into account. First of all, the parties will insist on an equal distribution of basic liberties, for there is no reason to expect that, at least under normal social conditions, inequalities of these liberties would benefit even those with lesser liberties. Secondly, "if the parties assume that their basic liberties can be effectively exercised, they will not exchange a lesser liberty for an improvement in economic well-being" (TJ, 151f.). So they arrive at a more differentiated conception of justice consisting of *two principles*. The first requires an appropriate arrangement of equal basic civil rights and liberties, whereas the second, subordinate, principle concerns the society's arrangement regulating the distribution of the other primary social goods, including income and wealth.

Rawls' first, provisional statement of the second principle states that "social and economic inequalities are to be arranged so that they are both (a) reasonably expected to be to everyone's advantage, and (b) attached to positions and offices open to all" (TJ, 60). In order to transform this rather vague statement into the principle's final version with the fair equality of opportunity condition and the DP, he pursues his argument, as it appears in *A Theory of Justice*, along two parallel paths, one formal or deductive, and the other more informal or deliberative.

As for the *formal* path, Rawls makes a number of more or less daring assumptions in order to move from the rather weak requirement that inequalities shall be to *everyone's advantage* to the DP's much stronger requirement that they have to be to the *greatest benefit* of the *least-advantaged*. One of these assumptions is the empirical thesis that socio-economic inequalities are, in general, both "chain-connected" and "close-knit", so that any raise of more favored social positions that improves the prospect of the lowest position also raises the prospects of all positions in between (TJ, 80), and, furthermore, that any change in the prospects of the better off affects the prospects of the worst off in some way (TJ, 81ff.). Due to this thesis, Rawls thinks it possible to proceed from a state of affairs which is to the advantage of the worst off to one which is to everyone's advantage. A second assumption is his normative premise that the parties in the original position will apply the *maximin rule* for choice under uncertainty. This rule tells us to maximize the minimum, i.e. "to rank alternatives by their worst possible outcomes: we are to adopt the alternative the worst outcome of which is superior to the worst outcomes of the others" (TJ, 152f.). Rawls regards this highly conservative rule as plausible under three conditions, which he deems to be satisfied by the original position: (i) one cannot take account of the respective likelihoods of the possible alternatives in consideration, (ii) one does not care very much to gain more than the minimum which the maximin rule grants; and (iii) one can hardly accept the worst outcomes of the other alternatives (cf. TJ, 154). With this premise and further reasonings dedicated to the comparison of his principles with alternative conceptions of justice, Rawls narrows the indefinite requirement of some advantage for everyone down to that of the greatest benefit of the worst off. So he eventually arrives at the DP in a way for which, in *A Theory of Justice*, he claims deductive stringency.

Beside this alleged formal proof, Rawls also pursues a more *informal*, deliberative way of reasoning in favor of his principles, including the DP. While this argument was not yet highly developed in *A Theory of Justice*, it becomes dominant in his subsequent writings, including his monograph *Political Liberalism* (1993, quoted as PL). The basic elements of the informal argument are the following ideas: first, the idea of a *political conception of justice* according to which his conception is not a comprehensive moral doctrine claiming universal validity, but rather a "moral conception worked out for a specific kind of subject, namely, for political, social, and economic institutions" of modern societies in the form of constitutional democracy (PL, 11 ff.); second, the idea of *society as a fair system of cooperation*, whose members are characterized by two moral powers, namely a capacity for a sense of justice on the one hand, and a capacity for a conception of the good on the other (PL, 15 ff.); and third, the idea of the original position, whose parties are now understood as persons who not only have the two moral powers mentioned, but are also thinking of themselves and each other as free citizens in the sense that they all have particular conceptions of the good, are equally entitled to make claims on common social institutions, and are capable of taking responsibility for their ends (PL, 22 ff.). On the basis of these ideas and in view of the fact of reasonable pluralism of individual conceptions of the good, Rawls assumes that people will strive to achieve a generally acceptable conception of justice that is neutral to the various conceptions of the good and the surrounding comprehensive moral doctrines, or, as he puts it, a conception that finds support in an "overlapping consensus" (PL, 133 ff.). And he contends that his two principles should be preferred to any other conception, since only these principles could guarantee all citizens the social conditions essential for the full development and exercise of their two moral powers as free and equal persons. Yet, while he seeks to substantiate this contention extensively for the principle of equal liberty, he abstains from providing specific grounds for the particular features of the DP (cf. PL, 289 ff.).

However, in the final exposition of his theory in *Justice as Fairness: A Restatement* (2001), Rawls again takes up some pertinent elements of the original formal argument for the DP and integrates them, albeit in a somewhat modified manner, into the sketched deliberative considerations. The resultant reasoning for the principles differs from the original formal argument mainly by the fact that it now proceeds on the way of *balancing* the reasons that the parties in the original position may have for the two principles in comparison with alternative conceptions rather than claiming deductive strength. Accordingly, Rawls now calls the maximin rule "simply a useful heuristic device" not essential for the parties' reasoning in the original position (JF, 99).

The revised argument for Rawls' principles relies on *two fundamental comparisons*: The first comparison, in which the two principles, taken as a unit, are compared with the utilitarian principle demanding to arrange the society's basic structure so as to maximize the average welfare of all members, leads to a strong preference for a ramified conception of justice compound of two principles, the first of which calls for an appropriate scheme of equal basic liberties having priority over the striving for economic welfare (JF, 96, 101 ff.). Subsequently, the DP emerges from the second comparison in which the two principles "are compared with an alternative formed by substituting for the difference principle the principle of average utility (combined with a stipulated social minimum)", in order to select a principle for regulating economic and social inequalities (JF, 96). In this second comparison, which, as Rawls admits, "turns on a less decisive balance of reasons" (JF, 97), the maximin rule is relevant only insofar as the parties compare the various principles under consideration in regard to their respective worst outcomes and find the level of welfare guaranteed by the maximin rule fully satisfactory (JF, 120).

To this effect, Rawls argues, the parties would prefer the DP to the principle of utility with a social minimum against the background of the *ideas of publicity, reciprocity and stability* for the following reasons: first, the DP would be more determinate than the utility principle and, therefore, less likely to create disputes and mistrust; second, the DP would be easier to accept than the utility principle, because it would ask less of the more advantaged citizens (in favor of the less advantaged) than the utility principle asks of the less advantaged members (for the sake of the more advantaged); and, third, the DP would cause less "strains of commitment" arising from its realization than the utility principle with a social minimum, since it would guarantee all members a share of goods owed them as free and equal citizens, while the minimum of the utility principle covers only the needs essential for a decent life owed persons in virtue to their humanity (JF, 126 ff.). Furthermore, Rawls' exposition of this comparison presupposes the simplifying assumption that the society is divided in two groups only, i.e. the more advantaged on the one hand and the less advantaged on the other.

This concludes my summary of Rawls' defense of the DP. I shall now turn to its critical discussion. I will begin with some further questions concerning its interpretation that Rawls has left open, and then proceed to various objections against his main arguments for its justification.

3 Critical issues of the Difference Principle

The DP's exclusive focus on the benefit of the *least advantaged* in judging social and economic inequalities causes a number of problems. A simple problem already appears when we face a situation with several feasible distributive structures which equally provide the least advantaged group with the greatest possible welfare, but differ in the welfare levels of the social classes above whose members also may fare badly, such as those of the second or of the third worst-off classes. According to the DP, if taken literally, all these distributive structures would have to be judged as equivalent, which is contradictory to wide-spread intuition. In order to cope with this situation, Rawls adopts a proposition by Amartya Sen (1970, p. 138) to the effect that the DP ought to be understood as a "leximin principle" that demands to proceed as follows:

> first maximize the welfare of the worst-off representative man; second, for equal welfare of the worst-off representative, maximize the welfare of the second worst-off representative man, and so on until the last case, which is, for equal welfare of all the preceding n − 1 representatives, maximize the welfare of the best-off representative man (TJ, 83).

There is, however, a more serious problem arising from the DP's focus on the least advantaged. As I said before, Rawls' move from the rather weak general conception of distributive justice (demanding that social inequalities are to be to everybody's benefit) to the much stronger DP (with its demand for the greatest benefit of the least advantaged) relies on his assumption that the society's various social positions are interrelated through *close-knitness* and *chain-connection*. This is clearly an *empirical* assumption, which, by and large, may have some plausibility for modern well-ordered societies, but is certainly not a necessary truth. In fact, there seem to be cases which do not meet the conditions of close-knitness and chain-connection.

One such case is a situation where social inequalities have developed to such an extent that they have contributed to raise the welfare of worse-off social groups to its maximum level, so that a further improvement of their position is no longer possible, while it would still be possible to raise the welfare of the most advantaged through granting them further benefits that are not transferable and, therefore, would not reduce the welfare of the worse-off. This case gives rise to the question as to whether the DP admits or excludes an increase of social inequality resulting from a further raise of the welfare of the well-off that would neither improve nor worsen the welfare of the worse-off. Rawls does not provide a clear answer to this question (see Van Parijs 2003, pp. 202ff.).

A further case in which the conditions of close-knitness and chain-connection are not met is when a minor improvement of the position of a less advantaged group, e.g. unemployed people, may be achieved, but only at the price of a comparatively significant reduction of the welfare level of a social group whose members are slightly better off, such as, for example, unskilled workers with a job. Is it really clear that in such a case the only thing that counts is the maximum welfare level of the worse-off group with no consideration for the sacrifices that its achievement may impose on those who are slightly better off? I have doubts as to whether this is so easily possible without carefully balancing the advantages of the less advantaged against the costs of the more advantaged. These doubts may suggest a modification of the DP to the effect that it allows a *weighing up* between the additional benefits of less advantaged people and the losses of better-off groups in the case described. A promising guideline for such a modification appears to be the following proposition by Derek Parfit (2000, p. 101), which he names the *Priority View:* "Benefiting people matters more the worse off these people are". If the DP is modified in accordance with this view, it will take a weaker form that may be roughly stated as follows:

> Social and economic inequalities are justifiable up to the point at which they are benefiting the members of less advantaged social groups more the worse off these people are (under condition of fair equality of opportunity).

I deem this variant preferable to Rawls' DP, for it leads, I think, to the same results, if social inequalities satisfy the conditions of close-knitness and chain-connection, while it is more flexible in cases in which these conditions are not fulfilled.

In his reasoning for the DP, Rawls relies on the assumption that there is an appropriate *welfare index* that enables us to determine the overall welfare level of the various social positions. Yet, the search for such a welfare index encounters significant difficulties, even if the list of primary social goods that he deems to be subject to the DP were plausible. The variety of these goods makes it far more difficult to reduce them to a common denominator, as Rawls suggests. But this difficulty is a minor problem. The main problem with his list of primary goods is not that it contains too many kinds of goods, but rather that it covers too *few* because of the fact that it only refers to divisible goods and, thereby, misses a number of pertinent issues of social justice. The missing issues include the following: first, the *burdens of social cooperation*, i.e. the extent to which the members contribute to social production; second, *public goods* whose provision has significant distributive effects on particular social groups; and third, society's *common assets of its natural environment and cultural heritage*. These gaps in Rawls' design of the subject of social justice give rise to three grave objections to his approach on which the DP is based, irrespective of whether or not this principle itself is deemed to be right.

First of all, distributive social justice concerns the distribution of social goods *and burdens* rather than goods alone. It is true that Rawls' focus on primary social goods also implies some reference to social burdens, since these goods, when assigned to particular individuals, take the form of individual rights that go hand in hand with correlative duties. But this fact alone does not provide a sufficient basis for taking account of the individual burdens in social life. The cause of Rawls' failing to pay appropriate attention to these burdens lies in his conception of society as a system of social cooperation among its citizens who all are assumed to be "normal and fully cooperating members of society over a complete life" (PL, 20, 21, 183). Thus, he not only leaves aside all contingencies that "prevent people from being normal and fully cooperating members of society in the usual sense", such as physical disabilities, mental disorders and involuntary unemployment, but also omits to relate the distribution of the social goods subject to the DP to the members' relative contributions to social cooperation.

Secondly, a plausible conception of social justice should not only deal with the distribution of *divisible* social goods which the society's basic structure may assign to its members in the form of individual rights, such as their rights to civil liberty, political participation and private property, but it should also deal with the provision of *public goods* whose ways of provision exert significant distributive effects on individual members depending on their social position and personal abilities, such as the systems of public services, public infrastructure, public transport and public media. If, for instance, a country does not have a sufficient system of public transport, poor people who cannot afford a car will suffer from this failure much more than the wealthy. A particularly striking case of the distributive effects of public infrastructure is the situation of people with physical disabilities who need appropriate devices in streets, buses and buildings for their mobility (see Nussbaum 2007, p. 109).

Thirdly, Rawls does not take the goods provided by the society's *natural environment* and *cultural heritage* into account, such as the atmosphere, land, waters, wild animals, mineral resources, language, technical knowledge, writing, social traditions, and artistic achievements. Even though most of these goods do not occur in pure form, but are contained in human artifacts, the regulation of their accessibility and use is a pertinent matter of social justice, since they are not only essential ingredients of people's means of freedom and welfare, but also, in a sense, society's common assets to whose benefits all members are equally entitled. The society's common ownership of its natural environment and cultural heritage does not exclude that their goods are part of individual private property, but it requires an arrangement of the possession and use of those goods that is to the benefit of every member of society, even though such an arrangement may allow inequalities, if they are expected to increase everyone's benefit, at least in the long run.

To sum up, Rawls' fundamental assumptions concerning the nature of society and its primary goods are much too weak to provide a solid basis for his principles of justice, particularly the DP. His view of society as a system of cooperation to the mutual advantage of "fully cooperating members over a complete life" fails to do justice to those members who, for whatever reason, are prevented from full participation in social cooperation. This view is also not sufficient to back up his rather demanding egalitarian account of socio-economic justice, even if applied only to the small set of primary goods that Rawls takes into consideration. For if society is conceived of as nothing more than a system of cooperation to the mutual advantage of its members, it appears hardly plausible that the demand of distributive justice should extend to the totality of primary goods rather than only to that portion of those goods which would not be produced without cooperation (cf. Gauthier 1974, p. 14; Barry 1989, pp. 250 ff.).

As for Rawls' previously sketched arguments for the DP in particular, none of them are successful. The formal argument, relying on the maximin rule, is not effectual, because it presupposes certain assumptions about people's utility functions and risk-aversion that appear hardly acceptable (cf. Harsanyi 1975). This seems to be the reason why Rawls distanced himself from this argument in his later writings. Although his deliberative argument appears somewhat more plausible, it is no more conclusive. When he defends the DP through comparing it with the utility principle combined with a social minimum, the reasons that he advances for it appear hardly convincing: Neither is the DP, if we consider all its problems of interpretation and application, more determinate than the utility principle with a social minimum, nor is it clear that its realization causes less "strains of commitment" because of the fact that it guarantees all members of society a larger share of goods than they need for a decent life.

My critical discussion of Rawls' conception of justice in general and the DP in particular should not give the impression that I am rejecting them as a whole. On the contrary, in spite of the raised objections to Rawls' reasoning for the DP, I do subscribe to this principle, although in a slightly modified form. So I now come to present my own argument in its favor.

4 In defense of the Difference Principle Modified

In order to circumvent Rawls' elusive assumption that social positions are interrelated through a chain connection, I propose to modify his DP according to Parfit's Priority View so that it allows a gradual balancing of the relative welfare of different social positions rather than focusing on the last advantaged only. Accordingly, I suggest putting the *modified DP* as follows:

> Social and economic inequalities are justifiable if and only if they are necessary ingredients or unavoidable side-effects of a society's socio-economic order which, in general, increases the welfare of less advantaged members more the worse-off these members are (under condition of fair equality of opportunity).

This variant of the DP is equivalent with Rawls' version under the condition that social positions are interrelated through close-knitness and chain-connection, while it leads to different results, if this condition is not met. The social and economic inequalities to which the principle refers may be broadly understood in terms of the members' shares in certain kinds of primary social goods. In addition to those on Rawls' list (i.e. powers and prerogatives of social positions, income and wealth, and the social bases of self-respect), I would also count *natural and cultural values* and *public goods with distributive effects*. Furthermore, when the members' relative shares of these goods are compared, their relative *burdens* in social cooperation need also to be taken into consideration.

The contention that the totality of the primary goods just mentioned is subject to distributive justice requires *a more substantial conception of society* than Rawls' cooperation view. In my view, a sufficiently ordered society, such as a modern state, combines three *communal features* that give rise to various demands of distributive justice. First of all, it is to be understood as an *ownership community* in regard to the members' common ownership of the society's natural resources and cultural heritage. Because of this fact, every member of society has a claim to a fair share of the benefits emerging from its natural and cultural goods. Secondly, a society is a *cooperation community* whose members are not only required to play by its rules for the sake of a peaceful social order, but also expected to partake in the production of social welfare, provided that they are capable of doing so. Consequently, all members of society have a claim to equal access to its system of social cooperation and to a fair share of its benefits in consideration of their contributions. Insofar as individual members are prevented from realizing this claim through unavoidable effects of a generally beneficial socio-economic system, they have a derivative claim to appropriate compensation, as, for example, people who fall victim to unemployment in a market economy. And thirdly, societies are also to be regarded as *solidarity communities* whose members are mutually responsible for taking care of each other and providing those in need with appropriate support, so that everyone is insured against natural, social or individual contingencies, such as disasters, unemployment, sickness, old-age, and disability. Thus, all members of society who are prevented from satisfying their needs to a sufficient extent have a claim to appropriate social support that enables them to lead a decent life. Taken together, these three communal features give rise to a pretty demanding conception of distributive social justice that applies to all the primary social goods mentioned above.

For a first approximation to this conception, I suggest starting from a *general principle of distributive social justice* that is similar, though not identical, to Rawls' general conception: All members of society ought to have an equal share of primary social goods, unless inequalities appear justifiable for reasons acceptable to every member from an impartial viewpoint. This principle, which simply results from applying the general basic demand of distributive justice to organized societies, leads to the question as to which reasons, if any, may justify social inequalities and to what extent. Even though there are far-reaching disagreements on this question, most people agree on various reasons which, in principle, make social inequalities acceptable. These reasons center around three general arguments: the arguments from desert, from liberty, and from need.

The *argument from desert* refers to the relative merits, achievements or contributions of individuals to the system of social cooperation. According to this argument, social inequalities are deemed to be justifiable, if they are in proportion to the individuals' relative merits, achievements or contributions (cf. Miller 1999, pp. 131 ff.). Clearly, this argument appears plausible only under certain presuppositions: first of all, that there is sufficient agreement on the criteria by which people's performances are to be valued in order to determine their relative merits, achievements or contributions; and furthermore, that a larger share of the product of social cooperation is due only to those individuals whose performances generate a surplus value which is not taken by them alone, but is also to the benefit of all or most other members. One familiar argument why people exhibiting better or even extraordinary capacities may rightly claim a relatively larger share is the thesis these individuals need appropriate incentives that stimulate them to bring forth desirable or outstanding achievements to the general benefit. This thesis, which Rawls repeatedly maintains, may have some plausibility in view of the fact that, in social reality, people usually are more led by their selfish interests than by impartial considerations, but it is no good argument in the context of impartial moral discourse (cf. Cohen 1992). Thus, appropriate reasons for privileging people whose performances appear particularly valuable should rather refer to the special burdens of these people, such as the tasks, expenses, costs, hardships, responsibilities and risks of their jobs.

According to the *argument from liberty*, social inequalities appear to be justified if they emerge from free activities of individuals who all make use of their privately owned means within the limits of the respective rights granted to them. When, for instance, two siblings inherit the same amount of money, and the first uses her money for a secure investment, while the other carries his to the casino where he gambles it away, the second has certainly no reason to complain about the resultant inequality. Of course, the validity of this argument also has limitations as it relies on the condition that the individual activities leading to inequality are framed by a societal order that, by and large, operates to the benefit of all members. The paradigm example of individual liberties which generate social inequalities, are those based on private property rights, but many other individual liberties also result in differences. It is fairly obvious that a social order granting such rights and liberties may be to the benefit of all members, for they are necessary not only for individual freedom and self-determination, but also for an efficient economic system promoting social welfare. In this context, the reference to incentives is less problematic, since, here, the incentives mainly result from the individuals' opportunities to use their own resources to their benefit in a proper way (see Dworkin 2000, pp. 120 ff.).

Finally, the *argument from need* maintains that inequalities are justifiable, if they arise from rendering appropriate support to fellow-members who would otherwise suffer deprivation, so that they are able to meet their needs to a sufficient extent. Providing support to these members amounts to treating them *unequally* rather than equally, for they get a larger share of supportive means than those who are required to contribute to the provision of these means without needing support. This argument is also subject to various constraints: the relevant needs must be conceivable against the background of the society's current standard of living; furthermore, the extent of support to which members in need are entitled cannot be unlimited, but must be balanced against the sacrifices of those who have to render support. If we take an *impartial moral perspective* in which we have to imagine that we could be in the situation of any member of society, we are required to decide on a scheme of mutual support by balancing its benefits and costs for all cases of possible unfortunate contingencies that may concern us. Understood in this way, a balanced scheme of mutual support will be to the benefit of every member of society.

Although the three arguments offer different reasons for social inequalities, they have, upon closer inspection, a basic idea in common: the idea that social inequalities appear to be justifiable, if and only if they are to the *benefit of all members* of society, regarded from an impartial perspective. Thus, the basic idea underlying all three arguments may be expressed by the following *general principle for justifying social inequalities:* Social inequalities are justifiable, if and only if they are necessarily or unavoidably connected to a social order that is to the benefit of all members of society, including the worse-off. This principle is, by and large, equivalent with Rawls' first, unspecified version of his inequality principle leading to the DP.

Now, the question arises of how it may be possible to specify this relatively vague general principle in a way that leads to the DP in its modified form. How to move from the general principle's indeterminate demand that inequalities are to be to the benefit of *every* member to the much more specific requirement that they ought to benefit the members of *less-advantaged* social groups to a *greater* extent the worse-off they are? In my view, this is not a very difficult task, for I think there are some well-grounded reasons which together create a good case for the Priority View and, consequently, for the modified DP: (1) the decreasing marginal value of increasing shares of primary goods, (2) the significance of relative differences between unequal social positions, and (3) the negative effects of socio-economic inequalities on the worth of equal liberty to people.

First of all, the *decreasing marginal value of increasing shares of primary goods* means that one's benefit from possessing or using a portion of some particular primary goods gradually decreases as one's share of these goods increases. This thesis resembles the "law of diminishing marginal utility", which has played an influential role in economic thinking. Yet, it differs from this 'law' in an important respect: While the principle of diminishing marginal utility, understood as an empirical thesis, is not generally true, because people's actual utility functions are usually much more complex, it appears highly plausible in the context of *impartial moral reasoning* where it refers to the fundamental interests of individuals in general rather than to their contingent individual preferences. Therefore, the assumption that the marginal value of an individual's share in primary goods decreases with the share's increase is a sound reason in favor of the Priority View in general and the reading of DP according to this view in particular.

The second reason, the *significance of relative differences between unequal social positions*, maintains that, in social reality, people are not merely interested in the absolute size of their shares in social goods irrespective of how large the shares of others are. They also pay attention to the *relative* differences between their own shares in social goods and those of their fellows. Even if it may be expedient to construct the people in the original position as mutually disinterested persons striving only for their own shares in primary social goods in absolute terms, as Rawls suggests, there is no reason to prevent them from knowing the general fact that, in reality, most people also pay attention to their relative social positions and levels of well-being in comparison to others. Thus, social goods are not merely means for the pursuit of the individuals' separate lifeplans, but also *positional goods*, for which people compete in order to distinguish themselves from others or not to fall behind their fellows. People who, irrespective of their absolute level, fare worse than their fellows usually wish to keep the relative differences between them and the better-off as small as possible, as they expect that increasing inequalities may diminish their opportunities in future competition. As long as this attitude does not amount to envy that denies others any differential benefit even at the price of one's own disadvantage, it appears fully reasonable from an impartial perspective and, therefore, provides a sound reason for constraining social differences to the extent necessary for the increase of the welfare of worse-off people.

Last but not least, the Priority View finds additional support in the fact that socio-economic inequalities exert *negative effects on the worth of equal liberty* for individuals, i.e. their actual capacities to exercise and enjoy their civil rights, individual liberties and political rights. Since these capacities greatly depend on people's respective socio-economic situation, the worth of equal liberty to individuals will diverge more, the larger the existing socio-economic differences are. In addition, growing socio-economic inequalities do not only diminish the worth of equal liberty to worse-off groups, but also create significant dangers for democracy, because well-off groups may use their social powers and economic means to influence the political decision-making process in order to advance their particular interests. Consequently, a just social order ought to keep socio-economic inequalities as small as possible by restricting them to the level at which they necessarily or unavoidably result from an institutional arrangement that raises the welfare of lower classes the more the worse-off their members are.

As a result, all these considerations combined give strong support to the view that, within a generally beneficial socio-economic order that unavoidably generates inequalities, the benefits of less-advantaged members have increasingly more weight than those of better-off people the worse-off the former are. And this result gives rise to the demand that the socio-economic order of a society is to be arranged in a way that its emerging inequalities are not merely to some unspecified benefit of all members, but rather to the greater benefit of the less-advantaged groups, or, in other words, that the inequalities do not exceed the extent to which they are necessary to increase the life-time welfare of the worse-off members. So we arrive at the modified Difference Principle.

Bibliography

Barry, Brian (1989): *Theories of Justice*. London, Sydney, Tokyo: Harvester-Wheatsheaf.
Cohen, G.A. (1992): "Incentives, Inequality, and Community". In: Peterson, Grethe B. (Ed.): *The Tanner Lectures on Human Values*. Vol. 13, Salt Lake City: University of Utah Press, pp. 263–329.
Dworkin, Ronald (2000): *Sovereign Virtue. The Theory and Practice of Equality*, Cambridge, MA: Harvard University Press.
Gauthier, David (1974): "Justice and Natural Endowment: Toward a Critique of Rawls' Ideological Framework". In: *Social Theory and Practice* 3, pp. 3–26.
Harsanyi, John C. (1975): "Can the Maximin Principle Serve as a Basis for Morality? A Critique of John Rawls's Theory". In: *The American Political Science Review* 69, pp. 594–606.
Miller, David (1999): *Principles of Justice*, Cambridge, MA: Harvard University Press.
Nussbaum, Martha (2007): *Frontiers of Justice. Disability, Nationality, Species Membership*, Cambridge, MA: Harvard University Press.
Parfit, Derek (2000): "Equality or Priority?" [1997]. In: Clayton, Matthew/Williams, Andrew (Eds.): *The Ideal of Equality*. New York: St. Martin's Press, pp. 81–125.
Rawls, John (1971): *A Theory of Justice*, Cambridge, MA: Harvard University Press.
Rawls, John (1993): *Political Liberalism*, New York: Columbia University Press.
Rawls, John (2001): *Justice as Fairness: A Restatement*. Erin Kelly (Ed.). Cambridge, MA: Harvard University Press.
Sen, Amartya K. (1970): *Collective Choice and Social Welfare*. San Francisco: Holden-Day.
Van Parijs, Philippe (2003): "Difference Principles". In: Freeman, Samuel (Ed.): *The Cambridge Companion to Rawls*. Cambridge: Cambridge University Press, pp. 200–240.

Aysel Demir
Marxist Critiques of the Difference Principle

Abstract: This paper focuses on contradictions in John Rawls's theory of distributive justice and presents the Marxist critique regarding the distribution of goods on the basis of abilities and needs via the difference principle. The paper examines Rawls's unjust and non-egalitarian theory. In doing so, it pays special attention to significant gaps in his second principle. Rawls is criticized by Marxists, especially analytical Marxists, because of some gaps in his theory. In *A Theory of Justice*, the difference principle allows and identifies inequalities as acceptable in the distribution of goods only if those inequalities benefit the worst-off members of society. In this sense, Rawls legitimizes inequality with the difference principle which for him is the basis of distribution, whereas Marx's, and Marxist, theories of distributive justice advocate the principle "from each according to his ability, to each according to his needs". In these circumstances, Marxists claim that the difference principle is unacceptable. Therefore, analytical Marxists philosophers are in disagreement with Rawls.

Introduction

In *A Theory of Justice*, Rawls makes the case for how and why we should choose the principles of justice, arguing we should reach justice through liberty with equality of opportunity and the difference principle. There are many points on which Rawls could be criticized from a Marxist perspective, but the most important criticism, from analytic Marxists in particular, is that the weakest part of Rawls's theory concerns the conditions of distribution. Approaching the issue by focusing on the scientific explication of Marx's concepts, they claim that the difference principle has gaps in the way it ensures justice, taking issue with the Rawlsian framework as a whole, particularly with the difference principle. As a prelude to Marxist critiques of Rawls' *A Theory of Justice*, firstly we should look at what Marxism is, whether Marx has a theory of justice and what analytic Marxists say about Rawls' theory of justice. Marxism is a theory which advocates for the establishment of a classless and stateless socio-political order, the basis of which is the communal ownership of the means of production. Within the co-operative society based on common ownership of the means of production, the producers do not exchange their products. Marx argues that when capitalism is overcome and a 'society of freely associated producers' has been created, there will be no further need for thinking about justice (Freeman 2007, p. 359). This will bring an end to alienation and exploitation and create a situation in which everyone equally shares in society's wealth. The requirements for a society of freely associated producers is that there be no alienation and no exploitation (Freeman 2007, p. 362). Thus, each person will produce according to his ability and each person will have benefits from this according to need and in the end a just society will come to be. In this context, some analytic Marxists philosophers – such as Allen Wood, George Brenkert, Allan Buchanan, John McMurtry, Gerald Cohen, Jon Elster, Adam Przeworksi and John Roemer – discuss whether Marx's works could be read as a theory of justice based on the normative claim that Marx holds capitalism yields an unjust society.[1]

Although some Marxists argue that Marxism cannot be understood as a theory of justice, the analytical Marxists recognize Marxism as a theory that is capable of explaining revolution by means of the economic dynamics of capitalism and how the class interests of the proletariat is seriously compromised. They undertook an analysis of Marx's writings as 'Marx's theory of justice', which prompted an extensive debate over the relationship between Marx and justice. Certainly, Marx's social theory can be placed within a theory of justice, although Marx makes no attempt to classify justice directly. Marx viewed justice as having an economic and political background which is based on two categories of justice, both of which are distributive; one is justice for socialist society and the other for communist society, i.e., socialist justice and communist justice. The basic characteristic of the socialist justice is the ownership of the means of production. The abolition of ownership and exploitation will lead to the general ownership of the whole society and the workers will be the owners of the sources of production. The Marxian theory of justice is distributive, because according to this, all the benefits and burdens within the society will be properly distributed among all the members of the society and the proceeds of labour belong to all

---

[1] Analytical Marxism began as a development in the late 1970s and early 1980s among a group of scholars in philosophy and social sciences, all these scholars shared the belief that Marx's body of work still constitutes a framework within which questions can be asked to fruitful ends. It was associated with the September Group of academics. They attempted to discern, using analytic methods, what aspects of Marxism could be empirically verified. In the end, most of the 'metaphysical' aspects of Marxism were discarded as unverifiable (Mandle/Reidy 2014, p. 515). Analytical Marxism originated with the publication of Cohen's *Karl Marx's Theory of History: A Defence* (1978). According to Cohen, Marxism had some problems which were based on an incorrect understanding of anthropology, and the trouble is that under these circumstances it could not be inferred from the truths of logic. He used analytic techniques to interpret the Marxian theory.

members of the society which Marx calls fair distribution. Fair distribution is a right which all workers can claim. Because the proceeds are from their labour, naturally they have a legitimate claim to them through fair distribution. Thus, the legitimate claims and fair distribution are closely connected. If the fair distribution right is ignored, then justice would not exist in that society. For Marx, fundamental concepts of social justice were rooted in economic justice. In this sense, the existence of private property and economic inequality brought the social injustice.

Marx uses terms such as 'theft' and 'robbery' to describe the capitalist appropriation of surplus value, which indicates that he implicitly, employs a language of injustice. Cohen claims that Marx describes the labour relationship as a robbery and theft and criticizes the injustice of capitalism (Cohen 1983, pp. 440–445). On this point, Marx's objection to injustice is embedded in his analysis of the wage relation, showing evidence of an implicit theory of justice.

Since Marx uses a dialectic method, he presupposes some principle or theory of justice. The basic logic of his theory of justice is that the relations of distribution are to be interpreted not through political and legal concepts of fairness and justice, but through the relations of production (Xinsheng 2015, p. 8). Some analytic Marxists, like Cohen and Buchanan, claimed that Marx offered a theory of justice indirectly, referring to a just, communist society which would come after capitalism. Others, like Allen Wood claimed that there is no theory of justice in Marx's writings, which are merely an attempt at the analysis of capitalism (Wood 2004, p. 69). This discussion was clearly linked to the revival of normative political philosophy after the publication of John Rawls's *A Theory of Justice*. The analytical Marxists, however, largely rejected Rawls's point of view because his theory allows inequalities to arise from differences in talent.

This paper aims to examine the contradictory effects of Rawls's theory distributive justice from an Analytical Marxist perspective by laying out their criticisms of his theory on the unjust and unequal." In so doing, I pay special attention to the main gaps in his second principle. My discussion is divided into the following parts. I begin by outlining exactly what Rawls's difference principle is and what the problems are with this principle. Then I go on to look at the differences between Marxist theory and Rawls's theory concerning abilities, talents and luck. Where Marx and analytical Marxists focus on abilities and talents, Rawls sees the abilities and talents as a problem in the theory of distribution. In the following sections, I discuss how the distributive theory of justice is invalid and how it causes unequal distribution, exploitation and class distinctions. I conclude that Rawls's *A Theory of Justice*, which constructs a system that is based on equality and needs through the difference principle, is neither realistic nor just. I claim that the result of his theory of justice causes permanent and growing inequality.

The difference principle

In *A Theory of Justice*, Rawls described two principles of justice for a system that provides for liberty and equality, and these principles together create a basis for all discussions on social justice. He uses a "lexical priority" to order these principles. In the "lexical priority", the first principle, that of liberty, has priority over the second principle. The second principle is the fair equality of opportunity and the difference principle. The principle of fair equality of opportunity has lexical priority over the difference principle. The difference principle regulates economic inequalities and permits them only if they are to the advantage of the worst off (Rawls 1971, p. 178). The liberty principle is interested in the socio-political structure of society, whereas the difference principle is interested in the socio-economic structure of society.

Rawls's second principle of justice states that social and economic inequalities are to satisfy two conditions: Firstly, they are to be attached to offices and positions open to all under conditions of fair equality of opportunity. Secondly, they are to be of the greatest benefit to the least advantaged members of society. The second condition is the crucial part of the difference principle that permits economic inequalities only if they are to the advantage of the least advantaged members of society (Rawls 1971, p. 178).

Justice as fairness actually refers to distributive justice and Rawls emphasizes that there is no need to have an equal distribution of income; inequalities can be accepted if they give an advantage to the worst-off members of society (Rawls 1971, p. 178). In this configured theory of justice, a system will be prepared to minimize the inequalities by supporting individuals who have the lowest income level which won't in turn reduce the standards of the richest individuals. In this regard, Rawls's argument is that each person should accept the inequalities, which are allowed by the basic structure. The inequality occurs by way of the difference principle which should be useful for both sides, since it is a principle of mutual benefit (Rawls 1999, p. 88). According to Rawls, the difference principle provides an interpretation of the principle of fraternity (Rawls 1999, p. 90). Inequalities can be just, in Rawls's view, as long as they are to the benefit of the worst off. In the basis of the difference principle, there are similarities in context to the principle of mutual benefit, which has the logic of brotherhood and financial support from those who were born lucky and create their own chances to the less advantaged individuals. In this sense, the difference principle symbolizes fraternity.

One of the main problems with Rawls's theory concerns which principles will be accepted and how benefits will be shared in collaboration with the distribution of justice as fairness (Nozick 2006, p. 242). There is a contradiction in his theory: when the welfare of the worse-off group has reached a maximum, it is still possible to raise the welfare of the most advantaged group. Here the difference principle allows an increase in the welfare of the best off which means the situation of those worst off doesn't change exactly. Rawls thinks that he gave all the answers to the question of how to resolve the problem of justice in his own terms. However, although he thought that he had solved the problem of justice, analytical Marxists claim that there are gaps in the methodological and practical justification of the difference principle in his theory. Although Rawls gained a number of important insights from his work on social justice, he could not completely configure them in theory and practice and thus he ran into a contradiction with his claims.

The weakest point of the difference principle regards distribution, in particular distribution between the rich and poor people. Therefore, analytical Marxists think that Rawls's theory cannot be seen as a theory of justice because it has far too strong a focus on distribution. Marx and analytical Marxists are focused on production, whereas Rawls's theory concentrates on distribution, especially redistribution. Robert Paul Wolff criticizes Rawls and claims that:

> By focusing exclusively on distribution rather than on production, Rawls obscures the real roots of that distribution. As Marx says in his *Critique of the Gotha Program*, "Any distribution whatever of the means of consumption is only a consequence of the distribution of the conditions of production themselves. The latter distribution, however, is a feature of the mode of production itself" (Wolff 1977, p. 210).

Cohen and Buchanan also declare clearly that the difference principle is insufficient to ensure the justice and equality (Cohen 2008, p. 228; Buchanan 1976, p. 58).

The difference principle is criticized because it ignores people who deserve certain economic benefits in light of their actions and overlooks important explanations of how people come to be in the more or less advantaged groups. In addition, in the system which is presumed through the difference principle individuals who sell their labour and work hard, which results in alienation, should give some of their income to others who are less advantaged people. This situation is unjust and conflicts with Marxist ideas that people have the right to take free advantage of the products of their own labour and that everyone gets a share in proportion to their need from the total income in the economy. Accumulated total capital is distributed to everyone as equal.

In the difference principle, Rawls particularly aims to reduce the effects of the 'natural lottery' through social and judicial institutions. According to Rawls, some people were born luckier and gifted in terms of abilities and talents than others. Rawls thinks that he can solve this natural lottery problem via redistribution of income. Therefore, Rawls stipulates a number of regulations for these social and economic inequalities, with the intent of limiting the income of individuals who earn more through possessing greater abilities. As he argues:

> The naturally advantaged are not to gain merely because they are more gifted, but only to cover the costs of training and education and for using their endowments in ways that help the less fortunate as well. No one deserves his greater natural capacity nor merits a more favourable starting place in society. But, of course, this is no reason to ignore, much less to eliminate these distinctions. Instead, the basic structure can be arranged so that these contingencies work for the good of the least fortunate (Rawls 1999, p. 87).

According to Rawls, individuals who have greater abilities through the natural lottery are not more deserving than other, less naturally talented people. Rawls tries to remove the effect of ability and the income earned through ability in his theory, whereas Marx and the Marxist view follows this principle: 'From each according to his ability'. At this point, the Rawlsian and the Marxist view separate from each other.

From each according to his ability, to each according to his needs!

Marx opposed all systematic social inequalities and he thought that monetary exchange ignored the differential needs economically. Therefore, Marx actually emphasized a theory of distributive justice and even a communist principle of distribution which is supposed to guide the distribution of goods and services in a society. In his 1875 *Critique of the Gotha Program*, he writes, "[f]rom each according to his ability, to each according to his needs" (Marx 1970, p. 17). Intended as a solution to the problems of inequalities created by different needs, this statement can have a much wider scope.[2] This is a descriptive state-

---

[2] 'From each according to his ability, to each according to his needs' can rightly be called a principle of distributive justice. To the extent there is a Marxist theory of justice, it would seem to be best summed up in the communist distributive principle.

ment of how things will eventually be, but the main function of this principle consists in abolishing economic inequalities and injustice of the capitalist system. At the first stage, the motto of the principle of distribution is 'to each according to his contribution', in the final stages, which is communism, it is 'to each according to his needs'. This principle is also integral to Marx's notion of a just society (Geras 1984, p. 70).

For Marx, social justice means that people should do the best suited work for themselves and all people should have their economic needs supplied. According to this principle, not only all persons should work as hard as they can, but also each person should best develop their particular talent. In this sense, the 'from each' clause presumes the freedom to develop, exercise and choose among one's abilities; the 'to each' clause presumes the material conditions that would enable one to have what is needed to affect one's conception of self-realization (Mandle/Reidy 2014, p. 452). Indeed, Marx discusses here the competing ethical principles of payments and income distribution for a socialist economy, contrasting in particular the right to a social share in line with our 'needs' (Sen 2015, p. 80). At the same time, Marx's principle can be interpreted as an equal welfare principle. This equal welfare principle means that each person will produce according to his ability, and the collective income will gain from this production. All members of society can take whatever they need from the common stock of goods. Every person will have benefits from this according to need notwithstanding their ability. In other words, this justice principle refers to how we should carry out this distribution. According to Marx, distribution is not independent from the relations of production, which he considers to be fundamental (Freeman 2007, p. 358). Marx points out clearly that distribution links relations of production and consumption (Xinsheng 2015, p. 8).

Marx claims that revolution starts with the labourers coming to power. After that, socialism, which is based on the classless state, will follow. The last stage will be communism which goes from control out of necessity to the dominance of freedom. In this stage, we will not have a state; everyone's freedom will be a condition for another people's freedom. Marx describes a communist society in which agents freely engage in activities that are simultaneously oriented to the agent's individual self-realization and involve the production of goods that others will use for their self-realization (Mandle/Reidy 2014, p. 452). He argues that the principle: 'from each according to their ability and to each according to their needs' is of this kind, because it aims at an equal right of self-realization for all, even though Marx imagines it has occurred with the disappearance of the state and its coercive institutions of law (Freeman 2007, p. 343). In the end, everything will be taken according to people's ability, from everyone, and it will be distributed according to people's needs to each other. This will be made possible by providing goods and services such that there will be enough to satisfy everyone's needs.³ According to Marx, individuals live to sustain their existence, and to provide for their needs and to realize their ability in life. The produced goods are distributed according to the needs. They are also developing their own talents, composing a social consciousness among individuals (Brenkert 1998, p. 158).

Although Marx and Rawls are both interested in the question of what features should exist in a just society, their methodologies, viewpoints and attitudes are highly different regarding the relations of production and distribution. Rawls believes differences in distribution and readjustments in distribution can exist simultaneously. He looks for coherence based on capitalism as well as certain kinds of distributional equality through the principle of going beyond justice in a society based on class. For Marx, the transformation of the principle of distribution from reward to needs occurs historically, one after the other. Marx stresses agents' lives as producers and consumers, whereas Rawls stresses their lives as citizens engaged in maintaining a distributive just society (Mandle/Reidy 2014, p. 450). When Marx is compared with Rawls, the problem of difference between rich and poor only concerns the type of distribution.

Rawls believes that distribution is a necessary part of the difference principle and he objects to equal distribution and finds it unnecessary. He sees that inequality is acceptable to improve the situation of the worst off (Rawls 1971, p. 4). Rawls does not support advancement of individuals who have ability and talents unless the best off help the worst off directly. In *A Theory of Justice*, Rawls obviously allows tolerance to economic inequality among people in different positions and in different features via the difference principle, which is the basis of distribution, while Marx and the Marxists state that the coproduction of everybody should be shared equally according to everyone's needs. Crucially, the difference principle doesn't prescribe a distribution of resources according to need, but instead requires whatever distribution of resources will most effectively satisfy the needs of the worst off (Miller 1976, p. 48). The contradictions between Marx's and Rawls's distribution view emerge on account of the distribution conditions.

Elster and Geras claim that 'from each according to his ability, to each according to his needs' is a principle of distributive justice which can be complemented with a proper and reasonable account of needs. However, Rawls denies

---

[3] Marx claims that the principle of real justice which is 'from each according to his ability, to each according to his needs' can only be applied in the higher stage of communism, where society goes beyond "the narrow horizon of bourgeoisie right" (Marx/Engels 1976, p. 119).

this claim and avers that this principle of needs is only a descriptive principle in a society beyond justice (Stoian 2014, p. 123).

Inequality, class, exploitation and alienation

It seems that Rawls just defends the redistribution of income; therefore, according to Marxists, he is merely a redistributor: his purpose is only to strike a certain balance. Rawls says that it will come about by the supreme social value of accepting a guiding notion of distributive justice which ensures the needs of people who are in the worst-off situation. Rawls argues that just institutions only accept redistribution of people's income as opposed to redistribution of capital. This principle causes greater inequality due to condoning and legitimizing the inequality; even Nozick claims that this kind of distribution is a form of "hush money" so people who have less advantage make nothing of it (Nozick 2006, p. 200). At the same time, Nozick objects that if Rawls's theory is used to regulate society, then it will have the intolerable effect of requiring the state to interfere continually in people's doing (Kukathas/Pettit 1990, p. 88). According to Marxist critiques, to accept the redistribution of an individual's income, in contrast with the distribution of capital, is the most important weakness of Rawls's theory.

At the same time, the difference principle promotes factors which motivate individuals regarding their personal economic interests which are not ethical. Individuals think that when they sacrifice their income for worse-off members of society, somehow this will return to them to line their own pockets. This idea motivates them to share a part of their income with people who have needs. Cohen critiques this situation in his book *Rescuing Justice and Equality*, stating that, if people are motivated by personal interests, they never truly depend on justice and equality. According to him, the difference principle is merely an expedient measure to regulate a predominantly selfish type of character formed by a capitalist system and does not qualify as a basic principle of justice. At the same time, Cohen claims that fair equality of opportunity cannot rule out capitalism, since the great inequalities of capitalism are consistent with it (Cohen 2008 p. 385). Moreover, Cohen agrees with Marx that a society can never achieve the full development of human abilities when people are treated as equal citizens and unequal private persons. Cohen argues that the difference principle is an unsuccessful descriptive approach, while also being insufficient as a justice principle because it motivates individuals on the basis of interests more than needs (Cohen 2008, p. 166). Simply stated, Cohen thinks that the great weakness of the representative type of Rawlsian liberalism is that rapacious self-interest maximization can occur along with, and contrary to, the egalitarian intentions of state redistributive policy (Holt 2011, p. 237). Furthermore, Wolff indicates that "as long as implementation of Rawls's theory continues, he will only advocate the protection of the status quo of the basic structure" (Wolff 1977, p. 205) and, according to him, this does not reveal the problem of the inequality which takes place in the market economy, the private ownership and the capitalist social relations.

Rawls says that justice is the first virtue of social institutions and that the principles of justice are applied to the 'basic structure' of fundamental social institutions such as the judiciary and the economic and political structure. According to him, the state should institutionalize these, but society and its functions must be taken into account too (Rawls 1971, pp. 3–7). Unfortunately, Rawls fails to recognize this and is trying to solve issues of distribution only through institutions. This approach of Rawls is too narrow in scope. In particular, Cohen rejects the institutional process of the difference principle (Cohen 2000, p. 22). For Cohen, there is already an uncertainty in Rawls's description of the basic structure. It is not very clear what is being judged and which institutions are considered part of the basic structure, whereas, in Marxist theory, institutions are not required for a good society.[4] Even Buchanan, in *Marx and Justice*, says that there is no need for an institutional equality theory if conflicts are eliminated (Buchanan 1982, p. 57). Marx had already said that communism will be realized

---

4 The early Marx's concept of species-being (*Gattungswesen*) expresses the relation between self-realization and community in historical terms, thus it provides an appropriate context for a Marxist theory of justice. To have a species-being and to achieve self-realization, alienation is an important concept. Marx distinguishes among three major facets of alienation: alienated labour, alienated capital, and alienated needs (Jessop/Wheatley 1999, p. 495). In this sense, alienation has four stages especially for the labour-worker: at first, the worker is alienated from the object of production, secondly, the worker is alienated from productive activity, and then the worker is alienated from 'species-being', and finally, the worker is alienated from other people. The worker puts his life into the object; then it no longer belongs to him but to the object (Jessop/Wheatley 1999, p. 495). However, Marx explains 'species-being': "Man is a species-being not only in that he practically and theoretically makes his own species as well as that of other things his object, but also, and this is only another expression for the same thing, in that as present and living species he considers himself to be a universal and consequently free being" (Marx 1994, pp. 58–63). Even Terry Eagleton describes 'species-being' the following way: "In his early writings, Marx speaks of what he calls human 'species being' which is really a materialist version of human nature. Because of the nature of our material bodies, we are needy, labouring, sociable, sexual, communicative, self-expressive animals who need one another to survive, but who come to find a fulfilment in that companionship over and above its social usefulness" (Eagleton 2011, p. 81). Capitalism dehumanizes the species-being and destroys the good qualities, therefore such a system cannot be a provider of justice.

in a society which has no state,[5] and at the same time Marx speaks of 'higher standards' of right in communist societies, when Marx criticizes politico-juridical conceptions of right and justice, it seems that he actually was criticising precisely what he understood 'justice' in general to be. In the higher phase of communism, as Marx says, society will not need a principle of justice at all, because communist society is a society beyond justice (Geras 1984, p. 39).

Responses to some Marxist critics come not from Rawls but from Arthur Di Quattro, who tries to show that Rawls's theory of justice is misunderstood and that it is compatible with Marxist-Socialist ideas of social justice. However, in 2001 Rawls published *Justice as Fairness: A Restatement* as a direct answer to the Marxist critical approaches. Although the highest goal of Marxist theory is the elimination of private ownership and property, Rawls talks about property-owning democracy which he strikingly describes as "an alternative to capitalism" (Rawls 2001, pp. 135–136). In this kind of democracy, property is distributed widely to everyone, and people get their wealth from property. For him, the meaning of the equalization of resources is the expansion of the amount of private property. In other words, equality is provided by increasing private ownership.

Di Quattro claims that the Rawlsian theory of justice is based on the understanding of property-owning democracy, and, if property is distributed widely and people get their wealth from property, then it is impossible to talk about class distinctions and exploitations as a result of these distributions (Di Quattro 1983, p. 65). In this situation, Marxists' objections to equality being provided by increasing private ownership is quite acceptable because they already reject the possession of private property. According to Marxism, the existence of private property separates the workers from what they produce, and the private ownership of the means of production causes capitalist exploitation, alienation and the loss of self-realization. In a capitalist society, it is impossible to realize justice because of the exploitative nature of its relations of production. From Marx's and a Marxist point of view, the private ownership of the means of production is the cause of capitalist exploitation, therefore only the public ownership of the means of production can guarantee distributive justice. In short, distributive justice could never be achieved under the capitalist system.

The Analytical Marxist view claims that Rawls ignores the producer's way of justice and the inequality between employers and employees who affect the ap-

---

[5] In the German Ideology Marx declares: "Communism is for us not a state of affairs which is to be established, an ideal to which reality [will] have to adjust itself" (Marx/Engels 1976, vol. 5, p. 49; cf. p. 247).

plication of the public area. The difference principle reveals an inequality in every sphere, and it also contains capitalist, ideological and particularly exploitative qualities which run contrary to Marxism. Therefore, this theory is unacceptable for them.

According to Rawls, when a worse-off member of society is given advantages through being employed by another who has profit, it is not exploitation because both sides benefit from this situation. Since Rawls does not see exploitation as the central topic; he never explained it in detail in his theory. However, although he does not focus on it, this situation that constitutes exploitation according to analytical Marxists. In the distribution stage, when the income transfer is evaluated to the advantage of the worst-off members, they ignore that people who work hard and have good positions do not find the idea of sharing their income with people who do not work enough acceptable. Although Rawls thinks that this situation should develop within the logic of fraternity, this does not seem realistic and fair to people. The situation shows that hard working individuals have been exploited and consequently individuals who have advantages would lose motivation to work hard due to this exploitive situation and does not appear to support them. Accordingly, it seems that the best-off will take serious losses if the difference principles are implemented. In this context, the difference principle will promote and cause the protection of status quo as well. These results invalidate Rawls's theory of justice. Analytical Marxist critics emphasize that this so-called equality actually creates exploitation by allowing the distribution of income that is earned with ability (Christie 2012, p. 6).

Additionally, Marx is correct regarding the relationship between systematic class exploitation and the existence of false consciousness and ideology in a society (Wolff 1977, p. 128). In this context, Marxist critics claim that Rawls's theory of justice has an ideological structure; therefore, it has the characteristics of particular social classes. Although Rawls seems to object to the justice principles that are grounded in the interests of class, the difference principle particularly creates the interests of class. That means there are classes in Rawls's theory, and Rawls's theory of justice is ideological and accepts the social inequalities as legitimate.

Although Rawls and his supporters think that there are no class distinctions in *A Theory of Justice*, in fact Rawls's theory has some features which cause class conflicts. In his theory, Rawls refers to the class that has fewer advantages, not to individuals who have fewer advantages. Basically, Rawls describes the working class as having a low-income, no ability and opportunity. Rawls seems to already accept the class distinction when he configures his theory. Particularly, Rawls is endorsing class divisions by permitting inequality; however, Di Quattro claims that Rawls merely interprets class distinctions differently than Marx. He says "yes, there is a class distinction in society but this distinction is about single-class society, which is not mentioned by Marx" (Di Quattro 1983, p. 70).

Rawls's system of justice creates an exploitation that causes the loss of human dignity in the context of benefit and interest through the difference principle, despite that Rawls considers Kant's principle of respect for persons and respect for human beings as a primary aim. In this context, according to Nielsen, the difference principle, which helps to regularize the inequalities, is a different version of utilitarianism. There is nothing to prevent the upper classes from exploiting the lower classes in the expansion of benefits through inequalities to less advantaged groups (Nielsen 1980, p. 77). Meanwhile, the better off groups in society can raise their welfare. Rawls' use of utilitarian features, especially in the distribution stage of the difference principle, allows more comprehensive exploitation to take place.

In discussing differences between alienation and exploitation, Marx pointed to the relations of production and private ownership. According to Marx, 'workers' cannot achieve self-realization because of the social structure of production they are alienated from in the capitalist system. The alienated worker cannot see her/himself as properly engaged in the shared activities due to the miserable conditions of the capitalist work process (Mandle/Reidy 2014, pp. 456–465). Although Rawls does not talk about alienation directly, in his theory of distributive justice, the cause of alienation is the difference principle and institutions which he describes as the basic structure of society. For Rawls, an actually alienated 'citizen' cannot see her/himself as properly engaged in the shared activity of maintaining just institutions, and of giving and receiving justice (Mandle/Reidy 2014, p. 465).

Exploitation is one of the most central concepts of Marxism and a normatively laden concept suggestive of injustice. Marxists have always believed that exploitation is unfair and capitalism is a system of exploitation that enables the appropriation of the unpaid surplus labour of the worker (Mandle/Reidy 2014, p. 515). In this sense, Marxists hold that distributive justice can never be achieved under the conditions of the capitalist system. Taking the argument to Rawls, analytical Marxists claim he never challenges the capitalist social structure; rather, he simply tries to rescue capitalism by filling in the gaps. Capitalism is a system of exploitation in a specific sense, and exploitation belongs to the essence of capitalism, thus, reform is not possible.

Conclusion

Specifically, Rawls's theory seems theoretically weaker than Marx's theory. Rawls's theory of justice neglects the productive side of justice. By focusing exclusively on distribution rather than on production, he obscures the real roots of that distribution. The difference principle is to ensure 'the greatest benefit to the least-advantaged' but here again he has to revert to insisting that 'right has priority over good' to set limits for this principle. This 'retreat' reflects not only his liberal insistence on right but also his methodological difficulties (Xinsheng 2015, p. 20).

It is clear that it seems impossible to have a fair and equal society via the difference principle. The tension between distributive justice and equality is undeniable, and Rawls's view of distributive justice unavoidably results in serious inequality. Inequalities cause class conflicts, and, as long as these conflicts are unresolved, his theory does not provide equal rights and liberties. Rawls's theory of justice cannot realistically construct a system that is based on equality and needs through the difference principle. It does not address needs as such; it just addresses the needs of poor people. The difference principle seems rather far away from the real foundation of any social and economic order. Although Rawls tried to bring an important perspective to theories of justice with the aim of improving the situation of the poor through the difference principle, but his theory of justice causes a permanent and growing inequality because it pursues the principles of justice in the wrong way.

Rawls's theory of justice, especially the difference principle, brings out more widely comprehensive exploitation because of the existence of social classes. His theory is ideological because it legitimizes the classes, exploitation, alienation and social inequality. In this sense, applying the difference principle is not reliable and the difference principle of Rawls is not fair from a Marxist viewpoint which claims distribution should be applied according to people's needs in order to achieve equal distribution (Marx 1989, p. 87). Marx's ideal society follows the principle of 'from each according to his ability, to each according to his needs'. It seems impossible, however, that Rawls's theory of justice could accommodate this principle. The perception of justice of Marx and Marxists is irreconcilable with Rawlsian concepts of justice. Therefore, Marxist philosophers disagree with Rawls about his theory of justice and in particular with the difference principle.

Bibliography

Brenkert, G. George (1998): *Marxın Özgürlük Etiği*. Y. Alogan (Trans.). Istanbul: Ayrıntı Yay.
Buchanan, Allen (1979): "Exploitation Alienation and Injustice". In: *Canadian Journal of Philosophy* 9. No. 1, pp. 121–139.
Buchanan, Allen (1982): *Marx and Justice: The Radical Critique of Liberalism, Philosophy and Society*, Totowa, NJ; London: Rowman & Littlefield/Methuen.
Christie, Isham (2012): "A Marxist Critique of John Rawls' Theory of Justice". http://www.ndsu.edu/fileadmin/history/Marxist_Critique_of_Rawls.pdf, visited on 12 February 2012.
Cohen, Gerald A. (1983): "Review of Allen Wood's Karl Marx". In: *Mind* 92, pp. 440–445.
Cohen, Gerald A. (1988): *History Labour and Freedom: Themes from Marx*. Oxford: Oxford University Press.
Cohen, Gerald A. (2000): *Karl Marx's Theory of History: A Defence*. Expanded edition. Oxford: Oxford University Press.
Cohen, Gerald A. (2008): *Rescuing Justice and Equality*. Cambridge, MA: Harvard University Press.
Di Quattro, Arthur (1983): "Rawls and Left Criticism". In: *Political Theory* 11. No. 1, pp. 53–78.
Eagleton, Terry (2011): *Why Marx Was Right*. New Haven: Yale University Press.
Freeman, Samuel (Ed.) (2007): *John Rawls. Lectures on the History of Political Philosophy*, Cambridge, MA: Harvard University Press.
Geras, Norman (1989): "The Controversy about Marx and Justice". In: Callinicos, Alex (Ed.): *Marxist Theory*. Oxford: Oxford University Press, pp. 211–267.
Holt, Justin P. (2011): "The Limits of An Egalitarian Ethos: Gerald A. Cohen's Critique of Rawlsian Liberalism". In: *Science & Society* 75. No. 2, pp. 236–261.
Jessop, Bob/Wheatley, Russell (1999): *Karl Marx's Social and Political Thought*. London: Routledge.
Kukathas, Chandran/Pettit, Philip (1990): *Rawls: A Theory of Justice and Its Critics*. Stanford: Stanford University Press.
Mandle, Jon/Reidy, David (Eds.) (2014): *A Companion to Rawls*. Chichester: Wiley Blackwell.
Marx, Karl (1970): "Critique of the Gotha Programme". In: Marx, Karl/Engels, Frederick: *Selected Works*. Vol. 3. Moscow: Progress Publishers, pp. 13–30.
Marx, Karl (1994): "Economic and Philosophic Manuscripts". In: Marx, Karl: *Selected Writings*. Indianapolis: Hackett, pp. 58–63.
Marx, Karl/Engels, Friedrich (1976): *Collected Works*. New York: International Publishers.
Miller, David (1976): *Social Justice*. Oxford: Clarendon Press.
Nielsen, Kai (1980): "Rawls and The Left: Some Left Critiques of Rawls' Principles of Justice". In: *Analyse & Kritik* 2. No. 1, pp. 74–97.
Nozick, Robert (1974): *Anarchy State and Utopia*. New York: Basic Books.
Rawls, John (1971): *A Theory of Justice*, Cambridge, MA: Harvard University Press.
Rawls, John (1999): *A Theory of Justice*. Revised edition. Cambridge, MA: Harvard University Press.
Rawls, John (2000): *Lectures on the History of Political Philosophy*. Barbara Herman (Ed.). Cambridge, MA: Harvard University Press.
Rawls, John. (2001): *Justice as Fairness: A Restatement*. Erin Kelly (Ed.). Cambridge, MA: Belknap Press.

Sen, Amartya (2015): "The Idea of Justice: A Response". In: *Philosophy and Social Criticism* 41. No. 1, pp. 77–88.
Stoian, Valentine (2014): *Property Owning Democracy, Socialism and Justice: Rawlsian and Marxist Perspectives on the Content of Social Justice*. Budapest: Central European University.
Wolff, Robert P. (1977): *Understanding Rawls: A Reconstruction and Critique of A Theory of Justice*. Princeton: Princeton University Press.
Wood, Allen W. (2004): *Karl Marx*. New York: Routledge.
Xinsheng, Wang (2015): "A Fourfold Defence of Marx's Theory of Justice". In: *Social Sciences in China* 36. No. 2, pp. 5–21.

Part VII: **The Economic Perspective: Adam Smith**

Jeffrey Young
Justice, Equity, and Distribution: Adam Smith's Answer to John Rawls's Difference Principle

Abstract: John Rawls essentially dismissed Smith as having relevance for his Kantian, non-utilitarian, theory of justice. However, there is a considerable body of opinion that Smith's moral theory was actually not utilitarian. Furthermore, Smith has not usually been seen as having cared much about distributive justice, distributive equity being outside the scope of his concept of justice. Distributive equity in the form of the Difference Principle is one of the main things Rawls asserts would be agreed to in the original position by rational agents. However, building on previous work this article shows this view of Smith to be erroneous, and, that Smith did have a more extensive and more practical approach to the problem of distributive equity than is found in Rawls's work.

1 Introduction

Despite a recent claim that John Rawls "appropriated" Adam Smith's economics (Johnson 2010), Rawls himself seems to have received little, if any, inspiration or filiation of ideas from Smith's ethics in general or his conception of justice in particular. On the one hand, this is not surprising since, after liberty and fair equality of opportunity, Rawls elevated distributive justice to the status of one of the two foundational principles rational agents would agree to in the original position, and Smith is not usually thought to have cared much about distributive justice. On the other hand, Rawls lumped Smith together with Hume, Bentham, and Mill as the "great utilitarians" (1971, p. vii), and his *A Theory of Justice*, was avowedly non-utilitarian in its principles.[1] Whatever Rawls may have taken from his economics, Smith, the moral philosopher, had nothing to say to Rawls, or at least that is the impression one gets.

---

[1] D.D. Raphael has long argued that Smith's ethics are not utilitarian, a point which he tried to raise with Rawls (1972–73; 2007, p. 46). Amos Witztum and I, following Raphael's lead, have also argued extensively that Smith's *Theory of Moral Sentiments* does not present a utilitarian theory of ethics, and that Rawls has profoundly misunderstood Smith's book (2013, pp. 572–573). My concern in the present paper is confined to the issues relating to distributive justice in Smith and Rawls, not to re-evaluate Smith's rightful position in the history of moral philosophy.

https://doi.org/10.1515/9783110537369-031

The purpose of this paper is to argue that Rawls too hastily dismissed Smith's work. While I think a strong case could be made that Smith endorsed Rawls's equal liberty principle and some form of equality of opportunity, I wish to argue that we can find in Smith's moral and economic writing a much more thorough and less ambiguous approach to the well-being of the worst off members of society than Rawls's vague difference principle.

For Rawls, establishing a principle for distributive justice within the theory of justice was entirely unproblematic. However, the same cannot be said of Smith. In previous work Barry Gordon and I, and Amos Witztum and I, have argued extensively for the idea that Smith's theory of justice does allow for issues of distribution to come under the principles of justice. This, however, is a controversial position as John Salter, for example, has argued in an on-going debate over the status of distributive justice in Smith. In his most recent critique he summarizes the debate succinctly:

> It is not, therefore, a distortion of Smith's views to say that they display a concern with social or distributive justice, as these terms have come to be understood in the contemporary, post-Rawlsian, period; that is to say, as terms that are practically synonymous with fairness. However, the revisionist claims regarding Smith's discussion of justice are not confined to the uncontroversial observation that he regarded poverty as a matter of justice as it is currently *understood*. According to recent statements of the revisionist view, Smith regarded the needs of the poor as a matter of justice in the sense that *he* understood the term (Salter 2012, p. 560; emphasis in the original; see also Salter 1994, 1997; Young 1997a; Witztum 2013).

My co-authors and I have presented our case in several previous publications (Young/Gordon 1996; Young 1997a, 1997b; Witztum 1997; Witztum/Young 2006). However, in this paper I would like to skirt the issue (at least initially) in order to concentrate on Rawls's difference principle, which everyone now would agree is indeed a matter of justice, and the extent to which Smith can be seen as holding a similar conception of the welfare of the least advantaged members of society. The principle is one of two principles of justice that Rawls argues would be selected by rational agents behind the veil of ignorance in the original position:

(a) Each person has the same indefeasible claim to a fully adequate scheme of equal basic liberties, a scheme which is compatible with the same scheme of liberties for all; and
(b) Social and economic inequalities are to satisfy two conditions: first, they are to be attached to offices and positions open to all under conditions of fair equality of opportunity; and second, they are to be to the greatest benefit

of the least-advantaged members of society (the difference principle) (Rawls 2001, pp. 42–43).

Our concern here is with the second part of the second condition for just inequality: that it be to the "greatest benefit" of the poorest members of the population.[2] This is from the Restatement of the *Theory of Justice*, but the same idea runs through all the iterations from the original edition of 1971 through the Restatement of 2001, including *Political Liberalism* (1993–2005), which is itself a recasting of the original theory as explicitly a theory of political justice, not a comprehensive moral philosophy or world view (Rawls 2001). Now the problem with this principle, which has been expressed as a maximin criterion of welfare maximization (Arrow 1973), is that it is virtually impossible to know if in practice the difference principle is satisfied by any set of basic institutions. Moreover, it would be difficult given Rawls's definitions to determine the line between the least advantaged and the others. As Rawls himself noted in *Political Liberalism*:

> Whether the constitutional essentials covering the basic freedoms are satisfied is more or less visible on the face of constitutional arrangements and how these can be seen to work in practice. But whether the aims of the principles covering social and economic inequalities are realized is far more difficult to ascertain. These matters are nearly always open to wide differences of reasonable opinion; they rest on complicated inferences and intuitive judgments that require us to assess complex social and economic information about topics poorly understood (Rawls 2005, p. 229).

Along the same lines Samuel Fleischacker argued that the difference principle is conceivably so expansive as to sanction almost any political economy:

> If the Difference Principle, for instance, means only that policies must aim to "help" the worst-off as much as possible, however "help" is defined and whatever factual claims are added in to interpret the aim of the policy, then it brings Plato's hierarchical utopia and Marx's egalitarian one, Milton Friedman's laissez-faire complacency and Harold Laski's

---

[2] Manuel Knoll points out to me that Rawls's conception of the "least advantaged" cannot simply be equated with "the poor". Indeed Rawls's offers more than one definition, and with the revised edition stating: "To fix ideas, let us single out the least advantaged as those who are least favored by each of the three main kinds of contingencies" (1999, p. 83). Summarizing he elaborates these three as based on social class, natural endowments, and luck. As I will argue Smith's least advantaged is simply the majority of the population, those who live by wages. Smith's approach does not require maximization and it does not require determining who is least advantaged, but since his encompasses the majority it will surely more than overlap Rawls's "least advantaged".

stifling paternalism, too close together to have any bite. No polemic for or against current policies can easily be read off of Rawls's principles (Fleischacker 1999, p. 195).

Fleischacker also proposes that to look after the well-being of the least well off, a guaranteed minimum, which may be found in Smith, is a preferable standard to maximin (1999, p. 236). In what follows I will lay out my case that Smith can be seen as endorsing a specific type of society and specific principles and policies which go a long way toward obviating the "complicated inferences and intuitive judgments" Rawls admitted would be necessary to use the principle in practice.

I begin with a consideration of Smith's welfare criterion, i. e. the over-arching norm from which the laws and policies are to be judged. In the "Introduction and Plan" of the *Wealth of Nations* (WN), Smith claims that "According therefore, as this produce, ... bears a greater or smaller proportion to the number of those who are to consume it, the nation will be better or worse supplied with all the necessaries and conveniences for which it has occasion" (WN Intro.2). Then much later he defines political economy as

> ... a branch of the science of a statesman or legislator, [which] proposes two distinct objects; first, to provide a plentiful revenue or subsistence for the people, or more properly to *enable them to provide* such a revenue or subsistence for themselves; and secondly, to supply the state or commonwealth with a revenue sufficient for the publick services. It proposes to enrich both the people and the sovereign (WN IV.Intro.1; emphasis added).

Aside from the hint that the people should be viewed as independent, self-governing agents, which I will return to, economists have traditionally viewed Smith as taking a highly aggregative perspective: national wealth, the people, annual output divided by the whole population, per capita GDP in modern parlance, are Smith's categories for both positive and normative economic analysis. Kenneth Boulding's presidential address to the American Economic Association in 1968 is a good case in point:

> The major impact of economics on ethics, it can be argued, has come because it has developed broad, aggregative concepts of general welfare which are subject to quantification. We can see this process going right back to Adam Smith, where the idea of what we would today call per capita real income, as the principal measure of national well-being, has made a profound impact on subsequent thinking and policy (Boulding 1969, p. 7).

The idea that Smith was working with such highly aggregated conceptions of the general welfare of the nation supports the traditional view that Smith did not care much about distribution of the total. Per capita real income rises if one person's income rises and no one else's falls, regardless of where in the initial distribution that person falls. However, this needs to be placed in the following context: "No society can surely be flourishing and happy, of which the *far greater part* of the members are poor and miserable" (WN I.viii.36; emphasis added).

Perhaps it was sentiments such as these that caught Malthus's attention in 1798. In the first edition of the *Essay on the Principle of Population* he included a little-referenced chapter on Adam Smith which opens with this characterization of Smith's great work:

> THE professed object of Dr Adam Smith's inquiry is the nature and causes of the wealth of nations. There is another inquiry, however, perhaps still more interesting, which he occasionally mixes with it; I mean an inquiry into the causes which affect the happiness of nations, or the happiness and comfort of the lower orders of society, which is the most numerous class in every nation (Malthus [1798] 2008, p. 124).

It is the recognition of this "other ... more interesting" inquiry in which the "happiness of nations" is equated with that of the "lower orders", the majority of the population, which immediately brings to mind the difference principle. Thus, a nation as a whole may be better supplied with real output if its per capita income rises, but it will only be *happier* if the labouring majority, those who live by wages, are seeing their real income rise.

Smith's emphasis on the growth of real total output in his analytical work has perhaps lent support to the idea that he believed growth is good regardless of how output is distributed. However, as Sandra Peart and David Levy have persuasively argued Smith's and Malthus's focus on the happiness of the poor majority of the population was the standard utilitarian view among the 19th-century classical economists (Levy 1995; Peart/Levy 2005). They, therefore, argue that the correct understanding of the utilitarian welfare standard was median income, i.e. the income of the household in the middle, not the average (Levy 1995).[3] Revisiting and extending previous work, in this paper I hope to recover this "more interesting" inquiry in Smith, and show that it is more "occasional" than perhaps Malthus was aware.

---

[3] As previously explained, I do not think it correct to place Smith's moral theory in the utilitarian camp. However, I agree with Peart and Levy that he identified the welfare of the nation with the welfare of the majority. By way of further clarification: the median income is sensitive to distribution, but the mean is not. If the highest income increases the mean increases, but not the median. If the lowest income increases this would increase the median and the mean.

2 Political economy and the happiness of nations

In analysing the concepts "welfare of a nation" or a "system of political economy" which aim to enrich the "people" we need to establish what welfare consists in and who the "people" are.

Fundamentally, political economy, being a branch of the science of legislation, would be rooted in the constitution. Constitutions of government, says Smith in *The Theory of Moral Sentiments* (TMS), "... are valued only in proportion as they tend to promote the happiness of those who live under them. This is there sole use and end" (TMS IV.1.11). This statement is found in the middle of a long paragraph in which Smith is talking about what arouses "public spirit" in a person who seems to lack humanity. Smith's analysis in this section is complex, and space limitations do permit doing if full justice here. In the same paragraph Smith observes that

> if you would implant public virtue in the breast of him who seems heedless of the interest of the country, it will often be to no purpose to tell him, what superior advantages the subjects of a well-governed state enjoy; that they are better lodged, that they are better clothed, that they are better fed (TMS IV.1.11).

The latter is repeated almost verbatim in the *Wealth of Nations* (WN):

> No society can surely be flourishing and happy, of which the far greater part of the members are poor and miserable ... they who feed, cloath and lodge the whole body of the people, should have such a share of the produce of their own labour as to be themselves tolerably well fed, cloathed and lodged (WN I.viii.36).

I have already alluded to the first part of this passage, and I will return to the ellipsis below. Happiness, says Smith, consists in the quality and quantity of the basics of life: food, clothing, and shelter. Furthermore, we can be sure that the rich already enjoy these in abundance. It is the majority, those who live by wages, with which the public-spirited person should be concerned. Indeed, happiness is defined in such a way that it takes the rich out of the picture. In evaluating constitutions we should look to the well-being of the majority.

In short, constitutions are judged according to the happiness of the people, and happiness consists at least in the first instance in being tolerably well fed, clothed, and housed. Smith also suggests that anyone motivated to reform the constitution would be motivated by sympathy with the suffering of the people. These criteria are clearly meant to apply to the poor majority, not the rich.

Both the definition of happiness and the identification of suffering as the object of the law-givers' sympathy reinforce Smith's statement in the *Wealth of Nations* that no nation can be considered happy if the majority of the people are miserable. Specifically, this is found in Smith's analysis of a just labour market.

3 A just labour market and the liberal reward of labour

Smith never completed his proposed treatise on law and government, so scholars must rely on TMS and student lecture notes to intuit what would have been in Smith's unfinished book. I can only give the briefest account of a few key issues here. It is common to view Smith following closely the natural law tradition in the *Lectures on Jurisprudence* (LJ), the student notes of Smith's moral philosophy course, which have survived and been published. The issue is the distinction between commutative and distributive justice, here explained in terms of perfect and imperfect rights:

> The common way in which we understand the word right, is the same as what we have called a perfect right, and is that which relates to commutative justice. Imperfect rights, again, refer to distributive justice. The former are the rights which we are to consider, the latter not belonging properly to jurisprudence, but rather to a system of morals [sic] as they do not fall under the jurisdiction of the laws (LJ (A) i.15).

Smith appears to have drawn a strict line between the two, which serves to remove questions of distributive equity from the province of government since they are not questions of justice, properly understood. This is reinforced in a manuscript fragment on justice, which was published as an Appendix to the Glasgow Edition of *The Theory of Moral Sentiments*: "In the Schools it has been distinguished by the name of distributive Justice, as the former, which can alone properly be called Justice, has been denominated commutative Justice" (TMS Appendix II, 390). The important difference is that justice can "be extorted by force" while beneficence cannot (TMS Appendix II, 390). This is the basis of the claim that the needs of the poor are not a matter of justice. Seen in the light of the famous invisible hand passage in TMS, we reach the conclusion that Providence, not government, will take care of the poor:

> They [the rich] are led by an invisible hand to make nearly the same distribution of the necessaries of life, which would have been made, had the earth been divided into equal portions among all its inhabitants, and thus without intending it, without knowing it, advance the interest of the society, and afford means to the multiplication of the species. When Prov-

idence divided the earth among a few lordly masters, it neither forgot nor abandoned those who seemed to have been left out in the partition. These last too enjoy their share of all that it produces (TMS IV.1.10).

The traditional view, based on the above, is that Smith drew a strict line between distributive justice and commutative justice; only the latter was justice "proper". However, in previous work my co-authors and I have shown that the line between the two types of justice is not so strict, and that it evolves over time, that the needs of the poor may be seen as an element of justice, and that distributive equity along with justice proper are both welfare criteria in Smith's "science of the legislator".

Now, if there is one place where the two types of justice overlap it is in the operation of the labour market. In a commercial society, "Every man ... lives by exchanging, or becomes in some measure a merchant ..." (WN I.iv.1). Commutative justice is what governs exchange in the market, and so when we speak of a labour market being "just" we mean in the sense of commutative justice. Its operation would entail no injury with which an impartial spectator would sympathize.

The chapter in the *Wealth of Nations* on the wages of labour begins with a seemingly obvious point that, "The produce of labour constitutes the *natural recompence* or wages of labour" (WN I.viii.1; emphasis added). Before going on I wish to establish two points. First, wages are to be thought of in real, not nominal terms, a distinction Smith has already explained (WN I.v.9). Although it is not stated here, we know wages are actually paid in money. It is the ability of the labourer to purchase "produce" that really counts. Wages are not actually paid in produce, because the law requires them to be paid in money:

> Whenever the legislature attempts to regulate the differences between masters and their workmen, its counsellors are always the masters. When the regulation, therefore, is in favour of the workmen, it is always *just and equitable*; but it is sometimes otherwise when in favour of the masters. Thus the law which obliges the masters in several different trades to pay their workmen in money and not in goods is quite *just and equitable* (WN I.x.c.61; emphasis added).

This linkage between justice and equity I believe has been largely missed in the literature, and I shall consider it shortly. The point here is that since the masters control law-making we can be sure that any law that favours labour will be just, and those which favour the masters will be unjust. Hence, payment in money is just.

Secondly, the real value of the wage is the natural recompense for labour. Now this is natural law language, which I have argued reflects the natural law roots of Smith's value and distribution theory (Young 2008). The wage payment is rooted in a just claim on the revenue of the employers. Smith then goes on to discuss the forces at work to determine the level of wages in real terms and their likely trend depending upon whether the overall system is in a progressive, stationary, or declining state. However, I wish to jump ahead to the issue of wage inequality.

Smith attributes inequality in the labour market to two broad sources: the nature of the employments and the "policy of Europe". In other words inequalities may be either natural or artificial. Those which arise from the nature of the employments we may consider just, while those resulting from policy are unjust, although there is one case where the results are nonetheless beneficial. There are five broad categories of natural inequalities in the labour market:

> First the agreeableness or disagreeableness of the employments themselves; secondly, the easiness or cheapness, or the difficulty or expence of learning them; thirdly, the constancy or inconstancy of employment in them; fourthly, the small or great trust which must be reposed in those who exercise them; and fiftly [sic], the probability or improbability of success in them (WN I.X.b.1).

It is not necessary to go into these five cases to understand the point: "The five circumstances above mentioned, though they occasion considerable inequalities in the wages of labour ... occasion none in the whole of the advantages and disadvantages, real or imaginary, of the different employments ..." (WN I.x.b.39). And the conditions necessary to achieve this equalization among other things there must be "the most perfect freedom" (WN I.x.b.40). The labour market functioning under conditions of perfect freedom (itself a principle of justice) will establish equality in the whole of the rewards minus costs. For example, the expense of acquiring an education creates a just basis for additional compensation – an instance of retributive justice in practice.

That this does present a picture of a just labour market is evident from Smith's condemnation of certain practices, such as long apprenticeships, which the policy of Europe enforces.

> The property which every man has in his own labour, as it is the original foundation of all other property, so it is the most sacred and inviolable. The patrimony of a poor man lies in the strength and dexterity of his hands; and to hinder him from employing this strength and dexterity in what manner he thinks proper without injury to his neighbour, is a plain violation of this most sacred property. It is a manifest encroachment upon the just liberty both of the workman, and of those who might be disposed to employ him (WN I.x.c.12).

This hardly needs elaboration; freedom exercised within the rules of justice is just liberty, which all should enjoy. A labour market in which freedom equalizes the whole advantages and disadvantages of all employments is a just labour market. Interferences are violations of natural justice. As matters of policy they are, of course, enjoined by the positive law.

Thus, a just labour market will create equality at a point in time, not an equality of real wages but one of net advantages. What about the general level of wages? Here Smith is concerned about the conditions which, first, establish a minimum below which wages should not be allowed to fall, and, second determine the liberal reward of labour, or its deficiency.

Smith deploys a basic supply and demand analysis to explain the aggregate, macroeconomic level of wages. While he begins with a bargaining power idea he quickly notes that no matter how much the masters might want to conspire to lower wages there is a minimum below which they cannot go. He then invokes the population principle that Malthus used a generation later so effectively in demolishing Godwin's utopia.

> A man must live by his work, and his wages must at least be sufficient to maintain him. They must upon most occasions be somewhat more; otherwise it would be impossible for him to bring up a family, and the race of such workmen could not last beyond the first generation (WN I.viii.15).

Now this minimum became known as the subsistence wage in later classical economics. It was a wage below which population would fall as mortality increased and vice versa when the wage was above subsistence. As we will see, this seems to be the mechanism Smith has in mind governing the aggregate supply of labour in the long run. Calling this a "subsistence wage" is, however, potentially misleading. The classical economists always defined this subsistence as a socially determined, not a biological, minimum, and Smith is no different (Waterman 1991, p. 271; see also Waterman 2012). For Smith the minimum is the "lowest which is consistent with common humanity" (WN I.viii.16). "Humanity" being a moral virtue could be a throwback the man of humanity found in TMS.

Fortunately, in a progressive commercial society the labourer would generally have the advantage and be able to negotiate higher wages. This depends on the interaction of the supply mechanism with the factors determining demand. In the aggregate, demand is regulated by, "funds which are destined for the payment of wages" (WN I.viii.18). Here Smith identifies the progressive, stationary, and declining states, and it is the progressive state which, "is in reality the cheerful and the hearty state to all the different orders of the society" (WN I.viii.43). If the constitution is to promote happiness, then it should promote the progressive state, and Smith has already argued that the progressive state brings about the liberal reward of labour, which is a great public benefit. The economics of the argument are straightforward. In the progressive state the demand for labour, which depends on the rate of capital accumulation with a given technology, will outpace the supply, and the real wage will rise over time.

> Is this improvement in the circumstances of the lower ranks of the people to be regarded as an advantage or as an inconveniency to the society? The answer seems at first sight abundantly plain. Servants, labourers, and workmen of different kinds, make up the *far greater part* of every great political society. But what improves the circumstances of the greater part can never be regarded as an inconveniency to the whole. No society can surely be flourishing and happy, of which the far greater part of the members are poor and miserable. *It is but equity*, besides, that they who feed, cloath and lodge the whole body of the people, should have such a share of the produce of their own labour as to be themselves tolerably well fed, cloathed and lodged (WN I.viii.36; emphasis added).

Firstly, note that the reason Smith raises the question is that the mercantile policy, which aimed for a favourable balance of trade emphasized low wages, since it was thought that low wages would contribute to the "competitiveness" of the nation's economy allowing it to increase its exports. We do not need to go into how Smith reconciled high wages with free trade. For my present purposes there are two lines of inquiry I want to pursue from this passage in addition to the points already established – first, the connection between the liberal reward of labour, population growth, and public happiness, and, second, the meaning of equity as an additional point in favour of the high wage economy of the progressive state.

"The most decisive mark of the prosperity of any country is the increase of the number of its inhabitants" (WN I.viii.23). Regardless of one's beliefs about over-population today, in Smith's day this was a reasonable claim. Given the supply and demand mechanisms explained above, a rising real wage will cause a rising population. Now the point is that this will improve the happiness of the lowest members of society. Why? Because the population mechanism operates only among the poor, and high levels of infant mortality must make for a great deal of human misery.

> But poverty, though it does not prevent the generation, is extremely unfavourable to the rearing of children. ... It is not uncommon, I have been told, in the Highlands of Scotland for a mother who has borne twenty children not to have two alive (WN I.viii.38).
>
> ... but in civilized society it is among the inferior ranks of people that the scantiness of subsistence can set limits to the further multiplication of the human species; and it can do so in no other way than by destroying a great part of the children which their fruitful marriages produce (WN I.viii.40).

> The liberal reward of labour, therefore, as it is the effect of increasing wealth, so it is the cause of increasing population. To complain of it is to lament over the necessary effect and cause of the greatest publick prosperity (WN I.viii.42).

The misery associated with the operation of the population principle is borne disproportionately by the working class. In the stationary state of China infant mortality is so common that a specialized occupation has developed to perform the "horrid office" of disposing of infants that cannot be fed (WN I.viii.24). A rising real wage not only brings them more food, clothing and shelter, but also reduces infant mortality and the tragedy of parents having to bury their children. And it is their prosperity which is explicitly equated to public prosperity, since only they will experience rising population.

Now Smith also points out that this result is a matter of equity, but equity *per se* as an attribute of justice is not developed in *The Theory of Moral Sentiments*. To grasp what Smith might have meant by equity we must look at its occurrences in the *Lectures on Jurisprudence*. In a number of places Smith uses terms such as "equity" and "natural equity", which suggests a connection between distributive justice and justice "proper" and a connection with modern concepts of justice as fairness.

For example,

> ... one who has been guilty of a crime frees himself from the obligation he is under to the offended person by submitting himself to the punishment which is to be inflicted on that crime, whether it be required by the law of *nature and equity* or by the civil law of the country (LJ (A) ii.162; emphasis added).

A similar expression appears in a discussion of the laws governing the repayment of debts:

> *Justice and equity* plainly require that one should restore the same value as he received without regard to the nominal value of the money, and therefore he is to restore as much in the old coin or an equall value in the new as he receiv'd. But the civil government in all countries have constituted the exact contrary of this (LJ (A) ii.80–81; emphasis added).

Other instances may be cited, but they all point in the same direction. Equity is virtually synonymous with justice and fairness. In all of these cases the reference is to the operation of the impartial spectator prior to, or as a criticism of, civil government. In addition, many of these cases have in common that they are instances of retributive justice, either in a negative sense of paying evil for evil, or in a positive sense of fitting payments to the value received. We have already seen the principle of retributive justice at work in Smith's very first sentence about the wages of labour. Equity would seem to constitute a fairness norm in Smith's theory of justice. The upshot is that he could have just as easily said that "it is but justice besides that they who feed, cloath and lodge the whole body of the people, should have such a share of the produce of their own labour as to be themselves tolerably well fed, cloathed and lodged". A tolerable level of happiness for the majority of the population does indeed seem to be not just a matter of public prosperity, but also a matter of justice as Smith understood the term. Distributive justice and commutative justice do indeed seem to overlap in his evaluation of the progressive state.

4 Education and independence

Smith, however, is not concerned solely with the material happiness of the majority; he is also concerned with the formation of theirs minds and characters. Consider, for example, Smith's well-known advocacy of publicly subsidized education to counteract the harmful effects of the division of labour on the "intellectual, social, and martial virtues" of the "great body of the people", we see that once again it is the majority labouring class that constitutes the public, but now the concern is not so much with happiness or prosperity. Rather Smith is worried about the mental and social capacities of people who work all day at one narrow, repetitive task (WN V.i.f.50). Education will help prevent specialized workers from becoming as "stupid and ignorant as it is possible for a human creature to become" (WN V.i.f.50). In turn this will improve the labourer's ability to judge in matters of public deliberation (WN I.xi.p.9).

The just operation of the labour market, as shown above requires freedom, but it also requires the ability to reason and deliberate over matters of self-interest. Net advantages cannot be equalized unless the agents in the market can roughly calculate the benefits and costs of entering various occupations, and moving from one place to another. In short, it requires educated and independent workers, the kind that could also acquire a political voice. Education is a matter of concern for the state, but independence came as an unintended consequence of the decline of feudalism and the rise of commercial society.

Now one of the great advances that commercial society represents over its feudal and "uncivilized" past is the elimination of the servile state of the majority of the population. We have already hinted at the high value Smith places on independence in the definition of political economy, previously quoted, and in the negative moral judgement attached to most interferences with liberty. However, dependency and independence are central themes of Smith's analysis of the fall of feudalism and the rise of commercial society following the collapse of the western part of the Roman Empire. "Order and good government" was first introduced in the cities and towns (WN III.iii.12), but the spread of commerce and manufacturing, "gradually introduced order and good government, and with them, the liberty and security of individuals, among the inhabitants of the country, who had before lived almost in a continual state of war with their neighbours, and of servile dependency upon their superiors" (WN III.iv.4). The "individuals" who have secured the goods of liberty and security are clearly those who lived previously in "servile dependency". The rise of commerce brings with it the division of labour, and this, in turn, changes the nature of dependency between rich and poor in significant ways.

> A man of ten thousand a year ... generally contributes, however, but a very small proportion to that of each [workmen and their employers], to very few perhaps a tenth, to many not a hundredth, and to some not a thousandth, nor even ten thousandth part of their whole annual maintenance. Though he contributes, therefore, to the maintenance of them all, they are more or less independent of him, because generally they can all be maintained without him (WN III.iv.11).

In commercial society the labouring majority depends on the expenditure of the rich, but with the advanced division of labour of commercial society, no one person depends on no other single person. Each individual is no longer subservient to the beneficence of a wealthy patron. The people are left free to produce their own livelihood; feeding them is no longer left to Providence. With independence comes the responsibility to take care of oneself, the virtue of prudence.

The feudal lords in this way lost their ability to command their tenants in battle, and, "were no longer capable of interrupting the regular execution of justice, or of disturbing the peace of the country. ... A regular government was established in the country as well as in the city ..." (WN III.iv.15). Thus, "A revolution of the greatest importance to the publick happiness, was brought about by two different orders of people, who had not the least intention to serve the publick" (WN III.iv.17). Happiness, we may now conclude, entails being "tolerably well" fed, clothed, and housed, and being independent, enjoying the liberty of being one's own master. Moreover, it is the majority who were previously in a servile condition who constitute the public whose happiness has been increased. Commercial society improves the condition of the majority materially and morally. Materially they are better supplied with the means of subsistence and their infants no longer die quite so often. Morally, we see that

> A poor independent workman will generally be more industrious than even a journeyman who works by the piece. The one enjoys the whole produce of his own industry; the other shares it with his master. The one, in his separate independent state, is less liable to the

temptation of bad company, which in large manufactories so frequently ruin the morals of the people (WN I.viii.48).

These labourers, being independent, learn the virtue of prudence. Not falling into bad company and having their morals corrupted they will better fit Smith's description of agents who are sensitive to sense of duty and the operation of the moral conscience. In Kantian terms their circumstances make them better able to become autonomous moral agents. Once again these are benefits that contribute to social welfare because they accrue to the poorest majority of the population, those who live by wages.

5 Conclusion

In previous work I have also considered the equity effects of land ownership, British commercial policy (the "mercantile system"), taxation, and famines. Space does not permit revisiting these aspects of the argument here. Suffice it to say that, since government is originally instituted to protect the rich from the invasion of their property by the poor (WN V.i.b.2), it is not surprising that Smith would find that when government seeks to manage economic affairs it does so for the benefit of the rich and detriment to the poor. Nonetheless, Malthus is quite right there is a second narrative in Smith, which focuses on the welfare of the majority, and it is quite extensive and consistent over a wide range of topics.

Having followed Malthus's observation through Smith's work we see it is surprisingly robust. Smith may be seen as having a wide-ranging set of policy norms, which have the unifying theme of being a practical application of the Rawlsian difference principle in the context of late 18th-century British commercial policy. The values that pervade the entire text centre on the welfare of the least advantaged members of society. In Smith's day this was the majority of the population, so I have essentially equated the least advantaged with the majority. Seen in this way Malthus's other inquiry runs through both of Smith's published works, and provides an extensive and consistent application of Rawls's principle.

Smith's recommendations are actually quite Rawlsian (with the exception of Rawls's advocacy for universal health care). The elimination of welfare for the rich, a system of progressive taxation, and government subsidized education constitute the policies which would improve the condition of the majority. Smith would probably put more weight on the ability of the private sector to achieve these results, as his system of natural liberty would allow independent self-interested and moral agents the necessary freedom to bring about the progressive state, which is also vital to raising the majority out of poverty. I think where Smith improves upon Rawls is that his program is more transparent as it suggests much simpler metrics of success: population growth and median real income, whereas Rawls's difference principle is by his own admission very difficult to determine whether it is satisfied. Smith does not propose a metric for the educational attainment of the majority, but raising it, would clearly be consistent with a Smithian program for improving the happiness of the majority.

If Amos Witztum and I are correct that a right to a minimum level of subsistence is a matter of justice and should be insured by what Smith understands as the constitution of a state, given the full complement of riches consistent with the state's level of development, adding health care and some level of educational attainment to the list of goods would be a legitimate extension to the modern world of Smith's conception of being "tolerably well fed". Similarly, I would modify population growth as the objective measure of increasing happiness. In its place I would put declining infant mortality and the freedom of Smith's independent families to practice Malthus's moral checks, i.e. family planning. Surely these are the reasons why increasing population for Smith is a sure sign of increasing happiness. Given a choice I would opt for Smith's liberalism over Rawls's.

Obviously from a Rawlsian perspective these policy issues are matters of justice. The debate over the role of distributive justice in Smith's normative economics now comes down to whether the rights of the majority to a minimum consistent with "common humanity" was a matter of justice as he understood it. I believe I have assembled sufficient evidence that Smith's moral and economic theories contain a Rawlsian perspective on distributive justice, which is more than incidental. Regardless of Smith's formal definitions it would seem that commutative and distributive aspects of justice intertwine in the normative perspectives from which Smith attacks mercantile policy and promotes natural liberty.

Bibliography

Arrow, Kenneth J. (1973): "Some Ordinalist-Utilitarian Notes on Rawls's Theory of Justice by John Rawls". In: *The Journal of Philosophy* 70, pp. 245–263. Stable URL: http://www.jstor.org/stable/2025006.

Boulding, Kenneth E. (1969): "Economics as a Moral Science". In: *American Economic Review* 59. No. 1, pp. 1–12.

Fleischacker, Samuel (1999): *A Third Concept of Liberty: Judgment and Freedom in Kant and Adam Smith*. Princeton, NJ: Princeton University Press.

Fleischacker, Samuel (2004): *A Short History of Distributive Justice*. Cambridge, MA: Harvard University Press.

Hume, David ([1777] 1975): *Enquiries Concerning Human Understanding and Concerning the Principles of Morals*. Third edition. L.A. Selby-Bigge (Ed.). Revised by P.H. Nidditch. Oxford: Clarendon Press.

Johnson, David (2010): "John Rawls's Appropriation of Adam Smith". *Doispontos* 7, pp. 65–86. Available at: http://ojs.c3sl.ufpr.br/ojs/index.php/doispontos/article/viewFile/20170/13341, visited on 10 July 2018.

Levy, David (1995): "The Partial Spectator in the Wealth of Nations: A Robust Utilitarianism". In: *The European Journal of the History of Economic Thought* 2, pp. 299–326.

Malthus, T.R. ([1798] 2008): *An Essay on the Principle of Population*. Geoffrey Gilbert (Ed.). Oxford World Classics Edition. Oxford: Oxford University Press.

Peart, Sandra J./Levy, David M. (2005): *The "Vanity of the Philosopher" From Equality to Hierarchy in Postclassical Economics*. Ann Arbor: University of Michigan Press.

Raphael, D.D. (1972–73): "Hume and Adam Smith on Justice and Utility". In: *Proceedings of the Aristotelian Society*, New Series 73, pp. 87–103.

Raphael, D.D. (2007): *The Impartial Spectato: Adam Smith's Moral Philosophy*. Oxford: Clarendon Press.

Rawls, John (1971): *A Theory of Justice*. Cambridge, MA: Belknap Press of Harvard University Press.

Rawls, John (1999): *A Theory of Justice*. Revised edition. Cambridge, MA: Belknap Press of Harvard University Press.

Rawls, John (2001): *Justice as Fairness a Restatement*. Erin Kelly (Ed.). Cambridge, MA: Belknap Press of Harvard University Press.

Rawls, John (2005): *Political Liberalism*. Expanded edition. New York: Columbia University Press.

Raphael, D.D. (2007): *The Impartial Spectato: Adam Smith's Moral Philosophy*. Oxford: Clarendon Press.

Ross, Ian Simpson (1995): *The Life of Adam Smith*. Oxford: Clarendon Press.

Rothschild, Emma (1992a): "Adam Smith and Conservative Economics". In: *The Economic History Review* 45, pp. 74–96.

Rothschild, Emma (1992b): "Commerce and the State: Turgot, Condorcet, and Adam Smith". In: *The Economic Journal* 102, pp. 1197–1210.

Rothschild, Emma (2001): *Economic Sentiments: Adam Smith, Condorcet, and the Enlightenment*. Cambridge, MA: Harvard University Press.

Salter, John (1994): "Adam Smith on Justice and Distribution in Commercial Societies". In: *Scottish Journal of Political Economy* 41, pp. 299–313.

Salter, John (2012): "Adam Smith on Justice and the Needs of the Poor". In: *Journal of the History of Economic Thought* 34. No. 4, pp. 559–575.

Smith, Adam ([1790] 1976a): *The Theory of Moral Sentiments*. D.D. Raphael/A.L. Macfie (Eds.). Oxford: Clarendon Press.

Smith, Adam ([1776] 1976b): *An Inquiry into the Nature and Causes of the Wealth of Nations*. A.S. Skinner/R.H. Campbell (Eds.). Oxford: Clarendon Press.

Smith, Adam (1978): *Lectures on Jurisprudence*. R.L. Meek/D.D. Raphael/P.G. Stein (Eds.). Oxford: Clarendon Press.

Waterman, Anthony (1991): *Revolution, Economics and Religion; Christian Political Economy 1798–1833*. Cambridge: Cambridge University Press.
Waterman, Anthony (2012): "Adam Smith and Malthus on High Wages". In: *European Journal of the History of Economic Thought* 19, pp. 409–429.
Witztum, Amos (1997): "Distributive Considerations in Adam Smith's Conception of Economic Justice". In: *Economics and Philosophy* 13, pp. 242–259.
Witztum, Amos (2005): "Property Rights and the Rights to the Fruits of One's Labor: A Note on Adam Smith's Jurisprudence". In: *Economics and Philosophy* 21, pp. 279–289.
Witztum, Amos (2013): "Adam Smith and the Need of the Poor: A Rejoinder". In: *Journal of the History of Economic Thought* 35, pp. 257–262.
Witztum, Amos/Young, Jeffrey T. (2006): "The Neglected Agent: Justice, Power, and Distribution in Adam Smith". In: *History of Political Economy* 38, pp. 437–471.
Young, Jeffrey T. (1997a): *Economics as a Moral Science*. Cheltenham: Edward Elgar.
Young, Jeffrey T. (1997b): "Justice and Price: Reply to John Slater". In: *History of Political Economy* 29, pp. 685–689.
Young, Jeffrey T. (2001): "Justice versus Expediency: The Wealth of Nations as an Anti-Political Economy". In: Forget, Evelyn/Peart, Sandra (Eds.): *Reflecting on the Canon*. London: Routledge, pp. 148–167.
Young, Jeffrey T. (2006): "Unintended Order and Intervention: Adam Smith's Theory of the Role of the State". In: *History of Political Economy*, Suppl. Vol. 37: *The Role of Government in the History of Economic Thought*, pp. 337–350.
Young, Jeffrey T. (2008): "Law and Economics in the Protestant Natural Law Tradition: Samuel Pufendorf, Francis Hutcheson, and Adam Smith". In: *Journal of the History of Economic Thought* 30, pp. 283–296.
Young, Jeffrey T./Gordon, Barry (1992): "Economic Justice in the Natural Law Tradition: Thomas Aquinas to Francis Hutcheson". In: *Journal of the History of Economic Thought* 14, pp. 1–17.
Young, Jeffrey T./Gordon, Barry (1996): "Distributive Justice as a Normative Criterion in Adam Smith's Political Economy". In: *History of Political Economy* 28, pp. 1–26.

Barry Stocker
Statism and Distributive Injustice in Adam Smith

Abstract: This paper seeks to displace contemporary "progressive" attempts to bring Adam Smith into the fold of thinkers who support a form of state intervention favouring the welfare of its poorest members through distributive justice. The paper argues that despite the validity of pointing to Smith's support of those at the lowest economic level, it never amounts to redistribution of wealth, especially to the poorest. The state structure Smith proposes does favour those with the most at stake in maintaining a stable political structure. The paper argues that the real and genuine concern Smith shows for the poorest element, would be supported by the state through the development of a legal system that would prevent or hinder the bad behaviour of the upper classes and state craft that promotes broader economic development while promoting the better virtues of societies wealthier members. Though there are distributive elements of Smith's theory that favours the poor, they tend to be measures that prohibit attempts at distribution that could end up harming the poor. Thus, there is no basis for the assertions of egalitarian liberals who see in Smith's work support for state sponsorship of an ideal formula for resource distribution.

Distribution and the state

The issue of distributive justice is present in the writings of Adam Smith. It is, however, an error to infer from this that Smith favoured state-instituted schemes of redistribution of economic goods away from the rich to the poor. It is also true to say that Smith's writings show contempt for an obsession with luxuries. Again, it is an error to see any idea of state-enforced distribution of economic goods away from the rich as following from this concern, or as proposed by Smith. Smith did not believe that economics was everything in life, but then few have including the "conservatives" and "libertarians" that some "progressive" commentators on Smith have claimed distorted Smith's message. "Progressive" commentators are correct to note that Smith was neither a capitalist anarchist on the lines of Herbert Spencer (1851), at least with his regard to future development of society and Michael Huemer (2013), nor a believer in a pure minimal state that only acts in the spheres of criminal justice and national defence on the lines of Wilhelm von Humboldt (1993) and Robert Nozick (1974). However, the number of societies run along those lines is close to zero and to say that Smith does not advocate these positions does not distinguish him from libertarians or small government conservatives, as some egalitarian redistributivist commentators claim. Smith was not an anarchist or a minarchist, but the same applies to Friedrich Hayek (1960), Milton Friedman (2002), and James Buchanan (2005), as well as more current thinkers in the same classical liberal or libertarian tradition like David Schmidtz (2006), Jerry Gaus (2011) and Jacob Levy (2015). Smith believed that the poor are more benefitted where the state stops doing bad things than by schemes of state intervention. The objections to the sentiments of many of the wealthier members of society is a criticism of moral standards not a call for state-enforced removal of their wealth.

Egalitarian constructions of Smith I: Gavin Kennedy

The issue inherent in the assumption that libertarians have not read, or at least not properly understood, *The Theory of Moral Sentiments* (Smith 1982b) or *Lectures on Jurisprudence* (1982a) is that Smith's arguments there about virtue and justice contradict any preference for small government and minimally regulated market economies. Gavin Kennedy set up this kind of approach with *Adam Smith's Lost Legacy* (2005) which, while undertaking an admirable job of demonstrating the breadth of Smith's achievement, relies on a good deal of negative simplification of other views of Smith, as in criticisms of "laissez-faire libertarian neo-conservatives" (Kennedy 2005, p. 232). This in itself sums up a world of oversimplification and false equivalence. Neo-conservative, in the precise use of political terms, refers to those American right-wingers who are most motivated by a belief in American interventionism in the world, based on a strong military and aggressive foreign policy to remodel the world on American lines, with a moralistic understanding of the merits of a tradition of constitutional democracy (Kristol 2011). Though the "Neo-cons" are maybe more free market than statist in economics, many are "liberal Democrats" (or what would be mostly known as social democrats in other parts of the world) who realigned with the right on issues of international relations. They are by no means pure libertarians in economics and are certainly not pure libertarians in other fields, where they may tend towards social conservatism and certainly towards security state national conservatism. As a distinctive doctrine, libertarianism is liberal on social and national identity issues and sceptical of aggressive state policy in international relations, particularly if it requires the kind of large military establishment that significantly expands the size of the state.

The Kennedy approach, and some of the more recent egalitarian liberal scholarship on Smith, is sometimes influenced by this conflation of economic liberalism or libertarianism and conservatism, as if the more free market Smith commentators must be right-wing in every sense. Free market libertarian leaning scholarship on Smith by Craig Smith (2006), Daniel Klein (2007), Deirdre McCloskey (2005, 2008), Russ Roberts (2013) and others is strongly aware that Smith was not a strict minarchist, and gives comprehensive coverage to texts Smith wrote other than *An Inquiry into the Nature and Causes of the Wealth of Nations* (= *An Inquiry*). This current of scholarship is not dominated by an apologia for the New Right since the 1970s, as is often assumed, though it may prefer the economics of the New Right to the more statist elements of left thinking on economics. Preferring economic policies of one political current is not in itself an endorsement of non-economic aspects of that current, and is not even a full endorsement of the economics, which have generally been regarded by libertarian thinkers as sometimes the best available from a limited choice, rather than as an ideal arrangement. The qualified advocacy of the economic policies of some right of centre governments is not the same as an endorsement of philosophical conservatism, and for libertarians often goes with positions on open borders, cosmopolitanism in culture, moderate punishment of crime, social tolerance, and so on, at odds with thoroughgoing conservatism. This is certainly true of the classical liberal and libertarian thinkers noted above. Of course there are examples of overlaps between small government free market thinking and thoroughgoing conservatism, but rather less so than what some egalitarian liberal commentators appear to assume.

Egalitarian constructions of Smith II: Lisa Herzog and Deborah Boucaoyannis

Lisa Herzog refers to Smith as linking virtue to prosperity as the ideal outcome in Chapter 5 of *Inventing the Market* (2013), where she discusses *The Theory of Moral Sentiments*, with regard to mismatch between effort or moral worthiness and rewards in economic goods, something which Smith discusses for example at VI.III.30 (1982b, pp. 252–253), though Herzog (2013, p. 99) focuses on I.3,II.3 (Smith 1982b, p. 62). This passage in Smith refers to how we like to think of virtue being rewarded and how this leads to not very well grounded judgements, such as that we ignore Caesar's crimes because he won great battles, not a critique of the distribution of economic goods within market society. Herzog (2013, p. 91) also refers to VI.I.5.9 (Smith 1982b, p. 26) on these lines, but again this is about the strong human tendency to wish to believe that virtue is always what is rewarded, rather than anything else.

Herzog uses the libertarian writer Deirdre McCloskey as a supporting reference here to expand on Smith, without apparently noticing that McCloskey is a libertarian, but in any case using McCloskey's idea of bourgeois virtue to explain Smith. Herzog is referring to *Bourgeois Virtues* (2006), which is an influential book in libertarian circles. She then goes on (2013, p. 91) to look at how Hayek uses Smith's arguments and Hayek with regard to the role of virtues in the economy. Herzog does acknowledge (p. 97) that libertarian thinkers, and all liberals in the most general sense of the term, would be happy with her version of Smith on market place justice, but this leaves in place a way of setting up the argument which at least sometimes appears to oppose Smith to libertarianism.

Herzog gets a bit more tendentious a few pages later (Herzog 2013, p. 99) when she looks at Smith acknowledging that employers acting in co-operation have more power than employees in negotiations referring to *An Inquiry* I.VIII.12. However, Smith does not argue for state action to redress this but rather argues in a subsequent passage (pp. 15–24), which Herzog does not adequately acknowledge, that the surplus going to employers from holding down wages tends to flow back into the labour market in demand for labourers, so pushing wages up, and allowing workers to share in increasing national prosperity. What Herzog does acknowledge is limited circumstances in which demand may increase, such as in the colonies, overlooking the general point that Smith makes, though she does appear to acknowledge Smith's main point, if in rather vague terms, in a reference to "trickle down" (p. 107). In general, Herzog seems to waver between seeing Smith as close to the libertarian aligned thinkers with whom she disagrees from a point of view here articulated with reference to her reading of Hegel, and seeing Smith as saying something different which can be used against the libertarians.

However, in her paper, "Adam Smith on Markets and Justice" (2014), Herzog seems to be arguing that if Smith was alive today his more egalitarian concerns would have gone under the influence of egalitarian liberalism and some recent schools of economics to favour state and legal action to favour much flatter income distribution and dispersed ownership of economic wealth. What Herzog more precisely claims is that "given the current state of economic knowledge" (2014, p. 872) along with the work of egalitarian political and social theorists, Smith would have favoured more interventionist measures. This is however rather speculative and clearly just about all Austrian economists (as in the school which includes Hayek) and a significant proportion of neoclassical economists would dispute her view of what "economic knowledge" now shows.

Herzog here gives some weight to Deborah Boucoyannis' "The Equalizing Hand: Why Adam Smith Thought the Market Should Produce Wealth without Steep Inequality" (2013), a paper which argues that Smith's concerns with interest group capture of policy and law, along with institutional distortions of market outcomes, and basic concern with a share for the poor in increasing wealth, would have led him to institutional designs with "pre-distributive" goals, that is laws and institutions designed to spread wealth. The trouble with this is the assumption that if only Smith knew what we "know" that he would favour a bigger state is its disregard of small state libertarian aligned thinkers like Buchanan (2005) and Hayek (1960) who were deeply concerned with minimising interest group distortions while ensuring that laws, and markets under law, would serve genuine universal and public goods.

Jeffrey Young puts a less statist interpretation on Smith's concern with the condition of the poorest than Boucoyannis, Amartya Sen (2011), Herzog at times, and other egalitarian liberal commentators on Smith. His approach is, however, close on the question of distributive justice and state action to one of the leading egalitarian liberal Smith commentators, Fleischacker (2005), as both argue that Smith wished for a system to benefit the poorest, but that he was cautious about how far state action could be used. Both suggest that Smith's view of justice is part of a natural tradition going back to Aristotle, in which distributive justice concerns do not lead to much in the way of public action to assist the poor. Smith's twist on this tradition, as both Young and Fleischacker argue, is more for the state to stop doing things which harm the poor, and to favour the poor over the rich within a limited sphere of action. This is the way of understanding Smith's view of distributive justice, which is closest to what Smith argued himself, as libertarian and egalitarian liberal commentators are able to agree when working to the highest level of scholarship and argument.

Justice, sovereignty and property

The three concerns shaping Smith's view of distributive justice, that is in the emergence of views on distributive justice within various discussions, are the survival of the state, the limitations of the role the state plays in society, and the protection of property. The emphasis on the importance of the state maintaining itself and the emphasis on protecting property can combine to some degree since protection of property includes the property of the rich who have the strongest interest in the maintenance of a state that protects property.

Smith's view that a state system of justice in significant part exists to protect the rich from the poor is quite direct and well known. It forms the core of a discussion in of *An Inquiry* (1981), Book V, Part II (1981 vol. II, pp. 708–723) and certainly distinguishes him from the most radical forms of egalitarianism, even if it does not itself preclude all forms of downward distribution to stabilise the state. Of course Smith could be said to demonstrate some empathy for the poor who less obviously benefit from the law, but it is not plausible to read that passage as anything other than an examination in very direct terms of the necessity of an unequal distribution of property within law and civil government. Nevertheless it is sometimes taken out of context by those egalitarian commentators eager to present Smith as their precursor (Rothschild 2001, p. 69). Smith's hopes that such government and law also benefit the poor have more to do with the general growth of prosperity than a flattening out of property distribution.

The emphasis on the importance of the state limiting itself (Haakonssen 1981, p. 94) is both potentially conflicting and potentially harmonious with the state survival concern. The goal of state survival might push the state to go well beyond its desirable limits (as when the state spends and controls too much in the course of war). It can also be said that a commitment to limiting the state may prevent self-destructive state expansion. Smith's attitude towards these questions is in any case contextual rather than absolutist, and can be seen as part of the growth of the art of government that Michel Foucault (2003) identifies with Enlightenment liberalism and political economy. The limits of the state are constantly open to debate as is clear in *An Inquiry* V.

Smith's commitment to the idea that the state should first of all exist, so that it can provide benefits to all can also express itself in quite brutal statements discussing the role of the state in protecting property, along with the use of violence against those communities too lacking in civilised virtues to be part of civil society under law. As Foucault points out in *On the Government of the Living* (2014), the Enlightenment is also a time of a growing tendency to see the criminal as an enemy of the social contract, at war with society. Following Foucault, we could say that Smith has something in common with Rousseau, which is a wish for a society in which the criminal is clearly defined as the enemy of just laws necessary to civil society.

There is an aspect of Smith which did exhibit a clear and consistent concern that the poor should benefit from all the arrangements of laws and institutions, combining this with a disdain for the luxuries of the rich. The latter though, to some significant degree, can be seen in terms of Smith's Stoic- and Epicurean-influenced moral background, rather than any strong commitment to equality of income or wealth. There is nothing inherently egalitarian about Stoicism in economic terms. Seneca and Marcus Aurelius did not redistribute the wealth and power they possessed. There is a difference between deploring excessive enthusiasm for luxury and limiting the capacity of the rich to purchase luxury.

Smith certainly does not regard it as a priority of state policy to directly promote luxury for the richest, though such luxury is the inevitable outcome of commercial society. Equally, Smith certainly does not advocate confiscation of wealth or anything more than quite minor adjustment to laws and policy in an egalitarian direction. Minor certainly by the standards of egalitarian liberal thinkers. Smith's major concern is that commercial society should work so that everyone, including the poor, shares in the benefits of increasing wealth. This, however, does not reflect any belief that wealth for some must create poverty for others or that a society based on any planned limit to inequality would be a desirable goal.

Smith's ethical foundations

The Theory of Moral Sentiments (1982b) gives psychological and social bases for moral rules and judgements. Smith strongly resisted the idea of an egotistical reduction of ethics, but the development of moral sentiments and principles of justice as they appear in *The Theory of Moral Sentiments* and *Lectures on Jurisprudence* (1982a), does not establish a sharp distinction between self-regarding acts and altruistic acts, since the latter also involve some kind of search for some kind of esteem. That is not to say that Smith says there is no pure moral motivation, but he does recognise the persistent force of wishing to be well regarded, as well as to genuinely merit moral esteem. The famous phrase Part III, Section II "Man naturally desires, not only to be loved, but to be lovely" (Smith 1982b, p. 113) emphasises pure merit, but does so by acknowledging the supporting power of the wish to seem meritorious.

It should also be noted that Smith was sceptical of the merits of the most arduously demanding moral theories, as *The Theory of Moral Sentiments* Part VII survey of theories of virtue shows, where he briefly but significantly indicates appreciation for Epicureanism (1982b). His posture towards Stoicism has been described as fear of it as a complete social system (Griswold 1999, p. 309), as is suggested by critical comments on Stoicism in *The Theory of Moral Sentiments* (1982b, p. 143, p. 156, pp. 292–293). The significance of this for his views on equality and luxury is that there is no basis for claiming that Smith could have had Stoic reasons for advocating an equality of austerity in preference to a society, where there is luxury and the inequality that generally accompanies luxury, even if he did regard a devotion to luxury as morally deficient.

As can be seen particularly, but not only, in *Lectures on Jurisprudence*, ethics and justice on a collective level grows and improves over time, on the whole with the progress through hunting, pastoral, agricultural, and commercial stages of society for Smith. The idea of social and political justice emerges from the experience of institutions and state craft, rather than the creation of abstractly perfect schemes. Smith strongly criticises perfect schemes in *The Theory of Moral Sentiments*, in a well-known passage on the man of system (1982b, pp. 233–234).

Though this passage does not preclude modest steps in a more egalitarian direction, it certainly precludes the imposition of a scheme of distributive justice, prior to the distributive effects of commercial society under the rule of law. This is particularly the case if it strongly burdens any major section of society, regarding which Smith's wording certainly suggests inclusion of aristocratic, financial, and commercial concentrations of wealth.

It seems unlikely then that Smith would wish to implement a complete scheme for the redistribution of economic goods according to an ideal scheme of just reward, particularly when Smith does not regard distributive justice as primarily a matter of state action. The egalitarian aspect of Smith's thought flowed from thoughts about ethics and justice, which did not directly argue for a systematic view of distributive justice. Smith does not give us a fully explicit theory of how far state action and positive law should promote a view of distributive justice. If he says that justice as such leads us to concern for the poorest, that is not the same as demanding state action and positive laws to bring about the goals of natural justice.

Smith did not give very high standing to the stronger forms of egalitarian thinking (Raphael 2007, p. 123; Hanley 2009, p. 208), nor did he indicate a wish for increasing state action and legislation to implement his vision of justice and ethics, whether with regard to egalitarian thought or not. His vision of political economy as of civil institutions and law is that they should be based in "nature", which is why he uses the phrase "natural liberty", further suggesting some distance from ideas of expanding state action and legislation.

What Smith does say on the topic of distributive justice in *The Theory of Moral Sentiments* (1982b), and it is not something he ever presents as a central theme, strongly suggests two main commitments: some, but only some cautious modification of the distribution of economic goods resulting from the working of the market is desirable; distributive justice emerges more from removing the state from the workings of markets than state schemes of redistribution. Both commitments are strongly conditioned by arguments that injustice and economic failings result from state action. Importantly, economic success and justice are seen as interpenetrating in voluntary transactions under the rule of law. Public good constraints are allowed on market exchanges, but only of very general kinds to satisfy very general public goods which demonstrably provide common benefit. "Natural liberty" is the fundamental guide, not state-enforced distributive justice.

Key passages from *The Theory of Moral Sentiments* suggest two types of situation which may lead Smith to some consideration of distributive justice through legislation and state action, but they only suggest a limited scope. In Part V, Section IX, Smith considers the possibility that someone of bad character, a "knave", may have more success at farming than a "man of virtue". We may wish to correct for nature in this kind of case, as Smith suggest. Nature here appears to stand for luck and natural endowments. Smith seems to both suggest that nature produces its own correction, through the natural inherent punishments and rewards that vices and virtues bring, and that humans wish to compensate for the kind of harshness of natural luck mentioned above. In this type of situation (1982b, p. 168), Smith suggests that nature itself and deeply rooted reactions of the human sentiments, which can themselves be regarded as "natural", co-operate in reducing the extent to which the unjust may prosper more than the just.

The second type of situation in which distributive justice may come into play is the general application of charity and benevolence as part of justice. This might of course include the first type of situation, but the first type stands out as a situation where benefits are given to those who do not work hard if they are of generally good character. This is explicitly stated in the cited passage. It is perhaps a support of a general principle of beneficence that we have a tendency to help the good of character even where they do not seem so deserving. The second type of situation, discussed in Part VII, Section II of *The Theory of Moral Sentiments*, moves away from the a specific situation of beneficence in which we see how nature and sentiments interact to a general duty of benevolence. Neither the narrower nor the broader type of situation requires state directed schemes of redistribution. Perhaps they are compatible with state-enforced schemes of distributive justice, but as Smith emphasises individual action, they do not require state action.

It is not just in the natural law arguments of the *Lectures on Jurisprudence* or the moral arguments of *The Theory of Moral Sentiments* that Smith develops his views on distributive justice and it is certainly a mistake to think of *An Inquiry* as only concerned with economic efficiency to the exclusion of those issues. Recognition of this aspect should not lead us though to ignore the extent to which Smith is concerned with a model of commercial society in such a way as to be suspicious of much intrusion into natural processes. It is fundamentally important to note that for the most part what Smith says that has an egalitarian thrust is arguing that the state should withdraw, rather than that the state should do more.

Two aspects of distribution

Two major themes come out in the concerns with equality and distribution: injustice towards the poor and injustice between sectors of society. The first brings us closer to the purer forms of distributive justice questions, and the second closer to the state craft issues concerned with maintenance of the state. Smith sees injustice as resulting from collaboration between merchants in the same sector in a famous passage from *Wealth of Nations*, in Part I, Section X. This is where Smith argues that traders when gathered together for any purpose, including leisure, tend to engage in conspiracies against the public good (1981 vol. I, p. 145). This should not be taken as an argument for expanding state action to counteract a deficiency of markets. Smith goes on to argue that such conspiracies against the public good are assisted by state requirements for businesses to appear in official registers, which only encourages them to come together and then work against the public good.

As the quotation above shows, the abuse of the market by cabals of business people is more the consequence of state intervention than of free commerce in Smith's understanding, a point which is missed if the first sentence of the first paragraph quoted is isolated from the subsequent sentence and from the subsequent paragraph, as frequently happens. The state enabling, encouraging and even requiring enterprises to form corporate associations is the biggest reason for merchants conspiring against the public. This passage should then lead us to see Smith as suspicious of a greater regulatory role for the state and as arguing for some measures of deregulation as a means of preventing monopolistic exploitation of consumers.

The great injustices to the poor that Smith mentions in *An Inquiry* Part I, Section X, comes in part from the way the Poor Law tends to tie the poor to their locality of birth (1981 vol. I, p. 152), under suspicion that they might apply for public funds in a parish (that is the minimal unit of local government in Britain), where they lack previous connections. There is a concern here with the suffering of the poor, but also with the negative consequences for the economy of restricting labour mobility. A related concern is that lingering requirements from the Middle Ages for seven years of apprenticeship, before practising a craft, limits the chances for the poor to improve their economic situation. The poor are less able to offer skills to make a good living if faced with an artificial seven year delay before putting their skills out on the market. There is a concern for the condition and rights of the poor, combined with the negative consequences for consumers in general and the public good of measures harming the poor.

The concern for the condition of the poor in Smith is generally intertwined with other issues, as is concern about the excessive economic benefits gained through market manipulation. In both cases the issue is just as much one of economic efficiency and the most general public good as it is with the distribution of economics goods. Though there is recognition that some economic benefits come to business owners from market rigging, there is no suggestion that there ought to be a ceiling on wealth or income or even taxes that aim to shift the distribution of wealth and income. The call is for state inaction to avoid making situations which arise at times in the course of things more frequent and more damaging.

Another source of injustice for the poor in Smith is the application of taxes on the necessities of life, in which case the concern is more purely one for the condition of the poor. Smith's favours taxing luxuries rather than necessities, but he nowhere calls for graduated (progressive) taxes on income and wealth. Smith's view of taxation is *not* for progressive taxation on *income* and *wealth*, but for *consumption* taxes on luxury goods (1981 vol. II, pp. 869–871), and even so he expresses considerable reservations about the benefits (1981 vol. II, pp. 896–899). Smith refers to the disincentive effects on honest economic activity and the incentives generated for smuggling, which strongly suggests that Smith only favoured a moderate rate of taxation, even on the luxuries of the rich. There is no support for large scale redistribution in Smith's comments on taxation. Egalitarian liberal commentators on Smith tend to read his support consumption taxes on luxuries as general support for progressive taxes, but consumption tax on "luxury" is not a progressive income tax, so these are two different issues and cannot be brought together as it there was no real difference.

It is public debt more than the workings of the market which results in a distributive injustice for Smith, the understanding of which includes the assumption that "natural liberty" is a better basis for political economy than state intervention, as stated in *An Inquiry* Part IV, Section IX (1981 vol. II, pp. 687–688), which surely creates a burden of justification for those who wish to see Smith as an advocate of active state redistribution. There Smith puts forward "natural liberty" as an ideal, which does not seem at all compatible with redistributive schemes. A redistributive interpretation of Smith would have to stretch the commitment to the state maintaining "an exact system of justice" into a commitment to distributive justice, in which distribution is downward. There is, however, no such commitment in Smith, here or anywhere else, and no indication that he wishes to stretch definitions of justice in that direction. He does refer to the need for public institutions and works that could not be financed by individuals.

The evidence of Part V of *Wealth of Nations*, "On the Revenue of the Sovereign or Commonwealth", is that beyond the army, police, judiciary and penal system, Smith only awards a role for the state in transport infrastructure and education. Even in these cases, Smith prefers private investment and provision with charges, where possible. Nothing is said about redistribution of wealth or the construction of an extensive welfare system. The overall aim of Smith's thinking on law and public policy is to stay as close as possible to "natural liberty", that is the voluntary habitual interactions between private individuals and private corporations. His views on justice and social ethics come from a natural law tradition, in which property rights and voluntary action are central, particularly in comparison to state action on welfare and distribution of economic goods. Distributive justice, as understood by recent egalitarians, is hardly an issue. Just distribution in this tradition is understood as preservation of individual justice in the acquisition and transmission of property.

There might be an opening for egalitarians in Aristotle and Aquinas, Grotius and Pufendorf with regard to distribution as linked with social and institutional stability needs, along with mentions of provision for the poorest. However, this is not an opening Smith follows in the manner of recent egalitarians. There might be a further opening for egalitarians in the voluntaristic turn from natural law to political contract, but contract theory as understood in the seventeenth and eighteenth centuries was close to the natural law tradition. It was not influenced by egalitarian constraints with regard to economic distribution. Rousseau might be a partial exception on the issues of voluntarism and egalitarianism, but much less so than the popular image suggests. In any case, Smith neither suggests the kind of voluntarism for principles of property and distribution nor the egalitarian constraints that recent egalitarians have suggested. Extrapolation from the overlapping natural law and early modern contractual traditions in an egalitarian direction is legitimate if undertaken openly, but should not be confused with the understanding of what Smith, Grotius, Pufendorf, Locke et al themselves thought of as desirable and just.

Hume, Burke and the radicals

The point that forcible transfer of capital from one part of the economy is bad for national wealth can be extended with reference to Hume's comments on the disadvantage of transferring wealth from the poor to the rich, through public debt. Public debt leads to a forced transfer of income from the productive sectors of the economy to creditors, so expanding the financial sector of the economy to a degree which may make it parasitic. That includes a transfer also noted by

Hume, Smith's friend and more importantly a major influence on his economic thought, from tax payers of low income to rich holders of government bonds. Like Hume, Smith is critical to some degree of the financial sector of the economy, but of the way it is supported by government not its market place "natural" activities. Smith discusses these issues in a rather digressive way in *An Inquiry* Part V, Section III "of publick Debts", while David Hume provides a more concentrated argument with similar points in his essay "Of Public Credit".

> The taxes, which are levied to pay the interests of these debts, are apt either to heighten the price of labour, or to be an oppression on the poorer sort.
> ...The greater part of the public stock being always in the hands of idle people, who live on their revenue, our funds, in that view, give great encouragement to an useless and unactive life (Hume 1987, p. 355).

Egalitarian Smith scholars typically refer to negative externalities and asymmetries of power in the economy that are not addressed by Smith (Herzog 2014), which of course implicitly recognises that Smith was more concerned with correcting and limiting state activity not expanding it to reverse the consequences of market activity. He *might* have expanded the field of legitimate state action, if he had lived long enough to see those issues become of more concern in political life and in political thought. However, it is clearly important to situate Smith within the politics of his time, before attempting to situate Smith within the politics of our time.

Edmund Burke was a friend of Smith and an admirer of his ideas on political economy. Smith appears to have greatly appreciated Burke's own understanding of his economic work: "Burke is the only man I ever knew who thinks on economic subjects exactly as I do, without any previous communications having passed between us" (Rae 1895, p. 610). Furthermore, two pages later in the same book we receive the information that Smith was a supporter of the Rockingham Whigs (p. 612), so a supporter of the centre ground in the parliamentary politics of the time, which of course was the politics of different factions of oligarchy and aristocracy, hardly suggesting that Smith was a plausible prophet of the distinctly left leaning social democratic "egalitarian liberals" of the present age.

Friendship, including Smith's friendship with Burke, does not itself indicate agreement of ideas, and even admiration of ideas does not itself indicate agreement. Friends and admirers may stretch ideas they are interested in beyond recognition to suit their own interests. Nevertheless it is of some relevance that Smith had a marked influence on the one of the major conservative thinkers of the time, an admirer of hierarchy and inequality (Burke 1968). It is sometimes argued that Burke put community cohesion above free markets, and there is some evidence for that, but what he meant by cohesion clearly included hierarchy, property, tradition, landed aristocracy, deference, and inequality.

In this context, we should recall Smith was happy enough to accept recognition from the political establishment in the Britain of his time, who greatly admired him, that is the establishment based on aristocratic-oligarchic domination in politics with little interest in economic equality as an end in itself. Again this is not a decisive basis for interpreting Smith, who might have accepted recognition and a state sinecure from a radical egalitarian government, but still no one has ever found that Smith was arguing for, or hoping for, such a government. Arguments that he wanted such a thing are inferential if not wholly speculative, having no more than an indirect relation with what is stated in Smith's texts, or his recorded conversations.

The evidence is that he hoped for the evolution of the monarchical British state away from aristocratic, state monopoly and guild interests towards concerns with the most general kind of public good on the basis of "natural liberty" in the economy. It is true that Smith influenced late eighteenth-century "radicals", most obviously Sophie de Grouchy, who translated *The Theory of Moral Sentiments* into French and added eight letters of commentary. However, de Grouchy was not a "radical" in the sense of favouring state designs for equality in economic goods (Berges 2015) and that was not the "radical" position in the eighteenth century. Until well into the nineteenth century "radical" refers to advocates of free trade, equality in individual rights and removal of economic privileges, not state redistribution of economic goods within commercial society. A lot of literature on Smith as egalitarian "progressive" assumes that a radical in this sense must be taken as the precursor of radicalism in socialist or at least social democratic terms. This is a clear case of misusing concepts by ignoring their changing meaning, what can be called bad genealogy, even if it is a popular move.

Conclusion: Current libertarian thought

There is distributive justice in Smith in the sense that he favours the distribution that emerges from freedom in economic activities, and in the state measures he favours to benefit the poor rather than the rich. However, that is not the same as the kind of belief in a predetermined pattern of distribution of justice which egalitarian liberals in general favour. There are ways of extending Smith's arguments into more radical egalitarianism while remaining true to his small state vision. There are capitalist libertarians, like Roderick Long, who argue that it is possible to favour a flat income distribution without favouring a state designed plan of redistribution (2012), which may mean following the egalitarian norms proposed by John Rawls in *A Theory of Justice* (1971), as Gary Chartier suggests (2014), but not applying them through state mechanism.

These are ideas to be found in the writings of those who believe that markets and property exist best through voluntary protection and law enforcement agencies; that is without the power of a central state which monopolises violence, so that there is no strong force favouring large scale concentrations of property. In that case, state actions that favour financial services and large companies cannot exist and such economic entities would not exist. Without such large entities, there can only be a diverse and broadly equal range of small companies and the self-employed. This kind of analysis draws on elements of Smith and Hume discussed above, such as the tendency of state law to favour the existence of a property owning class and for the instruments of public finance to favour an investing class. To some degree Smith and Hume argue that unjust outcomes for the less propertied members of society can be eliminated, which can be taken further in a purely voluntarist direction though that is not what Hume and Smith favoured.

In another part of the libertarian spectrum, there are moderate "classical liberals", that is those whose ideas are closest to eighteenth-century arguments for limiting government rather than abolishing it, such as Jerry Gaus in *The Order of Public Reason* (2011) and John Tomasi in *Free Market Fairness* (2012). They advocate some measure of ameliorative redistribution to maintain the living conditions of the poorest, but not any attempt to erode the distributive pattern produced by profit creation and competition in a market based on property rights and contract, which on the whole they believe brings benefits to all.

If this paper has been successful, it has demonstrated that the work of the recent self-identified classical liberals is the closest position in the political thought of our time to Smith's own position. They share commitments to secure property rights, the benefits of economic equality arising in an open competitive market, state intrusion into the market purely and only for well-grounded claims to serve a public good, intervention for a common interest, only rather than a sectional interest, and an openness to state assistance for the poorest where it does not undermine the open market economy. An open market economy is seen as vital to individual liberty and general human flourishing, as well as economic growth. On this argument Smith and recent classical liberals, at the moderate end of the libertarian spectrum, have a common cause of opposing state provided economic privileges of all kinds, whether grounded on traditional social privilege or the expansion of the state beyond what is necessary for clearly defined basic public goods. Moral action is largely seen as part of the private sphere. The state exists to stabilise society allowing human capacities to flourish, not take society towards a supposedly morally perfect scheme of redistribution and intervention. The distribution of economic goods in an open rule governed market is understood to be intrinsically just, though given that there is no perfect justice in any sphere, some limited state activity is just where it assists those who at any moment in time are at the very bottom of the hierarchy of possession of economic goods. The movable changeable nature of this hierarchy in a society of liberty and markets is why no permanent pattern of allegedly perfect distribution can be successfully enforced.

Bibliography

Berges, Sandrine (2015): "Sophie de Grouchy on the Cost of Domination in the *Letters on Sympathy* and Two Anonymous Articles in *Le Républicain*". In: *The Monist* 98, pp. 102–112.

Boucoyannis, Deborah (2013): "The Equalizing Hand: Why Adam Smith Thought the Market Should Produce Wealth Without Steep Inequality". In: *Perspectives on Politics* 11, pp. 1051–1070.

Buchanan, James (2005): *Why I Too, am Not a Conservative: The Normative Vision of Classical Liberalism*. Cheltenham, Northampton, MA: Edward Elgar.

Burke, Edmund (1968): *Reflections on the Revolution in France*. Conor Cruise O'Brien (Ed.). Harmondsworth, New York, NY: Penguin.

Chartier, Gary (2014): *Radicalizing Rawls: Global Justice and the Foundations of International Law*. New York, NY: Palgrave Macmillan.

Ferguson, Adam (1996): *An Essay on the History of Civil Society*. Fania Oz-Salzberger (Ed.). Cambridge: Cambridge University Press.

Fleischacker, Samuel (2005): *On Adam Smith's Wealth of Nations: A Philosophical Companion*. Princeton, NJ: Princeton University Press.

Foucault, Michel (2003): *Society Must Be Defended: Lectures at the Collège de France, 1975–1976*. Mauro Bertani/Alessandro Fontana (Eds.). David Macey (Trans.). New York, NY: Picador (first published 1997).

Foucault, Michel (2014): *On the Government of the Living: Lectures at the Collège de France. 1979–1980*. Michel Senbellart (Ed.), under the direction of François Ewald and Allesandro Fontana. Graham Burchell (Trans.). Basingstoke: Palgrave Macmillan.

Friedman, Milton (2002): *Capitalism and Freedom*. Chicago, IL: University of Chicago Press.

Gaus, Gerald (2011): *The Order of Public Reason: A Theory of Freedom and Morality in a Diverse and Bounded World*. Cambridge, New York, NY: Cambridge University Press.

Griswold, Charles L., Jr. (1999): *Adam Smith and the Virtues of Enlightenment*. Cambridge: Cambridge University Press.

Haakonssen, Knud (1981): *The Science of a Legislator: The Natural Jurisprudence of David Hume and Adam Smith*. Cambridge: Cambridge University Press.

Hanley, Ryan Patrick (2009): *Adam Smith and the Character of Virtue*. Cambridge: Cambridge University Press.

Hayek, Friedrich (1960): *The Constitution of Liberty*. Chicago, IL: University of Chicago Press.

Herzog, Lisa (2013): *Inventing the Market: Smith, Hegel and Political Theory*. Oxford: Oxford University Press.
Herzog, Lisa (2014): "Adam Smith on Markets and Justice". In: *Philosophy Compass* 12, pp. 864–875.
Huemer, John (2013): *The Problem of Political Authority*. London, New York, NY: Palgrave Macmillan.
Humboldt, Wilhelm von (1993): *The Limits of State Action*. J.W. Burrow (Ed.). Indianapolis, IN: Liberty Fund.
Hume, David (1987): *Essays Moral, Political and Literary*. Eugene F. Miller (Ed.). Indianapolis, IN: Liberty Fund.
Kennedy, Gavin (2004): *Adam Smith's Lost Legacy*. Basingstoke, New York, NY: Palgrave Macmillan.
Klein, Daniel (2014): "Unfolding the Allegory of Market Communication and Social Error and Correction". In: *The Adam Smith Review 7*, pp. 250–275.
Kristol, Irving (2011): *The Neoconservative Persuasion: Selected Essays, 1942–2009*. New York, NY: Basic Books.
Levy, Jacob T. (2015): *Rationalism, Pluralism, and Freedom*. Oxford, London: Oxford University Press.
Long, Roderick T. (2012): "Left-Libertarianism, Market Anarchism, Class Conflict and Historical Theories of Distributive Justice". In: *Griffith Law Review* 21, pp. 413–441.
McCloskey, Deirdre (2005): "The Demoralization of Economics: Can we Recover from Bentham and Return to Smith?". In: Fineman, Martha/Dougherty, Terence (Eds.): *Feminism Confronts Homo Economicus*. Ithaca, NY: Cornell University Press, pp. 20–31.
McCloskey, Deirdre (2006): *The Bourgeois Virtues: Ethics for an Age of Commerce*. Chicago, IL: University of Chicago Press.
McCloskey, Deirdre (2008): "Adam Smith, the Last of the Former Virtue Ethicists". In: *History of Political Economy* 40, pp. 3–71.
Nozick, Robert (1974): *Anarchy, State, and Utopia*. New York, NY: Basic Books.
Rae, John (1895): *Life of Adam Smith*. London: Macmillan.
Raphael, D.D. (2007): *The Impartial Spectator: Adam Smith's Moral Philosophy*. Oxford: Clarendon Press.
Rawls, John (1971): *A Theory of Justice*. Cambridge MA: Harvard University Press.
Roberts, Russ (2014): *How Adam Smith Can Change Your Life: An Unexpected Guide to Human Nature and Happiness*. New York, NY: Portfolio/Penguin.
Rothschild, Emma (2001): *Economic Sentiments: Adam Smith, Condorcet, and the Enlightenment*. Cambridge MA: Harvard University Press.
Schmidtz, David (2006): *The Elements of Justice*. Cambridge, New York, NY: Cambridge University Press.
Sen, Amartya (2011): "Uses and Abuses of Adam Smith". In: *History of Political Economy* 43, pp. 257–271.
Smith, Adam (1981): *An Inquiry into the Nature and Causes of the Wealth of Nations*. 2 Vols. Indianapolis, IN: Liberty Fund.
Smith, Adam (1982a): *Lectures on Jurisprudence*. R.L. Meek/D.D. Raphael/P.G. Stein (Eds.). Indianapolis, IN: Liberty Fund.
Smith, Adam (1982b): *The Theory of Moral Sentiments*. D.D. Raphael/A.L. MacFie (Eds.). Indianapolis, IN: Liberty Fund.

Smith, Craig (2006): *Adam Smith's Political Philosophy: The Invisible Hand and Spontaneous Order*. Abingdon, New York, NY: Routledge.
Spencer, Herbert (1851): *Social Statics Or the Conditions Essential to Human Happiness Specified, and the First of Them Developed*. London: John Chapman.
Tomasi, John (2012): *Free Market Fairness*. Princeton, NJ: Princeton University Press.
Young, Jeffrey T. (2008): "Law and Economics in the Protestant Natural Law Tradition: Samuel Pufendorf, Francis Hutcheson, and Adam Smith". In: *Journal of the History of Economic Thought* 30, pp. 283–296.

Notes on Contributors

Tom Bailey is Associate Professor of Philosophy at John Cabot University in Rome. He works in political theory, ethics, and the history of philosophy, and his research has recently focused on the place of religion in liberal democratic politics. In that field, he has published *Engaging Post-Secularism: Rethinking Catholic Politics in Italy* (with M. Driessen, Constellations, 2017) and edited *Rawls and Religion* (with V. Gentile, Columbia University Press, 2015). Email: tbailey@johncabot.edu

Peter Caven attained his PhD in Philosophy and MA in Political Theory at The University of Sheffield, concentrating on moral disagreement, moral psychology and liberal political theory, but decided to leave academic philosophy to remain in Sheffield. He currently works at the University, supporting interdisciplinary research with a focus on international development. Email: p.caven@sheffield.ac.uk

Aysel Demir is Associate Professor of Philosophy at Kırıkkale University, Turkey. She is working on a number of ongoing projects at Oxford University as a Visiting Academic. Research interests: political theory and philosophy, critical theory, ethics, communication philosophy, in particular theories of justice, Plato, Aristotle, Hobbes, Rousseau, Kant, Marx and Rawls. Email: ayselmus1@hotmail.com

Maria Dimitrova is Professor in Social Philosophy, Department of Philosophy, Sofia University, Bulgaria. She is the editor of *In Levinas' Trace* (Cambridge Scholars Press, 2011) and *Sociality and Justice. Toward Social Phenomenology* (Ibidem, 2016). Email: midimitrov@phls.uni-sofia.bg

Annette Förster is Lecturer and Research Fellow at RWTH Aachen University and has received her PhD from the London School of Economics and Political Science. Research interests: international political theory, political philosophy, theories of justice, in particular John Rawls, human rights, torture and democracy, politics and law. Email: annette.foerster@rwth-aachen.de

Gerald Gaus is the James E. Rogers Professor of Philosophy and Professor of Political Economy and Moral Science at the University of Arizona. His most recent book is *The Tyranny of the Ideal: Justice in a Diverse Society* (Princeton University Press, 2016). He is currently writing a book on morality and complexity to be published by Oxford University Press. Email: jerry@gaus.biz

Giovanni Giorgini is Professor of Political Philosophy at the University of Bologna and Visiting Professor of Politics at Princeton University. He is also Life Member of Clare Hall College, Cambridge. The author of three books, numerous essays and translations, Giorgini's current research interests are ancient political thought and its revival in contemporary liberal theory; tyranny and totalitarianism; ancient and modern relativism; Machiavelli. Email: giovanni.giorgini@unibo.it

Michael Haus is Professor of Modern Political Theory at Heidelberg University, Institute for Political Science. Research interests: contemporary political philosophy (in particular communitarian thinking, theories of social justice, religion and politics), social theory, interpretative approaches to politics, urban politics and governance theories.
Email: michael.haus@ipw.uni-heidelberg.de. Website: http://www.uni-heidelberg.de/politik wissenschaften/personal/haus/haus.html

Christoph Horn holds the Chair of Ancient Philosophy and Practical Philosophy at the University of Bonn. He is author of *Plotin über Sein, Zahl und Einheit* (De Gruyter, 1995), *Augustinus* (Beck, 1995), *Antike Lebenskunst* (Beck, 1998), *Politische Philosophie* (WBG, 2003), *Philosophie der Antike* (Beck, 2013), and *Nichtideale Normativität* (Suhrkamp, 2014).
Email: chorn@uni-bonn.de

Elena Irrera is Senior Research Fellow in Political Philosophy at the University of Bologna (Campus of Forlì). She is also member of Instituto "Lucio Anneo Séneca" of Universidad Carlos III de Madrid. Research interests: ancient and contemporary political philosophy and ethics, particularly theories of happiness, justice, toleration and respect (Plato, Aristotle, Hobbes, Rawls). Email: elena.irrera2@unibo.it
elena.irrera@uniupo.it

Angela Kallhoff is Professor of Ethics with special emphasis on Applied Ethics and Chair of Ethics at the University of Vienna. She is also head of the research platform Nano-Norms-Nature at the University of Vienna. Research interests: ethics, political philosophy, environmental ethics, war ethics, in particular theories of public goods and of citizenship.
Email: angela.kallhoff@univie.ac.at. Website: http://homepage.univie.ac.at/angela.kallhoff

Manuel Knoll is Professor of Philosophy at Istanbul Şehir University and member of Instituto "Lucio Anneo Séneca" of Universidad Carlos III de Madrid. Research interests: ancient, modern and contemporary political philosophy and ethics, in particular ancient and contemporary theories of justice, Plato, Aristotle, Machiavelli, Nietzsche, Rawls and Walzer, social philosophy and critical theory. Email: manuelknoll@sehir.edu.tr. Website: www.manuelknoll.eu

Peter Koller is Professor Emeritus of Philosophy and Sociology of Law at The Karl-Franzens University of Graz (Austria). Research interests: legal theory, political philosophy, ethics and critical theory. Email: peter.koller@uni-graz.at.

Chandran Kukathas holds the Chair in Political Theory at the Department of Government at The London School of Economics and Political Science. Research Interests: history of liberal thought, contemporary liberal theory, and multiculturalism. Email: c.kukathas@lse.ac.uk

Chong-Ming Lim is a doctoral candidate at the Faculty of Philosophy, University of Oxford, and a Teaching Assistant at Nanyang Technological University, Singapore.
Email: chongming.lim@philosophy.ox.ac.uk Website: http://cmlim.info

Francisco L. Lisi is Professor Emeritus of Classical Philology and Director of the Instituto "Lucio Anneo Séneca" of Universidad Carlos III de Madrid. Research interests: ancient practi-

cal philosophy and its reception, especially philosophy of law, justice and freedom, history of Platonism and Aristotelianism. Email: flisi@hum.uc3 m.es.
Website: https://uc3 m.academia.edu/FranciscoLLisi

Michał Rupniewski is Assistant Professor of Law and Philosophy at the University of Lodz, Branch in Tomaszów Mazowiecki, Poland. He specializes in comparative law and political philosophy and jurisprudence. He is director of a research project *Human Dignity as the Foundational Value of Law: A Personalist Explanation*, pursued at the Faculty of Law and Administration of the University of Lodz (2017–2021). Email: michal.dru@gmail.com

Chad Van Schoelandt is Assistant Professor of Philosophy at Tulane University and Affiliated Fellow with the F.A. Hayek Program for Advanced Study in Philosophy, Politics, and Economics at George Mason University. Research interests: social and political philosophy, particularly in the public reason and social contract traditions. Email: cvanscho@tulane.edu. Website: http://www2.tulane.edu/liberal-arts/philosophy/cvanschoelandt.cfm

Eckart Schütrumpf is Professor Emeritus of Classics and Humanities at the University of Colorado at Boulder, USA, he is the author of a translation and commentary in four volumes on *Aristotle's Politics* (1991–2005), of monographs on *Aristotle's Poetics* (1970) and *Politics* (1980) and *Xenophon's On Revenues* (1982) and of some 70 papers. He edited the fragments of *Heraclides Ponticus* (2007). He received the Research Prize of the Humboldt Foundation (2005). Email: schutrum@colorado.edu

Alberto L. Siani is a Senior Researcher of Aesthetics at the Department of Civilizations and Forms of Knowledge at Università di Pisa. Previously, he has been a Humboldt Post-Doc Fellow at the University of Münster and an Associate Professor of Philosophy at Yeditepe University, Istanbul. Research interests: German Idealism (esp. Hegel and Kant), aesthetics, contemporary political philosophy. Email: alberto.siani@unipi.it. Website: https://people.unipi.it/alberto_siani/

Nurdane Şimşek is a doctoral candidate at the Department of Philosophy, İstanbul University. Research Interests: political philosophy, in particular ancient and political philosophy, ancient Greek theology. Email: nurdanesimsek@hotmail.com

Stephen Snyder is a Fulbright Fellow at Tbilisi State University and a Visiting Assistant Professor in the Philosophy Department at Boğaziçi University in Istanbul. Research interests: philosophy of art and social and political philosophy. He is author of *End-of-Art Philosophy in Hegel, Nietzsche and Danto* (Palgrave, 2018). Recent essays appear in *Michael Walzer: Sphären der Gerechtigkeit: Ein kooperativer Kommentar*, *Philosophy in the Contemporary World* and *Countertext*.
Email: Snyder.Stephen.D@gmail.com. Website: http://home.earthlink.net/~stephensnyder/

Ulrike Spohn is Project Manager at the Bertelsmann Stiftung in Germany. She earned her PhD in political theory from the University of Münster. Fields of work: secularism, pluralism, religion and politics, cultural diversity. Email: mail.spohn@gmail.com

Notes on Contributors

Ulrich Steinvorth is Professor Emeritus for Philosophy at the University of Hamburg. He has published in political theory, applied ethics, moral theory and metaphysics.
Email: ulrich.steinvorth@uni-hamburg.de

Barry Stocker is an Assistant Professor of Philosophy at Istanbul Technical University. He is also an honorary associate of the Department of Philosophy at University College London. Research interests: political philosophy, ethics, aesthetics, philosophy and literature, European Philosophy since Kant, Montaigne, Vico.
Email: Barry.Stokcer@itu.edu.tr. Website: www.stockerb.wordpress.com

Kok-Chor Tan is Professor of Philosophy at the University of Pennsylvania. His most recent book is *What is This Thing Called Global Justice?* (Routledge, 2017).
Email: kctan@sas.upenn.edu

Manon Westphal is Post-Doc Research Fellow at Münster University. Her research interests are political theory and democratic theory, pluralism, moral disagreement, political conflict, agonistic democracy, modus vivendi and compromise. She is particularly interested in 'realistic' forms of political theorizing, political challenges related to conflict regulation and questions of institutional design. Email: manon.westphal@uni-muenster.de

Bertjan Wolthuis is Assistant Professor at the Faculty of Law of the Vrije Universiteit Amsterdam. Research projects: the extension of John Rawls's theory of justice to the European Union; public reason and political oratory.
E-mail: a.j.wolthuis@vu.nl. Website: https://research.vu.nl/en/persons/aj-wolthuis

Bill Wringe is Assistant Professor of Philosophy at Bilkent University in Ankara. His areas of interest include social and political philosophy, ethics and philosophy of international relations. Much of his work deals with the role of social phenomena in our ethical and political life. He is currently working on a book on collective obligations, defending the view that non-agents can be the bearers of collective obligations. Email: wringe@bilkent.edu.tr

Jeffrey T. Young is the A. Barton Hepburn Professor of Economics at St. Lawrence University. His research interests include the economics and moral philosophy of Adam Smith and Malthusian population theory, and its role in modern economic and environmental thought. In addition to journal articles his publications include *Economics as a Moral Science: The Political Economy of Adam Smith* (1997) and, as editor, *The Elgar Companion to Adam Smith* (2009). Email: jyoung@stlawu.edu

Author Index

Abrams, Kathryn 400
Achilles 183f.
Agamemnon 183
Agar, Nicholas 316, 373f., 376–378
Aligica, Paul Dragoș 417
Ammer, Margit 319
Anderson, Elizabeth S. 75, 83, 406, 424, 434
Aquinas, Thomas 3, 151, 154, 534
Aristotle 1–9, 12f., 24, 26–30, 32f., 37, 39, 42, 45f., 54, 56, 59f., 66, 75f., 91, 93f., 96–100, 105f., 109, 111, 114f., 119–124, 133–148, 151–168, 177, 527, 534
Arneson, Richard J. 36, 424
Arrow, Kenneth J. 412, 507
Attfield, Robin 316
Aubenque, Pierre 134, 142f.
Audard, Cathrine 333, 337
Ayer, Alfred Jules 94f.

Babeuf, François-Noël 33, 35–37
Bader, Veit 254, 256
Baier, Kurt 413
Bailey, Tom 17, 449
Baker, John 9
Barker, Ernest 93
Barnes, Jonathan 121
Barry, Brian 332, 334, 479
Barry, Norman P. 1, 7f., 37
Bates, Clifford Angell, Jr. 6
Beitz, Charles R. 330f., 334, 352
Bell, Derek 317
Bellamy, Richard 233
Berges, Sandrine 536
Berlin, Isaiah 11, 35f., 53–55, 59f., 62, 66, 68f., 94, 251–253, 280
Bicchieri, Cristina 415f.
Birchall, Ian 33, 35
Bird, Colin 434
Birnbacher, Dieter 46, 372, 377
Blair, Robert James R. 302
Bobbio, Noberto 48

Bodéüs, Richard 134
Boettcher, James W. 228
Boettke, Peter J. 417
Bohman, James 365
Bornemann, Basil 71f.
Boucoyannis, Deborah 527
Boulding, Kenneth E. 508
Brenkert, G. George 488, 494
Brennan, Geoffrey 415
Brettschneider, Corey 385, 400
Brighouse, Harry 82–84, 86
Brown, Peter G. 315, 385
Buchanan, James M. 417, 488f., 491, 496, 524, 527
Burke, Edmund 534f.
Burns, Tony 134
Butera, Fabrizio 427

Caldera, E. O. 190
Camus, Albert 78
Caney, Simon 318, 321f.
Cantillon, Sara 9
Carens, Joseph 194
Carter, Ian 423, 425, 428–432, 434
Caven, Peter 14f., 41, 291
Ceva, Emanuela 430f.
Chartier, Gary 537
Chavez, Alex 416
Cherniss, Joshua 251f.
Christie, Isham 498
Chuska, Jeff 6
Cohen, Gerald A. 36, 74, 194, 284, 406, 424, 481, 488f., 491, 495f.
Cohen, Joshua 228
Collins, Stephanie 349
Connolly, William E. 272
Cooke, Maeve 452
Copp, David 347, 351
Costanza, Robert 316
Cranor, Carl 436
Curtis, William M. 250–252

D'Agostino, Fred 226, 404, 412, 415

Danto, Arthur 379
Darwall, Stephen 428, 430, 433–435
Dawson, Walter 86
Deloney, Amalia 190
Demir, Aysel 2, 17, 37, 487
DeSteno, David 303
Di Quattro, Arthur 497–499
Diamond, Jared M. 321
Dimitrova, Maria 16f., 441
Dobson, Andrew 317
Dreben, Burton 210, 216
Dworkin, Ronald 23, 36f., 47, 74, 194, 276, 424, 429, 482

Eagleton, Terry 496
Eberle, Christopher J. 452
Eckersley, Robyn 319
Engberg-Pedersen, Troels 144
Engels, Friedrich 40, 59, 494, 497
Enoch, David 227, 239, 412
Estlund, David 385, 406

Fabre, Cecile 187
Faulkner, Robert K. 134
Favor, Christi 168
Fehr, Ernst 415
Feinberg, Joel 376
Feldman, David Lewis 314
Ferrara, Alessandro 452
Fichte, Johann Gottlieb 33
Fichtner, Georg 48
Fieser, James 45, 48
Finnis, John 93
Fischbacher, Urs. 415
Fleischacker, Samuel 1, 3f., 33, 39, 507f., 527
Fogelin, Robert J. 24, 42
Forst, Rainer 173, 195, 389
Förster, Annette 15, 329
Foucault, Michel 528
Frankfurt, Harry 37, 75
Fraser, Nancy 195, 424
Freeman, Samuel 331, 333, 336, 462, 488, 493
French, Peter 31f., 80, 252, 347, 349, 536
Freyenhagen, Fabian 306
Friedman, Milton 78, 507, 524

Frohlich, Norman 337f.
Fumurescu, Alin 231
Funk, Carolyn L. 304

Gadamer, Hans-Georg 134, 143
Gagnon, Bernard 250
Gale, Trevor 82
Galeotti, Anna E. 423f., 426, 432–434
Galston, William A. 109f., 252
Gardiner, Stephen M. 318
Gaus, Gerald 16, 403, 413, 416f., 524
Gauthier, David 479
Gehrke, Hans-Joachim 30
George, Robert P. 93, 280, 488
Geras, Norman 34, 493f., 497
Gershenshon, Olga 190
Gerth, Bernhard 155
Gilbert, Margaret 347, 349
Giorgini, Giovanni 12, 26, 39, 91, 104, 114
Girardet, Klaus M. 134
Gölz, Walter 36
Goodin, Robert E. 352
Gordon, Barry 506
Gorgias 27, 60
Gosepath, Stefan 173
Gosseries, Axel 319
Gray, John 14, 243f., 248–257, 271
Green, Thomas Hill 93
Griffin, James 348
Griswold, Charles L., Jr. 529
Gutmann, Amy 83, 235f., 236, 389
Gutmann, Thomas 246

Haakonssen, Knud 528
Habermas, Jürgen 12, 16f., 23, 109, 111, 115–119, 122, 124, 278, 361–380, 409, 449–457, 459–462
Hacker, P.M.S. 97
Hampshire, Stuart 12, 25f., 39, 91, 93–105, 109f., 113–115, 117, 123
Hanley, Ryan Patrick 530
Hardy, Henry 251f.
Harris, John 373–378, 463
Harsanyi, John C. 479
Hart, Herbert L.A. 104, 178f., 369
Haus, Michael 10f., 23, 37, 72f.
Hayek, Friedrich 1, 202, 524, 526f.

Hayward, Tim   319
Heinimann, Felix   135
Henckel von Donnersmarck, Florian   106
Heraclitus   103
Herodotus   45
Herwig, Dagmar   25, 30, 39, 43, 53, 55, 58–62
Herzog, Lisa   525–527, 535
Heyd, David   385, 400
Hinsch, Wilfried   331f., 335
Hobbes, Thomas   54, 56, 59f., 197
Höffe, Otfried   120f., 173
Hollis, Martin   233
Holt, Justin P.   496
Honneth, Axel   72, 127
Horberg, Elizabeth J.   303
Horn, Christoph   13, 171f., 177
Horton, John   109, 248, 250f., 255, 259, 262
Huemer, John   523
Humboldt, Wilhelm von   278, 523
Hume, David   95, 101, 191–197, 306f., 505, 534f., 537
Hurrell, Andrew   338, 341
Hutchings, Kimberly   337

Inbar, Yoel   303
Irrera, Elena   16, 423
Irwin, Terence   152f., 155, 159, 161, 164f., 167
Isaacs, Tracy   347, 349
Ivison, Duncan   252

James, Aaron   228, 406, 524
Joachim, Harold H.   134, 159
Joas, Hans   252
Johnson, David   505
Jonas, Hans   365f., 373, 377–380
Jones, Peter   250, 252, 254, 431
Jubb, Robert   111

Kallhoff, Angela   15, 311, 315f.
Kant, Immanuel   9, 56, 59, 172, 218, 369f., 377, 443–445, 455f., 499
Kekes, John   9, 24, 37
Kennedy, Gavin   524f.
Kersting, Wolfgang   1, 38

Keyt, David   5f., 135, 152
Klein, Daniel   525
Knoll, Manuel   1–6, 8f., 11f., 23, 27–30, 32, 37, 46f., 71, 75, 127, 143, 177, 207, 259, 275, 345, 361, 385, 399, 442, 463, 507
Koller, Peter   2, 17, 172, 469
Kolnai, Aurel   430
Kompridis, Nikolas   378f.
Korsgaard, Christine Marion   74
Kraut, Richard   152, 154
Krebs, Angelika   37, 75, 172
Kreide, Regina   334, 336, 341
Kristol, Irving   524
Kühner, Raphael   155
Kukathas, Chandran   13, 187, 495
Kumar, Rahul   367f., 370
Kundera, Milan   106
Kutz, Christopher   349
Kuypers, Karel   142
Kymlicka, Will   23, 37, 74f., 77f., 424, 428

Laclau, Ernesto   72, 80, 82, 214, 263–266
Ladd, John   45
Laden, Anthony Simon   209, 212, 214
Lafont, Cristina   452
Lamont, Julian   168
Lapié, Paul   134
Larmore, Charles   216, 228, 406
Lassman, Peter   100
Lawford-Smith, Holly   349–351
Levine, John M.   427
Levy, David M.   509
Levy, Jacob T.   427, 524
Lim, Chong-Ming   13f., 225
Lisi, Francisco L.   12, 133, 136–138, 148
List, Christian   349
Lister, Andrew   226, 228, 231
Little, Margaret   151, 155
Locke, John   38, 54, 56, 59, 65, 408, 534
Long, Roderick T.   536
Lynch, Kathleen   9
Lyotard, Jean-François   42, 444

Machiavelli, Niccolò   53, 102
MacIntyre, Alasdair   76, 86, 93
Mackie, Gerry   415

Mackie, John L.   44, 46, 413,
Mahbubani, Kishore   190
Malthus, T.R.   509, 514, 519f.
Mandle, Jon   488, 493f., 499
Mansbridge, Jane   229
March, Andrew   385, 452
Margalit, Avishai   231f.
Maritain, Jacques   93
Marx, Karl   8, 17, 33–40, 55f., 58f., 62, 103, 220, 411, 487–489, 491–500, 507
Mason, Andrew   406, 412f.
May, Larry   347
May, Simon   232, 347
McCarthy, Thomas   461
McCloskey, Deirdre   525f.
Meckled-Garcia, Saladin   348
Meislik, Alyse   190
Mendieta, Eduardo   453
Mendus, Susan   385
Meyer, Kirsten   83
Meyer, Lukas H.   319, 377
Michelakis, Emmanuel M.   134
Mill, John Stuart   13, 32, 95, 129, 171–176, 178, 180f., 292, 505
Miller, David   1, 4, 7, 10, 33f., 36, 75, 77f., 390, 481, 494
Miller, Fred D. Jr.   6, 134f., 140, 152, 165
Mitchell, Don   190
Moore, George Edward   94
Moraux, Paul   134
Morris, Theresa   378f.
Mouffe, Chantal   14, 72, 80, 82, 214, 259f., 263–270, 272f.
Mulgan, Richard   3, 6
Mulhern, John J.   143
Muraca, Barbara   316

Nagel, Thomas   390, 408, 424
Nathanson, Stephen   82
Neufeld, Blain   407
Nichols, Shaun   416
Nida-Rümelin, Julian   44f.
Nielsen, Kai   194, 499
Nietzsche, Friedrich   26, 31f., 42, 69, 76, 251
Norton, Bryan G.   315

Nozick, Robert   3, 7, 10f., 24, 38, 53, 55f., 58, 60, 62, 65f., 68, 78, 127, 194, 286, 491, 495, 523
Nussbaum, Martha C.   3, 23, 93, 194, 280, 285, 347, 411, 478

Oberdiek, Hans   385
O'Neill, Onora   348
Oppenheimer, Joe A.   337f.
Ostrom, Elinor   417

Pangle, Thomas L.   152
Parfit, Derek   477, 480
Pavel, Carmen   251f.
Peart, Sandra J.   509
Penner, Barbara   190
Peter, Fabienne   227
Pettit, Philip   347, 349, 495
Plato   1, 4, 9, 12, 26–30, 32f., 42, 44–46, 53–56, 59f., 68f., 103, 121, 128f., 133f., 136–139, 146, 148, 151, 156f., 163, 165, 168, 177, 217, 393, 412, 507
Pogge, Thomas   15, 313, 330, 334f., 338–341, 347f., 356, 358
Pojman, Louis P.   45, 48
Polansky, Ronald   30
Posner, Eric   321f.
Protagoras   45, 134, 157
Pufendorf, Samuel   534
Pythagoras   100, 107

Quong, Jonathan   212, 228

Rae, John   535
Rand, Ayn   413
Raphael, D.D.   505, 530
Rawls, John   1–3, 7–18, 23f., 32, 34, 36–41, 46, 53, 55–58, 60, 62, 64, 67f., 71–74, 79–82, 84, 86, 91–93, 103, 109–114, 118, 122, 124, 127–129, 171f., 175f., 178, 180, 187f., 190f., 193f., 199, 202, 207–212, 214–223, 225–227, 229, 231, 236–238, 243–249, 259–262, 268, 275–288, 291f., 294–302, 304–307, 311–317, 319–325, 329–342, 363, 370, 378, 396, 398, 403–405, 407–414, 416, 429,

441–445, 447, 449–453, 457–463,
469–481, 483, 487, 489–492, 494–
500, 505–508, 519f., 537
Raz, Joseph   93f., 230, 280, 292
Rehg, William   365
Reidy, David   488, 493f., 499
Reisner, Andrew E.   230
Ribeiro, Brian   39, 42, 46–48
Riedel, Manfred   94
Riker, William   412
Ritter, Joachim   93f., 135
Roberts, Jean   134, 152
Roberts, Russ   525
Rorty, Mary V.   373
Ross, William David   95, 138, 159
Rothschild, Emma   528
Rupniewski, Michał   14, 41, 275
Russell, Paul   95
Ryle, Gilbert   94

Sabl, Andrew   400
Salomon, Max   134, 142
Salter, John   506
Sandel, Michael J.   2f., 187f., 286, 374f., 437
Sandler, Ronald L.   316
Sartre, Jean-Paul   252, 363, 379
Satz, Debra   83
Scanlon, Thomas M.   367f., 370, 385
Scerri, Andy   319
Schaub, Jörg   218f.
Scheffler, Samuel   385f., 390
Schlossberg, David   312
Schmidt, Jeremy J.   315
Schmidtz, David   410, 418, 524
Schnall, Simone   303
Schütrumpf, Eckart   3, 12, 151f., 155f., 160–163, 165, 167
Schutz, Alfred   445
Schwyzer, Eduard   153
Selg, Peeter   214
Sen, Amartya K.   74, 199f., 411, 413, 476, 493, 527
Shapiro, Ian   428
Shue, Henry   318, 320, 322, 352
Siani, Alberto L.   13, 127, 207, 212
Siegel, Harvey   24, 42, 48

Şimşek, Nurdane   1, 12, 47, 127
Singer, Peter   318, 339f.
Slaughter, Anne-Marie   67
Sleat, Matt   110, 293
Smith, Adam   11, 17f., 121f., 172, 505–517, 519f., 523–537
Smith, Craig   525
Snyder, Stephen   1, 9, 15f., 23, 71, 207, 237, 259, 345f., 361, 367, 385, 463
Socrates   68f., 137, 144, 148, 393
Sommer, Andreas Urs   23, 43
Spencer, Herbert   523
Spohn, Ulrike   13f., 243
Sreenivasan, Gopal   348
Steiner, Hillel   194
Steinvorth, Ulrich   7, 11, 25, 36, 38, 53, 66f.
Stern, Nicholas   324
Stevenson, C. Leslie   95
Stocker, Barry   18, 207, 523
Stoian, Valentine   495
Stojanov, Krassimir   84–86
Strawson, Peter F.   410
Swift, Adam   82–84, 86, 188f.

Tan, Kok-Chor   16, 385, 398, 401
Tarantino, Quentin   106
Taylor, Charles,   430
Taylor, Gabriele   14, 72, 80, 243–256
Testino, Chiara   424, 427
Thomas, Alan   3, 23, 60, 111, 151, 154
Thompson, Dennis   235f.
Thompson, Janna,   367, 372f., 376f.
Thrasher, John   416
Thrasymachus   53–56, 60, 68f.
Thucydides   30
Tocqueville, Alexis de   201f.
Tomasi, John   537
Tremmel, Joerg Chet   365
Trude, Peter   134
Tugendhat, E.   173
Tullock, Gordon   417
Turkheimer, Eric   304
Turner, Brian S.   251

Vallier, Kevin   226, 403, 415–417
Van Norden, B.W.   393

Van Parijs, Philippe 477
Van Schoelandt, Chad 16, 228, 403, 407, 417
Volpi, Franco 133

Waldron, Jeremy 23, 25, 41, 46–48, 109 f., 113–115, 117, 261 f., 286
Walker, Gordon 312, 324
Walsh, Judy 9
Walzer, Michael 3, 7, 9–11, 25, 27, 34, 40, 71, 73, 75, 79–81, 83–85, 87, 218, 367, 377, 437 f.
Warnke, Claudia 25, 40
Waterman, Anthony 514
Weber, Max 35, 251
Weber, Michael 417
Weinstock, Daniel 233
Welie, Jos V.M. 189
Wenar, Leif 297, 299, 301, 341
Wendt, Fabian 233, 273
Wesselingh, Anton 86
Westphal, Manon 13 f., 259, 463
Willems, Ulrich 249, 251, 253 f., 256

Williams, Bernard 109 f., 112, 293, 385 f., 429
Wissenburg, Marcel L.J. 317
Witztum, Amos 505 f., 520
Wolff, Christian 135
Wolff, Jonathan 2, 434, 438
Wolff, Robert P. 491, 496, 498
Wolterstorff, Nicholas 254, 257
Wolthuis, Bertjan 12, 23, 41, 109–111, 116, 119, 122
Wood, Allen W. 488 f.
Wringe, Bill 15, 345–349, 351, 353

Xiao, Erte 416
Xinsheng, Wang 489, 493, 500

Yack, Bernard 134
Young, Charles M. 152, 154
Young, I. Marion 194 f., 424
Young, Jeffrey T. 17 f., 505 f., 513, 527
Ypi, Lea 336

Zanetti, G. 134
Zuolo, Federico 430 f.

Subject Index

abortion 42, 45, 232, 243, 247, 253, 261f., 272, 301, 364, 457
agonism 272
anarchy 7, 10, 118f., 194
ancient régime 31f.
animal suffering 298
antagonism 30, 263–267, 272
anthropology 45, 488
– moral anthropology 192
anti-democratic 30, 117
aretê 5f., 28f., 157f., 160–164, 168
argument 1f., 5f., 10, 13, 15–17, 23f., 29f., 36, 39–47, 54, 58, 64, 68, 77f., 80, 91, 95f., 101–105, 112, 116–119, 122, 127f., 154, 166–168, 177, 181, 197, 201, 209, 213, 215–217, 222, 245, 250, 260–263, 268, 271, 273, 280, 291f., 300, 305, 320–322, 325, 331f., 335f., 338f., 342, 345–349, 351f., 354f., 361f., 364, 367, 374–377, 395, 397, 400, 403, 430, 435, 445, 451f., 454, 461, 469, 472–476, 479, 481–483, 490, 499, 515, 519, 524, 526f., 530–532, 535–537
– argument from deep disagreements 11, 23, 47
– argument from queerness 44, 47
– argument from relativity 44f.
aristocracy, aristocrats, aristocratic 4–6, 27–32, 100, 147, 160, 166, 530, 535f.
assemblage of identities 266
assessment of evidence 297f.
authority 1, 17, 68, 116, 119, 135, 165, 180, 201, 253, 277, 287, 293f., 395, 398, 423, 428, 430f., 433, 435–438, 442, 449f., 453, 456f., 459–463, 470
– moral authority 423, 425, 434f.
– political authority 292f.
– second-personal authority 435f.
autonomy 72–76, 79f., 82, 84, 86f., 182, 210, 219, 275f., 281, 298, 334, 337, 371f., 374–377, 399, 441, 444f., 447, 453
– equal autonomy 71f.

– moral autonomy 376

basic socio-economic system 469
basic structure of society 193, 211, 220, 278, 284, 332, 441, 471, 499
bifurcation of liberalism 78
bounds of justice 188
Buddhism 294
burden-of-proof argument 46f.
burdens of judgement 227, 277, 279f., 285–287, 291f., 296, 298–302, 304–307
burdens of social cooperation 1, 477

capitalism 56, 300, 488f., 494–497, 499
Catholicism 294, 296
census suffrage 31
Christian, Christianity 9, 31, 60f., 243, 246f., 252, 453, 456
church 269f., 301
citizen, citizenry 2–7, 9f., 14–16, 24f., 27–29, 31–33, 35, 38, 77f., 83, 92, 105–107, 109f., 112, 117f., 123, 127–129, 137, 145, 151, 154, 156–160, 165f., 175f., 207, 210–212, 214–216, 218, 220–223, 225–240, 245, 250, 254, 256, 259–271, 273, 275–288, 291–296, 299f., 306, 312, 315, 321f., 324, 331–334, 337f., 346f., 353, 355, 388, 394–399, 405, 423–425, 444–446, 449–452, 454f., 458f., 461–463, 472, 474f., 478, 494f., 499
citizenship 4, 78, 80f., 111, 119, 175, 188, 275f., 281, 321, 398
– democratic citizenship 287
civility 262, 275–277, 457
civil war 24, 29f., 47, 162–164
class (economic or social) 17, 31, 34, 40, 158, 173f., 221, 284f., 295, 364f., 376, 443, 476, 484, 489, 494f., 497–500, 507, 509, 516f., 523, 537
class interest 40, 53, 58f., 300, 488

Subject Index

climate change   47, 236, 240, 314, 318–321, 323 f., 347, 355
coexistence   213, 248, 250, 254 f., 264, 462
cognitivism   11, 23, 43, 47
commodity   13, 58, 63, 187
commonalism   55 f., 58, 60, 68
common humanity   514, 520
common property   56 f.
communicative action   115, 361 f., 375
communism   38, 56, 493 f., 496 f.
community   3, 6, 30, 76, 135, 138, 141–143, 146, 157, 200, 219, 238, 275 f., 278, 285, 288, 331, 336, 338, 363, 366, 369, 372, 377 f., 424, 426, 438, 453, 455, 496, 535
– civic community   275–278, 287
– cooperation community   480
– moral community   228, 365, 426
– ownership community   480
– political community   3, 5, 9 f., 28, 46, 83, 106, 118, 141, 152, 195, 198, 238, 244, 256, 266, 271, 277, 286, 347, 424 f., 432
compensation   24, 75, 79, 82 f., 86, 177, 340, 480, 513
compromise   14, 25, 53, 115, 118, 123 f., 163, 191, 201, 225, 228 f., 231–236, 238 f., 247–249, 253 f., 273, 288, 293, 342, 462
conceptualisation   75, 262 f., 270, 277
conceptual vagueness   297 f.
conflict   14, 17, 24–27, 36, 39, 42, 47 f., 58, 71, 75, 91, 97–104, 106, 109, 114, 118, 165, 191, 218 f., 221–223, 225, 227–229, 231, 233, 243 f., 247–251, 253, 255–257, 259, 261–268, 270, 272 f., 276 f., 282, 284, 286, 293 f., 297, 303 f., 387, 391–393, 395 f., 399, 408 f., 418, 443, 447, 450, 462 f., 491, 496, 498, 500
– moral conflict   39, 294, 391, 452
– normative conflict   297
– political conflict   11, 91, 244, 249–251, 253, 262, 272, 449, 24, 30, 48, 209 f., 253, 260
– value conflict   252, 423
consensus   10–16, 23–25, 36, 46 f., 71–73, 75, 79, 82, 87, 92 f., 110, 116, 118, 123, 127, 129, 199, 205, 207–213, 218, 225 f., 243–245, 247–251, 254–257, 259, 261, 263, 265, 267–270, 272 f., 275, 277, 283–289, 291, 293–295, 305, 375, 441–444, 449 f., 452, 457, 459–461
– conflictual consensus   14, 259 f., 264–271, 273
– constitutional consensus   284, 286 f.
– deep consensus   71 f., 75, 78, 82, 283
– overlapping consensus   13 f., 23 f., 41, 75, 82, 92, 127, 208, 211–213, 215 f., 223, 226, 243–251, 256, 259–262, 265, 267 f., 275–277, 281–288, 291, 296, 300–302, 306 f., 333, 342, 409, 474
– rule of law consensus   14, 275, 277, 287 f.
– universal consensus   209, 293, 295, 365, 451
consensus approach   12, 127 f.
conservatism   524 f.
considered convictions of justice   128
considered judgments   46, 128
constitutionalism   76
constitutional reforms   166
constitution, constitutional   12, 16, 31, 105 f., 112, 117 f., 120, 122 f., 127, 135, 138, 141–144, 146–148, 151 f., 160 f., 163–167, 214, 278 f., 280, 284, 286–288, 295, 302, 322, 372, 405, 416 f., 441 f., 451 f., 454, 474, 507, 510, 514, 520, 524
constructivism   212, 247, 279
contemporary philosophy   27, 172, 177
contexts of justice   188
contractarian method   128
contractarian tradition   73, 362, 366
contractualism, contractualist   16, 361 f., 366–367, 370 f., 442
cooperation   62, 121 f., 166, 196–198, 211, 220, 231, 233–235, 238–240, 260, 273, 278, 283, 286 f., 291, 294, 299 f., 307, 312, 314 f., 318, 321, 324 f., 332, 334–336, 338, 340 f., 377, 404 f., 407, 409, 417, 445, 474, 479 f.
– international cooperation   330, 333, 335 f., 339, 342

- social cooperation 1, 16, 278, 288, 336, 340, 404, 442, 445, 447, 451, 470–472, 477–481
cosmopolitanism 321, 337, 525
courage 148, 158
cultural heritage 93, 478–480
cultural imperialism 337
culture 16, 45f., 117f., 128, 226, 287, 303, 331, 337, 339, 361, 372, 377f., 424, 427, 431f., 437f., 442, 525
- political culture 41, 117, 128f., 295, 337, 408
- public political culture 128, 215, 226, 282, 296, 300

dedifferentiation 365
democracy, democratic, democrats 4–6, 14, 23, 27–31, 41, 47, 61, 71f., 104, 110f., 118, 123f., 127f., 147, 160–164, 166f., 201, 210, 214, 216, 218–223, 228, 235, 56f., 259–261, 264f., 267f., 270–273, 281f., 286f., 295f., 299f., 319, 361, 376, 424, 441f., 474, 484, 497, 451, 454, 461, 463, 524, 535f.
- green democracy 318
- liberal democracy 259, 264, 267f., 271, 318, 394
- modern democracy 256, 277
- social democracy 2f.
desert 3, 7, 10, 33f., 168, 410, 415, 425, 481
dialectic 120f., 489
difference in weighing 297f.
difference principle 2, 11, 15, 17, 37, 67, 82, 127, 223, 261, 322, 329f., 332–334, 336f., 341, 403, 410, 412, 416, 469, 472, 475f., 480, 484, 487, 489–492, 494–496, 498–500, 505–507, 509, 519f.
disagreement 11f., 23–26, 29f., 39–43, 45–48, 72–74, 79f., 109–117, 119–122, 124, 127, 129, 162, 166, 199, 208, 210f., 216f., 219, 222, 225–229, 232, 237, 247–251, 259–273, 275f., 278f., 284– 286, 292–294, 297–301, 305f., 398f., 407, 418, 481, 487
- deep disagreements 10f., 13f., 23–26, 30, 36, 38f., 41–44, 46–48, 119, 225, 267f., 399
- moral disagreements 44f., 47, 244, 260, 262, 272, 387
- overlapping disagreement 13, 207f., 210f., 213, 216, 219f., 223
- radical disagreement 110f., 124
- reasonable disagreement 41, 48, 110, 112, 285, 297f., 301, 305f., 398f., 407, 418
discourse 1, 17, 23, 71–74, 76f., 81, 85–87, 187f., 201f., 260, 263–265, 288, 363f., 366–368, 373, 375, 378f., 441–444, 454
- legal discourse 289
- moral discourse 363, 481
- political discourse 74, 80, 82, 299
- public discourse 84, 87, 289
- rational discourse 453
- world-disclosive discourse 362f., 368, 372, 380
distribution 1–12, 15–17, 26–33, 35–40, 46, 55f., 58, 63–65, 79–81, 83, 85, 119, 141, 147, 151f., 154–158, 160–168, 176f., 179, 182–184, 194, 311, 314f., 319–322, 325, 329, 334f., 345, 370f., 403, 423–425, 428f., 436–438, 443, 470–473, 478, 487-500, 505f., 508f., 511, 513, 523, 526, 528, 530, 532–534, 536, 538
- autonomous distribution 80, 85
- fair distribution 34, 223, 311f., 315, 318, 320f., 324, 329, 424, 489
- just distributions 26, 39f., 43, 75
distributive paradigm 15, 313f., 317f.
diversity 41, 45, 99, 107, 140, 197, 243–246, 251, 254–257, 259, 276, 280, 287, 294, 297, 320, 333, 337, 386–388, 397f., 411, 436f.
- moral diversity 45f., 243f., 255f.
- normative diversity 386f.
duty of assistance 15, 329–336, 338, 340–342

education 10, 28, 66f., 75, 81, 83–86, 99, 104–107, 129, 136f., 146f., 176, 192, 223, 228, 240, 284, 331, 424, 472, 492, 513, 517, 519, 534
educational practice 84f.
efficient cause 139
egalitarianism 8f., 28, 37, 39, 48, 71–73, 75f., 78f., 81, 83, 315f., 322, 424, 441, 446, 462f., 528, 534, 536
– individualist egalitarianism 79, 86
– liberal egalitarianism 12, 71, 75, 83, 87
– political egalitarianism 79, 81, 83, 86
egoism 40
elements of justice 188
empiricism 53, 94
endoxa 12, 109, 111, 115, 119, 121–124
entitlement theory of justice 7, 38
epistemology 24, 48
equal 4f., 8–11, 24–35, 37f., 42, 55, 57f., 60, 64f., 73, 75f., 78–81, 83, 85f., 92, 109–112, 122f., 127–129, 141, 147, 154, 157f., 161, 163–165, 175, 177, 183, 210f., 214, 216, 218, 220f., 227, 231, 245, 261, 272, 275f., 281, 283, 288, 294–296, 314, 329, 332, 337, 365, 370f., 376, 388, 400, 405, 411, 414, 417, 423–426, 428–430, 432, 434–438, 442f., 445, 462, 469f., 472–476, 480f., 483f., 490, 492–495, 500, 506, 511, 537
– equal treatment 17, 25, 60f., 399, 428f.
equality 2, 4f., 8f., 11, 23, 27–37, 39f., 42f., 60f., 64, 71–82, 87, 128, 141, 146f., 152, 160–164, 166–168, 177, 188f., 194, 200, 223, 247, 249, 259, 264–268, 270, 276f., 286, 304, 306, 330, 399, 424f., 427, 429, 431, 433, 442–445, 453, 461–463, 470, 487, 489–491, 494–498, 500, 506, 513f., 528f., 532, 536f.
– arithmetic equality 30, 162
– complex equality 11, 80f., 85
– educational equality 82f.
– geometrical equality 4, 27, 164
– numeric equality 27, 36
– proportional equality 10, 27f., 30, 34, 75, 161–163
– simple equality 26f.

equalization 17, 25, 60f., 497, 513
error theory 44
ethics 3f., 13, 29f., 41, 46f., 94–96, 105, 121, 133f., 138–140, 144f., 151, 158, 161f., 165, 167, 171f., 176, 189, 193, 256, 286, 361, 363f., 366, 371, 378f., 505, 508, 529f., 534
– virtue ethics 176f.
ethnology 45
ethos 84f., 250, 252, 255f., 454
euthanasia 45, 301

fact 10f., 28, 32, 34, 40–42, 44–48, 54, 56f., 60–64, 66, 72, 75, 80, 93–98, 103, 106f., 109, 116, 135, 144f., 152, 160, 165, 172, 179–184, 187, 192, 195, 209f., 213, 219, 221, 223, 237, 239, 245, 247f., 250, 252, 254f., 262–265, 267f., 270–272, 276–281, 286f., 293f., 297f., 301f., 306f., 312f., 324, 338f., 348–350, 354–356, 358, 386–388, 390, 393, 403–406, 411–413, 416, 424, 431, 443, 445, 458, 472, 474–481, 484, 498
– moral fact 26, 43–45, 293, 406, 411
factum of pluralism 316
fair equality of opportunity 82, 329, 333, 413, 469, 471, 473, 477, 480, 490, 495, 505f.
fairness 13, 15, 92, 101, 103f., 114, 159, 311, 315–324, 339, 457, 489, 506, 516f., 537
faith 23, 54, 118, 166, 285, 302, 394, 407, 449, 453–457, 459–463
fetishism 413f.
final cause 136, 139, 142
formal cause 139
Frankfurt School 40
freedom 4–6, 29, 72, 85, 91f., 95, 97, 107, 112, 115, 117, 120, 123f., 127, 147f., 160, 175, 194, 197, 219f., 232, 245, 247, 249, 259, 261, 276, 280–282, 284, 286, 292, 305, 312, 315, 322, 330f., 363f., 366, 377–380, 387, 400, 446, 451, 461–463, 470, 479, 482, 493, 507, 513f., 517, 520, 536
– equal freedom 73, 109, 124
– political freedom 112

Subject Index — 555

freedom of speech 262
freedom of thought 291, 295f.
French Revolution 31
functionalism 16, 403f., 411, 415, 417

genetic makeup 304f., 370, 376
genetic manipulation 361, 366
genetic modification 374
God 31, 77, 95, 135, 232, 246f., 280, 296, 371, 442
goods 1, 7, 9, 11, 16, 25f., 32f., 35, 37f., 56–58, 62–64, 66, 72, 74, 76, 79–81, 83–86, 140, 147, 168, 177, 179, 181f., 184, 191, 214, 250, 252–254, 293, 312, 315, 318, 324, 329, 331, 335, 341, 345, 370, 376, 411, 413, 425, 427, 429, 438, 470, 475, 477–480, 483f., 487, 492–494, 512, 518, 520, 533
– basic goods 33, 39, 84, 312, 315, 322
– common good 23, 45, 229, 287
– cultural goods 85, 480
– dominant good 85f.
– economic goods 523, 525f., 530, 533f., 536, 538
– environmental goods 312, 317, 321, 323
– external goods 84, 140
– internal goods 85
– moral goods 184
– natural goods 176f., 311f., 314–317, 319f.
– peripheral goods 184
– political goods 175
– primary goods 7, 9, 37f., 311f., 315, 320, 322, 410–413, 471, 477, 479f., 483
– public goods 478, 480, 527, 531, 537
– secondary goods 318, 320
– social goods 10f., 25, 31, 34, 40, 53, 58, 62, 64–68, 80f., 470f., 473, 477f., 480f., 483f.
– welfare goods 318
greenhouse gas emission 321f.

happiness 18, 100, 143, 148, 201, 411, 413, 509–511, 514f., 517f., 520
harm principle 56f., 67
health care 34, 66f., 189, 519f.
heteronomy 445

hierarchy, hierarchical 71f., 77, 116, 137, 146, 165, 251, 507, 535f., 538
history 1, 4, 15, 23, 25, 30, 33, 39, 43, 45, 47, 56, 58f., 75, 94, 99, 101–103, 176, 199, 202, 217, 219f., 223, 249, 269f., 377, 380, 427, 431, 455, 488, 505
human flourishing 6, 256, 537

ideal theory 112, 114, 193, 301, 403, 417
identity 91, 93, 101f., 107, 144, 244, 263, 265f., 276, 362f., 367f., 370–372, 378f., 396, 423, 425–428, 432f., 435–438
– national identity 524
– political identity 265f.
– immorality 182, 184, 301
impartiality 16, 112, 116, 177, 181, 188, 332, 441
index 16, 412, 471, 477
individualism 55
– compensatory individualism 79
– minimal individualism 65
– political individualism 38, 56, 58, 60, 65, 68
individuality 97–99, 202
individual recognition 423
inequality 5, 17, 32, 38, 43, 57, 65, 67, 76, 78, 80f., 146f., 162, 166, 192, 443, 477, 482f., 487, 489f., 494–498, 500, 507, 513, 527, 529, 535f.
– natural inequalities 2, 43, 513
– social inequalities 17, 26, 37f., 92, 469, 471f., 475–477, 481–483, 492, 498
initial choice situation 24
injustice 13, 16f., 30, 36, 54f., 66, 69, 141, 151, 153, 156, 159, 171, 173–175, 178–184, 187, 190f., 199, 322, 330, 339–341, 357f., 380, 427, 430f., 433, 446, 451, 489, 493, 499, 523, 530, 532f.
– distributive injustices 357f.
– subjective injustice 141
institutions 1, 7, 15, 25, 64f., 67f., 72, 84, 104, 109, 111, 128, 157, 175–177, 180, 187, 190, 193, 195, 198–200, 210, 212, 218–220, 223, 225f., 234, 236f., 244, 260f., 264, 269, 276, 278, 280f., 284,

289, 311, 315, 318, 323f., 331, 336–338, 345, 347, 354–358, 361f., 370, 376f., 397–400, 403f., 407, 410, 414, 416f., 423, 425–428, 430f., 433–436, 441, 445–447, 472, 474, 492f., 495f., 499, 507, 527f., 530, 533
– just international institutions   345
– liberal institutions   301
– unjust institutions   198, 355f., 358
intelligence   32, 62, 129, 140, 147f., 269, 412, 429, 443
interest   10, 40, 48, 54f., 58–60, 74, 82–84, 95, 99f., 104, 112, 161, 166, 174f., 178, 182, 191f., 197, 216, 222f., 226, 229, 233, 235, 248, 254f., 281, 285f., 293, 299, 301, 305, 313, 331, 333, 338f., 342, 350, 354, 364–368, 371–373, 377, 390, 408, 411, 414, 442, 472, 481, 483f., 495, 498f., 510f., 517, 527, 535–537
international relations   15, 48, 67, 407, 524
irreconcilable (conceptions)   11, 17, 26–28, 30, 35f., 42, 53–55, 58, 60f., 210, 213, 218f., 221–223, 250, 276, 278, 280, 282, 288, 500
irreducibly social value   57, 62, 64, 66

jurisdiction   198, 222, 275, 277, 407, 511
just   1, 3–5, 8–10, 12f., 17, 25f., 28–30, 32, 35f., 38–40, 42–44, 46, 54–56, 59f., 64, 68f., 75f., 79–81, 83f., 86, 93, 99, 103, 110, 112–114, 124, 128f., 134, 136f., 139–148, 151–168, 172, 175–177, 179–182, 189, 192–194, 197–199, 210, 212, 216f., 227, 233, 235, 245–248, 250, 261, 270, 273, 278f., 284f., 287f., 292, 302, 315f., 322, 324, 329, 331, 333f., 341, 348, 350, 354, 357f., 361, 363, 370, 379, 389f., 392f., 395, 397–400, 409, 415f., 437, 443, 453, 456, 459, 472, 480, 484, 489f., 495, 499f., 507, 511–514, 517, 526, 528, 530f., 533f., 538
– conventional just   134, 140f., 143
– political just   134, 140–143, 145
just by nature   133–135, 140, 143–145

justice   1–18, 23–48, 53–60, 62–69, 71–73, 75–80, 82–84, 86, 91, 93, 100–104, 106, 109–115, 117, 119, 122, 124, 127f., 133, 137, 140–142, 145–147, 151–161, 164–166, 168, 171–184, 187–202, 207–209, 214f., 220, 222f., 225, 228, 238, 243–246, 249, 253f., 259, 272, 278, 280–288, 291, 304, 311–325, 329–332, 334, 339f., 342, 345, 357, 361–364, 367, 369, 372f., 377f., 380, 396–399, 403–418, 424, 429, 433f., 438, 441–443, 445–447, 450, 460, 462f., 469, 472–476, 479–481, 487–500, 505f., 510–514, 516–518, 520, 523f., 526–528, 530–534, 536, 538
– absolute justice   30
– brewing justice (coffee trading justice)   190
– climate change justice   190
– climate justice   15, 190, 311f., 317–322, 324f.
– communist justice   488
– commutative justice   177, 511f., 517
– compensatory justice   319
– connective justice   177
– corrective justice   152, 177
– egalitarian justice   26, 28, 30–33, 36f., 425
– democratic political justice   128f.
– genome justice   190
– global justice   190
– health justice   190
– impartial justice   177
– inter-cultural justice   190
– intergenerational justice   16, 179, 190, 361–363, 366–368, 370, 376–378, 380
– international distributive justice   329f., 334f., 338, 341f.
– language justice   190
– liberal justice   91, 118, 397
– meritorious justice   177
– minimal justice   78
– objective justice   134, 141f., 144f., 147
– particular justice   3, 153, 155–157
– personal justice   176
– political justice   11f., 16, 23–32, 35f., 39–44, 46–48, 111, 116, 127–129, 137,

Subject Index — 557

142, 146, 159, 179, 212, 214, 220–222, 261–264, 267, 271f., 286, 314, 396f., 399, 507, 530
- proportional justice   26–28, 30–33, 36f., 39, 46
- recognitional justice   463
- restorative justice   319
- retributive justice   177, 513, 516
- sex-selection justice   190
- socialist justice   488
- social justice   1, 3, 17, 23, 33–38, 41, 71, 73f., 77, 79–82, 86, 188–190, 193, 300, 311f., 316, 321, 424, 472, 477f., 481, 489–491, 493, 497
- substantial justice   25f.
- universal justice   55
justice as even-handedness   188
justice as fairness   1, 7, 82, 113, 127, 188, 193f., 207f., 211–213, 215–217, 219–223, 245, 261, 281–284, 294, 313, 324, 441f., 445, 469, 474, 490f., 497, 516
justice as impartiality   177, 188
justice as utility maximizing   188
justice in childcare provision   190

knowledge   32, 43, 75, 86f., 91, 94–97, 102, 129, 148, 200, 226, 294, 307, 332, 365f., 368f., 412, 414, 436, 453–457, 459f., 478, 526f.

labor movement   56
law   1, 13, 15, 25, 27f., 47, 60f., 65–67, 92, 95, 105f., 109–113, 115, 117, 123, 133, 135, 137f., 141f., 144–148, 153, 155, 159, 163, 165, 168, 173, 179, 190, 197, 199, 214, 217, 236, 276f., 287f., 292, 295, 329f., 333, 336, 338, 340f., 369, 399, 404, 416, 427, 446, 456, 461, 483, 493, 508, 511f., 516, 527–530, 532, 534, 537
- natural law   12, 60, 93, 133–135, 138, 142, 145f., 148, 172f., 511f., 531, 534
- positive law   134f., 142, 514, 530
lawfulness   13, 181
least advantaged   2, 37f., 332, 469–473, 476, 490, 500, 506f., 519
legality   275f.

legitimacy   13f., 110, 135, 152, 166, 225, 227f., 234, 236, 238–240, 267, 292–295, 305
leximin principle   476
liberalism   12, 37, 106, 111–113, 188, 226, 244, 248, 253f., 283, 292f., 315, 495, 520, 525f., 528
- Kantian liberalism   296
- political liberalism   13, 15, 40, 109, 112f., 118, 123, 127f., 207–223, 226, 233, 243, 249, 260f., 265, 267, 276, 278–280, 282f., 285f., 288, 291f., 294, 296, 298f., 301, 305–307, 312, 333, 457, 462, 474, 507
- public reason liberalism   14, 225–229, 233f., 236, 238–240
libertarianism   524–526
liberty   1, 8f., 31, 37, 54–57, 60, 62, 64–66, 72, 178, 192, 200, 223, 264–268, 270, 292, 306, 332, 356, 400, 416, 427, 445, 470, 472–474, 478, 481–484, 487, 490, 505f., 513f., 517–520, 530f., 533f., 536–538
- negative liberty   66, 253
- political liberty   111, 129, 442
- positive liberty   66f.
logical positivism   94
lottery of nature   78, 84, 86
luxury   529, 533

Marxism, Marxist   2, 17, 40, 53, 59, 78, 93, 106, 487–489, 491f., 494–500
- analytical Marxism   488
material cause   136, 139
maximin principle   322
maximin rule   473–475, 479
maximum of liberty   54
meaning   1, 14, 25, 40, 43, 62, 74, 80–82, 85f., 100, 105, 107, 133–136, 138–140, 142f., 145, 171, 176, 221f., 247, 259f., 264–268, 288, 333, 364, 367, 372, 375, 392, 406, 428, 433, 442, 497, 515, 536
- social meanings   11, 25, 79
membership   9, 11, 14f., 78f., 83, 238, 336, 367, 369, 376–378, 428, 438

merit   4–10, 29f., 33, 37, 86, 92, 94, 151, 160f., 163f., 168, 177f., 481, 492, 524, 529
meritocracy, meritocratic   32, 36, 77, 83f., 86
merit principle   33, 35, 38
meta-ethics, meta-ethical   11, 23, 26, 43f., 95, 282
metapolitical task   217, 222
metrics   16, 403, 410–415, 520
minority   118, 180, 397, 399, 423–428, 431f., 434–438
mixed constitution   28, 123
modus vivendi   13f., 243f., 248–251, 253–257, 284, 287f., 293, 295f., 462
money   3, 16, 66, 81, 86, 191, 411, 413–415, 482, 495, 512, 516
monism   252–254
monopoly   85, 536
moral conversion   388f.
moral intuition   56, 67, 74, 173
morality   13, 43, 47, 65, 92, 96–102, 116, 174f., 179, 181–184, 192, 196f., 249–252, 261, 277, 282, 323, 361, 363f., 372, 378f., 391–393, 397, 407, 411, 413, 433
– descriptive morality   45
– relational morality   389–394
moral philosophy   43, 46, 95, 171f., 220, 404f., 411, 414f., 505, 507, 511
– analytic moral philosophy   93
moral purity   304
moral theory   91, 94–97, 99, 281f., 316, 377, 403, 405, 417, 505, 509
– analytic moral theory   94

nation   15, 67, 147, 198, 321–323, 334, 347, 353, 427, 508–512, 515, 525, 532, 534
natural endowments   24, 35, 38, 40, 374, 507, 531
natural environment   478f.
naturalistic fallacy   94
need, needs   1, 3, 6–8, 10, 13, 15, 17, 23f., 27f., 33–35, 37–39, 44f., 47f., 57, 62f., 65, 72, 78f., 83, 85–87, 92, 97, 110, 112f., 116, 118f., 121f., 124, 127–129, 134, 147, 153, 156–159, 167f., 174, 184, 187, 192–194, 199–201, 207f., 211–213, 216, 222, 229, 231, 234, 236f., 245, 248, 256, 259, 261, 265–268, 270f., 273, 279, 296f., 299–302, 312–325, 329–342, 345, 347f., 350, 352–354, 357, 362, 366f., 372, 374, 377f., 385–387, 390, 395, 397, 404, 406f., 411, 413f., 416, 418, 423–428, 435, 441f., 445, 451, 459, 461, 470, 475, 478–482, 487–490, 492–497, 500, 506, 508, 510–512, 514f., 533f.
needs principle   34
negative duties   174, 330, 339–341
negative essence   263
neo-Kantian   23, 363
noble birth   4–6, 29, 32
non-egalitarianism   71, 73, 75–77
norms of justice   192f., 195

objective circumstances of justice   15, 313f.
obligation   11, 13, 15–17, 102, 162, 173f., 179, 187, 191, 196, 316, 322f., 345–358, 361f., 366–368, 370f., 374, 378f., 391f., 433f., 445, 516
– collective obligation   15, 345–355, 357f.
– global collective obligations   345, 347, 357
oligarchy   4–6, 29f., 123, 147, 160f., 164, 167, 535
ontology   139, 443
opacity   423, 431–433, 436
opinion   32, 75, 95, 97, 103, 116–118, 120–123, 129, 140, 152, 219, 318, 321, 333, 505, 507
– public opinion   12, 109, 111, 115, 117–119
opportunity   8, 36, 54f., 62, 65, 82, 85, 165, 189, 199, 273, 372, 375f., 472, 487, 498, 506
– equal opportunity   32, 116
opposing images of humanity   42f., 48
original choice   379
original position   7, 17, 82, 92, 112, 128, 207, 209, 213, 246, 281f., 314, 332, 334, 336f., 363, 405, 442f., 461, 472–475, 483, 505f.
origins of justice   191

Subject Index

paradox of toleration   385–387, 389, 391, 395
performance principle   33–36, 38
person   2f., 7–10, 13, 24, 32f., 35–38, 41–43, 55, 57, 72–76, 80f., 83, 85, 101f., 105, 109, 113, 124, 137, 147, 151, 153–155, 157–159, 173–179, 195–198, 219, 247, 262, 276, 278f., 281–283, 285f., 299f., 312–319, 321–325, 332, 335, 339, 363, 365–368, 370–372, 379, 387, 390, 392–394, 396–398, 400, 408f., 411, 413f., 423–426, 428–430, 432–437, 441, 444, 446, 471f., 474f., 483, 488, 490, 493, 495, 499, 506, 508, 510, 516, 518
– moral person   8, 24, 109, 429
philosopher ruler   138
philosophy of mind   94–97
pluralism   26f., 35, 41, 53, 71, 91, 109f., 113f., 118, 208, 222, 228, 235, 250, 259–261, 263f., 268–271, 276–282, 284, 301f., 313, 332f., 341, 345, 399, 452
– agonistic pluralism   260, 263–265, 270, 272f.
– conflict-focused conception of pluralism   260
– contemporary pluralism   260
– radical pluralism   109
– reasonable pluralism   15, 92, 109f., 113, 219, 221, 223, 227, 245, 291f., 294–296, 301f., 311, 324, 333, 337, 474
– social pluralism   263
– value pluralism   14f., 36, 53–55, 66, 68, 243f., 251–255, 280, 313, 316f., 325, 391–393, 395
polis   5f., 8, 12, 30, 32, 56, 66, 119f., 139, 145, 152, 154, 156, 158–161, 163f., 167
political argumentation   119–122, 124
political commonality   259, 262f., 265, 268
political communalism   38
political conception of justice   11, 24, 36, 41, 110, 127, 212, 215, 219, 221, 226, 236, 238, 245, 260f., 278, 280f., 285f., 291, 296, 299, 301f., 306f., 474
political moralism   112

political offices   3–5, 9f., 27–29, 33, 123, 160, 424
political philosophy   3, 11, 13, 25, 46f., 53, 55f., 67, 91f., 152, 154, 166, 168, 171f., 176, 187f., 194, 207f., 210f., 213f., 216–221, 223, 277, 282, 307, 311, 317, 345–347, 423, 489
– contemporary political philosophy   277
political principles   189, 218, 264, 291, 293, 461
political system   5f., 27–30, 138, 144–148, 280f., 287, 294, 363
political theory   8, 25, 28–30, 72, 77, 79f., 82, 93, 109, 117, 133, 151f., 154, 166, 168, 187–189, 195, 200, 202, 222, 244, 248, 250, 253, 262, 265, 267f., 292, 306f., 454
– contemporary political theory   75, 78, 194
– modern political theory   71f.
political thought   23–25, 38f., 43, 47, 75, 93, 100, 136f., 171, 244, 246, 251, 535, 537
– Western political thought   11, 26f., 75, 103
politics   4–6, 12f., 29f., 45, 57, 59, 83, 91f., 97f., 100, 102, 105, 110–124, 134, 137, 139f., 142, 146f., 151f., 156, 158, 160–168, 177, 188, 194, 214, 217, 247, 249–251, 253–257, 260, 263–265, 267, 270–273, 282, 324, 347, 426, 434, 441, 449f., 452f., 460, 462f., 535f.
– domestic politics   48
– practical politics   24f.
positivism   134
postsecular modesty   17, 449f., 460–463
power   14, 16f., 28, 41, 54, 81, 85, 98, 103f., 109, 120, 128, 136f., 140–144, 146f., 151f., 154, 157f., 161, 165–167, 173, 201f., 214, 221, 227, 248, 255–257, 259, 272f., 277, 279, 281, 292f., 295, 312, 315, 323, 325, 341, 351, 364, 368, 370–374, 376, 378f., 413, 426, 431,

442, 462, 470–472, 474, 480, 484, 493, 514, 526, 529, 535, 537
- political power   4–7, 9f., 27–31, 81, 110, 112, 152, 154, 164f., 168, 225–227, 255, 269, 295
practical philosophy   133, 139f.
practical wisdom   97
precept of need   7f.
principles of justice   1, 8, 24, 40, 55, 67, 73, 92, 112, 114, 127f., 188, 207–210, 213, 215, 217, 281f., 286f., 311–314, 318, 320–322, 324, 329, 332f., 340, 355, 405, 412f., 416, 429, 443, 447, 471f., 479, 487, 490, 496, 500, 506, 529
private property   55, 364, 478f., 482, 489, 497
privilege   31f., 34f., 37, 60, 66, 76, 181, 341, 356, 536f.
proportionalism   28, 32, 48
prosperity   238, 278, 515–517, 525f., 528
psychology   303, 416
- moral psychology 15, 291f., 302, 305–307
public-private-distinction   270
public sphere   17, 104, 106, 117f., 316, 451–455

racial discrimination   128
racism   179, 388
radical orthodoxy   455
rationality   13, 17, 53, 91, 101, 103f., 107, 123, 197, 207–210, 216, 223, 281, 294, 371, 377f., 449, 451–453, 455–457, 460
- common rationality   209
- communicative rationality   372, 378
- human rationality   209
realism   46, 110, 293
- ethical realism   23, 43–46
- moral realism   11, 44, 47
reason   2–6, 8f., 15, 23f., 26, 28–32, 34f., 38–47, 54, 59f., 67, 76, 82, 91–94, 96f., 100, 102f., 109–111, 114–119, 121, 135, 137, 140, 145–148, 157, 162, 168, 175f., 179, 191f., 195, 198–200, 210f., 214, 218–222, 225–227, 229f., 232–240, 246, 249, 253f., 261, 264, 268, 272f., 275–277, 279–281, 284f., 287f., 294–296, 298–302, 304f., 307, 311, 314, 316f., 321, 333–336, 341f., 345–347, 350, 352, 355f., 358, 363f., 367, 369–371, 374, 376f., 379, 385, 387, 389, 395, 409–411, 414f., 417f., 429, 442, 451f., 455, 457–459, 461, 471, 473, 475, 479, 481–484, 492, 515, 517, 520, 529, 532
- communicative reason, communicative reasoning   23, 451, 461
- impartial reason   472
- instrumental reason   371
- liberal public reason   119
- liberal reason   118
- public reason   12, 14, 109–115, 118f., 121, 124, 207–209, 212–216, 220–222, 225–236, 238–240, 245, 260–262, 276, 278, 364, 415, 457f., 461, 537
reasonable goals   15, 320f.
recognition   3, 9, 27f., 33, 53f., 62–65, 68, 77, 91, 103, 107, 116, 195f., 209f., 216, 225, 231, 237, 288, 291f., 294, 298–300, 302, 307, 363, 369, 374, 423–426, 428, 430–438, 509, 531, 533, 535f.
- social recognition   11, 62–64, 66f., 81
reconciliation   11, 13, 207f., 213, 216–223, 255, 276, 278, 409
redistribution   2, 7, 18, 38, 79, 194, 299, 334–338, 371, 424, 491f., 495, 523, 530f., 533f., 536–538
redress   2, 15, 24, 427f., 431, 433, 526
reflective equilibrium   112, 128, 214
relativism   47f., 103, 136
- ethical relativism   26, 45
- ethico-political relativism   26, 47
- justice relativism   59
religion   17, 41, 54, 106, 118, 198, 219, 262, 377, 387f., 397, 399, 407, 424, 434, 449–457, 459–463
religious intolerance   128
research perspective   11, 23f.
resources   15, 33, 36–38, 56, 67, 74, 78, 82, 194, 256, 272f., 313–315, 317, 322–325, 331f., 334–338, 341, 345, 348, 361, 367, 403, 407, 428, 445, 449f.,

452, 458–463, 470, 478, 480, 482, 494, 497
– material resources 424, 427
– technological resources 330
resource wars 321
respect 9, 16, 28, 37, 42, 48, 65, 72f., 76, 80, 82f., 86, 93, 105, 107, 112, 118f., 123f., 146, 157, 175, 181f., 192, 200, 212, 225, 228, 235, 245, 254, 256, 259, 262, 276f., 280f., 283–285, 287f., 312f., 315–317, 323, 325, 330, 332, 337, 367, 377–379, 385, 387–389, 392, 394–398, 400, 411, 423–426, 428–430, 432–438, 451–454, 483, 499
– equal respect 60, 78, 256, 397, 423, 425f., 429, 431–434, 436f.
– mutual respect 17, 398f., 449, 451, 453, 457–461, 463
– opacity respect 423, 425, 428, 431, 436
– self-respect 8f., 38, 55, 62, 65, 312, 315, 331, 333, 412, 430, 432, 470–472, 480
responsibility 15, 17, 56, 74, 162, 312, 323, 334, 339, 346f., 369, 371f., 374, 376f., 441, 443, 445–447, 463, 470, 472, 474, 518
– moral responsibility 15, 410
revolution 29–32, 161, 164, 192, 264, 488, 493, 518
rhetoric 119–121, 124, 135, 145, 363
rights 1, 7–10, 31f., 38, 41, 55, 66, 68, 79, 119, 129, 159, 174–176, 179, 188, 195, 226, 245–247, 249, 261, 265, 312, 315f., 318, 322f., 331–333, 345, 347f., 352, 356, 364, 377, 389–392, 399, 428, 441, 446, 469f., 478, 482, 500, 511, 520, 533
– animal rights 45, 240
– civil rights 180, 275, 469, 473, 484
– cultural rights 243
– human rights 32, 65, 127, 249, 315, 318, 322, 330–332, 337f., 340–342, 356f.
– individual rights 38, 175, 194, 407, 478, 536
– moral rights 178, 180f., 392
– natural right 56, 58, 62–65, 133f., 140, 145 f., 148
– political rights 399, 470, 484

– property rights 78, 404, 534, 537
– water rights 315
rule of law 14, 275–277, 285, 287f., 331, 530

same-sex marriage 240
scarcity 418
– moderate scarcity 193, 313f., 317
– radical scarcity 314
security 10, 34, 64, 201, 269, 331, 341, 352, 518, 524
self-determination 262, 281, 334, 337, 341, 364f., 368, 371, 451, 482
sense of justice 8, 25, 30, 39, 46, 145, 280, 312f., 323, 370, 414, 429, 474
sex education 240
skepticism 26, 45, 47, 69, 200, 386, 461
– ethical skepticism 26, 45
– ethico-political skepticism 26, 47
skill, skills 2, 7, 157, 160, 437, 532
social contract theory 112
social position 16, 40, 72, 81, 92, 424, 471–473, 476–478, 480, 483f.
social stability 194, 275–277, 282, 288
society 1–3, 8f., 13, 16, 25f., 32–35, 37, 40, 43, 54, 56–58, 62–65, 67f., 72–75, 77–79, 81–84, 86, 92–94, 99f., 103, 112–114, 136–138, 142–144, 147, 158f., 166, 173, 175, 179, 184, 190–192, 194–202, 210f., 219–223, 226, 234, 236f., 243, 245, 247–249, 255, 260f., 263, 269, 271, 276–279, 281–284, 288, 291, 293–296, 302, 305–307, 311, 313, 315f., 331f., 334, 336–338, 362, 365, 372, 374, 376, 387, 396, 398, 403–405, 407f., 410–412, 414–418, 423, 427, 431, 438, 441–443, 458, 469–476, 478–484, 487–490, 492–500, 506–512, 514f., 517–519, 523f., 526–532, 536–538
– civil society 117f., 198, 281, 377, 528
– closed society 199
democratic society 41, 115, 128, 214, 216, 218f., 223, 259, 276, 278, 283f., 287, 333, 336, 377, 408, 441

- just society 8, 26, 33, 36, 38f., 46, 54, 81, 91–93, 175f., 193, 199, 245, 296, 418, 442, 488, 493f.
- liberal civil society 117, 119
- liberal democratic society 332
- modern society 444, 451
- pluralist society 24, 127, 265
- well-ordered society 24, 112, 114, 127, 227, 229, 246, 277, 279–281, 311, 324, 333, 405

sociology 45
sophists 9, 31, 60, 134, 136
sovereignty 127f., 232, 238, 356, 527
species-capacity 364f.
species-ethic 362–366, 371, 373, 377–380
spheres of justice 9, 40, 79, 188, 367
state 2f., 7, 10, 16, 18, 23, 25, 30–33, 36, 54, 56, 66–68, 74, 77f., 85, 94, 96, 100, 102, 105f., 122f., 129, 133–137, 140–148, 152f., 155–158, 160, 164f., 167, 171, 173, 176f., 182, 187, 189, 193f., 198, 201, 235, 244, 248f., 259, 269f., 272, 275, 281, 284, 292f., 295f., 303, 307, 313f., 317, 319–321, 330, 332, 335f., 338–340, 342, 345, 347f., 352f., 356, 385–389, 394, 396, 399–401, 406, 442, 446f., 451, 455f., 469, 473, 480, 490, 493–497, 508, 510, 513–518, 520, 523–538
- minimal state 38, 523
- welfare state 2f., 7–9, 33, 37–39, 176, 442

state power 67, 218, 221, 225, 236, 240, 281
stoics 9, 31, 60
subjective circumstance of toleration 386f., 389f., 393, 397
subjective paradox 385f., 389, 391, 395
superiority 59, 104, 144, 161f., 166f., 247

talent 2, 7, 9, 32, 36, 38, 54, 59–61, 84, 188, 374, 437, 489, 492–494
taxation 7, 38, 334f., 519, 533
temperament 136, 147f., 304, 411
theory of justice 1, 3, 7f., 15, 17f., 40, 58, 69, 71, 73, 91, 93f., 111–113, 127, 171, 175, 187, 190, 193f., 199f., 213, 216, 222, 278, 281, 294, 311–315, 320–322, 324f., 329, 332–334, 369, 379, 404, 409, 416, 428f., 462, 469, 471–474, 487–492, 494, 496–498, 500, 505–507, 517, 537
theory of moral sentiments 172, 505, 510f., 516, 524f., 529–531, 536
theory of rational choice 128
toleration, tolerance 16, 53f., 69, 107, 197, 292, 385–389, 391, 394–400, 430f., 462
- liberal toleration 16, 386, 395–400
transgenerational obligation 367
transgenerational polity 367
transsubjective 362, 364, 371
truth 45f., 48, 55, 68f., 86, 94f., 97, 111, 119f., 127, 162, 175f., 180, 190f., 196, 211, 214, 217, 225, 229f., 252, 280, 307, 313, 412, 446, 455–457, 476, 488
- moral truth 26, 43, 46, 278, 405, 407f., 412
- objective truth 43, 46f.
- universal truth 45, 53–55, 127
tyranny 6, 103, 106

universalism 91, 174, 366
utilitarianism 98, 171, 173–175, 294, 296, 391, 499

values 1, 8, 34–37, 39, 45f., 55, 59f., 62, 64, 92, 95, 106f., 112, 114, 118, 177, 191f., 195, 198, 200, 209, 211–213, 218f., 223, 226f., 230f., 238, 240, 244f., 248, 251–253, 259f., 262, 264f., 267f., 281f., 293–300, 303–307, 316f., 324f., 331, 368, 372, 377, 386f., 391–393, 398f., 406, 408–410, 413f., 417f., 427, 431, 437f., 461, 473, 480, 519
- liberal values 14, 107, 243, 247, 249f., 301, 305
- objective values 44–46
- political values 41, 216, 218, 220, 223, 225, 227, 229f., 288, 291, 299, 306, 316
- social values 8, 55, 57, 62, 64–66, 472
veil of ignorance 40, 92, 282, 314, 332f., 378, 441–443, 472, 506

Subject Index — **563**

virtue 4–7, 12f., 27–29, 31f., 63, 77, 93, 98–101, 104, 106, 111f., 140, 142, 146, 148, 151–154, 156, 158, 160f., 164f., 168, 173–176, 187, 190f., 193, 197f., 208, 223, 231f., 251f., 255, 298f., 316, 348, 353, 374, 386, 388, 406, 426, 429, 433, 437, 441, 475, 496, 510, 514, 517–519, 523–526, 528f., 531
– artificial virtue 101
– civic virtue 243, 249, 254f.
– ethical virtue 9, 42, 46, 151
– natural virtue 101
– political virtue 6f., 28, 43, 48, 386, 395, 398f.
virtue of justice 147, 193
virtuism 154, 164, 168

wealth 2, 4–9, 16, 18, 29, 31, 33–35, 37–39, 55, 62, 65, 81f., 85f., 123, 160, 162, 299, 312, 315, 334, 336–338, 411f., 424, 470–473, 480, 488, 497, 508–512, 516, 523–530, 532–534
welfare 2, 10, 12, 18, 34, 36, 175, 200, 427, 475–477, 479f., 482, 484, 491, 493, 499, 506–510, 512, 519, 523, 534
world-disclosure, world-disclosive 372, 378–380
worth 4, 7, 9, 24, 32, 37, 42, 59, 74f., 77, 129, 160, 165, 190, 200, 254, 269, 281, 388, 424, 435, 437, 456, 483f.

xenophobia 179

www.ingramcontent.com/pod-product-compliance
Lightning Source LLC
Chambersburg PA
CBHW021112300426

44113CB00006B/120